FUNDAMENTALS OF FINANCIAL ACCOUNTING

The Willard J. Graham Series in Accounting

Consulting Editor   ROBERT N. ANTHONY   *Harvard University*

GLENN A. WELSCH

College of Business Administration
The University of Texas at Austin

ROBERT N. ANTHONY

Graduate School of Business Administration
Harvard University

Third edition

FUNDAMENTALS OF FINANCIAL ACCOUNTING

1981

Richard D. Irwin, Inc.
Homewood, Illinois 60430
Irwin-Dorsey Limited
Georgetown, Ontario L7G 4B3

© RICHARD D. IRWIN, INC., 1974, 1977, and 1981

All rights reserved. No part of this publication may be
reproduced, stored in a retrieval system, or transmitted,
in any form or by any means, electronic, mechanical,
photocopying, recording, or otherwise, without the prior
written permission of the publisher.

ISBN 0-256-02473-1
Library of Congress Catalog Card No. 80–84323

Printed in the United States of America

1 2 3 4 5 6 7 8 9 0 K 8 7 6 5 4 3 2 1

LEARNING SYSTEMS COMPANY—
a division of Richard D. Irwin, Inc.—has developed a
PROGRAMMED LEARNING AID
to accompany texts in this subject area.
Copies can be purchased through your bookstore
or by writing PLAIDS,
1818 Ridge Road, Homewood, Illinois   60430.

To our wives,
Irma and Katherine

Preface

This Third Edition retains all of the features favorably commented upon by numerous faculty members who used the prior editions. It has been updated in all respects, and approximately 80 percent of the assignment material has been replaced or revised. Additional problems contribute a measure of greater depth and analytical substance.

The chapter sequence has been rearranged somewhat. Chapters 1 and 2 of the prior edition have been consolidated into one chapter. Consolidated statements now follows long-term investments (Chapters 13 and 14). Chapter 17, Financial Reporting and Changing Prices, has been completely rewritten to emphasize the underlying concepts of *FASB Statement No. 33*. The authors present a unique illustration of general price level restatement and current cost application especially designed to be understandable to beginning accounting students.

To lend an unusual level of flexibility in use and to increase readability, chapters have been divided into two or more separate parts. The objectives of each part are concisely delineated and the questions for discussion, exercises, and problems are grouped separately by part (both in the text and the Solutions Manual). [A complete list of *key words*, with specific page citations, is given at the end of each chapter.] The demonstration cases, with solutions, in the various chapters have been carefully selected and written to provide a comprehensive overview of the chapter.

Major portions of each chapter have been rewritten to incorporate the latest developments in financial accounting and to increase comprehension. Numerous illustrations are provided to supplement the written discussions. All of the new features significantly increase the level of flexibility of the text in use.

The prior extensive list of teaching and student aids has been expanded and revised. In addition to the textbook, these aids are:

Available to students:
1. Study Guide (coordinated with the sequence of each chapter; includes comprehensive outlines, illustrations, and sample examination questions with answers).
2. Working Papers (includes all forms, with captions, needed for solving all exercises and problems).

3. Practice Set (application of the complete accounting information processing system as discussed in the textbook).

Available to the instructor:

4. Comprehensive *Teachers Manual* (includes answers to all questions class discussion, exercises, and problems; also, includes suggested course plans and instructional ideas).
5. List of Check Figures (includes check figures for exercises and problems; available in quantity for distribution to students).
6. Bank of Examination Questions (coordinated by chapter).
7. Teaching Transparencies (as used by the senior author for mass sections).

Many accounting instructors prefer to divide the first course in accounting into two parts—the first semester or quarter focusing on financial accounting and the second on management accounting. Many texts, however, are not arranged so that such an approach is feasible with a single text.

This volume and its companion, *Fundamentals of Management Accounting*, are designed to provide material for a fully coordinated first course. As their titles indicate, this volume deals with the fundamentals of financial accounting, and its companion with the fundamentals of management accounting. Each volume can be used either for a one-semester or a one-quarter course. Both are designed to provide maximum flexibility for the instructor in the selection and order of materials for the classroom. They emphasize those aspects of accounting we believe essential for interpretation and use of accounting information. Mechanical and procedural details are minimized, while the conceptual, measurement, and communication aspects are emphasized.

This book is an introduction to **financial accounting,** which has as its primary subject the communication of relevant financial information to external parties. We strongly believe that a certain level of knowledge of the accounting model, the measuring processes involved, the data classifications, and terminology, is essential to the interpretation and effective use of financial statements. We have provided the necessary information in this volume. The key to effective use of financial statements is to understand what they do and do not say, the measuring approaches used, and the standards observed in their development. This is the case both for students who will continue their study of accounting and for those who will not. The materials are arranged to meet the requirements of a wide range of academic institutions and curricula.

This volume represents a significant departure from the traditional financial accounting textbook in several respects. First, it provides the instructor with comprehensive discussions of a broad range of subject areas rather than the bare minimum. This approach means that more materials are presented than generally can be covered in the *undergraduate* financial course in accounting (however, it is completely adequate for such a graduate course). Importantly, this coverage gives the instructor a great amount of flexibility to select those topics appropriate to the situation. In contrast, a textbook that provides only the minimum materials imposes on the instructor the unfortunate choice of having to *(a)* present a *de minimus* course or *(b)* devote considerable time developing supplementary textual and homework assignments. Secondly, this text discusses a number of topics not traditionally included in an elementary textbook. In our judgment, much of the traditional material is essential; however, the recent thrusts and changes in financial accounting make it imperative that certain significant topics be accorded comprehensive treatment. This volume avoids superficial treatment of these new directions by giving special emphasis to concepts, rationale, measurement, and reporting. Certain traditional procedural topics are presented in appendixes should coverage of them be desired.

The primary features of this book and the instructional materials that accompany it are as follows:

- At the outset, the characteristics of the environment in which the accounting process operates is emphasized.

- At the outset, the student is presented with a comprehensive description of the end products of the financial accounting process—the external financial statements and related disclosures. This volume presents the maximum amount of material that can ordinarily be covered in a one-semester undergraduate course. Therefore, some choices usually must be made by the instructor.

- Accounting is viewed as an information processing model designed to enhance communication by the entity to the users of its financial reports.

- The discussions emphasize concepts, standards, and generally accepted accounting principles as the rationale for the way certain things are done in accounting.

- Throughout the chapters, the measuring approaches used in accounting and in reporting to decision makers are emphasized.

- Throughout, the focus is on the corporation rather than on the sole proprietorship or the partnership. Actual case examples are utilized. As a consequence, income taxes, dividends, earnings per share, capital stock, the *APB Opinions*, and the *FASB Statements* are discussed.

- Relevant topics, not ordinarily treated in a first course, are discussed. These include cash flow, present value, consolidated statements, purchase versus pooling, statement of changes in financial position (both working capital and cash bases), compensating balances, price level effects, and current value.

- One or more *appendixes* follow some of the chapters. These appendixes focus on the clerical and mechanical aspects of the accounting process such as special journals, subsidiary ledgers, payrolls, and petty cash. Separation in appendixes facilitates their exclusion, or order of selection, without affecting the continuity of the course.

These features are of particular importance to nonaccounting majors since the first semester usually is their only exposure to the fundamentals of financial accounting. For example, most of the external financial statements coming to the attention of the nonaccounting majors, both in school and in real life, will be consolidated statements. Similarly, an understanding of the effects of general inflation and specific price changes on financial information is essential in these times to the interpretation of reported results.

Answers to questions such as how much time should be spent on each chapter, how much homework should be required, and what materials should be omitted, depend on the objectives of the particular course, the time constraints, and the backgrounds of the students. As mentioned above, we have arranged the topical materials to permit maximum flexibility in selecting among various options and in giving varying topical emphasis to fit practically all situations. Appendixes, parts of chapters, and even entire chapters may be omitted without adversely affecting the continuity of the course. The Solutions Manual includes comments and suggestions that are particularly helpful in selecting among a number of possible options.

The subject matter of the 17 chapters and 8 appendixes, which comprise this volume, has been arranged in what we believe to be a pedagogically sound sequence; nevertheless, considerable rearrangements can be made if the instructor so desires. Each chapter has a summary and almost all have a demonstration case, with a suggested solution. The purpose of the demonstration cases is to tie together the various subtopics discussed in the chapter. Following each chapter are study materials classified as (a) discussion questions, (b) short exercises (suitable for homework, class illustrations, and examinations), and (c) comprehensive problems and cases. Each of these groups of study materials is arranged to follow the topical sequence of the chapter.

The list of students and faculty members to whom the authors feel a sense of gratitude for ideas and suggestions is too long to enumerate here. With respect to this volume, we are particularly grateful to the following individuals who devoted considerable time in discussions, reviewing parts of the manuscript, and testing materials: Professors William H. Beaver, Stanford University; Wayne S. Boutell, University of California; Robert S. Eskew, Purdue University; John C. Fellingham, University of Texas at Austin; Walter T. Harrison, University of Texas at Austin; Robert L. Kellogg, University of Texas at Austin; and Daniel G. Short, University of Texas at Austin.

We also express thanks to the following students at The University of Texas at Austin: Petrea Sandlin, Robert J. Arogeti, Elesa J. W. Bentsen, Elizabeth A. Henke, Carol H. McGinnis, Mary Jane Sloan, Mary Madeline Balent, and Janet Ammenheuser.

We especially recognize the valuable editorial suggestions provided by Mary Anne Keely and Robert E. Nelson, graduate students, University of Texas at Austin. Our gratitude extends to Linda Marie Nelson for her excellence in typing manuscript, and for her dedication in performing many other tasks which were essential to completion of this revision.

Finally, we express our thanks to numerous users of the prior editions for their valuable suggestions.

Our thanks to the American Institute of Certified Public Accountants, American Accounting Association, Financial Accounting Standards Board, and the authors identified by citations, for permission to quote from their publications. To J. C. Penney Company, Inc., Houston Industries, Incorporated, Corning Glass Works, and Abbott Laboratories our special thanks for permission to use selected materials from their annual reports.

And, finally, sincere appreciation to I. L. Grimes, Jack Young, William H. Schoof, and the editors and staff at the Irwin Company who worked so diligently in putting the manuscript together. And perhaps the most important debt of gratitude is owed to Dick Irwin for suggesting and encouraging us to collaborate in developing these two volumes.

Suggestions and comments on the text and the related materials are invited.

Glenn A. Welsch
Robert N. Anthony

Contents

Perspectives—
Accounting objectives
and communication

The objective of this book and its companion volume, *Fundamentals of Management Accounting,*[1] is to develop your knowledge of, and your ability to use, accounting information. This volume, on **financial accounting,** focuses on the role of accounting information in the decision-making processes of parties external to the business; that is, owners, investors, potential investors, creditors, and the public at large. The second volume, on **management accounting,** focuses on the role of accounting information in the decision-making processes of managers with responsibilities inside the organization. Whether you ultimately become an owner, a manager, an investor, or a creditor, or even if your only interest in an organization is that of a concerned citizen, an understanding of accounting will enhance significantly your competence as a decision maker. As you study these two volumes you will develop an understanding of how accounting information is used in resource-allocation decisions in all types of organizations such as profit-making enterprises, nonprofit endeavors, governmental entities, and social programs. In practically all organizations, long-term success depends in large part on the quality of the resource-allocation decisions that are made. Accounting information, in the broad sense, is used to aid in the decision-making process and to measure the financial results after the decisions are made and implemented.

This book is designed for students who have had no prior academic study of accounting. The chapters usually are divided into parts to facilitate

---

[1] Robert N. Anthony and Glenn A. Welsch, *Fundamentals of Management Accounting,* 3d ed. (Homewood, Ill.: Richard D. Irwin, Inc., 1981). © 1981 by Richard D. Irwin, Inc.

study and to provide flexibility in priority selection of materials consistent with the time available. Appendixes to the chapters also are provided to permit flexibility; they include (1) more advanced discussion of selected topics and (2) strictly procedural aspects of selected topics.

PURPOSE OF THE CHAPTER

The purpose of this chapter is to present a broad perspective of the objectives of accounting and of the environment (i.e., the surroundings) in which it operates. To accomplish this purpose, the chapter is divided into two parts:

Part A: The objectives and environment of accounting

* Defines accounting with emphasis on its fundamental objective of providing financial information that is useful in making business and economic decisions.
* Describes the features of the environment that bear most directly on accounting.

Part B: Communication of accounting information

* Introduces periodic financial statements as the primary means of communicating financial information about an organization.

Behavioral and learning objectives for this chapter are provided in the *Teachers Manual.*

PART A: THE OBJECTIVES AND ENVIRONMENT OF ACCOUNTING

ACCOUNTING DEFINED

Accounting is an information system designed to **measure, record,** and **report** in monetary terms the flows of resources into (inflows) and out (outflows) of an organization, the resources controlled by the organization, and the claims against those resources. In doing this, accounting collects, processes, evaluates, and reports financial information that is considered to be particularly useful in decision making. In addition, accounting involves judgmental and interpretative roles in analyzing, reporting, and using the financial results.

Accounting serves those that use the information it provides in three related ways:

1. Accounting provides information that is helpful in making decisions. Most important decisions, regardless of the type of endeavor involved, are based, in part, upon complex financial or monetary considerations. **Accounting provides an important information base and a particular**

analytical orientation that help the decision maker assess the potential financial implications and potential outcomes of various alternatives that are being considered. The primary role of accounting is to facilitate decision making.

2. Accounting reports the results of past decisions. Once a decision is made and implementation starts, important and often subtle financial effects occur. These financial effects often are critical to the success of the endeavor. Thus, the evolving effects of the decision must be measured continuously and periodically reported so that the decision maker can be appropriately informed of continuing and new problems, and of successes, over time. **Accounting provides a continuing measurement of the financial effects of a series of decisions already made, the results of which are communicated to the decision maker by means of periodic financial statements.**

3. **Accounting keeps track of a wide range of items to meet the scorekeeping and safeguarding responsibilities imposed on all organizations.** These include how much cash is available for use; how much customers owe the company; what debts are owed by the organization; what items are owned, such as machinery and office equipment; and inventory levels on hand.

Economics has been defined as the study of how people and society end up choosing, with or without the use of money, to employ scarce productive resources that could have alternative uses to produce various commodities and distribute them for consumption, now or in the future, among various persons and groups in society.[2] This definition suggests a relationship to the definition of accounting. Like economics, accounting has a conceptual foundation. It focuses on the collection, measurement, and communication of information on the flows of scarce resources of specific entities. Accounting generally is viewed as encompassing the **financial planning process** (discussed in *Fundamentals of Management Accounting*), which focuses on the planning and projection of **future** flows of scarce resources. Thus, accounting collects data and measures, interprets, and reports on those human activities that are the focus of economics. Economics attempts to *explain* economic relationships primarily on a conceptual level, whereas accounting attempts to *measure* the economic relationships primarily on a practical level. However, accounting measurements must be made as consistent as is feasible with economic concepts. Accounting must deal with the complex problems of measuring the monetary effects of **exchange transactions** (i.e., resource inflows and outflows), the resources held, and the claims against those resources for each entity. Throughout these two volumes many of the theoretical and practical issues that arise in the measurement process will be discussed from the accounting viewpoint.

---

[2] Paul A. Samuelson, *Economics*, 9th ed. (New York: McGraw-Hill Book Co., 1975).

A COMPLEX ENVIRONMENT

In various ways we are associated with social, political, and economic organizations, such as businesses, churches, fraternal organizations, political parties, states, counties, schools, environmental groups (both public and private), chambers of commerce, and professional associations. Many of these organizations are complex and pose critical problems on which decisions must be made. The future quality of our society depends in large measure upon the collective decisions of the managers of such organizations. These organizations are essential to the workings of a society; indeed, they constitute much of what we call "society."

Fundamental to a dynamic and successful society is the ability of each organization to measure and report its accomplishments, to undergo critical self-analysis, and, by means of sound decisions, to renew itself and grow so that the individual organization and societal objectives are served best. Essentially, society, and the various organizations that comprise it, thrives in direct proportion to the efficiency with which it allocates scarce resources: human talent, materials, services, and capital. To accomplish this broad goal, organizations and persons interested in specific organizations need information about how the resources that the organization controls were generated and used. Accounting information is designed to meet this need.

Therefore, accounting is said to be a man-made art and continuously is undergoing change to meet the evolving needs of the society. Since the environmental characteristics of a society are diverse and complex, accounting always is facing new challenges. For example, the current inflationary spiral necessitates the development of accounting concepts and procedures that will report separately real-value and inflationary effects (see Chapter 17).

Throughout this textbook you will study how accounting is responding to the environment in the United States. In the next few paragraphs we will discuss two environmental characteristics—**measurements in dollars** and the **types of business entities**—because they have pervasive effects on accounting concepts and procedures.

Measurements in dollars

A monetary system is one way for the measurement and communication of the flow of resources in and out of an organization. In a monetary system, the unit of exchange (dollars in our case) is the common denominator of measurement, the medium of exchange, and a store of value. Thus, the monetary unit provides a basis for expressing, in large measure, the available resources and the resource flows of both the society as a whole and the various organizations that comprise society. Accounting is concerned directly with measuring and reporting available resources and their flows. Accounting provides monetary measurement of inputs (resources received) and outputs (goods produced and services rendered), and, as a consequence, it provides benchmarks for evaluating the efficiency of organizational performance. It also measures the available resources held and the claims against those resources.

Accounting measures the resources and resource flows of organizations within a society in terms of the monetary unit of that society. Thus, accounting uses the monetary system of each country within which it operates. One of the critical problems in accounting is the conversion of financial amounts from one monetary system to another monetary system in measuring resources and resource flows for multinational activities. Since accounting measures and reports financial resources in terms of each society's monetary unit, it is based on what is called the **unit-of-measure assumption** (see Exhibit 2–6). The common denominator or "meterstick" used for accounting measurements in the United States is the dollar; the assumption is that the dollar is a useful measuring unit.[3]

Types of business entities

This book will focus primarily on accounting for business entities. In our environment there are three main types of business entities. Since they will be referred to often throughout this volume, their primary characteristics are explained below.

A **sole proprietorship** is a business that is owned by one person. This type of business entity is common in the fields of services, retailing, and farming. Generally, the owner is also the manager. Legally, the business and the owner are not separate entities—they are one and the same. However, accounting views the business as a **separate entity** to be distinguished from its owner.

A **partnership** is an unincorporated business that is owned by two or more persons known as partners. The agreements between the owners are set forth in a partnership contract. The contract specifies such matters as division of profits each period and distribution of resources upon termination of the business. As in the case of a sole proprietorship, a partnership is not legally separate from its owners. Legally, each partner is responsible for the debts of the business (i.e., each general partner has what is called unlimited liability). However, accounting views the partnership as a separate business entity to be distinguished from its several owners.

A **corporation** is a business that is incorporated under the laws of a particular state, and whose owners are known as shareholders or stockholders. Ownership is represented by shares of capital stock that can be bought and sold freely. When a proper application is filed by the organizers, the state issues a charter which gives the corporation the right to operate legally as an entity, separate and apart from its owners. The owners enjoy what is called "limited liability"; that is, they are liable for the debts of

---

[3] The exchange unit (dollars) changes in purchasing power due to the effects of inflation and deflation; simply put, the dollar does not always command the same amount of *real* goods. Thus, money does not have the most basic element of any measurement unit, that is, uniformity in magnitude. During inflation and deflation the monetary unit is not uniform in magnitude because one unit will command fewer, or more, real goods respectively than before.

the corporation only to the extent of their investments. The charter specifies the types and amounts of capital stock that can be issued. Most states require a minimum of two or three shareholders and a minimum amount of resources to be contributed at the time of organization. The shareholders elect a governing board of directors, which in turn employs managers and exercises general supervision of the corporation.[4] Accounting for the business entity focuses on the corporation, not on the directors and managers as individuals.

As to economic importance, the corporation is the dominant form of business organization in the United States. The advantages of the corporate form include limited liability for the stockholders, continuity of life, ease in transferring ownership (stock), and opportunities to raise large amounts of money by selling shares to a large number of people. Because of these advantages, most large and medium-sized businesses (and many small ones) are organized as corporations. We shall emphasize, therefore, this form of business. Nevertheless, the accounting concepts, standards, and measurement procedures apply generally to the other types of business.

To reiterate, accounting measures and reports information in financial terms for all types of entities, not just business entities.

One of the essentials of any measurement process is a precise definition of specifically what is to be measured. Examples of specific things to be measured are the population of California, the rainfall in Michigan, the voter registrations in New York, and the bank deposits in Texas (each for a stipulated time). Similarly, in the measurement of resources and resource flows, accounting requires precise definition of the **specific entity** for which monetary or financial data are to be collected, measured, and reported. When a specific entity is defined carefully, it is often referred to as an **accounting entity.** The whole nation is a specific entity, so is each business unit, and so is each individual person. In any measurement scheme, the definition of that which is to be measured often involves difficult problems. For example, in measuring the population of California should the amount include service personnel? college students? jail inmates? long-term visitors? hotel guests? Similarly, in defining an accounting entity, there are important problems to be resolved. For example, if we are to account for, say, Adams Company, it is defined as a separate and specific accounting entity. The accounting entity has a specialized definition that is known as the **separate-entity assumption.**[5] The separate-entity assumption holds that for accounting measurement purposes, the particular entity being accounted for is distinguished carefully from all similar and related entities and persons. Under this assumption, an account-

---

[4] There are a number of specialized types of entities that we do not discuss, such as joint ventures, mutual funds, cooperatives, investment trusts, and syndicates. Consideration of these is beyond the scope of this book.

[5] A list of the fundamental assumptions and principles underlying accounting is summarized in Exhibit 2–6.

ing entity is held to be separate and distinct from its owner(s). An entity is viewed as *owning the resources* (i.e., *assets*) used by it and as *owing the claims* (or *debts*) against those assets. The assets, debts, and activities of the entity are kept completely separate, for measurement purposes, from those of the owners and other entities. For example, in the case of Adams Company, the personal activities of the owners are not included in the accounting measurements of the business itself.

THE USE OF ACCOUNTING INFORMATION IN THE DECISION-MAKING PROCESS

We have said that your role as a future decision maker is significant, whether you become a manager, investor, professional person, owner of a business, or simply an interested citizen. Decision makers use various approaches for selecting one alternative from among a set of alternative solutions to a given problem. Selection of the preferred alternative constitutes the basic decision. In the process of reaching decisions, the decision maker is concerned about the **future** since a decision cannot change the past; however, the effective decision maker does not neglect the past. Knowledge and interpretation of what has happened in the past aid in making decisions since history may shed considerable light on what the future is likely to hold. Thus, one of the fundamental inputs to decision making is dependable and relevant historical data. A large portion of historical data that are relevant to business decisions are expressed in monetary terms. They include costs (i.e., resources expended), revenues (i.e., resources earned), assets (i.e., things owned), liabilities (i.e., amounts owed), and owners' equity (i.e., total assets less total liabilities of the entity). Thus, accounting provides an important **information base** for decision making. The information provided by accounting must be understandable to the decision maker to preclude unwarranted interpretations in the decision-making process. This is a primary reason why measurements in accounting must adhere to certain standards and concepts.

On pages 2 and 3, three ways in which accounting serves decision makers were outlined briefly. At this point we will reemphasize that the information measurement and reporting encompassed in the accounting process are essential to *(a)* effective control of the entity, and *(b)* sound decision making by those individuals directly concerned with, and interested in, the endeavor.

Most entities, such as a business, a hospital, or a program to educate the disadvantaged, carry on their activities over an extended period of time during which resources are committed and used with the expectation that desirable outputs will result in the form of goods and services. During the period of continuing activity, those involved in the organization, be they owners, sponsors, or managers, must have information about the continuing amounts of resources committed, resources used, resources on hand, and outputs (goods and services); and this information must be reported, interpreted, and evaluated periodically. The accounting process is designed to provide a continuing flow of such information to all interested parties. A typical flow of accounting information in an entity is diagrammed in Exhibit 1–1. The **financial statements** constitute the primary means of communicating the relevant information on a continuing basis (information feedback).

Now, let's see examples of how the flow of accounting information may aid decision makers in three different kinds of entities. We will consider a business, a hospital, and a community educational program for a disadvantaged group.

A business. First, the purposes of the business are formulated by the organizers. Initially, the owners provide the funds, which often are supplemented by funds provided by creditors. These funds then are used by the managers to acquire machinery, inventory, services, and other re-

EXHIBIT 1–1
Accounting information flows in a decision and implementation cycle

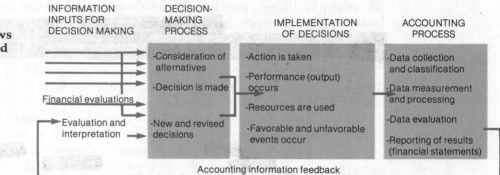

sources. The managers of the entity develop plans for operating the business. As the business operates, additional resources are generated from the sale of goods and services. Many other things happen, most of which involve either the inflow or outflow of resources. The managers of the business need information, on a continuing basis, that tells about the status of the resources. They want to know such things as sources and amounts of funds, revenues (sales and services sold), expenses, the amount invested in inventory, the cash situation, the amount being spent for research and development, and the amount of money being spent in the sales efforts.

The managers need answers to questions such as these for two fundamental reasons. First, accounting information in response to these and similar questions may aid importantly in making decisions about the entity to improve its effectiveness and efficiency. Second, accounting information tells the interested parties what the score was during the immediate past periods. This scorekeeping is important to the control and evaluation of performance. In Exhibit 1–1, **financial evaluations** are shown as one of the **information inputs** to the decision-making process. The exhibit also depicts the accounting process which involves data collection, measurement, evaluation, and reporting of the results. In the reporting phase, the accounting information is communicated as an aid in making new decisions and in revising prior decisions.

Now, consider a shareholder (an owner) who has a substantial amount of funds invested in the business but has little opportunity to directly influence the management. The shareholder often must decide whether to (1) retain the ownership interest, (2) expand or contract it, or (3) dispose of it completely. The shareholder also is interested in decisions that will lead to expansion of the business and raise its level of efficiency. As a consequence of these concerns, the shareholder would want to know such things as the trend of sales, the level of expenses, the amount of profits, earnings per share, the amount invested in various assets (such as inventory and machinery), the debts of the business, and the cash balance. In other words, the investors would be very interested in knowing how the **management** is allocating the scarce resources provided by the owners and the creditors. This information would be basic to taking one of the three actions listed above, to evaluate the management. The periodic financial reports provided on a continuing basis by the accounting process have as their primary objective the furnishing of information bearing on these questions. The accounting information thus provided should flow into the decision-making process of the shareholders' in ways similar to those depicted in Exhibit 1–1.

A hospital. Assume you are on the board of governors of a local hospital and, as a consequence, share the responsibility for the basic decisions and guidelines for its continued operation at an efficient level. Similar to the owner of a business, you have a wide variety of questions concerning its revenues, expenses, funds tied up in buildings and equipment, cost of charity services, and so on, that are in the scorekeeping category. You also are concerned with whether enough resources are being allocated to such activities as emergency care, sanitation, and nursing services. Before any sound decisions in these areas can be made for the future, you must have information about the past and current allocation of resources to them and what the output (quality and quantity of benefits) was. Thus, as a sponsor, you have many information needs that are important to your decisions for the future.

Now, consider the manager of the hospital. The manager needs accounting information about the operations of the hospital similar to that discussed above for the manager of a business, and for the same reasons. Typically, the manager will need more *detailed* accounting information than the sponsor. In any event, whether one is a sponsor or manager of the hospital, financial measurement and the reporting results should be continuing inputs to the decision-making process.

An educational program for a disadvantaged group. As with the business and the hospital, there are both sponsors and managers of the program. They are vitally concerned with its resource needs and uses, the level of operational efficiency, and the extent to which the entity is attaining the goals set out for it. In addition to the all-important dedication and efforts of those carrying out the day-to-day activities, the financial problems and related decisions command the major attention of both the sponsors and the management—how resources are being committed, are they being allocated to the most critical phases of the program, are they being used efficiently, and what additional resources are needed? These are indicative of the wide range of accounting information that is needed to make sound decisions and to direct the effort in a responsible way. The accounting process, if adequately designed for the situation, can provide, through the medium of continuing financial statements, information responses to many of these questions. The sponsors and the management, if they have a reasonable understanding of the financial considerations, can utilize the financial statements as important inputs to their decision-making process.

In summary, regardless of the type of endeavor or the position of the decision maker, a continuous flow of accounting information is useful to the decision maker. The flow of accounting information in the decision-making/implementation cycle, as depicted in Exhibit 1–1, is needed in practically all types of economic endeavors.

HISTORICAL PERSPECTIVES

Accounting is as old as the exchange processes (whether barter or monetary) that gradually developed with civilization. The earliest written records, including the Scriptures, contain references to what now is called accounting.

Accounting evolved in response to the economic needs of society. Prior to the 15th century it apparently followed no well-defined pattern except that it developed in answer to specific governing and trading needs of the era. The first known treatment of the subject of accounting was written in 1494, two years after the discovery of America. An Italian monk and mathematician, Fr. Luca Paciolo, described an approach that had been developed by the Italian merchants of the time to account for their activities as owner-managers of business ventures. Paciolo laid the foundations of the basic "accounting model" that is used to this day. As economic activity moved from the feudal system to agriculture and then to the Industrial Revolution, accounting adapted to the evolving needs. As business units became more complex and broader in scope, accounting evolved in response to the increased planning and control responsibilities of management. As governments increased in size and became more centralized, accounting was developed to meet the increased accountabilities.

In the 17th and 18th centuries, the Industrial Revolution in England provided the impetus for the development of new approaches in accounting. The impetus was particularly in the direction of management accounting and the accumulation of data concerning the cost of manufacturing each product. In the latter half of the 19th century, English accountants, small in numbers but large in competence, appeared on the American scene. By 1900 the lead in accounting developments, provided earlier by the English, began to shift to America. Since the turn of the century, spearheaded by the accounting profession in the United States, accounting has experienced dynamic, and sometimes controversial, growth.

The accounting profession today

In the period since 1900, accountancy has attained the stature of a profession similar to law, medicine, engineering, and architecture. As with all recognized professions, it is subject to licensing, observes a code of professional ethics, requires a high level of professional competence, is dedicated to service to the public, requires a high level of academic study, and rests on a "common body of knowledge." The accountant, in addition to meeting specified academic requirements, may be licensed by the state to be a **certified public accountant,** or **CPA.** This designation was first established in 1896. The primary objective was the attainment of high standards of professional competence. It is granted only upon completion of requirements specified by state statutes. Although the CPA requirements vary somewhat among states, generally they include a college degree with a major in accounting, good character, from one to five years specified experience, and successful completion of a three-day examination. The CPA examination, scheduled in each state simultaneously on a semiannual basis, is prepared by the American Institute of Certified Public Accountants and covers accounting theory, auditing, business law, and accounting practice.

As is common with physicians, engineers, lawyers, and architects, accountants (including CPAs) commonly are engaged in professional practice or are employed by businesses, government entities, nonprofit organizations, and so on.

Practice of public accounting

A CPA, practicing public accounting, is one who offers professional services to the public for a fee, as does the lawyer and physician. In this posture the accountant is known appropriately as an **independent CPA** because certain responsibilities also extend to the general public (third parties) rather than being limited to the specific business or other entity that pays for the services. Independent CPAs are not employees of their clients. This concept of independence from the client is a unique characteristic of the accounting profession. The consequences of this uniqueness are not so widely understood as perhaps they should be. For example, the lawyer and the physician, in case of malpractice or incompetence, generally are subject to potential liability (lawsuits) that may extend only to the client or patient involved (and the family). In contrast, the independent CPA, in case of malpractice or negligence in the audit function, is subject to potential liability that may extend to all parties (whether known to the CPA or not) that have suffered loss or failed to make a profit through reliance on financial statements "approved" by the CPA.

While a single individual may practice public accounting, usually two or more individuals organize an accounting firm in the form of a partnership (in some states incorporation is permitted). Firms vary in size from a one-person office, to regional firms, to the "big-eight" firms, which have hundreds of offices located around the world. Nearly all accounting firms render three types of services: auditing, management advisory services, and tax services.

Auditing. An important function performed by the CPA in public practice is the **audit** or **attest function.** Its purpose is to lend credibility to the financial reports; that is, to assure that they are dependable. Primarily this function involves an examination of the financial reports prepared by the management in order to assure that they are in conformance with *generally accepted accounting concepts and standards* (discussed in Part B). In carrying out this function the independent CPA examines the underlying transactions, including the collection, classification, and assembly of the financial data incorporated in the financial reports. In performing these tasks, established professional standards must be maintained and the information reported must conform to "generally accepted accounting principles" appropriate for the entity involved. Additionally, the CPA is responsible for verifying that the financial reports "fairly present" the resource inflows and outflows and the financial position of the entity. The magnitude of these responsibilities may be appreciated when it is realized that the number of transactions involved in a major enterprise such as General Motors runs into the billions each year. The CPA, of course, does not examine each one of these transactions; rather, professional approaches are used to ascertain that they were measured and reported properly.

Occasionally, the auditor may encounter attempts, for example, to increase reported profit by omitting certain expenses or to overstate financial position by omitting certain debts. There are many intentional and unintentional potentialities for preparing misleading financial reports. The audit function performed by an independent CPA is the best protection available to the public in this respect. Many investors have learned the pitfalls of making investments in enterprises that do not have their financial reports examined by an independent CPA.

Management advisory services. Many independent CPA firms also offer advisory or consulting services. These services generally are accounting based and encompass such activities as the design and installation of accounting, data processing, profit-planning and control (i.e., budget) systems; financial advice; forecasting; inventory controls; cost-effectiveness studies; and operational analyses. This facet of public practice is experiencing a rapid growth.

Tax services. CPAs in public practice usually are involved in rendering income tax services to their clients. This includes tax planning as a part of the decision-making process and also determination of the income tax liability (by means of the annual tax return). The increasing complexity of state and federal tax laws, particularly income tax laws, demands a high level of competence in this area. The CPA's involvement in **tax planning** often is quite significant. Virtually every major business decision carries with it significant tax impacts; so much so, in fact, that tax-planning considerations frequently govern the decision.

Employment by organizations

Many accountants, including CPAs and CMAs (Certified Management Accountants), are employed by profit-making and nonprofit organizations. A company or other organization, depending upon its size and complexity, may employ from one up to hundreds of accountants. In the business enterprise, the chief financial officer, usually a vice president or controller, is a member of the management team. This responsibility generally entails a wide range of management, financial, and accounting duties. Exhibit 1–2 shows a typical organizational arrangement of the **financial function** in a business enterprise. In the business entity, accountants typically are engaged in a wide variety of activities, such as general management, general accounting, cost accounting, profit planning and control (i.e., budgeting), internal auditing, and electronic data processing. A common pattern in

**EXHIBIT 1–2
Typical organization of the financial function**

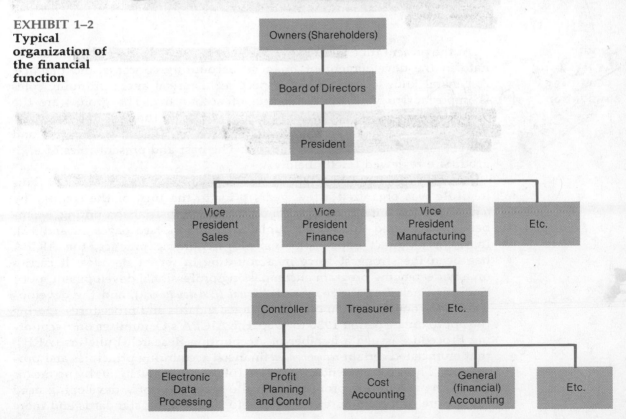

recent years has been the selection of a "financial expert" as the chief executive or president of the company. One primary function of the accountants in organizations is to provide data that are useful for managerial decision making and for controlling operations. In addition, the functions of external reporting, tax planning, control of assets, and a host of related responsibilities normally are performed by accountants in industry. The role of accountants within organizations is emphasized in *Fundamentals of Management Accounting* of this series.

Employment in the public sector

The vast and complex operations of governmental units, from the local to the international level, create a great need for accountants. Accountants employed in the public sector perform functions similar to those performed by their counterparts in private organizations. Additionally, the General Accounting Office (GAO) and the regulatory agencies, such as the Securities and Exchange Commission, Interstate Commerce Commission (ICC), Federal Power Commission (FPC), and Federal Communications Commission (FCC), utilize the services of accountants in carrying out their regulatory duties.

Finally, accountants are involved in varying capacities in the evolving programs of pollution control, health care, minority enterprises, and other socially oriented programs, whether sponsored by private industry or by government.

Groups involved in accounting innovation

At the present time, four important groups in the United States predominate in the development of financial accounting concepts and practice. A general knowledge of their respective historical and continuing roles is important to your understanding of accounting. The groups are the American Institute of Certified Public Accountants, the Financial Accounting Standards Board, the U.S. Securities and Exchange Commission, and the American Accounting Association. The past and present roles of each group are reviewed briefly below.

American Institute of Certified Public Accountants (AICPA). This institute was organized a few years prior to the turn of the century by a group of accountants engaged in public and industrial accounting. Membership is limited to certified public accountants (see pages 11 and 12). In terms of direct impact on financial accounting practice, the AICPA has been the strongest force in accounting in recent decades. It carries on a wide-ranging program encompassing professional development, publications (including the magazine *Journal of Accountancy*), and the development and communication of accounting standards and procedures. During the approximate period 1930 to 1950, the AICPA's Committee on Accounting Procedure issued a number of Accounting Research Bulletins (ARBs) that enunciated certain *recommended* financial accounting principles and procedures. These recommendations were followed by much, but by no means all, of the accounting profession. In the realization of a developing need for a more concentrated effort to develop accounting standards and more adherence to prescribed accounting guidelines, in 1959 the AICPA organized the Accounting Principles Board (APB) to replace the former committee. The APB issued 31 numbered *Opinions* during its existence from 1959 through 1973. Basically, accountants are **required** to follow the provisions of the *Opinions.* The *Opinions* dealt with many of the tough issues of financial accounting; as a consequence, many of them were highly controversial. Throughout this volume you will encounter a few references to the ARBs and numerous references to APB *Opinions.*

Financial Accounting Standards Board (FASB). This organization began operating June 1, 1973. It is appropriate to review its background. Accounting is a complex and frequently controversial professional activity. The intensity of the controversies in recent years is indicated by the fact that a wide range of interested individuals and special interest groups have committed significant amounts of resources and time in attempting to influence the setting of accounting concepts and standards. The controversy on occasion entered the political arena, which generally is viewed as an inappropriate forum in which to establish sound accounting concepts and standards. Accounting issues increasingly have been important in litigation in the courts.

As you study accounting you will realize that the economic results reported by financial accounting, such as asset valuations, profit, and earnings per share, may have impacts on the economy, on the capital markets (including the stock market), and on many major decisions of individuals, groups, and entities. You also may appreciate how the selection of a particular financial accounting approach frequently has a significant effect on the financial results reported through the accounting process (such as profit and earnings per share). In the light of these issues, the AICPA in 1972 decided to reassess the approaches to establishing financial accounting concepts and standards. As a consequence of this reassessment, the APB was discontinued, and in its place the Financial Accounting Standards Board was established and continues to function. The seven FASB members are appointed by an independent board of trustees and serve on a full-time basis. The FASB was organized to be independent. It has as its sole function the establishment and improvement of accounting concepts and standards. The accounting profession, through the FASB, intends to keep the standards-setting function in the private sector rather than to have the standards imposed by laws and governmental agencies.

Securities and Exchange Commission (SEC). This government regulatory agency operates under authority granted by the Securities Acts of 1933 and 1934. The acts gave the SEC authority to prescribe accounting guidelines for the financial reports required to be submitted by corporations that sell their securities in *interstate* commerce (i.e., registered companies). This includes most of the large, and some medium-sized, corporations. The SEC requires these corporations to submit periodic reports, which are maintained in the files of the Commission as a matter of public record. From the beginning, the SEC, as a matter of policy, generally followed the accounting concepts, standards, and procedures established by the accounting profession. The SEC published "Regulation S-X," which prescribes the special guidelines to be followed by registered companies in preparing the financial reports submitted in conformance with the Securities Acts. Throughout its existence the SEC has exerted a significant impact on accounting. Its staff has worked closely with the accounting profession on the evolution and improvement of accounting standards.

American Accounting Association (AAA). This association was organized during the World War I period by a group of college accounting professors. The Association sponsors and encourages the improvement of accounting teaching and accounting research (primarily on a theoretical plane), and publishes a magazine, *The Accounting Review.* Its committees issue reports that, coupled with the research activities of individual academicians, exert a pervasive influence on the development of accounting theory and standards.

PART B: COMMUNICATION OF ACCOUNTING INFORMATION

In this part of the chapter we will introduce the end product of an accounting system—the periodic financial statements. These statements are viewed as an important means of communication of financial information for the entity. Also this part emphasizes the purpose and nature of financial statements—not on how the various dollar amounts are derived. In Chapters 1 and 2 we introduce the basic financial statements prior to discussion of how they are derived to provide an initial overview of how the end product appears. The remaining chapters concentrate on the economic analyses, measurements, and recording of the transactions that necessarily precede financial statement preparation.

COMMUNICATION CONCEPTS AND APPROACHES

Communication consists of a flow of information from one party to one or more other parties. For communication to be effective, the recipient must understand what the sender intends to convey. In the process of communication there are numerous problems in understanding precisely the words, symbols, and sounds used by the parties involved. Accounting seeks to communicate by words and symbols financial information that is relevant to the types of decisions typically made by investors, creditors, and other interested parties. As we make decisions of varying sorts, we must rely upon certain information that often is unique to each type of decision. Often, we must make decisions without adequate information. Either the needed information is not available to us or the cost and time entailed in developing it is prohibitive when compared to its potential benefits.[6] The nature and form in which information is "packaged" and communicated sometimes affect the decision. For example, some individuals are more influenced by graphic than by quantitative presentations, others find narrative preferable to tabular expression, some prefer summaries rather than details, and still others object to technical presentations of any sort.

Financial information and the means of communicating it frequently have strong and pervasive **behavioral impacts**[7] upon decision makers. The behavioral impacts of accounting extend to both positive and negative motivations of people. The frequency, form, and quality of one's communications with others are often important to motivations.

The terminology and symbols of accounting were devised over a long period of time in the search for ways to communicate financial information effectively. As is common with other professions, such as law and medicine, the terminology and symbols of accounting are somewhat technical. Accounting has developed in direct response to the needs of people. As a consequence, it is continuously evolving new concepts, terminology, procedures, and means of communication. In the chapters to follow, one of our considerations will be the terminology of accounting.

OVERVIEW OF EXTERNAL FINANCIAL STATEMENTS

Financial statements often are classified as (1) internal (i.e., management accounting) statements and (2) external (i.e., financial accounting) statements. Internal financial statements are not distributed to parties outside the entity. Since they are used exclusively by, and are prepared under the direction of, the **managers** of the entity, they are prepared to meet specific internal policies and guidelines established by those managers.

In contrast, external financial statements are distributed to parties outside the entity (which include shareholders). External parties are unable to specify preparation guidelines for the statements. Therefore, the entity is required to conform to specific and well-known **generally accepted accounting principles** (often referred to as GAAP) which are developed by the accounting profession.

This textbook discusses the development of external financial reports.

---

[6] This suggests the concept of *benefit-cost analysis;* that is, a comparison of the cost of a particular course of action, compared with the economic benefits or advantages derived from that course of action.

[7] A behavioral impact is an individual's response to external forces. An individual may be motivated toward or away from certain courses of action by information or observations that come to his attention. For example, one may be motivated to purchase a large automobile rather than a small one for reasons of prestige. However, a financial report showing the relative costs of operating the two automobiles may motivate the individual to purchase the small automobile. Thus, the report exerts a significant behavioral impact on the decision maker.

The next several pages present an **overview** of the external financial statements required by GAAP.

A primary objective of the accounting process is the development of financial statements that communicate relevant information to decision makers. An understanding of financial statements at the outset places you in an excellent position to interpret them and to understand how the accounting process operates. The three primary financial statements for a profit-making entity for **external reporting** to owners, potential investors, creditors, and other decision makers are the—

1. Income statement (more descriptively, statement of revenues, expenses, and income).
2. Balance sheet (more descriptively, statement of assets, liabilities, and owners' equity).
3. Statement of changes in financial position (more descriptively, statement of working capital, or cash inflows and outflows; abbreviated SCFP).

These three statements summarize the financial activities of the business entity for each specific period of time. They can be produced at any time (such as end of the year, quarter, or month) and can apply to any time span (such as ten years, one year, one quarter, or one month). The heading of each statement contains a very specific statement of the **time dimensions** of the report. Although these three statements directly relate to each other, for convenience, at this point in your study, they will be considered separately. First, we will illustrate them for a simple business situation; the next chapter discusses and illustrates a more complex situation.

The income statement

The income statement is designed to report the profit performance of a business entity for a specific period of time, such as a year, quarter, or month. Profit, or net income, represents the difference between revenues and expenses for the specified period. An income statement presents the **results of operations;** that is, it reports, for a specific period of time in accordance with the time-period assumption (e.g., "For the Year Ended December 31, 1981"), the items that comprise the total revenue and the total expense and the resulting net income (see Exhibit 2–6).

Exhibit 1–3 presents the income statement for the first year of operations of Business Aids, Incorporated, an enterprise that renders professional secretarial, reproduction, and mailing services for a fee. Business Aids was organized by three individuals as a corporation. Each owner (who is called a shareholder or stockholder) received 1,000 shares of capital stock as evidence of ownership. The heading of the statement specifically identifies the name of the entity, the title of the report, and the period of time over which the reported net income was earned. Note that the date encompasses a period of time—in this case, one year. There are three major captions: *revenues, expenses,* and *net income.* The detail presented under each caption is intended to be sufficient to meet the needs of decision makers interested in Business Aids, Incorporated. This latter point is signif-

EXHIBIT 1–3

BUSINESS AIDS, INCORPORATED
Income Statement
For the Year Ended December 31, 1981

←Name of entity
←Title of report } HEADING
←Time

Revenues:		
Stenographic revenue	$30,000	
Printing revenue	20,000	
Mailing revenue	13,000	
Total revenues		$63,000
Expenses:		
Salary expense	30,750	
Payroll tax expense	1,100	
Rent expense for office space	2,400	
Rental payments for copiers	6,600	
Utilities expense	400	
Advertising expense	960	
Supplies expense	90	
Interest expense	100	
Depreciation expense on office equipment	600	
Total expenses (excluding income tax)		43,000
Pretax income		20,000
Income tax expense ($20,000 × 17%)		3,400
Net income		$16,600
Earnings per share (EPS) ($16,600 ÷ 3,000 shares)		$5.53

icant because the composition and the detail of a financial statement vary, depending on the characteristics of the business entity and the needs of the users.

Revenues. Revenues are the measure of goods sold or services rendered by the entity to others for which the entity will receive (or has received) cash or something else of value. When a business sells goods or renders services, if not on credit, it receives cash immediately. If on credit, it receives an **account receivable** which is collected in cash later. In either case, the business recognizes revenue for the period as the sum of the cash and credit sales and services rendered. Thus, revenue is measured in dollars as the bargained cash-equivalent price agreed on by the two parties to the transaction.[8] Various terms are used in financial statements to describe revenue, such as sales revenue, service revenue, rental revenue, and interest revenue. Revenues are discussed in more detail in Chapter 4.

Expenses. Expenses are the measure of resources used up or values lost by the entity during a period of time for which cash or other compensation was given (or will be given) to earn revenues. Expenses may require the immediate payment of cash or, in the case of credit, the payment of cash some time after the expense is incurred. In some cases cash is paid *before* the expense is incurred, as in the case of the payment of office rent

---

[8] Revenue sometimes is called "income," such as rent income, interest income, and royalty income, but this practice leads to confusion. *Income always should refer to the difference between revenue and expense.*

in *advance of occupancy.* For accounting purposes, an expense is recognized in the period in which it is incurred which is not necessarily the same as the period in which the cash is paid. **The period in which an expense is deemed to be incurred[9] is the period in which the goods are used or the services are received.**

An expense may represent the cost of **using** equipment or buildings that were purchased for continuing use in operating the business rather than for sale. Such items often have a high initial cost at the date of acquisition, and through use, each one is worn out (or becomes obsolete) over an extended period of time known as **useful life.** As they are used in operating the business, a portion of their cost becomes an expense. This kind of expense is known as **depreciation.** For example, on January 1, 1981, Business Aids purchased office equipment for its own use at a cost of $6,000. It was estimated that the office equipment would have a useful life of ten years. Therefore, the **depreciation expense** each year for using the equipment is measured as $6,000 ÷ 10 years = $600. The income statement for 1981 (Exhibit 1–3) reports this amount as an expense.[10] It also reports interest expense for one year on the $1,000, 10 percent note payable (i.e., $1,000 × 0.10 = $100). Since a corporation has a 17 percent income tax rate on the first $25,000 of income, Business Aids incurred income tax expense of $3,400 (i.e., $20,000 × 0.17 = $3,400). Observe that Business Aids reported both pretax and aftertax income.[11]

Net income. Net income (often called profit by nonaccountants) is the excess of total revenues over total expenses. If the total expenses exceed the total revenues, a **net loss** is reported. When revenues and expenses are equal for the period, the business is said to have operated at **breakeven.**

Earnings per share (EPS). The amount of earnings per share (EPS) is reported immediately below net income if the business is organized as a corporation. EPS is derived by dividing net income by the number of shares of common stock outstanding. Since Business Aids had 3,000 shares of stock outstanding (i.e., 1,000 shares were owned by each of the three shareholders) and a net income of $16,600, EPS was computed as $16,600 ÷ 3,000 shares = $5.53 per share for the year. Especially in recent years, EPS has been accorded an extensive amount of attention by security analysts and others. As a consequence, the accounting profes-

---

[9] Incurred, as used in this context, means that the amount involved should be accounted for (i.e., recorded in the accounting system) during the specific period.

[10] Accounting for depreciation is discussed in detail in Chapter 9.

[11] Corporations, except those that qualify under Subchapter S of the Internal Revenue Code, are required to pay income taxes as follows: 17 percent on the first $25,000 of income, 20 percent on the next $25,000, 30 percent on the next $25,000, 40 percent on the next $25,000, and 46 percent on all income in excess of $100,000. Sole proprietorships and partnerships, as business entities, and Subchapter S corporations are not subject to income taxes. In each of these situations, the owner, or owners, must report the income of the entity on their own individual income tax returns. For illustrative purposes, an average tax rate is used herein to ease the arithmetic.

sion has come to accept it as an important information input for investors. Specific accounting guidelines were prescribed in the APB in *Opinion No. 15* for computing and reporting EPS.

Some people view the income statement as the most important of the three required financial statements because it is designed to report the amount of net income and the details of how that amount was earned. They view the earning of income as the most important factor in a business. **The accounting model** for the income statement is:

$$\text{Revenues} - \text{Expenses} = \text{Net income (i.e., R} - \text{E} = \text{NI)}$$

The amount of net income for the period represents a net increase in resources (or a net decrease if a loss) that flowed into the business entity during that period.

The balance sheet

The purpose of the balance sheet is to report the **financial position** of a business at a particular **point** in time. Financial position refers to the amount of resources (i.e., assets) and the liabilities (i.e., debts) of the business on a specific date. As a consequence, this statement frequently is called the statement of financial position. A more descriptive title would be the statement of assets, liabilities, and owners' equity, since these are the three major captions on the statement.[12]

Exhibit 1–4 presents the balance sheet at the end of the first year of operations for Business Aids, Incorporated. Observe that the heading specifically identifies the name of the entity, the title of the report, and the specific date of the statement. Note the specific point in time—in this case, December 31, 1981—is stated clearly on the balance sheet. This contrasts with the dating on the income statement, which indicates a period of time (such as one year). After the statement heading, the **assets** are listed on the left and the **liabilities** and **owners' equity** on the right.[13] The result is that the two sides "balance" because the **accounting model for the balance sheet is:**

$$\text{Assets} = \text{Liabilities} + \text{Owners' equity (i.e., A} = \text{L} + \text{OE)}$$

As is the case with any equation, its elements may be transposed. For example, the model frequently is expressed to reflect the fact that owners' equity is a residual (i.e., the difference between the assets and liabilities of the entity), viz:

$$\text{Assets} - \text{Liabilities} = \text{Owners' equity (i.e., A} - \text{L} = \text{OE)}$$

---

[12] The designation "balance sheet" is unfortunate since it is not descriptive in any sense. It implies that the central fact is that it balances arithmetically, although this actually is an incidental feature. Because of the widespread use of the term, it will be used in this book.

[13] Owners' equity for a corporation generally is called shareholders' or stockholders' equity. Alternative formats for the balance sheet are discussed later.

EXHIBIT 1–4

BUSINESS AIDS, INCORPORATED
Balance Sheet
At December 31, 1981

Assets			Liabilities		
Cash		$13,600	Accounts payable		$ 900
Accounts receivable		13,000	Income taxes payable		500
Land		20,000	Note payable, short		
Office equipment	$6,000		term, 10%		1,000
Less: Accumulated			Total liabilities		$ 2,400
depreciation	600	5,400			
			Shareholders' Equity		
			Contributed capital:		
			Capital stock (3,000 shares, par value $10 per share)		$30,000
			Contributed capital in excess of par		3,000
			Retained earnings		16,600
			Total shareholders' equity		49,600
Total assets		$52,000	Total liabilities and shareholders' equity		$52,000

The accounting model is a basic building block in the total accounting process.[14] Next we will define and discuss each of the three variables in this model.

Assets. Fundamentally, assets are the resources owned by the entity. They may be tangible (physical in character) such as land, buildings, and machinery, or intangible (characterized by legal claims or rights) such as amounts due from customers (legal claims called accounts receivable) and patents (protected rights). In short, assets are the things of value, whether physical or not, owned by the entity.[15]

Observe in the balance sheet, given in Exhibit 1–4, that each of the assets listed has an assigned dollar amount. The **cost principle** states that assets generally should be *measured* on the basis of the *total cost incurred in their acquisition* (see Exhibit 2–6). To illustrate, the balance sheet for Business Aids reports "Land, $20,000"; this is the amount of resources that was paid for the land when it was acquired. It may well be that because of market changes, the market value of the land at December 31, 1981 (date of the balance sheet), actually was $35,000. Nevertheless, the balance sheet would report the land at its original acquisition cost. It follows that the

[14] The model also may be expressed as Assets = Equities. Equities is used to denote (1) liabilities or creditors' equity, which represent claims of creditors; and (2) owners' equity, which represents claims of the owners.

[15] Assets also include prepaid expenses and deferred charges, since these generally represent valid rights or claims for goods and services paid for in advance. These kinds of assets are considered in later chapters.

balance sheet does not necessarily show the current market value of the assets listed. This is called the **objectivity principle** (see Exhibit 2–6).

It is appropriate to inquire why accountants do not change the measurement of the assets for each subsequent balance sheet to reflect the then market value or price. This is not done because the acquisition cost is factually objective (i.e., not an estimate), whereas current market value of the assets owned by the entity would have to be estimated at the end of each year. The estimate would be very subjective since the assets are not sold each year-end.

Liabilities. Liabilities are debts or obligations owed by the entity to the creditors. They arise as a result of the purchase of goods or services from others on credit and through cash borrowings to finance the business. If a business fails to pay its creditors, the law may accord the creditors the right to force the sale of assets sufficient to meet their claims.[16]

Business entities frequently borrow money on **notes payable.** In this case, a liability known as notes payable is created. A note payable, which may be short term or long term, generally specifies a definite maturity or payment date and the rate or amount of interest charged by the lender. Also, many businesses purchase goods and services on open account that does not involve notes, thus creating a liability known as **accounts payable.** Income taxes frequently are paid, at least in part, several months after the end of the year. As a consequence, a liability to the government, **income taxes payable,** must be reported until the taxes are paid fully. You may observe in Exhibit 1–4 that Business Aids listed three liabilities and the amount of each. In respect to amounts, liabilities present few measurement problems since most liabilities are reported at the amount of the debt established by the parties to the transaction.

Owners' equity. The accounting model (page 21) shows owners' equity to be equal to the total assets minus the total liabilities of the business. Thus, the owners' equity is a **residual interest** or claim of the owners to the assets because creditor claims legally come first. Owners' equity sometimes is called net worth, capital, or proprietorship. However, the preferable designation is owner's equity for a sole proprietorship; partners' equity for a partnership; and shareholders' or stockholders' equity for a corporation. Owners' equity in a business derives from two sources: (1) **contributed capital,** which is the investment of cash or other assets in the business by the owner or owners; and (2) **retained earnings,** which is the amount of accumulated profits of the business less the losses and withdrawals. When the owners receive cash or other assets from the business through withdrawals (defined later), the total amount of owners' equity is reduced. When the business incurs a loss, owners' equity also is reduced.

In Exhibit 1–4, the shareholders' equity section reports the following:

---

[16] In case of dissolution or sale of all the assets of a business, legally the creditors must be paid first; any remainder goes to the owners.

1. **Contributed capital**—The three shareholders invested a total of $33,000 in the business and received 3,000 shares of capital stock having a par value of $10 per share (par value will be discussed in Chapter 12.) They invested $11 per share, or $1 above par value. The 3,000 shares issued are reported at their par value (3,000 × $10) as "Capital stock"; and the remainder, often called a premium (3,000 shares × $1 = $3,000), is reported as "Contributed capital in excess of par value."

2. **Retained earnings**—The accumulated amount of earnings less all losses and dividends declared or paid to shareholders since formation of the corporation is reported as "Retained earnings." During the first year the business earned $16,600, as shown on the income statement (Exhibit 1–3). This amount is reported on the balance sheet for Business Aids at this date as retained earnings since no dividends had been declared or paid to the shareholders.

3. **Total shareholders' equity** is the sum of the investment ($33,000) plus the retained earnings ($16,600) = $49,600. This amount may be verified in terms of the basic accounting model: Assets ($52,000) − Liabilities ($2,400) = Shareholders' equity ($49,600).

If, by contrast, a cash dividend of $6,000 had been declared and paid to the three shareholders, the balance sheet would have reflected cash of $7,600 ($13,600 − $6,000) and retained earnings of $10,600 ($16,600 − $6,000).

Statement of changes in financial position (SCFP)

In recent years the **financing activities** of businesses have become increasingly complex. The business entity of today requires substantial funds for operations and expansion. These funds come from three sources: (1) owner investment, (2) borrowings, and (3) by earning a profit or selling noncash assets. In recognition of the need by users of financial statements for information concerning the investing and financing activities of the business, the APB issued *Opinion No. 19* in March 1971. This *Opinion* requires a **statement of changes in financial position (SCFP)**[17] to accompany the income statement and the balance sheet.

The objective of the SCFP is to communicate to the user information about the inflows and outflows of cash (or, alternatively, working capital, defined later). Exhibit 1–5 presents a SCFP for Business Aids for a specific period of time (i.e., "For the Year Ended December 31, 1981"). At this point you need not be concerned about the derivation of the amounts. Rather, your attention is called to the two basic classifications: cash sources (inflows of cash) and cash uses (outflows of cash). The difference between them represents the increase, or decrease, in cash during the period. Since investors and creditors often think in terms of present and potential future cash flows, this statement provides an important information input to

---

[17] This statement is an outgrowth of an earlier "statement of sources and applications of fund," which was optional.

EXHIBIT 1–5

BUSINESS AIDS, INCORPORATED
Statement of Changes in Financial Position, Cash Basis
For the Year Ended December 31, 1981

Sources of cash (inflows):
From operations:
From revenues $50,000
Less: Cash used for expenses 44,400
Cash inflow from operations . . . . $ 5,600
From other sources:
Investment by owners (stock issued) 33,000
Loan—note payable 1,000
Cash generated from other sources 34,000
Total cash inflow during the year 39,600

Uses of cash (outflows):
To purchase office equipment 6,000
To purchase land 20,000
Total cash used during the year (outflows) 26,000
Change—increase in cash during the year $13,600

the decision-making process. The accounting model for this statement is:

$$\text{Cash inflows} - \text{Cash outflows} = \text{Net change in cash}$$
$$(\text{i.e., CI} - \text{CO} = \text{NC})$$

The statement, rather than being prepared on a cash basis, often is prepared on a working capital basis (discussed later).

The SCFP is derived from an analysis of the balance sheet and the income statement. For example, total revenue reported on Exhibit 1–3 (the income statement) of $63,000, less $13,000 of the revenue (mailing) extended on credit, equals $50,000, reported as the cash inflow from revenue on Exhibit 1–5. Similarly, total expenses of $46,400 (including income tax expense), shown on Exhibit 1–3, less the **noncash expenses** of $600 for depreciation, $900 for accounts payable, and $500 for income taxes payable, equals the $44,400 reported on Exhibit 1–5 as the cash used for expenses. Thus, the net income earned of $16,600 caused a cash inflow of $5,600. Additional shares of capital stock were sold that generated a cash inflow of $33,000, and a loan was obtained to secure another $1,000, giving a total cash inflow during the year of $39,600. During the year, $26,000 cash was expended for office equipment and land. Consequently, the statement reports that $13,600 more cash was received than was spent during the year.

A detailed discussion of the SCFP is deferred to Chapter 15 because its preparation requires special procedures that are best understood after your knowledge of accounting is substantial.

DEMONSTRATION CASE

At the end of each chapter one or more demonstration cases will be presented which provide an overview of the primary issues discussed.

Each case presented is followed by a recommended solution. The case should be read carefully; then you should try to prepare **your solution** prior to studying the recommended solution. This form of self-study is recommended highly.

The introductory case presented below is to start you thinking, in monetary terms, of some of the resource inflows and outflows of a business. It deals with reporting certain accounting information for the first year of a business entity that was organized by three individuals. See what you can do with the case before studying the recommended solution. (Hint: It will test your comprehension of Part B of the chapter and also your analytical competence.)

ABC Service Corporation

ABC Service Corporation was organized by three investors (Able, Baker, and Cain) on January 1, 1981. On that date as start-up cash, each investor bought 1,000 shares of the corporation's capital stock (par value $10 per share) and paid $12 per share. On the same day the corporation borrowed $10,000 from a local bank and signed a three-year note payable at 10 percent interest payable each December 31. On January 1, 1981, the corporation purchased two specially designed service trucks for $20,000 cash. Operations were started immediately.

At the end of 1981 the corporation had completed the following transactions (summarized):

REVENUES
a. Performed services and billed customers for $100,000, of which $94,000 was collected in cash by year-end.
b. Paid $55,000 cash for expenses (including the annual interest on the note owed to the local bank).
c. Paid $7,000 cash to the Internal Revenue Service for income taxes, and at the end of the year still owed the IRS $1,000 (the average tax rate is 20 percent).
d. Depreciated the two service trucks on the basis of a four-year useful life (disregard any residual or salvage value).

Required:

Complete the following two financial statements for 1981 by entering the correct amounts (show computations in the space provided):

Pretax income   Revenues
     ↓   − expenses
Before tax is paid

accumulative
NI = RETAINED EARNINGS − dividends

ABC Service Corporation
Income Statement

Date _Jan. 1, 1981 – Dec. 31, 1981_

Revenues:　　　　　　　　　　　　　　　　　　　　　　　Computations
　Service revenues . . . . $ _100,000_

goods sold, services rendered →

Expenses:
　Various expenses . . . . _55,000 - 1,000　54,000_
　Interest expense _10,000 × 10%_ _1,000_
　Depreciation expense _20,000 ÷ 4 yrs_ _5,000_
　　Total expenses . . . . $ _60,000_
Pretax income . . . _100,000 - 60,000_ _40,000_
　Income tax expense _7,000 + 1,000_ _8,000_
Net income . . . _40,000 - 8,000_ $ _32,000_
　Earnings per share . _32,000 ÷ 3,000_ $ _10.67_

ABC Service Corporation
Balance Sheet

Date _At Dec. 1, 1981_

Assets:
　Cash . . . . $ _58,000_
　Accounts receivable . . . . _6,000_ _100,000 - 94,000_
　Service trucks . . . . $ _20,000_
　　Less: Accumulated depreciation _5,000_ _15,000_ _20,000 ÷ 4 yrs_
Total assets . . . . $ _79,000_

Cash
12.00 × 3,000 =
36,000 - 20,000 =
16,000 + 94,000 =
110,000 + 10,000 =
120,000 - 55,000 =
65,000 - 7,000 =
58,000

Liabilities:
　Note payable . . . . $ _19,000_ 　BANK
　Income taxes payable . . . . _1,000_ 　owe IRS
　　Total liabilities . . . . $ _11,000_

Stockholders' Equity:
　Capital stock, par $ _10.00_ ;
　　shares _1,000 × 3 (3,000)_ _30,000_
　Contributed capital in excess
　　of par value _6,000_ 　$12 - $10 = $2, × $3000's
　Retained earnings . . . . _32,000_
　　Total stockholders' equity . . . . _68,000_
　　Total liabilities and
　　　stockholders' equity . . . . $ _79,000_

Suggested Solution:

ABC Service Corporation
Income Statement

Date *For the Year Ended December 31, 1981*

Revenues: Computations
  Service revenues .... $ 100,000   *Given*

Expenses:
  Various expenses .... $ 54,000   *Given*
  Interest expense ....   1,000 $10,000 x 10%
  Depreciation expense ....   5,000 $20,000 ÷ 4 years
    Total expenses .... $ 60,000
Pretax income   40,000
  Income tax expense ....   8,000 $40,000 x 20%
Net income .... $ 32,000
  Earnings per share .... $ 10.67 $32,000 ÷ 3,000 shares

ABC Service Corporation
Balance Sheet

Date _At December 31, 1981_

Assets: $36,000 + $10,000 + $94,000
  Cash .... $ 58,000   − $55,000 − $7,000 − $20,000
  Accounts receivable ....   6,000 $100,000 − $94,000
  Service trucks .... $ 20,000   *Given, cost of trucks*
    Less: Accumulated depreciation   5,000   15,000 $20,000 ÷ 4 years = $5,000
Total assets .... $ 79,000

Liabilities:
  Note payable .... $ 10,000   *Given, bank loan*
  Income taxes payable   1,000   *Given, amount unpaid*
    Total liabilities .... $ 11,000

Stockholders' Equity:
  Capital stock, par $ 10 ;
    shares 3,000   30,000   3,000 x $10
  Contributed capital in excess
    of par value   6,000   3,000 x ($12 − $10)
  Retained earnings   32,000   *From income statement* *
    Total stockholders' equity   68,000
    Total liabilities and
      stockholders' equity .... $ 79,000

* *Beginning RE ($ -0-) + Net income ($32,000) − Dividends ($ -0-) = Ending RE ($32,000).*

SUMMARY

Accounting interfaces with practically all aspects of the environment: social, economic, and political. Any open society is a complex one that is characterized by organizations—businesses, political parties, governmental entities, churches, social institutions, and private groups and associations. Each organization, whether local or international in scope, is an accounting entity. The essence of accounting is the measurement and reporting of financial information for an accounting entity. The measurement and reporting of the inflows and outflows of scarce resources and the financial position of each accounting entity is essential to (1) effective management of each such organization and (2) the understanding and evaluation of it by interested outside parties. Measurement of the financial characteristics of each such organization is essential because each of us is an important decision maker, both in respect to each one's economic interests and as a concerned citizen in the broader sense. Our decision-making potential is enhanced if we understand the financial impacts of alternative solutions to particular problems.

Part B of the chapter explained and illustrated the basic features of the three required **external** financial reports—the income statement, the balance sheet, and the statement of changes in financial position.

The income statement, as a statement of operations, reports revenues, expenses, and the net income for a stated **period** of time. Earnings per share (EPS), which expresses the relationship between net income and the number of shares of common stock outstanding, was illustrated.

The balance sheet, as a statement of financial position, reports dollar amounts for the assets, liabilities, and owners' equity at a specific **point** in time.

The statement of changes in financial position (SCFP), as a statement of the inflows and outflows of funds, reports those flows for a specific **period** of time.

The fundamental accounting model, **Assets = Liabilities + Owners' equity,** was introduced as the foundation for the balance sheet and the accounting process in general. The financial statements for a small company were illustrated. In the next chapter we will move one step forward and look at a more complex situation and, at the same time, add more concepts to your knowledge about the characteristics of the financial statements for a business entity.

IMPORTANT TERMS DEFINED IN THE CHAPTER (with page citations)

Financial (external) accounting— 1, 18
Management (internal) accounting—1, 17
Exchange transactions—3

Unit-of-measure assumption—5
Sole proprietorship—5
Partnership—5
Corporation—5
Accounting entity—6

QUESTIONS FOR DISCUSSION

Part A

1. What is meant by an accounting entity? Why is a business treated as a separate entity for accounting purposes?

2. Briefly distinguish among a sole proprietorship, a partnership, and a corporation.

3. What is the primary purpose of accounting, regardless of the type of entity?

4. Explain your general concept of the decision-making process. Refer to Exhibit 1–1.

5. Explain what is meant by the designation CPA.

6. Distinguish, in general terms, among the practice of public accounting and employment as an accountant in private organizations and in the public sector.

7. The independent CPA firm normally renders three services: auditing, management advisory, and tax. Briefly explain each.

8. In general, what are the duties of a controller in a business?

9. Explain the unit-of-measure assumption.

10. Explain the separate-entity assumption.

Questions
Part B

11. Financial statements are the end products of the accounting process. Explain.

12. Generally, how would you define communication?

13. The accounting process generates financial reports for both "internal" and "external" audiences. Identify some of the groups in each audience.

14. Complete the following:

Name of statement	A more descriptive name
a. Income statement	a. _____
b. Balance sheet	b. _____
c. Statement of changes in financial position (SCFP)	c. _____

15. What information should be included in the heading of each of the three required financial statements?

16. Explain why the income statement and the SCFP are dated "For the Year Ended December 31, 19XX," whereas the balance sheet is dated "At December 31, 19XX."

17. Define revenue.

18. Define expense.

19. Briefly define the following: net income, net loss, and breakeven.

20. What are the purposes of (a) the income statement, (b) the balance sheet, and (c) the SCFP?

21. Explain the accounting model for the income statement. What are the three major items reported on the income statement?

22. Explain the accounting model for the balance sheet. Define the three major components reported on the balance sheet.

23. Explain the accounting model for the SCFP. Explain the three major components reported on the statement.

24. Why is owners' equity referred to frequently as a residual interest?

25. What are the two primary sources of owners' equity in a business?

26. What are appropriate titles for owners' equity for (a) a sole proprietorship, (b) a partnership, and (c) a corporation?

EXERCISES

Part A

E1–1. Given below is a list of important abbreviations used in Part A of the chapter. These abbreviations also are used widely in business. For each abbreviation give the full designation. The first one is used as an example.

Abbreviation	Full designation
1. CPA	Certified Public Accountant
2. APB	
3. GAO	
4. AAA	
5. FPC	

6. CMA	
7. AICPA	
8. SEC	
9. FASB	
10. ICC	

E1–2. Review the chapter explanations of the income statement model and the balance sheet model. Apply these models in each independent case below to compute the two missing amounts for each case. Assume it is the end of 19A, the first full year of operations for the company.

(Relates to Exercise 1–2)

Independent Cases	Total Revenues	Total Assets	Total Expenses	Total Liabilities	Net Income (Loss)	Stockholders' Equity
A	$100,000	$150,000	$88,000	$90,000	$	$
B		110,000	60,000		9,000	70,000
C	80,000	92,000	88,000	25,000		
D	65,000			40,000	10,000	75,000
E			82,000	73,000	(6,000)	87,000

$$R - E = NI$$
$$A = L + OE$$
$$A - L = OE$$

Exercises
Part B

E1–3. Assume you are the owner of "The College Shop," which specializes in items of special interest to college students. At the end of January 19A you find that (for January only):

a. Sales, per the cash register tapes, totaled $70,000, plus one sale on credit (a special case) of $300.

b. With the help of a friend (who had majored in accounting) you determined that the goods sold during January had cost you $33,000 when they were purchased.

c. During the month, according to the checkbook, you paid $32,000 for salaries, utilities, supplies, advertising, and other expenses; however, you have not yet paid the $500 monthly rent on the store (including the fixtures).

On the basis of the data given, what was the amount of income for January (disregard income taxes)? Show computations. (Hint: A convenient form to use would have the following major side captions: revenue from sales, expenses, and difference—income before income taxes.)

E1–4. Dow Company, Inc., a small service organization, prepared the following report for the month of January 19A:

Required:

a. You have been asked by the owner (who knows very little about the financial side of business) to compute the "amount of cash that was generated in January by operations."

You decided to prepare a report for the owner with the following major side captions: cash inflows (collections), cash outflows (payments), and difference— net increase (or decrease) in cash. (Hint: There was a cash decrease; that is, a negative net cash flow.)

b. See if you can reconcile the "difference—net increase (or decrease) in cash" you computed in (a) with the income for January 19A.

E1–5. Duke Corporation was organized by five individuals on January 1, 19A. At the end of 19A, the following financial data are available:

Total revenues	$40,000
Total expenses (excluding income taxes)	30,000
Cash balance	12,000
Receivables from customers (all considered collectible)	6,000
Merchandise inventory (by inventory count at cost)	25,000
Payables to suppliers for merchandise purchased from them (will be paid during January 19B)	7,000

Assume a 17 percent tax rate on the income of this corporation; the income taxes will be paid during the first quarter of 19B.

(Relates to Exercise 1–4)

Services, Expenses, and Income

Services:		
Cash services (per cash register tape)	$35,000	
Credit services (per charge bills; not yet collected by end of January)	25,000	$60,000 ✓
Expenses:		
Salaries and wages (paid by check)	28,000	
Salary for January not yet paid	800	
Supplies (taken from stock, purchased for cash in December)	2,000	
Estimated cost of wear and tear on used delivery truck for the month (depreciation)	100	
Other expenses (paid by check)	8,100	39,000
Difference—pretax income		21,000
Estimated income taxes (to be paid next quarter)		4,000
Income for January		$17,000

Required:

Complete the following two statements for Duke Corporation:

DUKE CORPORATION
Income Statement
For the Month of January 19A

Total revenues	$_____
Less: Total expenses (excluding income tax) .	_____
Pretax income	_____
Less: Income tax expense	_____
Net income	$_____

DUKE CORPORATION
Balance Sheet
At January 31, 19A

Assets:
Cash	$_____
Receivables from customers	_____
Merchandise inventory ..	_____
Total assets	$_____

Liabilities:
Payables to suppliers	$_____
Income taxes payable	_____
Total liabilities	_____
Total stockholders' equity	_____
Total liabilities and stockholder's equity	$ 43,000

E1–6. Kyle Realty, Incorporated, has been operating for five years and is owned by three investors. S. T. Kyle owns 60 percent of the outstanding stock of 9,000 shares and is the managing executive in charge. On December 31, 19C, the following financial items for the entire year were determined: commissions earned and collected in cash, $150,000, plus $20,000 uncollected; rental service fees earned and collected, $20,000; salaries expense paid, $60,000; commissions expense paid, $45,000; payroll taxes paid, $4,000; rent paid, $2,200 (not including December rent yet to be paid); utilities expense paid, $700; promotion and advertising paid, $6,400; and miscellaneous expenses paid, $300. There were no other unpaid expenses at December 31. Kyle Realty rents office space for its own use but owns the furniture therein. The furniture cost $5,000 when acquired and has an estimated life of ten years. The average corporate income tax rate is 30 percent. Also, during the year, the company paid the owners "out of profit" cash dividends amounting to $10,000. You have been requested to complete the following income statement:

(Relates to Exercise 1–6)

Revenues:		
Commissions earned	$_____	
Rental service fees	_____	
Total revenues		$_____
Expenses:		
Salaries expense	_____	
Commission expense	_____	
Payroll tax expense	_____	
Rent expense	_____	
Utilities expense	_____	
Promotion and advertising	_____	
Miscellaneous expenses	_____	
Depreciation expense	_____	
Total expenses (excluding income taxes)		_____
Pretax income		_____
Income tax expense		_____
Net income		$ 49,490
Earnings per share (EPS)		$_____

Page 34

E1–7. The University Bookstore was organized as a corporation by Jane Nash and Roy Opel; each contributed $35,000 cash to start the business and each received 3,000 shares of common stock, par $10 per share. The store completed its first year of operations on December 31, 19A. On that date the following financial items for the entire year were determined: cash on hand and in the bank, $42,000; due from customers from sales of books, $6,100; store and office equipment, purchased January 1, 19A, for $40,000 (estimated useful life ten years); amounts owed to publishers for books purchased, $6,000; and a note payable, 10 percent, one year, dated July 1, 19A, to a local bank for $2,000. No dividends were declared or paid to the stockholders during the year.

Required:

a. You have been asked to complete the balance sheet at the end of 19A shown below.
b. What was the amount of net income for the year? $_____
c. Explain how the $100 liability for interest payable was computed. Why is it shown as a liability on this date?

E1–8. Rice Manufacturing Corporation is preparing the annual financial report for shareholders. A SCFP, cash basis, must be prepared. The following data on cash flows were developed for the entire year ended December 31, 19D; cash inflow from operating revenues, $270,000; cash expended for operating expenses, $190,000; sale of unissued Rice stock for cash, $30,000; cash dividends paid to shareholders during the year, $20,000; and payments on long-term notes payable, $40,000. During the year, three used machines were sold for $10,000 cash and $41,000 cash was expended for two new machines. The machines are used in the factory.

Required:

Prepare a SCFP, cash basis, for 19D. Follow the format illustrated in the chapter.

E1–9. On June 1, 1981, Rand Corporation prepared a balance sheet just prior to going out of business. The balance sheet totals reflected the following:

Assets (no cash)	$100,000
Liabilities	60,000
Stockholders' equity	40,000

(Relates to Exercise 1–7)

Assets		Liabilities	
Cash	$____	Accounts payable	$____
Accounts receivable	____	Notes payable	____
Store and office		Interest payable	100
equipment	$____	Total	
Less: Accumulated depreciation	____	liabilities	$____
		Stockholders' Equity	
		Common stock	____
		Contributed capital in excess of par	____
		Retained earnings	6,000
		Total stockholders' equity	____
		Total liabilities and stockholders' equity	$____
Total assets	$____		

Shortly thereafter, all of the assets were sold for cash.

Required:

a. How would the balance sheet appear immediately after the sale of the assets for cash for each separate case?

b. How should the cash be distributed in each separate case? (Hint: Creditors have a priority claim over owners upon dissolution.)

	To creditors	To stockholders	Total
Case A ...	$_____	$_____	$_____
Case B ...	_____	_____	_____
Case C ...	_____	_____	_____

(Relates to Exercise 1–9)

	Cash received for the assets	Balances immediately after sale		
		Assets	Liabilities	Stockholders' equity
Case A	$110,000	$_____	$_____	$_____
Case B	100,000	_____	_____	_____
Case C	90,000	_____	_____	_____

PROBLEMS

Part A:

P1–1. On January 1, 1981, three individuals organized TRI Service Company. Each individual invested $5,000 cash in the business. On December 31, 1981, they prepared a list of resources (assets) owned and a list of the debts (liabilities) to support a company loan request of $50,000 to a local bank. None of the three investors had studied accounting. The two lists prepared were as follows:

Company resources:

Cash	$ 3,000
Services supplies inventory (on hand)	5,000
Service trucks (four practically new)	60,000
Personal residences of organizers (three houses)	190,000
Service equipment used in the business (practically new)	24,000
Bills due from customers (for services already completed)	18,000
Total	$300,000

not a asset (handwritten annotation)

Debts of the company:

Unpaid wages to employees	$ 17,000
Unpaid taxes	6,000
Owed to suppliers	4,000
Owed on service trucks and equipment (to finance company)	41,000
Loan from Organizer T	12,000
Total	$ 80,000

Required:

a. If you were advising the local bank with respect to the two lists, what issues would you raise for consideration? Explain the basis for each question and include any recommendations that you have.

b. In view of your response to *(a)*, what do you think the amount of *net resources* (i.e., assets minus liabilities) of the company would be? Show your computations.

Problems
Part B

P1–2. Riser Company was organized as a corporation on January 1, 19A. At the end of 19A the company had not yet employed an accountant. However, an employee who was "good with numbers" prepared the following statements at that date:

plumber's helper for a large local plumbing company. After three years of hard work, Jack received a plumber's license, whereupon he decided to go into business for himself. He had saved $5,000 which he decided to invest in the business. His first

(Relates to Problem 1–2)

RISER COMPANY
December 31, 19A

Income from sales of merchandise	$180,000
Total amount paid for goods sold during 19A	(95,000)
Selling costs	(30,000)
Depreciation (on service vehicles used)	(15,000)
Income from services rendered	50,000
Salaries and wages paid	(60,000)
Income taxes (at tax rate of 17%)	(5,100)
Profit for the year 19A	$ 24,900

RISER COMPANY
December 31, 19A

Resources:		
Cash		$ 31,000
Merchandise inventory (held for resale)		44,000
Service vehicles		45,000
Retained earnings (profit earned in 19A)		24,900
Grand total		$144,900
Debts:		
Payables to suppliers		$ 15,000
Note owed to bank		20,000
Due from customers		12,900
Total		47,900
Residual:		
Supplies on hand (to be used in rendering services)	$12,000	
Depreciation (on service vehicles)	15,000	
Capital stock	70,000	
Total		97,000
Grand total		$144,900

Required:

The above statements have some items that are under the wrong caption, and the statement headings are incomplete. Prepare a correct income statement and balance sheet. (Hint: All figures [except totals] are correct; the balance sheet total should be $129,900.)

P1–3. Upon graduation from high school, Jack Kane immediately accepted a job as a

step was to transfer this amount from his savings account to a business bank account for "Kane Plumbing Company, Incorporated." His lawyer had advised him to start as a corporation. He then purchased, with cash, a used panel truck for $1,500 and tools for $800; rented space in a small building; inserted an ad in the local paper; and opened the doors on October 1, 19A. Immediately, Jack found himself very busy and, after one month, employed a helper. Although he knew practically nothing about the financial side of the business, Jack realized from his experience that a number of reports were required and that costs and collections had to be controlled carefully. Accordingly, at the end of the year, prompted in part by concern about his income tax situation (previously he only had to report salary), he recognized the need for financial statements. His wife, Jane, undertook "to develop some financial statements for the business." With the help of a friend, on December 31, 19A, she gathered the following data for the three months just ended: Deposits in the bank account of collections for plumbing services totaled $14,600. The following checks were written: plumber's helper, $1,000; payroll taxes paid, $65; supplies purchased and used on jobs, $6,000; oil, gas, and maintenance on truck, $715; insurance, $150; rent, $300; utilities and telephone, $150; and miscellaneous expenses, $400 (including advertising). In addition, there were uncollected bills to customers for plumbing services amounting to $1,400, and the rent for December amounting to $100 had not been paid. The income tax rate on this corporation may be assumed to be 17 percent. Also assume that the "wear and tear on the truck and tools due to use during the three months" was estimated by Jack to be $120.

Required:

a. Prepare an income statement for Kane Plumbing for the three months October–December 19A. Use the following main captions: revenues from services, expenses, pretax income, and net income. (Hint: Expenses, excluding income taxes, totaled $9,000.)
b. Do you visualize that Jack may have a need for one or more additional financial reports for 19A and thereafter? Explain.

P1–4. During the summer, between her junior and senior years, Mandy Walker was faced with the need to earn sufficient funds for the coming academic year. Unable to obtain a job with reasonable remuneration, she decided to try the lawn-care business for three months. After a survey of the market potential, Mandy acquired a used pickup truck on June 1 for $1,000. On each door she painted "Mandy's Lawn Service, Ph. XX." Additionally, she spent $500 for mowers, trimmers, and tools. To acquire these items she borrowed $2,000 cash on a note (endorsed by a friend) at 10 percent interest annum, payable at the end of the three months (ending August 31).

At the end of the summer Mandy realized that she had "done a lot of work and her bank account looked good," which prompted her to become concerned about how much profit the business had earned.

A review of the check stubs showed the following: Deposits in the bank of collections from customers totaled $6,470. The following checks were written: gas, oil, and lubrication, $620; pickup repairs, $115; repair of mowers, $60; miscellaneous supplies used, $80; helpers, $2,500; payroll taxes, $765; payment for assistance in preparing payroll tax forms, $50; insurance, $120; telephone, $60; and $2,050 to pay off the note including interest (on August 31). A notebook kept in the pickup, plus some unpaid bills, reflected that customers still owed her $600 for lawn services rendered and that she owed $100 for gas and oil (credit card charges), and income taxes (estimated tax rate 17 percent). She estimated that the "wear and tear" for use of the truck and the other equipment for three months amounted to $150.

Required:

a. Prepare an income statement for Mandy's Lawn Service covering the three months, June, July, and August 19A. Use the following main captions: revenues from services, expenses, pretax income, and net income. (Hint: Total revenues amounted to $7,070.)
b. Do you visualize a need for one or more additional financial reports for this company for 19A and thereafter? Explain.

P1–5. Western Realty Company was organized early in 1977 as a corporation by four investors, each of whom invested $5,000 cash. The company has been moderately successful, despite the fact that internal financial controls are inadequate. Although financial reports have been prepared each year (primarily in response to income tax requirements), sound accounting practice has not been followed. As a consequence, the financial performance of the company was known only vaguely by the four shareholders. Recently, one of the shareholders, with the agreement of the others, sold his shares to a local accountant. The new shareholder was amazed when handed the report below, which was prepared by a secretary for the last meeting of the board of directors. The accountant could tell at a glance that the reported profit was wrong and quickly observed that there was no interest expense shown on a $10,000, 12 percent note payable that had been outstanding throughout the year. Also, no recognition had been given to office equipment that was purchased on January 1, 1981, at a cost of $14,000 with an estimated five-year useful life.

WESTERN REALTY
Profit Statement
December 31, 1981

Commissions earned (all collected)	$130,000
Property management revenue (exclusive of $1,200 not collected)	8,000
Total	138,000
Salaries paid	31,000
Commissions paid	38,000
Payroll taxes paid	3,300
Office supplies expense	120
Rent paid	2,400
Utilities paid	500
Advertising (excluding the December bill for advertising of $4,000 not yet paid)	28,000
Miscellaneous expenses	400
Total	103,720
Profit for the year	$ 34,280

EPS: $34,280 ÷ 10,000 shares = $3.43.

Required:

You have been asked to redraft the income statement, including corrections. Assume an average income tax rate of 20 percent. (Hint: The correct EPS is $2.20.)

P1–6. Assume you are president of Joy Retailers, Incorporated. At the end of the first year (December 31, 19A) of operations the following financial data are available for the company:

Cash	$ 16,300
Receivables from customers (all considered collectible)	15,000
Inventory of merchandise (based on physical count and priced at cost)	78,000
Equipment owned, at cost (at year-end, the estimated value to the business for future use was 90% of cost)	20,000
Note payable, one year, 12% annual interest, owed to the bank (dated July 1, 19A)	20,000
Interest on the note through December 31, 19A (due to be paid to the bank on June 30, 19B)	1,200
Salary payable for 19A (on December 31, 19A, this was owed to an employee who was away because of an emergency; will return around January 10, 19B, at which time the payment will be made)	1,100
Total sales revenue	100,000
Expenses paid, including the cost of the merchandise sold (excluding income taxes at a 17% rate; the taxes will be paid during the first quarter of 19B)	70,700
Capital stock, 1,000 shares outstanding	80,000

Required (show computations):

a. Prepare a summarized income statement for the year 19A. (Hint: EPS is $2.075.)
b. Prepare a balance sheet at December 31, 19A.

P1–7. Aztec Rental Company was organized as a corporation in January 19A by five investors. Each investor paid in $12,000 cash, and each received 2,000 shares of $5 par value stock. Immediately thereafter, the company obtained a $15,000 loan from a local bank. Rental equipment costing $52,000 was purchased for cash, and operations began. Careful records were maintained during the year. As a consequence, the following correct amounts were available at the end of December 19A:

Rental revenue:
Cash (per cash register)	$72,000
Credit—not yet collected	3,000
Repair revenue—cash	10,000
Salaries and wages paid	29,200
Payroll taxes paid	1,600
Repair parts purchased and used	700
Rent paid (for 11 months)	2,200
December rent not yet paid	200
Utilities paid	400
Advertising expenditures paid	1,400
Insurance premiums paid for 19A	100
Miscellaneous expenses paid (including annual interest)	2,000
Depreciation for the year on rental equipment	10,000
Maintenance costs paid	200
Income tax rate (average rate)	22%
Cash on hand and in bank	26,560

Rental equipment (cost)	$52,000
Land for future building site	14,000
Other assets	10,000
Rent payable (December)	200
Income taxes payable	1,500*
Notes payable, long term	15,000
Capital stock	50,000
Cash dividends paid	10,000
Accounts receivable	3,000
Accumulated depreciation	10,000
Contributed capital in excess of par	10,000
Income tax expense	?

* Part of the income taxes was paid during the year.

Required:

You have been requested to use the above data to prepare an income statement and a balance sheet at the end of 19A. (Hint: The balance sheet total is $95,560.)

P1–8. At December 31, 19A, Big J Corporation had been in operation for one year. At the date of organization, each of the ten investors paid in $10,000 cash and each received 100 shares of capital stock. Due to a need for more capital, on January 1, 19A, the corporation also borrowed $90,000, at 12 percent interest per year, on a note from a local bank. Interest on the note is payable each December 31, and the loan matures December 31, 19D. On December 31, 19A, the income statement and the balance sheet (summarized) were as follows:

(Relates to Problem 1–8)

Income Statement
For the Year Ended December 31, 19A

Total revenue	$70,000
Total expenses	44,360
Pretax income.......................	25,640
Income tax expense ($25,640 × 20%)	5,128
Net income	$20,512

(Relates to Problem 1–8)

Balance Sheet
At December 31, 19A

Assets		Liabilities	
Cash	$ 24,154	Income taxes payable	$ 1,282*
Remaining assets	187,640	Notes payable, long term	90,000
		Stockholders' Equity	
		Capital stock (1,000 shares)	100,000
		Retained earnings	20,512
		Total liabilities and	
Total assets	$211,794	owners' equity	$211,794

* Three fourths of the income taxes was paid during the year on a quarterly basis (i.e., $5,128 × 0.25 = $1,282).

An independent CPA has audited the above amounts. The CPA found that the bookkeeper had neglected to include two transactions that occurred on December 31, 19A:

1. Payment of a cash dividend of $7.50 per share to each shareholder.
2. Cash payment of interest for one year on the long-term note payable owed to the bank.

Required:

Other than for these two transactions, the amounts were correct. Recast the income statement and the balance sheet to include the effects of these two transactions. Assume a 20 percent tax rate. (Hint: The corrected balance sheet total is $193,494.)

P1–9. At the end of 19A, Foster Corporation prepared the following annual income statement and balance sheet:

(Relates to Problem 1–9)

FOSTER CORPORATION
Income Statement
For the Year Ended December 31, 19A

Revenues	$280,000
Expenses	248,000
Income before taxes	32,000
Income taxes (average rate, 30%)	9,600
Net income	$ 22,400

FOSTER CORPORATION
Balance Sheet
At December 31, 19A

Assets

Cash		$ 18,000
Accounts receivable		22,000
Inventory (by count)		76,800
Fixtures	$25,000	
Less: Accumulated depreciation	7,000	18,000
Total assets		$134,800

Liabilities

Accounts payable	$ 8,000
Income taxes payable (one half unpaid)	4,800
Notes payable, 12% (due June 30, 19B)	20,000
Total liabilities	32,800

Shareholders' Equity

Common stock, par $10, 5,000 shares	$50,000	
Contributed capital in excess of par	10,000	
Retained earnings	42,000	
Total shareholders' equity		102,000
Total liabilities and shareholders' equity		$134,800

An independent audit of the above statements and underlying records revealed the following:

1. Depreciation expense included in total expense was $2,000 for 19A; it should have been $2,500.
2. A tentative order was received from a customer on December 31, 19A, for goods having a selling price of $10,000 and was included in sales revenue and accounts receivable. The goods were on hand (and included in the ending inventory), and it is likely a sale may not materialize; the customer will decide by January 20, 19B. This should not have been recognized as a sale in 19A.

Required:

Other than these two items, the amounts were correct. Recast the two statements to take into account the depreciation error and the incorrect recognition of the tentative order. Show computations and assume an average income tax rate of 30 percent. (Hint: Revised EPS is $3.01.)

Financial reporting and the fundamental accounting concepts

PURPOSE OF THE CHAPTER

Chapter 1 introduced the primary characteristics of the income statement, balance sheet, and statement of changes in financial position. This chapter expands that discussion of **external** financial statements to include the internal classifications used on the statements. It also introduces certain fundamental accounting concepts. Thus, the fundamental purpose of this chapter is to expand your background knowledge of the end result of the accounting process. This will facilitate your study and understanding of the succeeding chapters. To accomplish this purpose the chapter is divided into two parts.

Part A: Content of financial statements for external decision makers

* Discusses and illustrates the *subclassifications* of the financial information presented on external financial statements.

Part B: Use of financial information in decision making and the fundamental concepts of accounting

* Expands the discussion in Chapter 1 of the use of financial information in decision making.
* Presents the fundamental concepts that underlie the accounting for, and reporting of, information in the financial statements.

Behavioral and learning objectives for this chapter are provided in the *Teachers Manual.*

PART A: CONTENT OF FINANCIAL STATEMENTS FOR EXTERNAL DECISION MAKERS

External decision makers (that use financial statements) are quite varied as to background, education, experience, financial interests, and problems since they include investors, creditors, employees, governmental agencies, unions, customers, and other interested parties. Financial statements are prepared to serve the diverse needs of these groups; therefore, they often are referred to as **general-purpose financial statements.**

To enhance their understandability and usefulness to the wide range of decision makers (i.e., the users), **subclassifications** of the information presented are included on the financial statements.

In this part of the chapter the discussions will include a comprehensive illustration of the financial statements of a medium-sized company. We then will present and briefly discuss a more complicated set of **actual** financial statements as they were presented by a well-known company— J. C. Penney Company, Inc.

Throughout this chapter you should concentrate on understanding the nature of the classifications and the presentation of accounting information in the financial statements rather than on how the amounts shown were derived. At this time in your study of accounting, we do not anticipate that you will absorb all aspects of the financial statements that are presented; however, primary features of each statement should be understood. You also should appreciate the importance of the end product of the accounting process—the financial statements—and be able to maintain perspective in the chapters that follow when studying the details of information processing, measurement, and reporting in terms of the accounting model. As you study the subsequent chapters, you should return frequently to this one for reference points and further study. Also, the exhibits will be helpful as a guide in solving some of the assigned problems in subsequent chapters.

CLASSIFICATION OF ITEMS ON THE FINANCIAL STATEMENTS

To assist the user of financial statements, some standardization of classifications has evolved. As a basis for discussion of these classifications, this section presents the financial statements for Diamond's, Incorporated, a large department store that has been in business for more than 40 years. When classifications are included on the statements, they sometimes are referred to as **classified financial statements.** Classified financial statements vary in terminology and arrangement from those for Business Aids given in Chapter 1. These differences reflect the fact that financial statements are tailored to the **needs of a wide range of decision makers,** depending upon the type of company and the characteristics of the industry.

The income statement

Exhibit 2–1 presents an income statement for Diamond's.[1] It follows this basic model: **Revenues — Expenses = Net income.** Therefore, Exhibit 2–1, stripped of the detailed items, shows the following subclassifications:

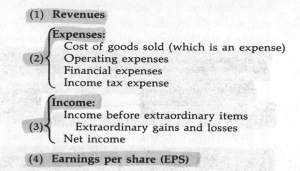

(1) **Revenues**

(2) **Expenses:**
   Cost of goods sold (which is an expense)
   Operating expenses
   Financial expenses
   Income tax expense

(3) **Income:**
   Income before extraordinary items
   Extraordinary gains and losses
   Net income

(4) **Earnings per share (EPS)**

We will discuss the meaning of each of these classifications.

Revenues. Revenues were defined in Chapter 1 (page 19). The revenue of a business that sells services is called **service revenue.** The revenue of a business that sells products or merchandise is called **sales revenue.** Merchandise sold and later returned by the customer represents **returned sales** and reduces revenue. Similarly, allowances granted to customers, say for a defect in the goods purchased from the store, reduce revenue. Such returns and allowances are **contra revenues** rather than expenses. Therefore, **gross sales** for the period must be reduced by these two amounts to derive the correct net revenue amount, or **net sales,** for the period. Observe the manner of reporting sales revenue in Exhibit 2–1.

Expenses. Expenses were defined in Chapter 1 (page 19). An income statement may be designed to reflect several classifications of expenses. These classifications tend to vary, depending upon the type of business. For a merchandising business, which is one that sells goods manufactured by others, the usual classifications of expenses are as follows:

1. Cost of goods sold. This expense reflects the amount that was incurred for the merchandise (or goods) sold during the period. For example, Diamond's sold goods during the period, at selling price, amounting to $3,-615,000 net. This merchandise, when purchased by Diamond's, cost $2,416,000 as reflected in Exhibit 2–1. The difference between these two amounts is known as the **gross margin on sales** (formerly called gross

---

[1] The income statement discussed and illustrated in this section sometimes is referred to as a *multiple-step* income statement since it shows several groupings of data and after each group (or step) shows a difference. Each such difference is appropriately labeled, such as gross margin on sales. In contrast, a single-step income statement would be similar to that illustrated in Chapter 1, Exhibit 1–3, since only two major categories (revenues and expenses) were shown and there were no "step" differences. Many published income statements follow the single-step format. The classifications illustrated for Diamond's are used frequently; however, they are not mandatory.

EXHIBIT 2–1

DIAMOND'S, INCORPORATED
Income Statement
For the Year Ended December 31, 1981

(1) **Rev.**	Gross sales revenue	$3,620,000	
	Less: Sales returns and allowances	5,000	
	Net sales revenue		$3,615,000
	Less: Cost of goods sold		2,416,000
	Gross margin on sales		1,199,000

Operating expenses:
Selling (distribution) expenses:

	Sales salaries	$399,000	
	Advertising and promotion	200,000	
	Depreciation, store equipment	15,000	
	Insurance	18,000	
	Taxes (excluding income tax expense) .	13,200	
	Warranty expense	3,000	
	Amortization of trademarks	2,000	
	Miscellaneous	9,800	
	Total selling expenses	660,000	

(2) **Exp.**
General and administrative expenses:

	Administrative salaries	170,000	
	Rent expense	9,000	
	Office supplies used	8,100	
	Estimated losses on doubtful accounts .	3,600	
	Depreciation, office equipment	1,000	
	Insurance	2,000	
	Taxes (excluding income tax expense) .	400	
	Miscellaneous	1,900	
	Total general and administrative expenses	196,000	
	Total operating expenses		856,000
	Income from operations		343,000

Financial expenses and financial revenues:

	Interest expense	56,000	
	Revenue from investments and funds	13,000	
	Net financial expense		43,000
	Pretax income		300,000
	Income tax on operations		138,000
	Income before extraordinary items		162,000

(3) **Inc.**
Extraordinary items:

	Gain on sale of land held for appreciation*	51,000	
	Less: Income tax on the gain	13,000	38,000
	Net income		$ 200,000

(4) **EPS**
Earnings per share (EPS) of common stock:

	Income before extraordinary items		$ 9.13
	Extraordinary items		2.54
	Net income		$11.67

* We have assumed that this transaction met the two criteria for an extraordinary item. The land was sold for $56,000 less it's very low cost of $5,000, resulting in a pretax gain of $51,000.

profit on sales). For Diamond's, the gross margin was $1,199,000. The gross margin indicates the markup on all of the goods sold during the period. To illustrate, the average markup *on cost* for Diamond's was $1,199,000 ÷ $2,416,000 = 49.6 percent; and *on selling price*, it was $1,199,000 ÷ $3,615,000 = 33.2 percent.

2. Operating expenses. These are the usual expenses that were incurred in operating the business during the period. Often they are subclassified further, as reflected in Exhibit 2–1, between **selling expenses** and **general and administrative expenses.** *Selling expenses* comprise all amounts incurred during the period in performing the sales activities. *General and administrative expenses* include the overall business expenses, such as the president's salary and the expenses of the accounting department.

3. Financial expenses. These are the expenses incurred as a result of borrowing money or for credit extended to the company. The cost of credit usually is referred to as **interest expense.** Since interest on debt is a **financing expense** rather than an operating expense, it is set out in a separate category from cost of goods sold and operating expenses.

Some businesses also collect interest for credit they have extended to others which is called **interest revenue** (discussed in a later chapter). When the amount of interest revenue is not substantial, instead of reporting it under the revenue caption along with sales and service revenue, it sometimes is offset against interest expense as shown on Exhibit 2–1. When interest revenue is under the revenue classification, "gross margin on sales" cannot be reported because that concept is disturbed. For this reason, and the desire to report both financial expenses and financial revenue under one caption, companies often report these as shown in Exhibit 2–1.

Extraordinary items. This special classification is used to report **nonoperating gains and losses.** Since these items are defined in accounting as being *both* (1) **unusual in nature** and (2) **infrequent in occurrence,** they are set out separately to aid the user in evaluating the profit performance of the business. To include them in the usual, regularly recurring revenue or expense categories would lead the user to believe extraordinary items are normal and will occur again in the future. Observe in Exhibit 2–1 that when there are **extraordinary items**, income amounts will be shown immediately before and immediately after the extraordinary items.[2]

Income tax expense. This is the amount of income tax expense incurred for the period encompassed by the income statement. The amount of income subject to tax is defined by the Internal Revenue Code and often

---

[2] AICPA, *APB Opinion No. 30*, "Reporting the Results of Operations" (New York, 1973), mandates that the following format be used at the bottom of the income statement when there are extraordinary items:

Income before extraordinary items.
Extraordinary items (net of any related income tax).
Net income.

Copyright (1973) by the American Institute of CPAs.

does not agree with the "accounting" income amount shown on the income statement. Detailed consideration of income taxes is beyond the scope of this book. However, we will use simplified tax rates and computations of income taxes to demonstrate appropriate reporting of the income tax expense and income taxes payable.

In Exhibit 2–1 observe that total income tax expense is $138,000 + $13,000 = $151,000. When there are extraordinary items, income tax expense must be reported in two parts:

1. Income tax based on normal operations is reported above the caption "Income before extraordinary items" ($138,000 in Exhibit 2–1).
2. Income tax based on the extraordinary items is reported with those items ($13,000 in Exhibit 2–1).

Income amounts. Observe that three separate "income" amounts are reported: pretax income (an optional step amount), income before extraordinary items (required when there are extraordinary items), and net income. Income before extraordinary items is the difference between "ordinary" revenues and expenses. Net income is always the last item (it is a difference) in the body of the income statement; as a result, it often is called the "bottom-line figure." It is after extraordinary items and has no qualifications—**it is the difference between total revenues and total expenses** (including extraordinary items).

Earnings per share (EPS). A corporation is required to report EPS amounts on the income statement for income before extraordinary items and for net income.[3] In Chapter 1 the computation of EPS was illustrated and discussed briefly. In that chapter, Business Aids, Incorporated, reported only one EPS amount since there were no extraordinary items. In contrast, Diamond's reported three EPS amounts since there was an extraordinary item.[4]

---

[3] AICPA, *APB Opinion No. 15,* "Earnings per Share" (New York, 1969), requires that the two EPS amounts be reported; viz, (1) on income before extraordinary items and (2) on net income. However, many companies also report an EPS amount for the extraordinary category as shown on Exhibit 2–1. *FASB Statement No. 21,* "Suspension of the Reporting of Earnings per Share and Segment Information by Nonpublic Enterprises" (Stamford, Conn., April 1978), suspended the EPS requirement for companies whose shares are not listed on the stock exchanges and for those not sold over the counter. Thus, it is required for most of the larger corporations.

[4] EPS amounts are computed only for **common** stock outstanding. At this point in your study you need not be concerned about the computation of EPS amounts when both common and nonconvertible preferred stock are outstanding. This will be discussed later. However, for those interested, the amounts on Exhibit 2–1 were computed as follows:

Income before extraordinary items:
($162,000 — $25,000, the dividend claim
of the nonconvertible preferred stock) ÷ 15,000 shares = $ 9.13
Extraordinary gain:
$38,000 ÷ 15,000 shares =   2.54
Net income:
($200,000 — $25,000) ÷ 15,000 shares = $11.67

EXHIBIT 2–2

DIAMOND'S, INCORPORATED
Balance Sheet
At December 31, 1981

Assets

Current assets:			
Cash			$ 150,000
Short-term investments			40,000
Accounts receivable	$425,000		
Less: Allowance for doubtful accounts	15,000		410,000
Notes receivable, short term			20,000
Merchandise inventory			1,510,000
Office supplies inventory			1,000
Prepaid insurance			4,000
Total current assets			$2,135,000
Long-term investments and funds:			
Stock of X Corporation			10,000
Sinking fund to pay bonds			150,000
Total long-term investments and funds			160,000
Operational assets:			
Store equipment	150,000		
Less: Accumulated depreciation	50,000	100,000	
Office equipment	16,000		
Less: Accumulated depreciation	4,000	12,000	
Total operational assets			112,000
Intangible assets:			
Trademarks			50,000
Other assets:			
Land acquired for future store site			68,000
Total assets			$2,525,000

Liabilities

Current liabilities:			
Accounts payable			$ 180,000
Notes payable, short term			100,000
Wages payable			16,000
Income tax payable			30,000
Estimated warranty obligations			24,000
Total current liabilities			$ 350,000
Long-term liabilities:			
Bank notes payable (maturity 1983)			100,000
Bonds payable (7%, maturity 1991)			500,000
Total long-term liabilities			600,000
Total liabilities			950,000

Stockholders' Equity

Contributed capital:		
Preferred stock, 5%, cumulative, nonconvertible, 5,000 shares outstanding, par $100	500,000	
Common stock, 15,000 shares outstanding, nopar	750,000	
Contributed capital in excess of par, preferred stock	50,000	
Total contributed capital	1,300,000	
Retained earnings (see statement of retained earnings below)	275,000	
Total stockholders' equity		1,575,000
Total liabilities and stockholders' equity		$2,525,000

DIAMOND'S, INCORPORATED
Statement of Retained Earnings
For the Year Ended December 31, 1981

Beginning balance, retained earnings, January 1, 1981 . . . . $220,000
Add net income for 1981   200,000
    Total   420,000
Less dividends declared and paid during 1981   145,000
Ending balance, retained earnings, December 31, 1981 . . . . $275,000

The balance sheet

Exhibit 2–2 presents a balance sheet for Diamond's. It follows the accounting model: Assets − Liabilities = Owner's equity (see Chapter 1, page 21). To assist decision makers, each of the three major categories of items—assets, liabilities, and owners' equity—is subclassified in terms of similar items. The following subclassifications usually are used:[5]

Balance Sheet

Assets	*Liabilities*
Current assets	Current liabilities
Long-term investments and funds	Long-term liabilities
Operational (i.e., fixed) assets	
Intangible assets	*Owners' equity*
Deferred charges	Contributed capital
Other assets	Retained earnings
	Unrealized capital

Exhibit 2–2 (Diamond's) presents the three major categories—assets, liabilities, and owners' equity—in a *vertical* arrangement which is called the **report format.** In contrast, the balance sheet for Business Aids (Exhibit 1–4, page 22) presented the major categories in a **horizontal format** with the assets to the left and the liabilities and owners' equity to the right which is called the **account format.** Both formats are used widely.

We will discuss each of the subclassifications on the balance sheet.

Current assets. Current assets are resources owned by the entity which are **reasonably** expected to be realized in cash or consumed within one year from the balance sheet date or during the **normal operating cycle** of the business, whichever is the longer. The normal operating cycle tends to vary for each business because it is the average time required for the cycle—cash to cash. For a merchandising company it may be represented graphically as in Exhibit 2–3.

Observe that Diamond's (Exhibit 2–2) reported seven different current assets starting with cash and ending with prepaid insurance. Current assets generally are listed on the balance sheet in order of decreasing liquidity. **Liquidity** refers to the average period of time required to convert a noncash

---

[5] The subclassification titles vary somewhat in actual practice. For example, operational assets often are called property, plant, and equipment.

resource to cash. In addition to cash, current assets include short-term or temporary investments, accounts receivable, inventories, and prepaid expenses.

Short-term investments are current assets because it is expected that they will be sold for cash within one year or one operating cycle, whichever is longer. Accounts receivable are amounts due the company on "open account" from customers and are current assets because they are expected to be collected in the near future. Observe the **contra amount** (contra because it is an offset), allowance for doubtful accounts. This contra amount will be discussed in Chapter 6. Notes receivable, short term, is a current asset for essentially the same reason as accounts receivable. Merchandise inventory is a current asset because it represents merchandise on hand which will be sold for cash or on short-term credit in the near future. Office supplies inventory represents items on hand which will be consumed (i.e., used) in the short term. **Prepaid expense** is a term widely used in business and in accounting. Prepaid expenses are goods or services paid for in advance of their use, such as a two-year insurance premium paid at the beginning of the term of the coverage. As each year of the coverage passes, a portion of the premium paid becomes expense. Since resources often are expended to attain goods or services prior to their actual usage and they will be used in the near future, they are classified on the balance sheet as current assets until used. To illustrate, assume a two-year insurance premium of $600 was paid on January 1, 1981. At the end of 1981, one half of the insurance period would have expired. Therefore, *insurance expense* for 1981 would be $300 and the remaining $300 would be reported on the balance sheet as a current asset because the

EXHIBIT 2–3
Operating cycle for a retail business

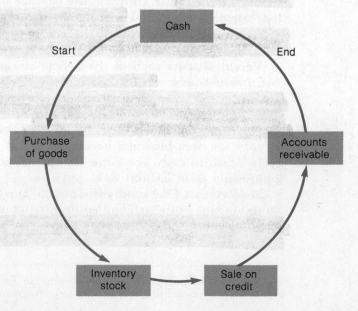

company still has insurance coverage due for one more year. Similarly, in 1982, insurance expense would be $300 and there would be no prepaid insurance on this policy at December 31, 1982.

Financial institutions and others who lend funds to a company are interested in the current assets of the borrower because such assets provide one indication of the short-term ability of the business to meet early maturing debts. Thus, a banker making a decision to grant short-term credit to Diamond's, for example, would consider the amount of each current asset at the date of the loan and throughout its term as an important information input to the lending decision. Such amounts also would be useful in making cash and income projections.

Long-term investments and funds. The second classification of assets reports the investments the company intends to hold for the long run (more than one year, or beyond the operating cycle, whichever is longer). Long-term investments include such items as the stocks and bonds of other companies that have been purchased as investments, investments in real estate, and so on. This classification also includes cash set aside in special funds (such as a savings account) for use in the future for a specified long-term purpose. The sinking fund to pay bonds reported in Exhibit 2–2 represents cash set aside for a special purpose. Eventually this fund will be expended to help retire (i.e., pay off) the bonds payable reported under "Long-term liabilities."[6] While the fund is in existence, it will earn interest revenue that will be reflected on the income statement as revenue from investments and funds (see "Revenue from investments and funds" on Exhibit 2–1).

Operational assets. This subcategory frequently is called **fixed assets** or property, plant, and equipment. It includes those assets having physical substance (i.e., they are tangible) that were acquired for use in **operating the business** rather than for resale as inventory items or simply held as investments. Typically, they include buildings owned; land on which the buildings reside; and equipment, tools, and furniture and fixtures used in operating the business. They are long-lived and are used in the production and/or sale of other assets or services. Operational assets, with the exception of land, are depreciated over time as they are used. Since their productive usefulness decreases as they are used, their initial cost is apportioned to expense over their estimated useful lives. This apportionment of cost over useful life is known as **depreciation.** Land is not depreciated because it does not wear out as do machinery, buildings, and equipment. The amount of depreciation computed for **each period** is reported on the income statement as an **expense,** and the **cumulative** (i.e., accumulated) amount of depreciation expense for all past periods since

---

[6] The term *sinking fund,* although widely used in accounting, is not descriptive. It simply refers to a cash fund set aside to pay a long-term debt at the maturity or due date, or for other future needs.

acquisition is **deducted** (as a contra amount) on the balance sheet from the cost of the asset to derive "book or carrying value." To illustrate, for Diamond's, the depreciation for office equipment was determined and reported as follows:

1. **Income statement (Exhibit 2–1)**—Depreciation expense on office equipment for 1981, $1,000. This was computed as follows:

$$\frac{\text{Cost of the equipment}}{\text{Estimated useful life}} = \frac{\$16,000}{16 \text{ years}}$$
$$= \$1,000 \text{ depreciation expense (each year)}$$

2. **Balance sheet (Exhibit 2–2)**—The amounts shown for office equipment represent the following:

Office equipment, cost when acquired on January 1, 1978	$16,000
Accumulated depreciation expense from January 1, 1978, to December 31, 1981 ($1,000 × 4 years)	4,000
Difference—book value; amount of equipment cost not yet allocated to depreciation expense	$12,000

The difference, $12,000, generally is referred to as the **book value** or **carrying value** of the office equipment. At the end of the 16th year, the book value of the office equipment will be zero. Depreciation expense on store equipment was computed on the basis of a ten-year life (i.e., $150,000 ÷ 10 years = $15,000). Depreciation is discussed in detail in Chapter 9.

Intangible assets. This classification includes those assets having **no physical existence** (i.e., they are intangible) and having a long life. Their value is derived from the rights and privileges that are incident upon ownership. Examples are patents, trademarks, copyrights, franchises, and goodwill. Intangible assets generally are not acquired for resale but rather are used by the business as a part of continuing operations. Thus, in this respect, they are akin to operational assets. Diamond's reported one intangible asset—trademarks (see Exhibit 2–2). Intangible assets are discussed in detail in Chapter 9.

Deferred charges. This is a classification for long-term **prepayments** for goods and services that are expected to contribute to the generation of revenue in the future. They are the same as prepaid expenses (defined above), except that the prepayment extends beyond one year or the operating cycle, whichever is longer. For example, the prepayment of a five-year insurance premium of $500 on January 1, 19A, theoretically would be reported as follows at December 31, 19A:

Income statement:	
Insurance expense for 19A	$100
Balance sheet:	
Prepaid expense	100
Deferred charge	300

When the amounts are relatively small (i.e., not material), the total amount of the prepayment often is reported as a prepaid expense. Observe in Exhibit 2–2 that Diamond's did not report any deferred charges.

Other assets. Some businesses own assets that do not fit reasonably into one of the preceding classifications. Thus, a miscellaneous category called **other assets** may be needed. For example, operational or fixed assets retired from service and held for disposal would be reported under this category as shown in Exhibit 2–2.

Current liabilities. Current liabilities are those debts at balance sheet date that are expected to be paid out of the current assets listed on the same balance sheet. Thus, they are short-term liabilities that are expected to be paid during the coming year or the operating cycle of the business whichever is longer (see page 49). Exhibit 2–2 shows that Diamond's reported five different current liabilities which sum to $350,000. Accounts payable of $180,000 represent amounts owed on open account to suppliers of merchandise purchased for resale; short-term notes payable evidence interest-bearing debt that will mature within the coming year (or operating cycle if it is longer); wages payable represent amounts due employees, not yet paid at balance sheet; and estimated warranty obligations represent future amounts that will have to be expended to make good guarantees on merchandise already sold and services already rendered.

Working capital is a widely used concept that is based on current assets and current liabilities. It can be expressed as a dollar amount or as a ratio as follows:

As a dollar amount:

Computation:	Total current assets	−	Total current liabilities	=	Working capital dollars
Example based on Diamond's:	$2,135,000	− $350,000		= $1,785,000	

As a ratio:

Computation:	Total current assets	÷	Total current liabilities	=	Working capital ratio
Example:	$2,135,000	÷ $350,000		= 6.10	

Thus, the working capital of Diamond's for 1981 was $1,785,000, and the amount of current assets was 6.10 times the amount of current liabilities. The significance of this ratio will be discussed in later chapters; however, we may note that it is a measure of the liquidity of the business, that is, its ability to pay its short-term debts and early maturities of its long-term debts.

Long-term liabilities. These are the liabilities that will not be paid within one year of the balance sheet (or within one operating cycle if it is longer). Thus, they are different from current liabilities because of an extended period before maturity. Exhibit 2–2 reports two long-term liabilities for Diamond's: "Bank notes payable," which are due two years hence; and "Bonds payable," which are due ten years from the balance sheet date.

Owners' equity. Owners' equity (called stockholders' equity for a corporation) represents the residual claim of the owners. This claim is the sum of the shareholders' investments (usually called **contributed capital**) plus the accumulated earnings of the company less the accumulated dividends declared (usually called **retained earnings**). Exhibit 2–2 reports these two categories of stockholders' equity. These two categories are intended to report the **sources** of owners' equity. Each class of capital stock is reported separately. Diamond's balance sheet reports two classes of capital stock:[7] (1) preferred stock, 5,000 shares outstanding; and (2) common stock, 15,000 shares outstanding.

The amount labeled "Contributed capital in excess of par, preferred stock," shows that the preferred stock initially was sold at an average price of $110 per share which was $10 per share above the par value of $100 per share since the "excess" was $10 × 5,000 shares = $50,000. The par value is reported as one amount, and the excess is reported separately. The sum of the two amounts represents the amount contributed by the stockholders when the stock was sold initially. The amount of owners' equity ($1,575,000) can be verified as total assets ($2,525,000) minus total liabilities ($950,000). The amount of owners' equity does not represent what the residual claim is worth in terms of current market value; it is the "book value" of the claim.

Statement of retained earnings

Below the balance sheet for Diamond's (Exhibit 2–2), a supplementary statement is presented with the title **"Statement of Retained Earnings."** This statement, although optional, generally is presented to provide "full disclosure." It explains the increases and decreases in retained earnings during the period. The statement starts with the balance of retained earnings at the beginning of the period. To that balance, net income for the year is added and dividends declared during the year are deducted. Dividends reduce retained earnings on the date they are **declared,** even if they have not yet been paid in cash. This is because a **legally enforceable obligation** to pay occurs on the declaration date. A dividend is **not an expense** on the income statement; rather it is a **distribution** of accumulated earnings. The result is the balance of retained earnings at the end of the period. Note that net income for the period ($200,000 for Diamond's) is

---

[7] Preferred stock is designated so because it has certain specified preferences over the common stock. In this particular case the preferred stock is reported as having two preferences: (1) a dividend preference of 5 percent—this means that dividends on the preferred stock must be paid each year equivalent to 5 percent of the par value per share of the preferred before any dividends can be paid on the common stock; and (2) a cumulative preference—this means that should dividends equivalent to 5 percent not be paid on the preferred stock for any year, the amount not paid will cumulate and must be paid in subsequent years before any dividends can be paid on the common stock. Capital stock is discussed in detail in Chapter 12.

carried to the statement of retained earnings, which in turn is carried to stockholders' equity on the balance sheet. Thus, each period net income increases stockholders' equity. After a number of years of operations, retained earnings becomes one of the primary sources of stockholder's equity in most corporations.

Statement of changes in financial position (SCFP)

The statement of changes in financial position (SCFP) was discussed briefly in Chapter 1, and a very simple situation was illustrated in Exhibit 1–5. In contrast, a more complex situation (Diamond's) is illustrated in Exhibit 2–4. The SCFP has as its primary purpose the reporting of all inflows (i.e., sources) of cash (or working capital if prepared on that basis) and all outflows (i.e., uses) of cash. This information is particularly useful to decision makers (such as stockholders and other potential investors in the business) in assessing the potential **future** amounts, timing, and uncertainty of net cash inflows to the business.

The SCFP for Diamond's is typical of many retail businesses. For example, the following analytical points may be observed:

1. Total cash inflows amounted to $371,700, and total cash outflows amounted to $263,000, which resulted in a net increase in cash of $108,700.
2. Of the total cash inflows of $371,700, 62 percent (i.e., $228,700 ÷ $371,700) came from operations. This statistic is especially important because it represents operations which are likely to continue into the future. In contrast, the $43,000 cash inflow from **extraordinary items,** since they are by definition unusual and infrequent, cannot be expected to continue into the future.
3. Of the total cash outflows of $263,000, 55 percent was for dividends to the owners. This outflow can vary depending upon the decision each year as to dividends by the board of directors of the corporation.

The SCFP illustrations in these first two chapters are to facilitate understanding of what the statement reports and how to interpret it in general. The ways in which the amounts are determined and some of the more complex issues, including preparation of the SCFP on a working capital (current assets minus current liabilities) basis, are discussed and illustrated in Chapter 15.

A MORE COMPLICATED SET OF FINANCIAL STATEMENTS

Up to this point you have studied two simplified sets of financial statements, stripped of much of the surrounding features. To complete this overview of financial statements for a business, we present a set of **published** financial statements for a well-known company, J. C. Penney. A corporation such as this one is said to "publish" its annual report because it is printed and distributed to each shareholder and to others upon request. Companies selling their stock on the stock exchanges (and some others)

EXHIBIT 2–4

DIAMOND'S, INCORPORATED
Statement of Changes in Financial Position, Cash Basis
For the Year Ended December 31, 1981

Sources of cash:
From operations:

Sales revenue	$3,615,000	
Revenue from investments	13,000	
	3,628,000	
Adjustments for *noncash* revenue for this period (deduction)	5,000* (a)	
Cash inflow from sale and investment revenues	3,623,000	
Expenses, including cost of goods sold	$3,466,000* (b)	
Adjustments for noncash expenses deduction	(71,700)* (c)	
Cash outflow for expenses	3,394,300	
Net cash inflow from continuing operations and investments		228,700
From extraordinary items (net of income taxes): Disposal of land ($56,000–$13,000)		43,000* (d)
From bank note, long term		100,000
Total cash generated (inflows during the year)		371,700

Uses of cash:
To pay dividends during the period:

On preferred stock	25,000	
On common stock	120,000	
To increase bond sinking fund	50,000	
To purchase land for future store site	68,000	
Total cash used (outflows during the year)		263,000
Increase in cash (during this period)		$108,700

Explanations:

* At this point in your study, there is no need to be concerned with the derivation of these amounts; however, they may be reconciled as follows:

(a) The adjustment of $5,000 to revenue was due to an increase in accounts receivable of that amount during the period, which means that this amount of cash will be collected later.

(b) Expenses from the income statement (Exhibit 2–1):

Cost of goods sold	$2,416,000
Operating expenses	856,000
Interest expense	56,000
Income tax expense	138,000
Total expenses (for this period)	$3,466,000

(c) Noncash expenses from the income statement (Exhibit 2–1):

Depreciation expense, store equipment	$15,000
Amortization of trademarks	2,000
Estimated losses on doubtful accounts	3,600
Depreciation expense, office equipment	1,000
Subtotal	21,600
Net change in accruals, deferrals, and accounts payable (data not given herein)	50,100
Total	$71,700

(The cash outflow related to the noncash expenses occurred before, or will occur after, this period.)

(d) The land was sold for $56,000 cash, of which $13,000 was paid for income taxes on the gain, leaving a net cash inflow of $43,000 from this source (also see Exhibit 2–1).

distribute such annual reports. The published annual report typically includes a number of features in addition to the financial statements, such as the president's letter to the shareholders, a list of the principal officers of the company, promotional data on the company's products (including pictures), and other information deemed by the management to be of interest.

The following components from the 1979 annual report of J. C. Penney are included in Exhibit 2–5 for your study:[8]

1. Consolidated statement of income.
2. Consolidated statement of retained (reinvested) earnings.
3. Consolidated balance sheet.
4. Consolidated SCFP (working capital basis).
5. Report of independent accountants.
6. Management's statement on financial information.
7. Summary of accounting policies.
8. Selected notes to the financial statements.

As recommended by the APB, **comparative** amounts are presented. That is, amounts for each item are reported for the current year and the preceding year.

There are a number of items reported on these statements you will not understand at this point in your study; however, you should understand most of them. Most of them will be discussed in subsequent chapters.

Income statement. The most recent statement of income is dated "52 weeks ended January 26, 1980." This means that the company uses a **fiscal year** which is different from the calendar year. The fiscal year for a business also is referred to as the natural business year since it ends when the business normally is at its lowest level of activity. The period selected by the business for its usual operating purposes also is used for accounting. It often is referred to as the **accounting period** as well as the fiscal year.

Statement of retained (reinvested) earnings. This statement is included to tie together the income statement and balance sheet and to provide details concerning owners' equity. It partially implements the full-disclosure principle.

Balance sheet. This most recent balance sheet is dated "January 26, 1980" and follows closely the classifications discussed previously.

SCFP. This statement is dated the same as the income statement and is prepared by this company on a working capital basis.

Accountants' report. The independent CPA firm, as the outside auditor,

---

[8] The statements are labeled "Consolidated Statements." These two words indicate that the parent company owns more than 50 percent of the outstanding voting stock of one or more other companies. This ownership gives the parent company a *controlling interest,* and the other companies are designated as subsidiaries. To prepare the statements on a *consolidated basis,* the financial statements of the subsidiaries are added on a line-by-line basis to those of the parent company. This subject is discussed further in Chapter 14.

EXHIBIT 2–5

J. C. PENNEY COMPANY, INC.

Statement of Income
Statement of Reinvested Earnings

(In millions except per share data)

J.C.Penney Company, Inc. and Consolidated Subsidiaries

1979   *1978*

Statement of Income	52 weeks ended January 26, 1980	52 weeks ended January 27, 1979
Sales	**$11,274**	$10,845
Costs and expenses		
Cost of goods sold, occupancy, buying, and warehousing costs	8,005	7,650
Selling, general, and administrative expenses	2,632	2,522
Interest, after deduction of income before income taxes of J.C.Penney Financial Corporation	254	208
Total costs and expenses	10,891	10,380
Income before income taxes and other unconsolidated subsidiaries	383	465
Income taxes	166	212
Income before other unconsolidated subsidiaries	217	253
Net income of other unconsolidated subsidiaries	27	23
Net income	**$ 244**	$ 276
Net income per share	**$ 3.52**	$ 4.12

Statement of Reinvested Earnings		
Reinvested earnings at beginning of year	**$ 1,613**	$ 1,456
Net income for the year	244	276
Changes in unrealized decline in value of equity securities	2	(1)
Dividends	(122)	(118)
Reinvested earnings at end of year	**$ 1,737**	$ 1,613

See Summary of Accounting Policies on page 14 and
1979 Financial Review on pages 18 to 25.

EXHIBIT 2–5
(continued)

J. C. PENNEY COMPANY, INC.

Balance Sheet
(In millions)

J.C. Penney Company, Inc. and Consolidated Subsidiaries

Assets	January 26, 1980	January 27, 1979
Current assets		
Cash and short term investments	$ 99	$ 78
Receivables, net	665	467
Merchandise inventories	1,749	2,046
Prepaid expenses	118	101
Total current assets	2,631	2,692
Investment in and advances to unconsolidated subsidiaries	579	498
Properties and property rights, net of accumulated depreciation and amortization of $641 and $569	1,823	1,609
Other assets	44	34
	$5,077	$4,833

Liabilities and Stockholders' Equity		
Current liabilities		
Accounts payable and accrued liabilities	$1,084	$1,077
Dividend payable	31	30
Income taxes	41	45
Deferred credits, principally tax effects applicable to installment sales	466	404
Total current liabilities	1,622	1,556
Long term debt and commitments under capital leases	836	841
Deferred credits, principally tax effects applicable to depreciation and capital leases, net	99	79
Stockholders' equity		
Preferred stock, without par value: Authorized, 5 million shares — issued, none		
Common stock, par value 50¢: Authorized, 100 million shares — issued, 69.7 million shares	783	744
Reinvested earnings	1,737	1,613
Total stockholders' equity	2,520	2,357
	$5,077	$4,833

See Summary of Accounting Policies on page 14 and
1979 Financial Review on pages 18 to 25.

Accountants' Report

To the Stockholders and Board of Directors of J.C. Penney Company, Inc.

We have examined the balance sheet of J.C. Penney Company, Inc. and consolidated subsidiaries as of January 26, 1980 and January 27, 1979, and the related statements of income, reinvested earnings, and changes in financial position for the 52 week periods then ended. Our examinations were made in accordance with generally accepted auditing standards, and accordingly included such tests of the accounting records and such other auditing procedures as we considered necessary in the circumstances.

In our opinion, the aforementioned financial statements present fairly the financial position of J.C. Penney Company, Inc. and consolidated subsidiaries at January 26, 1980 and January 27, 1979, and the results of their operations and changes in their financial position for the 52 week periods then ended, in conformity with generally accepted accounting principles applied on a consistent basis. Also, in our opinion, the accompanying statistical data on pages 26, 27, 28, and 29 present fairly the information shown therein.

345 Park Avenue
New York, N.Y.
March 18, 1980

Peat, Marwick, Mitchell & Co.

EXHIBIT 2–5
(continued)

J. C. PENNEY COMPANY, INC.

Statement of Changes in Financial Position

(In millions)

J.C. Penney Company, Inc. and Consolidated Subsidiaries

	52 weeks ended January 26, 1980	52 weeks ended January 27, 1979
Funds were generated from:		
Operations		
Net income	$ 244	$ 276
Deduct undistributed net income of unconsolidated subsidiaries	(87)	(66)
Depreciation and amortization	135	119
Deferred credits, principally tax effects applicable to depreciation and amortization	20	22
Stock issued for Company contributions to savings and profit-sharing and stock bonus plans	9	51
Total	321	402
External sources		
Disposition of properties	9	10
Increase in long term debt	10	100
Stock issued for employee contributions to savings and profit-sharing plan and exercise of options	30	31
Decrease in investment in and advances to unconsolidated subsidiaries	8	10
Total	57	151
Total funds generated	378	553
Funds were used for:		
Dividends	122	118
Capital expenditures	358	334
Retirement of long term debt	15	6
Change in other assets	10	7
Total funds used	505	465
Increase (decrease) in working capital	(127)	88
Increase in other deferred credits, principally tax effects applicable to installment sales	62	58
Increase (decrease) in working funds	$ (65)	$ 146

Analysis of Changes in Working Capital and Working Funds

Cash and short term investments	$ 21	$ 5
Receivables, net	198	(157)
Merchandise inventories	(297)	340
Accounts payable and accrued liabilities	(7)	(119)
Income taxes and deferred credits	(58)	(7)
Other	16	26
Increase (decrease) in working capital	(127)	88
Deferred credits, principally tax effects applicable to installment sales	62	58
Increase (decrease) in working funds	$ (65)	$ 146

See Summary of Accounting Policies on page 14 and
1979 Financial Review on pages 18 to 25.

EXHIBIT 2–5
(continued)

J. C. PENNEY COMPANY, INC.

Management's Statement on Financial Information

J C Penney Company, Inc and Consolidated Subsidiaries

The Company's management is responsible for the information presented in this Annual Report. The financial statements have been prepared in accordance with generally accepted accounting principles and are considered in the judgment of management to present fairly in all material respects the Company's results of operations, financial position, and changes in financial position. Certain estimated amounts are included in the financial statements, and these amounts are based on currently available information and management's judgment of current conditions and circumstances. Financial information elsewhere in this Annual Report is consistent with that in the financial statements.

The Company's system of internal accounting controls and procedures is supported by written policies and guidelines and supplemented by a staff of internal auditors. The system is designed to provide management with reasonable assurance, at appropriate cost, that assets are safeguarded and that transactions are executed in accordance with management's authorization and recorded and reported properly. The system is continually reviewed, evaluated, and, where appropriate, modified to accommodate current condi-

tions. Emphasis is placed on the careful selection, training, and development of professional managers.

An organizational alignment that is premised upon appropriate delegation of authority and division of responsibility is fundamental to this system. Communication programs are aimed at assuring that established procedures, policies, and guidelines are disseminated and understood throughout the Company.

The financial statements have been audited by independent public accountants whose report appears on page 16.

The Audit Committee of the Board of Directors is composed solely of directors who are not officers or employees of the Company. The Audit Committee is responsible for recommending to the Board the engagement of the independent public accounting firm for the purpose of conducting the annual examination of the Company's accounts. Company management, internal auditors, and the independent public accountants meet periodically with the Audit Committee to review financial statements and discuss auditing and financial reporting matters.

Summary of Accounting Policies

The dominant portion of JCPenney's business consists of selling merchandise and services to consumers through stores, including catalog operations.

Definition of Fiscal Year. JCPenney's fiscal year ends on the last Saturday in January. Fiscal year 1979 ended January 26, 1980; fiscal year 1978 ended January 27, 1979. Each year comprised 52 weeks. The accounts of several subsidiaries, including JCPenney Financial Services, are on a calendar year basis.

Basis of Consolidation. The consolidated financial statements present the results of all merchandising operations and those real estate subsidiaries whose properties are presently being utilized in merchandising operations. Not consolidated are J. C. Penney Financial Corporation, JCPenney Financial Services, and JCP Realty, Inc., which are accounted for on the equity basis.

The income before income taxes of J. C. Penney Financial Corporation is included in the statement of income as a reduction of interest expense. The combined income of all other unconsolidated subsidiaries is included as a single item in the statement of income.

Sales. Sales include merchandise and services, net of returns, and exclude sales and value added taxes.

Accounts Receivable. Finance charge income arising from customer accounts receivable is treated as a reduction of selling, general, and administrative expenses in the statement of income.

Merchandise Inventories. Substantially all merchandise inventories are valued at the lower of cost (last-in, first-out) or market, determined by the retail method.

Properties. Maintenance and repairs are charged to current operations as incurred, and improvements are capitalized.

Depreciation. The cost of buildings and equipment is depreciated on a straight line basis over the estimated useful lives of the assets. The principal annual rates used in computing depreciation are 3 per cent for store buildings, 2-1/2 per cent to 4 per cent for warehouse and office buildings, and 10 per cent for fixtures and equipment. Property rights under capital leases and improvements to leased premises are amortized on a straight line basis over the term of the lease or their useful life, whichever is shorter.

Income Taxes. JCPenney uses the "flow through" method whereby income taxes are reduced currently for the amounts of investment tax credits.

Deferred Charges. Expenses associated with the opening of new stores are written off in the year of store opening, except those of stores opened in January, which are written off in the following fiscal year. Catalog preparation and printing costs are written off over the estimated productive lives of the catalogs, not to exceed six months.

Pension Cost. The cost of pension benefits has been determined by the entry age normal method. Unfunded actuarial liabilities are amortized over a period not to exceed 30 years.

EXHIBIT 2–5
(continued)

J. C. PENNEY COMPANY, INC.

1979 Financial Review

Overview

Sales in 1979 were $11.3 billion, an increase of 4.0 per cent over the $10.8 billion in 1978. Following is a breakdown of the Company's sales:

(In millions)	1979	1978	Per cent increase — All units	Per cent increase — Comparative units
JCPenney stores	$ 9,322	$ 9,078	2.7	.1
Catalog	1,455	1,212	20.1	n/a
Other retail operations	1,688	1,525	10.7	9.6
Catalog sales centers	(1,191)	(970)	n/a	n/a
Total	$11,274	$10,845	4.0	1.3

Catalog merchandise sold through catalog sales centers located in the Company's stores is included in the sales of those stores. Total catalog sales shown above include sales by catalog sales centers, outlet stores, and mail. The duplication with respect to sales by catalog sales centers is eliminated in the line entitled catalog sales centers. Comparative units are those in operation throughout both 1979 and 1978. For further analyses of sales, see the discussion below and the Ten Year Operations Summary on page 27.

In the 10 years ended January 26, 1980, sales have grown at the compound annual rate of 11.2 per cent.

Net income was $244 million in 1979, a decline of 11.6 per cent from the $276 million earned in 1978. Net income per share, based on the weighted average number of shares outstanding, was $3.52 in 1979, a decline of 14.6 per cent from the $4.12 per share earned in 1978, when there were approximately 2.2 million fewer shares outstanding.

The lower of cost (last-in, first-out) or market retail method of inventory valuation reduced net income per share 70 cents in 1979 compared with a 17 cents per share reduction in 1978. On a per share basis, interest expense increased from $1.53 in 1978 to $1.89 in 1979.

In the 10 years ended January 26, 1980, net income per share has increased at the compound annual rate of 5.3 per cent.

The quarterly dividend was 44 cents per share in each quarter of 1979 and 1978, or an annual rate of $1.76 per share. Dividends declared totaled $122 million in 1979 compared with $118 million in 1978.

Assets

Receivables were as follows:

(In millions)	January 26 1980	January 27 1979
Customer receivables		
Regular charge	$2,118	$1,985
Time payment	756	644
	2,874	2,629
Less receivables sold to J. C. Penney Financial Corporation	2,465	2,420
	409	209
Due from J. C. Penney Financial Corporation	123	121
Other receivables	191	190
	723	520
Less allowance for doubtful accounts (2% of customer receivables)	58	53
Receivables, net	$ 665	$ 467

Customer receivables due after one year were approximately $552 million at year end 1979, compared with $477 million at year end 1978.

During February 1980, JCPenney entered into a 12-year agreement to sell on an ongoing basis approximately 10 per cent of its customer receivables to Citicorp Industrial Credit, Inc. (C.I.C.), a wholly owned subsidiary of Citicorp. Under the terms of the agreement, C.I.C. is committed to purchase up to $350 million of our customer receivables through November 30, 1980, and larger amounts thereafter, reaching $530 million after November 30, 1982. The initial sale totaled approximately $287 million.

Merchandise inventories at year end 1979 were $1,749 million, a decrease of 14.5 per cent from the $2,046 million at year end 1978. Substantially all inventories are valued at the lower of cost (last-in, first-out) or market, determined by the retail method. If the first-in, first-out method of inventory valuation had been used by the Company, inventories would have been $241 million higher at year end 1979 and $145 million higher at year end 1978.

For the Quarters (Unaudited) (In millions except per share data)	First 1979	First 1978	Second 1979	Second 1978	Third 1979	Third 1978	Fourth 1979	Fourth 1978
Sales	$2,335	2,175	2,481	2,433	2,764	2,705	3,694	3,532
Per cent increase from prior year	7.4	16.8	2.0	22.1	2.2	14.6	4.6	12.0
Cost of goods sold, occupancy, buying, and warehousing costs	$1,631	1,533	1,780	1,730	1,940	1,898	2,654	2,489
Net income	$ 35	33	16	40	60	68	133	135
Per cent increase (decrease) from prior year	6.4	15.7	(58.9)	21.2	(13.7)	(6.6)	(1.1)	(13.1)
Net income per share	$ .51	.50	.24	.58	.85	1.03	1.92	2.01
Dividends per share	$ .44	.44	.44	.44	.44	.44	.44	.44
Common stock price range								
(high)	$ 32	42	32	43	33	41	28	35
(low)	$ 28	33	28	36	25	32	24	30

EXHIBIT 2–5
(concluded)

J. C. PENNEY COMPANY, INC.

Properties and property rights at year end were as follows:

(In millions)	1979	1978
Land	$ 113	$ 111
Buildings		
Owned	628	524
Capital lease property rights	313	313
Fixtures and equipment	1,051	956
Leasehold improvements	189	169
Construction in progress and land held for future use	170	105
	2,464	2,178
Less accumulated depreciation and amortization	641	569
Properties, net	$1,823	$1,609

Capital expenditures in 1979 and 1978 are shown in the following tabulation:

(In millions)	1979	1978
Land	$ 4	$ 9
Buildings	105	99
Fixtures and equipment	159	194
Leasehold improvements	24	20
Construction in progress and land held for future use	66	12
Total capital expenditures	$358	$334

Liabilities and Stockholders' Equity

JCPenney's long term debt and commitments under capital leases are shown below:

(In millions)	January 26 1980	January 27 1979
8-7/8% sinking fund (commencing 1980) debentures due 1995	$141	$150
9% sinking fund (commencing 1984) debentures due 1999	150	150
8-1/2% guaranteed notes due 1983	100	100
5.778% mortgage notes on headquarters building	35	37
4-1/2% Eurodollar subordinated debentures due 1987, convertible at $83.96	35	35
5-1/2% note due 1980 (refinanced in 1980 with 9.75-9.875% notes dues 1985)	25	25
6% Eurodollar subordinated debentures due 1989, convertible at $54.50	11	11
9-3/8% note due 1984	10	—
Other	4	4
Total long term debt	511	512
Present value of commitments under capital leases	325	329
Total long term debt and commitments under capital leases	$836	$841

Supplementary Financial Data

Consumer purchases through JCPenney credit and bank cards totaled $4.6 billion in 1979, as compared with $4.3 billion in 1978.

JCPenney credit sales in 1979 rose to $4.5 billion, up 5.1 per cent from $4.3 billion in 1978. The proportion of credit sales to total sales increased to 43.0 per cent in 1979 from 42.2 per cent in 1978. In computing these percentages, sales in Belgium are excluded because the Company does not offer consumer credit in connection with those sales.

Approximately 81.8 per cent of total credit sales was made in accordance with the regular charge schedule, and the balance in accordance with the time payment schedule.

At year end, the number of accounts with outstanding balances was 12.3 million regular charge and 2.0 million time payment. Average account balances and average maturities were as follows:

	Average account balances		Average maturities (In months)	
	1979	1978	1979	1978
Regular	$172	$167	5.3	5.2
Time	371	356	9.7	9.8
All	201	192	6.1	5.9

Account balances in which any portion was three months or more past due represented 2.3 per cent of the amount of customer receivables at year end 1979, compared with 2.4 per cent at year end 1978.

The Company's policy is to write off accounts when a dollar amount equal to a scheduled minimum payment has not been received for six consecutive months, or if any portion of the balance is more than 12 months past due, or if it is otherwise determined that the customer is unable to pay. Collection efforts continue subsequent to write off, and recoveries are applied as a reduction of bad debt losses. Net bad debt losses increased in 1979 to $63 million, or 1.4 per cent of credit sales, from $54 million in 1978, or 1.3 per cent of credit sales.

The net cost of the retail credit operation increased in 1979, as shown below:

(In millions)	1979	1978
Finance charge income	$370	$326
Costs		
Administration and applicable store expenses	181	166
Interest on average receivables less applicable deferred taxes	217	161
Provision for doubtful accounts	68	62
Income taxes	(39)	(29)
	427	360
Net cost of credit	$ 57	$ 34
Net cost as per cent of credit sales	1.3%	.8%

is required to express an **opinion** on the financial statements or to state that an opinion cannot be expressed. The accountants' report on the statements of J. C. Penney states, in the first paragraph, the scope of the examination performed. In the second paragraph, the independent CPA has stated that in "our opinion, the aforementioned financial statements present fairly the financial position [i.e., the balance sheet], of J. C. Penney Company, Inc. and consolidated subsidiaries at January 26, 1980 and January 27, 1979, and the results of their operations [i.e., the income statement], and changes in their financial position [i.e., the SCFP] for the 52 week periods then ended, in conformity with generally accepted accounting principles applied on a consistent basis." The key words are "present fairly" and "generally accepted accounting principles." If the statements do not meet these standards, the independent CPA must explain why an unqualified opinion cannot be expressed. Since the accountants' opinion relates to the "fair presentation" of the financial statement in its entirety, the opinion is viewed as a necessary part of the financial report.

Summary of accounting policies. Because of its importance, this section is required by *APB Opinion No. 22.* Its purpose is to explain the accounting policies followed by the company. This information significantly aids the user in interpreting the amounts reported. Observe that this company explained its accounting policies in respect to ten different items.

Full disclosure. One of the broad fundamentals underlying accounting, listed in Exhibit 2–6, is the principle of full disclosure. This relates directly to the financial statements. It specifies that there should be complete and understandable reporting on the financial statements of all **significant information** relating to the economic affairs of the entity. To meet the requirements of this principle, the quantitative expressions in the financial statements frequently require narrative and detailed elaboration. As a consequence, practically all published financial statements will include a section often called "Notes to the Financial Statements" or "Financial Review." The notes are considered to be an integral part of the financial statements and are important to understanding and interpreting the amounts reported. To illustrate typical notes, several were selected from the J. C. Penney statements as shown in Exhibit 2–5.

PART B: USE OF FINANCIAL INFORMATION IN DECISION MAKING AND THE FUNDAMENTAL CONCEPTS OF ACCOUNTING

The external decision makers (see Chapter 1, page 18) do not participate directly in preparation of the financial statements they use nor in the development of guidelines (i.e., GAAP) used in the preparation of such statements. Rather, decision makers seek to elicit (select) information from the financial reports that will help them make better decisions than otherwise on specific problems they encounter.

In this part of the chapter the selection and analysis by decision makers of relevant information from the financial statements is introduced. This part also presents an outline of the fundamental concepts that underlie financial accounting and reporting. This outline is presented as a point of reference to be used throughout the chapters to follow.

FINANCIAL STATEMENTS RELATED TO THE DECISION PROCESS

The broad objective of financial reporting is to provide information that is useful in making decisions. This objective responds to the fact that the investors (i.e., the owners) and potential investors in a business are concerned primarily with the potential *future* cash returns they can reasonably expect to receive on their investments. The future returns are related to the profits (and losses) of the business and to the resources (assets) it owns and its liabilities. In a similar manner the creditors of the business are concerned about their future cash returns in the form of interest to be received and collection of the principals of the liabilities at maturity dates.[9] Decision makers must be concerned directly with the future rather than with the past; therefore, decision makers must make projections regarding the future. This means that the financial information they receive must have **qualitative characteristics** that focus on their decision-making needs. The information must be relevant to their needs; it must be reliable, not biased in any way, and be neutral with respect to all groups and individuals.

Recent past events and trends, if measured and reported appropriately, provide an important basis on which decision makers develop projections concerning potentials. Financial statements, since they report periodically on the revenues, expenses, incomes, resources, and liabilities of a business, provide invaluable data for most financial projections made by investors.

In addition to considering the data reported on the financial statements, decision makers must bring to bear in their projections knowledge of such factors as technological changes, environmental influences, competitive forces, behavioral considerations, general economic conditions, and the characteristics of the industry.

Throughout the chapters that follow you will learn more about how financial statements may help decision makers assess the **future prospects** of a business. At this time, only an introduction is possible. For this introduction we will refer to the financial statements of Diamond's presented in Part A of this chapter (Exhibits 2–1, 2–2, and 2–4).

In assessing the potential cash returns of Diamond's, a decision maker probably would want to carefully examine and analyze the company's recent financial statements, say, for the past three to five years. For example, the SCFP (Exhibit 2–4) would reveal trends as to the primary **sources**

---

[9] *FASB Statement of Financial Accounting Concepts No. 1*, "Objectives of Financial Reporting by Business Enterprises" (Stamford, Conn., November 1978), states: "Since investors' and creditors' cash flows are related to enterprise cash flows, financial reporting should provide information to help investors, creditors, and others assess the amounts, timing, and uncertainty of prospective net cash inflows to the related enterprise." Copyright © by the Financial Accounting Standards Board, High Ridge Park, Stamford, Conn. 06905, U.S.A. Quoted (or excerpted) with permission. Copies of the complete document are available from the FASB.

and **uses** of cash, such as the amount of cash generated by operations (62 percent) or from loans (27 percent), and the primary cash-demanding activities. A knowledge of each source and each use over several consecutive years would be helpful in projecting future sources and uses of cash.

In a similar manner a decision maker would make other analyses of the income statement and the balance sheet because they report past financial performance of the company. The income statement reports the basic operational activities that, if continued, would be expected to generate future cash inflows. The performance levels (i.e., efficiency) that can be projected will indicate future cash flows that may be expected reasonably from this primary source. In a similar manner, certain assets reported on the balance sheet provide a basis for projecting other potential cash inflows (such as from the sale of an investment or a tract of land), and the reported liabilities indicate significant future cash demands. All of this suggests the importance of understanding what financial statements say and what they do not say and, just as important, how to analyze them to maximize their usefulness in the decision-making process.

The analysis of financial statements will be emphasized in the various chapters with an overall view presented in Chapter 16. By way of introduction, the concept of **proportional relationships** is presented as one phase of such an analysis. Proportional analysis involves the selection of two important amounts from the financial statements that are related in a meaningful way. One, known as the **base amount,** is divided into the other to express the proportional relationship between them. The result may be expressed as a ratio, a percent, or sometimes as a dollar amount. Two examples already have been presented: (1) earnings per share (page 47) and (2) working capital (page 53). Three additional examples based on the financial statements of Diamond's, Inc., which focus on **profitability,** are presented below:

1. $$\text{Profit margin} = \frac{\text{Net income}}{\text{Net sales}} = \frac{\$162,000}{\$3,615,000} = 0.045$$

Thus, for the year, Diamond's earned 4.5 percent on each dollar of sales.[10]

2. Along with EPS the concept of **return on investment (ROI)** is widely used to measure profitability.

The concept of ROI is especially useful to decision makers. It is particularly significant since it expresses the relationship between **profit** and **investment.** The income statement provides the income amount, and the balance sheet provides the investment amount.

The concept of ROI is applied frequently by almost everyone in one way or another. To illustrate, suppose you invested $1,000 on January

---

[10] To compute profit margin when there are extraordinary items, income before extraordinary items rather than net income generally should be used to avoid the distortion caused by the unusual and infrequently recurring items.

1, 19A, and at the end of the year you got back $1,200. Disregarding income taxes, you may say that you earned $200 during the year on your investment. Based on these amounts, what would be your ROI (i.e., your return on investment)? You may calculate that your return for the year was $200 ÷ $1,000 = 20 percent on the investment. Similarly, the ROI for a **business** for a specific period of time may be computed as follows:

$$\frac{\text{Net income}}{\text{Investment (owners' equity)}} = \text{Return on investment (ROI)}$$

The ROI earned by Diamond's for 1981 would be computed as follows:[11]

$$\frac{\$162,000 \text{ (from Exhibit 2–1)}}{\$1,575,000 \text{ (from Exhibit 2–2)}} = 10.29\%$$

FUNDAMENTALS OF FINANCIAL ACCOUNTING AND REPORTING

Reporting to external parties (i.e., owners, creditors, and other decision makers) and financial accounting (which generates the external financial reports) must conform to specific concepts and guidelines formulated primarily by the accounting profession. These concepts and guidelines are intended to protect the interests of the external decision makers by assuring, to the extent practicable, that the external financial statements are reasonably complete and not misleading.

To accomplish this broad purpose the **fundamentals** of financial accounting and reporting have evolved. The fundamentals are man-made. They are in a process of continuing evolution to meet the changing needs of society and to keep the financial accounting measurements and reporting relevant to the current problems of external decision makers. The changes are initiated primarily because of such variables as inflation and expansion of international businesses. The evolving problems are the subject of much research by accountants (in academia, practice, and industry) and the groups involved in accounting innovations discussed in Chapter 1 (see page 14).

The fundamentals of financial accounting and reporting may be viewed as the objectives and qualitative characteristics of accounting, the assumptions that underlie accounting, the underlying principles, and finally (at the lowest level) the practices and procedures of accounting.

The accounting profession has not agreed upon a single listing of the fundamentals underlying accounting; therefore, throughout the literature of accounting you will find variation in terminology and definition. For purposes of this book we will use the list given in Exhibit 2–6. In this exhibit we list and define briefly each of these fundamentals for your

---

[11] Depending upon the nature of the problem and the preference of the decision maker, the income amount may be either (1) income before extraordinary items or (2) net income. Similarly, investment may be either (1) owners' equity or (2) total equity (i.e., liabilities plus owners' equity). When total equity is used, interest expense (net of tax) should be added back to income (see Chapter 16).

EXHIBIT 2–6
Summarization of the fundamentals underlying financial accounting and reporting

Fundamentals	Chapter	Page	Brief Explanation
1. **Objectives of financial accounting and reporting (to external parties)**	1 2	1, 5, 7–10, 65	The basic objective is to provide information that is useful in making business and economic decisions.
2. **Qualitative characteristics of financial accounting and reporting**	2	68–69	There are four qualitative characteristics of accounting—relevance, reliability, neutrality, and comparability. They are criteria used by the accounting profession to assure that financial accounting and reporting choices (of accounting policies, principles, and procedures) tend to produce the most useful financial information for decision making.
3. **Underlying assumptions:** *a.* Separate-entity assumption	1	6	Accounting is concerned with a specifically defined entity. Thus, for accounting purposes, an enterprise is assumed to be an accounting unit separate and apart from the owners, creditors, and other entities.
b. Continuity assumption	9		In accounting, an enterprise is assumed to be a "going concern." That is, for accounting purposes, it is assumed that the entity will not liquidate in the foreseeable future but will continue to carry out its business objectives in an orderly way.
c. Unit-of-measure assumption	1	5	With many diverse items and transactions to be accounted for, it is necessary that a single unit of measure be adopted. Accounting assumes the monetary unit—the dollar—as the common denominator in the measurement process.
d. Time-period assumption	1 4	18 143	Financial data must be reported for relatively short time periods: months, quarters, years. Society imposes this calendar constraint on accounting. Thus, accounting assumes that financial results must be reported for short time periods. This leads to the necessity for the accrual and deferral of revenues and expenses.
4. **Underlying principles:** *a.* Cost principle	1	22	Cost (i.e., the resources given up in the acquisition of other goods and services) is the appropriate basis for initial recording and subsequent accounting for assets, liabilities, revenues, and expenses.
b. Revenue principle	4	144	Revenue is the consideration received for the aggregate of goods and services transferred by an entity to its customers. Under this principle, revenue is realized (i.e., earned and recognized) when ownership to the goods sold is transferred and when services are rendered.

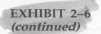

EXHIBIT 2–6
(continued)

Fundamentals	Chapter	Page	Brief Explanation
c. Matching principle	4	146	In conformity with the revenue principle the revenues of the period must be identified and recognized in the accounting process. Then, under the matching principle all of the costs incurred in generating that revenue, regardless of the period in which the costs were incurred, must be identified with the period in which the revenues are recognized. Thus, under this principle, the costs of generating particular revenues are matched with those revenues, period by period. This principle requires the accrual and deferral of many costs.
d. Objectivity principle	1	23	Accounting should be based on objective data and objective determinations to the fullest extent possible. It should be free from bias. The accounting data recorded and reported should be verifiable.
e. Consistency principle	7	0	The accounting process must apply all concepts, principles, standards, and measurement approaches on a consistent basis from one period to the next, in order to derive financial data that are comparable over time.
f. Full-disclosure principle	2	64	Financial reporting should be complete and understandable to the prudent user (i.e., the investor) and should include all significant information relating to the economic affairs of the entity.
g. Exception principle	8	0	Accounting is applied to a very diverse range of situations and transactions in the many companies and industries; therefore, a reasonable degree of flexibility is essential. As a consequence, certain exceptions to the basic concepts, standards, and procedures are necessary. There are three types of exceptions that are permitted: (i) Materiality—Amounts of small significance (i.e., relatively small amounts) need not be accorded strict theoretical treatment. (ii) Conservatism—Where more than one accounting alternative (or judgment) is permissible, the one having the least favorable immediate effect on owners' equity should be selected. (iii) Industry peculiarities—Unique characteristics of an industry may require the development and application of special accounting approaches in order to produce realistic financial results.

EXHIBIT 2–6
(concluded)

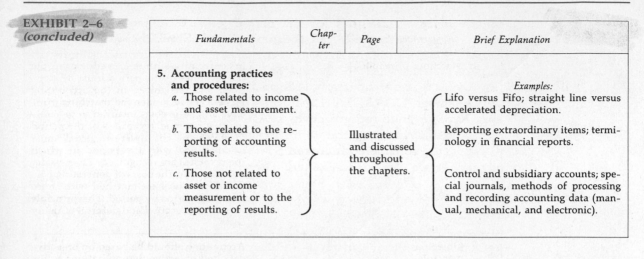

Fundamentals	Chapter	Page	Brief Explanation
5. Accounting practices and procedures:			*Examples:*
a. Those related to income and asset measurement.		Illustrated and discussed throughout the chapters.	Lifo versus Fifo; straight line versus accelerated depreciation.
b. Those related to the reporting of accounting results.			Reporting extraordinary items; terminology in financial reports.
c. Those not related to asset or income measurement or to the reporting of results.			Control and subsidiary accounts; special journals, methods of processing and recording accounting data (manual, mechanical, and electronic).

convenience in the chapters which follow. We also have listed the **chapter** and **page numbers** where each fundamental is introduced *first*. Throughout the discussions we often return to these fundamentals to explain the rationale for a particular accounting approach. Therefore, at this time you are not expected to comprehend fully their overall importance or the full meaning of each of them.

JUDGMENT IN ACCOUNTING

Financial accounting concepts and standards have been developed and articulated to increase the reliability and relevance of accounting measurements and reporting. Since accounting is man-made and must evolve to meet changing needs, it has a limited number of "provable" approaches. As you study accounting you will appreciate that it requires much professional judgment in application on the part of the accountant in order to capture the economic essence of transactions. Thus, accounting is stimulating intellectually; it is not a cut-and-dried subject. Rather, it is one that calls upon your intelligence, analytical ability, creativity, and judgment. Since accounting is a communication process involving an audience (users) of a wide diversity of knowledge, interest, and capabilities, it will call upon your ability as a communicator. The language encompasses concisely written phrases and symbols used to convey information about the resource flows measured for specific organizations.

ACCRUAL BASIS ACCOUNTING

The definition of revenues on page 19 states that revenue is considered **earned** (i.e., realized) in the period when the revenue transaction takes place rather than when the cash is collected. Therefore, the total amount of sales and service revenues on cash plus credit terms should be reported on the income statement for the period, even though the cash for the credit sales may be collected the next period. Similarly, when rent (for example) is collected in advance, rent revenue should be included on the income statement for the period in which occupancy occurred, rather in the period of cash collection. Assume rent revenue of $1,200 is collected on December 1, 19A, for 12 months' occupancy ending November 30, 19B. Rent revenue recognized in 19A would be $100 and in 19B, $1,100.

In a similar manner, the definition of expenses on page 19 states that expenses are considered **incurred** (i.e., used) in the period when the goods or services are used or consumed. Therefore, the total amount of expense incurred should be reported on the income statement. In some cases the expense-incurring services and goods are obtained on credit whereby the cash is paid in a later period, and in other cases the cash is paid in advance of use of the goods or services (as in the case of prepayment of a three-year insurance premium on a building). In each of these cases the cash flow is disregarded in determining the period for which the expense should be reported on the income statement.

The approach described above for determining when revenues are realized and when expenses are incurred is necessary to measure revenues properly for the period and to **match** expenses correctly with those revenues (see Exhibit 2–6, the matching principle). This method of measuring when revenues are to be recognized and when expenses are incurred is known as **accrual accounting.** It is required by generally accepted accounting principles (GAAP). In contrast, individuals and very small businesses sometimes use cash basis for their records, which means that all revenues are considered earned only when the cash is collected, and all expenses are considered incurred only when the cash is paid. This does not conform to GAAP because it incorrectly measures such revenues and expenses due to the fact that the related activities precede or lag the cash-flow dates.

SOME MISCONCEPTIONS

Some people naively confuse a bookkeeper with an accountant and bookkeeping with accounting. In effect, they confuse one of the minor parts with the whole of accounting. Bookkeeping involves the routine and clerical part of accounting and requires only minimal knowledge of the accounting model. A bookkeeper records the repetitive and uncomplicated transactions in most businesses and may maintain the simple records of a very small business. In contrast, the accountant is a professional competent in the design of information systems, analysis of complex transactions and economic events, interpretation and analysis of financial data, financial reporting, financial advising, auditing, taxation, and management consulting.

Another prevalent misconception is that all of the financial affairs of an entity are subject to precise and accurate measurement each period and that the accounting results reported, as reflected in the financial statements, are exactly what happened that period. For example, that accounting numbers are influenced by estimates in many respects will be illustrated in subsequent chapters. Many people believe that accounting should measure and report the value of the entity, but accounting does not attempt to do this. In order to understand financial statements and to interpret them wisely for use in decision making, the user must be aware of their limitations as well as their usefulness. One should understand what they do and do not attempt to accomplish.

As a student of accounting you must be wary of these misconceptions. To adequately understand financial statements and to be able to interpret the "figures" wisely, you must have a certain level of knowledge of the concepts and standards and the measurement procedures used in the accounting process. You must learn what accounting "is really like" and appreciate the reasons why certain things are done the way they are. This level of knowledge cannot be gained simply by reading a list of the "principles" and a list of the misconceptions. Neither can a generalized discussion of the subject matter suffice. A certain amount of involvement, primarily problem solving as used in mathematics courses, is essential in any study of accounting focused on the needs of the user. Therefore, we provide problems aimed at the desirable knowledge level for the user of financial statements.

SOCIAL AND ECONOMIC SIGNIFICANCE OF ACCOUNTING

The broad areas of public-policy formulation and the ranking of national priorities are important issues to many citizens. Even casual knowledge tells us that the financial implications of public-policy formulation are important considerations. Accounting information assists policy makers to bring the financial complexities into focus for study, evaluation, and selection of the more favorable alternatives. First and foremost, the financial information that underlies policy formulation must have credibility; that is, the financial information must be dependable. The **independent audit function** provided by the accounting profession, coupled with the expertise of the accountant in sorting out relevant financial analyses and relationships, helps to meet this need. Similarly, the credibility of financial reports on business units is indispensable in the conduct of the business, the administration of the taxation process, and the protection of the broad public interest. Inefficiencies, errors, and selfish interests could cause the whole system to break down if these reports were not reliable. In the federal government, the General Accounting Office was established to audit and report to the Congress on the administration of public funds. Regulatory bodies such as the SEC and the ICC were established by law to protect the public interest. These and similar agencies, in good measure, rely upon audited financial reports in carrying out their statutory missions.

The growth of business organizations in size, particularly publicly held corporations, has brought pressure from stockholders, potential investors, creditors, governmental agencies, and the public at large, for increased financial disclosure. The public's right to know more about organizations that directly and indirectly affect them (whether or not they are shareholders) is being increasingly recognized as essential. An open society is one that has a high degree of freedom at the individual level and typically evidences an effective commitment to measuring the quality of life attained. These characteristics make it essential that the members of that society be provided adequate, understandable, and dependable financial information from the major institutions that comprise it. Voters are asked to decide upon revenue-raising proposals, allocations of resources to many sources, and other questions. All of these decisions should be based upon adequate financial knowledge. Labor negotiations, environmental programs, economic opportunity programs, foreign aid, and education programs are but a few of the difficult problem areas important to all citizens that, for enlightened decision making, require extensive use of accounting information.

ACCOUNTING: AN INFORMATION SYSTEM

Accounting records the detailed financial history of the entity and, from that information, derives the financial statements. Thus, the **accounting process** involves the accumulation, analysis, measurement, interpretation, classification, and summarization of the results of each of the many business transactions that affected the entity during the year. After this processing, accounting then transmits or projects messages to potential decision makers. The messages are in the form of financial statements, and the decision makers are the users. Accounting generally does not generate the basic information (raw financial data); rather, the raw financial data result from the day-to-day transactions initiated, participated in, and completed by the employees of the enterprise. The accounting system includes procedures for collecting these data; and as an *information system,* the accounting process is designed to record these data and capture the **economic essence** of each transaction.[12]

An accounting system should be designed to classify financial information on a basis suitable for decision-making purposes and to process the tremendous quantities of data efficiently and accurately. The information system must be designed to report the results periodically, in a realistic and concise format that is comprehensible to users who generally have only a limited technical knowledge of accounting. The information system also must be designed to accommodate the special and complex needs

---

[12] The accounting information system should be viewed as a part of the overall information system that necessarily operates in every entity.

of the internal management of the entity on a continuing basis. These internal needs extend primarily to the planning and control responsibilities of the managers of the enterprise; they are discussed in *Fundamentals of Management Accounting*.

The accountant has the primary responsibility for developing an accounting information system that is essential for most entities, whether operating on a profit or nonprofit basis. In designing an information system, the accountant must consider the factors of (1) cost, (2) benefit, (3) timeliness (i.e., reports must be rendered early), and (4) requirements of various outside influences, such as governmental regulatory agencies (examples are the Securities and Exchange Commission and the Internal Revenue Service).

The accounting information processing system will be discussed in Chapters 4–6.

DEMONSTRATION CASE

ABC Corporation

ABC Service Corporation was organized by three investors on January 1, 1981. On that date as initial, or start-up, cash each investor bought 1,000 shares of ABC capital stock, par $10 per share, and paid $12 per share in cash. In addition, on January 1, 1981, the corporation borrowed $40,000 cash from a local bank and gave a three-year note payable due December 31, 1983. The note called for 10 percent annual interest payable each December 31. Operations started immediately.

On December 31, 1981, it was determined that service revenues amounted to $90,000, of which $20,000 will be collected in 1982. Expenses amounted to $50,000 excluding interest expense on the note and income taxes (assume a 20 percent income tax rate). On December 31, 1981, each shareholder was paid a cash dividend of $2 per share.

Required:

a. What were the sources and amounts of cash to start the business?
b. Prepare an income statement (summarized) for 1981.
c. Prepare the stockholders' equity section of the balance sheet at December 31, 1981.

Suggested solution:

Requirement (a):

Sources of cash	Amounts
From owners (1,000 shares × $12 × 3)	$36,000
From creditors (note payable $40,000, 10%, 3-year term)	40,000
Total start-up cash	$76,000

Requirement (b):

ABC CORPORATION
Income Statement
For the Year Ended December 31, 1981

Service revenue (including $20,000 on credit)		$90,000
Expenses (undesignated)	$50,000	
Interest expense ($40,000 × 10%)	4,000	54,000
Pretax income.....................................		36,000
Income tax expense ($36,000 × 20%)		7,200
Net income		$28,800
EPS: ($28,800 ÷ 3,000 shares)		$ 9.60

Requirement (c):

Stockholders' equity, balance sheet at December 31, 1981:	
Capital stock, par $10, 3,000 shares	$30,000
Contributed capital in excess of par ($12–$10) × 3,000 shares	6,000
Total contributed capital	36,000
Retained earnings (Note A)	22,800
Total stockholders' equity	$58,800

Note A—Computations:	
Beginning retained earnings, January 1, 1981	$ –0–
Add net income of 1981	28,800
Total	28,800
Deduct dividends declared in 1981 (3,000 shares × $2)	6,000
Ending balance, December 31, 1981	$22,800

SUMMARY

This chapter presented the commonly used subclassifications of financial information on the income statement, balance sheet, and statement of changes in financial position. You learned some of the analytical approaches used by the decision makers when relying on financial reports. You also learned to expect variations in the terminology and format of financial reports.

Financial reports of an existing company were presented to reinforce your understanding and for reference as you study the accounting process in the chapters to follow. The knowledge of financial statements, gained in Chapter 1 and in this chapter, should assure that in studying the details and complexities of accounting, you can maintain a broad view of accounting and keep in mind the nature of the end product—the periodic financial statements. We reemphasize this point because, not infrequently, students soon become immersed in details and lose the broad perspective of the end results—the financial statements and their use.

In Part B of the chapter a summarization of the fundamentals underlying financial accounting and reporting (i.e., for external decision makers) was presented. The fundamentals presented were identified as objectives of financial accounting, qualitative characteristics of accounting, underlying assumptions, underlying principles, and accounting practices and procedures. In essence, this is a summarization of the major considerations of the chapters that follow. It is presented at this time as a basic foundation to which your attention will be directed in the remaining chapters. It will serve as a basis for understanding much of the "why and how" of financial accounting and reporting. You should return to it often for this reason, and to maintain overall perspective.

We looked at a case where financial information exerted a significant impact on the decision maker. We will continue to focus on decision making because the overriding objective of accounting, as we have said, is to contribute to sound and realistic decisions.

IMPORTANT TERMS DEFINED IN THE CHAPTER (with page citations)

General-purpose financial statements—43
Classified financial statements—43
Revenues—44
Sales and service revenue—44
Returned sales—44
Gross sales—44
Net sales—44
Cost of goods sold—44
Operating expenses—46
Financial expenses—46
Extraordinary items—46
Income tax expense—46
Earnings per share (EPS)—47
Current assets—49
Normal operating cycle—49
Liquidity—49
Contra amount—50
Prepaid expenses—50
Long-term investments and funds—51
Operational assets—51

Fixed assets—51
Depreciation—51
Book value—52
Carrying value—52
Intangible assets—52
Deferred charges—52
Other assets—53
Current liabilities—53
Working capital—53
Long-term liabilities—53
Owners' equity—54
Statement of retained earnings—54, 57
Statement of changes in financial position (SCFP)—55, 56, 68
Report of independent accountants—57
Full disclosure—64
Proportional relationships—68
Profit margin—69
Return on investment (ROI)—69
Matching principle—65, 71
Accrual accounting—70

QUESTIONS FOR DISCUSSION

Part A

1. What is the primary purpose of subclassification of the information presented on financial statements?

2. What are the four major classifications on the income statement?

3. Distinguish between gross sales revenue and net sales revenue.

4. Explain the subclassification "Financial expenses and revenues" on the income statement.

5. What are extraordinary items? Why should they be reported separately on the income statement?

6. Explain EPS. What EPS amounts should be reported on the income statement?

7. Briefly explain how income tax expense is reported on the income statement when there are extraordinary items.

8. What are the six subclassifications of assets that are reported on a balance sheet?

9. Briefly define (a) current assets, (b) current liabilities, and (c) working capital.

10. What is a prepaid expense?

11. Distinguish between a prepaid expense and a deferred charge.

12. On a balance sheet, investments may be reported under either (a) current assets or (b) long-term investments and funds. Explain.

13. In respect to operational assets, as reported on the balance sheet, briefly explain (a) cost, (b) accumulated depreciation, (c) book value, and (d) carrying value.

14. What are the subclassifications of liabilities on a balance sheet?

15. Briefly explain the two major subclassifications of owners' equity for a corporation.

16. What is the purpose of a statement of retained earnings?

17. What are the three major subclassifications on a SCFP?

18. What is meant by a comparative financial statement? Why are comparative financial statements desirable?

19. Briefly, what does the independent auditors' report encompass?

20. What is proportional analysis? Why is it often useful in interpreting financial statements?

21. Explain (a) profit margin and (b) ROI.

Questions

Part B

22. What is the basic objective of financial accounting and reporting?

23. What are the four qualitative characteristics of financial accounting and reporting?

24. Explain the basic difference between cash basis accounting and accrual basis accounting.

25. Distinguish between accounting and book-keeping.

26. Explain why a major part of accounting may be viewed as an information system.

EXERCISES

Part A

E2–1. The accounting records of Doyle Corporation reflected the following summarized data for the year ended December 31, 19B: sales revenue, $100,000; gross margin rate (markup on selling price), 52 percent; financial (interest) expense, $2,000; extraordinary gain, $5,000; average income tax rate (on all items), 20 percent; operating expenses, $30,000; common stock outstanding, 10,000 shares; and dividends declared and paid, $3,000.

Required:

a. You have been asked to prepare a detailed income statement for 19B. Show your computations. (Hint: EPS on net income is $2 per share.)

b. You also have been asked to compute the amount of retained earnings at the end of 19B (the January 1, 19B, balance was $11,000). Show your computations.

E2–2. The following is a list of major classifications and subclassifications on the balance sheet. Number them in the order in which they normally appear on a balance sheet.

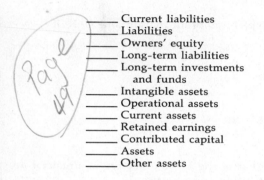

_____ Current liabilities
_____ Liabilities
_____ Owners' equity
_____ Long-term liabilities
_____ Long-term investments and funds
_____ Intangible assets
_____ Operational assets
_____ Current assets
_____ Retained earnings
_____ Contributed capital
_____ Assets
_____ Other assets

E2–3. EPS Corporation has just completed the 1981 income statement (there were no extraordinary items), except for the EPS computations. Net income has been determined to be $165,000. Common stock outstanding during the year was 40,000 shares, and preferred stock, nonconvertible, 5 percent ($10 par value) outstanding was 10,000 shares. Compute the EPS amount for the income statement. (Hint: First subtract the preferred dividends of $100,000 × 5% = $5,000.)

E2–4. Risk Corporation (common stock, 5,000 shares outstanding) is preparing the income statement for the year ended December 31, 19D. The pretax operating income has been determined to be $80,000, and there was a $20,000 pretax loss on earthquake damages to one of the plants properly classified as an extraordinary item. Total income tax expense has been determined correctly to be $24,000 on the basis of a 40 percent tax rate on operations and on the storm loss. You have been requested to complete the in-

come statement starting with pretax operating income. (Hint: EPS on income before extraordinary items was $9.60.)

E2–5. Candy Corporation was organized in 1970 by ten investors. Each investor paid in $12 cash per share and received 1,500 shares of $10 par-value common stock. In 1975, to raise more capital, Candy Corporation issued 5,000 shares of 7 percent preferred, nonparticipating, cumulative stock, par $20 per share, and received $125,000 cash for them. On December 31, 1981, retained earnings amounted to $75,000. Prepare the stockholders' equity section of the balance sheet at December 31, 1981.

E2–6. On July 1, 1981, Risky Company paid $4,800 cash for a two-year insurance premium. The premium was for a new insurance policy covering all of the assets owned. It is now December 31, 1981, and you are asked to respond to the following questions (show your computations):

a. How much should be reported for *insurance expense* on the income statement for year ended December 31, 1981?

b. What amount of *prepaid insurance* should be reported on the December 31, 1981, balance sheet? How should it be classified?

E2–7. Investor Manufacturing Corporation is preparing its annual financial statements at December 31, 1981. The company has two investments in shares of other corporations:

a. Common stock of M Corporation: 1,000 shares purchased for $80,000 during 1975. M Corporation is a supplier of parts to Investor Corporation; therefore, the latter "intends to hold the stock indefinitely." The shares acquired represented 2 percent of the total shares outstanding. M stock was selling at $95 at the end of 1981.

b. Common stock of N Corporation: purchased 500 shares at a cost of $60 per share on August 15, 1981. Investor made this investment to "temporarily use some idle cash that probably will be needed next year." N stock was selling at $70 at the end of 1981.

You have been requested to illustrate and explain the basis for the classification and amount that should be reported for each investment on the 1981 balance sheet of Investor Corporation.

E2–8. Scott Company is preparing the balance sheet at December 31, 1981. The following assets are to be reported:

1. Building, purchased 15 years ago (counting 1981); original cost, $180,000, estimated useful life, 20 years from date of purchase, and no residual value.
2. Land, purchased 15 years ago (counting 1981); original cost, $9,000.

Required:

a. You are requested to show how the two assets should be reported on the balance sheet.
b. What amount of depreciation expense should be reported on the 1981 income statement? Show computations.

E2–9. The amounts listed below were selected from the annual financial statements for Lazar Corporation at December 31, 19C (end of the third year of operations):

Required:

You have been asked to analyze the below data on the 19C financial statements by responding to the following questions. Show computations.

a. How much was the gross margin on sales? $_____
b. What was the amount of EPS? $_____
c. What was the amount of working capital? $_____
d. What was the working capital ratio? _____
e. What was the average sales price per share of the capital stock? _____
f. Assuming no dividends were declared or paid during 19C, what was the beginning balance (January 1, 19C) of retained earnings? $_____

E2–10. This exercise is designed to aid in your understanding of the contents of published financial statements and to observe differences in form and terminology. The year ended January 27, 1979, is labeled 1978, and the year ended January 26, 1980, is labeled 1979. You are to refer to the financial statements of J. C. Penney presented in this chapter and respond to the following:

a. Income statement:
   1. What title was used?

(Relates to Exercise 2–9)

From the 19C income statement:
Sales revenue	$300,000
Cost of goods sold	(180,000)
All other expenses (including income tax)	(90,000)
Net income	$ 30,000

From the December 31, 19C, balance sheet:
Current assets	$ 90,000
All other assets	275,000
Total assets	$365,000
Current liabilities	$ 50,000
Long-term liabilities	89,000
Capital stock, par $10	150,000
Contributed capital in excess of par	15,000
Retained earnings	61,000
Total liabilities and stockholders' equity	$365,000

2. Is it a comparative statement? Explain.
3. Were any extraordinary items reported?
4. What was the profit margin for each year?
5. Did EPS increase?
6. What was the average income tax rate for 1978 and 1979?

b. Statement of retained earnings:
7. What amounts were carried to the balance sheets?
8. What amounts were carried from the income statements?
9. What was the amount of dividends each year?

c. Balance sheet:
10. What was the amount of working capital at the end of each year?
11. Was accumulated depreciation reported on the balance sheet?
12. How many shares of each kind of stock were issued? What was the number of shareholders?

d. Statement of changes in financial position (SCFP):
13. Was this statement prepared on a working capital basis or on a cash basis?
14. What was the largest source of working capital funds each year?
15. What was the largest use of working capital funds each year?

16. Did working capital increase or decrease each year?

e. Accountants' report:
17. Did the independent CPAs believe that the statements "present fairly" the results of operations and financial position? Were there any exceptions on this point?

f. Summary of accounting policies:
18. How many accounting policies were explained? List them.
19. What is the primary method of depreciation used by the company?

g. Notes to the financial statements:
20. What was the percent of sales attributable to catalog sales each year?
21. What was the annual dividend rate (dollars) per share each year?
22. What was the net cost of the credit operation as a percent of credit sales in each year?
23. What was the average balance in accounts receivable each year?

Exercises
Part B

E2–11. At the end of the accounting year, December 31, 19B, the records of Simple Corporation reflected the following summarized data:

(Relates to Exercise 2–11)

Revenues for the year (net)	$150,000
Expenses for the year (including $3,000 income taxes)	(138,000)
Net income	$ 12,000
Total assets (including current assets of $48,000)	$200,000
Liabilities (including current liabilities of $20,000)	$ 90,000
Stockholders' equity (including capital stock, par $10, $80,000)	110,000
Total liabilities and stockholders equity	$200,000

Required:

For analytical and interpretative purposes you have been asked to complete the following tabulation:

Relates to Exercise 2–11)

Item	Computation	Briefly, What Does It Mean?
a. Average income tax rate		
b. Profit margin c. EPS d. Working capital amount		
e. Working capital ratio f. ROI		

E2–12. The accounting records of XY Service Company reflected the amounts shown below:

(Relates to Exercise 2–12)

	19A	19B	19C
Service revenue:			
Cash	$40,000	$50,000	
On credit	10,000	12,000	
19C revenue collected in advance of 19C (not included in the $50,000)		1,000	
Additional cash collections for:			
19A service revenue	6,000	4,000	
19B service revenue	1,000	8,000	$3,000
Expenses:			
Paid in cash	25,000	30,000	
On credit	5,000	7,000	
19C expenses paid in advance of 19C (not included in the $30,000)		1,000	
Additional cash payments for:			
19A expenses	3,000	2,000	
19B expenses	1,000	3,000	3,000

Required:

Complete the following tabulation (show computations):

	19A	19B
a. Service revenue that would be reported:		
Accrual basis	$_____	$_____
Cash basis	$_____	$_____

	19A	19B
b. Expenses that would be reported:		
Accrual basis	$_____	$_____
Cash basis	$_____	$_____

E2–13. Refer to Exhibit 2–6 and match the following:

(Relates to Exercise 2–12)

	Fundamental		Brief explanation
1. _____	Objective of financial statements	A.	Relevance, reliability, neutrality, and comparability.
2. _____	Unit-of-measure assumption	B.	The monetary unit is used as the common denominator in accounting measurements.
3. _____	Revenue principle	C.	Materiality, conservatism, industry peculiarities.
4. _____	Accounting practices and procedures	D.	To provide information useful in making business decisions.
5. _____	Qualitative characteristics	E.	Revenue is realized when ownership to goods sold passes and when services are rendered.
6. _____	Exception principle	F.	Straight-line versus accelerated depreciation.

PROBLEMS

Part A

P2–1. Flat Tire Company is developing the annual financial statements for 19D. The following amounts have been determined to be correct: sales, $300,000; selling expenses, $37,000; interest expense, $3,000; administrative expenses, $20,000; extraordinary loss, $10,000; sales returns and allowances, $3,000; cost of goods sold, $160,000; and interest revenue, $1,000.

Prepare a classified income statement for 19D. Assume 20,000 shares of common stock outstanding during the year and an average income tax rate on all items of 20 percent. (Hint: EPS on net income is $2.72 per share.)

P2–2. Ace Jewelers is developing the annual financial statements for 19C. The following amounts have been determined to be correct at December 31, 19C: cash, $41,200; accounts receivable, $19,000; merchandise inventory, $110,000; prepaid insurance, $600; investment in stock of Z Corporation (long term), $31,000; store equipment, $50,000; used store equipment held for disposal, $9,000; allowance for doubtful accounts, $800; accumulated depreciation, store equipment, $10,000; accounts payable, $43,000; long-term notes payable, $40,000; income taxes payable, $7,000; retained earnings, $50,000; and common stock, 100,000 shares outstanding, par $1 per share (originally sold at $1.10 per share).

You have been requested to prepare a classified balance sheet at December 31, 19C. (Hint: The balance sheet total is $250,000.)

P2–3. PM Corporation is developing the annual financial statements for 1981. The information given below has been verified as correct. The company sells merchandise to retail outlets only. Note that in some instances only totals are provided to shorten the solution.

(Relates to Problem 2–3)

Financial information, 1981

Income Statement		Balance Sheet	
Sales	$273,000	Cash	$ 31,000
Selling expenses	44,700	Accounts receivable	30,000
Interest expense	2,200	Allowance for doubtful accounts..........	1,000
Administrative expense	23,300	Accounts payable	61,000
Sales returns	3,000	Retained earnings	72,000
Cost of goods sold	130,000	Merchandise inventory	138,000
Extraordinary loss (earth-		Investment in stock of K Corp.	
quake)	10,000	(long term)	4,000
Income tax expense on		Income taxes payable	5,000
operations (30%) $21,000		Accumulated depreciation	16,600
Tax savings on extraor-		Store equipment	70,000
dinary loss (30%) 3,000	18,000	Used equipment held for disposal	44,600
Revenue from divi-		Common stock, par $10 per share	100,000
dends on stock in-		Long-term notes payable	46,000
vestment, K Corp.	200	Contributed capital in excess of par	16,000

Required:

a. On the basis of the listed data, you have been asked to prepare a classified income statement and a balance sheet for the year ended December 31, 1981.

b. Compute the average markup earned on cost, the amount of working capital, and the working capital ratio. Briefly interpret each.

(Hint: EPS on net income is $4.20.)

P2–4. Tasty Bakery is developing its annual financial statements for 1981. The following cash-flow data have been determined to be correct for the year: sales revenue (including $12,000 not collected), $300,000; expenses, $270,000 (including $21,000 of noncash items); cash received from sale of used machine, $1,000; cash received for extraordinary item, $900; cash borrowed on a five-year note payable, $20,000; cash disbursement for dividends, $12,000; cash expenditure to purchase two new delivery trucks, $9,900; and cash paid on $5,000 mortgage payable. You have been requested to prepare a statement of changes in financial position on the cash basis for 1981. (Hint: Cash increased $34,000.)

P2–5. Although Baker's Retail Store has been operating for only four years, the sales volume increase each year has been excel- lent; apparently it was occasioned by the location, a friendly atmosphere in the store, and a large stock for customer selection. Despite this appearance of success, the company has continually experienced a severe cash shortage, and a recent analysis by a consultant revealed significant inventory overstocking in numerous lines. Baker's Retail Store was organized as a corporation by Samuel Baker (now president) and four additional investors. Each owner invested $41,000 cash and received 4,000 shares of common stock (par value $10 per share). Although Sam Baker is recognized as an excellent retailer, he exhibits very little interest in the financial reports. At a recent meeting of the board of directors, the inadequacy of the financial reports was raised. The board voted to engage an independent CPA "to examine the accounting system, submit audited financial statements, analyze the financial situation, and make appropriate recommendations to the Board." The independent CPA has just been handed the following reports prepared for the last board meeting by the "store bookkeeper" (to simplify this case, assume that all of the figures are correct; also, only representative amounts have been included):

(Relates to Problem 2–5)

BAKER'S RETAIL STORE
Profit Statement
December 31, 1981

Revenues

Sales for the year	$572,000	
Interest collected on charge accounts	1,000	
Dividends received on stock of Y Corporation	200	$573,200

Costs and expense

Salaries, sales	66,500	
Salaries, administrative	36,000	
Depreciation, office equipment	1,200	
Depreciation, store equipment	6,000	
Store rent	18,000	
Office supplies used	800	
Store supplies used	1,900	
Cost of goods sold for the year	340,000	
Bad debt losses (estimated)	300	
Promotion costs	60,000	
Interest on debts	5,000	
Loss on earthquake damage (extraordinary loss)	1,200	
Insurance and taxes (two-thirds selling and one-third administrative)	6,000	
Miscellaneous expenses, sales	2,000	
Miscellaneous expenses, administrative	700	
Sales returns	8,000	
Income taxes on operations $8,000, less tax saving on earthquake loss $400; net taxes	7,600	561,200
Profit		$ 12,000

Balance Sheet

Assets		Liabilities	
Cash	$ 3,500	Accounts payable	$ 20,000
Accounts receivable (offset for allowance for bad debts $500)	33,500	Notes payable, short term	10,000
Merchandise inventory (at cost)	269,200	Notes payable, long term	80,000
Office supplies inventory	300	Rent due (for December 1981)	1,500
Store supplies inventory	1,600	Income taxes owed	4,600
Prepaid insurance	1,200		
Stock investment in Y Corporation, long term	5,000	*Capital*	
Store equipment (offset for accumulated depreciation, $25,600)	36,800	Stock, par $10	200,000
		Excess paid over par	5,000
		Retained earnings	36,000
Office equipment (offset for accumulated depreciation, $6,000)	6,000		
	$357,100		$357,100

Required:

a. Recast the income statement and balance sheet using preferred subclassfications and terminology. (Hint: EPS on income before extraordinary items is $0.64.)

b. Compute the amount of working capital and the working capital ratio. Show computations. Explain the meaning of the results. Do they appear to you to be favorable? Explain.

P2–6. Ready Repair Company, a successful local automobile repair shop, is preparing the 19E financial statements. On January 1, 19E, the company acquired a substantial quantity of new shop equipment (and related tools) for use in its testing and repair operations. The equipment involved a cash expenditure of $18,000. On the basis of experience, the owner estimated the useful life of the new equipment to be five years, at which time it would sell for approximately 20 percent of the original cost.

Your advice is requested on two questions: (a) How much depreciation should be reported on the 19E income statement? (b) How should the new equipment be reported on the December 31, 19E, balance sheet? Show your computations and explanations. (Hint: Residual value is 20 percent and should not be depreciated since it will be recovered at the time of disposal. Analyze this situation and try to derive a logical approach for the computation of depreciation expense.)

P2–7. This problem is designed to aid you in understanding the content of published financial statements and to observe differences in form and terminology. (Note: The year ended January 27, 1979, is labeled 1978, and the year ended January 26, 1980, is labeled 1979.)

You are to refer to the financial statements of J.C. Penney presented in this chapter and respond to the following:

a. Income statement:
1. Is this a comparative statement? Explain.
2. Is this a consolidated statement? Explain.
3. Are there any extraordinary items?
4. What was the average income tax rate each year?
5. What were the profit margins?
6. What EPS amounts were reported?

b. Statement of retained earnings:
7. What amount was carried from the income statement each year?
8. What amount was carried to the balance sheet each year?
9. What caused retained earnings to change during 1979?

c. Balance sheet:
10. What was the working capital at the end of 1979?
11. What was the amount of accumulated depreciation and amortization at the end of each year?
12. What was the amount of unpaid income taxes at the end of 1979? How does this compare with income tax expense of 1979?
13. What percent of total assets was "provided" by shareholders by the end of 1979?
14. At the end of 1979 how many classes of capital stock had been issued? How many shares of each are authorized and how many issued?
15. At the end of 1979, what percent of stockholders' equity was represented by prior earnings retained in the business?

d. Statement of changes in financial position (SCFP):
16. Can you tell from the heading whether it is based on working capital or on a cash basis?
17. How much working capital was provided by operations during 1979?
18. In which year did working capital increase by the greater amount?
19. In 1979, what item generated the largest amount of working capital? What item used the largest amount of working capital?
20. In which year did the company expend the most cash to retire long-term debt?

e. Accountants' report:
21. Who were the independent CPAs?
22. May this particular "accountants' report" presumably increase the

reliability of the financial statements? Explain why.

f. Summary of accounting policies:

23. How many accounting policies are explained? List them.
24. How are the inventories valued?
25. Over how many years is the goodwill being amortized?

g. Notes to the financial statements:

26. What was the percentage increase of 1979 sales over 1978 sales?
27. What and when were the highest and lowest stock prices during the 1978–79 period?
28. During 1979 what percent of the buildings used were leased?
29. By what percent did the 1979 merchandise inventories change from 1978?
30. What rate is used for estimating bad debts?

Problems

Part B

P2–8. On December 31, 19D, Short Corporation prepared the annual financial statements. The income statement and balance sheet amounts are summarized below:

(Relates to Problem 2–8)

Income Statement
For the Year Ended December 31, 19D

Sales revenue	$200,000
Cost of goods sold	(120,000)
All other operating expenses	(60,000)
Income tax expense	(3,400)
Net income	$ 16,600

Balance Sheet
At December 31, 19D

Current assets		$ 66,000
Operational assets (cost $210,000)		180,000
All other assets		34,000
Total assets		$280,000
Current liabilities		$ 30,000
Long-term liabilities		80,000
Total liabilities		110,000
Capital stock, par $10 10,000 Share	$100,000	
Contributed capital in excess of par	30,000	
Retained earnings	40,000*	170,000
Total liabilities plus stockholders' equity		$280,000

*During 19D a $5,000 dividend was declared and paid which has been subtracted from this amount.

Required:

For analytical and interpretative purposes you have been asked to compute each of the following. Show computations and briefly explain what each means.

a. Profit margin.
b. Gross margin.
c. Average income tax rate.
d. EPS.
e. Working capital amount.
f. Working capital ratio.
g. ROI.
h. Average sales price of the capital stock.
i. January 1, 19D, balance (beginning) of retained earnings.
j. Accumulated depreciation at December 31, 19D.

P2–9. You are considering making a $20,000 investment in the common stock of either X Corporation or Y Corporation. The companies operate in different industries, and their managements have followed different financing policies. In reviewing the latest financial statements you observe the following data:

amount of revenues ($93,800), and (3) the same net income ($36,000). However, as part of your analysis, you decide to compare the following: profit margin, return on stockholders' investment (owners' equity), EPS, and the aftertax, or net, interest rate.

Required:

a. Compute the above amounts for each company based on owners' equity. Show computations. (Hint: The pretax interest rate is 8 percent. Interest expense is deductible for income tax; therefore, the aftertax rate would be less. See if you can determine this lower rate by logical analysis.)
b. Which company would you select for the investment? Explain the basis for your choice.

P2–10. You are considering investing $50,000 in either A Corporation or B Corporation. Both companies have been operating in the same industry for a number of years. Your decision model calls for an evaluation and interpretation of the financial statements for the last five years; how-

(Relates to Problem 2–9)

	X Corporation		Y Corporation	
From the balance sheets:				
Total assets		$240,000		$240,000
Total liabilities		100,000		10,000
Shares outstanding		5,000		10,000
From the income statements:				
Revenues		$ 93,800		$ 93,800
Expenses:				
Interest expense (rate 8%)	$ 8,000		$ 800	
Income tax expense (rate 40%)	24,000		24,000	
Remaining expenses	25,800	57,800	33,000	57,800
Net income		$ 36,000		$ 36,000

From these amounts you observe that the two companies have (1) the same total amount of assets ($240,000), (2) the same

ever, you have obtained the statements for last year only. Those statements provided the following data:

Profitability
Finance
EPS

(Relates to Problem 2–10)

	A Corporation	B Corporation
Sales	$500,000	$700,000
Gross margin on sales	210,000	301,000
Income before extraordinary items	50,000	49,000 ✓
Net income	20,000	63,000 ✓
Total assets	300,000	400,000
Total liabilities (average interest rate 8%)	100,000	100,000
Owners' equity (total)	200,000	300,000
Shares outstanding	10,000	30,000
Income tax rate (average)	40%	40%

Required:

a. Based upon the above data (aside from other factors), what analytical steps would you suggest? Provide computations for each suggestion.

b. On the basis of your analytical results only, which company appears preferable as the investment choice? Explain why.

P2–11. The financial statements at the end of the fiscal year for Watts Corporation are summarized below at June 30, 1981:

Income Statement

Sales	$800,000
Cost of goods sold	460,000
Gross margin on sales	340,000
Operating expenses and income taxes	292,000
Income before extraordinary items	48,000
Extraordinary gain (net of income taxes)	60,000
Net income	$108,000

Balance Sheet

Current assets	$ 98,000
Investments	90,000
Operational assets (net)	330,000
Other assets	70,000
Total assets	$588,000
Current liabilities	$ 98,000
Long-term liabilities	40,000
Total liabilities	138,000
Capital stock, 8,000 shares	400,000
Contributed capital in excess of par	3,000
Retained earnings	47,000
Total stockholders' equity	450,000
Total liabilities and stockholders' equity	$588,000

Required:

Several important investment decisions are under consideration by a large shareholder. Among the analytical data needed are certain financial ratios. Accordingly, assume you have decided to compute the following ratios:

Profit margin:
1. Profit margin based on net income.
2. Profit margin based on income before extraordinary items.

Return on investment (ROI):
3. ROI based on net income and total stockholders' equity.
4. ROI based on income before extraordinary items and total stockholders' equity.

Earnings per share (EPS):
5. EPS based on net income.
6. EPS based on income before extraordinary items.

For each of the three categories select those that you would deem most important and explain the basis for your choice.

P2–12. Refer to Exhibit 2–6 and match the following (a blank may require more than one response):

(Relates to Problem 2–12)

Fundamental	*Brief explanation*

1. _____ Objectives of financial statements

2. _____ Qualitative characteristics

3. _____ Separate-entity assumption

4. _____ Unit-of-measure assumption

5. _____ Time-period assumption

6. _____ Cost principle

7. _____ Revenue principle

8. _____ Matching principle

9. _____ Objectivity principle

10. _____ Consistency principle

11. _____ Exception principle

12. _____ Accounting practices and procedures

13. _____ None of the above Explain

A. Reporting extraordinary items.

B. Apply accounting principles the same from period to period.

C. Measure revenue, then relate to it all costs incurred in generating that revenue.

D. An enterprise is assumed to be separate and apart from its owners.

E. To provide information that is useful in making business and economic decisions.

F. Straight-line versus accelerated depreciation.

G. Use the accounting alternative that has the least favorable immediate effect on owners' equity.

H. Include all significant information relating to the economic affairs of the entity.

I. Relevance, reliability, neutrality, and comparability.

J. Financial data must be reported for short time periods such as one year.

K. Cost at acquisition is appropriate basis for recording assets, liabilities, revenues, and expenses.

L. An enterprise is assumed to be a "going concern."

M. Financial reporting should be complete and understandable to a prudent user.

N. Accounting should be based on objective data.

O. Revenue is considered earned (realized) is when ownership to the goods sold is transferred and when services sold are rendered.

P. The monetary unit is used as the common denominator in accounting measurements.

Q. Small amounts need not be accorded strict theoretical treatment in accounting.

P2–13. Art Little Company (not a corporation) prepared the income statement given below including the two footnotes:

(Relates to Problem 2–13)

ART LITTLE COMPANY
Income Statement, Cash Basis
For the Year Ended December 31, 19B

Sales revenue (does not include $10,000 sales on credit because collection will be in 19C)	$90,000
Expenses (does not include $8,000 expenses on credit because payment will be made in 19C)	75,000
Profit	$15,000

Additional data:

a. Depreciation on operational assets (a company truck) for the year amounted to $4,000. Not included in expenses above.

b. On January 1, 19B, paid a two-year insurance premium on the truck amounting to $400. This amount is included in the expenses above.

Required:

a. Recast the above income statement on the *accrual basis* in conformity with GAAP. Show computations and explain each change.

b. Explain why the cash basis does not measure as well as the accrual basis on the income statement.

Transaction analysis

PURPOSE OF THE CHAPTER

In Chapters 1 and 2 we discussed the fundamentals of financial accounting and studied the end product—the financial statements. We now turn our attention to the accounting process; the way in which the ongoing transactions are recorded, analyzed, and classified in a form from which the periodic financial statements can be generated. In this chapter we will learn the fundamentals of the accounting model and the analysis of transactions to determine and capture quantitatively their economic impacts on that model.

To accomplish these purposes, this chapter is divided into two parts as follows:

Part A: The accounting model and transaction analysis

Part B: The accounting information processing cycle

Behavioral and learning objectives for this chapter are provided in the *Teachers Manual.*

PART A: THE ACCOUNTING MODEL AND TRANSACTION ANALYSIS

NATURE OF TRANSACTIONS

Accounting focuses on certain events that have an economic impact on the entity. Those particular events are recorded in the accounting process and generally are referred to as **transactions.** This is a broad view of transactions and includes (1) those events that involve an exchange of resources (assets) and/or obligations (liabilities) between the business (i.e., the accounting entity) and one or more parties other than the entity; and

90

(2) certain events (or economic occurrences) that are not between the entity and one or more parties but yet have a direct and measurable effect on the accounting entity.[1] Examples of the first category of transactions include the purchase of a machine, the sale of merchandise, the borrowing of cash, and the investment in the business by the owners. Examples of the second category of transactions include (1) **economic events,** such as a drop in the replacement cost of an item held in inventory and a flood loss; and (2) **time adjustments,** such as depreciation of an operational asset (as a result of use) and the "using up" of prepaid insurance. Throughout this book the word "transaction" will be used in the broad sense to include both types of events.

Most transactions are evidenced by an original business document of some sort; in the case of a sale on credit, a charge ticket is prepared, and in the case of a purchase of goods, an invoice is received. In certain other transactions, such as a cash sale, there may be no document other than the cash register tape. The documents that underlie, or support, transactions usually are called **source documents.** The important requirement, from the accounting point of view, is that there must be specified procedures to capture the raw economic data on each **transaction as it occurs.** Once this has been done, the data processing characteristics of the **accounting model** move the economic impact of each transaction on the entity from initial recording to its final resting place—the periodic financial statements.

The fundamental feature of most transactions with **external parties** is that the business entity both gives up something and receives something in return. For example, in the case of a sale of merchandise for cash, the entity gives up resources (the goods sold) and receives in return another resource (cash). In the case of a credit sale of merchandise, the resource received at the time of sale is an account receivable (an asset). Later, another transaction occurs when the account receivable is collected; here, the resource relinquished is the receivable and the resource received is cash. As another example, in the purchase of an asset (either merchandise for resale or a truck purchased for use in the business) the entity acquires the asset and gives up cash, or, in the case of a credit purchase incurs a liability. In the case of a credit purchase, another transaction occurs later when the debt is paid. At that time, the entity gives up a resource (cash) and "receives" satisfaction of the debt. The sale or purchase of services can be analyzed in the same way. Thus, transactions have a **dual economic effect** on the accounting entity. We will return to this dual effect when we consider the accounting model in Part B of this chapter.

---

[1] A narrow definition of a transaction limits it to the first category; that is, events between the entity and one or more parties other than the entity. This definition is useful in certain circumstances and is conceptually correct. However, since accounting recognizes a number of events that are not transactions in the strict sense, we have defined the term in the broader sense to generalize our terminology.

THE FUNDAMENTAL ACCOUNTING MODEL

The fundamental accounting model expresses in algebraic format the status of the assets, debts, and owners' claims of an accounting entity at any specific point in time. In Chapters 1 and 2 you learned the **fundamental accounting model** when you studied the balance sheet (the position statement), viz:

$$\text{Assets} = \text{Liabilities} + \text{Owners' equity}$$

You also learned that owners' equity is (1) increased by investments (i.e., contributions) by the owners, (2) decresed by withdrawals by owners (such as dividends), (3) increased by revenues, and (4) decreased by expenses.[2] Thus, we can expand the fundamental accounting model as follows:

$$\text{Assets} = \text{Liabilities} + \text{Owners' equity}$$

	Increased by:	*Decreased by:*
	Investments	Withdrawals
	Revenues	Expenses

The fundamental accounting model, since it is a broad economic description of an accounting entity, accommodates the *recording* of each transaction that directly affects the enterprise. The **dual economic effect** of each transaction (discussed below) is recorded in terms of this expanded accounting model. The dual effect is captured by the accounting process, whether the processing system is handwritten, mechanized, or computerized.

To illustrate how specific transactions are analyzed and how the dual economic effect is recorded in terms of the fundamental accounting model, let's consider a simple but realistic situation. Throughout the example you should note particularly that (1) each transaction is recorded separately; (2) in recording each transaction the integrity of the fundamental accounting model is maintained (that is, assets will always equal liabilities plus owners' equity); and (3) the **dual effect,** as discussed in the preceding section, is recorded separately for each transaction.

The
fundamental
accounting
model
illustrated

B. Bass and three friends started a dry cleaning business on January 1, 19A, by investing a total of $20,000 cash from their personal savings accounts. Each investor was issued 200 shares of capital stock. Remember that the accounting entity, Bass Cleaners, Incorporated, is to be distinguished from the four investors. Exhibit 3–1 lists a series of transactions for the year 19A and illustrates the dual effect of each transaction in terms of the accounting model for the business. It also provides the information for developing the income statement and balance sheet shown

---

[2] Owners' equity frequently is referred to as equity capital and, sometimes, net worth. The latter term is not recommended because it implies that owners' equity on the balance sheet states what the owners' claim is actually worth, which is not the case.

in Exhibit 3–2. This illustration should be studied carefully as you read the next few paragraphs.

On the balance sheet, since this is a corporation, owners' equity is represented by the two sources: contributed capital and retained earnings. Retained earnings represents the accumulated earnings of the corporation to date, less all dividends declared to date. This aspect of the balance sheet was explained and illustrated in Chapter 1 (page 23) and in Chapter 2 (page 54).[3]

From this simple situation you can view the broad perspective of the **accounting process.** Transactions occur that create raw economic data. Each transaction is subjected to **transaction analysis** and then each is recorded in terms of its **dual effect** on the fundamental accounting model. Finally, the financial statements at the end of the period are constructed from data accumulated in the accounting model.

This illustration, as reflected in Exhibits 3–1 and 3–2, indicates two primary data processing problems:

1. An efficient method is needed for keeping track of (i.e., recording) the **amounts** of each kind of asset (cash, accounts receivable, equipment, inventory, etc.); each kind of liability (accounts payable, notes payable, bonds payable, etc.); and each category of owners' equity (capital stock, dividends paid, revenues, and expenses).

2. An efficient and systematic method of checking is needed to assure accuracy during the recording process.

The account. These two data processing problems led early accountants to develop a series of **accounts.** A separate account is used for each kind of asset, liability, and owners' equity. **An account is simply a standardized arrangement for recording data by categories.** Thus, in most accounting systems, you will find separate accounts, individually labeled, for each asset, such as cash, inventory, accounts receivable, equipment, land; for each liability, such as accounts payable, notes payable, taxes payable; and for each element of owners' equity, such as capital stock, sales revenue, service revenue, and various kinds of expenses. For example, the **Cash account** for Bass Cleaners may appear as in Exhibit 3–3.

The **balance** in the Cash account is:

Total debits ($66,000) − Total credits ($36,700) = $29,300 (debit)

Now we will discuss and illustrate how accounts are used in an important phase of resolving these two data processing problems.

1. **Keeping track of the amounts for each item**—To do this a separate account is set up for each item that will be reported on the financial

---

[3] If Bass Cleaners were a sole proprietorship or a partnership instead of a corporation, owners' equity would be shown as "capital, owners' name" for each owner (see page 23).

EXHIBIT 3–1

BASS CLEANERS, INCORPORATED
Transaction Analysis—19A

Fundamental accounting model

Transactions	Assets	=	Liabilities	+	Stockholders' equity
a. Bass Cleaners received $20,000 cash invested by owners; 800 shares ($25 par value) of stock issued to the four owners	Cash + $20,000				Capital stock (400 shares) + $20,000
b. Borrowed $5,000 cash on 12% note payable	Cash + 5,000		Note payable + $5,000		
c. Purchased delivery truck for cash at cost of $8,000	Cash − 8,000 Delivery truck + 8,000				
d. Cleaning revenue collected in cash, $40,000	Cash + 40,000				Cleaning revenue + 40,000
e. Cleaning revenue earned in 19A but the bill is not collected, $4,000	Accounts receivable + 4,000				Cleaning revenue + 4,000
f. Operating expenses paid in cash, $25,800	Cash − 25,800				Operating expenses − 25,800
g. Operating expenses incurred in 19A but not paid, $2,000			Accounts payable + 2,000		Operating expenses − 2,000
h. Paid 12% interest on the $5,000 note payable, (b) above, with cash ($5,000 × 12% = $600)	Cash − 600				Interest expense − 600
i. Depreciation expense for one year on truck ($8,000 ÷ 5 years = $1,600)	Truck − 1,600				Operating expenses, depreciation − 1,600
j. Cash dividend of $1,800 declared and paid to shareholders	Cash − 1,800				Dividends paid (retained earnings) − 1,800
k. Collected $1,000 cash on accounts receivable in (e)	Cash + 1,000 Accounts receivable − 1,000				
l. Paid $500 cash on accounts payable in (g)	Cash − 500		Accounts payable − 500		
Totals (end of accounting period)	Total assets $38,700	=	Total liabilities $6,500	+	Total stockholders' equity $32,200

Observe how these items and their respective *ending balances* flow into the *financial statements*, Exhibit 3–2.

EXHIBIT 3–2

BASS CLEANERS, INCORPORATED
Income Statement
For the Year Ended December 31, 19A

Cleaning revenue ($40,000 + $4,000)		$44,000
Operating expenses ($25,800 + $2,000 + $1,600)	$29,400	
Interest expense	600	30,000
Net income		$14,000
EPS ($14,000 ÷ 800 shares)		$17.50

Note: To simplify the illustration, income taxes are disregarded.

BASS CLEANERS, INCORPORATED
Balance Sheet
At December 31, 19A

Assets

Cash ($20,000 + $5,000 − $8,000 + $40,000 −		
$25,800 − $600 − $1,800 + $1,000 − $500)		$29,300
Accounts receivable ($4,000 − $1,000)		3,000
Delivery truck	$ 8,000	
Less: Accumulated depreciation	1,600	6,400
Total assets		$38,700

Liabilities

Notes payable	5,000	
Accounts payable ($2,000 − $500)	1,500	
Total liabilities		$ 6,500

Stockholders' Equity

Contributed capital:		
Capital stock (800 shares)	20,000	
Retained earnings (beginning retained earnings, $–0–, plus net income,		
$14,000, minus dividends declared, $1,800)	12,200	
Total stockholders' equity		32,200
Total liabilities and stockholders' equity		$38,700

Observe that these items and their respective amounts were developed by the *transaction analysis* illustrated in Exhibit 3–1.

statements. Each account is designed so that all increases are entered in one location (i.e., on the left side of the Cash account in Exhibit 3–3) and all decreases are entered in another location (i.e., on the right side of the Cash account in Exhibit 3–3). To illustrate the increased efficiency possible, compare the list of plus and minus amounts on

EXHIBIT 3–3
Ledger Account
(T-account form)

Cash

Left or Debit Side		Right or Credit Side	Acct. No. 101
(Increases)		(Decreases)	
Investment by owners	20,000	To purchase truck	8,000
Loan from bank	5,000	Operating expenses	25,800
Cleaning revenue	40,000	Interest expense	600
Collections on accounts		Dividends paid	1,800
receivable	1,000	Payment on accounts payable	500
	66,000		36,700

the cash line of Exhibit 3–2, and also imagine thousands or millions of such increases and decreases during the year in a typical business. In contrast, the Cash account shown in Exhibit 3–3 reflects a left side total of $66,000 and a right side total of $36,700; the difference, $29,300, is the ending cash balance (as reported on the balance sheet in Exhibit 3–2). When the total amount on the decrease side of the Cash account is larger than the total amount on the increase side, a cash deficit (bank overdraft) is indicated. The account system is very flexible; for example, instead of being set up in T-account form (as in Exhibit 3–3) it can be set up in columnar form as in Exhibit 3–7. The account system can use either (or a combination of) handwritten, mechanical, or computerized approaches.

2. **Providing a systematic method of checking for accuracy during the recording process**—To do this the account was designed to provide a dual set of balances as follows:

a. Based on the fundamental accounting model } Assets = Liabilities + Owners' equity

b. Based on an algebraic relationship between account increases and decreases } Debits = Credits

The fundamental accounting model, **Assets = Liabilities + Owners' equity,** itself is an algebraic model of the economic position of an entity at any point in time. By definition, it always balances and can be rearranged mathematically (e.g., Assets − Liabilities = Owners' equity). Observe in Exhibit 3–1 that the analysis of each transaction, and the cumulative effects, were always in balance in terms of this algebraic model (as shown in the balance sheet in Exhibit 3–2). Thus, the first check for accuracy listed above, is applied continuously throughout the accounting information process.

Now we will consider the second accuracy test listed above, **Debits = Credits.** In this context, it is useful to think of an account as having two sides (i.e., parts), the left side, which in accounting is called the **Debit** side, and the right side, which in accounting is called the **Credit** side. These designations are shown in Exhibit 3–3.[4]

The Debits = Credits feature in accounting. The algebraic relationships in the two accuracy checks must be systematic, complementary, and flexible. Recall from Chapter 1 that in 1494 a mathematician (Paciolo) first described the fundamental accounting model used today. Perceiving the problem of attaining accuracy, and after designing the T-account (as illustrated above for cash), Paciolo applied an algebraic concept that has

---

[4] Handwritten or manually maintained accounts in the formats shown here generally are used only in small businesses. Highly mechanized and computerized systems retain the concept of the account but not this format. T-accounts are useful primarily for instructional purposes.

proven to be of great significance in decreasing the errors made in carrying out the accounting process. The fundamental accounting model, **Assets = Liabilities + Owners' equity,** itself is an algebraic model that balances and can be rearranged mathematically. Paciolo added another algebraic balance feature to it to accommodate the recording of increases and decreases in each account. Let's see how it was done.

Paciolo perceived that having designed the T-account with two sides to reflect increases and decreases, he could add still another algebraic **balancing feature** by simply *reversing* the position in the account of the "increases" and "decreases" on the *opposite sides* of the equal sign. To illustrate the point, he incorporated this second algebraic balance feature, which is still used to this day; it has the "+" and "−" *in reverse order* on the opposite sides of the equal sign as follows:

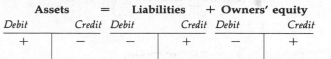

Assets		=	Liabilities		+ Owners' equity	
Debit	*Credit*		*Debit*	*Credit*	*Debit*	*Credit*
+	−		−	+	−	+

Observe that the debit and credit positions do not change; only the plus and minus signs change positions. The addition of this algebraic concept resulted in the second "balancing" feature; that is, **debits always equal credits.** Thus, the system used for recording increases and decreases in the accounts may be conveniently tabulated as follows:

	Increases	*Decreases*
Assets...................	Debit	Credit
Liabilities................	Credit	Debit
Owners' equity	Credit	Debit

Another way to view the Debits = Credits feature is in terms of the algebraic relationship: "The signs reverse on opposite sides of the equal sign."[5]

Debits and credits for revenues and expenses—Owners' equity is increased by credits and decreased by debits. Revenues increase owners' equity; therefore they are recorded as credits. Expenses decrease owners' equity; therefore they are recorded as debits. In other words, the debit/credit relationship for owners' equity accounts is applied to revenues and expenses as follows:[6]

---

[5] Historically, and continuing to the present, accountants refer to the left side as the debit side and to the right side as the credit side. For accounting purposes, the terms *debit* and *credit* have no other meanings. The words "to debit" and "to credit" should not be confused with "increase" or "decrease" as will become clear in the next few paragraphs. Contrary to what some people think, there is no implication of "goodness" attached to credits or "badness" attached to debits (or vice versa). Although rearranged, Exhibit 3–7 still maintains the Debits = Credits feature.

[6] To "charge an account" is a frequently used expression meaning to *debit* an account. Thus, the word "debit" is used as both a verb and a noun.

Revenues are recorded as credits.
Expenses are recorded as debits.

Dividends (withdrawals by owners) decrease owners' equity; hence, they are recorded as debits. It follows that for each transaction, and for all transactions, the debit amounts always will equal the credit amounts. To summarize, the two balancing features of the fundamental accounting model are:

1. Assets = Liabilities + Owners' equity
2. Debits = Credits

The next section of this chapter illustrates the use of accounts and emphasizes application of the fundamental accounting model and its dual balancing feature.

TRANSACTION ANALYSIS

Information processing in an accounting system involves the **collection** of economic data on each transaction, **analysis** of the data in terms of the fundamental accounting model (often called **transaction analysis**), **recording** (entering) the results of the analysis in the accounting system (i.e., the accounts discussed above), and finally, **preparing** the periodic financial statements. This section introduces transaction analysis.

Transaction analysis is a term used frequently to describe the process of studying each transaction to determine its dual effect on the entity in terms of the accounting model. In transaction analysis a careful distinction is made between the cash basis and the accrual basis methods. In Chapter 2, pages 70 and 71, the distinction between *cash basis accounting* and *accrual basis accounting* was discussed. Recall that the accrual basis is required by GAAP. The concept of **accrual accounting** requires that revenues and expenses be measured and reported in the accounting period in which they occur rather than when the related cash is received or paid.

Now, let's see how **each transaction** is subjected to transaction analysis to determine (1) the dual economic effect on the entity and (2) how that dual effect is recorded in the accounts (i.e., in the fundamental accounting model).

Recall that for each transaction recorded, **two separate balances** must be maintained, viz: (1) Assets = Liabilities + Owners' equity and (2) Debits = Credits. Bass Cleaners, Incorporated, will be used to demonstrate, on the next few pages, transaction analysis and the basic recording process. You should analyze each transaction (listed in Exhibit 3–1) and trace the manner in which the dual effect is recorded in the accounting model by using T-accounts (rather than simple plus and minus as in Exhibit 3–1). The transactions are entered in Exhibit 3–4 in T-accounts and are keyed with letters for ready reference.

EXHIBIT 3–4
Use of T-accounts

a. **Received $20,000 cash invested by the four owners and issued 800 shares of capital stock (par value $25 per share).**

Transaction analysis—This transaction increased the company's cash by $20,000, which is recorded in the **Cash** account as a debit (increase); liabilities were unaffected; and owners' equity was increased by $20,000, which is recorded in the **Capital Stock** account as a credit (increase). The entry (recording) in the accounting system may be summarized conveniently as follows (credits are listed last and also are indented for easy identification):

> Cash (asset) .... 20,000 (debit)
>   Capital stock (owners' equity) ....   20,000 (credit)

The two *accounts* would appear as follows:

	Cash (asset)				**Capital Stock (owners' equity)**	
	Debit	*Credit*			*Debit*	*Credit*
(a)	20,000			*(a)*		20,000

Dual check for accuracy—The entry meets both tests: Assets (+$20,000) = Liabilities (–0–) + Owners' equity (+$20,000), and Debits ($20,000) = Credits ($20,000).

b. **Borrowed $5,000 cash from the bank on a 12 percent note payable.**

Transaction analysis—This transaction increased cash by $5,000, which is recorded in the **Cash** account as a debit (increase); liabilities were increased by $5,000, which is recorded in **Notes Payable** as a credit (increase); and owners' equity was unchanged. The entry in the accounting system may be summarized as follows:

> Cash (asset) 5,000
>   Notes payable (liability)   5,000

The *accounts* affected would appear as follows:

	Cash (asset)				**Notes payable (liability)**	
	Debit	*Credit*			*Debit*	*Credit*
(a)	20,000			*(b)*		5,000
(b)	5,000					

Dual check for accuracy—The entry meets both tests: Assets (+$5,000) = Liabilities (+$5,000) + Owners' equity (–0–), and Debits ($5,000) = Credits ($5,000).

c. **Purchased a delivery truck for cash at a cost of $8,000.**

Transaction analysis—This transaction increased the asset, **Delivery Truck,** by $8,000, which is recorded in that account as a debit (increase); and the cash was decreased by $8,000, which is recorded in the **Cash** account as a credit (decrease). Liabilities and owners' equity were not affected. The entry in the accounting system may be summarized conveniently as follows:

EXHIBIT 3–4
(continued)

| Delivery truck (asset) | 8,000 | |
| Cash (asset) | | 8,000 |

The two *accounts* affected would appear as follows:

| | Delivery Truck (asset) | | | | Cash (asset) | | |
	Debit	Credit			Debit	Credit
(c)	8,000			(a)	20,000	·(c) 8,000
				(b)	5,000	

Dual check for accuracy—The entry meets both tests: Assets (delivery truck, +$8,000 and cash, −$8,000) = Liabilities (–0–) + Owners' equity (–0–), and Debits ($8,000) = Credits ($8,000).

d. Cleaning revenue collected in cash, $40,000.

Transaction analysis—This transaction increased cash by $40,000, which is recorded in the asset account **Cash** as a debit (increase); liabilities were unaffected; and owners' equity was increased by $40,000 as a result of earning revenue. Owners' equity is credited (increased) for $40,000. A separate owners' equity account, **Cleaning Revenue,** is used to keep track of this particular revenue. The entry may be summarized as follows:

| Cash (asset) | 40,000 | |
| Cleaning revenue (owners' equity) ... | | 40,000 |

The two *accounts* affected would appear as follows:

| | Cash (asset) | | | Cleaning Revenue (owners' equity) | |
	Debit	Credit		Debit	Credit
(a)	20,000	(c) 8,000		(d)	40,000
(b)	5,000				
(d)	40,000				

Dual check for accuracy—The entry meets both tests: Assets (+ $40,000) = Liabilities (–0–) + Owners' equity (+$40,000), and Debits ($40,000) = Credits ($40,000).

e. Cleaning revenue earned, but the cash not collected, $4,000.

Transaction analysis—This transaction increased the company's asset, **accounts receivable,** by $4,000, which is recorded as a debit (increase) to that account; liabilities were unaffected; and owners' equity was increased by $4,000. Owners' equity is credited (increased) by using a separate account, **Cleaning Revenue,** which is used to keep track of this particular revenue. The entry in the accounting system may be summarized as follows:

| Accounts receivable (asset) | 4,000 | |
| Cleaning revenue (owners' equity) ... | | 4,000 |

EXHIBIT 3–4
(continued)

The effect on the two *accounts* would appear as follows:

Accounts Receivable (asset)		Cleaning Revenue (owners' equity)	
Debit	*Credit*	*Debit*	*Credit*
(e) 4,000		(d) 40,000	
		(e) 4,000	

Dual check for accuracy—The entry meets both tests: Assets (+$4,000) = Liabilities (–0–) + Owners' equity (+$4,000), and Debits ($4,000) = Credits ($4,000).

f. Expenses paid in cash, $25,800.

Transaction analysis—This transaction decreased cash by $25,800, which is recorded in the **Cash** account as a credit (decrease); liabilities were unaffected; and owners' equity was decreased by $25,800 as a result of paying expenses. Owners' equity is decreased by debiting a separate account **Operating Expenses,** which is used to keep track of this particular expense. The accounting entry may be summarized as follows:

> Operating expense (owners' equity) 25,800
> Cash (asset) 25,800

The effect on the two *accounts* would appear as follows:

Operating Expenses (owners' equity)		Cash (asset)	
Debit	*Credit*	*Debit*	*Credit*
(f) 25,800		(a) 20,000	(c) 8,000
		(b) 5,000	(f) 25,800
		(d) 40,000	

Dual check for accuracy—The entry meets both tests.

g. Expenses incurred, but the cash not paid, $2,000.

Transaction analysis—This transaction increased the company's liabilities by $2,000, which is recorded as a credit (increase) to **Accounts Payable;** assets were unaffected; and owners' equity was decreased by debiting a separate account, **Operating Expenses.** The entry summarized is:

> Operating expenses (owners' equity) 2,000
> Accounts payable (liability) 2,000

The two *accounts* affected would appear as follows:

Operating Expenses (owners' equity)		Accounts Payable (liability)	
Debit	*Credit*	*Debit*	*Credit*
(f) 25,800			(g) 2,000
(g) 2,000			

Dual check for accuracy—The entry meets both tests.

EXHIBIT 3–4
(continued)

h. Paid cash interest on note payable in *(b)* ($5,000 × 12% = $600).

Transaction analysis—This transaction decreased cash by $600, which is recorded as a credit (decrease) in the **Cash** account; the amount of the related liability ($5,000) was unchanged; however, owners' equity was decreased by the amount of the interest ($600) since the payment of interest (but not principal of the note) represents an expense. Owners' equity is decreased by debiting a separate account, **Interest Expense,** which is used to keep track of this particular type of expense. The entry summarized is:

Interest expense (owners' equity)	600	
Cash (asset)		600

The two *accounts* affected would appear as follows:

Interest Expense (owners' equity)			Cash (asset)			
Debit	*Credit*		*Debit*		*Credit*	
(h) 600		*(a)*	20,000	*(c)*	8,000	
		(b)	5,000	*(f)*	25,800	
		(d)	40,000	*(h)*	600	

Dual check for accuracy—The entry meets both tests.

i. Depreciation expense for one year on the truck ($8,000 ÷ 5 years = $1,600).

Transaction analysis—This transaction is caused by the internal utilization of an asset owned for operating purposes. Such use gives rise to depreciation expense. Owners' equity was decreased by this expense, which is recorded as a debit to a separate account for this type of expense, **Operating Expenses.** Assets (i.e., the delivery truck) was decreased because a part of the cost of the asset was "used up" in operations. Instead of directly crediting (decreasing) the asset account, Delivery Truck, a related *contra account,* **Accumulated Depreciation, Delivery Truck,** is credited so that the total amount of depreciation can be kept separately. This will be explained and illustrated in detail in Chapter 9. The entry summarized is:

Operating expenses (owners' equity)	1,600	
Accumulated depreciation, delivery truck (asset contra)		1,600

The two *accounts* affected would appear as follows:

Operating Expenses (owners' equity)			Accumulated Depreciation, Delivery Truck (asset contra)		
Debit	*Credit*		*Debit*	*Credit*	
(f) 25,800				*(i)* 1,600	
(g) 2,000					
(i) 1,600					

Dual check for accuracy—The entry meets both tests: Assets (−$1,600) = Liabilities (−0−) + Owners' equity (−$1,600), and Debits ($1,600) = Credits ($1,600).

EXHIBIT 3–4
(continued)

j. Paid cash dividends to stockholders, $1,800.

Transaction analysis—This transaction decreased the company's cash by $1,800, which is recorded in the **Cash** account as a credit (decrease); liabilities were unaffected; owners' equity was decreased by $1,800 as a result of the resources (cash) paid out of the business to the stockholders. Owners' equity is debited (decreased) by using a separate account, **Dividends Paid**, which is used to keep track of this kind of decrease in owners' equity. Dividends paid is not an expense, rather it represents a distribution of "profits" to the owners. The entry summarized is:

Dividends paid (owners' equity)	1,800	
Cash (asset)		1,800

The two accounts *affected* would appear as follows:

Dividends Paid (owners' equity)				**Cash (asset)**			
Debit		*Credit*		*Debit*			*Credit*
(j)	1,800		(a)	20,000	(c)	8,000
			(b)	5,000	(f)	25,800
			(d)	40,000	(h)	600
					(j)	1,800

Dual check for accuracy—The entry meets both tests.

k. Collected $1,000 cash on accounts receivable in *(e)*.

Transaction analysis—This transaction increased cash by $1,000, which is recorded as a debit (increase) in the **Cash** account; another asset, **Accounts receivable,** was decreased, which is recorded as a credit (decrease) of $1,000. Liabilities and owners' equity were unaffected because there was a change in two assets with no change in total assets. The entry summarized is:

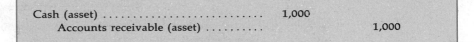

Cash (asset)	1,000	
Accounts receivable (asset)		1,000

The two accounts *affected* would appear as follows:

Cash (asset)				**Accounts Receivable (asset)**			
Debit		*Credit*		*Debit*			*Credit*
(a)	20,000	(c)	8,000	(e)	4,000	(k)	1,000
(b)	5,000	(f)	25,800				
(d)	40,000	(h)	600				
(k)	1,000	(j)	1,800				

Dual check for accuracy—The entry meets both tests.

EXHIBIT 3–4
(concluded)

l. **Paid $500 cash on accounts payable in** *(g).*

Transaction analysis—This transaction decreased cash by $500, which is recorded as a credit (decrease) in the **Cash** account; the $500 decrease in liabilities is recorded as a debit (decrease) to the **Accounts Payable** account. Owners' equity was unaffected since there was no revenue or expense involved in this transaction, merely the payment of a debt. The entry summarized is:

Accounts Payable (liability)	500	
Cash (asset)		500

The two accounts *affected* would appear as follows:

	Accounts Payable (liability)				Cash (asset)		
	Debit		*Credit*		*Debit*		*Credit*
(l)	500	*(g)*	2,000	*(a)*	20,000	*(c)*	8,000
				(b)	5,000	*(f)*	25,800
				(d)	40,000	*(h)*	600
				(k)	1,000	*(j)*	1,800
						(l)	500

Dual check for accuracy—The entry meets both tests.

Observe in Exhibit 3–4 that each transaction affected a minimum of two different accounts. This is because the economic position of the entity, in terms of the fundamental accounting model—Assets = Liabilities + Owners' equity—always is affected in at least two ways. This dual-effect characteristic of the model is the reason its application often is referred to as a double-entry information processing system.

Now we may summarize the fundamental accounting model and the mechanics of the debit-credit concept in T-account format as follows, where + means increase and − means decrease:

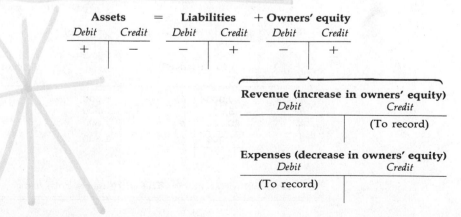

Note particularly that an increase in **revenue** (a credit) represents an **increase** in owners' equity and an increase in **expense** (a debit) represents a **decrease** in owners' equity. When a revenue is earned, the resources (i.e., assets) of the business are increased and, because of the dual effect, owners' equity is increased by the same amount. In contrast, when an expense is incurred, the net resources of the business are decreased (i.e., assets are decreased and/or liabilities increased), and because of the dual effect, the owners' equity is decreased by the same amount.

PART B: THE ACCOUNTING INFORMATION PROCESSING CYCLE

The accounting information processing cycle is repeated each period. It involves a series of **sequential** phases (steps), starting with the transactions and extending through the accounting records and finally to the required financial statements: income statement, balance sheet, and statement of changes in financial position. In this part, we will consider the primary sequential phases in the information processing cycle in the order in which they usually are accomplished, viz: (1) collecting raw data, (2) analyzing transactions, (3) recording transactions in the **journal**, (4) transferring data from the journal to the **ledger**, (5) preparing a **trial balance**, and (6) preparing the required financial statements.

PHASE 1—RAW DATA COLLECTION

The initial phase in the accounting information processing cycle is the collection of raw economic data on each transaction affecting the entity. Such economic data must be collected continuously throughout the accounting period as transactions occur. Transactions involving external parties usually generate documents that provide essential data. Examples are sales invoices, cash register tapes, purchase invoices, and signed receipts. Documentation must be generated **internally** for certain economic effects such as depreciation and the using up of office supplies already on hand. It is important to realize that most of the raw data (and the supporting documents) entered into an accounting system are not generated by the accounting function but through the various **operating** functions of the business. Since the quality of the outputs of an information processing system is determined primarily by the quality (and timeliness) of the inputs of raw data based on transactions, a carefully designed and controlled data collection system is necessary. Thus, the initial data collection procedure constitutes an integral and important subsystem of an accounting information processing system.

PHASE 2—TRANSACTION ANALYSIS

This phase in the accounting information processing system was exemplified on pages 99 through 104. Recall that it is a mental process having as its objective determination of the economic effects on the entity of each transaction in terms of the basic accounting model: Assets = Liabilities + Owners' equity. When transaction analysis is completed on a transaction, the economic effects then are entered **formally** in the accounting system.

PHASE 3—THE JOURNAL

The economic effect of each transaction immediately after transaction analysis is **formally** entered in the accounting system in a record known as the **journal.**

In a simple situation one could record the transactions of a business entity directly in the separate accounts as was done for Bass Cleaners. However, in more complex situations, it is essential, as each transaction is analyzed, that its dual economic effect on the accounting model (i.e., the resultant entry) be recorded in one place in its **chronological order** (i.e., in order of date of occurrence). The accounting record designed for this particular purpose is known as the **journal.** Typically, the dual effects are recorded first in the journal and later are transferred, or **posted,** to the appropriate accounts (refer to the T-accounts used for Bass Cleaners in Part A).

The journal contains a chronological listing of the entries for each of the transactions. The format of the entry in the journal for each transaction is designed so that the dual effects on the accounting model and the debit and credit features are linked physically. For example, transaction (a) for Bass Cleaners would appear in the **journal** in the following format in which the debit always is listed first and the credit is listed *last* and *indented* for easy identification.

		Debit	Credit
(Date) Cash		20,000	
Capital stock			20,000
To record investment of cash by owners.			

Observe that for instructional purposes on pages 99 through 104, this same format was used to summarize the required entry for each transaction. The physical linking of the dual effects of each transaction in the journal is in contrast to the separate accounts, where each entry is separated physically between two or more accounts. For example, you will recall (pages 99 and 104) that the dual effect of the above entry for Bass Cleaners would appear in the separate accounts as follows:

Cash		Capital Stock	
(Date) 20,000		(Date) 20,000	

The journal, as the place of formal entry of the dual economic effects of each transaction, serves three useful purposes:

1. It provides for the initial and orderly listing (by date) of each transaction immediately after the transaction is subjected to transaction analysis.
2. It provides a single place to record all of the economic effects of each transaction without any further subclassifications of the data.
3. It facilitates later tracing; checking for possible errors; and reconstruction of a transaction, its analysis, and its recording.

Knowledge of the approximate date very often is used in these activities; the journal is the only place in the accounting system where all of the dual economic effects of each entry are linked physically.

To facilitate your understanding, let's see how the journal might appear in a manually maintained system. The first three transactions for Bass Cleaners have been entered in a typical journal shown in Exhibit 3–5.

EXHIBIT 3–5

		Journal			Page ___1___
Date	Account Titles and Explanation	Folio	Debit	Credit
Jan. 1	Cash	101	20,000	
	Capital stock	301		20,000
	Investment of cash by owners			
Jan. 3	Cash	101	5,000	
	Note payable	202		5,000
	Borrowed cash on 12% note			
Jan. 6	Delivery truck	111	8,000	
	Cash	101		8,000
	Purchased delivery truck for use in the business			

Recording the transactions in the journal in this manner is known as **journalizing.** In summary, you should observe in particular that (1) each transaction and event is first recorded in the journal as a separate entry; (2) each entry is dated, and entries are recorded in chronological order; (3) for each transaction the debits (accounts and amounts) are entered first, the credits follow and are indented; and (4) as a consequence, for each transaction the effects on the accounting model and the debits and credits are linked in one entry. These features, since they provide an "audit or tracing trail," facilitate subsequent examination of past transactions and in the location of errors, and simplify subsequent accounting (as will be demonstrated later). Because it is the place of first recording of each transaction, the journal sometimes is referred to as a **book of original entry.**

PHASE 4—THE LEDGER

In the preceding illustration for Bass Cleaners (pages 99 through 104) a **separate account** was maintained for each kind of asset, liability, and owners' equity. Thus, it is apparent that an accounting system typically will contain a large number of such accounts. Collectively, the accounts are contained in a record known as the **ledger.** The ledger may be organized in numerous ways. Handwritten accounting systems may use a loose-leaf ledger—one page for each account. In the case of a "machine" account-ing system, a separate machine card is maintained for each account. In the case of a computerized accounting system, the ledger is maintained on magnetic tape or similar electronic storage devices, but there are still separate accounts as in the other systems (each account is identified by an assigned number).

Exhibit 3–6 shows the ledger for Bass Cleaners in handwritten T-account form. The ledger (i.e., the accounts contained in it) is the result of transfer-ring the information contained in the journal. In the preceding phase (the journal) we stated that the data for each entry recorded in the journal are transferred, or **posted,** to the appropriate accounts in the ledger. This transfer from the chronological arrangement in the journal to the account format in the ledger is a very important reclassification of the data since the ledger reflects the data classified (by separate accounts) as assets, liabili-ties, and owners' equity rather than chronologically.

In a business using a manual handwritten system, one may expect the entity to record the transactions in the journal each day and to post to the ledger less frequently, say every few days. Of course, the timing of these **information processing activities** varies with the size and complexity of the entity.

The T-account format was illustrated on page 95 and in Exhibit 3–6 (which is useful for instructional purposes). However, the typical account format used is columnar as illustrated in Exhibit 3–7. It maintains the

EXHIBIT 3–6

BASS CLEANERS, INCORPORATED
LEDGER (at December 31, 19A)

ASSETS	=	LIABILITIES	+	OWNERS' EQUITY

Cash

(a)	20,000	(c)	8,000
(b)	5,000	(f)	25,800
(d)	40,000	(h)	600
(k)	1,000	(j)	1,800
		(l)	500

(Net debit balance, $29,300)

Notes Payable

		(b)	5,000

Capital Stock

		(a)	20,000

Dividends Paid†

(j)	1,800	

Accounts Receivable

(e)	4,000	(k)	1,000

(Net debit balance, $3,000)

Accounts Payable

(l)	500	(g)	2,000

(Net credit balance, $1,500)

Cleaning Revenue

		(d)	40,000
		(e)	4,000

(Net credit balance, $44,000)

Delivery Truck

(c)	8,000	

Operating Expenses

(f)	25,800
(g)	2,000
(i)	1,600

(Net debit balance, $29,400)

Accumulated Depreciation, Delivery Truck*

		(i)	1,600

Interest Expense

(h)	600	

Totals	$38,700	=	$6,500	+	$32,200

Note: The accounting model, Assets = Liabilities + Owners' equity, given at the top of this exhibit, and the totals at the bottom are shown only for your convenience in study; they would not appear in an actual ledger.

* Accumulated depreciation is a negative, or contra, asset account. For further explanation see Chapter 9.

† Dividends paid represents a decrease in owners' equity since it shows the amount that was paid out as dividends to the stockholders. For further explanation see Chapter 12.

debit-credit concept but is arranged to provide columns for date, explanation, folio (F), and running balances.

In posting, the debits and credits reflected in the journal entries are transferred directly as debits and credits to the indicated accounts in the ledger. In both the journal (Exhibit 3–5) and ledger (as in the Cash account, Exhibit 3–7), you can observe that there is a **"folio"** column, which is included to provide a numerical cross-reference between the journal and

EXHIBIT 3–7
Ledger account (account form)

Account Title _Cash_   Account Number _101_

Date	Explanation	F	Debit	Credit	Balance
Jan. 1	Investments	1	20,000		20,000
3	Borrowing	3	5,000		25,000
6	Truck purchased	3		8,000	17,000
7	Cleaning revenue	4	40,000		57,000
8	Operating expenses	4		25,800	31,200
10	Interest expense	5		600	30,600
15	Payments to owners	7		1,800	28,800
16	Collections on receivables	8	1,000		29,800
17	Payments on accounts payable	8		500	29,300

the ledger (this is often said "to provide an audit trail"). For example, the journal shown in Exhibit 3–5 shows a folio number of 101 for Cash, which indicates the account in the ledger to which that amount was posted. You will recall that this is the account number assigned to cash in Exhibit 3–3. Similarly, if you look at the ledger account for Cash, as shown in Exhibit 3–7, you will see on the first line of the account a folio number of 1, indicating that the particular amount posted came from page 1 of the journal. Folio numbers are entered during the **posting** process; therefore, they indicate whether posting has been accomplished. Transferring amounts from the journal to the ledger is called *posting*. Since the data ends up in the **ledger**, it sometimes is referred to as the **book of final entry.**

PHASE 5—THE TRIAL BALANCE

At the end of the accounting period, as a matter of convenience, a **trial balance** is prepared from the ledger. A trial balance is simply a listing, in ledger-account order, of the ledger accounts and their respective net debit or credit balances. The net balance shown for each account is the difference between the total of the debits and the total of the credits in each ledger account. Exhibit 3–8 shows the trial balance of Bass Cleaners at December 31, 19A. It was prepared directly from the ledger given in Exhibit 3–6.

EXHIBIT 3–8

BASS CLEANERS, INCORPORATED
Trial Balance
December 31, 19A

Account titles	Balance Debit	Credit
Cash	$29,300	
Accounts receivable	3,000	
Delivery truck	8,000	
Accumulated depreciation, delivery truck		$ 1,600
Notes payable		5,000
Accounts payable		1,500
Capital stock (800 shares)		20,000
Dividends paid	1,800	
Cleaning revenues		44,000
Operating expenses	29,400	
Interest expense	600	
Totals	$72,100	$72,100

A trial balance serves two purposes in the accounting information processing cycle:

1. It provides a check on the equality of the debits and credits as reflected in the ledger accounts at the end of the period (or whenever taken).
2. It provides data in a convenient form for development of the financial statements.

PHASE 6—FINANCIAL STATEMENTS

At the end of the accounting period (1) all transactions for the period will have been analyzed and entered in the journal by order of date, (2) all amounts in the journal will have been posted (transferred) to the ledger accounts, and (3) a trial balance will have been prepared from the ledger.

The next phase is completion of the three required financial statements which were discussed and illustrated in Chapters 1 and 2. The trial balance provides the basic data needed to prepare the financial statements at the end of the period. The income statement and balance sheet for Bass Cleaners, prepared from the trial balance shown in Exhibit 3–8, were illustrated in Exhibit 3–2.

The demonstration case that follows is an important tool in understanding this chapter—you should study it carefully.

DEMONSTRATION CASE—THE ACCOUNTING
INFORMATION PROCESSING SYSTEM

La Paloma
Apartments,
Incorporated

This case illustrates the complete information processing cycle discussed in this chapter. (Try to resolve the requirements before proceeding to the suggested solution that follows.)

We have selected this case of a small business to demonstrate the complete **accounting information processing cycle** from the initial capture of the raw economic data to the financial statements developed at the end of the accounting year. Only representative and summary transactions have been selected to keep the length of the case within reason. Low amounts are used to simplify the illustration. You should study each step in the solution carefully since it reviews the concepts, principles, and procedures introduced in the chapters to this point.

On January 3, 1978, M. Hall and P. Garza formed a corporation to build and operate an apartment complex called La Paloma. At the start, each one invested $40,000 cash and received 3,000 shares of $10 par value stock. Therefore, at that date the following entry was recorded in the accounts:

January 3, 1978:

Cash..	80,000	
Capital stock, par $10 (6,000 shares)		60,000
Contributed capital in excess of par......................		20,000

Shortly thereafter, land was acquired for $30,000 and a construction contract was signed with a builder. The first apartments were rented on July 1, 1979. The owners decided to use a *fiscal year* of July 1 through June 30 for business purposes (instead of a fiscal year which agrees with the calendar year). It is now June 30, 1981, and the occupancy rate during the year has been over 96 percent due to the quality of the apartments and the excellent management by Hall and Garza.

Since this is the end of the second year of operations, certain accounts in the ledger will have balances carried over from June 30, 1980. A complete list of the accounts in the ledger that will be needed for this case, with the balances carried over from the previous fiscal year, is given on page 113. Ledger account (folio) numbers are provided at the left.

Typical transactions (most of them summarized) for the 12-month fiscal year—July 1, 1980, through June 30, 1981—are listed below. To facilitate tracing, instead of using dates, we will use the letter notation to the left of each transaction.

a. On November 1, 1980, paid $3,000 cash for a two-year insurance premium covering the building, its contents, and liability coverage.

b. Rental revenue earned: collected in cash, $105,500; and uncollected, $2,000.

c. Paid accounts payable (amount owed from last year for expenses), $6,000.

d. Purchased a tract of land, at a cost of $35,000, as a planned site for another apartment complex to be constructed in "about three years."

LA PALOMA APARTMENTS
Ledger Balances
July 1, 1980 (start of Year 2)

Account No.	Account titles	Balance Debit	Balance Credit
101	Cash	$ 18,000	
103	Accounts receivable (or rent receivable)		
105	Supplies inventory	2,000	
112	Prepaid insurance		
121	Land (apartment site)	30,000	
122	La Paloma apartment building	200,000	
123	Accumulated depreciation, apartment building		$ 10,000
125	Furniture and fixtures	60,000	
126	Accumulated depreciation, furniture and fixtures		12,000
131	Land for future apartment site		
201	Accounts payable		6,000
202	Property taxes payable		
203	Income taxes payable		
204	Mortgage payable, 10% (apartment building)		180,000
205	Note payable, long term, 10%		
301	Capital stock (par $10, 6,000 shares)		60,000
302	Contributed capital in excess of par		20,000
303	Retained earnings (accumulated earnings to June 30, 1980)		22,000
401	Rent revenue		
521	Utilities and telephone expense		
522	Apartment maintenance expense		
523	Salary and wage expense		
524	Insurance expense		
525	Property tax expense		
526	Depreciation expense		
527	Miscellaneous expenses		
531	Interest expense		
532	Income tax expense		
	Totals	$310,000	$310,000

Cash amounting to $5,000 was paid, and a long-term note payable (10 percent interest per annum, interest payable each six months) was signed for the balance of $30,000.

e. Operating expenses incurred and paid in cash were:

Utilities and telephone expense	$23,360
Apartment maintenance expense	1,200
Salary and wage expense	6,000

f. At the end of the fiscal year (June 30, 1981) the following bills for expenses incurred had not been recorded or paid: June telephone bill, $40; and miscellaneous expenses, $100.

g. Paid interest for six months on the long-term note at 10 percent per annum. (Refer to item [d].) (Hint: Interest = Principal × Rate × Time.)

h. An inventory count at the end of the fiscal period, June 30, 1981, showed remaining supplies on hand amounting to $400. Supplies used are considered a miscellaneous expense.

i. By the end of the fiscal period, June 30, 1981, one third (8 months out of 24 months) of the prepaid insurance premium of $3,000 paid in transaction *(a)* had expired.

j. Depreciation expense for the year was based on an estimated useful life of 20 years for the apartment and 5 years for the furniture and fixtures (assume no residual or salvage value).

k. The property taxes for the year ending June 30, 1981, in the amount of $2,700 have not been recorded or paid.

l. Cash payment at year-end on the mortgage on the apartment was:

On principal....................	$20,000
Interest ($180,000 × 10%)	18,000
Total paid	$38,000

m. Income tax expense for the year ending June 30, 1981, was computed to be $6,000 (i.e., a 20 percent average rate). Assume that this obligation will be paid in the next period.

Required:

Complete the accounting information processing cycle by solving each of the following:

1. Set up a ledger with T-accounts that includes all of the accounts listed above; include the account numbers as given. Enter the July 1, 1980, balances in each account in this manner:

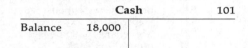

Cash		101
Balance 18,000		

2. Analyze, then journalize (i.e., enter in the journal), each transaction listed above for the period July 1, 1980, through June 30, 1981. Number the journal pages consecutively.
3. Post all entries from the journal to the ledger; utilize the folio columns.
4. Prepare a trial balance at June 30, 1981.
5. Prepare a classified income statement for the fiscal year ending June 30, 1981.
6. Prepare a classified balance sheet at June 30, 1981.

Suggested solution:

Requirement 1—Ledger (see pages 117 and 118):

Requirement 2—Journal:

JOURNAL   Page __1__

Date 1980–81	Account titles and explanation	Folio	Debit	Credit
a.	Prepaid insurance	112	3,000	
	Cash	101		3,000
	Paid insurance premium for two years in advance (Explanatory note: An asset account, Prepaid Insurance, is debited because a future service, insurance coverage, has been paid for in advance.)			
b.	Cash	101	105,500	
	Accounts receivable (or rent receivable)	103	2,000	
	Rent revenue	401		107,500
	To record rent revenues earned for the year, of which $2,000 has not yet been collected.			
c.	Accounts payable	201	6,000	
	Cash	101		6,000
	Paid obligation carried over from previous year.			
d.	Land for future apartment site	131	35,000	
	Cash	101		5,000
	Note payable, long term (10%)	205		30,000
	Purchased land as a site for future apartment complex. (This is a second tract of land acquired; the present apartment building was constructed on the first tract.)			
e.	Utilities and telephone expense	521	23,360	
	Apartment maintenance expense	522	1,200	
	Salary and wage expense	523	6,000	
	Cash	101		30,560
	Paid expenses.			
f.	Utilities and telephone expense	521	40	
	Miscellaneous expenses	527	100	
	Accounts payable	201		140
	Expenses incurred, not yet paid.			

Requirement 2 (continued):

JOURNAL   Page 2

Date 1980–81	Account titles and explanation	Folio	Debit	Credit
g.	Interest expense	531	1,500	
	Cash	101		1,500
	Paid six months' interest on long-term note ($30,000 × 10% × 6/12 = $1,500).			
h.	Miscellaneous expenses	527	1,600	
	Supplies inventory	105		1,600
	To record as expense supplies used from inventory during the year. (Explanatory note: Supplies are bought in advance of use; hence, at that time they are recorded as an asset, Supplies Inventory. As the supplies are used from inventory, the asset thus used becomes an expense. Refer to Supplies Inventory account [$2,000 − $400 = $1,600].)			
i.	Insurance expense	524	1,000	
	Prepaid insurance	112		1,000
	To record as an expense the cost of the insurance that expired ($3,000 × 8/24 = $1,000).			
j.	Depreciation expense	526	22,000	
	Accumulated depreciation, apartment building	123		10,000
	Accumulated depreciation, furniture and fixtures	126		12,000
	Depreciation expense for one year.			
	Computation: Apartment: $200,000 ÷ 20 years = $10,000. Furniture and fixtures: $60,000 ÷ 5 years = $12,000.			
k.	Property tax expense	525	2,700	
	Property taxes payable	202		2,700
	Property taxes for the year not yet paid.			
l.	Mortgage payable (10%)	204	20,000	
	Interest expense	531	18,000	
	Cash	101		38,000
	Payments on principal of mortgage payable plus interest expense.			
m.	Income tax expense	532	6,000	
	Income tax payable	203		6,000
	Income tax for the year.			

Requirements 1 and 3—Ledger:

LEDGER

Cash 101

Date	F	Amount	Date	F	Amount
Balance		18,000	(a)	1	3,000
(b)	1	105,500	(c)	1	6,000
			(d)	1	5,000
			(e)	1	30,560
			(g)	2	1,500
			(l)	2	38,000

(Net debit balance, $39,440)

Accounts Receivable 103

	F	Amount			
(b)	1	2,000			

Supplies Inventory 105

Date		Amount		F	Amount
Balance		2,000	(h)	2	1,600

Prepaid Insurance 112

	F	Amount		F	Amount
(a)	1	3,000	(i)	2	1,000

Land (Apartment Site) 121

Date		Amount			
Balance		30,000			

La Paloma Apartment Building 122

Date		Amount			
Balance		200,000			

Accumulated Depreciation, Apartment Building 123

			Date	F	Amount
			Balance		10,000
			(j)	2	10,000

Furniture and Fixtures 125

Date	F	Amount	Date	F	Amount
Balance		60,000			

Accumulated Depreciation, Furniture and Fixtures 126

			Date	F	Amount
			Balance		12,000
			(j)	2	12,000

Land for Future Apartment Site 131

	F	Amount			
(d)	1	35,000			

Accounts Payable 201

	F	Amount	Date	F	Amount
(c)	1	6,000	Balance		6,000
			(f)	1	140

Property Taxes Payable 202

				F	Amount
			(k)	2	2,700

Income Taxes Payable 203

				F	Amount
			(m)	2	6,000

Mortgage Payable (apartment building) 204

	F	Amount	Date		Amount
(l)	2	20,000	Balance		180,000

Requirements 1 and 3 (continued):

Note Payable, Long Term					205
Date	F	Amount	Date	F	Amount
			(d)	1	30,000

Insurance Expense					524
Date	F	Amount	Date	F	Amount
(i)	2	1,000			

Capital Stock		301
Balance		60,000

Property Tax Expense		525
(k)	2	2,700

Contributed Capital in Excess of Par		302
Balance		20,000

Depreciation Expense		526
(j)	2	22,000

Retained Earnings		303
Balance		22,000

Miscellaneous Expenses		527
(f)	1	100
(h)	2	1,600

Rent Revenue		401
(b)	1	107,500

Interest Expense		531
(g)	2	1,500
(l)	2	18,000

Utilities and Telephone Expense		521
(e)	1	23,360
(f)	1	40

Income Tax Expense		532
(m)	2	6,000

Apartment Maintenance Expense		522
(e)	1	1,200

Salary and Wage Expense		523
(e)	1	6,000

Requirement 4:

LA PALOMA APARTMENTS
Trial Balance
June 30, 1981

Account no.	Account titles	Balance Debit	Credit
101	Cash	$ 39,440	
103	Accounts receivable	2,000	
105	Supplies inventory	400	
112	Prepaid insurance (16 months)	2,000	
121	Land (apartment site)	30,000	
122	La Paloma apartment building	200,000	
123	Accumulated depreciation, apartment building		$ 20,000
125	Furniture and fixtures	60,000	
126	Accumulated depreciation, furniture and fixtures		24,000
131	Land for future apartment site	35,000	
201	Accounts payable		140
202	Property taxes payable		2,700
203	Income taxes payable		6,000
204	Mortgage payable (apartment building)		160,000
205	Note payable, long term		30,000
301	Capital stock (par $10, 6,000 shares)		60,000
302	Contributed capital in excess of par		20,000
303	Retained earnings (accumulated earnings to June 30, 1980)		22,000
401	Rent revenue		107,500
521	Utilities and telephone expense	23,400	
522	Apartment maintenance expense	1,200	
523	Salary and wage expense	6,000	
524	Insurance expense	1,000	
525	Property tax expense	2,700	
526	Depreciation expense	22,000	
527	Miscellaneous expenses	1,700	
531	Interest expense	19,500	
532	Income tax expense	6,000	
	Totals	$452,340	$452,340

Requirement 5:

LA PALOMA APARTMENTS
Income Statement
For the Year Ended June 30, 1981

Revenue:
Rent revenue		$107,500*

Operating expenses:
Utilities and telephone expense	$23,400	
Apartment maintenance expense	1,200	
Salary and wage expense	6,000	
Insurance expense	1,000	
Property tax expense	2,700	
Depreciation expense	22,000	
Miscellaneous expenses	1,700	
Total operating expenses		58,000
Income from apartment operations		49,500

Financial expense:
Interest expense	19,500
Pretax income	30,000
Income tax expense	6,000
Net income	$ 24,000
EPS (24,000 ÷ 6,000 shares)	$4.00

* Notes:
a. These amounts were take directly from Requirement 4, the trial balance.
b. Since no products are sold by this business, gross margin cannot be reported.

Requirement 6:

LA PALOMA APARTMENTS
Balance Sheet
At June 30, 1981

Assets

Current assets:
Cash		$ 39,440*
Accounts receivable		2,000
Supplies inventory		400
Prepaid insurance		2,000
Total current assets		$ 43,840

Operational assets:
Land, apartment site		30,000	
La Paloma apartment building	$200,000		
Less: Accumulated depreciation, building	20,000	180,000	
Furniture and fixtures	60,000		
Less: Accumulated depreciation, furniture and fixtures	24,000	36,000	
Total operational assets			246,000

Other assets:
Land acquired for future apartment site†	35,000
Total assets	$324,840

Liabilities

Current liabilities:
Accounts payable	$ 140	
Property taxes payable	2,700	
Income taxes payable	6,000	
Total current liabilities		$ 8,840

Long-term liabilities:
Mortgage payable	160,000	
Note payable, long term	30,000	
Total long-term liabilities		190,000
Total liabilities		198,840

Stockholders' Equity

Contributed capital:
Capital stock, par $10 (6,000 shares)	60,000	
Contributed capital in excess of par	20,000	
Total contributed capital	80,000	
Retained earnings (beginning balance $22,000 + net income $24,000)	46,000	
Total stockholders' equity		126,000
Total liabilities and stockholders' equity		$324,840

* These amounts were taken directly from Requirement 4, the trial balance.

† Classified as "other" rather than "operational" because this land is not being used currently for operating purposes.

SUMMARY

This chapter discussed the fundamental accounting model and the accounting information processing system; the latter is outlined for study purposes in Exhibit 3–9. We discussed the nature of transactions that provide the raw economic data for input into the accounting information system. We learned that the fundamental accounting model—Assets = Liabilities + Owners' equity—provides the basic framework for transaction analysis. The accounting model provides for recording the dual effect of each transaction. It encompasses two balancing features, the conditions of which must be met with respect to each transaction and event recorded, viz: (1) assets equal liabilities plus owners' equity and (2) debits equal credits. After analysis, the transactions are recorded (journalized) first in the journal, the resultant dual effect (i.e., the amounts debited and credited) is posted to the ledger. The ledger reflects a separate account for each kind of asset, liability, and owners' equity. Normally, asset accounts will have debit balances, whereas liability accounts will have credit balances. Owners' equity accounts normally will show credits for the capital stock and retained earnings accounts—expenses will show debit balances, and revenues will show credit balances. The accounting information processing system, as a consequence, generates the data needed to develop the periodic financial statements: the income statement, balance sheet, and statement of changes in financial position (SCFP).

EXHIBIT 3-9
The sequential phases in an accounting information processing system

(1) ORIGINAL SOURCE DOCUMENTS

(to capture the raw economic data of each transaction)

↓

(2) TRANSACTION ANALYSIS

(to determine economic effects of each transaction on the entity)

↓

(3) JOURNALS
(a record where the economic effects of each transaction on the accounting models are recorded in chronological order)

↓

(4) LEDGER

(a record that lists each asset, liability, and owners" equity account)

↓

(5) TRIAL BALANCE

(a listing of account balances to facilitate preparation of financial reports)

↓

(6) FINANCIAL REPORTS

(the reports to decision makers [users] of the economic impact of the transactions of the period on the entity.)

DAILY BUSINESS TRANSACTIONS

Invoices | Vouchers | Bills | Etc.

ECONOMIC ANALYSIS
(effect on the enterprise)

JOURNALIZING

Journal 1

POSTING

CASH 101

DEVELOPING

Trial Balance
Account | Debit | Credit

PREPARING

Income statement | Balance sheet | Statement of changes in financial position | Special reports

The discussions in this chapter establish the basis for the accounting information processing cycle for a business entity. It represents a cycle because it is **repeated** each accounting period (usually one year). The sequential phases in the information processing cycle may be outlined as follows:

Phase 1 **Raw data collection**—Economic data are collected for each transaction at the time of occurrence. Sales invoices, charge tickets, freight bills, notes, signed receipts, and so on, are source documents used in this step.

Phase 2 **Transaction analysis**—Each transaction undergoes transaction analysis to determine how it affects the fundamental accounting model: Assets = Liabilities + Owners' equity.

Phase 3 **Journalizing**—Each transaction is recorded *chronologically* in the journal, which indicates the date, accounts to be debited and credited, amounts, and an explanation.

Phase 4 **Posting**—Each amount entered in the journal is transferred, or posted, to the appropriate account in the ledger.

Phase 5 **Trial balance**—At the end of the accounting period the balance in each account (i.e., the net debit or credit balance) in the ledger is determined. The balance of each ledger account then is listed on a trial balance. The equality of debits and credits is checked.

Phase 6 **Financial statements**—The information on the trial balance is utilized to develop the periodic financial statements composed of the income statement, balance sheet, and statement of changes in financial position.

As we progress in our study, additions to and elaborations of this information processing cycle will be introduced.

IMPORTANT TERMS DEFINED IN THE CHAPTER (with page citations)

Transactions—90
Source documents—91
Dual economic effect—92, 93
Fundamental accounting
  model—92, 96
Transaction analysis—93, 94, 98, 106
Ledger account—93, 95, 109, 117
Debit—96, 97
Credit—96, 97

Accrual accounting—98
Accounting information
  processing cycle—105, 122
Journal—106
Journalizing—108
Ledger—108, 109, 117
Posting—108
Trial balance—110

QUESTIONS FOR DISCUSSION

Part A

1. Define a business transaction. Why does accounting focus on the individual business transaction?

2. Give the fundamental accounting model and briefly explain each variable included in it, including revenues, expenses, and investments and withdrawals by owners.

3. Explain why revenues increase and expenses decrease owners' equity.

4. What is the meaning of "to debit" and "to credit"?

5. Complete the following matrix by entering either debit or credit in each cell.

Item	Increases	Decreases
Assets		
Liabilities		
Owners' equity		
Revenues		
Expenses		

6. Complete the following matrix by entering either increase or decrease in each cell.

Item	Debit	Credit
Assets		
Liabilities		
Owners' equity		
Revenues		
Expenses		

Questions
Part B

7. Briefly explain what is meant by transaction analysis.

8. Define the journal. What purposes does it serve?

9. Define the ledger. What purpose does it serve?

10. Distinguish between the book of original entry and the book of final entry.

11. Distinguish between journalizing and posting.

12. What is the purpose of the *folio* notations in the journal and ledger accounts?

13. What is a trial balance? What purposes does it serve?

14. What does the term "audit trail" imply?

15. Define what is meant by fiscal period as used in accounting.

16. Briefly outline the accounting information processing system for a business.

EXERCISES

Part A

E3–1. XY Corporation has been operating for one year. At the end of the first year the financial statements have been prepared. Below are a series of separate and independent cases based on the required statements. For each independent case you are to supply the missing item and its amount.

(Relates to Exercise 3–1)

Case	Data	Missing Item	Amount
Example	Assets, $70,000; owners' equity, $40,000	Liabilities	$30,000
A	Revenues, $99,000; expenses, $62,000		
B	Liabilities, $32,000; owners' equity, $50,000		
C	Cash inflows, $75,000; increase in cash, $20,000		
D	Liabilities, $42,000; assets, $81,000		
E	Net income, $35,000; expenses, $63,000		
F	Net income, $33,000; revenues, $93,000		
G	Expenses, $80,000; revenues, $80,000		
H	Revenues, $82,000; expenses, $90,000		
I	Increase in cash, $15,000; cash outflows, $60,000		
J	Cash outflows, $55,000; cash inflows, $48,000		

E3–2. For each transaction below indicate the effect upon assets, liabilities, and owners' equity by entering a plus for increase and a minus for decrease.

service fees performed on credit in (c) above.

f. Paid cash, $2,000, on the operating expenses that were on credit in (d) above.

(Relates to Exercise 3–2)

Transaction	Effect upon		
	Assets	Liabilities	Owners' equity
a. Issued stock to organizers for cash			
b. Borrowed cash from local bank			
c. Purchased equipment on credit			
d. Earned revenue, collected cash			
e. Incurred expenses, on credit			
f. Earned revenue, on credit			
g. Paid cash for (e)			
h. Incurred expenses, paid cash			
i. Earned revenue, collected three fourths cash, balance on credit			
j. Theft of $100 cash			
k. Declared and paid cash dividends			
l. Collected cash for (f)			
m. Depreciated equipment for the period			
n. Incurred expenses, paid four fifths cash, balance on credit			
o. Paid income tax expense for the period			

E3–3. Jiffy Service Company, Inc., was organized by four investors. The following transactions were completed:

a. The investors paid in $40,000 cash to start the business. Each one was issued 1,000 shares of capital stock, par value $10 per share.

b. Equipment for use in the business was

g. Investor A borrowed $10,000 from a local bank and signed a one-year, 10 percent note for that amount.

Required:

Set up a format similar to the following and enter thereon each of the above transactions that should be recorded by Jiffy. Transaction (a) is entered as an example.

(Relates to Exercise 3–3)

Transactions	*Assets*	*= Liabilities +*	*Owners' equity*
a. Investment of cash in the business	Cash + $40,000		Capital stock + $40,000

purchased at a cost of $8,000, one half was paid in cash and the balance is due in six months.

c. Service fees were earned amounting to $54,000, of which $6,000 was on credit.

d. Operating expenses incurred amounted to $33,000, of which $3,000 was on credit.

e. Cash was collected for $4,000 of the

Also determine the total amounts for assets, liabilities, and owners' equity after completing the recording.

E3–4. Snappy Service Company Inc., was organized with the issuance of 10,000 shares of stock for $30,000 cash. The following transactions occurred during the current accounting period:

a. Received the cash from the organizers.
b. Service fees earned amounted to $35,000, of which $25,000 was collected in cash.
c. Operating expenses incurred amounted to $23,000, of which $17,000 was paid in cash.
d. Bought two machines for operating purposes at the start of the year at a cost of $9,000 each; paid cash.
e. One of the machines was destroyed by fire one week after purchase; it was uninsured. The event to be considered is the fire. (Hint: Set up a fire loss expense account.)
f. The other machine has an estimated useful life to Snappy of ten years (and no residual value). The event to be considered is the depreciation of the equipment since it was used for one year in rendering services.
g. Stockholder Able bought a vacant lot (land) for $5,000 cash.

ble, Machines, Accumulated Depreciation, Accounts Payable, Service Fees Earned, Operating Expenses, Fire Loss Expense, Depreciation Expense, and Capital Stock.
b. Complete the following by entering the correct totals:

Assets . . . . $_____
Liabilities . . . . $_____
Owners' equity . . . . $_____
Debits . . . . $_____
Credits . . . . $_____

Exercises
Part B

E3–5. The following T-accounts for Home Service Company, Inc., reflect five different transactions (entries). You are requested to prepare a journal entry for each transaction and write a complete description of each transaction.

(Relates to Exercise 3–5)

Cash			
(a)	50,000	(c)	7,000
(b)	13,000	(e)	1,000
(d)	2,000	(f)	5,000

Accounts Payable		
(e)	1,000	(c) 2,000

Capital Stock, Par $10	
	(a) 50,000

Accounts Receivable		
(b)	3,000	(d) 2,000

Note Payable	
	(f) 15,000

Service Revenue	
	(b) 16,000

Equipment	
(f)	20,000

Operating Expenses	
(c) 9,000	

Required:

a. Set up appropriate T-accounts and enter in them the dual effects on the accounting model of each of the above transactions that should be recorded by Snappy. Key the amounts to the letters starting with *(a)*. Number the following accounts consecutively starting with 101 for Cash: Cash, Accounts Receiva-

E3–6. On January 1, 1981, Nancy Boyd and Donna Nance organized the B&N Service Company, Inc. The transactions of the company for the first 45 days are stated below. You are requested to analyze each transaction and enter it in a journal similar to the one illustrated in Exhibit 3–5.

1981

Jan. 1 Cash invested by the organizers was Boyd, $30,000 (for 3,000 shares); and Nance, $10,000 (for 1,000 shares).

3 Paid monthly rent, $500.

15 Purchased equipment for use in the business costing $18,000; paid one third down and signed a 12 percent note payable for the balance. Monthly payments (24) comprised of part principal and part interest are to be paid on the note.

30 Paid cash for operating expenses amounting to $18,000; in addition, operating expenses of $2,000 were incurred on credit.

30 Service fees earned amounted to $30,000, of which $5,000 was collected and the balance was on credit.

Feb. 10 Collected $1,500 on account for service fees previously performed which were on credit.

12 Paid $1,000 on the operating expenses previously incurred which were on credit.

15 Paid $565 on the equipment note, including $120 interest expense.

E3–7. Stern Air Conditioning Service Company, Incorporated, has been operating for three years. A. T. Stern, the majority shareholder, has built it up from a one-person organization to an operation requiring ten people. Few records have been maintained; however, Stern now realizes the need for a complete accounting system. The size and complexity of the business is partially indicated by the following selected transactions completed during the first five months of 1981:

Jan. 15 Purchased three new service trucks at $9,000 each; paid a third down and signed a 12 percent one-year note for the balance. Twelve monthly payments, including interest, are to be made on the note.

Jan. 31 Service revenue earned in January amounted to $74,000, which included $3,000 on credit (due in 90 days).

31 Operating expenses incurred in January amounted to $58,000, which included $4,000 on credit (payable in 60 days).

Feb. 5 Dividends declared of $1,000; paid in cash to the shareholders. (Hint: This decreases owners' equity.)

15 Paid $1,600 on the truck note, which included $180 interest.

Apr. 15 Paid 1980 taxes on business property, $150; this amount was recorded in 1980 as a liability (property taxes payable).

May 1 Collected $2,400 of the services extended on credit in January.

Required:

a. Journalize the above transactions in a form similar to that illustrated in Exhibit 3–5. Number the journal pages consecutively, starting with 51.

b. Post to T-accounts in the ledger; utilize the folio columns and enter dates. Number the ledger accounts as follows: Cash, 101; Accounts Receivable, 102; Trucks, 103; Accounts Payable, 104; Note Payable, 105; Property Taxes Payable, 106; Dividends Paid, 107; Service Revenue, 108; Operating Expenses; 109; and Interest Expense, 110. As you post, keep in mind that there would be prior amounts carried over from 1980 in some of the ledger accounts.

E3–8. The bookkeeper of Careless Company prepared the following trial balance at December 31, 1981:

Account titles	Debit	Credit
Notes receivable	$ 4,000	
Supplies inventory		$ 200
Accounts payable	800	
Land	16,000	
Capital stock		20,000
Cash	7,000	
Interest revenue	200	
Notes payable		5,000
Operating expenses ...	19,000	
Interest expense		800
Other assets	9,583	
Service revenues		30,583
Total	$56,583	$56,583

The independent CPA (auditor) casually inspected the trial balance and concluded there were several errors on it. You have been requested to draft a correct trial balance. (Hint: All of the amounts are correct.)

E3–9. Dunn Service Company is in a situation where a considerable amount of credit is typical. For some time after it was organized by A. D. Dunn and two friends, the only records maintained were for cash receipts and cash payments. Dunn (the company president) stated, "I watched my cash balance to see how I was doing; if cash went up I assumed a profit, and, to the contrary, if cash went down I assumed a loss." As the company expanded and became involved in more credit, Dunn realized that "I must look at the revenue earned and the expenses incurred on an accrual basis, as well as the cash situation." Illustrative of the current situation is the following information for Dunn Company for the month of January 1981:

Service revenues:
Cash collected for services performed in January 1981 ...... $36,000
Services performed in January 1981 on credit 4,000
Operating expenses:
Cash paid for expenses incurred in January 1981 17,000
Expenses incurred in January 1981 on credit 25,000

(Disregard income taxes.)

Required:

a. Prepare a special statement on a cash basis to reflect cash inflows, cash outflows, and the change in cash occasioned by the above summarized transactions.

b. Prepare an income statement (accrual basis) to show computation of revenues earned, expenses incurred, and the net income or loss for January 1981.

c. Explain why the cash and accrual results were different.

d. Basically, what does this suggest as to the inappropriateness of the cash basis to reflect profit performance?

PROBLEMS

Part A

P3–1. Listed below are the ledger accounts of the AAA Rental Company, Incorporated.

a. Cash.
b. Accounts receivable.
c. Common stock.
d. Bonds payable.
e. Rent revenue.
f. Prepaid insurance premiums.
g. Interest revenue.
h. Investments, long term.
i. Interest expense.
j. Machinery and equipment.
k. Patents.
l. Income tax expense.
m. Property taxes payable.
n. Loss on sale of operational assets.
o. Land, plant site (in use).
p. Contributed capital in excess of par.
q. Supplies inventory.
r. Notes payable, short term.
s. Retained earnings.
t. Short-term investments.
u. Other assets.
v. Operating expenses.
w. Income taxes payable.
x. Gain on sale of operational assets.
y. Land held for future plant site.
z. Revenue from investments.
aa. Wages payable.
bb. Accumulated depreciation.
cc. Merchandise inventory.

(Relates to Problem 3–1)

	Type of account			Usual balance	
Item	Asset	Liability	Owners' equity (including revenues and expenses)	Debit	Credit
a. Etc.	✓	....		✓	

Complete a tabulation similar to the following (enter two check marks for each item above):

P3–2. The following transactions were completed by Duster Service Company during the year 19X:

1. The organizers paid in cash and received 10,000 shares of capital stock.
2. Duster borrowed cash from the local bank.
3. Duster purchased a delivery truck, paid three fourths cash, and the balance is due in six months.
4. Earned revenues, collected cash in full.
5. Expenses incurred, paid cash in full.
6. Earned revenues, on credit (cash not collected in 19X).
7. Expenses incurred, on credit (cash not paid in 19X).
8. Declared and paid cash dividend to stockholders.
9. Collected half of the amount on credit in 6.
10. Paid all of the credit amount in 7.
11. A spare tire was stolen from the delivery truck (not insured).
12. During the period the delivery truck depreciated ($ amount).

Required:

Below is given a tabulation. For each transaction given above enter in the tabulation a D for debit and a C for credit to reflect the effects on the assets, liabilities, and owners' equity (separate groups are given for owners' equity).

P3–3. Super Service Company has been operating for three years. At the end of 19C the accounting records reflected assets of $300,000 and liabilities of $100,000. Dur-

(Relates to Problem 3–2)

Accounting Model	Transactions											
	1	2	3	4	5	6	7	8	9	10	11	12
a. Assets												
b. Liabilities												
Owners' equity: c. Investments												
d. Revenues												
e. Withdrawals												
f. Expenses												

(Note: In some cases there may be both a D and C in the same box.)

ing the year 19D the following summarized transactions were completed:

a. Revenues of $150,000, of which $10,000 was on credit.
b. Issued 1,000 shares of additional capital stock, par $10 per share, for $10,000 cash.
c. Purchased equipment that cost $15,000, paid cash $10,000, and the balance is due next year.
d. Expenses incurred were $110,000, of which $15,000 was on credit.
e. Collected $8,000 of the credit amount in (a).
f. Paid cash dividends to stockholders of $15,000.
g. Paid $11,000 of the credit amount in (d).
h. Borrowed $10,000 cash from a local bank (at the end of 19D), payable June 30, 19E.
i. Cash amounting to $500 was stolen (not covered by insurance).
j. Depreciation on equipment was $1,000 for 19D.

Required:

a. Compute the amounts for assets, liabilities, and owners' equity as of the end of 19D. Use the following format for your response:

The accounts are numbered for identification. Below the accounts is a series of transactions. For each transaction indicate the account(s) to be debited and credited by entering the appropriate account number(s) to the right.

1. Cash.
2. Accounts receivable.
3. Supplies inventory.
4. Prepaid insurance.
5. Equipment.
6. Accumulated depreciation, equipment.
7. Patents.
8. Accounts payable.
9. Notes payable.
10. Wages payable.
11. Income tax payable.
12. Capital stock, par $10.
13. Contributed capital in excess of par value.
14. Service revenues.
15. Operating expenses.
16. Income tax expense.
17. Interest expense.
18. None of the above (explain).

(Relates to Problem 3–3)

	Assets		Liabilities		Owners' equity	
	Debit	Credit	Debit	Credit	Debit	Credit
Balance, Jan. 1, 19D						
Transactions:						
a. Revenues						
b. Etc.						
Balance, Dec. 31, 19D						

b. What was the amount of net income for 19D? Show computations.

P3–4. Listed below is a series of accounts for Quality Service Company, Incorporated, which has been operating for three years.

(Relates to Problem 3–4)

Transactions	Debit	Credit
a. Example—Investment by shareholders to start the business; cash was received for stock in excess of the par value.	1	12,13
b. Purchased equipment for use in business; paid half cash and gave note payable for balance.	5	1,9
c. Paid cash for salaries and wages.		
d. Collected cash for services performed this period.		
e. Collected cash for services performed last period.		
f. Performed services this period on credit.		
g. Paid operating expenses incurred this period.	15	1
h. Paid cash for operating expenses incurred last period.		
i. Incurred operating expenses this period, to be paid next period.		
j. Purchased supplies for inventory; paid cash.		
k. Used some of the supplies from inventory for operations.		
l. Purchased a patent; paid cash.		
m. Made a payment on the equipment note (b) above; the payment was in part on principal and in part interest thereon.		
n. Collected cash on accounts receivable for services previously performed.		
o. Paid cash on accounts payable for expenses previously incurred.		
p. Paid three fourths of the income tax expense for the year; the balance to be paid next period.		
q. On last day of current period, paid in cash an insurance premium covering the next two years.		

P3–5. Listed below is a series of accounts for Ready Service Company, Inc. The accounts are numbered for identification.

1. Cash.
2. Accounts receivable.
3. Service supplies inventory.
4. Trucks and equipment.
5. Accumulated depreciation.
10. Accounts payable.
11. Notes payable.
12. Income tax payable.
20. Capital stock, par $10 per share.

21. Contributed capital in excess of par.
25. Service revenues.
26. Operating expenses.
27. Depreciation expense.
28. Interest expense.
29. Income tax expense.
30. None of the above (explain).

During 19X the company completed the selected transactions given below.

Required:

To the right indicate the accounts (by identification number) that should be debited and credited and the respective amounts. The first transaction is used as an example.

(Relates to Problem 3–5)

Transaction	Debit		Credit	
	Acct. No.	Amount	Acct. No.	Amount
Example: Investment by organizers to start the business, $60,000 cash for 5,000 shares, par $10 per share.	1	60,000	20 21	50,000 10,000
a. Purchased panel truck for use in the business for $8,000; paid one fourth cash and signed 10% note for the balance.				
b. Service revenues earned, $100,000, of which $10,000 was on credit.				
c. Operating expenses incurred, $75,000, of which $15,000 was on credit.				
d. Purchased service supplies, $500, paid cash (placed in supplies inventory).				
e. Collected $9,000 of the credit amount in (c).				
f. Paid $13,000 of the credit amount in (d).				
g. Used $200 of the service supplies (taken from inventory) for service operations.				
h. Depreciation on the truck for the year, $1,600.				
i. Paid six months' interest on the note in (a).				
j. Income tax expense for the year, $4,000, paid three fourths cash, balance payable by April 1 of next year.				

Problems
Part B

P3–6. The ledger accounts for Ball Real Estate Agency, a corporation (organized three years previously) provided the annual trial balance shown below at March 31, 1981 (the end of the annual fiscal period).

Trial Balance
At March 31, 1981

Account titles	Debit	Credit
Cash	$ 33,000	
Accounts receivable ..	48,800	
Office supplies inventory	200	
Automobiles (company cars)	6,000	
Accumulated depreciation, automobiles ...		$ 4,000
Office equipment	2,000	
Accumulated depreciation, office equipment		1,000
Accounts payable		2,000
Income tax payable ...		
Salaries and commissions payable		1,000
Notes payable, long term		20,000
Capital stock (par $10, 3,000 shares)		30,000
Contributed capital in excess of par		3,000
Retained earnings (on April 1, 1980)		5,000
Dividends declared and paid during the fiscal year	10,000	
Sales commissions earned		70,000
Management fees earned		6,000
Operating expenses (detail omitted to conserve time)	40,000	
Depreciation expense (on autos and office equipment)	500	
Interest expense	1,500	
Income tax expense ..	.	
Totals	$142,000	$142,000

Required:

a. Prepare a classified, multiple-step income statement for the year ended March 31, 1981. The above trial balance does not include income taxes. Assume an average corporate tax rate of 25 percent and that the income tax will be paid later. (Hint: EPS is $8.50.)

b. Prepare a classified balance sheet at March 31, 1981. (Hint: For both requirements refer to Chapter 2 for examples of classified statements. Total assets are $85,000.)

P3–7. Box Home Repair Service was organized two years ago by M. E. Box and three friends. By the end of the second year, three crews were operating and Box (the company president) felt that the business was a success. Although prices charged were high, the customers appeared pleased in view of the quality of the work done and the efficiency with which repairs were completed. The following account balances were reflected by the ledger on January 1, 1981:

(Relates to Problem 3—7)

Account No.	Account titles	Debit	Credit
101	Cash	$ 6,550	
105	Accounts receivable	3,700	
110	Building supplies inventory (for use on repair jobs)	1,500	
120	Trucks	15,000	
121	Accumulated depreciation on trucks		$ 6,000
200	Accounts payable		3,000
201	Income tax payable		
205	Note payable, short term		5,000
210	Wages payable		250
220	Note payable, long term		10,000
300	Capital stock, par $1 per share		2,500
400	Service revenue		
501	Operating expenses		
502	Depreciation expense		
503	Interest expense		
504	Income tax expense		
	Totals	$26,750	$26,750

During 1981 the following transactions occurred:

a. Paid the $250 wages payable carried over from 1980.

b. Purchased, for cash, additional building supplies for future use, $1,100 (debit the Building Supplies Inventory account).

c. Purchased an additional truck for $9,500 cash.

d. Collected $2,800 cash on the accounts receivable.

e. Paid the $5,000 short-term note, plus six months' interest at 12 percent per annum.

f. The stockholders' invested an additional $10,000 cash in the business and were issued 10,000 shares.

g. Repair fees earned in 1981, $97,000, which included $7,000 earned in 1981 but uncollected (i.e., on credit).

h. Paid operating expenses of $60,000 cash. Additional operating expenses of $4,000 were incurred; the cash will be paid for these in 1982.

i. According to an inventory count of the building supplies at December 31, 1981, unused supplies amounted to $800. (Hint: Supplies used should be debited to Operating Expenses: Sup-

plies used = Amount on hand at start + Additional purchased − Ending inventory.)

j. Depreciation on the three trucks was computed on the basis of an estimated useful life of five years. The new truck will not be depreciated in 1981 since it was acquired near the end of the year.

k. Paid $6,000 on the long-term note, plus 12 percent interest on the $10,000 for one year.

l. Paid $5,000 on accounts payable.

m. Income tax expense $5,340 (20 percent rate), all paid in cash.

Required:

1. Set up the ledger accounts listed above and enter the beginning balances; label these as "Balance."
2. Analyze each transaction, then enter it directly in the ledger accounts (you will not need additional accounts). Key your entries with the letter designation (in place of a date). No journal is required; however, it may be helpful to form each journal entry on scratch paper before entering it in the ledger.
3. Prepare a trial balance at December 31, 1981. (Hint: Trial balance total, $124,500.)

4. Prepare an income statement. Assume an average income tax rate of 20 percent which results in income taxes of $5,340.

P3–8. Quality Stenographic and Mailing Service, Incorporated, was organized by three individuals during January 19A. Each investor paid in $5,000 cash, and each received 400 shares of $10 par value stock. During 19A the transactions listed below occurred. The letters at the left of each item will serve as the date notation.

a. Received the $15,000 investment by the organizers and issued the shares.

b. Purchased office equipment which cost $6,000; paid cash.

c. Paid $400 cash for a two-year insurance premium on the office equipment (debit Prepaid Insurance).

d. Purchased a delivery truck at a cost of $8,000; paid $7,000 down and signed a $1,000, 90-day, 12 percent, interest-bearing note payable for the balance.

e. Purchased office supplies for cash to be used in the stenographic and mailing operations, $2,000. The supplies are for future use (therefore, debit Office Supplies Inventory).

f. Revenues earned during the year were:

	Cash	On credit
Stenographic fees	$55,000	$6,000
Mailing fees	8,000	1,000

g. Operating expenses incurred during the year were:

Cash	$26,000
On credit	14,000

h. Paid the $1,000 note on the panel truck. Cash paid out was for the principal plus the interest for three months.

i. Purchased land for a future building site at a cost of $20,000; paid cash.

j. Depreciation on the truck for 19A, was computed on the basis of a five-year useful life; on the office equip-

ment, useful life of ten years was assumed (compute full-year depreciation on each and assume no residual value).

k. By December 31, 19A, insurance for one year had expired. Prepaid Insurance should be decreased, and an expense recorded.

l. An inventory of the office supplies reflected $300 on hand at December 31, 19A. Supplies Inventory should be reduced, and an expense recognized.

Required:

1. Analyze and prepare a journal entry for each transaction listed. Use a form similar to Exhibit 3–5 and include a brief explanation after each transaction.

2. Prepare an income statement that reports total revenues, total expenses, pretax income, income taxes (assume an average 20 percent corporate tax rate which results in income tax of $5,174), and net income. (Hint: Since no ledger is required, you can do this by either (a) selecting and aggregating amounts from the entries made in Requirement 1, or (b) setting up the needed T-accounts on scratch paper. Net income is $20,696.)

3. What is the ending balance of cash? Show computations. Why is it different than net income?

P3–9. Hasty Delivery Service was organized as a corporation on June 1, 1980. The management decided that the fiscal year for the company would be June 1 to May 31. The following transactions were selected from the first year for case purposes; for convenience, use the letter identification to the left as the date notation.

a. Cash invested was $15,000, and 1,000 shares of $10 par value capital stock were issued.

b. Three new delivery vehicles were purchased at a total cost of $24,000;

$14,000 was paid in cash, and a 12 percent note payable was signed for the balance.

c. Operating supplies which cost $450 were purchased for cash. These supplies were placed in operating supplies

(Relates to Problem 3–9)

Account No.	Account titles
101	Cash
102	Accounts receivable
103	Office supplies inventory
104	Prepaid insurance
105	Delivery vehicles
106	Accumulated depreciation, delivery vehicles
201	Accounts payable
202	Note payable

inventory (debit) and will be used gradually.

d. Delivery revenues earned amounted to $80,000, of which $11,000 was on credit.

e. Operating expenses incurred amounted to $54,000, of which $8,000 was on credit.

f. Paid cash for a two-year insurance premium in advance to insure the delivery vehicles, $600.

g. Collected $9,000 on the credit extended for delivery services (item [d] above).

h. Paid $7,000 on the obligations for operating expenses (item [e] above).

i. An inventory count showed that two thirds of the operating supplies purchased ([c] above) had been used by May 31, 1981.

j. Paid $2,000 on the principal of the note given on the delivery vehicles ([b] above), plus six months' interest on $10,000.

k. Computed depreciation on the delivery vehicles for one year (up to May 31, 1981), assuming a five-year useful life and no residual value.

l. On May 31, 1981, insurance for one year had expired.

m. Disregard income taxes.

Required:

1. Set up a journal similar to Exhibit 3–5, then journalize each item.
2. Post the journal entries to the following ledger accounts:

Account No.	Account titles
301	Common stock
302	Contributed capital in excess of par
303	Retained earnings
401	Delivery revenue
501	Operating expense
502	Interest expense
503	Depreciation expense

3. Prepare a trial balance at May 31, 1981. (Hint: The trial balance totals are $108,800.)
4. Compute the ending cash balance and pretax income. How much do they differ? Why do they differ?

P3–10. Able, Baker, and Cain organized ABC Realty as a corporation to conduct a real estate and rental management business. Each contributed $20,000 cash and received 1,500 shares of stock (par value $10 per share). They commenced business on January 1, 19A. The transactions listed below, representative of those during the first year, were selected from the actual transactions for case purposes.

Assume for case purposes that these transactions comprise all of the transactions for the year. This case demonstrates the information processing cycle from the capture of raw economic data to the final output—the financial statements. Use the numbers at the left as the date notation.

1. Received $60,000 cash invested by shareholders and issued 4,500 shares of stock. See the list of accounts given below.
2. On January 1, 19A, purchased office equipment that cost $6,000; paid one-

third cash and charged the balance (one third due in 6 months, remainder due in 12 months). Credit Accounts Payable for the amount not paid in cash.

3. Purchased land for future office site, cost, $20,000; paid cash.

4. Paid office rent in cash, 11 months at $200 per month. Beginning with this transaction, set up separate accounts for each type of expense.

5. Sold nine properties and collected sales commissions of $56,000. Set up an account, "Realty Commissions Revenue."

6. Paid salaries and commissions to salespersons amounting to $52,000 and miscellaneous expenses amounting to $1,000.

(Relates to Problem 3–10)

Account No.	Account titles
101	Cash
102	Accounts receivable
103	Office equipment
104	Accumulated depreciation, office equipment
105	Land for future office site
201	Accounts payable
202	Rent payable
203	Income tax payable
301	Capital stock, par $10
302	Contributed capital in excess of par
401	Realty commission revenue

13. Additional commissions earned during 19A on sale of real estate amounted to $64,000 of which $14,000 was uncollected at year-end.

14. Paid the installment of $2,000 on the office equipment (see 2 above).

15. Assume an average corporate income tax rate of 30 percent; 19A tax expense of $21,450 will be paid in 19B.

Required:

a. Analyze, then journalize, each of the above entries in chronological order. Number the journal pages consecutively, starting with 1.

b. Post each transaction from the journal to the ledger; use T-accounts as follows:

Account No.	Account titles
402	Rental management revenue
501	Rent expense
502	Salary and commission expense
503	Miscellaneous expense
504	Utilities expense
505	Auto rental expense
506	Advertising expense
507	Depreciation expense
508	Income tax expense

7. Collected rental management fees, $20,000. Set up an account, "Rental Management Revenue."

8. Paid utilities, $1,400.

9. Paid auto rental fees (auto rented for use in business), $3,600.

10. Paid for advertising, $7,500.

11. At year-end, the December rent had not been paid (credit Rent Payable).

12. The estimated life of the office equipment was ten years; assume use for the full year in 19A and no residual value.

Use folio cross-references when posting.

c. Prepare a trial balance from the ledger; check the equality of debits and credits. (Hint: Trial balance total is $224,250, including cash of $94,300.)

d. Use the data on the trial balance to prepare a classified income statement and balance sheet. Refer to Chapter 2 for examples of classified statements. Because of its complexity, we will defer preparing a statement of changes in financial position until a later chapter. (Hint: EPS, $11.12.)

P3–11. SD Moving and Storage Company, Inc., was organized four years ago by O. Snow and R. P. Dean. Each contributed $20,000 cash initially and was issued 2,000 shares of capital stock, par $10 per share. Since that time, a good portion of the earnings has been left in the business for growth. SD owns a large warehouse and 11 hauling vans. At the beginning, few financial records were maintained; however, it now has one person who devotes full time to records and reports. Disagreements with the Internal Revenue Service prompted the company to approach an independent CPA for advice. As a consequence, the first audit was performed for 1980. For purposes of this case, we will utilize only representative accounts and transactions to minimize the time requirements. Assume that the accounts for SD showed the following balance on January 1, 1981 (the fiscal and calendar years agree):

a. Purchased land for future office building at a cost of $13,000; paid cash.

b. Revenues earned:

	Cash	Credit
Trucking	$220,000	$40,000
Storage	30,000	2,000

c. Paid $1,600 cash for a two-year insurance premium covering the trucks and warehouse. This payment was made on January 2, 1981 (debit Prepaid Insurance).

d. Purchased additional supplies for use in operations for cash, $1,600; these supplies are to be used as needed. Debit Account No. 110.

e. At end of 1981 paid $10,000 on the principal of the long-term note payable, plus 10 percent interest on the $30,000 for 12 months.

f. Operating expenses incurred:

Cash	$195,000
On credit	23,000

(Relates to Problem 3–11)

Account No.	Account titles	Debit	Credit
101	Cash	$ 21,500	
103	Accounts receivable	15,000	
110	Supplies inventory	2,500	
112	Prepaid insurance		
131	Land (on which warehouse is located)	10,000	
133	Warehouse	80,000	
134	Accumulated depreciation, warehouse		$ 16,000
135	Moving vans	75,000	
136	Accumulated depreciation, moving vans		30,000
151	Land for future office building		
201	Accounts payable		10,000
202	Income tax payable		
210	Notes payable, long term (10%)		30,000
301	Capital stock, par $10 (4,000 shares)		40,000
302	Retained earnings		78,000
303	Dividends declared and paid		
401	Trucking revenues		
402	Storage revenues		
501	Operating expenses		
502	Depreciation expense		
505	Interest expense		
506	Income tax expense		
	Totals	$204,000	$204,000

Representative transactions for 1981 follow (use the letter notation at the left for dating purposes):

g. Collections on part of accounts receivable (for trucking and storage services on credit), $38,000 (see [b] above).

h. Payments on part of accounts payable (expenses and services previously incurred on credit), $20,000 cash.

i. Declared and paid cash dividend of $33,000 in December 1981 (debit Account No. 303).

j. A full year's depreciation expense for 1981 was computed on the basis of the following useful lives: warehouse, 20 years; and moving vans, 5 years (assume no residual values). Debit Account No. 502.

k. On December 31, 1981, an inventory showed supplies remaining on hand (unused) amounting to $1,800. Reduce Supplies Inventory and recognize an expense (Account No. 501).

m. Income tax expense (30 percent rate), $14,670; paid in cash except for one fourth which will be paid during April 1982.

Required:

1. Set up T-accounts for each account listed above (the above list includes all of the accounts needed) and enter therein the beginning balances given in the following manner:

	Cash	101
Balance	21,500	

2. Set up a journal similar to Exhibit 3–5 and enter each of the transactions. Use the letter designation for dating and include a short explanation after each entry. Number the journal pages consecutively starting with 1.

3. Post each transaction entered in the journal to the ledger accounts; complete the folio columns in both the journal and ledger.

4. Prepare a trial balance from the ledger accounts at December 31, 1981. (Hint: The trial balance total is $511,667, including cash of $21,297).

5. Prepare a classified income statement and balance sheet. See Chapter 2 for examples of classified statements. To

support the balance sheet, prepare a statement of retained earnings as follows:

Appropriate Heading

Balance, January 1, 1981	$_____
Add: Net income for 1981	_____
Total	_____
Deduct: Dividends declared and paid in 1981	_____
Balance, December 31, 1981 (reported on balance sheet)	$_____

(Hint: EPS is $8.56.)

P3–12. (Note: This is a special case to test your analytical skills.) Simon Lavoie, a local attorney, decided to sell his practice and retire. He has had discussions with an attorney from another state who desires to relocate. The discussions have entered the complex stage of agreeing on a price. Among the important factors have been the financial statements on Lavoie's practice. Lavoie's secretary, under his direction, maintained the records. Each year they developed a "Statement of Profits" on a cash basis from the incomplete records maintained, and no balance sheet was prepared. Upon request, Lavoie provided the other attorney with the following statement for 1981 prepared by his secretary:

S. LAVOIE
Statement of profits
1981

Legal fees collected		$62,000
Expenses paid:		
Rent for office space .	$ 3,900	
Utilities	360	
Telephone	2,900	
Office salaries	19,000	
Office supplies	900	
Miscellaneous expenses	1,600	
Total expenses . .		28,660
Profit for the year		$33,340

Upon agreement of the parties, you have been asked to "look into the financial figures for 1981." The other attorney appeared to question the figures, especially since they appear to him "to be on a 100 percent cash basis." Your investigations have revealed the following additional data at December 31, 1981:

a. Of the $62,000 legal fees collected in 1981, $18,000 was for services performed prior to 1981.

b. At the end of 1981, legal fees of $7,000 for services performed during the year were uncollected.

c. Office equipment owned and used by Lavoie cost $3,000 and had an estimated useful life of ten years.

d. An inventory of office supplies at December 31, 1981, reflected $200 worth of items purchased during the year that were still on hand. Also, the records for 1980 indicate that the supplies on hand at the end of that year were approximately $125.

e. At the end of 1981 a secretary, whose salary is $7,200 per year, had not been paid for December because of a long trip that extended to January 15, 1982.

f. The phone bill for December 1981, amounting to $300, was not paid until January 11, 1978.

g. The office rent paid of $3,900 was for 13 months (it included the rent for January 1982).

Required:

On the basis of the above information, prepare an income statement for 1981 on an accrual basis. Show your computations for any amounts changed from those in the statement prepared by Lavoie's secretary. (Suggested solution format with four columns: items; Per Lavoie Statement, $; Explanation of Changes; and Corrected to Accrual Basis, $.)

Matching of expenses
with revenue each period

PURPOSE OF THE CHAPTER

Net income is one of the more significant single amounts developed through the accounting process. In this chapter we will focus on several critical issues involved in the measurement of net income. We will examine some of the complications posed when the lifespan of a business is divided into a series of equal time periods, such as one year. We will consider the problem of realistically identifying **revenues** within the selected time period and then identifying the **expenses** that were incurred in order to generate the revenues for that period.

Behavioral and learning objectives for this chapter are provided in the *Teachers Manual*.

RELATIONSHIPS AMONG FINANCIAL STATEMENTS

In the preceding chapters the three periodic financial statements required for external reporting were discussed; however, the relationships among them were considered only indirectly. In Chapter 2 we stated that the three statements, plus the accompanying notes and the auditors' opinion, should be viewed as a single reporting package for the selected time period. The entire reporting package usually is needed to understand the overall financial aspects in many business decision-making situations. Exhibit 4–1 presents the basic relationships among the three financial statements for a fiscal year, such as January 1 through December 31, 1981. In this exhibit you can visualize the starting point as the financial position as reported in the balance sheet at the end of the *prior* year and the ending point as the financial position reflected in the balance sheet at the end

EXHIBIT 4–1
Interrelationships among financial statements

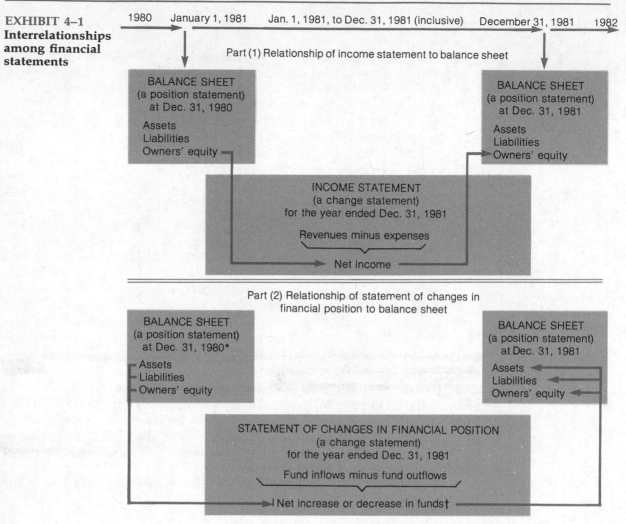

1980   January 1, 1981   Jan. 1, 1981, to Dec. 31, 1981 (inclusive)   December 31, 1981   1982

Part (1) Relationship of income statement to balance sheet

BALANCE SHEET
(a position statement)
at Dec. 31, 1980

Assets
Liabilities
Owners' equity

BALANCE SHEET
(a position statement)
at Dec. 31, 1981

Assets
Liabilities
Owners' equity

INCOME STATEMENT
(a change statement)
for the year ended Dec. 31, 1981

Revenues minus expenses

Net income

Part (2) Relationship of statement of changes in financial position to balance sheet

BALANCE SHEET
(a position statement)
at Dec. 31, 1980*

Assets
Liabilities
Owners' equity

BALANCE SHEET
(a position statement)
at Dec. 31, 1981

Assets
Liabilities
Owners' equity

STATEMENT OF CHANGES IN FINANCIAL POSITION
(a change statement)
for the year ended Dec. 31, 1981

Fund inflows minus fund outflows

Net increase or decrease in funds†

* This also is the balance sheet at the beginning of 1981.
† For this statement, funds are measured as either cash or working capital.

of the *current* year. The changes in financial position between the starting and ending points are communicated to the users by two different change statements:

1. **Income statement**—The income statement reports changes in owners' equity during the period as a result of operations. Net income increases owners' equity, and this is graphically shown in Exhibit 4–1, Part (1). The detailed amounts of revenue, expense, and extraordinary items that caused this change in owners' equity (or financial position) during the period are reported on the income statement for the period. Therefore, the income statement reports detailed information to explain **one major category of changes** in financial position during the selected

time period. The changes are those resulting from operations and extraordinary items.

2. **Statement of changes in financial position (SCFP)**—This statement is designed to report, or explain, all the **causes** of changes in financial position (i.e., assets, liabilities, and owners' equity) during the period that result from the financing activities (funds inflows) and investing activities (funds outflows). It explains how funds (measured as cash or working capital) were generated and used by the entity during the selected time period.

TIME-PERIOD ASSUMPTION

Each financial statement should include in its heading a specific statement as to the **time dimension** of the report (see Chapter 1, pages 18, 21, and 24). Exhibit 4–1 reemphasizes the fact that the time dimension of the balance sheet is **at a specific date** (such as "At December 31, 19XX"). In contrast, the two "change" statements cover **a specified period of time** (such as, "For the Year Ended December 31, 19XX").

The lifespan of most business entities is indefinite. Society in general "lives by the calendar." These facts require that the lifespan of an entity be divided into a series of short time periods, such as one year, for many measurement financial reporting purposes. The business community assumes that the activities of a business can be divided into a series of equal time periods. This is the **time-period assumption** (see Exhibit 2–6), and it is fundamental to the accounting process and financial reporting.

Because annual periods tend to be dominant throughout our society, the accounting period generally is viewed as being 12 consecutive months. As a consequence, we focus on the **annual** financial statements. Many companies use a year that corresponds to the natural cycle of the business, such as July 1 through June 30, rather than to the calendar year. An accounting year that does not correspond to the calendar year is known as a **fiscal year.** In addition to the annual financial statements, many businesses prepare and publish quarterly financial reports for external distribution. These usually are called **interim reports.** Monthly financial statements frequently are prepared; however, they are used exclusively for **internal management** purposes.

Dividing the lifespan of a business into short time periods, such as a year, for measurement purposes often poses complex accounting problems because some **transactions start in one accounting period and are,** in effect, **concluded in a subsequent period.** This continuity of a transaction may occur for all classifications; for example:

a. **Assets**—A machine which is purchased in one year will be depreciated over the next five years.

b. **Liabilities**—A note payable is signed which requires interest payments

> each of three years and payment of the principal at the end of the third year.

c. **Owners' equity**—Shares of stock are sold in one year with a cash down payment plus two equal annual installment payments and issuance of the shares at the date of the last installment.

e. **Revenues**—Rent is collected in one year for six months in advance, and two of the occupancy periods (months) extend into the next year.

f. **Expenses**—An insurance premium on property is paid in advance for two years of coverage.

PERIODIC RECOGNITION OF REVENUES AND EXPENSES

Earning **revenues** through sales and services and the incurring of **expenses** necessary to generate those revenues is a **continuous process.** Since some transactions cover an extended period of time between their initiation and completion and financial reports must be made for a specific time period, such as a month, quarter, or year, there must be a careful **cutoff** among the selected time periods so that the revenues and expenses for each such period can be measured accurately.

Frequently, it is difficult to identify a specific revenue and/or expense with a particular accounting period. In response to this problem, the **revenue principle** and the **matching principle** were evolved as two of the broad fundamentals underlying accounting (see Exhibit 2–6, page 64). These two principles focus on the measurement of net income for each period. **The revenue principle takes a timing precedence over the matching principle in the measurement process.** First, the revenue earned for the period from the sales of goods and services is measured; next, the matching principle is applied to measure the expenses incurred in generating that revenue. To reemphasize, for accounting measurement purposes, the revenue and matching principles require a careful cutoff of revenues and expenses at the end of each accounting period.

The revenue principle.   The revenue principle was defined in Chapter 2, Exhibit 2–6. This principle holds that revenue should be measured (and recognized as revenue in the accounting system) in the period in which it is *earned* or *realized*. In identifying revenues with a specific period for measurement purposes, one must look to *when* the various transactions occur, rather than to the period in which the related cash inflows occur. The income statement for each particular period must report all of the revenue earned, or realized, in the period covered but must not report any revenue earned in a prior or following period.

The general guideline is that revenue is earned when a sales transaction is made (consummated) or when services are rendered. In the case of sales or services for cash, this guideline is easy to apply; however, in the case of credit sales or services, problems often arise. Sales or services made on a normal **short-term** credit basis follow the general rule, regardless of whether there is a cash down payment. In contrast, sales and services made on a long-term credit basis, and with little or no down payment, pose the question of the **risk** that full payment will not be made ultimately (a default and/or repossession may occur). For such situations, the accounting profession has developed exceptions to the general guideline. For example, in the case of land development companies, one common practice is to sell undeveloped land for a down payment of approximately 5 percent with a 10- to 30-year payout period. Because of the risk of default, for this particular industry a current guideline is that sales revenue should not be recognized until the period in which the total cash collected reaches at least 10 percent of the sales price. (There are some related accounting complexities in this industry that are beyond the scope of this book.)

Many companies sell large items of merchandise (such as a television set) on the **installment plan.** The usual characteristics of an installment plan are (1) a relatively small down payment is required; (2) the payment period is long and calls for monthly payments of principal plus interest; (3) the seller retains conditional title to the goods until full payment is made; and (4) bad debt losses that cannot be estimated reasonably. When all of these characteristics exist in combination, there is a relatively high risk of reclamation of merchandise because of nonpayment (default). The installment method of accounting is used in this situation. Under this method the revenue is recognized as the **cash is collected.** As a consequence, this method is close to cash basis accounting.

Another difficult problem arises in respect to **long-term construction contracts.** For example, assume a building contractor signs a contract to build a large plant at a cost of $3,500,000 and the construction period is three years, starting January 1, 19A. Assume further that the cost of the plant is estimated to be $3,200,000 to the contractor; that is, an estimated profit of (1) $300,000. The question is: Should the profit be reported as (1) earned in 19C or (2) allocated on an estimated basis to each of the three years? One accounting method used is called the **completed contract method.** Under this method all of the income (profit) is recognized in the accounting system as earned in the year of completion. It is a conservative method because recognition of income is deferred until its actual amount is known. Another accounting method used is called the **percentage of completion method.** It permits **allocation** of revenue to each of the three construction periods based on estimates (usually based on the ratio of actual costs incurred during the period to total costs for the project) covering the three-year period. Thus, a portion of the estimated $300,000 would be recognized as revenue each year.

At the present time a contractor is permitted to select either method of accounting for long-term construction contracts. Many accountants believe that this choice between two accounting alternatives for the same set of facts is not sound. They believe that the profit should be allocated to each of the three periods based upon percentage of completion of the building by years (generally estimated by the architects). Of course, other accountants prefer the completed contract method. Lack of agreement as to the best measurement approach primarily is the reason for the approval of alternatives. There are a number of other areas of accounting where measurement and recognition alternatives are permitted for the same set of facts. The accounting profession is striving to eliminate such alternative accounting choices.

The matching principle. Expenses were defined in Chapter 1 (pages 19 and 65). The matching principle focuses on the measurement of expenses and the matching of them with the periodic revenues earned during the period. **The matching principle holds that all of the expenses incurred in generating revenue should be identified, or matched, with the revenue earned, period by period.**

In measuring and matching expenses with revenue, one must look to the **purpose** for which the expenses were incurred. If the purpose was to generate specific revenue, as is the usual case, the expenses should be identified with the period in which that revenue was recognized as earned. In this way the expenses are matched with the revenues of each period so that income for each period is measured correctly. Expenses incurred in generating the revenue earned for the period should be reported in that period. Resources expended in one period to generate revenues in other periods should be apportioned to those other periods.

Application of the revenue and matching principles is to effect the cutoff among consecutive accounting periods. This requires that a special type of end-of-the-period accounting entries be made. Collectively, such entries generally are referred to as **adjusting entries.**

ADJUSTING ENTRIES

Adjusting entries are required by the revenue and matching principles to effect a precise cutoff of revenues and expenses among consecutive accounting periods because transactions are recorded when they are consummated, and during subsequent accounting periods, certain economic events happen which alter the previously recorded economic impacts on the enterprise. This means that adjusting entries are necessary to change certain account balances at the end of the accounting period, not because of errors but to reflect **new** economic effects due to the passage of time. To illustrate, assume a company purchased a machine on January 1, 19A, that cost $50,000 with an estimated useful life of five years (no residual value). On January 1, 19A (date of consummation), an asset account— machinery—was debited (increased) for $50,000. However, by December 31, 19A (end of the accounting period), the machine has depreciated to $40,000. Therefore, due to an economic event (use of the machine) an **adjusting entry** must be made to *(a)* decrease the book value of the asset by $10,000 and *(b)* record depreciation expense of $10,000.

Adjusting entries possess three fundamental characteristics as follows:

1. An income statement account balance (revenue or expense) is changed.
2. A balance sheet account balance (asset or liability) is changed.
3. They usually are recorded at the end of the accounting period.

Adjusting entries are required by four types of transactions as follows:

Revenues (revenue principle applied):

1. **Recorded revenue collected in advance**—Revenue collected in advance of being earned must be apportioned (deferred) to the periods in which it will be earned. Example: Rent collected in advance of the accounting period in which occupancy will occur.
2. **Unrecorded revenue**—Revenue not collected nor recorded but earned in the current accounting period (the related cash will be collected in a subsequent period) should be recorded as earned in the current period. Example: Rent occupancy provided in the current period but collection not received by the end of the current accounting period (i.e., past due rent).

Expenses (matching principle applied):

3. **Recorded expense paid in advance**—Expense paid in advance of use of the services or goods (i.e., incurred) must be apportioned (deferred) to the periods in which such services or goods will be used. Example: Payment of a two-year insurance premium on property.
4. **Unrecorded expense**—Expense neither paid nor recorded but incurred (the services or goods used) in the current accounting period (the related cash will be paid in a subsequent period) should be recorded as expense in the current period. Example: Wages earned by an employee in the current period, neither recorded nor paid by the end of the current accounting period.

At the end of each accounting period, after the regular entries are completed, the accountant must make a careful check of the records and supporting documents to determine whether there are any situations such as those listed above for which **adjusting entries** should be made. One or more such entries invariably will be required at the end of each accounting period. If any adjusting entries are overlooked, revenue for the period may be measured incorrectly and expenses may not be matched with revenues earned during the period. In either instance, the result would be incorrect measurement of amounts on both the income statement and the balance sheet.

Adjusting entries are not unusual. They require no additional competence, only a knowledge of the actual facts in respect to each item. In Chapter 3 the illustrations, exercises, and problems include several adjusting entries (depreciation expense, prepaid insurance, supplies used, and accrued or unpaid wages) routinely made without special identification or concern.

The two technical terms "accrued" (or to accrue) and "deferred" (or to defer) frequently are used in accounting. A straightforward and practical definitional statement for our purposes is: **Accrued,** in the case of expenses, means not yet paid; and in the case of revenues, not yet collected. **Deferred,** in the case of expenses means paid in advance (prepaid); and in the case of revenues, collected in advance. To summarize:

	Item	*Brief definition*
1.	Deferred revenue.	A revenue collected, not yet earned.
2.	Accrued revenue.	A revenue earned, not yet collected.
3.	Deferred expense.	An expense paid, not yet incurred.
4.	Accrued expense.	An expense incurred, not yet paid.

ADJUSTING ENTRIES ILLUSTRATED

An example was given of each of the four general types of adjusting entries discussed above. In this section we will examine these and other examples, analyze them, and give the **adjusting entry** that should be made at the end of the accounting period. These illustrations will increase your understanding of the application of the accounting model, measurement of periodic revenues and expenses, and determination of income. Throughout the examples to follow, we will refer to High-Rise Apartments and will assume that the **current** annual accounting period ends December 31, 1981.

Recorded revenue collected in advance

Some businesses collect cash in advance of earning the revenue from the sale of services or goods (sometimes called unearned revenue). In such situations the revenue must be apportioned to the period in which the services are rendered or the sale is completed in accordance with the revenue principle (see pages 144 and 145). This type of situation requires an adjusting entry at the end of the period to recognize (1) the correct amount of revenue earned during the current period and (2) the obligation in the future to provide the related goods or services. We will analyze one such situation for High-Rise Apartments that occurs because a few tenants pay their rent on the 15th of each month. (Note: Each entry is letter coded for reference in the illustrations to follow.)

Rent revenue collected in advance. On December 11, 1981, two tenants paid rent for the month December 11, 1981, through January 10, 1982, in the amount of $1,500. The sequence of entries would be:

December 11, 1981—date of consummation of the transaction:

Cash	1,500	
Rent revenue		1,500
To record one month's rent for the period December 11, 1981, through January 10, 1982.		

December 31, 1981—end of the accounting period:

Analysis—The $1,500 cash collected included rent revenue for 1981 of $1,500 × 20/30 = $1,000 and rent revenue collected in advance for 1982 of $1,500 × 10/30 = $500. Therefore, an adjusting entry is required on December 31, 1981, to *(a)* reduce the balance in rent revenue by $500 and *(b)* record the obligation to furnish occupancy in 1982 for one third of a month which was paid in advance of that year. This is a **current liability** which will be paid in January 1982 by providing occupancy rights.[1]

a. December 31, 1981 (end of the accounting period)—adjusting entry:

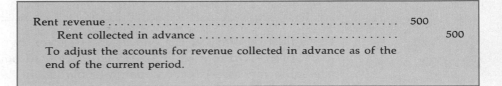

```
Rent revenue .............................................     500
    Rent collected in advance ...............................            500
    To adjust the accounts for revenue collected in advance as of the
    end of the current period.
```

Unrecorded and uncollected revenue

At the end of the current period, there may be revenue that has been **earned** (in accordance with the revenue principle), not yet recorded and not yet collected (sometimes called accrued revenue). Such revenue must be entered in the accounting system in the period in which it was earned. This recording is accomplished by making an adjusting entry at the end of the current period to recognize *(a)* a receivable for the amount earned but not collected, and *(b)* the amount of revenue earned. We will analyze a typical situation for High-Rise Apartments.

Rent revenue unrecorded. On December 31, 1981, the manager of High-Rise Apartments, upon checking the rental records, found that one tenant had not paid the December rent amounting to $600. The sequence of entries would be:

b. December 31, 1981 (end of the accounting period)—adjusting entry:

---

[1] Observe that the entry at collection date, December 11, 1981, could have been recorded in a way that would preclude the need for an adjusting entry later, viz:

```
Cash .....................................................  1,500
    Rent revenue .........................................            1,000
    Rent collected in advance ............................              500
```

Alternatively, it could be accounted for as follows with the same end result:

December 11, 1981:

```
Cash .....................................................  1,500
    Rent collected in advance ............................            1,500
```

December 31, 1981—adjusting entry:

```
Rent collected in advance ................................  1,000
    Rent revenue .........................................            1,000
```

```
Rent revenue receivable .......................................   600
    Rent revenue .............................................          600
    To record rent revenue earned in 1981 but not collected by year-
    end.
```

January 1982—date of collection:

```
Cash ......................................................   600
    Rent revenue receivable ..................................          600
    To record collection of receivable for 1981 rent revenue.
```

The adjusting entry at the end of 1981 served two measurement purposes: (1) to record rent revenue earned in 1981 of $600 and (2) to record a receivable (an asset) for occupancy provided in 1981 for which $600 cash will be collected in January 1982. Rent revenue receivable is reported on the December 31, 1981, balance sheet as a current asset.

Recorded expenses paid in advance

A company frequently must make an expenditure of cash or incur a liability for assets or services that will help generate revenue in the current period and also in one or more future accounting periods. When such a transaction occurs, an **asset** is increased (debited) which usually is called a **prepaid expense.** As the future periods pass, the asset cost is apportioned to *expense* so that there is a matching of expense with revenue for each of the periods affected. For High-Rise Apartments we will analyze three such transactions that occurred in 1981.

Prepaid insurance. On January 1, 1981, High-Rise paid in advance a two-year insurance premium of $2,400 on an apartment building. The sequence of entries for this **prepaid expense** would be:

January 1, 1981—date of the transaction:

```
Prepaid insurance (an asset account) ..........................   2,400
    Cash ...................................................          2,400
    To record payment of a two-year premium.
```

December 31, 1981—end of the accounting period:

Analysis—The $2,400 cash paid on January 1, 1981, was for insurance coverage for two full years; therefore, insurance **expense** for each year will be $1,200. At the end of 1981 an adjusting entry must be made to *(a)* reduce prepaid insurance by $1,200 and *(b)* record insurance expense of $1,200 for 1981, viz:

c. December 31, 1981 (end of the accounting period)—adjusting entry:

Insurance expense 1,200
    Prepaid insurance   1,200
To record insurance expense for 12 months
($2,400 × 12/24).

The latter entry would be repeated at the end of 1982. The adjusting entry serves two measurement purposes: (1) it apportions insurance expense to the current period for **matching** purposes and (2) it adjusts (reduces) the Prepaid Insurance account to the correct asset amount for the **unexpired** insurance at the end of 1981. That is, at the end of 1981 the company was still entitled to one year of insurance protection and hence had a current **asset** amounting to $1,200.

Depreciation. On January 1, 1980, a contractor completed an apartment building for High-Rise. The contract price of $360,000 was paid in cash. The building has an estimated useful life of 30 years and an estimated $60,000 **residual value** at the end of the 30 years. The sequence of entries would be:

January 1, 1980—date of transaction:

Apartment building..................................... 360,000
    Cash   360,000
To record full payment for building construction.

d. December 31, 1981 (end of the accounting period)—adjusting entry:

Depreciation expense................................... 10,000
    Accumulated depreciation, building   10,000
To record depreciation expense for one year ($360,000 −
$60,000) ÷ 30 years = $10,000.

The adjusting entry would be repeated at the end of each year over the life of the building. The **estimated** amount expected to be recovered when the asset finally is sold or disposed of is known as the **residual value** (sometimes it is called scrap or salvage value). For computing depreciation, the cost of the asset must be reduced by the residual value. The difference ($360,000 − $60,000 = $300,000) is the amount to be depreciated over the estimated useful life. Thus, the annual depreciation expense on the apartment building would be ($360,000 − $60,000) ÷ 30 years = $10,000.[2] The residual value of $60,000 is deducted since it is expected

---

[2] This example assumes straight-line depreciation; that is, an equal amount of depreciation expense is apportioned to each period. Other methods of depreciation will be discussed in Chapter 9.

to be recovered at the end of the useful life to the company. The adjusting entry serves two measurement purposes: (1) it **allocates** a part of the cost of the building to expense for the current period for matching purposes and (2) it adjusts (reduces) the amount of the asset to represent the unexpired cost of the asset. The credit to "Accumulated Depreciation, Building" could have been made directly to the building account with the same effect; however, it is desirable, for reporting purposes, to keep the balance of the asset account "Apartment Building" at original cost. This is accomplished by setting up a **contra,** or **offset,** account entitled "Accumulated Depreciation, Building." You will recall from Chapters 2 and 3 that on the balance sheet the building would be shown on one line at cost with a deduction on the next line for accumulated depreciation (see Exhibit 2–2). The difference between the cost and accumulated depreciation amounts often is referred to as the book value, or carrying value, of the asset. The book or carrying value does not represent the current **market** value of the asset because accounting for depreciation is a **cost** allocation process rather than a market valuation process.

Supplies inventory. On January 1, 1981, the inventory of maintenance supplies was $100; these were unused supplies on hand carried over from the previous year. High-Rise purchases maintenance supplies, not for resale but for use as needed; they are kept in a small storeroom pending use. On March 18, 1981, additional supplies were purchased at a cost of $500 and were placed in the storeroom. No accounting entry is made when the supplies are used. To determine the amount of supplies used during the period, an inventory of the supplies remaining on hand is taken. At December 31, 1981, the inventory of the supplies in the storeroom showed $200 in supplies on hand. The sequence of entries would be:

March 18, 1981—date of purchase of supplies:

Inventory of maintenance supplies (an asset)	500	
Cash		500
To record purchase of maintenance supplies for addition to inventory.		

e. December 31, 1981 (end of the accounting period)—adjusting entry:

Maintenance expense	400	
Inventory of maintenance supplies		400
To record the amount of supplies used from inventory ($100 + $500 − $200 = $400).		

Analysis: The balance in the Inventory of Maintenance Supplies account on this date is $600 (i.e., beginning inventory, $100, plus the purchase, $500); however, the actual inventory count at this date reflected $200, which means that usage of supplies was $400 (i.e., $100 + $500 − $200 = $400). An adjusting entry is required to *(a)* reduce the inventory account by $400 (so that the asset, inventory, will be reflected as $200) and *(b)* to record an expense for the amount of supplies used, $400. The adjusting entry would be as shown above.

Unrecorded and unpaid expenses

Most expenses are incurred and paid for during the same period; however, at the end of the accounting period there usually are some expenses that have been **incurred** (i.e., the goods and/or services that already have been used) but are not recorded, usually because payment has not been made. Such unpaid expenses generally are referred to as **accrued expenses.** We will analyze three different transactions for High-Rise Apartments, each of which requires an adjusting entry because *(a)* an expense and *(b)* a related liability must be recorded.

Salary expense. On December 31, 1981, the manager of High-Rise was on a trip and due to return January 10, 1982. As a consequence, the manager's December salary of $900 was not paid or recorded by December 31, 1981. The sequence of entries for the accrued salary expense (disregard payroll taxes at this time) would be:

f. December 31, 1981 (end of the accounting period)—adjusting entry:

Salary expense	900	
Salaries payable (or accrued salaries payable)		900
To record salary expense and the liability for December salary not yet paid.		

January 10, 1982—date of payment:

Salaries payable	900	
Cash		900
To record payment of a December 1981 salary.		

The adjusting entry serves two measurement purposes: (1) to record an expense incurred in 1981 and (2) to record the liability for the salary owed at the end of 1981.

Property tax expense. On December 30, 1981, a tax bill amounting to $5,700 was received from the city for 1981 property taxes. The taxes are due on February 15, 1982; hence they were unpaid and unrecorded at the end of 1981. The sequence of entries would be:

g. December 31, 1981 (end of the accounting period)—adjusting entry:[3]

Property tax expense 5,700
    Property tax payable   5,700
To record 1981 property taxes incurred and the related liability.

The adjusting entry serves the same two measurement purposes enumerated above for salaries. When the taxes are paid, Cash will be credited and Property Tax Payable debited for $5,700.

Interest expense. On November 1, 1981, High-Rise borrowed $30,000 cash from a local bank on a 90-day note with an annual interest rate of 12 percent. The principal plus interest is due in three months. The sequence of entries is:

November 1, 1981—date of transaction:

Cash 30,000
    Note payable, short term   30,000
To record a three-month, 12 percent loan from the bank.

December 31, 1981 (end of the accounting period):

Analysis—At this date two months have passed since the note was signed; therefore, interest expense for two months has accrued on the note because interest legally accrues with the passage of time, notwithstanding the fact that the interest is payable in cash at the maturity date. This also means that there is a liability for interest for the two months at the end of 1981. Since this expense and the related liability have not been recorded, an adjusting entry is necessary to *(a)* debit interest expense for $600 (i.e., $30,000 \times 12\% \times 2/12 = $600) and *(b)* to credit interest payable for the same amount. The adjusting and payment entries would be:

h. December 31, 1981 (end of the accounting period)—adjusting entry:

Interest expense 600
    Interest payable (or accrued interest payable)   600
To record accrued interest expense for two months on note payable
($30,000 \times 12\% \times 2/12 = $600).

---

[3] This is an example of a situation where there may or may not be an adjusting entry. For example, assume the tax bill was received on December 5, 1981. At that date a *current entry* may have been made identical to the adjusting entry given above. Obviously, under these circumstances, an adjusting entry at December 31, 1981, would not be needed.

January 31, 1982—maturity date:

Note payable, short term	30,000	
Interest payable (per adjusting entry)	600	
Interest expense (1982—$30,000 × 12% × 1/12)	300	
Cash		30,900
To record payment of principal plus interest on note payable at maturity date.		

Recording adjusting entries. The above examples of adjusting entries demonstrate application of the revenue and matching principles at the end of the accounting period. They also reflect the three characteristics of adjusting entries given on page 147. If they are not made, both the income statement and balance sheet will be incorrect. Development of adjusting entries requires an analysis to **allocate** revenue and expense between the current and one or more future periods so that expenses are matched properly with revenues each accounting period. It is important to remember that an adjusting entry, when needed, results from a transaction that started in one period and, in effect, continues into one or more subsequent periods. This means that an analysis to determine whether an adjusting entry is needed, and if so, how it should be made, must be based on the **sequence** of related events covering the periods affected. Demonstration Case B at the end of the chapter illustrates how the situation affects the adjusting entries.

Adjusting entries first are entered in the journal (dated the last day of the accounting period) immediately after all of the regular transactions are recorded. They then are posted from the journal to the ledger accounts in the usual way. This is necessary because, in substance, they are full-fledged economic events and their effects must be processed through the accounting information system and into the financial statements in the same manner as the regular transactions. These procedures are illustrated in the next chapter.

In some instances, it is difficult to draw a distinct line between regular and adjusting entries. There are no real reasons for the distinction, other than the fact that they *(a)* are made at the end of the accounting period and *(b)* update certain income statement and balance sheet accounts. The important point is that adjusting entries (as well as many other entries) are necessary to appropriately measure periodic revenues and to match expenses with those revenues which were earned during the period.

Two demonstration cases follow in this chapter. Demonstration Case A illustrates the effects of adjusting entries on the income statement and balance sheet. Demonstration Case B illustrates the relationship between related initial and adjusting entries.

DEMONSTRATION CASE A

(Try to resolve the requirements before proceeding to the suggested solution that follows.)

New Service Corporation is owned by three stockholders and has been in operation for one year, 19A. Cash flow and expenses are critical problems. Recordkeeping has been kept at a minimum to keep expenses low. One secretary performs both the secretarial and recordkeeping functions. Because of a loan made to the corporation, the bank has requested an income statement and balance sheet. Accordingly, the secretary prepared the following (summarized for case purposes):

Profit Statement
Annual—December 31, 19A

Revenues:	
Service	$ 78,500
Expenses:	
Salaries and wages	(43,200)
Utilities	(1,800)
Miscellaneous	(4,000)
Net income	$ 29,500

Balance Sheet
At December 31, 19A
Assets

Cash	$ 4,000
Accounts receivable	35,500
Supplies inventory	8,000
Equipment	40,000
Other assets	16,000
Total assets	$103,500

Liabilities

Accounts payable	$ 9,000
Income taxes payable	
Note payable, one year, 12%	10,000

Stockholders' Equity

Capital stock, par $10	50,000
Contributed capital in excess of par	5,000
Retained earnings	29,500
Total liabilities and stockholders' equity	$103,500

After reading the two statements, the bank requested that a CPA examine them. The CPA found that the secretary used inappropriate headings and terminology and did not include the following data (i.e., the adjusting entries):

a. Supplies inventory on hand at December 31 amounted to $3,000.
b. Depreciation for 19A. The equipment was acquired during January 19A; estimated useful life, ten years, and no residual value.

c. The note payable was dated August 1, 19A, and the principal plus interest are payable at the end of one year.

d. Rent expense of $3,600 was included in miscellaneous expense.

e. Income taxes; assume an average tax rate of 17 percent.

Required:

1. Recast the above statements to incorporate the additional data and preferred format.

2. Prepare the adjusting entries (in journal form) for the additional data at December 31, 19A.

3. Comment on any aspects of this situation that the bank loan officer should note in particular if they appear to be unusual.

Suggested Solution:

Requirement 1:

NEW SERVICE CORPORATION
Income Statement
For the Year Ended December 31, 19A

	Amounts reported	Effects of adjusting entries*	Corrected amounts
Revenue:			
Service revenue	$78,500		$78,500
Expenses:			
Salaries and wages	43,200		43,200
Utilities	1,800		1,800
Supplies expense		(a) + 5,000	5,000
Depreciation expense		(b) + 4,000	4,000
Interest expense		(c) + 500	500
Rent expense		(d) + 3,600	3,600
Miscellaneous expense	4,000	(d) − 3,600	400
Total expenses	49,000		58,500
Pretax income	$29,500		20,000
Income tax expense ($20,000 × 17%)		(e) + 3,400	3,400
Net income			$16,600
EPS ($16,600 ÷ 5,000 shares)			$3.32

NEW SERVICE CORPORATION
Balance Sheet
At December 31, 19A

	Amounts reported	Effects of adjusting entries*	Corrected amounts
Assets			
Cash	$ 4,000		$ 4,000
Accounts receivable	35,500		35,500
Supplies inventory	8,000	(a) − 5,000	3,000
Equipment	40,000		40,000
Accumulated depreciation		(b) − 4,000	(4,000)
Other assets	16,000		16,000
Total assets	$103,500		$94,500

* Computations shown under Requirement 2.

Requirement 1 (continued)

	Amounts reported	Effects of adjusting entries*	Corrected amounts
Liabilities			
Accounts payable	$ 9,000		$ 9,000
Income taxes payable		*(e)* + 3,400	3,400
Interest payable		*(c)* + 500	500
Note payable, one year, 12%	10,000		10,000
Total liabilities	19,000		22,900
Stockholders' Equity			
Capital stock, par $10 (5,000 shares)	50,000		50,000
Contributed capital in excess of par	5,000		5,000
Retained earnings	29,500	−29,500 + 16,600	16,600
Total liabilities and stockholders' equity	$103,500		$94,500

* Computations shown under Requirement 2.

Requirement 2:

Adjusting entries at December 31, 19A:

a. Supplies expense 5,000
      Supplies inventory 5,000
      To reduce supplies inventory to the amount on hand December 31, 19A, $3,000, and to record supplies expense, $8,000 − $3,000 = $5,000.

b. Depreciation expense 4,000
      Accumulated depreciation 4,000
      Depreciation for one year, $40,000 ÷ 10 years = $4,000.

c. Interest expense 500
      Interest payable 500
      To record interest expense and the interest accrued (a liability) from August 1 to December 31, 19A ($10,000 × 12% × 5/12 = $500).

d. Rent expense 3,600
      Miscellaneous expense 3,600
      To record rent expense in the proper account.

e. Income tax expense 3,400
      Income tax payable 3,400
      To record income tax expense and the liability for unpaid tax as computed on the income statement.

Requirement 3:

The loan officer should note particularly the following:

a. The overstatement of net income (by 78 percent; i.e., $29,500 ÷ $16,600) and total assets (by 10 percent; i.e., $103,500 ÷ $94,500) suggests either (1) an attempt to mislead or (2) the need for better accounting.
b. The very high amount in accounts receivable compared to cash and total assets. This suggests inadequate evaluation of credit and/or inefficiency in collections.
c. Inclusion of rent expense in miscellaneous expense.

DEMONSTRATION CASE B

(Try to resolve the requirements before proceeding to the suggested solution that follows.)

This case is presented to illustrate why and how adjusting entries are influenced directly by the manner in which an *initial entry* made in one period and its economic effects carry over to one or more subsequent accounting periods (see pages 146 and 147). To determine whether an adjusting entry is needed, and if so, how it should be made, requires a careful analysis of the situation.

General situation: On July 1, 19A, Company K paid a two-year insurance premium of $1,200. The annual accounting period ends on December 31.

Required:

1. How much of the premium should be reported as expense in the 19A, 19B, and 19C income statements?
2. What is the amount of prepaid insurance on December 31, 19A? How should this amount be reported on the 19A financial statements?
3. Company K could have recorded the $1,200 payment on July 1, 19A, in one of three ways as follows:

Case A:

| Prepaid insurance | 1,200 | |
| Cash | | 1,200 |

Case B:

| Insurance expense | 1,200 | |
| Cash | | 1,200 |

Case C:

Prepaid insurance	900	
Insurance expense	300	
Cash		1,200

For each case, give the appropriate adjusting entry (at December 31, 19A) in journal form and then post to ledger T-accounts. If no adjusting entry is required, explain why.

Suggested solution:

Requirement 1:

Insurance expense: 19A—$1,200 \times$ 6/24 = \$300 (½ year)
19B—$1,200 \times$ 12/24 = 600 (1 year)
19C—$1,200 \times$ 6/24 = 300 (½ year)

Requirement 2:

Prepaid insurance on December 31, 19A—$1,200 \times 18/24 = \$900$. This amount should be reported on the balance sheet at December 31, 19A, as a current asset. Theoretical strictness suggests that \$300 of the \$900 should be reported as a deferred charge (a noncurrent asset); however, this usually is not done in practice because the effect is not material as in this case.

Requirement 3:

Adjusting entry at December 31, 19A:

JOURNAL   LEDGER

CASE A

Adjusting entry:

Insurance expense	300	
Prepaid insurance		300

To reduce prepaid insurance to \$900, and to record insurance expense for 19A, \$300.

Prepaid Insurance

Initial entry	1,200	Adj. entry	300

Insurance Expense

Adj. entry	300		

CASE B

Adjusting entry:

Prepaid insurance	900	
Insurance expense		900

To record prepaid insurance at the end of 19A, \$900, and to reduce insurance expense to \$300 for 19A.

Insurance Expense

Initial entry	1,200	Adj. entry	900

Prepaid Insurance

Adj. entry	900		

CASE C

Adjusting entry:	Prepaid Insurance

No adjusting entry is needed at December 31, 19A, because the correct amounts for both prepaid insurance at December 31, 19A, $900, and insurance expense for 19A, $300 were recorded on the transaction date, July 1, 19A. An adjusting entry would be needed at the end of 19B.

Prepaid Insurance

Initial entry	900	

Insurance expense

Initial entry	300	

SUMMARY

This chapter focused on the revenue and matching principles. Matching expenses with revenue for the period is critical because the lifespan of an enterprise, although indefinite in length, must be divided into a series of short time periods (usually one year) for periodic performance measurements. Primary among those performance measurements are the economic effects reported in the periodic financial statements.

In the measurement of net income, the **revenue principle** holds that revenues earned in the period through sale of goods or performance of services must be identified, measured, and reported for that period. The **matching principle** holds that the expenses incurred in generating those revenues must be identified, measured, and matched with revenues earned in the period to determine periodic net income. To implement the matching principle, certain transactions and events whose economic effects extend from the current period to one or more future accounting periods must be analyzed at the end of the accounting period. This analysis is the basis for allocating their expense effects to the future periods during which they will aid in the generation of revenues. The allocation of some revenues and expenses to two or more accounting periods requires the use of **adjusting entries.** Adjusting entries follow the same concepts and procedures as entries for the usual transactions except that they are made at the end of the accounting period. At the end of the accounting period they are entered first in the journal and then are posted to the ledger in the same manner as are other entries.

IMPORTANT TERMS DEFINED IN THE CHAPTER (with page citations)

QUESTIONS FOR DISCUSSION

1. Identify the two *change* statements and briefly explain why they are so designated.

2. Explain the time-period assumption.

3. What is an interim report?

4. What is fiscal year and the natural business year for a business? How does it relate to accounting?

5. What revenue and expense recognition problems are caused by the time-period assumption?

6. Explain the revenue principle and the matching principle.

7. Contrast the completed contract method with the percentage of completion method of recognizing revenues for long-term construction contracts.

8. What is an adjusting entry? Why are such entries necessary?

9. What are the three distinct characteristics of adjusting entries?

10. Briefly define each of the following: accrued expense, accrued revenue, deferred expense, and deferred revenue.

11. In general, what two purposes are served by an adjusting entry for revenues?

12. In general, what two purposes are served by an adjusting entry for expenses?

13. AB Company collected $600 rent for the period December 15, 19A, to January 15, 19B. The $600 was credited to Rent Revenue Collected in Advance on December 15, 19A. Give the adjusting entry required on December 31, 19A (end of the accounting period).

14. Explain "estimated residual value." Why is it important in measuring depreciation expense?

15. Explain why adjusting entries are entered in the journal on the last day of the period and then are posted to the ledger.

EXERCISES

E4–1. Super Construction Company, Incorporated, specializes in major commercial construction. In April 19A the company signed a contract to build a large warehouse. The contract price was $900,000, and the estimated construction cost was $750,000. Construction was started on June 1, 19A, and completed March 31, 19B. Actual construction costs were 19A, $600,000; and 19B, $120,000.

Required:

a. Complete the following tabulation for each separate case. Assume income recognition under percentage of completion is allocated on the basis of actual costs incurred to total estimated costs.

(Relates to Exercise 4–1)

| | | Pretax income to be recognized | |
		19A	19B
Case	Method		
A	Completed contract	$	$
B	Percentage of completion		

b. Which method would you recommend for Super? Explain the basis for your choice.

E4–2. It is December 31, 19B, end of the annual accounting period for TT Service Company. Below are listed five independent transactions (summarized) that affected the company during 19B. The transactions are to be analyzed in terms of their effects on the balance sheet and income statement for 19B.

a. On January 1, 19A, the company purchased a machine that cost $10,000 cash (estimated useful life five years and no residual value).

  1. How should the machine be reported on the 19B balance sheet?
  2. How should the 19B income statement report the effects of the machine under the *(a)* revenue principle or *(b)* matching principle?

b. On September 1, 19A, the company signed a $10,000, 12 percent, one-year note payable. The principal plus interest is payable on maturity date.

  1. How should the liability be reported on the 19B balance sheet?
  2. How should the effects of the note be reported on the 19B income statement under the *(a)* revenue principle or *(b)* the matching principle?

c. During 19B service revenues of $90,000 were collected of which $10,000 was collected in advance.

  1. How should the $10,000 be reported on the 19B income statement?
  2. How should the 19B income statement report the effects of the transaction in terms of the *(a)* revenue principle or *(b)* matching principle?

d. In 19B expenses paid in cash amounted to $60,000 of which $5,000 was paid for expenses yet to be incurred (prepaid).

  1. How should the 19B balance sheet report the $5,000?
  2. What should be reported on the 19B income statement under the *(a)* revenue principle or *(b)* matching principle?

e. In 19B, $85,000 cash revenues were collected and in addition revenues of $5,000 were on credit.

  1. How should the $5,000 be reported on the 19B balance sheet?
  2. How should the 19B income statement report the revenues under the *(a)* revenue principle or *(b)* matching principle?

f. In 19B expenses amounting to $56,000 were paid in cash and in addition expenses of $3,000 were on credit.

  1. How should the $3,000 be reported on the 19B balance sheet?
  2. How should the expenses be reported on the 19B income statement under the *(a)* revenue principle or *(b)* matching principle?

E4–3. Rich Department Store is in the process of completing the accounting process for the year just ended, December 31, 19B. The current entries have been journalized and posted. The following data in respect to adjusting entries are available:

a. Office supplies inventory at January 1, 19B, was $120. Office supplies purchased and debited to Office Supplies Inventory during the year amounted to $360. The year-end inventory showed $80 of supplies on hand.

b. Wages earned during December 19B but unpaid and unrecorded at December 31, 19B, amounted to $1,400. (The last payroll was December 28, and the next payroll will be January 6, 19C.)

c. Three fourths of the basement of the store is rented to another merchant, J. B. Smith, who sells compatible, but not competitive, merchandise. On November 1, 19B, the store collected six months' rent in advance from Smith amounting to $4,800, which was credited in full to Rent Revenue when collected.

d. The rest of the basement is rented to Spears Specialty; at $360 per month, payable monthly. On December 31, 19B, the rent for November and December 19B was neither collected nor recorded. Collection is expected January 10, 19C.

Required:

Give the adjusting entry for each situation that should be entered in the records at December 31, 19B.

E4–4. The information processing cycle for the fiscal year ended December 31, 19B, has been completed for all of the current entries by Teddy Retailers, a men's store. Additional information from the records and related documents revealed the following:

a. Delivery equipment which cost $21,000 was being used by the store. Estimates in respect to equipment were (1) useful life five years and (2) residual value at the end of five years' use, $1,000. Assume depreciation for a full year for 19B.

b. On July 1, 19B, a two-year insurance premium amounting to $1,000 was paid in cash and debited to Prepaid Insurance.

c. Teddy rents one half of the building occupied by the store to another merchant, Brand Ladies Shop. The rent of $600 per month is payable six months in advance, each September 1 and March 1. The rent collection on Sep-

tember 1, 19B, was credited in full to Rent Revenue.

d. Teddy operates an alteration shop to meet its own needs. In addition, the shop does alterations for Brand. At the end of December 31, 19B; Brand had not paid for alterations completed amounting to $450; this amount has not been recorded as Alteration Shop Revenue.

Required:

Give the adjusting entry for each situation that should be entered in the records at December 31, 19B.

E4–5. Rye Company, on August 1, 19B, to meet a cash shortage, obtained an $8,000, 15 percent loan from a local bank. The principal, plus interest, was payable at the end of 12 months. The annual accounting period for Rye ends on December 31, 19B.

Required:

a. Give the journal entry on date of the loan, August 1, 19B.

b. Give the adjusting entry required on December 31, 19B.

c. Give the journal entry on date of payment, July 31, 19C.

E4–6. On April 1, 19B, May Corporation received a $10,000, 15 percent note from a customer in settlement of a $10,000 open account receivable. According to the terms, the principal of the note, plus the interest, was payable at the end of 12 months. The annual accounting period for May ends on December 31, 19B.

Required:

a. Give the journal entry for receipt of the note on April 1, 19B.

b. Give the adjusting entry required on December 31, 19B.

c. Give the journal entry on date of collection, March 31, 19C.

E4–7. Kay Company is in the process of making adjusting entries for the year ended December 31, 19B. In developing information for the adjusting entries, we learned that on September 1, 19B, a two-year insurance premium of $2,400 was paid.

Required:

a. What amount should be reported on the 19B income statement for insurance expense?
b. What amount should be reported on the December 31, 19B, balance sheet for prepaid insurance?
c. Give the adjusting entry at December 31, 19B, under each of two cases:

Case 1—Assume that when the premium was paid on September 1, 19B, the bookkeeper debited the full amount to Prepaid Insurance.

Case 2—Assume that when the premium was paid September 1, 19B, the bookkeeper debited Insurance Expense for the full amount.

(Hint: In Case 2 be sure you end with the same amount in the Prepaid Insurance account as in Case 1.)

E4–8. Wise Manufacturing Company uses a large amount of shipping supplies which are purchased in large volume, stored, and used as needed. At December 31, 19B, in collecting information as a basis for making the adjusting entries, the following data relating to shipping supplies were obtained from the records and supporting documents:

Shipping supplies on hand, January 1, 19B	$ 2,000
Purchases of shipping supplies during 19B	13,000
Shipping supplies on hand, per inventory, December 31, 19B	4,000

Required:

a. What amount should be reported on the 19B income statement for shipping supplies expense?

b. What amount should be reported on the December 31, 19B, balance sheet for shipping supplies inventory?
c. Give the adjusting entry at December 31, 19B, assuming the purchases of shipping supplies were debited in full to Shipping Supplies Inventory ($13,000).
d. What adjusting entry would you make assuming the bookkeeper debited Shipping Supplies Expense for the $13,000 supplies? (Hint: In solving (c) and (d), be sure that each solution ends up with the same amount remaining in the Shipping Supplies Inventory account.)

E4–9. On December 31, 19B, Ransom Company prepared an income statement and balance sheet and failed to take into account three adjusting entries. The income statement, prepared on this incorrect basis, reflected a pretax income of $18,000. The balance sheet reflected total assets, $75,000; total liabilities, $25,000; and owners' equity, $50,000. The data for the three adjusting entries were:

1. Depreciation for the full year on equipment that cost $44,000; estimated useful life, ten years, and residual value, $4,000.
2. Wages amounting to $10,000 for the last three days of December 19B not paid and not recorded (the next payroll will be on January 10, 19C).
3. Rent revenue of $1,500 was collected on December 1, 19B, on office space for the period December 1, 19B, to February 28, 19C. The $1,500 was credited to Rent Revenue when collected.

Required:

Complete the following tabulation (indicate deductions with parentheses):

(Relates to Exercise 4–9)

Item	Pretax income	Total assets	Total liabilities	Owners' equity
Balances reported	$18,000	$75,000	$25,000	$50,000
1. Effects of depreciation	____	____	____	____
2. Effects of wages	____	____	____	____
3. Effects of rent revenue	____	____	____	____
Correct balances	=====	=====	=====	=====

E4–10. Supreme Auto Rentals, Inc., completed its first year of operations on December 31, 19A. Since this is the end of the annual accounting period, the company bookkeeper prepared the following tentative income statement:

(Relates to Exercise 4–10)

Income Statement

Rental revenue		$98,000
Expenses:		
Salaries and wages	$26,000	
Maintenance expense	10,000	
Rent expense (on location)	6,000	
Utilities expense	3,000	
Gas and oil expense	2,000	
Miscellaneous expense (items not listed above)..........................	1,000	
Total expenses		48,000
Income		$50,000

An independent CPA, engaged to perform an audit, developed additional data as follows:

1. Wages for the last three days of December amounting to $600 have not been recorded or paid (disregard payroll taxes).
2. The telephone bill for December amounting to $200 has not been received or paid.
3. Depreciation on rental autos amounting to $10,000 for 19A has not been recorded.
4. Interest on a $10,000, one-year, 12 percent note payable dated November 1, 19A, has not been recorded. The 12 percent interest is payable on maturity date.
5. Rental revenue includes $2,000 rental revenue collected in advance of January 1, 19B.
6. Maintenance expense includes $1,000, which is the cost of maintenance supplies still on hand (per inventory) at December 31, 19A.
7. Assume the income tax rate is 20 percent. Assume payment in 19B.

Required:

a. Prepare a corrected income statement for 19A assuming 10,000 shares of stock are outstanding. Show computations.
b. Give the adjusting entry at December 31, 19A, for each of the additional data items. If none is required explain why.

E4–11. On December 15, 1981, the bookkeeper for Tobin Company prepared the income statement and balance sheet given on page 167 (summarized) but neglected to consider three of the adjusting entries.

(Relates to Exercise 4–11)

	As prepared	Effects of adjusting entries	Corrected amounts
Income statement:			
Revenues	$92,000	_____	_____
Expenses	(81,000)	_____	_____
Income tax expense		_____	_____
Income	$11,000	_____	_____
Balance sheet:			
Assets			
Cash	$17,000	_____	_____
Accounts receivable	16,000	_____	_____
Rent receivable		_____	_____
Equipment*	40,000	_____	_____
Accumulated depreciation	(8,000)	_____	_____
	$65,000		

* Acquired January 1, 1979; ten-year life, no residual value.

	As prepared	Effects of adjusting entries	Corrected amounts
Liabilities			
Accounts payable	$10,000	_____	_____
Income taxes payable		_____	_____
Owners' Equity			
Capital stock	40,000	_____	_____
Retained earnings	15,000	_____	_____
	$65,000		

Data on the three adjusting entries:

1. Depreciation on the equipment not recorded for 1981.
2. Rent revenue of $800 for December 1981 neither collected nor recorded.
3. Income taxes for 1981 not paid or recorded; assume an average rate of 17 percent.

Required:

a. Prepare the three adjusting entries (in journal form) that were omitted.
b. Complete the two columns to the right on the above tabulation.

E4–12. (Analytical) TK Company's comparative balance sheets for 19A and 19B reported the following selected amounts:

(Relates to Exercise 4–12)

	19A	19B
Assets:		
Prepaid insurance premium	$ 600	$ 700
Liabilities:		
Rent revenue collected in advance	1,000	500

The 19B income statement reported the following amounts:

	19B
Expenses:	
Insurance expense	$ 800
Revenues:	
Rent revenue	7,500

Required:

a. Compute the total amount of insurance premium that was paid during 19B. Show computations.

b. Compute the total amount of rent revenue that was collected during 19B. Show computations.

PROBLEMS

P4–1. The following information was provided by the records and related documents of Apache Garden Apartments (a corporation) at the end of the annual fiscal period, December 31, 19B:

(Relates to Problem 4–1)

Revenue:

1. Rental revenue collected in cash during 19B for occupancy in 19B (credited to Rent Revenue) $497,000
2. Rental revenue earned for occupany in December 19B but not collected until 19C 8,000
3. In December 19B, collected rent revenue in advance for January 19C 6,000

Salary expense:

4. Cash payment made in January 19B for salaries incurred (earned) in December 19A 3,000
5. Salaries incurred and paid during 19B (debited to Salary Expense)... 58,000
6. Salaries earned by employees during December 19B but not to be paid until January 19C 2,000
7. Cash advance to employees in December 19B for salaries to be earned in January 19C 4,000

Supplies used:

8. Maintenance supplies on hand (Inventory) on January 1, 19B 2,000
9. Maintenance supplies purchased for cash during 19B (debited to Maintenance Supplies inventory when purchased).................................. 8,000
10. Maintenance supplies on hand (Inventory) on December 31, 19B 1,500

Required:

Under the revenue and matching principles, what amount should be shown on the 19B, income statement for *(a)* rent revenue, *(b)* salary expense, and *(c)* maintenance supplies expense? Show computations with explanations for each numbered item.

P4–2. (Analytical) Sims Service Company has completed its financial statements for the year ended December 31, 19A. The balance sheet reported the following selected items and amounts:

(Relates to Problem 4–2)

Assets:
1. Prepaid insurance (one-year premium was purchased and paid for on May 1, 19A; debited Prepaid Insurance) .... $ 480
2. Service truck (purchased on January 1, 19A) $7,700
   Accumulated depreciation (no residual value) 1,100   6,600

Liabilities:
3. Rent collected in advance (cash collected for annual rent on October 1, 19A; credited Rent Revenue) 600
4. Salaries payable (monthly salary for J. Doe was not yet paid) 1,500

Required:

a. What was the amount of insurance premium paid on May 1, 19A? Give the adjusting entry that was made on December 31, 19A.
b. What was used as the estimated useful life for the service truck? Give the adjusting entry that was made on December 31, 19A.
c. What was the amount of cash collected for rent on October 1, 19A? Give the adjusting entry that was made on December 31, 19A.
d. What was J. Doe's total annual salary? How much of it was paid in cash during 19A? Give the adjusting entry that was made on December 31, 19A.

P4–3. Jackson Service Company is preparing the adjusting entries for the year ended December 31, 19B. On that date the bookkeeper for the company assembled the following data:

1. On December 31, 19B, salaries earned by employees not yet paid amounted to $6,000.
2. Depreciation is to be recognized on a service truck that cost $9,000 on July 1, 19B (estimated useful life six years and no residual value).
3. Cash of $1,000 was collected on December 28, 19B, for services to be rendered during 19C (Service Revenue was credited).
4. On December 27, 19B, Jackson received a tax billing from the city of $200 for 19B property taxes (on service

equipment) which is payable (and will be paid) during January 19C.
5. On July 1, 19A, the company paid $840 cash for a two-year insurance policy on the service truck (2 above).
6. On October 1, 19B, the company borrowed $10,000 from a local bank and signed a 12 percent note for that amount. The principal and interest are payable on maturity date, September 30, 19C.

Required:

a. The bookkeeper has asked you to assist in preparing the appropriate adjusting entries at December 31, 19B. For each situation above, give the appropriate adjusting entry with a brief explanation. If none is required, explain why.
b. Based on your entries given in Requirement (a), complete the following schedule to reflect the amounts and balance sheet classifications:

(Relates to Problem 4–3)

			Balance sheet classification (one check on each line)		
Item No.	Accounts	19B amount	Assets	Liabilities	Owners' equity
1.	Salaries payable	$ _____	_____	_____	_____
2.	Accumulated depreciation	_____	_____	_____	_____
3.	Revenue collected in advance	_____	_____	_____	_____
4.	Property tax payable	_____	_____	_____	_____
5.	Prepaid insurance	_____	_____	_____	_____
6.	Interest payable	_____	_____	_____	_____

P4–4. Slow Transportation Company is at the end of the accounting year December 31, 19B. The adjusting entries are to be prepared for entry into the accounting system. The following data that must be considered have been developed from the records and related documents:

1. On July 1, 19B, a three-year insurance premium on equipment was paid amounting to $900 which was debited in full to Prepaid Insurance on that date.

2. During 19B, office supplies amounting to $1,000 were purchased for cash and debited in full to Supplies Inventory. At the end of 19A, an inventory of supplies showed $200. The inventory of supplies on hand at December 31, 19B, showed $300.

3. On December 31, 19B, B&R Garage completed repairs on a truck at a cost of $650; the amount is not yet recorded and is payable by January 30, 19C.

4. In December 19B, a tax bill on the trucks owned for 19B amounting to $1,400 was received from the city. The taxes, which have not been recorded, are due and will be paid on February 15, 19C.

5. On December 31, 19B, Slow completed a hauling contract for an out-of-state company. The bill was for $7,500 payable within 30 days. No entry has been made for this transaction.

6. On July 1, 19B, Slow purchased a new hauling van at a cash cost of $21,600. The estimated useful life of the van was ten years, with an estimated residual value at that time of $1,600. Compute depreciation for six months in 19B.

7. On October 1, 19B, Slow borrowed $6,000 from the local bank on a one-year, 15 percent note payable. The principal plus interest is payable at the end of 12 months.

Required:

a. Give the adjusting entry required on December 31, 19B, related to each of the above transactions. Give a brief explanation with each entry.

b. Assume Slow Transportation Company had prepared a tentative income statement for 19B that did not include the effect of any of the above items and that the tentative pretax income computed was $30,000. Considering the above items, compute the *correct* pretax income for 19B. Show computations.

P4–5. This case, taken from the experiences of May's Department Store, has been selected to give you an opportunity to test your analytical ability in transaction analysis and in developing the adjusting entries where there are both notes receivable and notes payable. The annual fiscal period ends on December 31, 19B. Each of the two situations otherwise is independent.

Situation A—May's arranged a line of credit whereby a local bank will provide them cash for short-term working capital needs. Repayment will vary from 60 to 90 days. Occasionally, the company also borrows a substantial amount on a long-term basis. On October 1, 19B, May's borrowed $40,00 on a one-year, 12 percent note. The principal plus interest are payable at the end of 12 months.

Situation B—May's sells approximately 40 percent of their goods on credit; accounts are due at the end of the month in which the sale is made. From time to time, special efforts must be made to collect an account. J. Doe was such a case. Doe owed $1,000 on an account that the store has been unable to collect. Finally, on November 1, 19B, Doe gave them a 15 percent note for the $1,000 coupled with a mortgage on two personal automobiles. The note was for two years. At the end of the first full year, Doe agreed to pay one half of the principal ($500) plus interest on the amount of principal outstanding during the year. Final payment of principal and interest was due at the end of the second year.

Required:

a. What amount should be shown on May's income statement for 19B for (1) interest expense and (2) interest revenue?

b. What items and amount(s) should be shown on the balance sheet at December 31, 19B?

c. Give the adjusting journal entry required for each situation at December 31, 19B. Show computations.

d. What would be the amount of error in 19B pretax income if the two adjusting entries were omitted? Explain.

P4–6. Rapid Service Company has completed preparation of its annual financial statements for the year ended December 31, 19C. The income statement (summarized) reflected the following:

Revenues:	
Service	$95,600
Rental (office space)	2,400
Total revenues	98,000
Expenses:	
Salaries and wages	44,000
Service supplies used	2,600
Depreciation expense	2,000
Maintenance of equipment	2,000
Rent expense (service building)	8,400
Oil and gas for equipment	1,800
Insurance expense	200
Utilities expense	800
Other expenses	6,200
Total expenses	68,000
Pretax income	$30,000

An audit by a CPA of the records and statements revealed the following:

1. Service revenue of $700 earned yet not collected on December 31, 19C, was not included in the $95,600 on the income statement.

2. The $2,600 of service supplies used included $600 of service supplies still on hand in the supplies storeroom on December 31, 19C.

3. Rent revenue of $100 that was collected in advance and not yet earned by December 31, 19C, was included in the $2,400 on the income statement.

4. Property tax for 19C of $400 was billed during December 19C, but will be due and paid during January 19D (not included in the above amounts on the income statement).

5. A two-year insurance premium of $400 was paid on July 1, 19B; none was paid in 19C.

Required:

a. Recast the above income statement to include, exclude, or omit each of the items identified by the CPA. Use a format similar to the following:

Items	Amounts as reported	Corrections	Amounts that should be reported

b. The owner of the company asked you to explain the following:

1. Since no insurance premium was paid in 19C, why was insurance expense reported?
2. Since the company paid no cash for depreciation expense, why was the $2,000 included in 19C expenses?

P4–7. You are developing the adjusting entries for Robin Service Company at December 31, 19B. Three items are of special concern. Data at hand concerning the three items are:

Cash inflows and outflows:
Prepaid insurance—cash spent
during 19B .... $ 600
Interest expense—cash spent
during 19B 700
Service revenue—cash collected
during 19B 6,700

	Dec. 31, 19A	Dec. 31, 19B
Balance sheet amounts:		
Prepaid insurance (asset—debit)	$100	$400
Interest payable (liability—credit)	300	200
Service revenue collected in advance (liability—credit)	300	500

Required:

How much should be reported on the 19B income statement for (show computations):

1. Insurance expense?
2. Interest expense?
3. Service revenue earned?

P4–8. Modern Service Company is completing the information processing cycle at the end of its fiscal year, December 31, 19B. Below is listed the balance for each account at December 31, 19B *(a)* before the adjusting entries for 19B and *(b)* after the adjusting entries for 19B.

(Relates to Problem 4–8)

	Account balance, December 31, 19B			
	Before adjusting entries		After adjusting entries	
	Debit	Credit	Debit	Credit
a. Cash	$ 8,000		$ 8,000	
b. Service revenue receivable			400	
c. Prepaid insurance	300		200	
d. Operational assets	120,200		120,200	
e. Accumulated depreciation, equipment		$ 21,500		$ 25,000
f. Income taxes payable .				5,500
g. Capital stock		70,000		70,000
h. Retained earnings, January 1, 19B		14,000		14,000
i. Service revenue		60,000		60,400
j. Salary expense	37,000		37,000	
k. Depreciation expense .			3,500	
l. Insurance expense			100	
m. Income tax expense ...			5,500	
	$165,500	$165,500	$174,900	$174,900

Required:

  a. By comparing the amounts in the columns before and after the adjusting entries, reconstruct the four adjusting entries that were made in 19B. Provide a brief explanation of each.

  b. Compute the amount of income assuming (1) it is based on the amounts, "before adjusting entries" and (2) it is based on the amounts, "after adjusting entries." Which income amount is correct? Explain why.

P4–9. (Comprehensive) Morris Transportation Corporation has been in operation since January 1, 19D. It is now December 31, 19D, the end of the annual accounting period. The company has not done well financially during the first year, although hauling revenue has been fairly good. The three stockholders manage the company, and they have not given much attention to recordkeeping. In view of a serious cash shortage, they asked a local bank for a $10,000 loan. The bank requested a complete financial statement. The statements below were prepared by a clerk and then were given to the bank.

MORRIS TRANSPORTATION
CORPORATION
December 31, 19D

Income Statement

Hauling revenue	$90,000
Expenses:	
Salaries	20,000
Maintenance	15,000
Other expenses	25,000
Total expenses	60,000
Net income	$30,000

Balance Sheet

Assets

Cash	$ 1,000
Receivables	4,000
Inventory of maintenance	
supplies	5,000
Equipment	30,000
Other assets	37,000
Total assets	$77,000

Liabilities

Accounts payable	$ 7,000

Capital

Capital stock	40,000
Retained earnings	30,000
Total liabilities and	
capital	$77,000

After briefly reviewing the statements and "looking into the situation," the bank requested that the statements be redone (with some expert help) to "incorporate depreciation, accruals, inventory counts, income taxes, and so on." As a consequence of a review of the records and supporting documents, the following additional information was developed:

1. The inventory of maintenance supplies should be $2,000, instead of the $5,000 shown on December 31, 19D. (Hint: Increase Maintenance Expense.)

2. Prepaid insurance at December 31, 19D, amounted to $1,000. This insurance premium had been debited to Other Expenses in full when paid.

3. The equipment cost $30,000 when purchased January 1, 19D, and has an estimated useful life of five years (no residual value).

4. Unpaid salaries at December 31, 19D, amounted to $1,500 (have not been recorded).

5. At December 31, 19D, hauling revenue collected in advance was $3,000. This amount was credited to Hauling Revenue when the cash was collected earlier.

6. Assume an income tax rate of 20 percent.

Required:

  a. Give the six adjusting entries (in journal form) required by the above additional information for December 31, 19D.

  b. Recast the above statements after taking into account the adjusting entries. You do not need to use subclassifications on the statements. Suggested form for the solution:

| | | Changes | | |
Items	Amounts reported	Plus	Minus	Correct amounts
(List here each item from the two statements)				

(Hint: Correct balance sheet total is $69,000.)

c. Compute the amount of the error in (1) net income and (2) total assets due to the omission of the adjusting entries. Draft a brief nontechnical report for the bank explaining causes of the differences.

P4–10. (Comprehensive) Small Company is completing the information processing cycle for the annual accounting period that ended on December 31, 1981. All of the current entries for 1981 were entered correctly in the accounting system. A list of all of the ledger accounts and their respective balances (i.e., an unadjusted trial balance) was prepared immediately after the last current entry was journalized and posted.

The accountant was away for the next few days. During this time, a new assistant to the president requested that the bookkeeper prepare an income statement and balance sheet immediately "for our use" despite a suggestion by the bookkeeper that "the adjustments have to be determined by the accountant." Consequently, the following statements (summarized for case purposes) were prepared forthwith by the bookkeeper and given to the assistant.

Income Statement
For the Year Ended December 31, 1981

Revenues:
Sales	$240,000
Service	50,000
Total revenues	290,000

Expenses:
Cost of goods sold	150,000
Salaries and wages	65,000
Utilities	18,000
Other expenses	7,000
Total expenses	240,000
Net income	$ 50,000

Balance Sheet
At December 31, 1981

Assets
Cash	$ 23,000
Accounts receivable	61,000
Inventory	130,000
Prepaid insurance	6,000
Equipment*	100,000
Accumulated depreciation, equipment	(30,000)
Other assets	10,000
Total assets	$300,000

Liabilities
Accounts payable	$ 41,000
Income taxes payable	
Notes payable, one year, 15%	20,000

Stockholders' Equity
Capital stock, par $10, 15,000 shares	150,000
Contributed capital in excess of par	15,000
Retained earnings	74,000
Total liabilities and stockholders' equity	$300,000

* Acquired January 1, 1978; estimated ten-year life and no residual value.

After returning, the accountant immediately prepared another set of statements by including the following data:

a. The inventory at the end of December 1981 should have been $120,000 instead of $130,000. (Hint: Correct inventory and cost of goods sold.)

b. The prepaid insurance amount of $6,000 was the total premium paid on July 1, 1981, which covered a two-year period from payment date. (The $6,000 was debited to Prepaid Insurance.)

c. Depreciation for 1981. (Hint: Refer to the balance sheet.)

d. Interest on the note payable. The note was dated November 1, 1981, and the principal plus interest is payable at the end of one year.

e. Corporation income taxes. Assume an average tax rate of 20 percent.

Required:

a. Prepare the appropriate adjusting entry, in journal form, for each item of additional data.

b. Recast the income statement and balance sheet to incorporate the additional data. Suggested format:

Items	Amounts reported	Changes		Correct amounts
		Plus	Minus	
Income statement:				
Balance sheet:				

c. Draft a brief nontechnical explanation for the management to adequately explain why the second set of statements should replace the first set. (Hint: Correct EPS is $1.49.)

P4–11. This is a case to test your ability to analyze a specific situation and to determine whether an adjusting entry is required and, if so, what the entry should be.

General situation: On December 1, 19A, the company collected cash, $4,000, which was for some office space rented to an outsider. The rent collected was for the period December 1, 19A, through March 31, 19B. The annual accounting period ends on December 31.

Required:

a. How much of the $4,000 should be reported as revenue on the 19A annual

income statement? How much of it should be reported as revenue on the 19B income statement?

b. What is the amount of rent revenue collected in advance as of December 31, 19A? How should this amount be reported on the 19A financial statements?

c. On December 1, 19A, the company could have recorded the $4,000 collection in one of three different ways as follows:

Case A:

Cash	4,000	
Rent revenue . .		4,000

Case B:

Cash	4,000	
Rent revenue collected in advance		4,000

Case C:

Cash	4,000	
Rent revenue . .		1,000
Rent revenue collected in advance		3,000

For each case, give the appropriate adjusting entry (in journal form) at December 31, 19A. If no adjusting entry is required, explain why.

d. Do you believe one approach is better than the other two? Which one? Explain.

5

Information processing
in an accounting system

PURPOSE OF THE CHAPTER

In Chapter 3, Part B, the accounting information processing cycle was introduced. Chapter 4 discussed one important phase of that cycle—adjusting entries. The purpose of this chapter is to expand those discussions to include all of the phases and procedures in the accounting information processing cycle. This cycle is repeated each accounting period because it is a systematic approach to periodic recording, measuring, and classifying of financial data and generating periodic financial statements.

For those students interested in majoring in accounting, knowledge of accounting information processing is essential from the professional and technical points of view. For other students, particularly those interested in careers in management, a general knowledge of the information processing cycle is important because, as managers, they should be able to assess such things as (1) the capabilities and limitations of such a system, (2) the basic adaptations that should be expected for different types and sizes of entities, (3) cost-benefit relationships (i.e., the benefit of financial information versus the cost of generating the information), (4) the internal control implications of the system, and (5) the relationship of the accounting information processing system to the overall information system of the entity.

This chapter includes the following appendix:

Appendix: Reversing entries

Behavioral and learning objectives for this chapter are provided in the *Teachers Manual*.

MANUAL, MECHANICAL, AND ELECTRONIC DATA PROCESSING

Information processing refers to the order and ways in which the *accounting* work is accomplished in collecting the source (business) documents, recording their effects in the accounting system in terms of the accounting model, classifying the data collected, and, finally, in preparing the periodic financial statements. In most entities an extremely large amount of accounting data must be handled. Although information processing can be time consuming and costly to the enterprise, a well-designed processing system provides a smooth, uninterrupted, and efficient flow of data from the points of occurrence of the transactions to the financial statements. The processing of accounting data may be performed in one of three ways, or, as is the usual case, by a combination of them. The three approaches may be briefly described as follows:

1. **Manual data processing**—When this approach is used, the accounting work is performed manually (that is, by hand). In the discussion and illustrations up to this point, manual processing of accounting data has been employed. The manual approach is used extensively in small entities. Also, in large and medium-sized businesses, certain parts of the information process often are performed manually. The manual approach is quite useful for illustrating the application of accounting principles and measurement procedures. It also is convenient for explaining and illustrating the accounting process because the learner can readily see what is being done. One cannot see what is going on inside a computer.

2. **Mechanical data processing**—Mechanical data processing often is used in accounting to record repetitive transactions that occur in large numbers. Mechanical processing of accounting data employs accounting machines that vary widely in type and application. They encompass mechanical devices, some of which display a combination typewriter-adding machine keyboard. They encompass not only the strictly mechanical devices, such as posting machines, but also punched-card equipment. The latter consists of (1) key-punch machines, on which cards are punched to record the transactions; (2) sorting machines, which sort the cards in a predetermined order; and (3) tabulating machines, which print the output, such as a listing of the expenses for the period. Although mechanical data processing is used today, it is being superseded rapidly by electronic data processing.

3. **Electronic data processing**—Electronic processing of accounting data uses electronic computers. When electronic data processing is employed, the use of manual and mechanical activities in an accounting system is reduced to a minimum. Because of the large capability to store data and the speed with which such data can be manipulated and recalled, electronic data processing is widely used in accounting. Electronic data processing involves the use of "hardware" and "software." The com-

puter and equipment related to it (usually called peripheral equipment) constitute the **hardware. Software** includes *(a)* the computer programs that must be designed as instructions to the computer and *(b)* other items related to the operation of the system. Other items include materials used in operating the system, training materials, and studies of various sorts. Electronic data processing is applied widely to such accounting problems as payrolls, billings for goods and services, accounts receivable, accounts payable, and inventories.[1]

EXPANDING THE ACCOUNTING INFORMATION PROCESSING CYCLE

The discussions to follow in this chapter will expand on the accounting information processing cycle that was introduced in Chapter 3, Part B. You should review that introductory material (particularly Exhibit 3–8) before proceeding further.

The accounting information processing cycle is expanded in this chapter to encompass the **four additional phases** indicated by an **asterisk** in the listing below. The end-of-the-period phases are set off by a screen. Each of the phases in a complete accounting information processing cycle is outlined below in the chronological (timing) order in which each usually is implemented.

PHASES OF THE ACCOUNTING INFORMATION PROCESSING CYCLE

Currently during the accounting period

1. Collection of raw economic data generated by the transactions of the entity.
2. Analysis of all current transactions (as they occur) to determine their economic effects on the entity in terms of the accounting model. <u>This phase is called transaction analysis.</u>
3. Journalizing the results of the analysis of the current transactions. This phase encompasses recording the entries in chronological order in the journal.
4. Posting the current entries from the journal to the respective accounts in the ledger.

debit/credit ⟵

Only at the end of the accounting period

5. Preparation of an unadjusted trial balance from the ledger.
*6. Preparation of an accounting worksheet:
   a. Collection of data for adjusting entries and analysis of the data in the context of the accounting model.

---

[1] This subject is discussed in more depth in Robert N. Anthony and Glenn A. Welsch, *Fundamentals of Management Accounting,* 3d. ed. (Homewood, Ill.: Richard D. Irwin, Inc., 1981). © 1981 by Richard D. Irwin, Inc.

   b. Separation of the data among the income statement, balance
      sheet, and statement of changes in financial position.
7. Preparation of financial statements:
   a. Income statement.
   b. Balance sheet.
   c. Statement of changes in financial position (SCFP; discussed
      in Chapter 15).
*8. Adjusting entries (at the end of the period):
   a. Recorded in the journal.
   b. Posted to the ledger.
*9. Closing the revenue and expense accounts in the ledger:
   a. Entered in the journal.
   b. Posted to the ledger.
*10. Preparation of a post-closing trial balance.

Only at the start of the next period

11. Optional reversing entries (see chapter Appendix).

The four phases added (6, 8, 9, and 10 above) are information processing phases only and involve no new accounting concepts or principles beyond those that you have already learned in the first four chapters. These four added phases are designed to provide an orderly flow of the data processing work **at the end of the accounting period** and generally are quite helpful in completion of the financial statements with minimum effort. They also tend to decrease the potential for errors and omissions. The phases discussed in Chapter 3 will be reviewed. The four added phases will be discussed and illustrated in detail. In the illustrations, a manual system is employed for instructional purposes.

**Phase 1—
Collection of
raw economic
data generated
by transactions**

This is a necessary continuing activity that collects source documents for transactions as they occur. The collection process involves all functions of the entity and a large number of employees. The source documents provide the data to be analyzed and recorded in the accounting system. The source documents (such as sales invoices) must be timely and provide accurate data.

**Phase 2—
Analysis of
transactions**

This is a mental activity performed by accountants that identifies and measures the economic impact of each transaction on the entity in terms of the basic accounting model: Assets = Liabilities + Owners' equity. The analysis also involves determination of the **specific** asset, liability, and owners' equity accounts that should be increased and/or decreased to properly reflect the economic impacts. Analysis of transactions requires, for each transaction, the source document(s) and often other related information.

Journalizing is used to denote the process of entering the results of **transaction analysis** in the **journal** in the debit-credit format. Thus, the economic impacts of each transaction on the entity are recorded first in the journal in chronological order.

**Phase 4—
Posting**

The accounting data, having first been recorded in the journal, next are transferred or posted to the **ledger** to reclassify and aggregate the information in terms of the fundamental accounting model—Assets = Liabilities + Owners' equity. The ledger is composed of a number of separate accounts—one for each kind of asset, liability, and owners' equity. Thus, posting to the ledger reorders the data from a chronological order to the classifications explicit within the fundamental accounting model. The ledger is viewed as the basic accounting record since it provides the economic data for the entity appropriately classified for use in completing the remaining phases of the accounting information processing cycle (including preparation of the periodic financial statements).

**Phase 5—
Preparation of
an unadjusted
trial balance**

At the end of the period, after all current transactions are recorded in the journal (journalized) and then posted to the ledger, a **listing of all ledger accounts** and their balances is prepared. This listing is called an **unadjusted** trial balance since (1) it serves to check the equalities of the accounting model (A = L + OE and Debits = Credits) and (2) it does not include the effects of a particular group of end-of-the-period entries called adjusting entries which were discussed and illustrated in Chapter 3.

Chapter 3 illustrated the use of a trial balance to prepare the periodic financial statements. However, that chapter did not discuss or illustrate the **remaining** phases of the accounting information processing cycle. The **detailed** discussions and illustrations that follow relate to the remaining phases which are **end-of-the-period phases.**

**Phase 6—The
worksheet**

The outline on page 178 lists six different phases at the end of the accounting period, including a **worksheet.** The end-of-the-period phases involve numerous related details and the consequent possibility of errors. The worksheet has been designed (a) to facilitate handling of the details and (b) to minimize the potential for errors. It is an optional procedure that results in a comprehensive worksheet which is not a part of the basic accounting records. It is an optional facilitating device and generally is prepared in pencil (for ease in revision) since it is not presented to the management or to other parties. Once completed, it provides in one place all of the data that are needed to complete the remaining end-of-the-period phases in the accounting information processing cycle. It accomplishes this broad purpose by bringing together in one place, in an orderly way, the (1) unadjusted trial balance, (2) adjusting entries, (3) income statement, (4) statement of retained earnings, (5) balance sheet, and (6) the closing entries (explained later).[2]

Preparing the worksheet. The simplified case used in Chapter 4 (pages 148–155) for High-Rise Apartments will be used to illustrate the preparation of a typical worksheet at the end of the accounting year, December 31, 1981. To facilitate explanation, two exhibits are presented:

Exhibit 5–1—Preparation of the worksheet format with inclusion of the **unadjusted** trial balance.

Exhibit 5–2—Completion of the worksheet to reflect the income statement, statement of retained earnings, and balance sheet.

The steps involved in developing the worksheet are:

Step 1—Set up the worksheet format by entering the appropriate column headings. This step is illustrated in Exhibit 5–1, which includes in the left column the account titles (taken directly from the ledger) and six separate pairs of debit/credit money columns. The six money columns basically reflect the end-of-the period phases of the accounting information processing cycle.

Step 2—Develop the **unadjusted** trial balance as of the end of the accounting period directly in the first pair of money columns. When all of the current entries for the period (excluding the adjusting entries) have been recorded in the journal and posted to the ledger, the amounts for the unadjusted trial balance are the balances of the respective ledger accounts therein. Before proceeding to the next step, the equality of the debits and credits in the unadjusted trial balance should be assured. Note that when a worksheet is used there is no need to develop a **separate** unadjusted trial balance (Phase 5).

Step 3—The second pair of money columns, headed "Adjusting Entries," is completed by developing and then entering the adjusting entries directly on the worksheet. The adjusting entries for High-Rise Apartments shown in Exhibit 5–1 were illustrated (with the same letter codes) and discussed in detail in Chapter 4. They are repeated for convenience in Exhibit 5–2. To facilitate examination (for potential errors), future reference, and study, the adjusting entries usually are coded on the worksheet as illustrated in Exhibit 5–1. Some of the adjusting entries may require the addition of one or more account titles below the original trial balance listing. This was done for the last four accounts on the worksheet. After the adjusting entries are completed on the worksheet, the equality of debits and credits for those entries is checked (totals $19,900).

---

[2] This entire section on the worksheet can be omitted without affecting the remaining chapters.

EXHIBIT 5-1

HIGH RISE APARTMENTS, INC.
Worksheet for the Year Ended December 31, 1981

Account Titles	Unadjusted Trial Balance		Adjusting Entries		Adjusted Trial Balance		Income Statement		Retained Earnings		Balance Sheet	
	Debit	Credit	Debit	Credit	Debit	Credit	Debit	Credit	Debit	Credit	Debit	Credit
Cash	2,297											
Prepaid insurance	2,400			(c) 1,200								
Inventory of maintenance supplies	600			(e) 400								
Land	25,000											
Apartment building	360,000											
Accumulated depreciation, building		10,000		(d) 10,000								
Notes payable		30,000										
Rent collected in advance				(a) 500								
Mortgage payable		238,037										
Capital stock, 500 shares		50,000										
Retained earnings, Jan. 1, 1981		24,960										
Dividends paid	12,000											
Rent revenue		128,463	(a) 500	(b) 600								
Advertising expense	500											
Maintenance expense	3,000		(e) 400									
Salary expense	17,400		(f) 900									
Interest expense	19,563		(h) 600									
Utilities expense	34,500											
Miscellaneous expenses	4,200											
Insurance expense			(c) 1,200									
Depreciation expense			(d) 10,000									
Salaries payable				(f) 900								
Property tax expense			(g) 5,700									
Property taxes payable				(g) 5,700								
Interest payable				(h) 600								
Rent revenue receivable			(b) 600									
	481,460	481,460	19,900	19,900								

EXHIBIT 5-2

HIGH RISE APARTMENTS, INC.
Worksheet for the Year Ended December 31, 1981

Account Titles	Unadjusted Trial Balance Debit	Unadjusted Trial Balance Credit	Adjusting Entries* Debit	Adjusting Entries* Credit	Adjusted Trial Balance Debit	Adjusted Trial Balance Credit	Income Statement Debit	Income Statement Credit	Retained Earnings Debit	Retained Earnings Credit	Balance Sheet Debit	Balance Sheet Credit
Cash	2,297				2,297						2,297	
Prepaid insurance	2,400			(c) 1,200	1,200						1,200	
Inventory of maintenance supplies	600			(e) 400	200						200	
Land	25,000				25,000						25,000	
Apartment building	360,000				360,000						360,000	
Accumulated depreciation, building		10,000		(d) 10,000		20,000						20,000
Notes payable		30,000				30,000						30,000
Rent collected in advance				(a) 500		500						500
Mortgage payable		238,037				238,037						238,037
Capital stock, 500 shares		50,000				50,000						50,000
Retained earnings, Jan. 1, 1981		24,960				24,960				24,960		
Dividends paid	12,000				12,000				12,000			
Rent revenue		128,463	(a) 500	(b) 600		128,563		128,563				
Advertising expense	500				500		500					
Maintenance expense	3,000		(e) 400		3,400		3,400					
Salary expense	17,400		(f) 900		18,300		18,300					
Interest expense	19,563		(h) 600		20,163		20,163					
Utilities expense	34,500				34,500		34,500					
Miscellaneous expenses	4,200				4,200		4,200					
Insurance expense			(c) 1,200		1,200		1,200					
Depreciation expense			(d) 10,000		10,000		10,000					
Salaries payable				(f) 900		900						900
Property tax expense			(g) 5,700		5,700		5,700					
Property tax payable				(g) 5,700		5,700						5,700
Interest payable				(h) 600		600						600
Rent revenue receivable			(b) 600		600						600	
	481,460	481,460	19,900	19,900	499,260	499,260	97,963	128,563				
Income tax expense†			(i) 6,120		6,120		6,120					
Income tax payable				(i) 6,120		6,120						6,120
Net income‡							24,480			24,480		
							128,563	128,563	12,000	49,440		
Retained earnings, Dec. 31, 1981§									37,440			37,440
									49,440	49,440	389,297	389,297

* Explanation of adjusting entries is provided in Exhibit 5-3.

† Revenues, $128,563 − Pretax expenses, $97,963 = $30,600; $30,600 × tax rate, 20% = $6,120.

‡ Pretax income, $30,600 − Income tax, $6,120 = $24,480.

§ $49,440 − $12,000 = $37,440.

The steps to complete the worksheet are reflected by a screen in Exhibit 5–2; these steps are:

Step 4—The pair of money columns headed "Adjusted Trial Balance" is completed. Although not essential, they are used for ensuring accuracy. They simply represent, line by line, the combined amounts of the unadjusted trial balance, plus or minus the amounts entered as adjusting entries in the second pair of columns. For example, the Rent Revenue account reflects a $128,463 credit balance under Unadjusted Trial Balance. To this amount is *added* the *credit* amount, $600, and *subtracted* the *debit* amount, $500, giving a combined amount of $128,563, which is entered as a *credit* under **Adjusted** Trial Balance. For those accounts that were unaffected by the adjusting entries, the Unadjusted Trial Balance amount is simply carried across to the Adjusted Trial Balance column. After each line has been completed, the equality of the debits and credits under Adjusted Trial Balance is checked (total $499,260).

Step 5—The amount on each line, under Adjusted Trial Balance, is extended horizontally across the worksheet and entered *(a)* as a debit, if it was a debit under Adjusted Trial Balance, or as a credit, if it was a credit under Adjusted Trial Balance; and *(b)* under the financial statement heading (income statement, retained earnings, or balance sheet) on which it must appear. You can see that each amount extended across (1) was entered under *only one* of the six remaining columns, and (2) that debits remain debits and credits remain credits in the extending process.

Step 6—At this point, the two Income Statement columns are summed (subtotals). The difference between the two subtotals represents the pretax income (or loss). Income tax expense then is computed by multiplying this difference by the tax rate. In Exhibit 5–2, the computation was (pretax revenues, $128,563 − pretax expenses, $97,963) × tax rate, 20% = $6,120. The **adjusting entry** for income tax then was entered at the bottom of the worksheet (we call this a "loopback"). Income tax expense and income tax payable now can be extended horizontally to the Income Statement and Balance Sheet columns. Net income is entered as a balancing **debit** amount in the Income Statement column and as a credit (i.e., increase) in Retained Earnings.

Step 7—The two Retained Earnings columns are summed, and the difference is the ending balance of retained earnings. This balance is entered as a balancing debit amount and also as a balancing credit amount (i.e., an addition to owners' equity). At this point the two Balance Sheet columns should sum to equal amounts. The continuous checking of equality of debits and credits in each pair of money columns helps to assure the correctness of the worksheet. However, the balancing feature does not provide absolute proof that the worksheet contains no errors. For example, if an expense amount (a debit) were extended to either Retained Earnings as a debit or to the Balance Sheet debit column, the worksheet would balance in all respects, however, at least two money columns would be in error. Therefore, special care must be exercised in the horizontal extension process.[3]

The completed worksheet, Exhibit 5–2, will provide all of the data needed to complete the remaining phases of the accounting information processing cycle as follows (refer to page 179):

Phase	Designation	Source on worksheet
7	Preparation of income statement	Income Statement columns
	Preparation of balance sheet	Balance Sheet columns
	Preparation of statement of retained earnings	Retained Earnings columns
8	Record adjusting entries in journal and post to ledger	Adjusting Entries Columns
9	Record closing entries in journal and post to ledger	Income Statement and Retained Earnings columns
10	Post-closing trial balance	Prepare from ledger and check with Balance Sheet columns.

Phase 7—Preparing financial statements from the worksheet

The completed worksheet provides all the amounts needed, in convenient form, to prepare the income statement, balance sheet, and statement of retained earnings. The statement of retained earnings, although not listed as a required statement, generally is prepared by corporations (see pages 49 and 58 for examples). It ties together the income statement and the stockholders' equity section of the balance sheet. For example, the statement of retained earnings for High-Rise Apartments would be as follows:

HIGH-RISE APARTMENTS, INC.
Statement of Retained Earnings
For the Year Ended December 31, 1981

Retained earnings balance January 1, 1981	$24,960
Add net income of 1981	24,480
Total	49,440
Less dividends paid in 1981	12,000
Retained earnings balance, December 31, 1981	$37,440

In a similar manner, the task of preparing the income statement and balance sheet is simply one of classifying the data provided by the worksheet.

---

[3] The number of paired columns on a worksheet can be reduced by omitting both, or either, the Adjusted Trial Balance columns and the Retained Earnings columns. Also, the number of columns can be reduced further by using only one money column for each set instead of separate debit and credit columns (for example, the credits can be indicated by parentheses).

Since classified statements were illustrated in Chapter 3, they will not be repeated here.

The worksheet described above does not provide data for the statement of changes in financial postion. This statement requires special analytical procedures; as a consequence, a special worksheet must be used to develop it. The special worksheet will be discussed and illustrated in Chapter 15.

Phase 8— Recording adjusting entries in the accounting records

Next the adjusting entries reflected on the completed worksheet are entered in the journal and then posted to the ledger. They are "dated" at the last day of the period. This is a clerical task since they merely are copied from the worksheet. The adjusting entries for High-Rise Apartments, showing a folio notation for posting completed, are illustrated in Exhibit 5–3. The ledger, with the adjusting entries posted (in color to facilitate your identification), is shown in Exhibit 5–5. This phase is done to enter the economic effects of the adjusting entries into the accounting system.

Phase 9— Closing the temporary accounts

In our study of the fundamental accounting model, we have emphasized that the **revenue** and **expense** accounts are subdivisions of retained earnings which is a part of **owners' equity.** The revenue and expense accounts are "income statement accounts," whereas the remainder of the accounts can be viewed as "balance sheet accounts." The revenue and expense accounts are often called **temporary** or **nominal** accounts in the sense that data are collected in them for the current accounting period only. At the end of each period their balances are transferred, or closed, to the Retained Earnings account. This periodic clearing out, dumping, or closing of their balances into Retained Earnings serves two purposes: (1) it transfers net income (or loss) to retained earnings (i.e., owners' equity) and (2) it establishes a zero balance in the revenue and expense accounts to start the new accounting period. In this way, the income statement accounts are ready to serve their temporary periodic collection function for the next period.

In contrast, the balance sheet accounts (assets, liabilities, and owners' equity) are not closed; therefore, they are often called **permanent** or **real** accounts. The only time a permanent account has a zero balance is when the item represented (such as machinery or notes payable) is no longer owned or is fully depreciated. The balance at the end of the period in each balance sheet account is carried forward in the ledger as the beginning balance for the next period.

The clearing out, or **closing,** at the end of the accounting period of all revenue and expense accounts is simply a mechanical phase. To close an account means to transfer its balance to another designated account by means of an entry. For example, an account that has a credit balance

EXHIBIT 5-3
Adjusting entries
(High-Rise
Apartments)

JOURNAL   Page 6

Date 1981	Account Titles and Explanation	Folio	Debit	Credit
Dec. 31	(a) Rent revenue	340	500	
	Rent collected in advance	204		500
	To adjust the accounts for revenue collected in advance (see pages 148–149).			
31	(b) Rent revenue receivable	102	600	
	Rent revenue	340		600
	To adjust for rent revenue earned in 1981, but not yet collected (see page 150).			
31	(c) Insurance expense	356	1,200	
	Prepaid insurance	103		1,200
	To adjust for insurance expired during 1981 (see pages 150–151).			
31	(d) Depreciation expense	360	10,000	
	Accumulated depreciation, building	113		10,000
	To adjust for depreciation expense for 1981 (see page 152).			
31	(e) Maintenance expense	351	400	
	Inventory of maintenance supplies	104		400
	To adjust for supplies used from inventory during 1981 (see page 152).			
31	(f) Salary expense	352	900	
	Salaries payable	206		900
	To adjust for salaries earned yet not recorded or paid (see page 153).			
31	(g) Property tax expense	361	5,700	
	Property tax payable	207		5,700
	To adjust for 1981 property tax incurred, but not yet recorded or paid (see page 154).			
31	(h) Interest expense	353	600	
	Interest payable	209		600
	To adjust for accrued interest expense for two months on note payable ($30,000 $\times$ 12% $\times$ 2/12 = $600) (see page 154).			
31	(i) An adjusting entry for income tax expense will be computed on the worksheet when the pretax income is computed thereon (see pages 158 and 184). The entry will be:			
	Income tax expense	370	6,120	
	Income tax payable	208		6,120

(such as a revenue account) would be closed by *debiting* that account for an amount equal to its balance and crediting the account to which the balance is to be transferred. In the closing process a credit balance is always transferred to the other account as a credit, and similarly a debit is always transferred as a debit for the same amount. The closing entries are dated the last day of the accounting period and are entered in the journal in the usual debit-credit format. They are immediately posted to the ledger.

Another temporary account, called "Income Summary," often is used to facilitate the procedure. To illustrate the closing procedure, assume the following summarized data from the accounts of XYZ Corporation at December 31, 19X, end of the accounting period.

Stockholders' equity accounts

Capital stock, 5,000 shares, par $10	$ 50,000
Retained earnings beginning balance January 1, 19X	15,000
Total revenues earned during 19X	100,000
Total expenses incurred during 19X	80,000
Total dividends declared and paid during 19X	10,000

The four closing entries required would be dated December 31, 19X, and would appear in the journal as follows:

a. Revenue 100,000

    Income summary   100,000

    To close the revenue amount into Income Summary.

b. Income summary 80,000

    Expenses   80,000

    To close the expense amount into Income Summary.

c. Income summary 20,000

    Retained earnings   20,000

    To close the income summary amount (i.e., net income) into Retained Earnings.

d. Retained earnings 10,000

    Dividends paid   10,000

    To close the dividends paid amount into Retained Earnings.

Posting of the above closing entries is diagrammed, and their effects on the **temporary and permanent ledger accounts** are shown below:

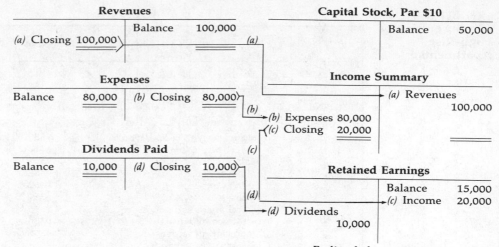

Ending balance, $25,000

In the above example, only one revenue and one expense account were used for illustrative purposes. All revenue and expense accounts must be closed at the end of the period using the procedure illustrated above. Also, the above example assumed that dividends paid were recorded previously as a debit to a temporary account, Dividends Paid, rather than as a debit to Retained Earnings. Therefore, the temporary account, Dividends Paid, was closed into Retained Earnings. When this temporary account is not used, a closing entry for it is not needed.

Now, let's return to High-Rise Apartments and apply the same closing mechanics. The closing entries are shown in Exhibit 5–4 as they would be entered in the journal; the posting notation (folio) to the ledger also is indicated. Observe that all of the revenue and expense accounts are closed, and in the process their balances are transferred into Retained Earnings. Also, the Dividends Paid account is closed into Retained Earnings.

The ledger accounts with (1) the trial balance totals, (2) the adjusting entries posted (in color), and (3) the closing entries posted (in black boxes) are shown in Exhibit 5–5 in T-account format. The colors and boxes are used to facilitate your study of the mechanics of each step. You should observe that all of the adjusting and closing amounts are verifiable directly on the completed worksheet (Exhibit 5–2).

There is one additional point that should be emphasized. The closing entry in the journal for expenses (and for revenues when there is more than one) is a compound entry, which saves closing time and space (of course, a separate closing entry could be made for each separate expense

EXHIBIT 5–4
**Closing entries for
High-Rise
Apartments**

JOURNAL

Page 7

Date 1981	Account Titles and Explanation	Folio	Debit	Credit
Dec. 31	Rent revenue	340	128,563	
	Income summary	330		128,563
	To transfer revenues into Income Summary.			
31	Income summary ($97,963 + $6,120)	330	104,083	
	Advertising expense	350		500
	Maintenance expense	351		3,400
	Salary expense	352		18,300
	Interest expense	353		20,163
	Utilities expense	354		34,500
	Miscellaneous expenses	355		4,200
	Insurance expense	356		1,200
	Depreciation expense	360		10,000
	Property tax expense	361		5,700
	Income tax expense	370		6,120
	To transfer expense amounts into Income Summary.			
31	Income summary	330	24,480	
	Retained earnings	305		24,480
	To transfer Net Income into Retained Earnings.			
31	Retained earnings	305	12,000	
	Dividends paid	306		12,000
	To transfer Dividends Paid into Retained Earnings.			

account). Notice that the total debit to Income Summary in that entry is taken from the worksheet.

After the closing process is completed, observe that all of the temporary (i.e., the income statement) accounts are closed and are ready for reuse during the next accounting period for accumulating the revenues and expenses of that period. The Retained Earnings account now has an ending balance of $37,440, which will be reported on the December 31, 1981, balance sheet as a part of stockholders' equity.[4]

---

[4] A common bookkeeping approach to "ruling a permanent T-account" with a carry-forward balance is as follows:

Retained Earnings			305
Dividends (1981)	12,000	Jan. 1, 1981, balance	24,960
Balance carried forward to 1982	37,440	Net income (1981)	24,480
	49,440		49,440
		Jan. 1, 1982, balance	37,440

EXHIBIT 5–5
Ledger for High-Rise Apartments, Inc.

LEDGER

Cash	101
2,297	

Rent Revenue Receivable	102
(b) 600	

Prepaid Insurance	103
2,400	(c) 1,200

Inventory of Maintenance Supplies	104
600	(e) 400

Land	110
25,000	

Apartment Building	111
360,000	

Accumulated Depreciation, Building	113
	10,000
	(d) 10,000

Notes Payable	201
	30,000

Rent Collected in Advance	204
	(a) 500

Salaries Payable	206
	(f) 900

Property Tax Payable	207
	(g) 5,700

Income Tax Payable	208
	(i) 6,120

Interest Payable	209
	(h) 600

Mortgage Payable	251
	238,037

Capital Stock	301
	50,000

Retained Earnings	305
(7) 12,000	24,960
	(7) 24,480

Dividends Paid	306
12,000	(7) 12,000

Income Summary	330
(7) 104,083	(7) 128,563
(7) 24,480	

Rent Revenue	340
(a) 500	128,463
(7) 128,563	(b) 600

Advertising Expense	350
500	(7) 500

Maintenance Expense	351
3,000	(7) 3,400
(e) 400	

Salary Expense	352
17,400	(7) 18,300
(f) 900	

Interest Expense	353
19,563	(7) 20,163
(h) 600	

Utilities Expense	354
34,500	(7) 34,500

Miscellaneous Expenses	355
4,200	(7) 4,200

Insurance Expense	356
(c) 1,200	(7) 1,200

Depreciation Expense	360
(d) 10,000	(7) 10,000

Property Tax Expense	361
(g) 5,700	(7) 5,700

Income Tax Expense	370
(i) 6,120	(7) 6,120

For illustrative purposes:
· Unadjusted balances are in black.
· Adjusting entries are in color.
· Closing entries are enclosed in boxes.

Phase 10—Post-closing trial balance

Despite the guidance provided by the worksheet, occasional errors are made in the adjusting and closing mechanics. After the completion of these two phases, it is desirable to retest the equality of the ledger account balances. This normally is accomplished by using the computer or simply running an adding machine tape on the ledger—the debits can be entered as plus and the credits as minus, and the resultant total should be zero; any difference is the amount of the error(s). Instead, some individuals prefer to prepare another formal trial balance, called a **post-closing trial balance,** before starting the new period. Since all of the revenue and expense accounts have been closed to retained earnings, the post-closing trial balance will reflect account balances *only* for the assets, liabilities, and owners' equity. These balances should be identical with those shown in the last two columns of the worksheet. Observe that the ending balances reflected in the ledger accounts, after the closing process, will be the beginning balances for the next period.

REVERSING ENTRIES

Some accountants add one more phase to the accounting informaion processing cycle, which is known as **reversing entries.** This phase is dated as of the first day of the next period and is used for the sole purpose of *simplifying* certain subsequent entries in the accounts. Reversing entries are related only to certain adjusting entries already made in the accounts. When appropriate, such adjusting entries are reversed on the first day of the next period (i.e., the debits and credits simply are reversed). Reversing entries are strictly optional and involve only bookkeeping mechanics rather than accounting concepts and principles. The Appendix at the end of this chapter discusses and illustrates reversing entries for those who desire to become familiar with this optional facilitating technique.

PREPARATION OF INTERIM FINANCIAL STATEMENTS

Many companies prepare interim financial statements during the accounting year for each month or each quarter. **Monthly** interim statements, when prepared, almost always are for internal management uses only. In contrast, many larger companies prepare **quarterly** financial statements for internal management use and also present summarized versions of them to their shareholders and other parties.

With monthly or quarterly interim financial statements the company does not go through the process of recording in the journal and posting to the ledger accounts **interim** adjusting and closing entries. The formality of journalizing and posting adjusting entries is used **only** at the end of the annual accounting period.

Therefore, the worksheet serves another very useful purpose when interim monthly or quarterly financial statements are prepared. At the end of each interim period an unadjusted trial balance is taken from the ledger accounts and entered directly on an interim (say monthly) worksheet. The worksheet then is completed on the interim basis by entering the interim adjusting entries thereon and extending the adjusted amounts to the Retained Earnings, Income Statement, and Balance Sheet columns. The interim statements (say monthly) are prepared on the basis of the worksheet. The phases of the accounting information processing cycle (adjusting entries recorded, closing entries recorded, and post-closing trial balance) are not completed at the end of the interim period.

SUMMARY

This chapter focused on the accounting information processing cycle which must be accomplished in situations where periodic financial statements for both external and internal users are developed. The cycle captures raw economic data on transactions as they occur and processes the economic effects on the entity to the final effective communication by means of the periodic financial statements. The information system must be designed to measure net income, financial position, and funds flow accurately and effectively. An information system also must be designed to fit the characteristics of the entity.

We cannot emphasize too strongly that the worksheet, the closing entries, and the post-closing trial balance steps are only mechanical data processing procedures and do not involve any new accounting principles or measurement approaches.

The ten phases discussed above constitute the accounting information processing cycle repeated each accounting period in all accounting information systems. It is a processing model that captures the economic essence of all transactions at their points of incurrence and carries those effects to the end result—the periodic financial statements. Numerous adaptations of the procedures used to implement the cycle are to be found because entities have different characteristics such as size, type of industry, complexity, and sophistication of the management.

Implementation of the cycle and organization of the information processing activities in a particular entity can be efficient, effective, and timely in terms of the outputs (the financial statements) or the opposite, depending on the competence of those performing the data processing tasks and the importance attached by the management and owners to measurement of operating results and financial position. In this context, the information processing system of an entity is significant to all parties interested in the entity because the end results—the financial statements—are important in their decision-making models.

APPENDIX: REVERSING ENTRIES

After completion of Phase 10 of the accounting information processing cycle (i.e., the post-closing trial balance), an *optional phase* may be added as Phase 11 (see page 179). This final phase is known as "reversing entries." Reversing entries are dated at the beginning of the *next period* and relate *only* to certain adjusting entries made at the end of the immediate prior period. Certain adjusting entries may be reversed on the first day of the next period **solely** to simplify or facilitate the recording of subsequent related entries. Unlike most of the phases in the accounting information processing cycle already discussed, reversing entries are strictly **optional** and involve only bookkeeping mechanics rather than accounting principles or concepts.

The reversing entry phase is presented because (1) it introduces a common data processing technique used in most companies, whether the system is manual, mechanical, or computerized; and (2) a knowledge of the circumstances under which it may be used gives some additional insight into certain relationships in the efficient processing of accounting information.[5]

Reversing entries are given this name because they reverse, at the start of the next accounting period, the effects of certain adjusting entries made at the end of the previous period. Reversing entries are always the opposite of the related adjusting entry. It may be desirable to "reverse" certain adjusting entries; the other adjusting entries should not be reversed.

To illustrate reversing entries and the type of situation where a reversing entry will simplify the subsequent accounting entry, assume that Day Company is in the process of completing the information processing cycle at the end of its accounting period, December 31, 1981. To place the reversing entry in context, Exhibit 5–6 presents a situation which shows (1) an adjusting entry on December 31, 1981; (2) the reversing entry that could be made on January 1, 1982; and (3) the subsequent entry on January 13, 1982, that was simplified. To demonstrate the facilitating effect of a reversing entry, we also have presented entries in the tabulation reflecting the same situation assuming no reversing entry. You should study carefully the two sets of entries and the explanatory comments in Exhibit 5–6. The reversing entry is shown in color for emphasis.

Another example is given below of a situation where a reversing entry simplifies recording of a subsequent related entry. This example will illustrate both the journal entries and the related ledger accounts.

Situation: On September 1, 19A, Company X loaned $1,200 on a one-year, 10 percent, interest-bearing note. On August 31, 19B, the company will collect the $1,200 principal plus $120 interest revenue. The annual accounting period ends December 31.

The related journal entries, explanations, and ledger accounts are given on page 196. Study them carefully. The reversing entry is shown in color for emphasis.

---

[5] Knowledge of reversing entries is of importance primarily to those students who plan to study accounting at the advanced level. This knowledge is not significant for study of the remaining chapters in this book.

EXHIBIT 5–6
Purpose of reversing entries illustrated

DAY COMPANY

a. The preceding adjusting entry: The payroll was paid on December 28, 1981; the next payroll will be on January 13, 1982. At December 31, 1981, there were wages earned of $3,000 for the last three days of the year that had not been paid or recorded.

With reversing entry   *Without reversing entry*

December 31, 1981, adjusting entry to record the $3,000 accrued (unpaid) wages:

Wage expense..... 3,000		Wage expense..... 3,000	
Wages payable		Wages payable	
(a liability)..	3,000	(a liability)..	3,000

b. The closing entry: The revenue and expense accounts are closed to Income Summary after the adjusting entries are completed and posted to the ledger.

December 31, 1981, closing entry:

Income summary .. 3,000		Income summary .. 3,000	
Wage expense .	3,000	Wage expense .	3,000

c. The reversing entry: The information processing cycle in 1981 is complete. All closing entries have been posted, and the post-closing trial balance has been verified. At this point in time, January 1, 1982, the accountant should decide whether it is desirable to make any reversing entries to simplify the *subsequent entries*. Question: Would a reversing entry on January 1, 1982, simplify the entry to be made on January 13, 1982, when the wages are paid?

January 1, 1982, reversing entry:

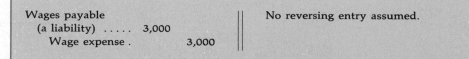

Wages payable		No reversing entry assumed.	
(a liability) 3,000			
Wage expense .	3,000		

d. The subsequent entry that was facilitated: The payroll of $25,000 was completed and paid on January 13, 1982. This subsequent payment entry is to be recorded. Question: Did the reversing entry simplify this entry?

January 13, 1982, payroll entry:

Wage expense ... 25,000		Wages payable .. 3,000	
Cash	25,000	Wage expense ... 22,000	
		Cash	25,000

Explanation—Observe that when the reversing entry was used, this last entry required only one debit, contrasted with two debits when no reversing entry was made. This difference was due to the fact that the reversing entry served to (1) clear out the liability account, "Wages Payable," and (2) set up a temporary *credit* in the Wage Expense account. After the last entry, to record the payment of the payroll, both accounts affected—Wage Expense and Wages Payable—are identical in balance under both approaches. If the reversing entry is not made, the company must go to the trouble of identifying how much of the $25,000 paid on January 13, 1982, was expense and how much of it was to pay the liability set up in the adjusting entry at the end of the prior period ([a] above).

JOURNAL

a. September 1, 19A—To record the loan:

> Note receivable . 1,200
>   Cash   1,200

b. December 31, 19A (end of the accounting period)—Adjusting entry for four months' interest revenue earned but not collected ($1,200 × 10% × 4/12 = $40):

> Interest receiv-
>   able   40
> Interest
>   revenue . .   40

c. December 31, 19A—To close interest revenue:

> Interest revenue   40
> Income
>   summary   40

d. January 1, 19B—To reverse adjusting entry of December 31, 19A:

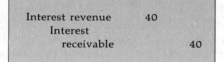

> Interest revenue   40
> Interest
>   receivable   40

Observe that after this entry, the Interest Receivable account reflects a zero balance and Interest Revenue reflects a *debit* balance of $40 (four months interest).

e. August 31, 19B—Subsequent entry; to record collection of note plus interest for one year:

> Cash   1,320
> Note
>   receivable   · 1,200
> Interest
>   revenue . .   120

LEDGER

Cash

	x,xxx	*(a)* 9/1/19A 1,200
(e) 8/31/19B	1,320	

Note Receivable

(a) 9/1/19A	1,200	*(e)* 8/31/19B 1,200

Interest Receivable

(b) 12/31/19A	40	*(d)* 1/1/19B 40

Interest Revenue

(c) 12/31/19A	40	*(b)* 12/31/19A 40
(d) 1/1/19B	40	*(e)* 8/31/19B 120

Income Summary

	(c) 12/31/19A 40

Note: To demonstrate the facilitating feature, assume the reversing entry *(d)* was not made. The August 31, 19B, entry would be more complex, viz:

> Cash   1,320
>   Note receivable   1,200
>   Interest receivable . . .   40
>   Interest revenue   80

Observe that after this entry the Note Receivable account has a zero balance and the Interest Revenue an $80 balance which represents eight months' interest revenue earned in 19B.

The facilitating feature is clear if we observe that without the reversing entry on January 1, 19B, the collection entry on August 31, 19B, would be more complex, as demonstrated on page 195.

In the above discussion it was indicated that **certain** adjusting entries could be reversed to simplify subsequent entries and that certain adjusting entries would not be reversed. How does one decide the entries that may be reversed to advantage? There is no inflexible rule that can be provided. The accountant must analyze each situation and make a rational choice. In general it can be said that short-term accruals and deferrals are candidates for reversal.

The adjusting entry to record depreciation and entries of this type should never be reversed. In these situations the adjusting entry is not followed by a subsequent "payment" entry; therefore, it would be not only pointless to reverse it but would also introduce an error into the accounts because the accumulated depreciation account would reflect a zero balance throughout the period. Thus, most adjusting entries are not candidates for reversal, and those that are candidates are easily identified if one considers the nature of the subsequent related entry.

Perhaps the most compelling reason for reversing entries is to increase the likelihood that the effects of certain adjusting entries will **not** be overlooked when recording the next related transaction in the following period.

IMPORTANT TERMS DEFINED IN THE CHAPTER (with page citations)

Manual data processing—177
Mechanical data processing—177
Electronic data processing—177
Computer hardware—178
Computer software—178
Accounting information
   processing cycle—178, 179

Worksheet—180
Closing entries—186, 188, 190
Temporary (nominal) accounts—
   186
Permanent (real) accounts—186
Post-closing trial balances—192
Reversing entries—192, Appendix

QUESTIONS FOR DISCUSSION

1. Briefly explain an accounting information processing system.

2. Distinguish among manual, mechanical, and electronic data processing. How does each relate to accounting information processing?

3. Briefly identify, in sequence, the ten phases of the accounting information processing cycle.

4. Contrast transaction analysis with journalizing.

5. Compare journalizing with posting.

6. Explain in what way posting reflects a change in classification of the data.

7. Contrast an unadjusted trial balance with an adjusted trial balance. What is the basic purpose of each?

8. What is the purpose of the worksheet?

9. Why are adjusting entries entered on the worksheet?

10. Why are adjusting entries recorded in the journal and posted to the ledger even though they are entered on the worksheet?

11. What are the purposes of closing entries? Why are they recorded in the journal and posted to the ledger?

12. Distinguish among (a) real, (b) nominal, (c) permanent, and (d) temporary accounts.

13. Explain why the income statement accounts are closed but the balance sheet accounts are not.

14. What is a post-closing trial balance? Is it a useful part of the accounting information processing cycle? Explain.

15. What are reversing entries? When are they useful? Give an example of an adjusting entry that (a) should be reversed and (b) that should not be reversed (based on the Appendix).

EXERCISES

E5–1. Simple Company prepared the unadjusted trial balance given below at the end of the accounting year, December 31, 19B. To simplify the case, the amounts given are in thousands of dollars.

	Debit	Credit
Cash	$ 19	
Accounts receivable	22	
Prepaid insurance	3	
Machinery (ten-year life, no residual value)	30	
Accumulated depreciation, machinery		$ 3
Accounts payable		2
Wages payable		
Income tax payable		
Capital stock, nopar (1,000 shares)		40
Retained earnings		5
Dividends declared and paid during 19B	2	
Revenues (not detailed)		56
Expenses (not detailed)	30	
Totals	$106	$106

Other data not yet recorded at December 31, 19B:

1. Insurance expired during 19B, $1.
2. Depreciation expense for 19B.
3. Wages payable, $2.
4. Income tax rate, 20 percent.

Required:

(Note: A worksheet may be used but is not required.)

a. Complete the income statement and balance sheet given below for 19B.
b. Give the adjusting entries for 19B.
c. Give the closing entries for 19B.

Income Statement

Revenues (not detailed)	$_____
Expenses (not detailed)	_____
Pretax income	_____
Income tax expense	_____
Net income	$_____
EPS	$_____

(Relates to Exercise 5–1)

Balance Sheet

Assets		Liabilities	
Cash	$_____	Accounts payable	$_____
Accounts receivable	_____	Wages payable	_____
Prepaid insurance	_____	Income tax payable	_____
Machinery	_____		
Accumulated		*Owners' Equity*	
depreciation	_____	Capital stock	_____
		Retained earnings	_____
Total	$_____	Total	$_____

Know *(handwritten)*

E5–2. Assume that the worksheet at December 31, 19B, for Toby Realty Corporation has been completed through "Adjusted Trial Balance" and you are ready to extend each amount to the several columns to the right. These columns that will be used are listed below with code letters:

Write out to remember (handwritten)

Code	Columns
a	Income Statement, debit
b	Income Statement, credit
c	Retained Earnings, debit
d	Retained Earnings, credit
e	Balance Sheet, debit
f	Balance Sheet, credit

Below are listed representative accounts to be extended on the worksheet. You are to give, for each account, the code letter that indicates the proper worksheet column to the right of "Adjusted Trial Balance" to which the amount in each account should be extended. Assume normal balances.

Account titles	Code
1. Cash	
2. Inventory of office supplies	
3. Interest payable	
4. Capital stock	
5. Commissions earned	
6. Rent revenue collected in advance	
7. Salary expense	
8. Return sales	
9. Retained earnings, beginning balance (a credit)	
10. Building	
11. Mortgage payable	
12. Income tax payable	
13. Sales commissions receivable	
14. Accumulated depreciation on building	
15. Contributed capital in excess of par	
16. Dividends paid	
17. Income tax expense	
18. Prepaid insurance	

19. Net income amount (indicate both the debit and credit)
20. Net loss amount (indicate both the debit and credit)
21. Retained earnings, ending balance amount (indicate both the debit and credit)

E5–3. Stone Company is completing the annual accounting information processing cycle at December 31, 19B. The worksheet, as shown below, has been started (to simplify, amounts given are in thousands of dollars).

Account numbers and titles	Unadjusted trial balance Debit	Credit
101 Cash	$ 20	$
102 Accounts receivable	38	
103 Inventory	22	
104 Prepaid insurance	3	
110 Equipment (10-year life, no residual value)	70	
111 Accumulated deprecia- tion, equipment		7
119 Accounts payable		11
120 Wages payable		
121 Income tax payable		
122 Revenue collected in advance		
123 Note payable, long term (10% each Dec. 31)		20
130 Capital stock, par $10 ...		60
131 Contributed capital in excess of par		10
140 Retained earnings		15
141 Dividends paid	8	
145 Revenues		99
146 Expenses	61	
147 Income tax expense		
	$222	$222

Data not yet recorded for 19B:

a. Insurance expense, $1.
b. Depreciation expense.
c. Wages earned by employees yet not paid, $2.
d. Revenue collected by Stone yet not earned, $3.
e. Income tax rate, 20 percent.
(Note: No accrued interest is recorded because interest is paid on each December 31.)

Required:

Complete the worksheet in every respect (you may use account numbers instead of account titles). Set up appropriate column headings for Adjusting Entries, Adjusted Trial Balance, Income Statement, Retained Earnings, and Balance Sheet. Enter all revenues and expenses (except income tax) in the two accounts given (145 and 146).

E5–4. Brown Corporation, a small company, is completing the annual accounting information processing cycle at December 31, 19B. The worksheet, as reflected below, has been started.

Account Titles	Unadjusted Trial Balance	
	Debit	Credit
Cash	17,000	
Accounts receivable	15,000	
Equipment	20,000	
Accumulated depreciation		6,000
Other assets	54,500	
Accounts payable		9,000
Long-term note payable		15,000
Capital stock, par, $10		30,000
Contributed capital in excess of par		1,500
Retained earnings		18,000
Dividends paid	3,000	
Revenues		80,000
Expenses	50,000	
	159,500	159,500
Income tax expense		
Net income		

Data not yet recorded for 19B:
a. Depreciation expense, $2,000.
b. Income tax rate, 20 percent.

Required:

Complete the worksheet in all respects. Set up appropriate column headings for Adjusting Entries, Adjusted Trial Balance, Income Statement, Retained Earnings, and Balance Sheet.

E5–5. All-Purpose Service Company is in the process of completing the information processing cycle at the end of the fiscal year, December 31, 19B. The worksheet and financial statements have been prepared, and the next step is journalization of the adjusting entries. The two trial balances given below were taken directly from the completed worksheet.

(Relates to Exercise 5–5)

| Account Titles | December 31, 19B | | | |
| | Unadjusted Trial Balance | | Adjusted Trial Balance | |
	Debit	Credit	Debit	Credit
a. Cash	$ 8,000		$ 8,000	
b. Accounts receivable			700	
c. Prepaid insurance	300		250	
d. Equipment	120,200		120,200	
e. Accumulated depreciation, equipment		$ 21,500		$ 25,500
f. Income tax payable				4,000
g. Capital stock, par $10		50,000		50,000
h. Retained earnings, January 1, 19B		14,000		14,000
i. Service revenues		60,000		60,700
j. Salary expense	17,000		17,000	
k. Depreciation expense			4,000	
l. Insurance expense			50	
m. Income tax expense			4,000	
	$145,500	$145,500	$154,200	$154,200

Required:

By examining the amounts in each trial balance, reconstruct the four adjusting entries that were made between the unadjusted trial balance and the adjusted trial balance. Give a brief explanation of the reason for which each adjusting entry was made.

E5–6. The accountant for Z Corporation has just completed the following worksheet for the year ended December 31, 19D (note the shortcuts used by the accountant to reduce the size of the worksheet):

202

(Relates to Exercise 5—6)

Account Titles	Unadjusted Trial Balance (credits)	Adjusting Entries		Income Statement (credits)	Balance Sheet (credits)
		Debit	Credit		
Cash	15,000				15,000
Prepaid insurance	300		100		200
Accounts receivable	20,000				20,000
Machinery	80,000				80,000
Accumulated depreciation	(24,000)		8,000		(32,000)
Other assets	13,700				13,700
Accounts payable	(7,000)				(7,000)
Rent collected in advance			200		(200)
Interest payable			450		(450)
Income tax payable			3,375		(3,375)
Notes payable, long term	(10,000)				(10,000)
Capital stock, par $10	(50,000)				(50,000)
Retained earnings	(18,000)				(18,000)
Revenues	(80,000)	200		(79,800)	
Expenses (not detailed)	60,000	100		60,100	
Depreciation expense		8,000		8,000	
Interest expense		450		450	
Income tax expense		3,375		3,375	
Net income				7,875	(7,875)
Totals	-0-	12,125	12,125	-0-	-0-

Required:

a. Prepare the adjusting entries in journal form for December 31, 19D. Write a brief explanation with each entry.

b. Prepare the closing entries for December 31, 19D.

E5—7. (Based on the Appendix) B Company has completed the accounting information processing cycle for the year ended December 31, 19A. Reversing entries are under consideration now (for January 1, 19B) for two different accounts. For case purposes, the relevant data are given in T-accounts, viz:

(Relates to Exercise 5—7)

Prepaid Insurance

| 1/1/19A Balance | 600 | (a) 12/31/19A Adj. entry | 400 |

Insurance Expense

| (a) 12/31/19A Adj. entry | 400 | (c) 12/31/19A Closing entry | 400 |

Accrued Wages Payable

	(b) 12/31/19A Adj. entry 1,000

Wage Expense

Paid during 19A	18,000	(d) 12/31/19A Closing	
(b) 12/31/19A Adj. entry	1,000	entry	19,000

Income Summary

12/31/19A Closing entries		12/31/19A	
(c)	400	Closed to Retained	
(d)	19,000	Earnings	19,400

Required:

Would a reversing entry on January 1, 19B, facilitate the next related entry for (a) Prepaid Insurance and (b) Accrued Wages Payable? Explain why.

PROBLEMS

P5–1. General Services Company, Inc., a small service company, maintains its records without the help of an accountant. Using considerable effort, an outside accountant prepared the following trial balance as of the end of the annual accounting period, December 31, 19C:

(Relates to Problem 5–1)

Account Titles	Debit	Credit
Cash	$ 24,900	
Accounts receivable	33,000	
Service supplies inventory	500	
Prepaid insurance	600	
Service trucks (5-year life, no residual value)	20,000	
Accumulated depreciation, service trucks		$ 8,000
Other assets	10,000	
Accounts payable		1,000
Wages payable		
Income tax payable		
Note payable (3 years, 10% each December 31)		10,000
Capital stock, par $10		30,000
Contributed capital in excess of par		3,000
Retained earnings		8,000
Dividends paid	1,000	
Service revenues		70,000
Expenses (not detailed)*	40,000	
Income tax expense		
	$130,000	$130,000

* Excludes income tax expense.

Data not yet recorded at December 31, 19C:

1. The supplies inventory count on December 31, 19C, reflected $200.
2. Insurance expired during 19C, $200.
3. Depreciation expense for 19C.
4. Wages earned by employees yet not paid on December 31, 19C, $500.
5. Income tax rate, 20 percent.

Required:

Note: A worksheet may be used but is not required.

a. You have been asked to complete the statements given below (show computations) for 19C.
b. Give the 19C adjusting entries.
c. Give the 19C closing entries.

P5–2. Darby, Inc., was organized on January 1, 19A. At the end of the first year of operations, December 31, 19A, the bookkeeper prepared the following two trial balances (amounts in thousands of dollars):

(Relates to Problem 5–1)

Income Statement

Service revenues		$ _____
Expenses (not detailed)	$ _____	
Supplies expense	_____	
Insurance expense	_____	
Depreciation expense .	_____	
Wage expense	_____	
Total expenses .		_____
Pretax income		_____
Income tax expense . . .		_____
Net income		$ _____
EPS		$ _____

Balance Sheet

Assets			*Liabilities*		
Cash	$ _____		Accounts payable	$ _____	
Accounts receivable	_____		Wages payable	_____	
Service supplies inventory	_____		Income tax payable	_____	
Prepaid insurance	_____		Note payable, long term	_____	
Service trucks	_____		Total liabilities	_____	
Accumulated depreciation, trucks	_____		*Stockholders' Equity*		
Other assets	_____		Capital stock, par $10	_____	
			Contributed capital in		
			excess of par	_____	
			Retained earnings	_____	
			Total stockholders' equity	_____	
			Total liabilities plus		
Total assets	$ _____		stockholders' equity	$ _____	

(Relates to Problem 5–2)

Account Titles	Unadjusted trial balance		Adjusted trial balance	
	Debit	Credit	Debit	Credit
Cash..................................	$ 30	$	$ 30	$
Accounts receivable......................	25		25	
Prepaid insurance	3		2	
Rent receivable.........................			1	
Operational assets	48		48	
Accumulated depreciation, operational assets				6
Other assets	4		4	
Accounts payable		11		11
Wages payable				2
Income tax payable				2
Rent revenue collected in advance				3
Note payable, 10% (dated January 1, 19A) .		30		30
Capital stock, par $10 per share		50		50
Retained earnings				
Dividends paid..........................	2		2	
Revenues (total)........................		92		90
Expenses (total)	71		80	
Income tax expense			2	
Totals	$183	$183	$194	$194

Required:

Note: A worksheet may be completed, but is not required.)

a. Based upon inspection of the two trial balances give the 19A adjusting entries developed by the bookkeeper (provide brief explanations).

b. Based upon the above data give the 19A closing entries with brief explanations.

c. Respond to the following questions (show computations):

1. How many shares of stock were outstanding at year-end?

2. What was the estimated useful life of the operational assets assuming no residual value?

3. What was the amount of interest expense included in the total expenses?

4. What was the balance of Retained Earnings on December 31, 19A?

5. What was the average income tax rate?

6. How would the two accounts (a) Rent Receivable and (b) Rent Revenue Collected in Advance be reported on the balance sheet?

7. In general, explain why cash increased by $30,000 during the year despite the fact that net income was very low comparatively.

8. What was the amount of EPS for 19A?

9. What was the selling price of the shares?

10. When was the insurance premium paid and over what period of time did the coverage extend?

P5–3. Rattle Corporation has partially completed the following worksheet for the year ended December 31, 19E:

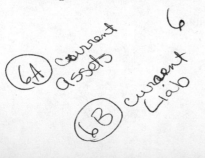

(Relates to Problem 5–3)

Account Titles	Unadjusted Trial Balance		Adjusting Entries	
	Debit	Credit	Debit	Credit
Cash	18,770			
Accounts receivable	25,680			
Supplies inventory	180			(a) 110
Interest receivable			(b) 300	
Long-term note receivable, 10%	6,000			
Equipment	75,000			
Accumulated depreciation		30,000		(c) 7,500
Accounts payable		11,000		
Short-term notes payable, 12%		8,000		
Interest payable				(d) 320
Income tax payable				(e) 4,000
Capital stock, par $10		40,000		
Contributed capital in excess of par		2,000		
Retained earnings		7,000		
Service revenue		67,680		
Interest revenue				(b) 300
Expenses (not detailed)	40,050		(a) 110	
Depreciation expense			(c) 7,500	
Interest expense			(d) 320	
Income tax expense			(e) 4,000	
Totals	165,680	165,680	12,230	12,230

Required:

a. Add appropriate columns for Unadjusted Trial Balance, Income Statement, Retained Earnings, and Balance Sheet and complete the worksheet.

b. Give the 19E adjusting and closing entries.

c. Explain why the adjusting and closing entries must be journalized and posted.

P5–4. Most Corporation is completing the accounting information processing cycle for the year ended December 31, 19C. The unadjusted trial balance, taken from the ledger, was as follows:

(Relates to Problem 5–4)

Account No.	Account titles	Unadjusted Trial Balance	
		Debit	Credit
101	Cash	$ 43,550	
103	Accounts receivable (net)	17,000	
105	Prepaid insurance	450	
107	Interest receivable		
120	Long-term note receivable, 12% ...	6,000	
150	Equipment	90,000	
151	Accumulated depreciation		$ 20,000
170	Other assets	30,000	
201	Accounts payable		14,000
203	Wages payable		
205	Interest payable		
210	Long-term note payable, 15%		10,000
300	Capital stock, par $10		80,000
301	Contributed capital in excess of par		12,000
310	Retained earnings		24,000
311	Dividends paid during 19C	8,000	
320	Service revenue		150,000
322	Interest revenue		
350	Expenses (not detailed)*	115,000	
351	Depreciation expense		
360	Interest expense		
370	Income tax expense		
207	Income tax payable		
		$310,000	$310,000

* Includes wage and insurance expense.

Additional data for adjusting entries:

a. Expired insurance during 19C was $150.

b. Interest on the long-term note receivable (dated September 1, 19C) is collected annually each August 30.

c. The equipment was acquired on January 1, 19A (assume no estimated residual value).

d. At December 31, 19C, wages earned yet not paid or recorded amounted to $3,000.

e. Interest on the long-term note payable (dated May 1, 19C) is paid annually each April 30.

f. Assume a 20 percent average income tax rate.

Required:

a. Complete a worksheet for the year ended December 31, 19C. Key the adjusting entries with letters. (Hint: Net income is $16,872.)

b. Prepare a single-step income statement, a statement of retained earnings, and an unclassified balance sheet.

c. Write a brief explanation of each adjusting entry reflected on the worksheet.

d. Give the closing entries in journal form. Explain why they must be journalized and posted to the ledger.

P5–5. Quick Service Company was organized as a corporation three years ago by three individuals. During the first two years, practically no records were kept. In June 1981, it employed a college student on a part-time basis who was majoring in accounting "to get an accounting system going." With the advice of an accounting professor, the student has been able to establish a simple and efficient system that will provide monthly financial statements for internal purposes and financial statements for the stockholders at the end of each year. The

(Relates to Problem 5–5)

Debits		Credits	
Cash	$ 28,700	Accumulated deprecia-	
Accounts receivable	6,000	tion	$ 4,500
Supplies inventory	1,200	Accounts payable	1,900
Prepaid insurance	800	Income tax payable	
Land (future building site)	20,000	Service revenue collected in advance	100
Equipment	25,000	Interest payable	400
Salary expense	30,000	Note payable, long term	10,000
Rent expense	4,800	Capital stock, par $10	30,000
Insurance expense	500	Retained earnings	1,800
Advertising expense	1,000	Service revenue	73,000
Utilities expense	900		
Depreciation expense	1,500		
Interest expense	1,200		
Income tax expense			
Miscellaneous expenses	100		
	$121,700		$121,700

shortened list of accounts (and simplified amounts) used in this case are representative of operations of 1981. The first set of financial statements will be prepared for the year ended December 31, 1981. The student has worked diligently to gather the raw data for the year and to record it in the newly designed information processing system.

This case starts with the worksheet, which has been completed through the columns headed "Adjusted Trial Balance, December 31, 1981." However, income tax has not been recorded; assume a 30 percent average tax rate. You are to start there and complete the requirements listed below. The Adjusted Trial Balance columns on the worksheet are shown above.

Required:

a. Set up a worksheet starting with the Adjusted Trial Balance columns given above and complete the worksheet in every respect (you may omit the Retained Earnings columns).

b. Prepare an unclassified income statement, statement of retained earnings, and balance sheet based upon the worksheet.

c. Based upon the worksheet, prepare the closing entries in journal form. Date and provide a brief explanation for each entry.

P5–6. (Note: This is an extended case selected to review Chapters 2, 3, 4, and 5.) W&P Moving and Storage Service, Incorporated, has been in operation for several years. Revenues have increased gradually from both the moving and storage services. The *annual* financial statements prepared in the past have not conformed to GAAP. The newly employed president decided that starting at the end of 1981, correct and complete balance sheet and income and cash-flow statements would be prepared. The first step was to employ a full-time bookkeeper and engage a local CPA firm for assistance. It is now December 31, 1981, the end of the current fiscal year. The bookkeeper has developed a trial balance. A member of the staff of the CPA firm will advise and assist the bookkeeper in completing the accounting information processing cycle for the first time. The unadjusted trial balance at December 31, 1981, is shown on the next page.

(Relates to Problem 5–6)

Debits		Credits	
Cash	$ 25,880	Accumulated depreciation	$ 18,000
Accounts receivable	2,030	Accounts payable	6,000
Office supplies inventory	150	Wages payable	
Prepaid insurance	600	Interest payable	
Land for future building site	6,000	Revenue collected in advance	
Equipment	68,000	Income tax payable	
Other assets (not detailed)	27,000	Note payable (12%)	30,000
Salary expense	74,000	Capital stock, par $10	20,000
Advertising expense	1,000	Retained earnings, Janu-	
Utilities expense	1,270	ary 1, 1981	21,600
Maintenance expense	6,500	Hauling revenue	106,400
Miscellaneous expenses	570	Storage revenue	14,000
Insurance expense			
Wage expense			
Depreciation expense			
Interest expense			
Income tax expense			
Dividends paid	3,000		
	$216,000		$216,000

Examination of the records and related documents provided the following additional information that should be considered for adjusting entries:

a. A physical count of office supplies inventory at December 31, 1981, reflected $40 on hand. Office supplies used are considered to be a miscellaneous expense. No office supplies were purchased during the year.

b. On July 1, 1981, a two-year insurance premium was paid amounting to $600.

c. The equipment cost $68,000 when acquired. It is estimated to have a ten-year useful life to the company and an $8,000 residual value.

d. Unpaid and unrecorded wages at December 31, 1981, amounted to $1,200.

e. The $30,000 note payable was signed on October 1, 1981, for a 12 percent bank loan, principal and interest due at the end of 12 months from that date.

f. Storage revenue collected and recorded as earned before December 31, 1981, included $400 collected in advance from one customer for storage time in 1982. (Hint: Reduce storage revenue.)

g. Gasoline, oil, and fuel purchased for the vehicles and used during the last two weeks of December 1981 amounting to

$300 have not been paid for nor recorded (this is considered maintenance expense).

h. The average income tax rate is 20 percent which produces income tax expense of $5,600.

Required:

a. Enter the unadjusted trial balance on a worksheet; then, based on the above data, enter the adjusting entries. Complete the worksheet. (Hint: The adjusted trial balance total is $230,000.)

b. Using the worksheet, prepare a single-step income statement, statement of retained earnings, and balance sheet. (Hint: The balance sheet total is $105,400.)

c. Using the worksheet, enter the 1981 adjusting entries in the journal.

d. Using the worksheet, prepare 1981 closing entries in journal form.

P5–7. (Note: This is an extended case selected to review Chapters 2, 3, 4, and 5.) Charter Air Service, Incorporated, was organized to operate a charter service in a city of approximately 350,000 population. The ten organizers were issued 7,500 shares of $10 par-value stock for a total of $75,000 cash. To obtain facilities to operate the Charter service, the company rents from the city hangar and office space at the city airport for a flat monthly rental. The business has prospered because of the excellent service and the high level of maintenance on the planes. It is now December 31, 1981, end of the annual fiscal period, and the accounting information processing cycle is in the final phases. Following are representative accounts and unadjusted amounts selected from the ledger at December 31, 1981, for case purposes:

and office space was paid during the year and recorded as Rent Expense. This included rent paid in advance amounting to $2,000 for January and February 1982. The total amount was recorded as Rent Expense in 1981.

f. The inventory of maintenance parts at December 31, 1981, showed $7,000. All parts purchased are debited to Maintenance Parts Inventory when purchased.

g. For case purposes, assume an average income tax rate of 20 percent which results in income tax expense of $6,000.

(Relates to Problem 5–7)

Debits		Credits	
Cash	$ 24,600	Accumulated depreciation, aircraft	$ 60,000
Prepaid insurance	6,000	Notes payable, 12%	100,000
Maintenance parts inventory	18,000	Capital stock, par $10	75,000
Aircraft	260,000	Retained earnings, January 1, 1981	20,600
Salary expense	90,000	Charter revenue	262,400
Maintenance expense	24,000		
Fuel expense	63,000		
Advertising expense	2,000		
Utilities expense	1,400		
Rent expense	14,000		
Dividends paid	15,000		
	$518,000		$518,000

For the adjusting entries, the following additional data were developed from the records and supporting documents:

a. On January 1, 1981, the company paid a three-year insurance premium amounting to $6,000.

b. The aircraft, when purchased on January 1, 1978, cost $260,000; and the estimated useful life to the company is approximately ten years. The equipment has an estimated residual value of $60,000.

c. On July 1, 1981, the company borrowed $100,000 from the bank on a five-year, 12 percent loan. Interest is payable annually starting on June 30, 1982.

d. Charter revenue, on occasion, is collected in advance. On December 31, 1981, collections in advance amounted to $1,000; when collected this amount was recorded as Charter Revenue.

e. Rent amounting to $14,000 on hangar

Required:

a. Enter the above accounts and unadjusted balances from the ledger on a worksheet. (The following accounts should be added at the bottom of the worksheet because they will be needed for the adjusting entries: Insurance Expense, Depreciation Expense, Interest Expense, Interest Payable, Revenue Collected in Advance, Prepaid Rent Expense, Income Tax Expense, and Income Tax Payable.)

b. Based on the additional data given above, enter the 1981 adjusting entries on the worksheet.

c. Complete the worksheet. (Hint: The adjusted trial balance total is $550,000.)

d. Based on the worksheet, prepare a single-step income statement, a statement of retained earnings, and a classified balance sheet. (Hint: The total on the balance sheet is $217,600.)

e. Journalize the 1981 adjusting entries.

f. Journalize the 1981 closing entries.

P5–8. (Based on the Appendix)   Alvin Corporation has completed all information processing including the annual financial statements at December 31, 19D. The adjusting entries recorded at that date were as follows:

a. Insurance expense   150
      Prepaid insurance   150

b. Interest receivable   200
      Interest revenue   200

c. Supplies expense   80
      Supplies inventory . . .   80

d. Depreciation expense   2,000
      Accumulated depreci-
          ation   2,000

e. Wage expense   500
      Wages payable   500

f. Interest expense   300
      Interest payable   300

g. Income tax expense   4,000
      Income tax payable . . .   4,000

Required:

For each of the above adjusting entries indicate whether it usually would be reversed. Give the reversing entry in each instance (if none, so state) and explain the basis for your response.

P5–9. (Based on the Appendix)   BV Corporation was organized in January 19A. The annual accounting period ends December 31. The following transactions occurred during 19C:

1. January 1, 19C—BV Corporation purchased a special machine at a cash cost of $24,000. The estimated useful life is three years and no residual value.
2. September 1, 19C—BV Corporation paid a $480 two-year insurance premium on equipment used in operations.
3. October 1, 19C—BV Corporation borrowed $10,000 on a two-year, 12 percent, interest-bearing note dated October 1, 19C. Interest is payable on September 30, 19D, and 19E; the principal is payable on September 30, 19E.

Required:

Give entries, in journal form, on the following dates:

a. January 1, 19C, September 1, 19C, and October 1, 19C—to record each of the three transactions; provide an explanation of each entry.

b. December 31, 19C—to record the required 19C adjusting entry for each item at the end of the accounting period; include an explanation of each adjusting entry. If no adjusting entry is required, so state and explain why.

c. January 1, 19D—to record an appropriate reversing entry for each item. If no reversing entry is appropriate, so state. Explain the basis for your treatment of each item.

d. September 30, 19D—to record payment of the annual interest on the $10,000 note; include an explanation.

e. December 31, 19D—to record the required 19D adjusting entry for each item; include an explanation.

6

Accounting for sales revenue and cost of goods sold

PURPOSE OF THE CHAPTER

The dominant features of many business entities are the purchasing and selling functions, whether the business is a retail, wholesale, or manufacturing entity. Decision makers who use financial reports focus considerable attention on the marketing successes and failures of a business. Retail and wholesale merchandising businesses devote much of their energies to buying and selling goods. Practically all manufacturing businesses also devote significant efforts and resources to purchasing and selling activities. Generally, a manufacturing business purchases raw materials for conversion into finished products, which then are sold. It is not uncommon for a service business also to sell some merchandise. For example, a retail appliance store frequently includes a combined sales-and-service-type operation.

Although the discussions and illustrations in the preceding chapters relating to the measurement of assets, liabilities, income, and cash flows are as appropriate for merchandising and manufacturing companies as for service businesses, for instructional reasons they usually were limited to **service** businesses. Recall that Business Aids, Incorporated, was a service business (Exhibit 1–3, page 19). However, Diamond's, Incorporated (Exhibit 2–1, page 45), and J. C. Penney Company, Inc. (Exhibit 2–5, pages 58–63) were **retail** merchandising businesses.

Two distinguishing features on the **income statement** of retail, wholesale, and manufacturing businesses (as opposed to service businesses) are (1) sales revenue and (2) a **special expense,** which usually is called **cost** of goods sold.[1] For example, Diamond's income statement (Exhibit 2–1) reported cost of goods sold of $2,416,000 (which was 67 percent of net sales revenue), and J. C. Penney's income statement (Exhibit 2–5) reported cost of products sold of $371,506,000 (which was 66 percent of net sales revenue).

The income statement of retail, wholesale, and manufacturing businesses can be outlined for our purposes in this chapter as follows:

		Illustrative amounts	
A.	*Revenue:*		
	1. Sales revenue	$10,000,000	100%
B.	*Expenses:*		
	2. Cost of goods sold	6,500,000	65
	3. Gross margin on sales	3,500,000	35
	4. Operating expenses (detailed)	3,000,000	30
C.	*Income:*		
	5. Pretax income........................	500,000	5
	6. Income tax expense (assumed 40% rate) ..	−200,000	2
	7. Net income	$ 300,000	3%
	8. EPS ($300,000 ÷ 100,000 shares)	$3.00	

This chapter will discuss and illustrate the **two directly related** measuring, recording, and reporting problems of retail, wholesale, and manufacturing businesses as follows:

Part A: Accounting for sales revenue (which includes credit sales and bad debts)

Part B: Accounting for cost of goods sold (which includes inventories)

This chapter includes the following Appendixes:

Appendix A: Data processing—controlling accounts and subsidiary ledgers

Appendix B: Aging accounts receivable

Aside from these two directly related problems, this chapter will not consider manufacturing activities. That topic is discussed in the other volume of this series, *Fundamentals of Management Accounting.*

Behavioral and learning objectives for this chapter are provided in the *Teachers Manual.*

PART A: ACCOUNTING FOR SALES REVENUE

Accounting for sales revenue requires careful measurement of the economic effects of each sale of goods in accordance with the revenue principle.

---

[1] Similar titles sometimes used are cost of sales and cost of products sold. Regardless of title, it is accounted for as an expense.

Sales may be for cash or on credit and also may involve the trade in of noncash assets. Determination of the net sales price and the appropriate period in which sales revenue should be recognized sometimes pose special problems. The **revenue principle** holds that sales revenue is *(a)* measured as the **market value** of the considerations received, or the market value of the item sold, whichever is the more clearly determinable, and *(b)* recognized in the accounting period when ownership of the goods passes from the seller to the buyer (see Exhibit 2–6, pages 64, 65, and 66). Problems in implementing this principle will be discussed and illustrated in this part of the chapter.

For illustrative purposes the income statement given in Exhibit 6–1 will be used to emphasize the selling and purchasing activities of a small business.[2]

EXHIBIT 6–1

CAMPUS CORNER
Income Statement (multiple-step format)
For the Year Ended December 31, 1981

	Amount	Percentage analysis
Gross sales	$108,333	
Less: Sales returns and allowances	8,333	
Net sales	100,000	100
Cost of goods sold	60,000	60
Gross margin on sales	40,000	40
Operating expenses:		
Selling expenses (detailed) ... $15,000		
Administrative expenses (detailed) ... 10,000	25,000	25
Pretax income	15,000	15
Income tax expense	3,000	3
Net income	$ 12,000	12
EPS ($12,000 ÷ 10,000 shares)	$1.20	

In Exhibit 6–1 observe that the expense, cost of goods sold, is set out separately from the remaining expenses which makes it possible to report a step difference called **gross margin on sales.**[3] This difference between net sales revenue and cost of goods sold reflects the average maintained **markup** on all goods sold during the period. It is expressed in dollars on the income statement ($40,000) and often is reported as a percent (cost of goods sold, $40,000 ÷ net sales revenue, $100,000 = 0.40, or 40 percent).

---

[2] In this chapter, to simplify the illustrations, we ordinarily shall not show the detailed operating expenses. In the single-step format for the income statement, revenues would be reported as above under a major caption "Revenues." However, all expenses, including cost of goods sold, would be reported under a major caption "Expenses." Therefore, in the single-step format, gross margin on sales is not reported.

[3] This often is called gross profit on sales or simply gross margin or gross profit. In the *Accounting Terminology Bulletins* the AICPA recommended against use of the term *profit* in this context.

This relationship is called the gross margin ratio (or percent). For Campus Corner, it can be said that *(a)* for each $1 of net sales the average gross margin was $0.40, or *(b)* the average markup maintained on sales was 40 percent of sales.[4]

RECORDING SALES REVENUE

When ownership to goods passes from the seller to the buyer, the seller must record sales revenue. Under the revenue principle the sales price, net of any trade discounts and other offsets, is the measure of the amount of revenue realized. If the sale is for cash, the amount of cash received is the measure of revenue. If the sale is on credit, the revenue is the cash equivalent to be received **excluding** any financing charges (i.e., interest). If the sale is for noncash items (such as the sale of goods for other goods) the cash equivalent (i.e., market value) of the goods received or given up, whichever is the more clearly determinable, measures the amount of revenue to recognize. Thus, under the revenue principle, Campus Corner would recognize a sale in 1981 (i.e., when ownership passes) as follows:

a. Cash sales for the day per the cash register tapes:

Jan. 2	Cash	2,000
	Sales revenue	2,000

b. Credit sales for the day per all charge tickets:

Jan. 2	Accounts receivable	1,000
	Sales revenue	1,000

Alternatively, if it is desired to maintain a **separate sales revenue** account in the ledger for the sales of each department, the two entries could be as follows:[5]

Jan. 2	Cash	2,000	
	Accounts receivable	1,000	
	Sales, Department 1		1,000
	Sales, Department 2		1,500
	Sales, Department 3		500

---

[4] This percent is based on sales revenue rather than cost. The markup percent on *cost* would be $40,000 \div $60,000 = 66\frac{2}{3}$ percent.

[5] See Appendix A to this chapter for an applicable data processing procedure.

Credit sales. A substantial portion of the sales made by some businesses are on credit. When merchandise is sold on credit, the terms of payment should be definite so there will be no misunderstanding as to the amounts and due dates. In fact, credit terms usually are printed on each credit document. Frequently, credit terms are abbreviated by symbols such as, "n/10, EOM," which means the net amount (i.e., the sales amount less any sales returns and no discount) is due not later than ten days after the end of the month (EOM) in which the sale was made. In other cases the terms may be "n/30," which means that the net amount is due 30 days after the date of the invoice (i.e., after date of sale). In still other cases, **sales discounts** (often called cash discounts) are granted to the purchaser for early payment. For example, the credit terms may be "2/10, n/30," which means that if payment is made within 10 days from the date of sale, the customer (debtor) may deduct 2 percent from the invoice price; however, if not paid within the 10-day discount period, the full sales price (less any returns) is due in 30 days from date of sale.

When a cash discount is granted, a customer is motivated to pay within the discount period because by doing so the savings are substantial. For example, with terms 2/10, n/30, 2 percent is saved by paying 20 days early, which equates to approximately 37 percent annual interest. As a consequence, the **usual case** is that credit customers take advantage of the sales discount. A favorable economic effect may result even when cash must be borrowed so that the cash discount can be taken.

To account for sales discounts, the usual case should govern the accounting procedure. The revenue principle holds that sales revenue is measured by the cash or cash equivalent received (or to be received) for the sales of goods. Since the sales discount almost always will be taken, to measure revenue properly the Sales Revenue account should be credited (i.e., increased) for the cash that probably will be received rather than for the gross sales amount. To illustrate, assume a sale by Campus Corner was made for $1,000 with terms 2/10, n/30. The sequence of entries would be as follows:[6]

a. January 18, date of sale on credit:

---

[6] In this type of situation some persons prefer to record sales revenue at date of sale at the gross amount of $1,000. If payment is *within* the discount period, a debit of $20 to a "Sales Discount Revenue" account would be recorded at date of collection. The total sales discount amount is deducted from sales revenue on the current income statement. This procedure clearly is conceptually deficient since it often overstates both sales revenue and accounts receivable and fails to recognize interest earned on amounts not collected within the discount period. Its continued use can be traced to precedent which was not soundly based and is defended on the assumption that the annual amounts are not material in most cases. Such an assumption appears unrealistic for companies that extend relatively large amounts of credit on which discounts are given. Also, because most collections are made within the discount period (for pure economic reasons), it incorrectly treats the unusual case in the simple way and complicates recording sales returns. Thus, it fails on both conceptual and practical grounds.

Accounts receivable 980
    Sales revenue... 980
  Terms: 2/10, n/30 ($1,000 × 0.98 = $980).

b. January 27, date of collection **within** the discount period (the usual case):

Cash 980
    Accounts receivable 980

Alternatively, assuming the collection is after the discount period, entry b would be:

January 31, date of collection **after** the discount period (the unusual case):

Cash 1,000
    Sales discount revenue* 20
    Accounts receivable 980
   * Interest revenue sometimes is used because conceptually it is in the nature of interest revenue earned.

Cash discounts should be distinguished from **trade discounts**. A cash discount is a price concession given to encourage early payment of an account. A trade discount is a device sometimes used by vendors for quoting sales prices; the amount *after* the trade discount is the sales price. For example, an item may be quoted at $10 per unit subject to a 20 percent trade discount on orders of 100 units or more; thus, the price for the large order would be $8 per unit.

In recent years there has been a trend toward more credit sales, particularly at the retail level. However, the use of cash discounts appears to be declining. In some jurisdictions, they are not legal in certain situations because the effect is to charge the cash customers more than the credit customers who pay within the discount period. The discount **not taken** by credit customers is a hidden financing charge.

The extension of credit usually entails a significant increase in the amount of recordkeeping required. Unless the business has its credit sales handled by a credit card company, which charges a fee for this service, detailed records must be maintained for each credit customer. The fee paid to the credit card company is recorded as a collection expense (and not a sales discount; see footnote 6). Appendix A discusses some aspects of the detailed records maintained for credit customers.

Measuring bad debt losses. When goods and services are sold on credit, despite careful credit investigation, there will be a few customers who do not pay their obligations. When an account receivable proves uncollectible, the business incurs a **bad debt loss.** Businesses that extend substantial amounts of credit do so with the expectation that there will be a certain **average rate** of bad debt losses on credit sales. As a matter of fact, an unusually low rate of losses due to uncollectible accounts may give evidence of too tight a credit policy. If the credit policy is too restrictive, many credit customers who would pay their bills may be turned away. In the measurement of net income for the period, the bad debt expense (losses) of that period must be measured.

To account for bad debt losses, the **matching principle** requires that the bad debt expense be matched with the period's sale revenues that gave rise to those losses. This requirement is difficult to implement because a bad debt loss may not materialize until one or more years after the particular sale was made.

To satisfy the matching principle in credit situations, the **bad debt allowance method** was developed to measure bad debt expense. It recognizes that bad debt losses really are incurred in the year in which the sales that generated those losses were made. Since there is no way of telling in advance which individual accounts ultimately will prove worthless, the method is based upon the concept of **estimating** in each accounting period what the probable amount of bad debt losses due to uncollectible accounts will be during the collection period. The estimate is made on an aggregate basis (i.e., based on total credit sales for the period) because the individual accounts that will be bad will not be known in the period of sale. The question is: What percent of the aggregate credit sales for the period probably will become bad debts?

Estimating the probable amount of losses due to uncollectible accounts generally is neither complex nor fraught with major uncertainties. For a company that has been operating for some years, experience provides a sound basis for projecting probable future bad debt losses related to credit sales. For example, an analysis of accounting data on aggregate **credit** sales and aggregate uncollectible accounts for the past five years by Campus Corner indicated an average bad debt loss of 1.2 percent of aggregate credit sales, viz:

Year	Bad debt losses	Credit sales
1976	$ 640	$ 54,000
1977	680	57,000
1978	620	53,000
1979	800	66,000
1980	860	70,000
	$3,600	$300,000

Aggregate: $3,600 ÷ $300,000 = 1.2 percent average loss rate for the five-year period 1976–80.

The 1.2 percent bad debt loss rate could be used by Campus Corner for 1981, or alternatively, assuming more care will be exercised in credit granting and more efficient collection efforts, the rate may be estimated at 1 percent.

Now, let's see how the allowance method would be applied to the above example. Assuming net **credit** sales in 1981 of $40,000, we would record bad debt expense of $40,000 × 1% = $400 **in 1981.** This would require the following *adjusting entry* at the end of the accounting period, December 31, 1981:

Bad debt expense 400
    Allowance for doubtful accounts (or bad debts)   400
    To adjust for the 1981 estimated bad debt loss based on credit sales and an average expected loss rate of 1 percent ($40,000 × 1% = $400).

Bad debt expense of $400 would be reported on the 1981 income statement as an expense and thus would be matched with the sales revenue of the year in which the credit was granted (1981 in this case). The Bad Debt Expense account is closed at the end of each accounting period along with the other expense accounts.

In the above entry, rather than crediting the Accounts Receivable account, the credit was made to a **contra account** descriptively titled "Allowance for Doubtful Accounts" because there is no way of knowing *which* account receivable is involved. Other acceptable titles are "Allowance for Bad Debts" and "Allowance for Uncollectible Accounts." The balance in Allowance for Doubtful Accounts is **always** considered as a contra amount to Accounts Receivable. Thus, the two accounts would be reported on the balance sheet, under current assets, as follows:

CAMPUS CORNER
Balance Sheet
At December 31, 1981

Current assets:
Cash $34,000
Accounts receivable $100,000
    Less: Allowance for doubtful accounts 2,400*   97,600

* This amount assumes a balance of $2,000 carried forward prior to the above entry.

Allowance for Doubtful Accounts carries a cumulative **credit** balance; and since it is a balance sheet account, it is not closed. It is sometimes described as a contra account, an asset reduction account, an offset account, or a negative asset account, but more frequently as a **valuation account.** These descriptions, particularly the last one, derive from the fact its cumulative credit balance is the total of the accounts receivable that are estimated to be uncollectible. Thus, the difference between the balances of Accounts Receivable and the allowance account measures the estimated net realizable value of accounts receivable. In the above example, the difference between the two accounts—$97,600—represents the **estimated net realizable value** of accounts receivable (also called the book value of accounts receivable).

In the above illustration the bad debt estimate was based on **credit sales.** Occasionally, a company bases the loss rate on total sales (i.e., cash plus credit sales), which is illogical because (1) it is impossible to have a bad debt loss on a cash sale (except in the case of a "hot" check which is uncollectible), and (2) a shift in the relative proportion between cash and credit sales would cause a combination rate to be meaningless. Since the total amount of credit sales for each period can be determined (because they are recorded in Accounts Receivable as debits), there is no reason for not using credit sales as the base. Another method of estimating bad debt losses is known as "aging accounts receivable"; this method is explained and illustrated in Appendix B to this chapter.

Writing off a bad debt. When a particular account receivable (say, $100 owed by J. Doe) ultimately is determined to be uncollectible (i.e., bad), the amount should be removed from the Accounts Receivable account with an offsetting debit to the allowance account. This entry does not record a bad debt loss (expense) because the estimated expense recorded in the adjusting entry of the period of sale (one or more years earlier) recognized the loss and the related allowance account was established to absorb the later write-off. To illustrate, assume Campus Corner sold J. Doe merchandise on credit in 1979 amounting to $100 (which was properly credited to 1979 Sales Revenue and debited to Accounts Receivable). At the end of 1981 Campus Corner decided that it would never collect the $100; accordingly, they made the following entry:

December 31, 1981:

Allowance for doubtful accounts	100	
Accounts receivable (J. Doe)		100
To write off a receivable from J. Doe determined to be uncollectible.		

Observe that the above entry did not affect the income statement since the expense already had been recorded (when the adjusting entry was made). Also, the entry did not change the net realizable value (i.e., the book value) of the accounts receivable. The **difference** between Accounts Receivable and the allowance account remains the same as before the entry, viz:

	Before write-off	After write-off
Accounts receivable	$100,000	$99,900
Less: Allowance for doubtful accounts	2,400	2,300
Difference—estimated net realizable value	$ 97,600	$97,600

Actual write-offs compared with estimates. The uncollectible accounts actually written off seldom will agree exactly in amount with the estimates previously recorded. If the accounts actually written off are less than the allowance provided, the Allowance for Doubtful Accounts will continue with a credit balance.[7]

If an account is written off as bad and the customer subsequently pays it, the write-off entry should be reversed and the collection should be recorded in the usual way.

Terminology. The caption "Accounts receivable" often appears on the balance sheet under current assets without additional descriptive terms; however, a more descriptive designation such as "Receivables from trade customers" is preferable. Receivables from other than the regular trade customers, such as loans to officers or employees, should not be included in the accounts receivable category. Rather, such nontrade receivables should be reported as separate items.

Sales returns and allowances. Many businesses permit customers to return unsatisfactory or damaged merchandise and receive a cash or credit refund. In some cases, rather than taking back such merchandise, a cash or credit adjustment may be given to the customer. To measure correctly sales revenue, such transactions must be recorded, whether or not the goods are returned. In effect, the sales entry must be reversed. Although the Sales account could be debited (i.e., reduced) in recording these reductions in sales, for management control purposes (that is, so that management will be informed of the volume of returns and allowances), a separate account entitled "Sales Returns and Allowances" often is used. If cash is refunded, the Cash account must be credited. Alternatively, if a credit adjustment is given, accounts receivable of the customer must be credited. The Sales Returns and Allowances account always is considered as a deduction from gross sales revenue as shown in Exhibit 6–1 because it is a contra revenue account. To illustrate, assume a customer, F. Fox, bought five units of Merchandise A from Campus Corner for $500, terms, 2/10, n/30. Fifteen days after the purchase, and after payment (within the discount period), Fox returned one unit that was damaged. The sequence of entries by Campus Corner would be:

Date of sale:

Accounts receivable (F. Fox)	490	
Sales revenue		490
To record sale; terms, 2/10, n/30 ($500 × 0.98 = $490), net.		

---

[7] On the other hand, if the amount written off is more than the allowance balance, there will be a temporary debit balance in the allowance account. This situation will be resolved when the next "allowance entry" is made. It indicates that the estimated loss rate used may be too low.

Date of sale return:[8]

Sales returns and allowances	98	
Cash*		98
To record sale return, 1 unit ($490 ÷ 5 units = $98).		
* If payment had not been made this credit would be to Accounts Receivable.		

PART B: ACCOUNTING FOR COST OF GOODS SOLD (WHICH INCLUDES INVENTORIES)

The income statement shown in Exhibit 6–1 (Campus Corner) reported an expense called cost of goods sold, which is unique to nonservice types of businesses. Cost of goods sold, as an expense, is a relatively simple concept. Sales revenue is the merchandise sold during the accounting period valued at **sales price**, whereas cost of goods sold is the same merchandise valued at **cost**. Thus, revenue and expense are matched on the income statement in conformity with the **matching principle** (see Exhibit 2–6, pages 64, 65, and 66). Cost of goods sold relates to all (and only to) merchandise sold during the period; therefore, it excludes all merchandise remaining on hand at the end of the accounting period (i.e., the ending merchandise inventory).

Typically, a business will start each accounting period with a stock of merchandise on hand for resale which is called the **beginning** (or initial) **inventory (BI)**. The merchandise on hand at the end of an accounting period is called the **ending** (or final) **inventory (EI)** for that period which, by definition, becomes the beginning inventory for the next period.

During the accounting period the beginning inventory usually is supplemented by the purchase or manufacture of additional merchandise. The sum of the beginning inventory and the purchases (P) during the period represents the **goods available for sale** during that period. If all of the goods available for sale were sold during the period, there would remain no ending inventory. Typically, all of the goods available for sale are not sold; therefore, a quantity of goods remains on hand which is the ending inventory for the period. From these facts we can state the cost of goods sold (CGS) model as follows:

$$BI + P - EI = CGS$$

To illustrate, Campus Corner reported cost of goods sold of $60,000 (Exhibit 6–1), which was determined as follows:

Beginning inventory (January 1, 1981)	$40,000
Add purchases of merchandise during 1981	55,000
Goods available for sale	95,000
Deduct ending inventory (December 31, 1981)	35,000
Cost of goods sold	$60,000

[8] If the receivable had been recorded at gross (see footnote 6), an illogical credit of $2 to Sales Discount Revenue would be necessary.

To compute cost of goods sold, three amounts must be known: (1) beginning inventory, (2) purchases of merchandise during the period, and (3) ending inventory. **The ending inventory of one accounting period is the beginning inventory of the succeeding period.** Therefore, the beginning inventory amount always will be available from the preceding period. The amount of purchases for the period will be accumulated in the accounting system. Determining the amount of the **ending inventory** presents a special problem.

There are two distinctly different systems that are used in measuring the ending inventory. They are:

1. **Periodic inventory system**—Under this system, no detailed record of inventory is maintained during the year. An **actual physical count** (i.e., an inventory count) of the goods remaining on hand is required at the **end of each period.** The number of units of each type of merchandise on hand then is multiplied by the purchase cost per unit to compute the dollar amount of the ending inventory. Thus, the balance of goods on hand (i.e., the ending inventory) is not known until the last day of the period when the inventory count is completed. Also, the amount of cost of goods sold cannot be determined until the inventory count is completed.

2. **Perpetual inventory system**—This system involves the maintenance of detailed inventory records in the accounting system. For each type of goods stocked, a detailed record is maintained that shows *(a)* units and cost of the beginning inventory, *(b)* units and cost of each purchase, *(c)* units and cost of the goods for each sale, and *(d)* the units and amount on hand at any point in time. This continuous record is maintained on a transaction-by-transaction basis throughout the period. **Thus, the inventory record provides both the amount of ending inventory and the cost of goods sold for the period.**

PERIODIC INVENTORY SYSTEM

For various reasons some companies use a periodic inventory system. One of the primary reasons is the nature of the business. For example, a variety store or a grocery store could experience considerable difficulty, and additional cost, in trying to keep track of the number of units and cost per unit of each purchase and sale of the number of low-priced items stocked (as would be necessary if a perpetual inventory system were used). For example, when such small items are sold for cash (as in a grocery store), usually no record is made at the cash register of the quantity and cost of each item (rather the total sales price is entered into the cash register). The two primary disadvantages of a periodic inventory system are *(a)* the necessity (and cost) to take a complete physical count of all merchandise on hand at the end of each period for which financial statements are to be prepared and *(b)* lack of inventory control (for purchasing purposes and measurement of theft). Nevertheless, many companies use the periodic system either for all items offered for sale or for only the small, low-cost items.[9]

A periodic inventory system applies the cost of goods sold model given on page 222 as follows:

Model:	Beginning inventory	+	Purchases of the period	−	Ending inventory	=	Cost of goods sold
Source:	Carried over from prior period		Accumulated in the Purchase account		Measured at end of period by physical inventory count		Computed as a residual amount

A periodic inventory system may be outlined sequentially as follows:

1. **Record all purchases**—During the period, the **purchase cost** of all goods bought is accumulated in an account called **Purchases** (or Merchandise Purchases). Thus, a credit or cash purchase would be recorded as follows:

January 14, 1981:

```
Purchases .............................................    9,000
    Accounts payable (or Cash) ..........................            9,000
```

2. **Record all sales**—During the period, the **sales price** received for all goods sold is accumulated in a Sales Revenue account. Thus, a credit or cash sale would be recorded as follows:

January 30, 1981:

```
Accounts receivable (or Cash) ............................    8,000
    Sales revenue ........................................            8,000
```

3. **Count the number of units on hand**—At the end of the period, the **Inventory account** balance still reflects the inventory amount carried over from the prior period since **no entries** are made to the Inventory account during the current period. Thus, to measure the ending inventory for the current period, a physical inventory count must be made of all goods on hand. This count must be made at the end of each period for which financial statements are to be prepared. A physical count is necessary because, under the periodic inventory system, a trans-

---

[9] Because of these important disadvantages, large chain stores now have computerized perpetual inventory systems tied in directly to the cash registers.

action-by-transaction unit and cost record is not maintained for purchases, cost of goods sold, and the inventory balance. Taking a physical inventory count is discussed later.

4. **Compute the dollar valuation of the ending inventory**—The **dollar amount** of the ending inventory quantities is computed by multiplying the number of units found as determined by the inventory count (3 above) to be on hand times their unit purchase cost. The dollar amounts, thus determined for all of the types of goods stocked, are summed to measure the total ending inventory valuation for the company.

5. **Compute cost of goods sold**—After the ending inventory valuation is measured, as in 4 above, cost of goods sold for the period can be computed as follows:

CAMPUS CORNER
Schedule of Cost of Goods Sold
For the Year Ended December 31, 1981*

Beginning inventory (carried over from the last period in the Inventory account) $40,000
Add purchases for the period (accumulated balance in the Purchases account) 55,000
Goods available for sale 95,000
Less ending inventory (determined by physical count, per above) 35,000
Cost of goods sold (as shown in Exhibit 6–1) $60,000

* Based on the data given on page 222, except for CGS.

PERPETUAL INVENTORY SYSTEM

A perpetual inventory system may involve a considerable amount of clerical effort; however, it is very effective in measuring inventory and cost of goods sold and in maintaining inventory control. The maintenance of a separate inventory record for each type of goods stocked on a transaction-by-transaction basis can be time consuming and costly. In businesses stocking very few items, a manual system may be feasible; however, to minimize these difficulties, most perpetual inventory systems are computerized. Whether manual, mechanical, or computerized, the data that are recorded and reported are the same. For instructional purposes let's look at a manual approach. For example, assume for this illustration only, that Campus Corner stocks and sells only one item, called Super X. The following events apply to 1981:

Jan.   1 Beginning inventory—8 units, at unit cost of $5,000.
July 14 Purchased—11 additional units, at unit cost of $5,000.
Nov. 30 Sold—13 units, at unit sales price of $8,333.
Dec. 31 Return sale—1 unit (returned to stock and refunded sales price).

The perpetual inventory record for this single item stocked is shown in Exhibit 6–2.[10]

[10] Measuring inventories and cost of goods sold when there are different *unit* purchase costs is deferred to Chapter 7.

PERPETUAL INVENTORY RECORD

Item **Super X** Code **No. 33** Minimum stock **10**
Location **Storage No. 4** Valuation basis **Cost** Maximum stock **20**

Date	Explanation	Goods Purchased			Goods Sold			Balance on Hand		
		Units Rec'd	Unit Cost	Total Cost	Units Sold	Unit Cost	Total Cost	Units	Unit Cost	Total Cost
Jan. 1	Beginning inventory							8	5,000	40,000
July 14	Purchase	11	5,000	55,000				19	5,000	95,000
Nov. 30	Sale				13	5,000	65,000	6	5,000	30,000
Dec. 31	Return sale				(1)	5,000	(5,000)	7	5,000	35,000
Recap: Total purchases		11		55,000						
Total cost of goods sold					12		60,000			
Ending inventory								7		35,000

The beginning inventory, purchases, cost of goods sold, and ending inventory amounts on the above perpetual inventory record agree with the amounts computed on page 225 using the periodic inventory system. In the absence of errors and other differences, the two systems will produce the same end results. However, as already indicated they will serve the company in different ways because the periodic system provides no details regarding the inventory changes whereas the perpetual system provides all of the details on a continuing basis.

When the perpetual inventory system is computerized, the computer does exactly what was done manually in Exhibit 6–2; however, a computerized system does it with tremendous speed and has considerable capacity to handle voluminous data. This is one reason why the perpetual inventory system is used widely in large, medium, and even small companies.

A perpetual inventory system may be outlined sequentially as follows:

1. **Record all purchases**—During the period, the purchase cost of each type of goods bought is entered in the **Inventory** ledger account as an increase and in a detailed perpetual inventory record (Exhibit 6–2). Thus, a cash or credit purchase of goods for resale would be recorded as follows (refer to Exhibit 6–2):

July 14, 1981:

```
Inventory* (Super X, code 33) ........................... 55,000
    Accounts payable (or Cash) ..........................          55,000
    * Also entered in the perpetual inventory record as shown in Exhibit 6–2.
```

2. **Record all sales**—During the period, each sale is recorded by means of **two companion entries.** One entry is to record the **sales revenue at sales price,** and the other entry is to record the **cost of goods sold at purchase cost.** The sales revenue is accumulated in the Sales Revenue account, and the cost of goods sold is accumulated in the Cost of Goods Sold account. Thus, a credit or cash sale would be recorded as follows (refer to Exhibit 6–2).

November 30, 1981:

a. To record the sales revenue at the sales price of $8,333 per unit:

```
Accounts receivable (or Cash) ....................... 108,329
    Sales revenue (13 units @ $8,333) ..............          108,329
```

b. To record the cost of goods sold (at cost per the perpetual inventory record—Exhibit 6–2):

```
Cost of goods sold  ................................. 65,000
    Inventory (13 units @ $5,000)* ..................          65,000
    * Also entered in the perpetual inventory record as shown in Exhibit 6–2.
```

3. **Record all returns**—During the period, **purchase returns** and **sales returns** are recorded in the Inventory account and on the perpetual inventory record at cost. For example, the return by a customer of one unit of Super X on December 30 requires companion entries to reverse the two sale entries above (only for the number of units returned). The return would be recorded as follows (refer to Exhibit 6–2):

a. To record the sale return at sales price:

```
Sales returns and allowances (1 unit @ $8,333) ........... 8,333
    Accounts receivable (or Cash) .......................          8,333
```

b. To record the return of the unit to inventory:

> Inventory (1 unit @ $5,000) 5,000*
>   Cost of goods sold 5,000
> * This amount was provided by the perpetual inventory record; it also is restored to the perpetual inventory record as shown in Exhibit 6–2.

4. **Use cost of goods sold and inventory amounts**—At the end of the period, the balance in the Cost of Goods Sold accounts provides the total amount of that expense that is reported on the income statement. No computations would be needed of cost of goods sold like those shown on page 225 because under the perpetual inventory system cost of goods sold is not computed as a residual. Similarly, the Inventory account would reflect the ending inventory amount that would be reported on the balance sheet. The sum of all the inventory balances in the various perpetual inventory records should equal the balance in the Inventory account in the ledger each point in time.

This illustration demonstrates that when a perpetual inventory system is used, it is not necessary to take a physical inventory count of the merchandise remaining on hand at the end of the accounting period in order to measure the inventory amount and cost of goods sold. However, since clerical errors, theft, and spoilage may occur, a physical inventory should be taken from time to time to check upon the accuracy of the perpetual inventory records. When an error is found, the perpetual inventory records and the Inventory account are adjusted to agree with the physical count.

To summarize, there are two basic differences between periodic and perpetual systems:

1. Inventory:
   a. Periodic—During the period, the Inventory account is not changed; thus, it reflects the beginning inventory amount. During the period, each purchase is recorded in the Purchases account. As a consequence, the ending inventory each period must be measured by physical count, then "costed" at unit purchase cost.
   b. Perpetual—During the period, the Inventory account is increased for each purchase and decreased (at cost) for each sale. Thus, at the end of the period, it measures ending inventory.

2. Cost of goods sold:
   a. Periodic—During the period, no entry is made for cost of goods sold. At the end of the period, after the physical inventory count, cost of goods sold is measured as:

$$\frac{\text{Beginning}}{\text{inventory}} + \text{Purchases} - \frac{\text{Ending}}{\text{inventory}} = \frac{\text{Cost of}}{\text{goods sold}}$$

b. Perpetual—During the period, cost of goods sold is recorded at the time of each sale and the Inventory account is reduced (at cost). Thus the system measures the cost of goods sold amount for the period.

The perpetual inventory system is used widely because of the following advantages over the periodic inventory system:

1. It provides continuous inventory amounts (units and dollar valuation for each item).
2. It provides the cost of goods sold amount without the necessity of taking a periodic inventory count.
3. It provides continuing information necessary to maintain minimum and maximum inventory levels by appropriate timing of purchases.
4. It provides continuing information about the quantity of goods on hand at various locations.
5. It provides a basis for measuring the amount of theft.
6. It provides cost of goods sold information needed to record sales at both selling price and cost.
7. It is readily adaptable to the use of computers to process quickly large quantities of inventory data.

For these reasons there has been an increase in the use of the perpetual inventory system and a decrease in use of the periodic inventory system.

SOME ISSUES IN MEASURING PURCHASES

In accordance with generally accepted accounting principles, goods purchased for resale are recorded at the date that ownership passes to the buyer. Normally, ownership is considered to pass when the goods are received constructively and not when the purchase order is placed. Goods purchased should be recorded at their **cash equivalent cost** in accordance with the **cost principle.** Cost includes the cash equivalent price paid to the vendor plus other amounts paid for freight and handling in order to get the goods to their intended location. Cost does not include financial expenditures, such as interest paid on funds borrowed to make the purchase. In accounting for purchases, several measurement problems frequently are encountered; they are discussed below.

Purchase returns and allowances. Goods purchased may be returned to the vendor because they do not meet specifications, arrive in unsatisfactory condition, or are otherwise unsatisfactory. When the goods are returned or when the vendor makes an allowance because of the circumstances, the effect on the cost of purchases must be measured. The purchaser will receive a cash refund or a reduction in the liability to the vendor for the purchase. To illustrate, assume Campus Corner returned to Company B, for credit, unsatisfactory goods that cost $1,000. The return would be recorded by Campus Corner as follows:

Accounts payable 1,000
    Purchase returns and allowances* 1,000
* Inventory is credited when the perpetual inventory system is used.

Purchase returns and allowances are accounted for as a deduction from the cost of purchases.

Transportation-in. Under the cost principle, assets acquired should be measured and recorded at their **cash equivalent cost**. Thus, the **purchase cost** of goods acquired for resale should include all freight and other transportation-in costs incurred by the purchaser. When a perpetual inventory system is used, transportation costs paid on goods purchased should be included in the inventory cost amount entered in the perpetual inventory if feasible. When a periodic inventory system is used, such costs should be entered as a debit (i.e., increase) to the Purchases account. However, for control and reporting purposes, and because of problems of apportioning a freight bill to the several items it may cover, it may be more practical to use a separate ledger account entitled "Transportation-In," or "Freight-In." Thus, in this situation the journal entry to record a payment for transportation charges upon delivery of merchandise acquired for resale would be:

Jan. 17 Transportation-in 3,000
          Cash 3,000

At the end of the period, the balance in the Transportation-In account would be reported as an addition to the cost of purchases.

Assuming freight-in and purchase returns, cost of goods sold may be reflected as follows on the income statement when periodic inventory procedures are used (refer to Campus Corner, page 225):

Cost of goods sold:
  Beginning inventory $40,000
  Purchases $53,000
    Add: Freight-in 3,000
    Deduct: Purchase returns and allowances . . . . (1,000)
  Net purchases   55,000
    Goods available for sale   95,000
    Less: Ending inventory   35,000
      Cost of goods sold $60,000

Purchase discounts. Recall the discussion of cash discounts on sales (page 216). Essentially, a corresponding situation occurs when merchandise is purchased for resale—except that the cash discount is **received** rather than given. When merchandise is purchased on credit, terms such as 2/

10, n/30 sometimes are specified. This means that if payment of the purchase invoice cost is made within ten days from date of purchase, a 2 percent discount is granted. If payment is not made within the discount period, then the full purchase invoice cost is due 30 days after purchase. To illustrate, assume Campus Corner purchases goods from a number of suppliers. The company always pays cash at date of purchase or within the discount period. On January 17 the company purchased goods from Vendor B that had a $1,000 invoice price with terms, 2/10, n/30. Under these terms, Campus Corner, following its own payment policy, will pay $980 for the goods. Therefore, the purchase should be recorded on the net basis by Campus Corner as follows:[11]

January 17—date of purchase:

Purchases*	980	
Accounts payable		980
*Inventory is debited when a perpetual inventory system is used.		

January 26—date of payment, within the discount period:

Accounts payable	980	
Cash		980

If for any reason Campus Corner did not pay within the ten-day discount period, the following entry would result:

Feb. 1 Accounts payable	980	
Purchase discounts lost (or Interest expense)	20	
Cash		1,000

Purchase discounts lost should be reported on the income statement as a *financial expense* along with regular interest expense.

Taking a physical inventory. We explained above that whether a periodic or perpetual inventory system is used, a physical inventory count

---

[11] Some persons prefer to record the transaction at the date of purchase at the gross amount, that is, at $1,000. In this instance, payment within the discount period would result in credit to an account called Purchase Discounts, $20. The purchase discount credit would then be reported as a revenue, or as a deduction from purchases. This credit is not revenue and if deducted in full from purchases on the income statement would tend to misstate both inventory and purchases. Also, in contrast, the net basis has the distinct advantage in that recording the *purchase discount lost* calls direct attention to inefficiency— failure to take the discount. The gross approach conceptually and practically is deficient for reasons similar to those cited in footnote 6.

must be taken from time to time. When a periodic inventory system is used, the inventory must be counted (and costed) at the **end of each period** because the financial statements cannot be prepared without this key amount. When a perpetual inventory system is used, the inventory count may be scheduled at various times to verify the perpetual inventory records. The two steps in taking a *physical inventory count* are:

1. **Quantity count**—The **count** of merchandise is made after the close of business on the inventory date. Normally, it would be difficult to count the goods accurately during business hours when sales are taking place. A physical count is made of all items of merchandise on hand and entered on an appropriate form. For example, an **inventory sheet**, such as the one shown in Exhibit 6–3, may be used. The **quantity** determined to be on hand by actual count is recorded in a quantity column as shown in the exhibit. Special care must be exercised in the quantity count to be sure that all of the merchandise owned by the business is included, wherever located, and that all items for which the entity does not have legal ownership are excluded. Occasionally, a business will have possession of goods it does not own (see discussion of consignments in Chapter 7).

2. **Inventory costing**—After the physical count to determine the quantity of goods on hand has been completed, each kind of merchandise must be assigned a **unit cost**. The quantity of each kind of merchandise is multiplied by the unit purchase cost to derive the **inventory amount**

EXHIBIT 6–3

Campus Corner
PHYSICAL INVENTORY SHEET

Date of Inventory _12/31/81_ Department _Hand last_ Taken by _M. R._

Location	Identification of Merchandise	Quantity on Hand	Date Purchased	Unit Cost	Unit Market Price*	Unit Cost (LCM)	Inventory Amount
1	Headsets #8-16	20	12/2/81	$ 20	$ 21	$ 20	$ 400
2	Television sets #17-961	7	11/5/81	300	300	300	2,100
2	Radios #23-72	4	10/26/81	52	50	50	200
	Total Department Inventory						6,000
	TOTAL INVENTORY VALUE—ALL DEPARTMENTS 12/31/81						$35,000

* Price that would have to be paid if the item were being purchased on the inventory date (see lower of cost or market discussion in Chapter 7).

as illustrated in Exhibit 6–3. The sum of the inventory amounts for all merchandise on hand measures the total ending inventory amount for the business. Exhibit 6–3 reflects computation of the ending inventory shown on the income statement for Campus Corner (see page 214). In costing inventory quantities, the cost principle is applied; therefore, unit purchase cost, as defined above, must be used. However, there are several ways to identify unit purchase cost for inventory purposes such as the *first-in, first-out (Fifo), last-in, first-out (Lifo),* or *average cost* approaches. These alternative approaches to costing inventories are discussed in detail in Chapter 7.

Inventories, because they frequently represent large amounts of tied-up resources (cash), often present management with complex planning and control problems. For example, decisions should be made as to the maximum and minimum levels of inventory that should be maintained; when to reorder; how much to reorder; and the characteristics of the items to stock, such as size, color, style, and specifications. Some of these issues are discussed in *Fundamentals of Management Accounting.* From the viewpoint of the investor, creditor, and other interested parties, the investment in inventory frequently is important in decision making. Thus, explanatory footnotes related to inventories frequently are included in the financial reports.

DATA PROCESSING—CLOSING ENTRIES FOR SALES REVENUE, COST OF GOODS SOLD, AND MERCHANDISE INVENTORY

In this chapter some new accounts related to the selling and purchasing functions were introduced. Usually no adjusting entries are needed for these accounts; however, because they are temporary accounts, closing entries are required.

The Sales Revenue account, and its related contra account, Sales Returns and Allowances, are closed to the Income Summary account in the usual manner. Similarly, Bad Debt Expense and Sales Discount Revenue (see page 217) are closed to the Income Summary account.

In contrast, the closing entries for cost of goods sold (an expense) and the merchandise inventory amounts depend upon the inventory system (periodic versus perpetual) used.

Closing entries when a periodic inventory system is used. When a periodic inventory system is used, there is no Cost of Goods Sold account for accumulation of this type of expense. However, the merchandise inventory requires two directly related closing entries: (1) an entry to close the **beginning inventory** amount to the Income Summary account and (2) an entry to transfer the **ending inventory** amount from the Income Summary account to the Inventory account. Campus Corner (see page 225) would make two closing entries for the merchandise inventories as follows:

December 31, 1981

a. To close (transfer) the **beginning** merchandise inventory amount into Income Summary:

Income summary	40,000	
Merchandise inventory (beginning)		40,000

b. To transfer the **ending** merchandise inventory amount from the Income Summary account to the Merchandise Inventory account:

Merchandise inventory (ending)	35,000	
Income summary		35,000

The effects of these two entries are *(a)* to replace the beginning inventory amount with the ending inventory amount in the Merchandise Inventory account and *(b)* to enter the beginning inventory amount in the Income Summary account as an **expense** (a debit) and to remove the ending inventory amount from the Income Summary account (a credit) as a cost transfer to the asset account, Merchandise Inventory.

In addition, the Purchases account is closed to Income Summary as follows:

c. Income summary	55,000	
Purchase		55,000

The reason for the two closing entries for merchandise inventories under the **periodic inventory system** can be understood if you recall that under this system the ending inventory of the **prior year** (say 1980) automatically is the beginning inventory for the current year (say 1981) and that the Inventory account balance is unchanged throughout the year (because all purchases of merchandise are debited to the **Purchases account** rather than to the Inventory account). Therefore, at the end of the current year the beginning inventory amount ($40,000 for Campus Corner) is still in the Inventory account at December 31, 1981. Simply, it must be transferred out as an expense. It must be replaced with the December 31, 1981, ending inventory amount, which under the periodic inventory system is determined at that date by a physical inventory count ($35,000 for Campus Corner). The offsetting credit in the second entry above, which records the **ending** inventory, is made to Income Summary because its cost is included in the **purchases amount** (a debit in the Income Summary account). After completion of these closing entries, the Merchandise Inventory, Purchases, and Income Summary accounts for Campus Corner would appear as follows:

Periodic Inventory System
Merchandise Inventory

12/31/80 (beginning)	40,000	(a) 12/31/81 To close	40,000
(b) 12/31/81 (ending)	35,000		

Purchases

12/31/81 (balance)	55,000	(c) 12/31/81 To close	55,000

Income Summary

Operating expenses (not shown)		Revenues (not shown)	
(a) 12/31/81 (beginning inventory)	40,000	(b) 12/31/81 (ending inventory)	35,000
(c) 12/31/81 (purchases)	55,000		

(Note that these three amounts net to $60,000, the amount of cost of goods sold.)

These closing entries, along with all the other closing entries, are illustrated in the demonstration case (Rote's Appliance Store) at the end of this chapter.[12] This demonstration case should be studied carefully because it ties together all of the parts discussed in this chapter.

Closing entries when a perpetual inventory system is used. When a perpetual inventory system is used, the Merchandise Inventory account and Cost of Goods Sold account are maintained on a cumulative day-to-day basis. Therefore, at the end of the accounting period each of these accounts will reflect the correct up-to-date balance. Consequently, no adjusting or closing entries are needed for the Merchandise Inventory account; it reflects the inventory amount that will be reported on the balance sheet. Because the Cost of Goods Sold account is an expense account, it will be closed. For example, Campus Corner would record the following closing entry under the perpetual inventory system:

December 31, 1981:

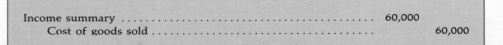

```
Income summary ........................................... 60,000
    Cost of goods sold ...................................        60,000
```

Inventory shrinkage. Inventory shrinkage (i.e., loss) occurs as a result of theft, breakage, spoilage and incorrect measurements. The measurement

---

[12] There are several mechanical variations in how the closing entries can be made; all of them give the same end results. For example, some persons prefer to record the two inventory entries as adjusting, rather than closing, entries. Also, some persons prefer to use a temporary Cost of Goods Sold account in the closing process under a periodic inventory system; in this approach the two inventory amounts and purchases are first transferred to the Cost of Goods Sold account, which is then closed to Income Summary.

of inventory shrinkage is important for internal management purposes and, if large, is a major issue to investors and creditors. The amount of shrinkage is reported on *internal* financial statements, but seldom if ever are such amounts reported **separately** on *external* financial statements. Accurate measurement of this loss is related directly to the inventory system used.

When a periodic inventory system is used, measurement of shrinkage loss often is difficult, and may be impossible. The inventory, as counted at the end of the period, does not, in itself, provide a basis for measurement of shrinkage. Under this system, since cost of goods sold is a residual amount (i.e., Beginning inventory + Purchases − Ending inventory = Cost of goods sold), shrinkage loss necessarily is buried in the cost of goods sold amount.

Alternatively, a perpetual inventory system will provide data on shrinkage loss. The inventory record provides both cost of goods sold and the ending inventory. These data make it possible to measure shrinkage loss. To illustrate, assume the perpetual inventory records show cost of goods sold for the period, 12 units, $60,000 (Exhibit 6–2), and ending inventory of 7 units, $35,000. Assume further that an inventory count is taken at the end of the period which shows 6 units on hand. In the absence of clerical error, an inventory shrinkage would be reported as 1 unit, $5,000 (assuming no insurance recovery). Further investigation may convince the management that the shrinkage was due to theft. The entry to record the shrinkage, assuming a perpetual inventory system, would be:

Inventory shrinkage (or Loss due to theft)*	5,000	
Inventory		5,000
* Closed to Income Summary.		

DEMONSTRATION CASE

Rote's Appliance Store

(Try to resolve the requirements before proceeding to the suggested solution that follows.)

Rote's Appliance Store has been operating for a number of years. It is a relatively small but profitable retail outlet for major appliances, such as refrigerators and air conditioners. Approximately 40 percent of the sales are on short-term credit. This case has been selected and simplified to demonstrate information processing when there are significant selling activities; the service activities have been deleted. The case has been structured to illustrate the application of both perpetual and periodic inventory systems with the same data. The annual accounting period ends December 31, 1981. Two independent cases will be assumed:

Case A—Perpetual inventory system is assumed.

Case B—Periodic inventory system is assumed.

The trial balance derived from the ledger at December 31, 1981, was:

| | Unadjusted trial balance | | | |
| | Case A—Perpetual inventory system used | | Case B—Periodic inventory system used | |
Account titles	Debit	Credit	Debit	Credit
Cash	$ 34,100		$ 34,100	
Accounts receivable	5,000		5,000	
Allowance for doubtful accounts		$ 1,000		$ 1,000
* Merchandise inventory:				
January 1, 1981			20,000	
December 31, 1981	16,000			
Store equipment	30,000		30,000	
Accumulated depreciation, store				
equipment		9,000		9,000
Accounts payable		8,000		8,000
Income tax, payable				
Capital stock, par $10		40,000		40,000
Retained earnings, January 1, 1981		9,000		9,000
Sales revenue		102,000		102,000
Sales returns and allowances	2,000		2,000	
* Cost of goods sold	60,000			
* Purchases			57,000	
* Purchases returns and allowances				1,000
Expenses (not detailed)	21,900		21,900	
Depreciation expense				
Income tax expense				
	$169,000	$169,000	$170,000	$170,000

* These account balances are different between the cases because of the effects of the inventory system used.

Data developed as a basis for the adjusting entries at December 31, 1981, were:

a. Credit sales in 1981 amounted to $40,000; the average loss rate for bad debts is estimated to be 0.25 percent of credit sales.
b. The store equipment is depreciated on the basis of an estimated ten-year useful life with no residual value.
c. On December 31, 1981, the periodic inventory count of goods remaining on hand reflected $16,000.
d. The average income tax rate is 20 percent.
e. The beginning inventory, January 1, 1981, was as shown on the trial balance (Case B).

Required:

a. Based upon the above data, complete a worksheet at December 31, 1981, similar to that shown in Exhibit 5–2. If you prefer, you may omit the columns for Adjusted Trial Balance. **Prepare a separate worksheet for each separate case.**
b. Based upon the completed worksheets, present an income statement

for each case. Use a single-step format for Case A and a multiple-step format for Case B.

c. Based upon the two worksheets, present, in parallel columns, the adjusting entries for each case at December 31, 1981.

d. Based upon the two worksheets, present, in parallel columns, the closing entries for each situation at December 31, 1981.

In preparing the worksheet when a **perpetual inventory system** is used, no new complications are presented. The inventory amount is extended across the worksheet as an asset since the balance in the Inventory account reflects the ending inventory when a perpetual inventory system is used. The expense—cost of goods sold—is extended to the Income Summary debit column along with the other expenses. See Exhibit 6–4.

Requirement (a):

EXHIBIT 6–4

Worksheets compared for perpetual and periodic inventory systems

ROTE'S APPLIANCE STORE
Worksheet, December 31, 1981
Case A—Assuming **Perpetual Inventory System** Is Used

Account Titles	Trial Balance		Adjusting Entries*		Income Statement		Retained Earnings		Balance Sheet	
	Debit	Credit	Debit	Credit	Debit	Credit	Debit	Credit	Debit	Credit
Cash	34,100								34,100	
Accounts receivable	5,000								5,000	
Allowance for doubtful accounts		1,000		(a) 100						1,100
Merchandise inventory Dec. 31, 1981	16,000								16,000	
Store equipment	30,000								30,000	
Accumulated depreciation, equipment		9,000		(b) 3,000						12,000
Accounts payable		8,000								8,000
Income tax payable				(c) 3,000						3,000
Capital stock		40,000								40,000
Retained earnings, Jan. 1, 1981		9,000						9,000		
Sales revenue		102,000				102,000				
Sales returns and allowances	2,000				2,000					
Cost of goods sold	60,000				60,000					
Expenses (not detailed)	21,900		(a) 100		22,000					
Depreciation expense			(b) 3,000		3,000					
	169,000	169,000			87,000	102,000				
Income tax expense†			(c) 3,000		3,000					
Net income					12,000			12,000		
			6,100	6,100	102,000	102,000	–0–	21,000		
Retained earnings, Dec. 31, 1981							21,000			21,000
							21,000	21,000	85,100	85,100

* Note that a *simplifying mechanical change* is used—the "Adjusting Entries" total is not entered until *after* the income tax is computed and entered.

† ($102,000 − $87,000) × 20% = $3,000 income tax expense.

Requirement (a) (continued):

EXHIBIT 6–4 *(continued)*

ROTE'S APPLIANCE STORE
Worksheet, December 31, 1981
Case B—Assuming **Periodic Inventory System** Is Used

Account Titles	Trial Balance		Adjusting Entries*		Income Statement		Retained Earnings		Balance Sheet	
	Debit	Credit	Debit	Credit	Debit	Credit	Debit	Credit	Debit	Credit
Cash	34,100								34,100	
Accounts receivable	5,000								5,000	
Allowance for doubtful accounts		1,000		(a) 100						1,100
Merchandise inventory, Dec. 31, 1980	20,000				20,000					
Store equipment	30,000								30,000	
Accumulated depreciation, equipment		9,000		(b) 3,000						12,000
Accounts payable		8,000								8,000
Income tax payable				(c) 3,000						3,000
Capital stock		40,000								40,000
Retained earnings, Jan. 1, 1981		9,000						9,000		
Sales revenue		102,000				102,000				
Sales returns and allowances	2,000				2,000					
Purchases	57,000				57,000					
Purchases returns and allowances		1,000				1,000				
Expenses (not detailed)	21,900		(a) 100 (b) 3,000		22,000 3,000					
Depreciation expense										
Merchandise inventory, Dec. 31, 1981						16,000			16,000	
	170,000	170,000			104,000	119,000				
Income tax expense †			(c) 3,000		3,000					
Net income					12,000			12,000		
			6,100	6,100	119,000	119,000	–0–	21,000		
							21,000			21,000
							21,000	21,000	85,100	85,100

* Note that a *simplifying mechanical change* is used—the "Adjusting Entries" total is not entered until *after* the income tax is computed and entered.
† ($119,000 − $104,000) × 20% = $3,000 income tax expense.

Requirement (b):

ROTE'S APPLIANCE STORE
Income Statement
For the Year Ended December 31, 1981
Case A—Perpetual Inventory System and Single-Step Format

Revenues		
Sales	$102,000	
Less: Sales returns and allowances	2,000	
Net sales		$100,000
Expenses:		
Cost of goods sold	60,000	
Expenses (not detailed for case purposes)	22,000	
Depreciation expense	3,000	85,000
Pretax income		15,000
Income tax expense ($15,000 × 20%)		3,000
Net income		$ 12,000
EPS ($12,000 ÷ 4,000 shares)		$3.00

ROTE'S APPLIANCE STORE
Income Statement
For the Year Ended December 31, 1981
Case B—Periodic Inventory System and Multiple-Step Format

Gross sales		$102,000
Less: Sales returns and allowances		2,000
Net sales		100,000
Cost of goods sold:		
Inventory, January 1, 1981	$ 20,000	
Purchases	57,000	
Purchase returns and allowances	(1,000)	
Goods available for sale	76,000	
Less: Inventory, December 31, 1981	16,000	
Cost of goods sold		60,000
Gross margin on sales		40,000
Operating expenses:		
Expenses (not detailed for case purposes)	22,000	
Depreciation expense	3,000	25,000
Pretax income		15,000
Income tax expense ($15,000 × 20%)		3,000
Net income		$ 12,000
EPS ($12,000÷ 4,000 shares)		$3.00

Requirement (c):

Adjusting Entries
December 31, 1981

	Case A		Case B	
	Perpetual inventory		*Periodic inventory*	
a. Expenses (bad debt loss)	100		100	
Allowance for doubtful accounts .		100		100
Bad debt loss estimated, $40,000 \times$ 0.25% = $100.				
b. Depreciation expense	3,000		3,000	
Accumulated depreciation, store equipment		3,000		3,000
Depreciation for one year, $30,000 \div$ 10 years = $3,000.				
c. Income tax expense	3,000		3,000	
Income tax payable		3,000		3,000
Income taxes for year, $15,000 \times$ 20% = $3,000.				

SAles

       | xxxx

SALes RET + ALLow

xxxx |

Requirement (d):

Closing Entries
December 31, 1981

	Case A		Case B	
	Perpetual inventory		*Periodic inventory*	
1. Sales revenue	102,000		102,000	
Sales returns and allowances		2,000		2,000
Income summary		100,000		100,000
To transfer the revenue amounts to Income Summary.				
2. Income summary	(Not applicable)		56,000	
Purchase return and allowances			1,000	
Purchases				57,000
To transfer purchase amounts to Income Summary.				
3. Income summary	(Not applicable)		20,000	
Merchandise inventory (beginning)				20,000
To transfer beginning inventory to Income Summary.				
4. Merchandise inventory (ending)	(Not applicable)		16,000	
Income summary				16,000
To transfer ending inventory from Income Summary.				
5. Income summary	60,000		(Not applicable)	
Cost of goods sold		60,000		
6. Income summary	28,000		28,000	
Expenses (not detailed)		22,000		22,000
Depreciation expense		3,000		3,000
Income tax expense		3,000		3,000
To transfer expense amounts to Income Summary.				
7. Income summary	12,000		12,000	
Retained earnings		12,000		12,000
To transfer net income to Retained Earnings.				

In preparing the worksheet with a **periodic inventory system,** both the beginning and ending inventory amounts must be used. First, the **beginning inventory** amount must be extended horizontally as a debit to the Income Statement column (because it now is an expense). A special line, "Merchandise inventory, ending" is added to the bottom of the worksheet and the **ending inventory** amount (determined by physical count) is entered on this line under Income Statement, credit. Also, this amount is entered on the same line under Balance Sheet, debit (because it is an asset).[13]

SUMMARY

This chapter discussed the measuring, recording, and reporting of the effects on income of the selling and purchasing activities of various types of businesses. Another expense on the income statement was discussed: "Cost of goods sold." It measures the *cost* of the merchandise; the **sales amount** for the same merchandise is recorded in the Sales Revenue account. In conformity with the matching principle, the total cost of the goods sold during the period must be matched with the sales revenue earned during the period. When cost of goods sold is deducted from sales revenue for the period, the difference is called gross margin on sales. From this amount, the remaining expenses must be deducted to derive income.

The chapter also discussed and illustrated the effect on cost of goods sold of the beginning and ending inventory amounts. We observed that the ending inventory of one period is the beginning inventory of the next period. Two inventory systems were discussed for measuring the merchandise remaining on hand at the end of the period (ending inventory) and cost of goods sold for the period: (1) the perpetual inventory system, which is based on the maintenance of detailed and continuous inventory records for each kind of merchandise stocked; and (2) the periodic inventory system, which is based upon a physical inventory count of the goods remaining on hand at the end of each period.

APPENDIX A: DATA PROCESSING—CONTROLLING ACCOUNTS AND SUBSIDIARY LEDGERS

This appendix explains an accounting procedure designed to facilitate recordkeeping and internal control in situations where a large number of similar transactions recur continuously. It does not involve accounting theory, principles, or standards but deals only with the mechanics of data processing. The use of **control accounts** and **subsidiary ledgers** will be explained and illustrated for accounts receivable; however, the procedure is also applicable in any situation that involves numerous transactions that are similar and require detailed recordkeeping, such as accounts payable and operational assets.

In the preceding discussions and illustrations, charge sales and services

---

[13] There are several mechanical ways of handling the inventories on the worksheet when a periodic inventory system is used. Some accountants view the inventory entries as closing rather than adjusting entries. The various approaches arrive at the same net result, and each has its particular mechanical advantages and disadvantages.

244

GENERAL LEDGER

Date 1981	Cash #101	Folio	Debit	Credit	Balance
Jan. 12		3	1 000		

	Accounts Receivable Control #102	Folio	Debit	Credit	Balance
Jan 5		1	2 400		2 400
7		2		140	2 260
12		3		1 000	1 260

	Sales #610	Folio	Debit	Credit	Balance
Jan 5		1		2 400	2 400

	Sales Returns #620	Folio	Debit	Credit	Balance
Jan 7		2	140		140

were credited to a revenue account with the corresponding debit to an account designated *"Accounts Receivable."* Subsequently, upon payment, the Accounts Receivable account was decreased (a credit). We did not illustrate the manner in which the account receivable for each *individual customer* was maintained. Some businesses carry thousands of individual customers on a credit status. The business could maintain some kind of "filing system" that would show (1) the amount of sales and services provided each customer on credit, (2) the cash collections from each customer on credit previously extended, and (3) the balance owed by each customer at each point in time. Alternatively, it could maintain a separate receivable account for each customer in the *general ledger.* This would require, in the above example, several thousand such accounts in that ledger.

A more efficient procedure involves the use of a single *control account* in the general ledger for Accounts Receivable and a separate *subsidiary ledger* that carries an individual account for each credit customer. Thus, in the above example, the general ledger would include Accounts Receivable as a *single control account* and the *subsidiary ledger* would include several thou-

SUBSIDIARY LEDGER

		Adams, J. K. 102.1					
Jan.	5		1	740			740
	7	Return	2		140		600
	12		3		400		200

		Baker, B. B. 102.2					
Jan.	5		1	120			120

		Ford, C. E. 102.3					
Jan.	5		1	340			340
	12		3		340		-0-

		Moore, W.E. 102.4					
Jan.	5		1	320			320
	12		3		220		100

		Price, V. T. 102.5					
Jan.	5		1	430			430
	12		3		40		390

		Ward, B. L. 102.6					
Jan.	5		1	450			450

sand *individual receivable accounts*. At any given point, the *sum* of the *individual account balances* in the receivable subsidiary ledger, in the absence of error, would equal the *single balance* in the *Accounts Receivable control account* in the general ledger. The Accounts Receivable account in the general ledger is called a control account because it controls the subsidiary ledger. The individual customer accounts, as subdivisions of it, are subsidiary to the control account; thus the designation, subsidiary ledger.

To illustrate data processing with a control account and a subsidiary ledger for Accounts Receivable, we will assume several transactions for the Mayo Department Store. Although most businesses that have a large volume of transactions such as these will use a computerized system, we will illustrate a manual system for instructional purposes. First, assume that on January 5, 1981, credit sales were made to six different customers. These sales could be recorded in the general journal as follows:

GENERAL JOURNAL   Page 1

Date	Account Titles and Explanation	Folio	Debit	Credit
Jan. 5	Accounts receivable	102	2,400	
	Sales	610		2,400
	To record the following credit sales:			
	Adams, J. K. .... $ 740	102.1		
	Baker, B. B. 120	102.2		
	Ford, C. E. 340	102.3		
	Moore, W. E. 320	102.4		
	Price, V. T. 430	102.5		
	Ward, B. L. 450	102.6		
	Total $2,400			

Posting of the above journal entry to the control account in the general ledger is indicated by entering the account numbers in the folio column in the usual manner, and posting to the individual customer accounts in the subsidiary ledger is indicated by entering an individual customer's account number in the folio column of the journal. Thus, we posted the total amount to the control account, Accounts Receivable (a debit total of $2,400), and we posted the several single amounts to the subsidiary ledger as illustrated below. Note that the debit-credit-balance form is used rather than the T-account form that often is used for instructional purposes.

Now, assume that on January 7 one customer, J. K. Adams, returned as unsatisfactory some of the goods purchased on January 5. Mayo accepted the goods and gave Adams a credit memorandum. The resultant journal entry was:

GENERAL JOURNAL   Page 2

Date	Account Titles and Explanation	Folio	Debit	Credit
Jan. 7	Sales returns	620	140	
	Accounts receivable	102		140
	To record the return of goods:			
	Adams, J. K. $140	102.1		

The folio column reveals that the above entry has been posted in total to the control account in the general ledger and that the single amount has been posted to the individual customer account in the subsidiary ledger.

Now, let's complete the example by assuming subsequent collections on accounts from some of the customers. The collections are recorded in the journal entry given below. The folio column indicates that the entry has been posted in total to the control account and each single amount to the individual customer accounts in the subsidiary ledger.

GENERAL JOURNAL   Page 3

Jan. 12	Cash	101	1,000	
	Accounts receivable	102		1,000
	To record collections on accounts as follows:			
	Adams, J. K. .... $ 400	102.1		
	Ford, C. E. 340	102.3		
	Moore, W. E. 220	102.4		
	Price, V. T. 40	102.5		
	Total $1,000			

The subsidiary ledger should be reconciled frequently with the control account. This is accomplished by summing the balances in the subsidiary ledger to determine whether that total agrees with the total shown by the control account in the general ledger. This check can be done simply by running an adding machine tape from the subsidiary ledger or by preparing a schedule or listing of the individual customer account balances. When there are a large number of credit sales and collections, a frequent reconciliation is advisable. A reconciliation schedule for Mayo follows:

MAYO DEPARTMENT STORE
Schedule of Accounts Receivable
January 28, 1981

No.	Customer	Amount (per subsidiary)
102.1	Adams, J. K.	$ 200
102.2	Baker, B. B.	120
102.4	Moore, W. E.	100
102.5	Price, V. T.	390
102.6	Ward, B. L.	450
102	Total accounts receivable (per control account) ...	$1,260

In this instance the subsidiary ledger total agrees with the balance in the control account. If there is disagreement, of course, an error is indicated; however, the mere fact of agreement does not necessarily mean there are no errors. One could post a debit or credit to the wrong individual account and the two ledgers would still reconcile in total.

In the above situation, the *Sales* account also could have been established as a control account supported by a subsidiary ledger that would contain separate accounts for the sales of *each department* or for *each product*. A very common application also relates to *accounts payable* when there are numerous purchases on credit.

Another common application relates to *operational assets.* For example, the Office Equipment account is included in the general ledger, usually as a control account. In such instances, the control account is supported by a subsidiary ledger of office equipment that incorporates an account for each different kind of office equipment, such as copiers, typewriters, calculators, and furniture. You can appreciate from these examples that the control account/subsidiary ledger procedure is an important element of the accounting information processing system of most enterprises.

A particular advantage of the use of subsidiary ledgers in a manual system is that it facilitates the subdivision of work. A person can be trained in a short time to maintain a subsidiary ledger since a knowledge of the broad field of accounting is not required for such routine recordkeeping tasks.

In the journal entries given above, the individual amounts relating to each individual customer account were listed in the "Explanation" column of the journal and then were posted to the subsidiary ledger. There are two approaches to simplifying this particular phase of the recordkeeping. Obviously, one could transfer directly from the charge tickets and credit memoranda to the subsidiary ledger accounts and thus avoid the detailed listing in the journal entry. This approach is used sometimes by small companies that use a manual system. Another approach involves the use of a related procedure known as *special journals.* This procedure is explained and illustrated in Appendix B to Chapter 8.

Although our illustration used a manual approach to subsidiary ledgers, such is not the usual case. Most companies of any size apply the procedure by means of accounting machines or electronic computers. The computer can be programmed to process credit sales, returns, collections on account, reconciliation of account balances, and a printout of monthly bills to be mailed to the customers.

APPENDIX B: AGING ACCOUNTS RECEIVABLE

Generally the older an account receivable, the greater the probability of its uncollectibility (i.e., its status as a bad debt). Therefore, an analysis of accounts receivable, in terms of "age," provides management with valuable information in respect to probable cash inflows, losses due to uncollectible accounts, and the general effectiveness of the credit and collection activities of the entity. Aging analysis of accounts receivable also is used by some companies to provide information needed to make the *adjusting entry* at the end of each period for estimated **bad debt expense.**

Instead of estimating bad debt expense on the basis of credit sales for the period, as illustrated on pages 217–221, an aging method sometimes is used that relates bad debt losses to the uncollected accounts (i.e., the balance in Accounts Receivable) at the end of each period. The accounts receivable aging method involves an aging analysis of the individual accounts receivable balances to *estimate* the amount of bad debts. The amount estimated to be uncollectible is the **balance** that should be in the account "Allowance for Doubtful Accounts" at the end of the period. The *difference* between the **actual balance** in that account and the **estimated balance** is the amount recorded as bad debt expense in the adjusting entry at the end of the period.

To illustrate, assume the general ledger for Macon Appliance Store, whose fiscal year ended December 31, 1981, reflected the following account balances:

Accounts receivable...................	$ 40,000 (debit balance)
Allowance for doubtful accounts........	900 (credit balance)
Sales on credit for 1981................	200,000

The adjusting entry for bad debt *expense* must be made at December 31, 1981. The company uses the **accounts receivable aging method** for determining the amount of the adjusting entry to record estimated bad debt expense. Consequently, the following aging analysis of accounts receivable was completed:

Aging Analysis of Accounts Receivable, December 31, 1981						
Customer	Total	Not Yet Due	1–30 Days Past Due	31–60 Days Past Due	61–90 Days Past Due	Over 90 Days Past Due
Adams, A. K.	$ 600	$ 600				
Baker, B. B.	1,300	300	900	100		
Cox, R. E.	1,400			400	900	100
Day, W. T.	3,000	2,000	600	400		
Zoe, A. B.	900					900
Total	$40,000	$17,200	$12,000	$8,000	$1,200	$1,600
Percent	100%	43%	30%	20%	3%	4%

The management, on the basis of experience and knowledge of specific situations, can use the above analysis as a basis for realistically estimating the probable *rates of uncollectibility for each age group.* Assume the management **estimated** the following probable bad debt loss rates: not yet due, 1 percent; 1–30 days past due, 3 percent; 31–60 days, 6 percent; 61–90 days, 10 percent; over 90 days, 25 percent. The following **estimating** schedule can be prepared:

Estimate of Probable Uncollectible Accounts, December 31, 1981			
Age	Amount of Receivable	Percent Estimated to Be Uncollectible	Balance Needed in Allowance for Doubtful Accounts
Not yet due	$17,200	1	$ 172
1–30 days past due	12,000	3	360
31–60 days past due	8,000	6	480
61–90 days past due	1,200	10	120
Over 90 days past due	1,600	25	400
Total	$40,000		$1,532

The resultant adjusting entry on December 31, 1981, would be:

Dec. 31	Bad debt expense	632	
	Allowance for doubtful accounts		632

To adjust Allowance for Doubtful Accounts to estimated balance needed.

Computations:
Balance needed (per schedule above). $1,532
Balance before adjustment (page 249) 900
Difference—adjustment needed (increase). . . . . . . $ 632

Some persons argue that this approach to estimating the amount of bad debt expense does not comply with the *matching principle* as effectively as the allowance method discussed in the chapter. There the estimate was based only on the amount of credit sales for the period from which uncollectible accounts ultimately will occur. The allowance method matches bad debt expense with the current period's sales revenues.

In contrast, the aging method, since it is based on the ending balance in Accounts Receivable, tends to match bad debt expense with credit sales for a number of periods; hence the matching principle may not be served well each period. However, it produces a good measurement of the **net realizable value** of accounts receivable since it takes into account probable losses by actual age distribution of the amounts in each account.

In practice, the allowance method (based on credit sales) appears to be used more widely.

IMPORTANT TERMS DEFINED IN THE CHAPTER (with page citations)

Revenue principle—214
Gross margin on sales—214
Markup—214
Sales discount—216
Trade discount—217

Bad debt loss—217
Bad debt allowance method—218
Contra account—219
Net realizable value—220
Sales returns and allowances—221

QUESTIONS FOR DISCUSSION

Part A

1. In a company characterized by extensive selling and purchasing activities, the *quantity* of goods included in sales revenue also must be included in a particular *expense* amount. Explain the basis for this statement.

2. Explain the difference between gross sales and net sales.

3. What is gross margin on sales? How is the gross margin ratio computed?

4. Explain what is meant by sales discount. Use 1/10, n/30 in your explanation.

5. When merchandise, invoiced at $1,000, is sold on terms, 2/10, n/30, the vendor must make the following entry:

Accounts receivable . . . .
    Sales revenue . . . .

What amounts should be used in this entry? Explain the basis for your decision.

6. A sale is made for $500; terms are 2/10, n/30. At what amount should the sale be recorded? Give the required entry with an explanation. Also, give the collection entry assuming it is after the discount period.

7. Since the actual time of cash collection is not relevant in determining the date on which a sale should be given accounting recognition, what factor is relevant?

8. Why is an estimate used instead of the actual amount of bad debts as the measure of periodic bad debt expense?

9. What is a contra account? Give two examples.

10. Define the book value of accounts receivable.

11. Why should estimated bad debt losses be based on credit sales rather than on total sales for the period?

12. What is the distinction between sales allowances and sales discount?

Questions
Part B

13. Define goods available for sale. How does it differ from cost of goods sold?

14. Define beginning inventory and ending inventory.

15. Briefly distinguish between a perpetual and a periodic inventory system. Basically, how does each measure (a) inventory and (b) cost of goods sold?

16. What model is applied when the periodic inventory system is used? Explain the *source* of each variable.

17. Why is it necessary to take an actual physical inventory count at the end of the period when the periodic inventory system is used?

18. Under the cost principle, at what amount should a purchase be recorded?

19. What is the purpose of a perpetual inventory record for each item stocked?

20. What accounts are debited and credited for a purchase of goods for resale (a) when a perpetual inventory system is used and (b) when a periodic inventory system is used?

21. What accounts are debited and credited for a sale of goods on credit *(a)* when perpetual inventory system is used and *(b)* when a periodic inventory system is used?

22. Why is there no purchases account when the perpetual inventory system is used?

23. Why is transportation-in considered to be a cost of purchasing merchandise?

EXERCISES

Part A

E6–1. Supply the missing dollar amounts for the 19B income statement of Ace Retail Company for each of the following independent cases:

Pretax income	$10,000
Income tax rate, 17%	
Shares of stock outstanding	1,000

(Relates to Exercise 6–1)

	Case A	Case B	Case C	Case D	Case E
Sales	$900	$900	$900	$?	$?
Selling expenses	?	190	160	220	180
Cost of goods sold	?	480	?	500	510
Income tax expense	?	30	30	20	40
Gross margin	400	?	?	?	390
Pretax income	100	140	?	80	?
Administrative expenses	100	?	80	100	90
Net income	80	?	120	?	80

E6–2. The following data were taken from the records of Slick Appliances, Incorporated, at December 31, 19D:

Sales	$150,000
Administrative expenses	$ 15,000
Distribution (selling) expenses	$ 20,000
Income tax rate	20%
Gross margin rate	40%
Shares of stock outstanding	5,000

Required:

Prepare a complete income statement for Slick. Show all computations. (Hint: Set up side captions starting with sales and ending with earnings per share: rely on the percents given.)

E6–3. The following data were taken from the records of Sound Center, Incorporated, at December 31, 19B:

Gross margin (40% rate)	$24,000
Selling (distribution) expenses	$ 9,000
Administrative expenses	?

Required:

Prepare a complete multiple-step income statement for Sound Center. Show all computations. (Hint: Set up the side captions starting with sales and ending with earnings per share; rely on the percents given.)

E6–4. The following data were taken from the records of Reo Corporation on December 31, 19B:

Sales of merchandise for cash	$252,000
Sales of merchandise for credit	150,000
Sales returns and allowances	2,000
Selling expenses	100,000
Cost of goods sold	242,000
Administrative expenses	40,500

Items not included in above amounts:
  Estimated bad debt loss, 1% of net credit sales.
  Average income tax rate, 17%.
  Number of shares of common stock outstanding, 20,000.

Required:

a. Based on the above data, prepare a multiple-step income statement. There were no extraordinary items. Include a column for percentage analysis.

b. How much was the gross margin? What was the gross margin rate? Explain what these two amounts mean.

E6–5. The following summarized data were provided by the records of Melody's Music Store, Incorporated, for the year ended December 31, 19B:

Sales of merchandise for cash	$124,000
Sales of merchandise on credit	80,000
Cost of goods sold	120,000
Distribution expenses	30,800
Administrative expenses	20,000
Sales returns and allowances	4,000

Items not included in above amounts:
Estimated bad debt loss, 1½% of credit sales.
Average income tax rate, 20%.
Number of shares of common stock outstanding, 10,000.

Required:

a. Based upon the above data, prepare a multiple-step income statement. Include a Percentage Analysis column.

b. What was the amount of gross margin? What was the gross margin rate? Explain.

E6–6. During the months of January and February, the WZ Corporation sold goods to two customers. The sequence of events was as follows: SELLER

Jan. 6 Sold goods for $800 to J. Doe and billed that amount subject to terms, 2/10, n/30.

6 Sold goods to R. Roe for $600 and billed that amount subject to terms, 2/10, n/30.

14 Collected cash due from J. Doe.

Feb. 2 Collected cash due from R. Roe.

28 Sold goods for $1,000 to B. Moe, and billed that amount subject to terms, 2/10, n/30.

Required:

a. Give the appropriate entry for each date. Assume a periodic inventory system is used.

b. Explain how each account balance as of February 28 should be reported, assuming that this is the end of the accounting period.

E6–7. The following transactions were selected from among those completed by Dawson Retailers:

November 25, 19B, sold 20 items of merchandise to Customer A at an invoice price of $2,000 (total); terms 3/10, n/30.

November 28, 19B, sold ten items of merchandise to Customer B at an invoice price of $1,000 (total); terms, 3/10, n/30.

November 30, 19B, Customer B returned one of the items purchased on the 28th; the item was defective and credit was given to the customer.

December 6, 19B, Customer B paid the account balance in full.

December 30, 19B, Customer A paid in full for the invoice of November 25, 19B.

Required:

a. Give the appropriate entry for each of the above transactions assuming Dawson uses the periodic inventory system.

b. Assume it is December 31, 19B, end of the accounting period. Show how the various account balances would be reported.

E6–8. MK Company started business on January 1, 19A. During the year, 19A, the company records indicated the following:

Sales on cash basis	$200,000
Sales on credit basis	100,000
Collections on accounts receivable	70,000

The manager of MK Company is concerned about accounting for the bad debts. At December 31, 19A, although no accounts were considered bad, several customers were considerably overdue in paying their accounts. A friend of the manager, who lived in another city in the region, suggested a 1 percent bad debt rate on sales, which the manager decided to use at the start.

Required:

a. Assume you have been employed, on a part-time basis, to assist with the recordkeeping for MK Company. The manager told you to set up bad debt expense of $3,000. Give the required entry.

b. Assume you were concerned about how the $3,000 was determined and the manager told you it was from another manager "who knew his business" and used 1 percent of sales. Do you agree with the $3,000? If you disagree, give the correct entry and explain the basis for your choice.

c. Show how the various accounts related to credit sales should be shown on the December 31, 19A, income statement and balance sheet.

E6–9. During 19G, Mae's Ready-to-Wear Shop sold merchandise amounting to $110,000, of which $40,000 was on credit. At the start of 19G, Accounts Receivable reflected a debit balance of $12,000 and the Allowance for Doubtful Accounts, a $600 credit balance. Collections on accounts

receivable during 19G amounted to $33,000.

Data during 19G:

1. December 31, 19G, an account receivable (J. Doe) of $700 from a prior year was determined to be uncollectible; therefore, it was written off immediately as a bad debt.
2. December 31, 19G, on the basis of experience, a decision was made to continue the accounting policy of basing estimated bad debt losses on 1 percent of credit sales for the year.

Required:

a. Give the required entries for the two items on December 31, 19G (end of the accounting period).

b. Show how the amounts related to accounts receivable and bad debt expense would be reported on the income statement and balance sheet for 19G. Disregard income tax considerations.

c. On the basis of the data available does it appear that the 1 percent rate used is too high or too low? Explain.

Exercises
Part B

E6–10. Supply the missing dollar amounts for the 19B income statement of Joplin Retailers for each of the following independent cases:

(Relates to Exercise 6–10)

Case	Sales	Beginning Inventory	Purchases	Total Available	Ending Inventory	Cost of Goods Sold	Gross Margin	Expenses	Pretax Income or (Loss)
A	900	100	700		200	?	?	200	?
B	900	180	750		?	?	?	100	0
C	900	140	?		300	650	?	100	?
D	900	?	600		210	?	?	150	50
E	900	?	650		100	?	100	?	(50)

E6–11. Supply the missing dollar amounts for the 19D income statement of Swazey Company for each of the following independent cases:

ary 19B, through the caption "Gross margin on sales" and show the details of cost of goods sold. The December 31, 19A, inventory of merchandise was

(Relates to Exercise 6–11)

	Case A	Case B	Case C
Sales	6,000	6,000	6,000
Sales returns and allowances	150	?	?
Net sales	?	?	?
Beginning inventory	9,000	9,500	8,000
Purchases	5,000	?	5,300
Freight-in	?	120	120
Purchase returns	40	30	?
Goods available for sale	?	14,790	13,370
Ending inventory	10,000	9,000	?
Cost of goods sold	?	?	5,400
Gross margin	?	110	?
Expenses	690	?	520
Pretax income	1,000	(500)	-0-

E6–12. The following list of transactions involving College Store were selected from the records of January 19B:

1. Sales: cash, $130,000; and on credit, $40,000 (terms, n/30).
2. Merchandise sold on credit in 1 and subsequently returned for credit, $800.
3. Purchases: cash, $80,000; and on credit $15,000 (terms, n/60).
4. Merchandise purchased and subsequently returned for credit: $500.
5. Shipping costs paid in cash on the merchandise purchased, $400 (debit Freight-In).
6. Bad debt losses, on the basis of experience, are estimated to be one half of 1 percent of credit sales net of sales returns and allowances.
7. An account receivable amounting to $150 was written off as uncollectible. The sale was made two years earlier.

Required:

a. Give the journal entry that would be made for each transaction, assuming the company uses a periodic inventory system.
b. Prepare an income statement for Janu-

$75,000; and the physical inventory count of merchandise taken on January 31, 19B, amounted to $90,000.

E6–13. Swift Sport Shop sells merchandise on credit terms of 2/10, n/30. A sale invoiced at $800 was made to K. Williams on February 1, 19B. In due time the account was paid in full.

Required:

a. Give the entry to record the credit sale.
b. Give the entry assuming the account was collected in full on February 9, 19B.
c. Give the entry assuming, instead, the account was collected in full on March 2, 19B.

On March 4, 19B, Swift purchased from a supplier, on credit, sporting goods invoiced at $6,000; the terms were 1/10, n/30.

Required:

d. Give the entry to record the purchase on credit. Assume periodic inventory system.

e. Give the entry assuming the account was paid in full on March 12, 19B.

f. Give the entry assuming, instead, the account was paid in full on March 28, 19B.

E6–14. Palmer Company uses a perpetual inventory system. Since it is a small business and sells only five different high-cost items, a perpetual inventory record is maintained for each item. The following selected data relate to Item A for the month of January:

1. Beginning inventory—quantity 5, cost $77 each.
2. Purchased—quantity 4, cost $72 each; paid $20 total freight.
3. Sold—quantity 6, sales price $150 each.
4. Returns—one sold in (3) was returned for full credit.

Required:

a. Give the journal entries for the above transactions assuming a perpetual inventory system and cash transactions.

b. Prepare the perpetual inventory record to Item A.

c. For January, give the following amounts for Item A:

    a. Sales revenue ...... $_____
    b. Cost of goods
       sold .... $_____
    c. Gross margin
       on sales .... $_____
    d. Ending inventory ... $_____

d. Was there any inventory shrinkage? Explain.

E6–15. Rose Company uses a perpetual inventory system that provides amounts for the

period for *(a)* cost of goods sold and *(b)* ending inventory. Physical inventory counts are made from time to time to verify the perpetual inventory records. On December 31, 19B, the end of the accounting year, the perpetual inventory record for Item No. 18 showed the following (summarized):

	Units	Unit cost	Total cost
Beginning inventory	500	$2	$1,000
Purchases during the period	900	2	1,800
Sales during the period (sales price $3.50)	800		

Required:

a. Give the entry to record the purchases for cash during the period.

b. Give the entry to record the sales for cash during the period.

c. Assume a physical inventory count was made after the above transactions and it reflected 590 units of Item No. 18 on hand. Give any entry required.

d. Give the following amounts for 19B related to Item No. 18:

    1. Ending inventory .... units _____ $_____
    2. Cost of goods sold .. units _____ $_____
    3. Shrinkage loss........ units _____ $_____

e. As a manager, would you investigate in this situation? How?

E6–16. During 19B, XY Corporation's records reflected the following for one product stocked:

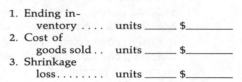

(Relates to Exercise 6–16)

1. Beginning inventory ..... 1,000 units, unit cost $2
2. Purchases .... 8,000 units, unit cost $2
3. Sales .... 7,000 units, unit sales price $3
4. Purchase returns .... 10 units, for $2 per unit refund from the supplier
5. Sales returns .... 5 units, for $3 per unit refund to the customer

Required:

a. All transactions were cash; give the entries for the above transactions assuming:

Case A—A perpetual inventory system.

Case B—A periodic inventory system.

b. How would the amount of cost of goods sold be determined in each case?

E6–17. The trial balance for Variety Store, Incorporated, at December 31, 19B (the end of the accounting year), is given below. Only selected and summary accounts are given in order to shorten the case. Also, the amounts have been simplified for this same purpose. The company uses a periodic inventory system. With the exception of the ending inventory, all of the accounts (before adjusting and closing entries) that you will need are listed in the trial balance.

Data developed as a basis for the adjusting entries at December 31, 19B, were:

a. Estimated bad debt expense for 19B was 1 percent of net credit sales of $12,000.

b. An inventory of store supplies on hand taken at December 31, 19B, reflected $50.

c. Depreciation on the store equipment is based on an estimated useful life of ten years and no residual value.

d. Wages earned up to December 31, 19B, yet not paid or recorded amounted to $500.

e. Inventories: The beginning inventory is shown in the above trial balance. A physical inventory count of merchandise on hand and unsold, at December 31, 19B, reflected $2,000.

f. Assume an average income tax rate of 20 percent.

Required:

Set up a worksheet similar to the one in the demonstration case. If desired, you may omit columns for Adjusted Trial Balance and Retained Earnings. Enter the trial balance, adjusting entries, ending inventory, and complete the worksheet.

E6–18. The trial balance for Home Appliances, Incorporated, at December 31, 19B (end of the accounting year), is given below. Only selected items have been used in order to shorten the case. The company uses a perpetual inventory system. All of the accounts you will need are listed in the trial balance.

(Relates to Exercise 6–17)

Debits		Credits	
Cash	$ 7,600	Allowance for doubtful	
Accounts receivable	3,000	accounts	$ 150
Merchandise inventory,		Accumulated	
January 1, 19B	4,000	depreciation	900
Store supplies inventory	250	Accounts payable	5,000
Store equipment	3,000	Wages payable	
Sales returns	150	Income tax payable	
Purchases	6,000	Capital stock, par $10	6,000
Bad debt expense		Retained earnings	1,870
Depreciation expense		Sales	13,000
Freight-in		Purchases returns	80
(on purchases)	100		
Income tax expense			
Other operating			
expenses	2,900		
	$27,000		$27,000

Trial Balance
December 31, 19B

Account titles	Debit	Credit
Cash	$ 6,800	
Accounts receivable . .	12,000	
Allowance for doubt-ful accounts		$ 700
Merchandise inventory, ending	64,000	
Operational assets . . .	40,000	
Accumulated depreciation		12,000
Accounts payable . . .		8,000
Income tax payable. . .		
Capital stock, par $10		60,000
Retained earnings, January 1, 19B		14,300
Sales		105,000
Sales returns and allowances	1,200	
Cost of goods sold . . .	56,000	
Expenses (not detailed)	20,000	
Bad debt expense		
Depreciation expense		
Income tax expense . .		
	$200,000	$200,000

Additional data developed for the adjusting entries:

a. Estimated bad debt expense is 2 percent of net credit sales. Net credit sales for 19B amounted to $35,000.
b. The operational assets are being depreciated $4,000 each year.
c. The average income tax rate is 20 percent.

Required:

Set up a worksheet similar to the one in the demonstration case. If desired, you may omit columns for Adjusted Trial Balance and Retained Earnings. Enter the trial balance, adjusting entries, and complete the worksheet.

PROBLEMS

Part A

P6–1. The following data were taken from the year-end records of Alvin-Eric Company. You are to fill in all of the missing amounts. Show computations.

(Relates to Problem 6–1)

P6–2. Red Equipment Company, Inc., sells heavy construction equipment. There are 10,000 shares of capital stock outstanding. The annual fiscal period ends on December 31. The following condensed trial

		Independent cases		
Income statement items		Case A		Case B
Gross sales		$102,000		$205,000
Sales returns and allowances		?		5,000
Net sales		?		?
Cost of goods sold	(62%)	?		?
Gross margin on sales		?	(40%)	?
Operating expenses		18,000		?
Pretax income		?		35,000
Income tax expense (20%)		?		?
Income before extraordinary items . .		?		?
Extraordinary items	(gain)	5,000	(loss)	10,000
Less: Income tax (20%)		?		?
Net income		?		?
EPS (10,000 shares)		2.00		?

balance was taken from the general ledger on December 31, 19D:

Account titles	Debit	Credit
Cash	$ 11,000	
Accounts receivable . .	20,000	
Allowance for doubt-		
ful accounts		$ 1,000
Inventory (ending) . . .	90,000	
Operational assets. . . .	40,000	
Accumulated de-		
preciation.		8,000
Liabilities		17,000
Capital stock		100,000
Retained earnings,		
January 1, 19D		20,000
Sales		204,000
Sales returns and		
allowances	4,000	
Cost of goods sold . . .	120,000	
Selling expenses	37,000	
Administrative ex-		
penses	10,000	
Interest expense	3,000	
Extraordinary loss,		
unusual and in-		
frequent storm		
damage	5,000	
Income tax expense* .	10,000	
	$350,000	$350,000

* Assume a 40 percent average tax rate on both operations and the extraordinary loss.

Required:

a. Prepare a multiple-step income statement similar to the format in Exhibit 2–1. (Hint: Reflect the income tax effect of the extraordinary loss as is done with the extraordinary item in Exhibit 2–1.)
b. Prepare the following ratio analyses:
   1. Gross margin on sales ratio.
   2. Profit margin ratio (see Chapter 2).
   3. Return on investment on owners' equity (see Chapter 2).
c. To compute (b) 2 and (b) 3, what amount did you use as the numerator? Explain why.
d. Briefly explain the meaning of each of the three ratios computed in (b).

P6–3. New Corporation is a local grocery store organized seven years ago as a corporation by three individuals. At that time, a total of 10,000 shares of common stock

was issued to the organizers. The store is in an excellent location, and sales have increased each year. At the end of 19B the bookkeeper prepared the following statement (assume all amounts are correct; also note the inappropriate terminology and format):

NEW's
Profit and Loss
December 31, 19B

	Debit	Credit
Sales		$301,000
Cost of goods		
sold	$169,500	
Sales returns and		
allowances	1,000	
Selling expenses	60,000	
Administrative and		
general expenses . .	30,000	
Interest expense	500	
Extraordinary loss . . .	4,000	
Income tax expense		
(on operations		
$12,000 less $1,200		
saved on the		
extraordinary loss) .	10,800	
Net profit	25,200	
	$301,000	$301,000

Required:

a. Prepare a multiple-step income statement similar to Exhibit 2–1. Assume an average 30 percent income tax rate.
b. Prepare the following ratio analyses:
   1. Profit margin on sales ratio (see Chapter 2).
   2. Gross margin on sales ratio.
   3. Return on investment on owners' equity of $150,000 (see Chapter 2).
c. In computing ratios (b) 1 and (b) 3, what amount did you use for income? Explain why.
d. Generally, it is conceded that of the three ratios in (b), return on investment has the highest information content for the typical investor? Why?

P6–4. The data below were selected from the records of Barr Company for the year ended December 31, 19C.

Balances January 1, 19C:
Accounts receivable (various
customers) $40,000
Allowance for doubtful
accounts 4,000

Transactions during 19C:

1. Sold merchandise for cash, $150,000.

Sold merchandise and made collections, on credit terms, 2/10, n/30, in the order given below (assume a unit sales price of $1,000 in all transactions):

2. Sold merchandise to T. Smith; invoice price, $18,000.

3. Sold merchandise to K. Jones; invoice price, $30,000.

4. T. Smith returned one of the units purchased in 2 above, two days after purchase date and received account credit.

5. Sold merchandise to B. Sears; invoice price, $20,000.

6. T. Smith paid his account in full within the discount period.

7. Collected $32,000 cash from customer sales on credit in prior year, all within the discount periods.

8. K. Jones paid the invoice in 3 above within the discount period.

9. Sold merchandise to R. Roy, invoice price, $10,000.

10. Three days after paying the account in full, K. Jones returned one defective unit and received a cash refund.

11. Collected $5,000 cash on an account receivable on sales in prior year, after the discount period.

12. Barr wrote off a 19A account of $1,920 because it was concluded that the amount would never be collected.

13. The estimated bad debt rate used by Barr is 1 percent of *net* credit sales.

Required:

a. Record the above entries, including the bad debt write-off and the adjusting entry for estimated bad debts. Do not consider any cost of goods sold entries. Show computations for each entry. (Hint: Set up T-accounts on scratch paper for Accounts Receivable by customer, Cash, Allowance for Doubtful Accounts, Sales, Sales Returns, Sales Discount Revenue, and Bad Debt Expense; this will provide the data needed for the next requirement.)

b. Show how the accounts related to the above sale and collection activities should be reported on the 19C income statement and balance sheet.

P6–5. (Based on Appendix B) Reed Equipment Company uses the aging approach to estimate bad debt expense at the end of each accounting year. Credit sales occur frequently on terms, n/60. The balance of each account receivable is aged on the basis of three time periods as follows: *(a)* not yet due; *(b)* up to one year past due; and *(c)* more than one year past due. Experience has shown that for each age group the average loss rate on the amount of the receivable at year-end due to uncollectibility is *(a)* 1 percent, *(b)* 5 percent, and *(c)* 20 percent.

At December 31, 19F (end of the current accounting year), the Accounts Receivable balance was $50,500 and the Allowance for Doubtful Accounts balance was $2,000. To simplify, only five accounts are used; the details of each on December 31, 19F, follow:

A. Able—Account Receivable

Date	Explanation	Debit	Credit	Balance
3/11/19E	Sale	15,000		15,000
6/30/19E	Collection		5,000	10,000
1/31/19F	Collection		3,000	7,000

C. Carson—Account Receivable

Date	Explanation	Debit	Credit	Balance
2/28/19F	Sale	21,000		21,000
4/15/19F	Collection		10,000	11,000
11/30/19F	Collection		3,000	8,000

M. May—Account Receivable

Date	Explanation	Debit	Credit	Balance
11/30/19F	Sale	18,000		18,000
12/15/19F	Collection		8,000	10,000

T. Tyler—Account Receivable

Date	Explanation	Debit	Credit	Balance
3/2/19D	Sale	5,000		5,000
4/15/19D	Collection		5,000	-0-
9/1/19E	Sale	12,000		12,000
10/15/19E	Collection		10,000	2,000
2/1/19F	Sale	19,000		21,000
3/1/19F	Collection		1,000	20,000
12/31/19F	Sale	1,500		21,500

Z. Ziltch—Account Receivable

Date	Explanation	Debit	Credit	Balance
12/30/19F	Sale	4,000		4,000

Required:

a. Set up an aging analysis schedule and complete it; follow the illustration given in Appendix B to the chapter.

b. Compute the amounts estimated uncollectible for each age category and in total.

c. Give the adjusting entry for bad debt expense at December 31, 19F.

d. Show how the amounts related to accounts receivable should be presented on the 19F income statement and balance sheet.

Problems

Part B

P6–6. This problem is designed to demonstrate the accounting for cash discounts by both the seller and purchaser. Observe the consistency between both parties to the same transactions—one party's sales discount is another party's purchase discount.

Assume the following summarized transactions between Company A, the vendor, and Company B, the purchaser. Use the letters to the left as the date notations. Assume each company uses a periodic inventory system.

1. Company A sold Company B merchandise for $10,000; terms, 2/10, n/30.

2. Prior to payment, Company B returned $1,000 (one tenth) of the merchandise for credit because it did not meet B's specifications.

Required:

Give the following entries in parallel for each party:

a. The sale/purchase transaction.

b. The return transaction.

c. Payment in full assuming it was made within the discount period.

d. Payment in full assuming, instead, it was made after the discount period.

Use a form similar to the following:

4. Other vendors, invoice price, before deduction of cash discount 115,000

5. Purchased equipment for use in the store; paid cash 1,800

6. Purchased office supplies for future use in the store; paid cash 600

7. Freight on merchandise purchased; paid cash (set up a separate account for this item) 500

8. Accounts payable paid in full during the period as follows: May Supply Company, paid after the discount period .... 4,000 Other vendors, paid within the discount period 98,000

Required:

a. Prepare journal entries for each of the above items.

(Relates to Problem 6–6)

Date	Accounts	Co. A—vendor		Co. B—purchaser	
		Debit	Credit	Debit	Credit

P6–7. College Shop, Incorporated, is a "student co-op." It has been operating successfully for a number of years. The board of directors is composed of faculty and students. On January 1, 19X, when this case starts, the beginning inventory was $200,000; the Accounts Receivable debit balance was $3,000; and the Allowance for Doubtful Accounts credit balance was $400. A periodic inventory system is used.

The following transactions (summarized) have been selected from 19X for case purposes:

1. Merchandise sales for cash $220,000

2. Merchandise returned by customers as unsatisfactory, for cash refund .... 1,400 Merchandise purchased from vendors on credit; terms, 2/10, n/30:

3. May Supply Company, invoice price, before deduction of cash discount 4,000

b. Give the closing entry required at December 31, 19X, for:
1. Beginning inventory.
2. Ending inventory (assume $210,000).

c. Prepare a partial income statement through gross margin on sales.

d. Did you record merchandise purchases at net or at gross? Explain why.

P6–8. The transactions listed below have been selected from those occurring during the month of January 19D for OK Department Store, Incorporated. A wide line of goods is offered for sale. Credit sales are extended to a few select customers; however, the usual credit terms are n/EOM. Selected transactions (summarized for January) are:

(Relates to Problem 6–8)

1. Sales to customers:
   Cash $350,000
   On credit 20,000
2. Unsatisfactory merchandise returned by customers:
   Cash 4,000
   Credit 1,000
   Merchandise purchased from vendors on credit; terms, 1/20, n/30:
3. AB Supply Company, amount billed, before deduction of cash
   discount 1,000
4. From other vendors, amount billed, before deduction of cash
   discount 120,000
5. Freight paid on merchandise purchased; paid cash (set up a
   separate account for this item) 2,000
6. Collections on accounts receivable 17,000
   The accounts payable were paid in full during the period as
   follows:
7. AB Supply Company, paid after the discount period 1,000
8. Other vendors, paid within the discount period 118,800
9. Purchased two new typewriters for the office; paid cash 900
10. An account receivable from a customer from a prior year amounting
    to $300 was determined to be uncollectible and was written off.
11. At the end of January the adjusting entry for estimated bad debts is
    to be made. The loss rate, based on experience, is one half of
    1% of net credit sales for the period (i.e., on credit sales less credit
    returns).

Relevant account balances on January 1, 19D, were Accounts Receivable, $3,200 (debit); and Allowance for Doubtful Accounts, $900 (credit). Total assets at the end of the period, $250,000.

Required:

a. Prepare journal entries for the above items assuming a periodic inventory system.
b. Show how the following amounts should be reported on the January 19D income statement and balance sheet. Show computations.
   1. Bad debt expense.
   2. Balance in accounts receivable.
   3. Balance in allowance for doubtful accounts.
c. Explain why bad debt expense for January should not be debited for the $300 bad debt.

P6–9. Strong Distributing Company uses a perpetual inventory system for the ten different kinds of items it sells. The following selected data relate to a small but high-cost item stocked during the

month of January 19B. To simplify, refer to this item as Item 10.

1. Beginning inventory—quantity, 70; cost, $50 each.
2. Purchases—quantity, 90; cost, $48 each plus $180 total freight-in.
3. Sales—quantity, 120; sales price, $95 each.
4. Returns—Strong accepted a return of two of the items sold in 3 because they were not needed by the customer and they had not been used.
5. At the end of January 19B a physical inventory count showed 37 items remaining on hand.

Required (assume all transactions were cash):

a. Prepare the perpetual inventory record for Item 10.
b. Give entries for each of the above transactions.
c. Prepare the income statement for January 19B through gross margin on sales as it relates to Item 10. What was the gross margin ratio on sales?

d. As the responsible manager, would you investigate the inventory shrinkage? How? What alternatives would you consider for corrective action?

e. Assume also that you observe quite often that the required items are out of stock. How can a perpetual inventory system be helpful in avoiding this problem?

P6–10. MRW Company uses a perpetual inventory system. During the month of January 19D the perpetual inventory record for Item A, which is one of the 23 items stocked, is shown below (summarized):

Required:

a. Complete the above perpetual inventory record.
b. Give the journal entry for each transaction reflected above (assume transactions are cash).
c. Complete the following:

Income statement:
Sales . . . . $_____
Cost of goods sold . . _____
Gross margin on
sales . . . . _____
Gross margin ratio . . _____

Balance sheet:
Inventory . . . . _____

d. How should the inventory shortage be reported?

e. As the responsible manager, would you investigate this situation? How? What alternatives would you consider for corrective action?

f. Assume "stockout" has been a problem. What would you recommend?

P6–11. The following transactions, relating to one product sold by Robbins Company, were completed in the order given during January:

a. Purchased—quantity, 100; cost, $20 each.
b. Sold—quantity, 80; $30 each.
c. Purchase return—returned one of the units purchased in *(a)* because it was the wrong size.
d. Sales return—accepted two units from a customer that were sold in *(b)*. The customer did not need them, and they were not damaged.
e. Inventories:
Beginning inventory, January 1—30 units at total cost of $600.

(Relates to Problem 6–10)

PERPETUAL INVENTORY RECORD

Date	Explanation	Goods Purchased		Goods Sold		Balance	
		Units	Total Cost	Units	Total Cost	Units	Total Cost
1	Beginning inventory					40	3,200
2	Purchase (at $80 each)	20					
3	Sale (sales price $150 each)			31			
4	Purchase return (one unit)						
5	Purchase (at $80 each)	30					
6	Sale return (one unit)						
7	Sale (sales price $150 each)			29			
8	Inventory shortage (two units)						

Ending inventory, January 31—per periodic inventory count, 51 units @ \$20 = \$1,020.

f. Cost of goods sold for January—78 units @ \$20 = \$1,560.

Required:

You are to compare the journal entries that would be made for the above transactions assuming: Case A—a perpetual inventory system is used; and Case B—a periodic inventory system is used. To do this, set up the following form (assume cash transactions):

P6–12. Long Retailers' Inc., is completing the accounting information processing cycle for the year ended December 31, 19D. The worksheet given below has been completed through the adjusting entries. (An optional column "Adjusted Trial Balance," may be helpful in completing the requirements.)

Required:

a. Complete the worksheet on page 266 (periodic inventory system is used). Assume an average income tax rate of 20 percent.

b. Give the closing entries at December 31, 19D.

(Relates to Problem 6–11)

		Amounts			
		Perpetual		*Periodic*	
Date	Explanation	Debit	Credit	Debit	Credit
a.	To record the purchase				
b.	To record the sale				
c.	To record the purchase return				
d.	To record the sales return				
e.	To record the closing entries for inventories				
f.	To record the closing entry for cost of goods sold				
g.	To close purchases and purchase returns				

(Relates to Problem 6–12)

LONG RETAILERS, INC.
Worksheet—December 31, 19D

Account Titles	Trial Balance		Adjusting Entries		Income Statement		Retained Earnings		Balance Sheet	
	Debit	Credit	Debit	Credit	Debit	Credit	Debit	Credit	Debit	Credit
Cash	25,700									
Accounts receivable	12,000									
Allowance for doubtful accounts		300		(a) 400						
Merchandise inventory Jan. 1, 19D	30,000									
Equipment	22,500									
Accumulated depreciation, equipment		7,500		(b) 1,500						
Other assets	20,000									
Accounts payable		8,000								
Interest payable				(c) 300						
Note payable, long term, 12%		10,000								
Capital stock, par $10		50,000								
Contributed capital in excess of par		7,500								
Retained earnings, Jan. 1, 19D		13,000								
Dividends paid	6,000									
Sales revenue		95,000								
Sales returns and allowances	1,000									
Purchases	52,000									
Freight-in	2,000									
Purchase returns and allowances		1,100								
Operating expenses (not detailed)	20,300									
Bad debt expense			(a) 400							
Depreciation expense			(b) 1,500							
Interest expense	900		(c) 300							
Merchandise inventory, Dec. 31, 19D ($32,000)										
	192,400	192,400								
Income tax expense										
Income tax payable										
Net income										
Retained earnings, Dec. 31, 19D										

P6–13. (Note: This is an extended problem designed to review Chapters 3, 4, 5, and 6.) Quality Furniture Store, Inc., has been in operation for a number of years and has been quite profitable. The losses on uncollectible accounts and merchandise returns are about the same as for other furniture stores. The company uses a perpetual inventory system. The annual fiscal period ended December 31, 1981, and the end-of-the period accounting information processing cycle has been started. The following trial balance was derived from the general ledger at December 31, 1981:

(Relates to Problem 6–13)

Account titles	Debit	Credit
Cash	$ 28,880	
Accounts receivable	36,000	
Allowance for doubtful accounts		$ 4,600
Merchandise inventory (ending)	120,000	
Store equipment	20,000	
Accumulated depreciation		8,000
Accounts payable		10,000
Income tax payable		
Interest payable		
Notes payable, long term (12%)		50,000
Capital stock, par $10		70,000
Retained earnings, January 1, 1981		11,400
Sales revenue		441,000
Sales returns and allowances	25,000	
Cost of goods sold	213,350	
Selling expenses	102,700	
Administrative expenses	49,070	
Bad debt expense		
Depreciation expense		
Interest expense		
	$595,000	$595,000
Income tax expense		
Net income		

Data for adjusting entries:

a. The bad debt losses due to uncollectible accounts are estimated to be $6,000.

b. The store equipment is being depreciated over an estimated useful life of ten years with no residual value.

c. The long-term note of $50,000 was for a two-year loan from a local bank. The interest rate is 12 percent, payable at the end of each 12-month period. The note was dated April 1, 1981. (Hint: Accrue interest for nine months.)

d. Assume an average 20 percent corporate income tax rate.

Required:

a. Based upon the above data, complete a worksheet similar to the one illustrated in the chapter for the demonstration case. If you prefer, you may omit columns for Adjusted Trial Balance and Retained Earnings. The company uses a perpetual inventory system. (Hint: Net income is $30,704.)

b. Based upon the completed worksheet, prepare a multiple-step income statement and classified balance sheet.

c. Based upon the completed worksheet, prepare the adjusting and closing entries for December 31, 1981.

P6–14. (Note: This is an extended problem designed to review the materials discussed in Chapters 3, 4, 5, and 6.) Central Appliances, Incorporated, is owned by six local investors. It has been operating for four years and is at the end of the 1981 fiscal year. For case purposes, certain accounts have been selected to demonstrate the information processing activities at the end of the year for a corporation that sells merchandise rather than services. The following trial balance, assumed to be correct, was taken from the ledger on December 31, 1981. The company uses a periodic inventory system.

(Relates to Problem 6–14)

Debits		Credits	
Cash	$ 18,000	Allowance for doubtful	
Accounts receivable	28,000	accounts	$ 600
Merchandise inventory,		Accumulated	
January 1, 1981	80,000	depreciation	12,000
Prepaid insurance	300	Accounts payable	15,000
Store equipment	40,000	Notes payable,	
Sales returns	3,000	long term (12%)	30,000
Purchases	250,000	Capital stock, par $10	40,000
Freight-in	11,000	Retained earnings,	
Operating expenses	76,300	January 1, 1981	2,000
		Sales	400,000
		Purchase returns	7,000
	$506,600		$506,600

Additional data for adjusting entries:

a. Credit sales during the year were $100,000; based on experience a 1 percent loss rate on credit sales has been established.

b. Insurance amounting to $100 expired during the year.

c. The store equipment is being depreciated over a ten-year estimated useful life with no residual value.

d. The long-term note payable for $30,000 was dated May 1, 1981, and carries a 12 percent interest rate per annum. The note is for three years and interest is payable at April 30 each year.

e. Assume an average tax rate of 30 percent.

f. Inventories:

Beginning inventory, January 1, 1981 (per above trial balance), $80,000.

Ending inventory, December 31, 1981 (per physical inventory count), $75,000.

Required:

a. Prepare a worksheet at December 31, 1981, similar to the one shown in the demonstration problem in the chapter. If you prefer, you may omit columns for Adjusted Trial Balance and Retained Earnings. In order to save time and space, all operating expenses have been summarized. However, you

should set up additional expense accounts for depreciation, bad debts, interest, and income tax. Also, you will need additional liability accounts for interest payable and income tax payable. (Hint: Net income is $37,940.)

b. Based upon the completed worksheet, prepare a multiple-step income statement and classified balance sheet.

c. Based upon the completed worksheet, prepare the adjusting and closing journal entries at December 31, 1981.

P6–15. (Related to Appendix A) Town's Department Store, Incorporated, is a large department store located in a midwestern city with a population of approximately 200,000 persons. The store carries top brands and attempts to appeal to "quality customers." Approximately 80 percent of the sales are on credit. As a consequence, there is a significant amount of detailed recordkeeping related to credit sales, returns, collections, and billings. Some years ago the accounts receivable records were maintained manually. A change was made to a mechanized system, and now the store is considering computerizing this phase of the accounting information system. Included in the general ledger is a control account for Accounts Receivable. Supporting the control account is an accounts receivable subsidiary ledger which has individual accounts for more than 20,000 customers. For case purposes, a few accounts and transactions with simplified amounts have been selected. The case requirement is intended to indicate the nature of the data processing work that is to be computerized; however, here it will be completed manually.

On January 1, 1981, the Accounts Receivable control account (No. 52), in the general ledger, reflected a debit balance of $4,000 and the subsidiary ledger reflected the following balances:

52.1	Akins, A. K.	$400
52.2	Blue, V. R.	700
52.3	Daley, U. T.	900
52.4	Evans, T. V.	300
52.5	May, O. W.	800
52.6	Nash, G. A.	100
52.7	Roth, I. W.	600
52.8	Winn, W. W.	200

During the month of January, the following transactions and events relating to sales activities occurred (use notation at left for date):

a. Sales of merchandise on credit:

Akins, A. K.	$300
Blue, V. R.	250
Winn, W. W.	730
May, O. W.	140
Daley, U. T.	70
Roth, I. W.	370
Evans, T. V.	410

b. Unsatisfactory merchandise returned:

Roth, I. W.	$ 30
Winn, W. W.	70
Akins, A. K.	20

c. Collections on accounts receivable:

Winn, W. W.	$800
May, O. W.	940
Akins, A. K.	200
Roth, I. W.	700
Blue, V. R.	750
Daley, U. T.	600

d. The account with G. A. Nash has been inactive for several years. After an investigation, the management decided that it was uncollectible; therefore, it is to be written off immediately.

e. The bad debt losses are based on credit sales; the estimated loss rate is 2 percent of net credit sales (i.e., on credit sales less returns for credit).

Required:

a. Set up the general ledger control account for Accounts Receivable. Also, set up the general ledger account for Allowance for Doubtful Accounts (No. 53) with a credit balance of $600. Indicate the beginning balance as "Bal." and for convenience use T-accounts.

b. Set up an accounts receivable subsidiary ledger in good form; use three columns—Debit, Credit, and Balance. Enter the beginning balances with the notation "Bal."

c. Prepare journal entries for each of the above transactions. Include a folio number for posting to both the control account and the subsidiary ledger. Assume periodic inventory.

d. Post the entries prepared in (c) to the Accounts Receivable control account. Allowance for Doubtful Accounts, and the subsidiary ledger. Use folio numbers.

e. Prepare a schedule of accounts receivable to show how much each customer owed at the end of January.

f. Show how accounts receivable and the related allowance would be reported in the January balance sheet.

7

Costing methods for measuring inventory and cost of goods sold

PURPOSE OF THE CHAPTER

To measure the amount of inventory at a given date, whether a perpetual or periodic inventory system is used, the following basic questions must be considered:

1. What items should be included in the inventory and in cost of goods sold?
2. What cost should be assigned to those items included in the inventory and in cost of goods sold?

This chapter discusses the generally accepted accounting answers to these two questions and their implementation in an information processing system.[1] The discussions and illustrations will be presented in two parts as follows:

Part A: Measuring the dollar amounts of the ending inventory and cost of goods sold with a periodic inventory system

Part B: Application of a perpetual inventory system and selected inventory costing problems

Behavioral and learning objectives for this chapter are provided in the *Teachers Manual.*

---

[1] *Fundamentals of Management Accounting* discusses inventory measurement in a manufacturing business.

PART A: MEASURING THE DOLLAR AMOUNTS OF THE ENDING INVENTORY AND COST OF GOODS SOLD WITH A PERIODIC INVENTORY SYSTEM

INVENTORY EFFECTS ON THE MEASUREMENT OF INCOME

Inventory often is the largest single asset owned by a business. Its measurement directly affects the amount of income reported for the period. The amount of inventory, measured at the end of the accounting period, affects not only the income for that period but also the amount of income for the **following period**. This two-period effect is due to the fact that the ending inventory for one period is the beginning inventory for the next period. To illustrate these effects, assume that the 19A and 19B income statements for Company X reflected pretax incomes of $5,000 and $6,500, respectively, measured as follows:

	19A		19B	
Sales		$100,000		$110,000
Cost of goods sold:*				
Beginning inventory	$ -0-		$10,000	
Purchases	70,000		58,000	
Goods available for sale	70,000		68,000	
Ending inventory	10,000		-0-	
Cost of goods sold		60,000		68,000
Gross margin		40,000		42,000
Expenses		35,000		35,500
Pretax income		$ 5,000		$ 6,500

* See Chapter 6: BI + P − EI = CGS.

Observe that the ending inventory, as measured and reported at December 31, 19A, amounted to $10,000. This amount also is reported as the **beginning** inventory of 19B.

To illustrate inventory effects on pretax income, assume that there was an error in measuring the ending inventory at December 31, 19A, and that the correct amount was determined to be $11,000 (i.e., $1,000 more than shown above). The $1,000 error in the ending inventory could have been due to either one or a combination of the following factors:

1. In physically counting the inventory items, some items were left out incorrectly. They had a cost of $1,000.
2. Although the physical count of items was correct, in applying the **unit costs,** a higher purchase cost should have been used. This higher cost would have increased the amount of the inventory by $1,000.

We now will see how this $1,000 understatement of the 19A ending inventory affected the income amounts for each of the two years. The income statements may be restated to reflect the correct inventory amount as follows:

	19A		19B	
Sales		$100,000		$110,000
Cost of goods sold:				
Beginning inventory	$ -0-		$11,000	
Purchases	70,000		58,000	
Goods available for sale	70,000		69,000	
Ending inventory	11,000		-0-	
Cost of goods sold		59,000		69,000
Gross margin		41,000		41,000
Expenses		35,000		35,500
Pretax income		$ 6,000		$ 5,500

Observe that, in comparison with the preceding income statements, pretax income for 19A is greater by $1,000 and less by the same amount for 19B. Thus, a comparison of the two sets of income statements demonstrates the following generalizations:

1. **In the period of the change**   An increase in the amount of the ending inventory for a period increases pretax income for that period by the same amount. To the contrary, a decrease in the amount of inventory decreases pretax income for that period by the same amount.
2. **In the next period**   An increase in the amount of the ending inventory for a period decreases the pretax income of the *next period* by the same amount. To the contrary, a decrease in the amount of the ending inventory for a period increases pretax income of the *next period* by the same amount.

Observe that in any period there is a direct relationship between ending inventory and pretax income. Conversely, there is an inverse relationship between beginning inventory and pretax income.

The above illustration was presented to indicate the importance of careful measurement of inventory. Care must be exercised in (1) measuring the **quantity** of items that should be included in the inventory and (2) applying the dollar **unit cost** to the units included in the ending inventory.

WHAT ITEMS SHOULD BE INCLUDED IN INVENTORY

Inventory usually is represented by tangible personal property that is held for sale in the ordinary course of business or is to be consumed in the near future in producing goods or services for sale. Inventory is reported on the balance sheet as a current asset because it normally will be consumed or converted into cash within one year or within the next operating cycle of the business, whichever is the longer. It usually is listed below accounts receivable because it is less liquid (i.e., less readily convertible to cash).

The kinds of inventory normally held depend upon the characteristics of the business:[2]

Retail or wholesale business:

Merchandise inventory—goods (or merchandise) held for resale in the ordinary course of business. The goods usually are acquired through purchase as completely manufactured and ready for sale without further processing.

Manufacturing business:

Finished goods inventory—goods manufactured by the business, completed and ready for sale.

Work in process inventory—work (or goods) in the process of being fabricated or manufactured but not yet completed as finished goods. Work in process inventory, when completed, becomes finished goods inventory.

Raw materials inventory—items acquired by purchase, growth (such as food products), or extraction of natural resources for the purpose of processing into finished goods. Such items are accounted for as raw materials inventory until used. When used, they are included in the cost of manufacturing along with labor and factory overhead.

The discussions which follow focus on merchandise and finished goods inventories.

In measuring the **physical quantity** of goods in the inventory, a company should include all items to which it has **legal ownership,** regardless of their locations. In business transactions involving inventories and cost of goods sold, accounting focuses on the passage of legal ownership. When ownership passes, one party has made a sale and the other party has made a purchase. In a purchase/sale transaction, the basic guideline is that ownership to the goods passes at the *time intended by the parties* to the transaction. Generally, ownership passes when the goods are delivered by the seller to the buyer; however, there are situations in which this is not the case.

In some situations the intentions of the parties as to the time of passage of ownership are not clear. In such situations, all of the circumstances must be assessed and judgment applied as to when the buyer and seller intended ownership to pass. For example, goods may be sold on credit and the buyer may request the vendor to hold the goods pending shipping instructions. In this instance, ownership appears to have passed, irrespective of the delivery date. A similar question arises when a third party, usually a transportation company, has physical possession of the goods for a period of time. The issue is: Who owns goods during the period of transit? If the terms of the sale provide that the buyer must pay the

---

[2] Supplies on hand are reported as prepaid expenses.

transportation charges (known as FOB shipping point), then ownership generally is assumed to pass when the vendor delivers the goods to the transportation agent. In contrast, if the terms of the sale are FOB destination (i.e., the seller must pay the freight), ownership generally is assumed to pass when the goods are delivered to the buyer at destination.[3]

The passage-of-ownership guideline is a facet of the revenue principle previously discussed (Exhibit 2–6). The passage-of-ownership guideline has a legal basis and prevails in the accounting process with respect to both the sale and purchase of goods. In the absence of the passage-of-ownership guideline, the financial statements could be manipulated to overstate income by entering all **sales orders** received up through the last day of the period, regardless of the fact that ownership to the goods ordered may not have passed to the buyer. Conversely, purchases intentionally may not be recorded even though ownership to the goods has passed.

A company may have possession of goods that it does not own; these should be excluded from the inventory. The usual situation here is when goods are **on consignment** for sale on a commission basis. When goods are on consignment, the supplier (known as the consignor) legally retains ownership to the goods although they are in the physical possession of the party that will sell them (known as the consignee). The consignor, although the goods are not in his or her physical possession, should include them in the ending inventory. The consignee, although having possession of the goods, should exclude them from the ending inventory since ownership still resides with the consignor.

In summary, in identifying the goods to be included in the ending inventory at a specific date, ownership, rather than physical possession, is controlling. The inventory should include only, but all of, the goods to which the entity has legal ownership.

INVENTORY COST

In Chapter 6 we discussed the application of the cost principle to the purchase of goods for resale. Goods in inventory are costed in accordance with the *cost principle*. Its application to inventories has been stated authoritatively as follows:

> The primary basis of accounting for inventory is cost, which has been defined generally as the price paid or consideration given to acquire an asset. As applied to inventories, cost means, in principle, the sum of the applicable expenditures and charges directly or indirectly incurred in bringing an article to its existing condition and location.[4]

[3] FOB stands for "free on board"; it is used in business to indicate who is responsible for paying the transportation charges: FOB destination, seller pays the freight; FOB shipping point, buyer pays the freight.

[4] AICPA, *Accounting Research Bulletin No. 43* (New York, 1961), chap. 4, statement 3. Copyright (1961) by the American Institute of CPAs.

We also explained that in accordance with the cost principle, indirect expenditures related to the purchase of goods, such as freight, insurance, and storage, conceptually should be included in measuring the purchase cost of the goods acquired. When any of those goods remain in inventory, these elements should be included in measuring the inventory cost. However, since these incidental amounts frequently are not *material in amount* (see the materiality concept, Exhibit 2–6) when related to the total purchase cost, and since there often is no convenient method of apportioning such costs to each item of goods, they may not be assigned to the inventory cost. Thus, for practical reasons, some companies use the *net invoice price* when assigning a unit cost to goods included in the ending inventory.

Chapter 6 discussed the assignment of **dollar cost** to *(a)* the ending inventory and *(b)* cost of goods sold in situations in which there were no changes in unit purchase (or manufacturing) cost during the period (including the beginning inventory). This chapter expands those discussions to the typical situation in which the cost per unit of the goods stocked changes during the annual accounting period. To illustrate the typical situation, assume **one product** which is stocked by Summer's Retail Store reflected the beginning inventory, merchandise purchases, and sales data given in Exhibit 7–1.

EXHIBIT 7–1

SUMMER'S RETAIL STORE
Illustrative Data—Beginning Inventory, Purchases, and Sales

Transactions	Symbol	Number of units	Unit cost	Total cost	
Beginning inventory (carried over from last period)	BI	100	$6		$ 600
Purchases during the year:					
January 3, first purchase	P	50	7	$ 350	
June 12, second purchase	P	200	8	1,600	
December 20, third purchase	P	120	9	1,080	
Total purchases		370			3,030
Goods available for sale during the year		470			3,630
Sales during the year:					
January 6 (unit sales price, $10)	S	40			
June 18 (unit sales price, $12)	S	220			
December 24 (unit sales price, $14)	S	60			
Total sales		320			?
Ending inventory (units 470 − 320)	EI	150			?

Assuming 320 units of this item were sold during the year, the accounting problem that must be resolved before the financial statements can be prepared is: Of the $3,630 total cost, how much should be apportioned to cost of goods sold (i.e., for the 320 units sold) and how much should be apportioned to the ending inventory (i.e., 470 units − 320 units = 150 units). Alternatively, the answer to this problem necessarily involves assignment of the four unit cost amounts ($6, $7, $8, and $9), or some combination of them, to the ending inventory and to cost of goods sold. This part of the chapter discusses the alternative methods used for making this assignment of unit costs.

Also in Chapter 6, two different **inventory systems** were discussed. These two systems were presented as **alternative systems** used to accumulate data in the accounting information processing system to facilitate determination of *(a)* the ending inventory and *(b)* cost of goods sold. The **unit cost problem** cited immediately above must be recognized and resolved in applying each of the two different inventory systems. To review, the two alternative inventory systems are:[5]

1. **Periodic inventory system**—This system accumulates total merchandise acquisition cost, and at the **end of the accounting period,** the ending inventory is measured by means of a physical inventory count of all goods remaining on hand. The units counted on hand then are valued (costed) in dollars by using appropriate unit purchase cost amounts (for example, from above, some combination of $6, $7, $8, and $9). The periodic inventory system measures cost of goods sold as a residual amount; that is:

$$BI + P - EI = CGS$$

2. **Perpetual inventory system**—This system maintains a detailed daily inventory record throughout the period for each item stocked. This record includes *(a)* each purchase (including the beginning inventory), *(b)* each issue (i.e., sales), and *(c)* a continuous (perpetual or running) balance of the inventory. Thus, this system measures cost of goods sold and ending inventory without the necessity for a physical inventory count at the end of the accounting period. Under this system the ending inventory can be viewed as a residual amount; that is:

$$BI + P - CGS = EI$$

Conceptually, both systems will produce the same ending inventory and cost of goods sold amounts. Nevertheless, in practical application (procedural) they sometimes produce somewhat different dollar amounts (illustrated in Part B of this chapter).

The discussions which follow in this part of the chapter consider the several alternative inventory costing methods that generally are used. They also assume that the **periodic inventory system** is used. Part B of the chapter discusses these methods with a perpetual inventory system. The four generally accepted **inventory costing methods** commonly used are:

[5] Often a single company will use one of the systems for certain items stocked, and the other system for the remaining items. The choice usually depends upon such factors as the nature of the item (size), unit cost, the number stocked, and cost to implement the system.

1. Weighted average.
2. First-in, first-out *(Fifo).*
3. Last-in, first-out *(Lifo).*
4. Specific identification.

In the discussions to follow we must remember constantly that the central objective is not solely to measure the amount of goods on hand in order to obtain the balance sheet amount, but it also is to measure cost of goods sold, which is an important expense on the income statement in the measurement of income.

APPLICATION OF THE INVENTORY COSTING METHODS (WITH PERIODIC INVENTORY SYSTEM)

In reiteration, the four inventory costing methods listed above are **alternative** allocation methods for apportioning the total amount of goods available for sale (BI + P) between *(a)* ending inventory (reported as an asset at the end of the period) and *(b)* cost of goods sold (reported as an expense for the period). For illustration, refer to the data for Summer's Retail Store given in Exhibit 7–1. The allocated amounts, using the weighted average inventory costing method (explained below), are as follows:

	Units	Amount
Goods available for sale (total amount to be apportioned)	470	$3,630
Cost allocation:		
Ending inventory (determined by inventory count and then costed at weighted average unit cost)	150	1,158
Cost of goods sold (residual amount)	320	$2,472

Observe that goods available for sale ($3,630) was allocated between ending inventory ($1,150) and cost of goods sold ($1,158), and that the sum of these two amounts (and the related units as well) necessarily must be the same as goods available for sale. The cost allocation procedure also is protrayed graphically in Exhibit 7–2.

The total amount to be allocated (goods available for sale) is provided directly by the accounting records under **either** the periodic inventory system or the perpetual inventory system. Recall that the **periodic inventory system** requires computation of the ending inventory by means of a physical count of the goods remaining on hand (which then are costed in dollars by applying one of the inventory costing methods) and cost of goods sold is computed as a residual amount as illustrated above (also see page 276). In contrast, the perpetual inventory system (discussed in Part B of this chapter) views the ending inventory as the residual amount.

EXHIBIT 7–2

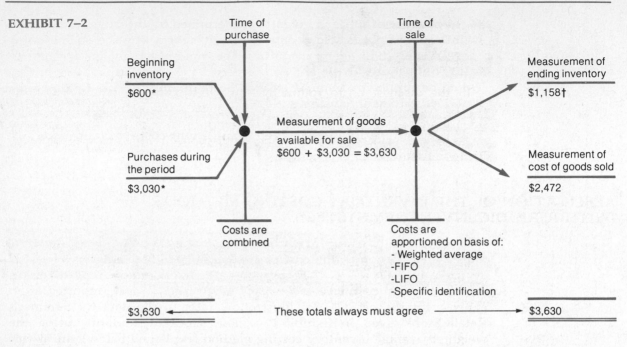

* Data from Exhibit 7–1.
† Based on the weighted average cost method.

Each of the four inventory costing methods listed above will be discussed and illustrated using the data for Summer's Retail Store given in Exhibit 7–1.

Inventory costing methods   A choice among the inventory costing methods is necessary only when there are different unit costs in the beginning inventory and/or purchases during the current period. These are **cost allocation** methods and do not necessarily relate to the physical flow of goods on and off the shelves. Although the actual *physical flow* of goods usually is first-in, first-out, a company can use any of the four inventory costing methods. Generally accepted accounting principles only require that the inventory costing method used be "rational and systematic."

A company is not required to use the same inventory costing method for all inventory items. Therefore, it is not unusual for a company to use several of the methods for different inventory items. No particular justification is required for selection of one or more of the acceptable methods. However, a **change in method** is viewed as significant and requires special disclosures as in footnotes to the financial statements.

Weighted average inventory costing method. This method requires computation of the weighted average unit cost of the goods available for sale. In a periodic inventory system, the unit cost computed is applied to the **number of units** in inventory determined by the physical inventory count. Cost of goods sold is determined by subtracting the ending inventory amount thus determined from the amount of goods available for sale. To illustrate, at the end of the period the weighted average method would be applied by Summer's Retail Store (Exhibit 7–1) as follows under a periodic inventory system.[6]

Step 1—To compute the weighted average unit cost for the period:

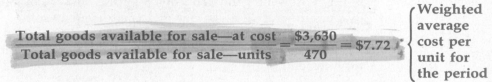

$$\frac{\text{Total goods available for sale—at cost}}{\text{Total goods available for sale—units}} = \frac{\$3,630}{470} = \$7.72 \left\{ \begin{array}{l} \text{Weighted} \\ \text{average} \\ \text{cost per} \\ \text{unit for} \\ \text{the period} \end{array} \right.$$

Step 2—Allocation of the cost of goods available for sale:

	Units	Amount
Goods available for sale (Exhibit 7–1)	470	$3,630
Ending inventory (150 units × $7.72)	150	1,158*
Cost of goods sold (residual amount)	320	$2,472†

* Reported on the balance sheet.

† Reported as expense on the income statement. This amount can be verified as 320 units × $7.72 = $2,470 (a $2 rounding error).

The weighted average cost method is used often since it is rational, systematic, easy to apply, and not subject to manipulation. It weights the number of units purchased and unit costs during the period (including the beginning inventory). Thus, it is representative of costs during the entire period (including the beginning inventory) rather than of the cost only at the beginning, end, or at one point during the period.[7] Representative costs are reported on both the balance sheet (ending inventory) and the income statement (cost of goods sold).

First-in, first-out inventory costing method. This method, frequently referred to as *Fifo,* assumes that the oldest units (i.e., the first costs in) are the first units sold (i.e., the first costs out). In other words, the units in the beginning inventory are treated as if they were sold first, the units

---

[6] When an average cost is used, uneven unit cost amounts usually are rounded to the nearest cent. The rounded unit cost amount is used to compute the ending inventory amount which allocates any rounding error to cost of goods sold. Under the perpetual inventory system, a moving average unit cost (rather than the weighted average unit cost) usually is used (see Part B).

[7] A weighted average unit cost rather than a simple average of the unit costs must be used. For example, ($6 + $7 + $8 + 9) ÷ 4 = $7.50 would be incorrect because it does not consider the number of units at each unit cost.

from the first purchase sold next, and so on until the units left in the ending inventory all come from the most recent purchases. It follows that the oldest unit costs are apportioned to cost of goods sold and the latest unit costs apply to the ending inventory.

Frequently, *Fifo* is justified on the basis that it is consistent with the actual physical flow of the goods. It is said that the first goods placed in stock tend to be the first goods sold. However, the method is applied regardless of the actual physical inflow and outflow of goods because it is not a flow of goods concept but is a **cost allocation** procedure used to measure ending inventory and cost of goods sold.

To illustrate, at the end of the period the *Fifo* method would be applied by Summer's Retail Store (Exhibit 7–1) as follows under a periodic inventory system:

	Units	Unit cost	Total cost
Goods available for sale (Exhibit 7–1)	470		$3,630
Valuation of ending inventory *(Fifo):*			
At latest unit costs, 150 units:			
From December 20 purchase (latest)	120	$9	$1,080
From June 12 purchase (next latest)	30	8	240
Valuation, *Fifo* basis	150		1,320*
Cost of goods sold (residual *Fifo* amount) ...	320		$2,310†

* Report on balance sheet.

† Report as expense on income statement. This amount can be verified as follows: Units sold at oldest costs—100 units @ $6 = $600, plus 50 units @ $7 = $350, plus 170 units @ $8 = $1,360, which sum to $2,310.

The *Fifo* method is used widely since it is rational, systematic, easy to apply, and not subject to manipulation. On the balance sheet, under *Fifo*, the ending inventory amount is at the most **recent unit costs** and, therefore, it is likely to be a realistic valuation prevailing at the balance sheet date. In contrast, on the income statement, cost of goods sold is at the oldest unit costs, which may be an unrealistic valuation. The significance of the impact of *Fifo* on the income statement (i.e., cost of goods sold and income) and the balance sheet (i.e., the inventory amount under current assets) depends on the extent to which unit costs increase or decrease during the period. Comparative effects are illustrated later.

Last-in, first-out inventory costing method. This method, frequently referred to as **Lifo,** assumes that the most recently acquired goods are sold first. Regardless of the physical flow of goods, *Lifo* treats the **costs** of the most recent units acquired as cost of goods sold. This leaves the unit costs of the beginning inventory and the earliest purchases in the ending inventory. Thus, the *Lifo* method attains results that are inverse to *Fifo*. That is, under *Lifo*, the total ending inventory cost is measured at the oldest unit costs and cost of goods sold is measured at the newest unit costs.

To illustrate, at the end of the period the *Lifo* method would be applied by Summer's Retail Store (Exhibit 7–1) as follows under a periodic inventory system:

	Units	Unit cost	Total cost
Goods available for sale (Exhibit 7–1)	470		$3,630
Valuation of ending inventory *(Lifo):*			
At earliest unit costs, 150 units:			
From beginning inventory (oldest)	100	$6	$600
From January 3 purchase (next oldest)	50	7	350
Valuation, *Lifo* basis	150		950*
Cost of goods sold (residual *Lifo* amount)	320		$2,680†

* Report on balance sheet.

† Report as expense on income statement. This amount can be verified as follows: Units sold at latest costs—120 units @ $9 = $1,080, plus 200 units @ $8 = $1,600, which sums to $2,680.

The *Lifo* method is acceptable since it is deemed rational and systematic. However, it is amenable to manipulation by buying, or not buying, goods at the end of a period when unit costs have changed, which makes it possible to affect cost of goods sold and, hence, reported income. On the income statement under *Lifo*, cost of goods sold is based on the latest unit costs, which is a realistic valuation. In contrast, on the balance sheet the ending inventory amount is based on the earliest unit costs which may be an unrealistic valuation. The comparative impact of *Lifo* will be discussed later.[8]

Specific identification inventory costing method. Another way of allocating the cost of goods available for sale to cost of goods sold and the ending inventory is to keep track of the units of the beginning inventory and each separate purchase—that is, specific identification of the purchase cost of each item. This is done simply either by coding the purchase cost on each unit before placing it in stock or by keeping a separate record of the unit and identifying it with a serial number. When a sale is made, the cost of that specific unit is identified and recorded by means of an item-by-item choice. For example, using the data given in Exhibit 7–1, if the 40 units sold on January 6 were selected specifically as, say, units that were purchased at $6 each (i.e., from the beginning inventory), the

---

[8] This discussion and the illustration of *Lifo* assume an item-by-item application of the method and costing of goods sold currently throughout the period. For income tax purposes *Lifo* costing must be done at the end of the taxable year. Although the concepts are the same, many companies use an application known as dollar-value *Lifo*, and the costing is at the end of the year. These complexities are beyond the scope of this book. See Welsch, Zlatkovich, and Harrison, *Intermediate Accounting*, 5th ed. (Homewood, Ill.: Richard D. Irwin, Inc., 1979). © 1979 by Richard D. Irwin, Inc.

cost of goods sold amount for that particular sale would be measured as 40 units × $6 = $240. Alternatively, if 20 of the units were selected from those that cost $6 each (from the beginning inventory) and the other 20 from those that cost $7 each (from the January 3 purchase), cost of goods sold would be measured as (20 units × $6) + (20 units × $7) = $260.

The specific identification method would be rather tedious and impractical where (1) unit costs are low, (2) unit costs change frequently, or (3) a large number of different items are stocked. On the other hand, where there are "big-ticket" items such as automobiles and expensive jewelry, it is especially appropriate since each item tends to be different from the other items. In such situations, it is rational because the *selling price* generally is based on a markup over specific cost. However, the method may be unsystematic when the units are identical because one can manipulate the cost of goods sold and the ending inventory amounts simply by "picking and choosing" from among the several available unit costs, even though the goods are identical in every other respect. To illustrate, in the above example, cost of goods sold was either $240 or $260, depending on the choices made. In that example, assuming identical items, income would be different by $20, depending on an arbitrary "identification."

Comparison of the inventory costing methods

Four alternative inventory costing methods were explained and illustrated in the preceding paragraphs. Each method is in accordance with generally accepted accounting principles, although each may produce significantly different income and asset (i.e., ending inventory) amounts.

To illustrate, the comparative results for Summer's Retail Store are as follows:

	Sales revenue	Cost of goods sold	Gross margin	Balance sheet (inventory)
Weighted average	$3,880	$2,472	$1,408	$1,158
Fifo..............................	3,880	2,310	1,570	1,320
Lifo (end of period)	3,880	2,680	1,200	950

A comparison of the results shown above for three of the **methods** will increase our understanding of their characteristics. First, we can perceive readily that in the case of a stable unit cost, all methods would provide the same income and the same inventory amounts. Second, in the case of **changing unit costs**, each method tends to give different income and different inventory amounts. On this point, observe that the difference in *pretax income* among each of the methods is the same as the difference in the inventory amounts. The method that provides the highest ending inventory amount also provides the highest income amount and vice versa. Third, the weighted average cost method tends to give income and inventory amounts that fall between the *Fifo* and *Lifo* extremes.

We will focus now on a comparison of the *Fifo* and *Lifo* methods since they usually represent the extreme, and opposite, effects. Note in the comparison above that unit costs were *increasing* and that *Lifo* provided the lower income and inventory amounts, whereas *Fifo* provided the higher income and inventory amounts. In comparing the effects of *Fifo* and *Lifo*, it is important to note that the comparative effects will depend upon the direction of change in unit cost. *When unit costs are rising, Lifo will result in lower income and a lower inventory valuation than will Fifo. Conversely, when unit costs are declining, Lifo will result in higher income and higher inventory valuation than will Fifo.* These effects occur because when **prices are rising Lifo** will cause the **higher (new)** unit costs to be reflected on the income statement whereas *Fifo* will cause the **lower (old)** unit costs to be reflected on the income statement, and the converse when prices are falling.

INCOME TAX EFFECTS

Let's turn our attention to the income tax effects for the moment. The effect of different inventory costing methods on income taxes to be paid in particular years often is significant. Of course, over the long term only the actual cost incurred for goods for resale is deductible as an expense for tax purposes. We have seen that income is allocated among periods in a different way by the several inventory costing methods. Thus, when prices are rising, **Lifo** often is used for income tax purposes since an early tax deduction is to be preferred to a later tax deduction. Due to the time value of money, the shifting of tax liability to later years becomes important.

Since all four methods are acceptable for income tax purposes, why have some businesses opted for **Lifo** in recent years? Clearly, the reason is that it tends to minimize early income tax payments. Prices have been rising; and with rising prices, *Lifo* charges higher costs to cost of goods sold. This in turn reduces income so the income tax bill is lower. Of course, the inventory effect suggests that should prices decline at some future date, those businesses may want to change from *Lifo* to *Fifo* to minimize income taxes on the downward trend of prices. It is difficult to obtain permission from the Internal Revenue Service to change the inventory costing method (except when the change is to *Fifo*).

To illustrate the income tax effects, assume the following for X Corporation for the year 19XX (when prices rose rapidly):

Fact situation

a. Sales revenue	$900,000
b. Cost of goods sold:	
Fifo basis	400,000
Lifo basis	600,000
c. Remaining expenses (excluding income taxes)	250,000
d. Average income tax rate	30%

Effect on income tax expense

	Inventory costing method	
	Fifo	Lifo
Revenue	$900,000	$900,000
Cost of goods sold	400,000	600,000
Gross margin	500,000	300,000
Less: Expenses (except income taxes)	250,000	250,000
Pretax income	250,000	50,000
Income tax expense (30% rate)	75,000	15,000
Net income	$175,000	$ 35,000
EPS (100,000 shares common stock outstanding)	$1.75	$0.35

Reduction in income tax expense. ($75,000 — $15,000) = $60,000.
Cash saved ($75,000 — $15,000) = $60,000.

In this situation, ending inventory, cost of goods sold, and pretax income all were different by $200,000 which was caused by the divergence between the *Fifo* and *Lifo* methods. Obviously, there was a significant difference between the "old" and "new" unit costs, and prices were rising. This difference, when multiplied by the 30 percent income tax rate, indicates a cash saving of $60,000 in 19XX—not an insignificant amount. The internal revenue code allows use of *Lifo;* however, if it is used on the income tax return it also must be used on the financial reports. It is well to keep in mind that this is not a permanent tax saving because (a) when inventory levels drop or (b) prices drop, the effect reverses and the income taxes deferred will have to be paid. The only advantage of deferring income taxes in such situations is due to the time value of money (i.e., interest).

WHICH METHOD OF INVENTORY COSTING IS THE BEST

No one method of inventory costing can be considered as the "best." It would be impractical to assume that the tax consequences are not important in the choice of method. Many observers believe that businesses, in setting selling prices, often do so within a *"Lifo* assumption" since the goods sold must be replaced on the shelf at the latest cost rather than at earlier cost.

Many accountants believe that the best inventory costing method is the one that best matches the sales pricing policy of the company. Companies do price units for sale in each of the ways implied by these four costing methods. These accountants believe that the only conceptually sound basis for selecting the best costing method for a particular company depends upon the sales pricing policy followed. Other accountants believe that the choice should be based upon whether the measurement emphasis should be on the income statement or on the balance sheet. Those who believe that the income statement should be accorded primary emphasis tend to defend *Lifo* since it matches the most recent purchase cost with current sales revenue. To the contrary, those who prefer to emphasize the balance sheet tend to prefer *Fifo* since it reports the inventory (an asset) at the most current cost price. Also, there is a problem when one is comparing companies in the same industry which use different methods. Because of these considerations, it is not difficult to understand why the accounting profession, and the income tax laws, have accepted several alternative inventory costing methods.

PART B: APPLICATION OF A PERPETUAL INVENTORY SYSTEM AND SELECTED INVENTORY COSTING PROBLEMS

Recall that in Chapter 6, Part B, the periodic and perpetual inventory systems were discussed and illustrated. Also, in Part A of this chapter (pages 276 and 277), these two inventory systems were discussed again. Regardless of which of the two alternative inventory systems is used, one or more of the inventory costing methods (discussed in Part A) must be applied. The discussions and illustrations in Part A of this chapter assumed a periodic inventory system (i.e., in this system the units in the ending inventory each period are determined by a physical inventory count, and then the units found to be on hand are valued in dollars by applying the inventory costing methods).

This part of the chapter discusses and illustrates **application of each of the inventory costing methods with a perpetual inventory system.** Separate discussion of the two systems is essential because:

a. Although, from a conceptual view, application of the several inventory costing methods is the same, the **timing** of the application of the inventory costing methods between the two systems causes somewhat different valuation amounts. The periodic inventory system **costs** inventory units at the end of the period, whereas the perpetual inventory system costs units on a day-to-day basis.
b. The accounting entries vary between the two systems.
c. The inventory controls possible are quite different as between the two systems.
d. The availability of computers of various capabilities has encouraged a high percent of large, medium, and even small businesses to use perpetual inventory systems for numerous items in their inventories.

APPLICATION OF THE INVENTORY COSTING METHODS WITH A PERPETUAL INVENTORY SYSTEM

Recall that a perpetual inventory system requires the maintenance of a detailed **perpetual inventory record** for each kind of goods or merchandise stocked and sold. This record is designed to show **units and dollar**

amounts, at all times, for *(a)* goods received (purchases), *(b)* goods sold (issues), and *(c)* balance of goods on hand (inventory), on a continuing day-to-day basis. Each purchase and each sale transaction is entered in the perpetual inventory record when it occurs. The perpetual inventory record may be maintained manually, mechanically, or by means of the electronic computer. The perpetual inventory record is designed so that cost of goods sold and the inventory are measured on a perpetual or continuous basis.

In the discussions to follow, a **perpetual inventory record** will be illustrated for each of the four inventory costing methods. To illustrate each application, we will use the data for Summer's Retail Store given in Exhibit 7–1. We also will use a manual system for instructional purposes. The beginning inventory of 100 units at a unit cost of $6 would have been carried over in the records from the prior period. Recall from Chapter 6 that each purchase would be recorded as follows and, at the same time, entered on the perpetual inventory record (see Exhibit 7–4):

Jan. 3	Inventory (50 units @ $7)	350
	Cash (or accounts payable)	350

Also recall that a sale generates *two* companion entries when a perpetual inventory system is used:

Jan. 6	Cash	400
	Sales revenue (40 units @ $10)	400
	Cost of goods sold (*Fifo* basis)	240
	Inventory (40 units @ $6)	240

Weighted average inventory costing method applied. When the weighted average cost method is applied with a perpetual inventory system, a **weighted moving average** unit cost usually is used. A weighted moving average is used because the cost of goods sold amount is measured and recorded at the **time of each sale.** Instead, if one were to apply the concept of an *annual* weighted average, the recording of costs of goods sold would be delayed until year-end at which time an annual average can be computed.

In applying a weighted moving average, a *new* average unit cost is computed during the period at the time of *each purchase.* Cost of goods sold and the remaining inventory are measured at the then prevailing moving average unit cost. An illustration of the perpetual inventory record on a weighted moving average basis for the data given in Exhibit 7–1 is shown in Exhibit 7–3. The weighted moving average was recomputed three times

EXHIBIT 7–3
Weighted moving average method—perpetual inventory system

PERPETUAL INVENTORY RECORD

Item _____ Item A _____   Cost Basis _____ Moving average _____
Location _____ 320 _____   Minimum Level _____
Code _____ 13 _____   Maximum Level _____

Date	Received (purchases)			Issued (sales)			Inventory Balance		
	Units	Unit Cost	Total Cost	Units	Unit Cost	Total Cost	Units	Unit Cost	Total Cost
1/1 Bal.							100	6.00	600
1/3	50	7.00	350				150	6.33*	950
1/6				40	6.33	253	110	6.33	697
6/12	200	8.00	1,600				310	7.41*	2,297
6/18				220	7.41	1,630	90	7.41	667
12/20	120	9.00	1,080				210	8.32*	1,747
12/24				60	8.32	499	150	8.32	1,248
Total cost of goods sold						2,382			
Total ending inventory									1,248

* New average computed.

during the period since there were three purchases. Units sold are removed from the inventory record at the then average unit cost. For example, the moving average was computed on the date of the first purchase as follows:

	Units	Cost
Beginning inventory	100	$600
Purchase, January 3	50	350
Totals	150	$950

Moving average unit cost: $950 ÷ 150 units = $6.33 per unit.

The companion entries for the sale on January 6 would reflect sales revenue of $400 and cost of goods sold of $253 (from the inventory record) as follows:

Jan. 6 Cash	400	
Sales revenue (40 units @ $10)		400
Cost of goods sold (moving average basis)	253	
Inventory		253
From Exhibit 7–3.		

Comparison of the resulting dollar valuations between the periodic inventory system (weighted annual average) and the perpetual inventory system (weighted moving average) reveals:

a. The perpetual system requires more clerical effort than the periodic system.
b. The periodic system requires a year-end physical inventory whereas the perpetual system does not.
c. The ending inventory and cost of goods sold amounts usually will be **different**, viz:

	Perpetual inventory system (weighted moving averate)	Periodic inventory system (annual weighted average)
Source	Exhibit 7–3	Page 279
Ending inventory	$1,248	$1,158
Cost of goods sold	2,383	2,472
Total goods available	$3,630	$3,630

It appears that both inventory systems are used widely when the weighted average inventory cost method is applied.

Fifo inventory costing method applied. When the *Fifo* method is applied with a perpetual inventory system, after each issue the remaining quantities on hand must be identified separately on the perpetual inventory record for *each unit cost.* These groups frequently are referred to as "inventory cost layers." The identification of inventory cost layers is necessary because goods are removed from the perpetual inventory record in *Fifo* order; that is, the oldest unit cost is taken off first. An illustration of the perpetual inventory record on a *Fifo* basis is shown in Exhibit 7–4. Each purchase and each sale of goods is entered in the record at the time of occurrence. At each time, the balance column on the perpetual inventory record is restated to show the units and amount on hand for each different unit cost. At the same time, each transaction would be recorded in the accounts. For example, the companion entries to record the sale of June 18 are:

June 18	Cash	2,640	
	Sales revenue (220 units @ $12)		2,640
	Cost of goods sold (*Fifo* basis)	1,590	
	Inventory		1,590
	From Exhibit 7–4, $360 + $350 + 880 = $1,590.		

Comparison of the application of the *Fifo* inventory costing method between the perpetual and periodic inventory systems reveals that (a) the perpetual system requires more clerical effort, (b) the periodic system requires an ending inventory count of units, and (c) that under *Fifo* they

EXHIBIT 7–4
Fifo method—
perpetual
inventory system

PERPETUAL INVENTORY RECORD
(heading—same as in Exhibit 7–3, except cost basis—*Fifo*)

Date	Received (purchases)			Issued (sales)			Inventory Balance		
	Units	Unit Cost	Total Cost	Units	Unit Cost	Total Cost	Units	Unit Cost	Total Cost
1/1 Bal.							100	6	600
1/3	50	7	350				100	6	600
							50	7	350
1/6				40	6	240	60	6	360
							50	7	350
6/12	200	8	1,600				60	6	360
							50	7	350
							200	8	1,600
6/18				60	6	360			
				50	7	350			
				110	8	880	90	8	720
12/20	120	9	1,080				90	8	720
							120	9	1,080
1/24				60	8	480	30	8	240
							120	9	1,080
Total cost of goods sold						2,310			
Total ending inventory									1,320

always produce the same ending inventory and cost of goods sold results. In contrast to the average cost method, *Fifo* produces the same results under either system because the **timing** of the costing (whether during the period or only at the end of the period) does not affect the unit costs allocated to each issue (sale). To illustrate, for Summer's Retail Store the perpetual inventory record (Exhibit 7–4) reflects ending inventory of $1,320 and cost of goods sold of $2,310, which are the same valuations shown under the periodic inventory system portrayed on page 280.

Lifo inventory costing method applied. When the *Lifo* method is applied with a perpetual inventory system, the inventory cost layers must be identified separately on the perpetual inventory record, as was the case with *Fifo*. This identification is necessary so that the *unit costs* for the number of units for **each sale** can be removed at that time from the inventory record in the **inverse order** that they came in; that is, the newest unit costs are removed from the perpetual inventory record on a **current basis** at the time of each issue (sale). This means that the **timing of costing is during the period rather than at the end of the period.** To illustrate, the perpetual inventory record on a *Lifo* basis is shown in Exhibit 7–5.

EXHIBIT 7–5
Lifo method
costed currently—
perpetual
inventory system

PERPETUAL INVENTORY RECORD
(heading—same as in Exhibit 7–3, except cost basis—*Lifo*)

Date	Received (purchases)			Issued (sales)			Inventory Balance		
	Units	Unit Cost	Total Cost	Units	Unit Cost	Total Cost	Units	Unit Cost	Total Cost
1/1 Bal.							100	6	600
1/3	50	7	350				100	6	600
							50	7	350
1/6				40	7	280	100	6	600
							10	7	70
6/12	200	8	1,600				100	6	600
							10	7	70
							200	8	1,600
6/18				200	8	1,600			
				10	7	70			
				10	6	60	90	6	540
12/20	120	9	1,080				90	6	540
							120	9	1,080
12/24				60	9	540	90	6	540
							60	9	540
Total cost of goods sold						2,550			
Ending inventory									1,080

Comparison of application of the *Lifo* inventory costing method between the perpetual and periodic inventory systems reveals that the ending inventory amounts and the cost of goods sold amounts each are different, viz:

	Perpetual inventory system (current costing)	Periodic inventory system (end-of-period costing)
Source	Exhibit 7–5	Page 281
Ending inventory	$1,080	$ 950
Cost of goods sold	2,550	2,680
Total goods available	$3,630	$3,630

The *Lifo* results are different between the perpetual and periodic systems because of the different time at which each issue (sale) is costed. For example, when costed currently (as is done under the perpetual system), the *Lifo* method required that the sale of the 40 units on January 6 be measured, recorded in the accounts, and removed from the perpetual inventory card (at that date) at the latest purchase price, which was $7 per unit. This is because the perpetual inventory system does not wait until the end of the year to cost issues (sales). In contrast, under the periodic inventory system, since all costing is deferred to year-end, the above sale would be costed at $9 per unit (i.e., out of purchases that occurred **after** the sale).[9]

Specific identification inventory costing method applied. When this method is applied with a perpetual inventory system, the item-by-item choice (for entry in the perpetual inventory record and in the accounts) should be made at the time of sale rather than later (which is probable under the periodic inventory system). Therefore, the valuation results between the two inventory systems for ending inventory and cost of goods sold could be different in dollar amounts. Application of the specific identification costing method in a perpetual inventory system is accomplished in a manner similar to the preceding illustrations.

To summarize, the four **inventory costing methods** (weighted average, *Fifo*, *Lifo*, and specific identification) are alternative methods of measuring the valuation of ending inventory and cost of goods sold. Each method assumes a different **flow of unit costs** during the accounting period; therefore, each method tends to produce different results. The periodic and perpetual inventory systems are two different accounting approaches for applying the inventory costing methods to measure cost of goods sold and ending inventory. The periodic inventory system assumes **cost allocation at the end of the accounting period** (using one of the four inventory costing methods), while the perpetual inventory system assumes **cost allocation currently during the accounting period.** Because of these two different timing assumptions the two systems tend to give different valuations of ending inventory and cost of goods sold under the weighted average, *Lifo*, and specific identification costing methods, but always the same under *Fifo*.

SELECTED INVENTORY COSTING PROBLEMS

The remaining discussions in this chapter relate to four issues which may directly affect the valuation of the inventory reported on the balance sheet and reported net income on the income statement; they are *(a)* lower of cost or market (LCM) valuation, *(b)* net realizable value, *(c)* estimating the ending inventory, and *(d)* consistency in accounting.

Inventories at lower of cost or market (LCM)

We have emphasized that inventories should be measured at their unit purchase cost in accordance with the **cost principle.** However, when the **new** goods remaining in the ending inventory can be replaced new at a

---

[9] It sometimes is asserted that even under the perpetual inventory system costing of issues (sales) can be deferred to year-end. Of course, under this assumption the perpetual and periodic systems always would produce the same results; however, it would defeat totally one objective of the perpetual inventory system—recording cost of goods sold (issues) on a current basis.

lower cost at inventory date, that lower unit cost should be used as the inventory valuation. This is known as measuring inventories on a **lower of cost or market (LCM) basis.** It is a departure from the cost principle in favor of the **exception principle**—conservatism (see Exhibit 2–6). It serves to recognize a "holding" loss in the period in which the replacement cost dropped, rather than in the period in which the goods actually are sold. The **holding loss** is the difference between purchase cost and the subsequent lower replacement cost. To illustrate, assume that an office equipment dealer has ten new electronic calculators remaining in the ending inventory. The calculators were purchased for $450 each about a year earlier and were marked to sell at $499.95. At the date of the ending inventory, however, the same new calculators can be purchased for $400 and will be marked to sell for $429.95. Under the LCM basis the ten calculators should be costed in the ending inventory at $400 each. In this context, market is defined as the **current market replacement cost** of the new item in the quantities usually purchased.

Let's look carefully at the effect of using a replacement cost of $400 against using the original purchase cost of $450 for the ten computers included in the ending inventory. By costing them at $50 per unit below their purchase cost, pretax income will be $500 (i.e., 10 × $50), less than it would have been had they been costed in the inventory at $450 per unit. This $500 loss in **economic utility** of the inventory (i.e., the holding loss) was due to a decline in the replacement cost. Because it is included in the cost of goods sold, pretax income will be reduced by $500 in the period in which the replacement cost dropped, rather than in the later period when the goods actually are sold. Thus, the holding loss is matched with the revenues generated in the accounting period in which the drop in economic utility occurred. These effects are demonstrated in Exhibit 7–6. LCM usually is applied to all inventories of new goods except those measured on a net realizable value basis.[10] The LCM rule usually is applied to merchandise inventory on an item-by-item basis rather than on the aggregate inventory as a whole.

Inventories at net realizable value

Merchandise on hand that is damaged, obsolete, or shopworn should not be measured and reported at original cost but at present **net realizable value when it is below cost.** Net realizable value is used, rather than replacement cost, because the replacement cost **new** would be inappropriate. Net realizable value is the *estimated amount* to be realized when the goods actually are sold in their deteriorated condition, less disposal costs.[11]

---

[10] In contrast, if the replacement cost had increased to, say, $500 each, there would have been a *holding gain* of 100 units × $50 = $500. Generally accepted accounting principles do not permit recognition of holding gains since revenue is recognized only at date of sale of the goods. Because of the unfavorable connotations, holding gains are called "windfall profits" in the political arena.

[11] Net realizable value is used to apply the LCM concept to merchandise which is either not new or not in its original condition. The difference in application occurs because

EXHIBIT 7–6
Effect of inventory measurement at LCM

| | Inventory measured at— | |
	Cost (Fifo)	LCM
Sales	$41,500	$41,500
Cost of goods sold:		
Beginning inventory	$ 5,000	$ 5,000
Add purchases	20,000	20,000
Goods available for sale	25,000	25,000
Less ending inventory		
(ten computers):		
At purchase cost of $450	4,500	
At LCM of $400		4,000
Cost of goods sold	20,500	21,000
Gross margin on sales	21,000	20,500
Expenses	15,000	15,000
Pretax income	$ 6,000	$ 5,500

For example, assume a company selling television sets has on hand two sets that have been used as demonstrators and cannot be sold as new sets (i.e., they are shopworn). When purchased, the sets cost $300 each. In the light of their present condition, realistic estimates are:

	Per set
Sales value in present condition	$175
Estimated selling costs	35
Estimated net realizable value	$140

On the basis of these estimates, the two television sets would be included in the inventory at $140 each, or a total of $280, rather than at the total original cost of $600. Net realizable value is used because it records the loss in the period in which it occurred rather than in the period of sale and does not overstate the asset.

If a periodic inventory system is used, the item simply is included in the ending inventory at estimated net realizable value and the loss is reflected in cost of goods sold. However, if a perpetual system is used, the following entry would be made:

Inventory of damaged goods (2 × $140)	280	
Loss on damaged goods (an expense) ($600 − $280)	320	
Inventory (2 × $300)		600

The perpetual inventory record also would be changed to reflect this entry.

new goods have an established wholesale market that provides replacement cost data. In contrast, usually there is no established wholesale market for damaged and deteriorated goods; therefore, net realizable value is used as a surrogate for replacement cost.

Estimating ending inventory and cost of goods sold

When a **periodic inventory system** is used, a physical inventory count must be taken each date on which financial statements are to be prepared. Taking a physical inventory at the end of each period for which financial statements are derived is a time-consuming task in many businesses. As a consequence, physical inventories may be taken only once a year. Nevertheless, the management of many businesses desire financial statements for internal use on a monthly or, at least, a quarterly basis. When a periodic, rather than a perpetual, inventory system is used, some businesses *estimate* the ending inventory for the monthly or quarterly financial statements. The **gross margin method** has been developed for this purpose. The method uses an **estimated gross margin ratio** as the basis for the computation.

Recall that the gross margin ratio is derived by dividing gross margin on sales by net sales (page 214). The gross margin method assumes that the *gross margin ratio* for the current period should be essentially the same as it was in the immediate past. Therefore, based on the *ratio* in the immediate past, a gross margin ratio is estimated for the current period. This estimated ratio then can be used to compute *estimated amounts* for (1) gross margin on sales, (2) cost of goods sold, and (3) ending inventory.

To illustrate the gross margin method, assume Patz Company is preparing *monthly* financial statements at January 31, 19D. The accounting records would provide the sales, beginning inventory, purchases, and expense amounts as listed below.

PATZ COMPANY
Income Statement
For the Month Ended January 31, 19D

Sales		$100,000 *
Cost of goods sold:		
Beginning inventory	$15,000 *	
Add purchases	65,000 *	
Goods available for sale	80,000	
Less ending inventory	?	
Cost of goods sold		?
Gross margin on sales		?
Expenses		30,000 *
Pretax income		$?

* Provided by the accounts.

The amount of the ending inventory each month is to be *estimated* rather than determined by physical count. Assume that the net sales for 19C amounted to $1,000,000 and gross margin was $400,000; therefore, the actual gross margin ratio for 19C was $400,000 ÷ $1,000,000 = 0.40. Now assume that the management decides that this ratio is a realistic estimate for 19D. Using the 0.40 as our estimate for 19D, we can compute an *estimated* inventory valuation. The computational steps, in lettered sequence, are shown below.

PATZ COMPANY
Income Statement
For the Month Ended January 31, 19D (estimated)

			Computations (sequence a, b, c)
Sales		$100,000	Per accounts
Cost of goods sold:			
Beginning inventory	$15,000		Per accounts
Add purchases	65,000		Per accounts
Goods available for sale	80,000		
Less ending inventory	20,000		c. $ 80,000 — $60,000 = $20,000
Cost of goods sold . .		60,000	b. $100,000 — $40,000 = $60,000*
Gross margin on sales		40,000	a. $100,000 × 0.40 = $40,000
Expenses		30,000	Per accounts
Pretax income		$ 10,000	

* Or alternatively, $100,000 × (1.00 — 0.40) = $60,000.

The balance sheet can be completed by reporting the $20,000 estimated ending inventory amount as a current asset.

The gross margin method (formerly called gross profit method) has several other uses apart from preparation of the monthly or quarterly financial statements. Auditors and accountants may use it to test the reasonableness of the amount of the inventory determined by other means. If the current gross margin ratio has changed materially from the recent past, it may suggest an error in the inventory determination. As another example, the method also is used in the case of a casualty loss, such as when an inventory of goods is burned and its valuation must be estimated for settlement purposes with an insurance company.[12]

The consistency principle in accounting

In this and the two preceding chapters, several alternative approaches in measuring cost of goods sold and ending inventory were discussed and illustrated. Some of these alternatives produce different income statement and balance sheet results under otherwise identical situations. In addition to these situations, there are accounting alternatives in other areas of accounting. Recall that in Chapter 2 we illustrated different accounting policies that were reported by J. C. Penney Company, Inc. Some of the policies reflected the company's choice of one of several alternatives available. In view of the **consistency principle** (Exhibit 2–6), a company cannot shift capriciously from one accounting alternative to another. **The consistency principle holds that in the accounting process all concepts, principles, and measurement approaches should be applied in a similar or consistent way from one period to the next in order to assure that the data reported in the financial statements are reasonably comparable**

[12] Another method, known as the retail inventory method, is used widely to estimate the ending inventory by department stores. It is essentially the same as the gross margin method, but differs in detail. Discussion of it is deferred to more advanced books.

over time. This principle prevents "willy-nilly" changes from one accounting or measurement approach to another. The consistency principle is not inflexible. It permits changes in accounting when the changes tend to improve the measurement of financial results and financial position. Consistency is a difficult concept to define precisely and poses troublesome problems in application.

In respect to inventories, a business is not permitted to change from one inventory costing method to another from period to period. Changing from one inventory costing method to another is a major event, and such a change requires full disclosure as to the reason for the change and the accounting effects.

DEMONSTRATION CASE A

Metal Products, Incorporated

(Try to resolve the requirements before proceeding to the suggested solution that follows:)

This case focuses on the effects of a misstatement of the ending inventory. It does not introduce any new accounting concepts or procedures.

Metal Products, Incorporated, has been operating for eight years as a distributor of a line of metal products. It is now the end of 19C and for the first time the company will undergo an audit by an independent CPA. The company uses a periodic inventory system. The annual income statements, prepared by the company, were:

	For the year ended December 31	
	19C	19B
Sales	$800,000	$750,000
Cost of goods sold:		
Beginning inventory	40,000	45,000
Add purchases	484,000	460,000
Goods available for sale	524,000	505,000
Less ending inventory	60,000	40,000
Cost of goods sold	464,000	465,000
Gross margin on sales	336,000	285,000
Operating expenses	306,000	275,000
Pretax income	30,000	10,000
Income tax expense (20%)	6,000	2,000
Net income	$ 24,000	$ 8,000

During the early stages of the audit, the independent CPA discovered that the ending inventory for 19B had been understated by $15,000.

Required:

a. Based on the above income statement amounts, compute the gross margin ratio on sales for each year. Do the results suggest the inventory error? Explain.

b. Reconstruct the two income statements on a correct basis.
c. Answer the following questions.
1. What are the correct gross margin ratios?
2. What effect did the $15,000 understatement of the ending inventory have on 19B pretax income? Explain.
3. What effect did it have on 19C pretax income? Explain.
4. How did the error affect income tax expense?

Suggested solution:

Requirement (a), gross margin ratios as reported:

19B: $285,000 ÷ $750,000 = 0.38
19C: $336,000 ÷ $800,000 = 0.42

The change in the gross margin ratio from 0.38 to 0.42 suggests the possibility of an inventory error in the absence of any other explanation for this significant change.

Requirement (b), income statements corrected:

	For the year ended December 31	
	19C	19B
Sales	$800,000	$750,000
Cost of goods sold:		
Beginning inventory	55,000*	45,000
Add purchases	484,000	460,000
Goods available for sale . . .	539,000	505,000
Less ending inventory	60,000	55,000*
Cost of goods sold	479,000	450,000
Gross margin on sales	321,000	300,000
Operating expenses	306,000	275,000
Pretax income	15,000	25,000
Income tax expense (20%)	3,000	5,000
Net income	$ 12,000	$ 20,000
* Increased by $15,000.		

Requirement (c):

1. Correct gross margin ratios:

19B: $300,000 ÷ $750,000 = 0.400
19C: $321,000 ÷ $800,000 = 0.401

The inventory error of $15,000 was responsible for the variation in the gross margin ratios reflected in Requirement *(a).* The inventory error in 19B affected gross margin for both 19B and 19C, in the opposite direction but by the same amount ($15,000).
2. Effect on pretax income in 19B: *Ending inventory understatement ($15,000)* caused an *understatement of pretax income* by the *same amount.*

3. Effect on pretax income in 19C: Beginning inventory *understatement* (by the same $15,000 since the inventory amount is carried over from the prior period) caused an *overstatement* of pretax income by the same amount.
4. Total income tax was the same ($8,000) regardless of the error. However, there was a shift of $3,000 ($15,000 × 20 percent) income tax expense from 19B to 19C.

An inventory misstatement in one year affects pretax ending income by the amount of the error and in the next year affects pretax income again by the same amount but in the opposite direction.

DEMONSTRATION CASE B

Balent Appliances, Incorporated

(Try to resolve the requirements before proceeding to the suggested solution that follows.)

This case presents the effects on ending inventory, cost of goods sold, and the related accounting entries of a periodic inventory system compared with a perpetual inventory assuming the *Lifo* inventory costing method is applied in each system.

Balent Appliances distributes a number of high-cost household appliances. One product, microwave ovens, has been selected for case purposes. Assume the following summarized transactions were completed during the period in the order given below (assume all transactions are cash).

	Units	Unit cost
a. Beginning inventory	11	$200
b. Sales (selling price $420)	8	?
c. Sales returns (can be resold as new)	1	200
d. Purchases	9	220
e. Purchase returns (damaged in shipment)	1	220

Required:

a. Compute the following amounts assuming application of the *Lifo* inventory costing method:

	Ending inventory		Cost of goods sold	
	Units	Dollars	Units	Dollars
1. Periodic inventory system (costed at end of period)	___	___	___	___
2. Perpetual inventory system (costed during period)	___	___	___	___

b. Give the indicated journal entries for transactions *(b)* through *(e)* assuming:
1. Periodic inventory system.
2. Perpetual inventory system.

Suggested Solution:

Requirement *(a):*

	Ending inventory		Cost of goods sold	
	Units	Dollars	Units	Dollars
1. Periodic inventory system (costed at end of period)	12	$2,420	7	$1,540
2. Perpetual inventory system (costed during period)	12	2,560	7	1,400

Computations:
Goods available for sale: (11 units @ $200 = $2,200) + (8 units @ $220 = $1,760) = $3,960.

1. Periodic inventory (costed at end):
   Ending inventory: (11 units @ $200 = $2,200) + (1 unit @ $220 = $220) = $2,420.
   Cost of goods sold: (Goods available, $3,960) − (Ending inventory, $2,420) = $1,540.
2. Perpetual inventory (costed during period):
   Ending inventory: (8 units @ $220 = $1,760) + (4 units @ $200 = $800) = $2,560.
   Cost of goods sold: 7 units @ $200 = $1,400.

Requirement *(b)—Journal entries:*

1. Periodic Inventory System	2. Perpetual Inventory System
b. Sales: Cash (8 × $420) .... 3,360 Sales 3,360	Cash .... 3,360 Sales .... 3,360 Cost of goods sold ... 1,600 Inventory (8 × $200) 1,600
c. Sales returns: Sales returns .... 420 Cash (1 × $420) 420	Sales returns .... 420 Cash .... 420 Inventory (1 × $200) .... 200 Cost of goods sold 200
d. Purchases: Purchases .... 1,980 Cash (9 × $220) 1,980	Inventory .... 1,980 Cash 1,980
e. Purchase return: Cash .... 220 Purchase returns 220	Cash .... 220 Inventory 220

SUMMARY

This chapter focused on the problem of measuring cost of goods sold and ending inventory. The inventory should include all the items remaining on hand for resale to which the entity has ownership. Costs flow into inventory when goods are purchased (or manufactured) and flow out (as expense) when the goods are sold or disposed of otherwise. When there are several unit cost amounts representing the inflow of goods for the period, one is confronted with the necessity of using a rational and systematic method to assign unit cost amounts to the units remaining in inventory and to the units sold (cost of goods sold). The chapter discussed and illustrated four different inventory costing methods and their applications in both a perpetual inventory system and a periodic inventory system. The methods discussed were weighted average cost, *Fifo, Lifo,* and specific identification. Each of the inventory costing methods is in accordance with the cost principle. The method of inventory costing used is particularly important since it will affect reported income, income tax expense (and hence cash flow), and the inventory valuation reported on the balance sheet. In a period of rising prices, *Fifo* gives a higher income than does *Lifo;* in a period of falling prices the opposite result occurs.

Damaged, obsolete, and deteriorated items in inventory should be assigned a unit cost that represents their current estimated net realizable value. Also, when market value (i.e., replacement cost) of new inventory items (not damaged, deteriorated, or obsolete) has declined below the actual cost of the goods remaining on hand, the ending inventory should be measured on a LCM basis.

This chapter featured another fundamental accounting principle (Exhibit 2–6) known as the consistency principle. This principle holds that in the accounting process all concepts, principles, and measurement approaches should be applied in a similar or consistent way from period to period so that the financial statements will be reasonably comparable over time.

IMPORTANT TERMS DEFINED IN THE CHAPTER (with page citations)

Merchandise inventory—273
Finished goods inventory—273
Work in process inventory—273
Raw materials inventory—273
Consignments—274
Periodic inventory system—276
Perpetual inventory system—276, 285
Weighted average inventory costing method—278, 286
First-in, first-out inventory costing method—279, 288
Last-in, first-out inventory costing method—280, 289

Specific identification inventory costing method—281, 291
Perpetual inventory record—285, 287
Weighted moving average inventory costing—286
Lower of cost or market (LCM)—291
Net realizable value—292
Gross margin method (estimating inventory)—294
Consistency principle—295

QUESTIONS FOR DISCUSSION

Part A

1. Assume the 19A ending inventory was understated by $100,000. Explain how this error would affect the 19A and 19B pretax income amounts. What would be the effects if the inventory were overstated by $100,000 instead of understated?

2. Match the type of inventory with the type of business in the following matrix:

Type of inventory	Type of business	
	Trading	Manufacturing
Merchandise		
Finished goods		
Work in process		
Raw materials		

3. Why is inventory an important item to both internal management and external users of financial statements?

4. Fundamentally, what items should be included in inventory?

5. In measuring cost of goods and inventory, why is passage of ownership an important issue? When does ownership to goods usually pass? Explain.

6. There are two parties to a consignment. Which party should include the goods on consignment in the inventory? Explain.

7. Explain the application of the cost principle to an item in the ending inventory.

8. When a perpetual inventory system is used, unit costs are known at the date of each sale. In contrast, when a periodic inventory system is used, unit costs are known at the end of the accounting period. Explain.

9. The periodic inventory model is BI + P − EI = CGS, and the perpetual inventory model is BI + P − CGS = EI. Explain the significance of the difference between these two models.

10. The chapter discussed four inventory costing methods: (a) weighted average cost, (b) Fifo, (c) Lifo, and (d) specific identification. Briefly explain each.

11. The four inventory costing methods may be applied with either a periodic inventory system or a perpetual inventory system. Briefly explain how the methods collectively are applied in each system.

12. Explain how income can be manipulated when the specific identification inventory costing method is used.

13. Contrast the balance sheet effects of Lifo versus Fifo on reported assets (i.e., the ending inventory) when (a) prices are rising and (b) prices are falling.

14. Contrast the income statement effect of Lifo versus Fifo (i.e., on pretax income) when (a) prices are rising and (b) prices are falling.

15. Contrast the effects on cash outflow and inflow between Fifo and Lifo.

Questions

Part B

16. What is the purpose of a perpetual inventory record? List the four main column headings and briefly explain the purpose of each.

17. When a perpetual inventory system is used, a *moving weighted average* is used. In contrast, when a periodic inventory system is used, an *annual weighted average* is used. Explain why the different averages are used.

18. Explain why the weighted average inventory costing method generally produces different results when a perpetual inventory system is used than when a periodic inventory system is used.

19. Explain briefly application of the LCM concept to the ending inventory and its effect on the income statement and balance sheet when market is lower than cost.

20. When should net realizable value be used in costing an item in the ending inventory?

21. The chapter discussed the gross margin method to estimate inventories. Briefly explain it and indicate why it is used.

22. Briefly explain the consistency principle. How might it relate to the inventory costing methods?

EXERCISES

Part A

E7–1. Small corporation prepared the two income statements given below (simplified for illustrative purposes):

(Relates to Exercise 7–1)

	First quarter 19B		Second quarter 19B	
Sales		$10,000		$12,000
Cost of goods sold:				
Beginning inventory	$ 2,000		$ 3,000	
Purchases	9,000		10,000	
Goods available for sale .	11,000		13,000	
Ending inventory	3,000		4,000	
Cost of goods sold . .		8,000		9,000
Gross margin		2,000		3,000
Expenses		1,000		1,000
Pretax income		$ 1,000		$ 2,000

During the third quarter it was discovered that the ending inventory for the first quarter should have been $2,500.

Required:

a. What effect did this error have on the combined pretax income of the two quarters? Explain.
b. Did this error affect the EPS amounts for each quarter? Explain.
c. Prepare corrected income statements for each quarter.
d. Set up a schedule which reflects the comparative effects of the correct and incorrect amounts. Indicate the self-correcting amounts.

E7–2. Teenie Company purchased 100 units of merchandise X and recorded a total cost of $2,940 determined as follows:

Invoice cost	$2,000
Less: Cash discount 2%	
Shipping charges	530
Import taxes and duties	110
Interest paid in advance (15%) on $2,000 borrowed to finance the purchase	300
	$2,940

Give the entry(s) to record this purchase assuming a periodic inventory system. Show computations.

E7–3. The records at the end of January 19B for N Company showed the following for a particular kind of merchandise:

	Units	Total cost
Inventory, December 31, 19A	30	$390
Purchase, January 9, 19B	60	900
Sale, January 11, 19B (at $35 per unit)	40	
Purchase, January 20, 19B	35	490
Sale, January 27, 19B (at $36 per unit)	41	

Required:

Assuming a periodic inventory system, compute the amount of (1) goods available for sale, (2) ending inventory, and (3) cost of goods sold at January 31, 19B, under each of the following inventory costing methods (show computations and round to the nearest dollar):

a. Weighted average cost.
b. First-in, first-out.
c. Last-in, first-out.
d. Specific identification (assume the sale on January 11 was "identified" with the purchase of January 9, the sale of January 27 was "identified" with the purchase of January 20, and any excess identified with the beginning inventory).

E7–4. Martin Company uses a periodic inventory system. At the end of the annual accounting period, December 31, 19B, the accounting records provided the following information for Product Z:

Transaction	Units	Unit cost
1. Inventory, December 31, 19A	2,000	$20
For the year 19B:		
2. Purchase, April 11	2,000	22
3. Sale, May 1 (@ $50 each) ..	3,000	
4. Purchase, June 1	6,000	24
5. Sale, July 3 (@ $52 each) ..	4,000	
6. Operating expenses (excluding income tax expense), $140,000.		

Required:

a. Prepare a separate income statement through pretax income that details cost of goods sold for:

Case A—Annual weighted average.
Case B—*Fifo.*
Case C—*Lifo.*
Case D—Specific identification assuming two thirds of the first sale was "selected" from the beginning inventory and the second sale was "selected" from the purchase of June 1, 19B.

For each case, show the computation of the ending inventory. (Hint: Set up adjacent columns for each case.)
b. For each case, compare the pretax amounts with the ending inventory amounts. Explain the similarities and differences.

E7–5. Use the data given in Exercise 7–3 for this exercise (assume cash transactions and a periodic inventory system).

Required:

a. Assume: Case A, *Fifo,* and Case B, *Lifo;* compute (1) goods available for sale, (2) cost of goods sold, and (3) ending inventory.
b. Give in parallel columns, journal entries for each of the transactions assuming a periodic inventory system for (1) *Fifo* and (2) *Lifo.* Set up captions as follows:

	Fifo		Lifo	
Accounts	Debit	Credit	Debit	Credit

c. Prepare an income statement through gross margin and explain why the *Fifo* and *Lifo* ending inventory, cost of goods sold, and gross margin amounts are different.
d. Which inventory costing method may be preferred for tax purposes? Explain.

E7–6. During January 19B, RN Company reported sales revenue of $400,000 for the one item stocked. The inventory for December 31, 19A, showed 7,500 units on hand, valued at $165,000. During January 19B, two purchases of the item were made: the first was for 1,500 units at $24 per unit; and the second was for 7,600 units at $25 each. The periodic inventory count reflected 8,600 units remaining on hand on January 31, 19B. Operating expenses for the month summed to $62,100.

Required:

a. On the basis of the above information, complete the 19B summary income statements under *Fifo* and *Lifo*. Use a single list of side captions including computation of cost of goods sold. Set

19A), 1,600 units @ $15; purchases, 6,000 units @ $18; expenses (excluding income taxes), $51,800; ending inventory per physical count at December 31, 19B, 1,800 units; sales price per unit, $33; and average income tax rate of 20 percent.

Required:

a. Complete income statements under the *Fifo, Lifo,* and weighted average costing methods. Use a format similar to the following:

(Relates to Exercise 7–7)

Income statement	Units	Inventory costing method		
		Fifo	Lifo	Weighted average
Sales.........................	_____	$_____	$_____	$_____
Cost of goods sold:				
Beginning inventory........	_____	_____	_____	_____
Purchases	_____	_____	_____	_____
Goods available for sale .	_____	_____	_____	_____
Ending inventory...........	_____	_____	_____	_____
Cost of goods sold ..	_____	_____	_____	_____
Gross margin	_____	_____	_____	_____
Expenses		_____	_____	_____
Pretax income................		_____	_____	_____
Income tax expense		_____	_____	_____
Net income		_____	_____	_____

up three separate column headings as follows: Units; *Fifo; Lifo.* Show your computations of the ending inventory.

b. Which method gives the higher pretax income? Why?

c. Which method gives the more favorable cash flow effects? By how much, assuming a 20 percent tax rate?

E7–7. MK Company uses a periodic inventory system. Data for 19B were: beginning merchandise inventory (December 31,

b. Comparing *Fifo* and *Lifo,* which method is preferable in terms of (1) net income and (2) cash flow? Explain.

c. What would be your answer to Requirement *(b)* assuming prices were falling? Explain.

E7–8. Following is a partial computation of cost of goods sold for the income statement under three different inventory costing methods assuming a periodic inventory system:

(Relates to Exercise 7–8)

	Fifo	Lifo	Weighted average
Unit sales price, $30.			
Cost of goods sold:			
Beginning inventory (480 units)	$ 9,600	$ 9,600	$ 9,600
Purchases (520 units)	13,000	13,000	13,000
Goods available for sale			
Ending inventory (530 units)			
Cost of goods sold			
Expenses, $2,000.			

Required:

a. Compute cost of goods sold under each inventory costing method.

b. Prepare an income statement through pretax income for each method. (Hint: Set up three money columns.)

c. Rank the three methods in order of favorable cash flow and explain the basis for your ranking.

Exercises
Part B

E7–9. Western Company uses a perpetual inventory system and *Fifo*. The record reflected the following for January 19B:

	Units	Unit cost
Beginning inventory, January 1	100	$1.00
Purchase, January 6	200	1.20
Sale, January 10 (at $2.40 per unit)	110	
Purchase, January 14	100	1.30
Sale, January 29 (at $2.60 per unit)	160	

Required:

a. Prepare the perpetual inventory record for January.

b. Give journal entries indicated by the above data for January (assume cash transactions).

c. Prepare a summary income statement for January through gross margin.

E7–10. At the end of the accounting period the inventory records of Able Company reflected the following:

Transactions (in order of date)	Units	Unit cost
Beginning inventory	500	$10
1. Purchase No. 1	600	12
2. Sale No. 1 (@ $23 per unit)	(700)	
3. Purchase No. 2	800	14
4. Sale No. 2 (@ $24 per unit)	(600)	
Ending inventory.....	600	

Required:

a. Compute goods available for sale in units and dollars.

b. Compute the (1) ending inventory valuation and (2) cost of goods sold assuming a *periodic* inventory system under the *Lifo* inventory costing method.

c. For comparative purposes compute the (1) ending inventory valuation and (2) cost of goods sold assuming a *perpetual* inventory system under the *Lifo* inventory costing method. To do this prepare a perpetual inventory record and cost each sale when made.

d. Compare the results of *(b)* and *(c)* and explain why the valuations of ending inventory and cost of goods sold are different as between the periodic and perpetual inventory systems.

E7–11. Use the data given in Exercise 7–3 for this exercise (assume cash transactions, a perpetual inventory system, and moving average cost).

Required:

a. Prepare the perpetual inventory record for January on a moving average basis. Round to the nearest cent on unit costs and the nearest dollar on total cost.

b. Give the journal entry to record the purchase of January 9.

c. Give the journal entries to record the sale on January 11.

d. Prepare a summarized income statement through gross margin for January.

e. Explain why a moving average rather than a weighted average for the period was used.

f. Would the ending inventory and cost of goods sold amounts usually be different between periodic and perpetual inventory systems? Explain why.

E7–12. XY Company uses a perpetual inventory system and applies *Fifo* inventory costing. The data below were provided by the accounting records for 19B:

(Relates to Exercise 7–12)

Transactions (in order of date)	Units	Unit cost	Total cost
Beginning inventory	100	$10	$1,000
1. Purchase No. 1	300	12	3,600
2. Sale No. 1 (@ $21 each)	(200)		
3. Purchase No. 2	400	14	5,600
4. Sale No. 2 (@ $23 each)	(300)		
Ending inventory	300		?

Required:

a. Compute the valuation of the (1) cost of goods sold and (2) ending inventory assuming a perpetual inventory system and application of the *Fifo* inventory costing method.

b. Give the entries to record transactions 1 and 2 assuming *(Fifo):*

(Relates to Exercise 7–13)

	TV set (Model 2–206)	Stereo (Model 112A)
Quantity damaged	1	2
Actual unit cost	$400	$300
Regular sales price	700	500
Estimated unit market value in present condition	380	250
Estimated unit cost to sell	60	35

Case A—A perpetual inventory system

Case B—A periodic inventory system

Use adjacent amount columns for each system and assume cash transactions.

c. Explain why the entries are different between the perpetual and periodic inventory systems.

E7–13. Keely Sound Company is preparing the annual financial statements at December 31, 19D. Two different items that were used as demonstrators remained on hand at year-end. These two items will be sold as damaged (used) merchandise; therefore, they must be removed from the ending inventory of new merchandise. The company uses a perpetual inventory system. These items will be included in the inventory of damaged goods. Data on the two items are:

Required:

a. Compute the valuation of each item that should be used for 19D inventory purposes. Show computations.

b. Give the required entry(s) to reflect the appropriate inventory valuations in the accounts.

E7–14. Miller Company is preparing the annual financial statements dated December 31, 19B. Ending inventory information about the five major items stocked for regular sale is:

(Relates to Exercise 7–14)

	Ending inventory, 19B		
Item	Quantity on hand	Unit cost when acquired (Fifo)	Replacement cost (market) at year-end
A	50	$20	$18
B	100	45	45
C	20	60	62
D	40	40	40
E	1,000	10	8

Required:

Compute the valuation that should be used for the 19B ending inventory using the LCM rule. For merchandise inventory the rule usually is applied on an item-by-item basis. (Hint: Set up columns for Item, Quantity, Total Cost, Total Market, and LCM Valuation.

E7–15. Nelson Retail Company prepares annual financial statements each December 31. The company uses a periodic inventory system. This system requires a detailed inventory count of all items on the store shelves, items stored in the basement, and items in a separate warehouse. However, the management also desires quarterly financial statements but will not take a physical inventory count four times dur-

4. Purchases		196,000
5. Freight-in		4,000
6. Operating expenses (excluding income tax expense)		50,000
7. Estimated average income tax rate, 25%.		
8. Estimated gross margin rate, 30%.		

Required:

Based on the above information prepare a detailed income statement for the first quarter of 19D. Show all computations.

E7–16. On November 2, 19C, a fire destroyed the inventory of Mason Retail Store. The accounting records were not destroyed; hence, they provided the following information:

(Relates to Exercise 7–16)

	19A	19B	19C to date of fire
Sales	$120,000	$142,000	$115,000
Cost of goods sold	73,200	85,200	?
Gross margin on sales	46,800	56,800	?
Expenses	34,800	42,800	37,000
Pretax income	$ 12,000	$ 14,000	?
Ending inventory	$ 20,000	$ 22,000	?
Purchases during year	70,000	87,200	68,000

ing the year. Accordingly, they use the gross margin method to estimated the ending inventory for the first three quarters.

At the end of the first quarter, March 31, 19D, the accounting records provided the following information:

1. Beginning inventory, January 1, 19D		$ 60,000
Data for the first quarter of 19D:		
2. Sales		305,000
3. Return sales		5,000

Required:

a. Based on the data available, prepare an estimated income statement for 19C up to the date of the fire. Show details for the cost of goods sold. Disregard income taxes and show computations.

b. What amount of loss on the inventory should be submitted to the insurance company (a casualty loss insurance policy is in effect)? Write a brief statement in support of the amount of indemnity claimed.

PROBLEMS

Part A

P7–1. The income statement for Mason Company summarized for a four-year period showing the following:

(Relates to Problem 7–1)

	1981	1982	1983	1984
Sales	$1,000,000	$1,200,000	$1,300,000	$1,100,000
Cost of goods sold	600,000	610,000	870,000	650,000
Gross margin	400,000	590,000	430,000	450,000
Expenses	300,000	328,000	362,000	317,000
Pretax income	100,000	262,000	68,000	133,000
Income tax expense (30%)	30,000	78,600	20,400	39,900
Net income	$ 70,000	$183,400	$ 47,600	$ 93,100

An audit revealed that in determining the above amounts, the ending inventory for 1982 was overstated by $50,000. The company uses a periodic inventory system.

Required:

a. Recast the above income statements on a corrected basis.
b. Did the error affect cumulative net income for the four-year period? Explain.
c. Did the error affect cash inflows or outflows? Explain.

P7–2. Alva Company has just completed a physical inventory count at year-end, December 31, 19B. Only the items on the shelves, in storage, and in the receiving area were counted and extended at cost on a *Fifo* basis. The inventory summed to $90,000. During the audit the independent CPA developed the following additional information:

a. Goods costing $400 were out on trial by a customer; hence, they were excluded from the inventory count at December 31, 19B.
b. Goods in transit on December 31, 19B, from a supplier, with terms FOB destination, cost, $700. Since these goods had not arrived, they were excluded from the physical inventory count.
c. On December 31, 19B, goods in transit to customers, with terms FOB shipping point, amounted to $900 (expected delivery date January 10, 19C). Since the goods had been shipped, they were excluded from the physical inventory count.
d. On December 28, 19B, a customer purchased goods for cash amounting to $1,500 and left them "for pickup on January 3, 19C." Alva had paid $800 for the goods and, since they were on hand, included the latter amount in the physical inventory count.
e. Alva Company, on the date of the inventory, received notice from a supplier that goods ordered earlier, at a cost of $2,400, had been delivered to the transportation company on December 27, 19B; the terms were FOB shipping point. Since the shipment had not arrived by December 31, 19B, it was excluded from the physical inventory.
f. On December 31, 19B, Alva shipped $750 worth of goods to a customer, FOB destination. The goods are expected to arrive at destination no earlier than January 8, 19C. Since the goods were not on hand, they were not included in the physical inventory count.
g. One of the items sold by Alva has such a low volume that the management planned to drop it last year. In order

to induce Alva to continue carrying the item, the manufacturer-supplier provided the item on a consignment basis. At the end of each month, Alva (the consignee) renders a report to the manufacturer on the number sold and remits cash for the cost. At the end of December 19B, Alva had five of these items on hand; hence, they were included in the physical inventory count at $1,500 each.

Required:

Begin with the $90,000 inventory amount and compute the correct amount for the ending inventory. Explain the basis for your treatment of each of the above items. (Hint: The correct amount is $85,250. Set up three columns: Item, Amount, and Explanation.)

P7-3. Vogel Company uses a periodic inventory system. At the end of the annual account-

Required:

Compute the amount of (1) goods available for sale, (2) ending inventory, and (3) cost of goods sold at December 31, 19E, under each of the following inventory costing methods (show computations and round to the nearest dollar):

a. Weighted average cost.
b. First-in, first-out.
c. Last-in, first-out.
d. Specific identification, assuming the April 1, 19E, sale was "selected" one third from the beginning inventory and two thirds from the purchase of February 20, 19E. Assume the sale of August 1, 19E, was "selected" from the purchase of June 30, 19E.

P7-4. At the end of January 19B, the records of Stanford Company showed the following for a particular item that sold at $15 per unit:

(Relates to Problem 7–4)

	Units	Amount
Inventory, January 1, 19B	500	$3,000
Sale, January 10	(400)	
Purchase, January 12	600	4,200
Sale, January 17	(550)	
Purchase, January 26	310	2,790
Purchase return, January 28 ...	(10) Out of Jan. 26 purchase	

ing period, December 31, 19E, the accounting records for item X (a regular item sold) showed:

Transaction	Units	Unit cost
Beginning inventory, January 1, 19E	300	$18
Transactions during 19E:		
1. Purchase, February 20 ..	500	22
2. Sale, April 1 (@ $40 each)	(600)	
3. Purchase, June 30	400	24
4. Sale, August 1 (@ $42 each)	(200)	
5. Return sale, August 5 (related to transaction 4) ..	10	

Required:

a. Assuming a periodic inventory system, prepare a summarized income statement through gross margin on sales under each method of inventory: (1) weighted average cost, (2) *Fifo*, (3) *Lifo*, and (4) specific identification. For specific identification, assume the first sale was out of the beginning inventory and the second sale was out of the January 12 purchase. Show the inventory computations in detail.

b. Between *Fifo* and *Lifo*, which method will derive the higher pretax income? Which would derive the higher EPS?

c. Between *Fifo* and *Lifo,* which method will derive the lower income tax expense? Explain, assuming a 20 percent average tax rate.

d. Between *Fifo* and *Lifo,* which method will produce the more favorable cash flow? Explain.

P7–5. Speculative Company sells one major item, Product X, which it acquires from a foreign source. During the year, 19W, the inventory records for Product X reflecting the following:

	Units	Unit cost	Total cost
Beginning inventory	10	$20,000	$200,000
Purchases	30	25,000	750,000
Sales (35 units @ $45,000)	20	28000	

The company uses the *Lifo* inventory costing method. On December 28, 19W, the unit cost of Product X was increased to $28,000. The price may increase to $28,500 during the first quarter of the next year.

Required:

a. Complete the following income statement summary using the *Lifo* method (show computations):

Sales	$_____
Cost of goods sold	_____
Gross margin	_____
Expenses	425,000
Pretax income	$_____
Ending inventory	$_____

b. The management, for various reasons, is considering buying 20 additional units before December 31, 19W, at $28,000 each. Restate the above income statement (and ending inventory) assuming this purchase is made on December 31, 19W.

c. How much did pretax income change because of the decision on December 31, 19W? Is there any evidence of income manipulation? Explain.

P7–6. Big Corporation reported the following summarized annual data at the end of 19X:

	(Millions)
Sales	$900
Cost of goods sold*	540
Gross margin	360
Expenses	200
Pretax income	$160

* Based on ending *Fifo* inventory of $150 million. On a *Lifo* basis this ending inventory would have been $80 million.

Before issuing the above statement the company decided to change from *Fifo* to *Lifo* for 19X because "it better reflects our operating results." The company has always used *Fifo.*

Required:

a. Restate the summary income statement on a *Lifo* basis.

b. How much did pretax income change due to the *Lifo* decision for 19X? What caused the change in pretax income?

c. If you were a shareholder what would be your reaction to this change? Explain.

P7–7. This case is designed to demonstrate the effect on pretax income of (a) rising prices and (b) falling prices in comparing *Fifo* with *Lifo.* Income is to be evaluated under four different situations as follows:

Prices are rising:
Situation A—*Fifo* is used.
Situation B—*Lifo* is used.

Prices are falling:
Situation C—*Fifo* is used.
Situation D—*Lifo* is used.

The basic data common to all four situations are sales, 600 units for $5,300; beginning inventory, 500 units; purchases, 500 units; ending inventory, 400 units; and operating expenses, $3,000. The following tabulated income statements for each situation have been set up for analytical purposes:

(Relates to Problem 7–7)

| | Prices rising | | Prices falling | |
	Situation A Fifo	Situation B Lifo	Situation C Fifo	Situation D Lifo
Sales	$5,300	$5,300	$5,300	$5,300
Cost of goods sold:				
Beginning inventory	1,000	?	?	?
Purchases	1,500	?	?	?
Goods available for sale	2,500	?	?	?
Ending inventory	1,200	?	?	?
Cost of goods sold	1,300	?	?	?
Gross margin	4,000	?	?	?
Expenses	3,000	3,000	3,000	3,000
Pretax income	1,000	?	?	?
Income tax expense (20%)	200	?	?	?
Net income	$ 800	?	?	?

Required:

a. Complete the above tabulation for each situation. In Situations A and B (prices rising), assume the following: beginning inventory, 500 units @ $2 = $1,000; and purchases, 500 units @ $3 = $1,500. In Situations C and D (prices falling), assume the opposite; that is, beginning inventory, 500 units @ $3 = $1,500; and purchases, 500 units @ $2 = $1,000. Use periodic inventory procedures.

b. Analyze the relative effects on pretax income and on net income as demonstrated by Requirement (a) when prices are rising and when prices are falling.

c. Analyze the relative effects on the cash position for each situation.

d. Would you recommend *Fifo* or *Lifo?* Explain.

Problems
Part B

P7–8. The income statements for four consecutive years for Wash Company reflected the following summarized amounts:

(Relates to Problem 7–8)

	1980	1981	1982	1983
Sales	$60,000	$70,000	$80,000	$65,000
Cost of goods sold	36,000	38,300	50,100	39,000
Gross margin	24,000	31,700	29,900	26,000
Expenses	15,000	16,700	19,100	15,800
Pretax income	$ 9,000	$15,000	$10,800	$10,200

Subsequent to development of the above amounts, it has been determined that the physical inventory taken on December 31, 1981, was overstated by $4,000.

Required:

a. Recast the above income statements to reflect the correct amounts, taking into consideration the inventory error.

b. Compute the gross margin ratio for each year (1) before the correction and (2) after the correction. Do the results lend confidence to your corrected amounts? Explain.

c. What effect would the error have had on the income tax expense assuming a 20 percent average rate?

P7–9. PCB Company has completed taking the periodic inventory count of merchandise remaining on hand at the end of the fiscal year, December 31, 19D. Questions have arisen concerning inventory costing for five different items. The inventory reflecting the following:

16 Sold 1,800 units at $10 per unit.
18 Purchased 2,300 units for $13,800.
24 Sold 600 units at $12 per unit.

Required (assume cash transactions):

a. Prepare a perpetual inventory record for January on (1) a *Fifo* basis and (2) a *Lifo* basis.
b. Give the entry for each basis for the purchase on January 10.

(Relates to Problem 7–9)

	Units	Original unit cost
Item A—The two units on hand are damaged because they were used as demonstrators. It is estimated that they may be sold at 20 percent below cost and that disposal costs will amount to $60 each.	2	$260
Item B—Because of a drop in the market, this item can be replaced from the original supplier at 10 percent below the original cost price. The sales price also was reduced.	20	70
Item C—Because of style change, it is highly doubtful that the four units can be sold; they have no scrap value.	4	20
Item D—This item no longer will be stocked; as a consequence it will be marked down from the regular selling price of $110 to $50. Cost of selling is estimated to be 20 percent of the original cost price.	3	80
Item E—Because of high demand and quality, the cost of this item has been raised from $120 to $144; hence, all replacements for inventory in the foreseeable future will be at the latter price.	15	120

The remaining items in inventory pose no valuation problems: their costs sum to $50,000.

Required:

Compute the total amount of the ending inventory. List each of the above items separately and explain the basis for your decision with respect to each item.

P7–10. Stover Appliance Store uses a perpetual inventory system. In this problem, we will focus on one item stocked, which is designated as Item A. The beginning inventory was 2,000 units @ $4. During January, the following transactions occurred that affected Item A:

Jan. 5 Sold 500 units at $10 per unit.
10 Purchased 1,000 units at $5 per unit.

c. Give the entries for each basis for the sale on January 16.
d. Complete the following financial statement amounts for each basis:

	January	
	Fifo	Lifo
Income statement:		
Sales	$?	$?
Cost of goods sold	?	?
Gross margin	?	?
Expenses	12,000	12,000
Pretax income	?	?
Balance sheet:		
Current assets:		
Merchandise inventory	?	?

e. Which method derives the higher pre-tax income? Under what conditions would this comparative effect be the opposite?

f. Assuming a 20 percent average tax rate, which method would provide the more favorable cash position? By how much? Explain.

g. Which basis would you recommend for Stover? Why?

P7–11. XY Company uses a perpetual inventory system. Below is a perpetual inventory record for the period for one product sold at $6 per unit.

Assumption	Cost of goods sold	Ending inventory
a. Fifo	_____	_____
b. Lifo (end of period)	_____	_____
c. Annual weighted average (for the period)	_____	_____

8. Assume a periodic inventory taken at the end of the period reflected 590 units on hand. Give any entry(s) required. (Disregard Requirement 7.)

9. Disregard Requirements 7 and 8 and assume that on date *(h)* 10 units of the beginning inventory were returned to

(Relates to Problem 7–11)

PERPETUAL INVENTORY RECORD

Date							
a.						400	1,200
b.	800	3.30				1,200	
c.			500		1,600	700	2,240
d.	300	1,050					3,290
e.			200			800	2,632
f.			300		987	500	
g.	100	3.65				600	

Required:

1. Complete the column captions for the perpetual inventory record.
2. What inventory costing method is being used?
3. Enter all of the missing amounts on the perpetual inventory record.
4. Complete the following:

the supplier and a cash refund of $2.90 per unit was recovered. Give the required entry.

P7–12. Clark Company executives are considering their inventory policies. They have been using the moving average method with a perpetual inventory system. They

(Relates to Problem 7–11)

	Units	Per unit	Amount
a. Beginning inventory	_____	_____	_____
b. Ending inventory	_____	_____	_____
c. Total purchases	_____	_____	_____
d. Total cost of goods sold	_____	_____	_____

5. Give the entry(s) for date *(b)*.
6. Give the entry(s) for date *(c)*.
7. Complete the following tabulation:

have requested an "analysis of the effects of using *Fifo* versus *Lifo.*" Selected financial statement amounts (rounded) for the month of January 19B based upon the moving average method are as follows:

	Units	Amounts
Income statement:		
Sales	180	$9,400
Cost of goods sold	180	5,710
Gross margin on sales		3,690
Less: Expenses		1,700
Pretax income		$1,990
Balance sheet:		
Merchandise inventory		$2,620

(Relates to Problem 7–13)

Sales	$290,000
Cost of goods sold:	
Beginning inventory .... $ 40,000	
Purchases 206,000	
Goods available for sale ... 246,000	
Ending inventory (*Fifo* cost) 50,000	
Costs of good sold ...	196,000
Gross margin	94,000
Operating expenses	58,000
Pretax income	36,000
Income tax expense (25%)	9,000
Net Income	$ 27,000

Transactions during the month were:

Beginning inventory 50 units @ $30

Jan. 6 Sold 40 units @ $50
9 Purchased 100 units @ $32
16 Sold 80 units @ $52
20 Purchased 110 units @ $33
28 Sold 60 units @ $54

Required:

a. Copy the above statement data and extend it to the right by adding columns for *Fifo* and *Lifo* (costed currently) using perpetual inventory system. This will provide one basis for analyzing the different results among the three inventory costing methods.
b. Which method produces the highest pretax income? Explain.
c. Between *Fifo* and *Lifo*, which one provides a more favorable cash position for 19B? Explain.

P7–13. Foxy Company prepared their annual financial statements dated December 31, 19B. The company uses a periodic inventory system and applies the *Fifo* inventory costing method. The unaudited 19B income statement is summarized below:

Assume you are participating in an audit of the 19B financial statements and have developed the following data relating to the 19B ending inventory:

Item	Quantity	Acquisition cost Unit	Acquisition cost Total	Current replacement unit cost (market)
A	2,000	$ 2	$ 4,000	$ 2
B	3,000	6	18,000	5
C	4,000	4	16,000	5
D	1,000	12	12,000	10
			$50,000	

Required:

a. Restate the above income statement to reflect LCM valuation of the 19B ending inventory. Apply LCM on an item-by-item basis and show computations.
b. Compare and explain the LCM effect on each amount that was changed in (a).

c. What is the conceptual basis for applying LCM to merchandise inventories?

d. Thought question: What effect did

(Relates to Problem 7–15)

P7–15. The president of DT Company has been presented with the March 19B financial statements. They reflect data for three months as summarized below:

| | Income statements | | | |
	January	February	March	Quarter
Sales	$100,000	$106,000	$90,000	$296,000
Cost of goods sold	61,000	59,360	?	?
Gross margin on sales . .	39,000	46,640	?	?
Expenses	32,000	33,500	32,000	97,500
Pretax income	$ 7,000	$ 13,140	$?	$?
Gross margin ratio	0.39	0.44	0.43 (estimated)	
Ending inventory	$ 14,000	$ 16,000		

LCM have on the cash flow of 19B? What will be the long-term effect on cash flow?

P7–14. Lowlands Company suffered a major flood on April 15, 19B. The entire merchandise inventory was damaged badly. However, Lowlands carried a casualty insurance policy that covered floods. The accounting records were not damaged; therefore, they provided the following information for the period January 1 through April 14, 19B:

Merchandise inventory, December 31, 19A	$ 21,000
Transactions through April 14, 19B:	
Purchases	70,000
Purchase returns	2,000
Freight-in	1,000
Sales	103,000
Sales returns	3,000

Required:

For insurance indemnity purposes you have been asked to estimate the amount of the inventory loss. Your analysis to date indicates that (1) a 40 percent gross margin rate is reasonable and (2) the damaged merchandise can be sold to a local salvage company for approximately $2,000 cash.

What amount should be presented to the insurance company as a claim for insurance indemnity? Show computations.

The company uses a periodic inventory system. Although monthly statements are prepared, a monthly inventory count is not made. Instead, the company uses the gross margin method for monthly inventory purposes.

Required:

a. Complete computations in the following form to estimate the results for March.

	Amounts	Computations
Cost of goods sold:		
Beginning inventory	$16,000	From records
Purchases	51,000	From records
Goods available for sale	?	?
Ending inventory	?	?
Cost of goods sold		?

b. Complete the income statements given above (March and quarter). Disregard income tax.

c. What level of confidence do you think can be attributed to the results for March? Explain.

d. Would you recommend continued use of the method for the company? Explain.

Cash, short-term investments in securities, and receivables

PURPOSE OF THE CHAPTER

This chapter discusses the measurement and reporting of a group of assets known as liquid assets: cash, short-term investments in securities, and receivables. They are designated as liquid assets because of a primary characteristic: they are either money or relatively close to conversion to money. Thus, they meet the definition of a current asset.

To explain comprehensively the features and accounting problems peculiar to liquid assets, this chapter is divided into three parts as follows:

Part A: **Safeguarding and reporting cash**

Part B: **Measuring and reporting short-term investments**

Part C: Measuring and reporting receivables

This chapter includes the following Appendixes:

Appendix A: Petty cash

Appendix B: **Special journals**

Behavioral and learning objectives for this chapter are provided in the *Teachers Manual.*

PART A: SAFEGUARDING AND REPORTING CASH

Cash is the most liquid of all assets. Cash includes money and any instrument, such as a check, money order, or bank draft, that banks normally will accept for deposit and immediate credit to the depositor's account. Following this definition, cash *excludes* such items as notes receivable, IOUs, and postage stamps (a prepaid expense). Cash usually is divided into three categories: cash on hand, cash deposited in banks, and other instruments that meet the above definition. It is not unusual for a business to have several bank accounts. Even though a separate cash account may be maintained for each bank account, all cash accounts are combined as one amount for financial reporting purposes.

Because cash is the most liquid asset and is generated and used continuously, it imposes heavy responsibilities on the management of an entity. These responsibilities may be summarized as follows:

1. Safeguarding to prevent theft, fraud, loss through miscounting, and so on.
2. Accurate accounting so that relevant reports of cash inflows, outflows, and balances may be prepared periodically.
3. Control to assure that a sufficient amount of cash is on hand to meet *(a)* current operating needs, *(b)* maturing liabilities, and *(c)* unexpected emergencies.
4. Planning to prevent excess amounts of idle cash from accumulating— idle cash produces no revenue. In many cases, idle cash is invested in securities to derive a return pending future need for the cash.

INTERNAL CONTROL OF CASH

Internal control refers to those policies and procedures of an entity designed primarily to safeguard the assets of the enterprise. Internal control should extend to all assets: cash, receivables, investments, operational assets, and so on. An important phase of internal control focuses on cash. Effective internal control of cash normally should include:

1. Complete separation of the *function* of receiving cash from the function of disbursing cash.
2. Definite and clear-cut assignment to designated *individuals* of the responsibilities for all activities related to cash handling and accounting for cash.
3. Establishment of definite and separate *routines* for *(a)* handling the inflow of cash, *(b)* handling the outflow of cash, and *(c)* the accounting process for both cash receipts and disbursements.
4. Separation of the physical handling of cash (in all forms) from the *accounting function.* Individuals that handle cash receipts or make cash disbursements (whether by cash or by check) should not have access

to the cash records. Similarly, those involved in maintaining the records should not have access to cash.

5. Requirement that all cash receipts be deposited in a bank daily. Keep cash on hand under strict controls.

6. Requirement that all significant cash payments be made by numbered checks with a separate approval requirement. For example, the person authorized to approve payments should be different from the person authorized to sign checks.

The separation of responsibilities and the use of prescribed routines are particularly important phases in the control of cash. A clear-cut separation of duties and responsiblities among persons would require collusion among two or more persons if cash is embezzled and the theft concealed in the accounting records. Prescribed routines are designed so that the work done by one individual automatically is checked by the results reported by other individuals. For example, the routine for handling cash received through the mail may be designed so that one designated person opens the mail and makes a list of the cash. Then the cash received must follow a prescribed channel to the bank deposit, and another channel is prescribed for the flow of the related cash forms and documents. Finally, the accounting process for cash is another prescribed routine accomplished by other persons. Thus, the individuals that handle the cash are separated at all times from those that maintain the related records in the cash-processing cycle.

To indicate how easy it is to conceal cash theft when internal control is lacking, two examples are used.

Example 1—Employee X handles both cash receipts and the recordkeeping. Cash amounting to $100 was collected from J. Doe in payment of an account receivable. Employee X pocketed the cash and made an entry for $100 crediting Accounts Receivable (J. Doe) and debiting Allowance for Doubtful Accounts.

Example 2—Occasionally Employee X would send a fictitious purchase invoice through the system. The resulting check, to a fictitious person, was cashed by Employee X (using a fictitious endorsement and perhaps a partner in crime).

All cash disbursements should be made with **prenumbered** checks. For cash payments there should be separate routines and responsibilities specified for (1) payment approvals, (2) check preparation, and (3) check signing. When procedures similar to these are followed, it is difficult to conceal a fraudulent cash disbursement without the collusion of two or more persons. The level of internal control, which is subject to close scrutiny by the independent auditor, increases the reliability that users can accord the financial statements of the business.

BANK STATEMENTS TO DEPOSITORS

When a depositor opens a bank account, a **signature card** must be completed that lists the names and signatures of persons authorized to sign checks drawn against the account. When a deposit is to be made, the depositor must fill out a **deposit slip** that includes the name of the account, the account number, and a listing of the coins, currency, and checks deposited. In recent years most banks have converted almost exclusively to personalized checks; that is, the name, address, and account number of the depositor is preprinted on each check. Obviously, this is an important safety feature for all parties concerned.

Each month the bank provides the depositor with a **bank statement** that lists (1) each deposit recorded by the bank during the period, (2) each check cleared by the bank during the period, and (3) a running balance of the depositor's account. The bank statement also will reflect any bank charges or deductions (such as service charges) made directly to the depositor's account by the bank. Also included with the bank statement are copies of the deposit slips and all checks that cleared through the bank during the period covered by the statement. A typical bank statement (excluding the deposit slips and canceled checks) is shown in Exhibit 8–1.

On Exhibit 8–1 there are three items that need explanation. First, observe that on June 20 there is listed under "Checks and Debits" a deduction for $18 coded with "NC."[1] This code indicates an "NSF check charge" (in slang, a "hot" or "rubber" check); NSF stands for Not Sufficient Funds. A check for $18 was received and deposited by J. Doe Company from a customer, say R. Roe. Capital National Bank processed it through banking channels to Roe's bank. Roe's account did not have sufficient funds to cover it; therefore, the bank used by Roe returned it to the Capital National Bank, which then charged it back to J. Doe Company. The NSF check is now a receivable; consequently, J. Doe Company must make an entry debiting Receivables (R. Roe) and crediting Cash for the $18.

The second item on Exhibit 8–1 that requires explanation is the $6 listed on June 30 under "Checks and Debits" and coded "SC." This is the code for **bank service charges.** Included with the bank statement was a memo prepared by the bank explaining this service charge (which was not supported by a check). J. Doe Company must make an entry to reflect this $6 decrease in the bank balance by debiting an appropriate expense account, such as Bank Service Expense, and crediting Cash.

The third item that needs explanation is the $100 listed on June 12 under "Deposits" and coded "CM" for "credit memo." In this instance, J. Doe Company had asked the bank to collect a note receivable held by Doe that had been received from a customer. The bank collected the

---

[1] These codes vary among banks.

EXHIBIT 8–1
Bank statement

Capital
National
Bank

7TH & COLORADO
AUSTIN, TEXAS 78789
PHONE: 512/476-6611

ACCOUNT NUMBER	STATEMENT DATE	PAGE NO.
877–95861	6–30–81	1

J. Doe Company
1000 Blank Road
Austin, Texas 78703

STATEMENT OF ACCOUNT

Please examine statement and checks promptly.
If no error is reported within ten days, the
account will be considered correct. Please
report change of address.

ON THIS DATE	YOUR BALANCE WAS	DEPOSITS ADDED		CHECKS AND DEBITS SUBTRACTED		SERVICE COST	RESULTING BALANCE
		NO.	AMOUNT	NO.	AMOUNT		
6-1-81	7 562 40	5	4 050 00	23	3 490 20	6 00	8 122 20

CHECKS AND DEBITS						DEPOSITS	DATE	DAILY BALANCE
							6-1-81	7 562 40
						3 000 00	6-2-81	10 562 40
							6-4-81	10 062 40
500 00		5 00		40 00			6-5-81	9 962 40
55 00						500 00	6-8-81	10 362 40
100 00		16 50		160 00			6-10-81	10 177 70
8 20		10 00				*100 00CM	6-12-81	8 177 70
2 150 00		15 30					6-16-81	8 094 90
7 50		1 50				150 00	6-17-81	8 208 40
35 00		15 00		6 00			6-18-81	8 147 20
40 20							6-20-81	8 129 20
*18 00NC		80 00		2 00			6-21-81	7 921 70
125 50						300 00	6-24-81	8 202 80
18 90		19 60					6-27-81	8 175 68
7 52		32 48					6-28-81	8 128 20
15 00							6-30-81	8 122 20
*6 00SC								

Code:
CM – Credit Memo--Customer note collected
NC – Insufficient funds
SC – Service charge

note and increased the depositor account in favor of J. Doe Company. The bank service charge mentioned above also included the collection service. J. Doe Company must record the collection by making an entry debiting Cash and crediting Note Receivable (customer's name) for the $100.

COMPANY LEDGER ACCOUNTS FOR CASH

Typically, a balance sheet reports **cash** as the first current asset because it is the most **current** of all assets. The amount of cash reported on a balance sheet is the **total amount** of cash at the end of the last day of the accounting period. The total amount of cash reported (as defined on page 317) is the end-of-the-period sum of—

1. Cash in all checking accounts **on deposit** with all banks holding such deposits (offset by any overdrafts).[2]

---

[2] Adjusted for deposits in transit and outstanding checks (discussed later).

2.) Cash on hand (not yet transmitted to a bank for deposit).
3.) Cash held in all petty cash funds.

Typically, a company will carry a separate account in the **ledger** for each separate bank account.[3] Often companies carry forward daily a minimum amount of **cash on hand.** Although such amounts are included in debits to the **regular Cash account,** they have not yet been deposited because they represent either, or a combination of, (a) amounts of cash received since the last deposit was made and (b) a stable amount of cash needed for making change to start the next day.

Frequently, a **petty cash system** is maintained for making separate **small cash payments** (not for making change) in lieu of writing a separate check for each such item. This system necessitates the use of another separate cash account, usually called Petty Cash (discussed later).

BANK RECONCILIATION

Bank reconciliation is a term generally used to identify the process of comparing (reconciling) the **ending** cash balance reflected in a **company's Cash account** and the **ending** cash balance reported by the bank on the monthly **bank statement.** A bank reconciliation serves two primary purposes from the accounting viewpoint:

a.) A check on the accuracy of both the company's Cash account and the bank statement.
b.) An identification of certain transactions that have not been recorded in the company's accounts, although they appear on the bank statement (or vice versa).

A bank reconciliation should be completed for each separate checking account (i.e., for each bank statement received from each bank) at the end of each month.

Normally, when the bank statement arrives, the ending cash balance shown on the bank statement will not agree with the ending balance shown by the related Cash ledger account on the books of the depositor. For example, assume the Cash ledger account at the end of June of J. Doe Company reflected the following (Doe has only one checking account):

Cash

| June 1 | Balance | 7,010.00* | June | Checks written | 3,800.00 |
| June | Deposits | 5,750.00 | | | |

(Ending balance, $8,960.00)

* Including $200 undeposited cash held for change.

---

[3] Larger companies often carry one Cash control account in the ledger which is supplemented with a series of separate cash subsidiary accounts for the depository banks. Refer to Chapter 6, Appendix A.

The $8,122.20 **ending cash balance** shown on the **bank statement** (Exhibit 8–1) is different from the $8,960.00 **ending book balance** shown on the **books of the J. Doe Company** because (1) some transactions affecting cash were recorded in the books of depositor Doe but were not recognized on the bank statement, and (2) some transactions were recognized on the bank statement but were not recorded in the books of the depositor, Doe. The most common causes of a difference between the ending bank balance and the ending book balance of cash are:

1. **Outstanding checks**—checks written by the depositor and recorded in the Cash account as credits (in the depositor's books) but have not cleared the bank (hence they have not been deducted from the bank statement). The **outstanding checks** are identified by comparing the canceled checks returned with the bank statement with the record of checks drawn (such as the check stubs) maintained by the depositor.

2. **Deposits in transit**—deposits taken or mailed to the bank by the depositor and recorded in the Cash account as debits (in the depositor's books) but not yet recorded by the bank (hence they have not been reflected on the bank statement). This usually happens when deposits are made one or two days before the close of the period covered by the bank statement. These are known as **deposits in transit** and are determined by comparing the deposits listed on the bank statement with the copies of the deposit slips retained by the depositor.

3. **Bank service charges**—explained above.

4. **NSF checks**—explained above.

5. **Errors**—both the bank and the depositor are susceptible to errors, especially when the volume of cash transactions is large.

In view of these several factors, a **bank reconciliation** should be made by the depositor (whether for a business or a personal account) immediately after each bank statement is received. A bank reconciliation is an important element of internal control and is needed for accounting purposes. To encourage bank reconciliation by depositors, many banks provide a format on the back of the bank statement for such purposes. Instructions for completing a bank reconciliation also may be given. A typical form is shown in Exhibit 8–2.

Bank reconcilation illustrated. The bank reconciliation for the month of June prepared by J. Doe Company to reconcile the ending bank balance (Exhibit 8–1, $8,122.20) with the ending book balance (page 321, $8,960), is shown in Exhibit 8–3. Observe on the completed reconciliation, Exhibit 8–3, that the **true** (correct) cash balance is $9,045, which is different from both the reported bank and book balances before the reconciliation.

Although the layout of a bank reconciliation can vary, the most simple and flexible one follows a balancing format with the "Depositor's Books," and the "Bank Statement" identified separately. This format starts with two different amounts: (1) the reported **ending** balance per books and (2) the reported **ending** balance per bank statement. Provision then is

EXHIBIT 8–2
Sample form and instructions for a bank reconciliation

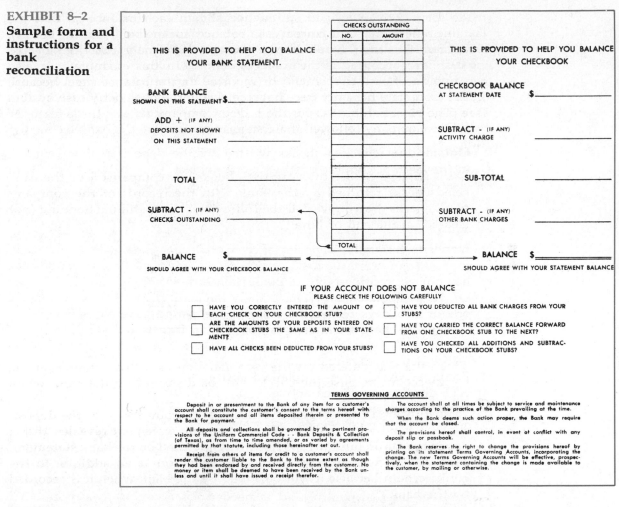

EXHIBIT 8–3

J. DOE COMPANY
Bank Reconciliation
For the Month Ending June 30, 1981

Depositor's Books			Bank Statement	
Ending cash balance per books		$8,960.00	Ending cash balance per bank statement	$ 8,122.20
Additions:			Additions:	
Proceeds of customer note collected by bank		100.00	Deposit in transit	1,800.00
Error in recording check No. 137		9.00	Cash on hand	200.00
		9,069.00		10,122.20
Deductions:			Deductions:	
NSF check of R. Roe	$18.00		Outstanding checks	1,077.20
Bank service charges	6.00	24.00		
True cash balance		$9,045.00	True cash balance	$ 9,045.00

made for additions to, and subtractions from, each balance so that the last line reflects the same correct cash balance (for the bank and the books). This correct balance represents the amount that finally *should be* reflected in the Cash account after the reconciliation. In this example it is also the amount of cash that should be reported on the balance sheet because J. Doe Company has only one checking account and no petty cash system (see page 321). Exhibit 8–3 for the J. Doe Company reflects these features.

J. Doe Company followed these steps in completing the bank reconciliation:

1. **Identification of the outstanding checks**—A comparison of the canceled checks returned by the bank with the records of the company of all checks drawn revealed the following checks still outstanding (not cleared) at the end of June:

Check No.	Amount
101	$ 145.00
123	815.00
131	117.20
Total	$1,077.20

This total was entered on the reconciliation as a deduction from the bank account because the checks will be deducted by the bank when they clear the bank.

2. **Identification of the deposits in transit**—A comparison of the deposit slips on hand with those listed on the bank statement revealed that a deposit made on June 30 for $1,800 was not listed on the bank statement. This amount was entered on the reconciliation as an addition to the bank account because it will be added by the bank when it is recorded by the bank.

3. **Cash on hand**—On the date of the bank statement, cash on hand (i.e., undeposited cash held for making change) amounted to $200. Since this amount is included in the company's Cash account but was not included in the bank statement balance (it was not deposited), it was entered on the reconciliation as an addition to the bank balance (as it would be, if deposited).

4. Items on bank statement not yet recorded in the books of J. Doe Company.

   a. Proceeds of note collected, $100 (explained on page 319)—entered on the bank reconciliation as an addition to the book balance; it already was included in the bank balance. A journal entry is required to increase the Cash account balance and decrease the Note Receivable balance for this item.

   b. NSF check of R. Roe, $18 (explained on page 319)—entered on the bank reconciliation as a deduction from the book balance; it already was deducted from the bank statement balance. A journal entry is required to reduce the Cash account balance for this item.

(c.) Bank service charges, $6 (explained above)—entered on the bank reconciliation as a deduction from the book balance; it already has been deducted from the bank balance. A journal entry is required to reduce the Cash account balance for this item.

5. **Error**—At this point J. Doe Company found that the reconciliation did not balance by $9. Since this amount is divisible by 9, they suspected a transposition. (A transposition, such as writing 65 for 56, always will cause an error that is divisible by 9.) Upon checking the journal entries made during the month, they found that a check was written by J. Doe Company for $56 to pay an account payable for that amount. The check was recorded in the company's accounts as $65. The incorrect entry made was a debit to Accounts Payable and a credit to Cash for $65 (instead of $56). Therefore, $9 (i.e., $65 − $56) must be added to the book cash balance on the reconciliation; the bank cleared the check for the correct amount, $56. The following correcting entry also must be made in the accounts: Cash, debit $9; and Accounts Payable, credit $9.

Note in Exhibit 8–3 that the "Depositor's Books" and the "Bank Statement" parts of the bank reconciliation now agree at a **true cash balance** of $9,045. This is the amount which will be included in the cash amount reported on a balance sheet prepared at the end of the period. The process of preparing a bank reconciliation illustrated above accomplishes the objective of checking the accuracy of the company's books and the bank statement (see page 323).

The bank reconciliation must be used to identify any transactions that are included on it which have not been entered into the accounts of the company (see the second objective listed on page 321). The explanations above of the development of the bank reconciliation cited such transactions. When the appropriate transactions are entered in the accounts the company's Cash account will agree with the true cash balance reflected on the bank reconciliation. Therefore, the following entries, taken directly from the bank reconciliation, must be entered in the company's records:

	Journal entries from bank reconciliation	
	Debit	*Credit*
Entries from the reconciliation:		
Cash	100	
Note receivable		100
To record note collected by bank.		
Accounts receivable (R. Roe)	18	
Cash		18
To record NSF check.		

Entries *(continued)*	Journal entries from bank reconciliation	
	Debit	Credit
Bank service expense	6	
Cash		6
To record bank service charges.		
Cash	9	
Accounts payable (name)		9
To correct transposition made in prior journal entry.		

Cash (after recording results of bank reconciliation)

June 1	Balance	7,010.00	June	Checks written	3,800.00
June	Deposits	5,750.00	June 30	NSF check	18.00
June 30	Note collected	100.00	June 30	Bank service charge	6.00
June 30	Correcting entry	9.00			

(True cash balance, $9,045.00)

Observe that all of (and only) the additions and deductions on the "Depositor's Books" side of the reconciliation require journal entries to update the Cash account. Otherwise, the cash amount reported on the balance sheet and reflected in the Cash account will not be the **true cash balance.** All other reconciling differences are adjustments to the "Bank Statement" side and will work out automatically when they clear the bank. The **balance sheet** should report the true cash balance of $9,045 (which includes the cash on hand) plus any balance in a Petty Cash account (and any other cash accounts).

The importance of the bank reconciliation procedure in generating entries to *update* the Cash account should not be overlooked. This feature is important in measuring the true cash balance that should be reported on the balance sheet.

CASH OVER AND SHORT

Regardless of the care exercised, when a large number of cash transactions is involved, errors in handling cash inevitably occur. These errors cause cash shortages or cash overages at the end of the day when the cash is counted and compared with the cash records for the day. Cash overages and shortages must be recognized in the accounts. To illustrate, assume that at the end of a particular day the cash from sales, as counted, amounted to $1,347.19 and the cash register tapes for sales totaled $1,357.19—a cash *shortage* of $10 is indicated. The sales for the day should be recorded as follows:

Cash	1,347.19	
Cash over and short	10.00	
Sales		1,357.19
To record cash sales and cash shortage.		

Alternatively, in the case of a cash *overage*, the Cash Over and Short account would be credited. It is important to note that sales revenue should be recorded for the correct amount reflected on the register tapes. Sometimes the bank reconciliation will divulge a cash shortage or overage which must be reflected under the "books" portion of the reconciliation and recorded in an accounting entry. At the end of the period, the Cash Over and Short account, in the case of a cumulative debit balance, usually is reported as miscellaneous expense. If a credit balance exists, it is reported as miscellaneous revenue.

PETTY CASH

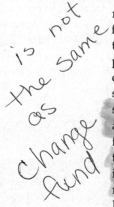

is not the same as Change fund

In the discussion of internal control we stated that all major disbursements of cash should be made by prenumbered checks. Many businesses find it quite inconvenient and costly in terms of paperwork and employee time to write checks for small payments for items such as taxi fares, newspapers, and small amounts of supplies. To avoid this inconvenience and cost, businesses frequently establish a **petty cash fund** to handle these small miscellaneous cash payments. To establish a petty cash fund a check should be drawn "Pay to the order of Petty Cash" for the amount desired and cashed. Small cash payments, supported by written receipts, are made from this fund. When the cash runs low and at the end of each period, the expenditures from the fund are summarized and an accounting entry is made to reflect the payments from the fund (debit expenses) and to record the check written to reimburse the fund for the total amount spent. For balance sheet reporting, the amount in the Petty Cash account must be added to the other cash balances. The details of accounting for a petty cash fund are discussed and illustrated in Appendix A to this chapter.

COMPENSATING BALANCES

An accounting issue related to cash is the disclosure of **compensating balances.** A compensating balance exists when the bank requires the business to maintain a minimum amount in its bank account. A minimum, or compensating balance, may be required by the bank explicitly (by a loan agreement), or implicitly (by informal understanding), as part of a credit-granting arrangement. Often, it is difficult for the independent auditor to know whether or not an informal understanding exists. Information on compensating balances is important to statement users because there are two major effects on the business: (1) a compensating balance requirement imposes a restriction on the amount of cash readily available in the checking account; and (2) if it arises in connection with a loan, the compensating balance increases the real rate of interest on the loan since not all of the cash borrowed can be used because some must remain on deposit.

Information concerning a compensating balance must be reported in the notes to the financial statements because of its importance to statement users.

DATA PROCESSING FOR CASH

In small businesses the processing of accounting information on cash inflows and cash outflows often is done manually. In medium-sized companies much of the cash information processing may be mechanized through use of various accounting machines. In the still larger businesses much of the cash information processing is accomplished by means of electronic computers. The nature of these data processing activities broadly is the same whether manual, mechanical, or electronic approaches are used. For instructional purposes their characteristics are viewed best in terms of a manual system. Appendix B to this chapter presents a data processing procedure known as "special journals." Two of these special journals relate to data processing for cash inflows and outflows. As you read the appendix, although a manual system is illustrated, mechanical or electronic computer applications should be apparent.

PART B: MEASURING AND REPORTING SHORT-TERM INVESTMENTS

To employ idle cash and for other business reasons, a company may invest in commercial paper (such as certificates of deposit), or in the capital stocks (equity securities) or bonds (debt securities) of another company. Such investments are facilitated because commercial paper is sold by local banks, and the stocks and bonds of most of the large corporations are "listed" on the New York or American stock exchanges. Capital stock of smaller unlisted companies frequently can be bought and sold "over the counter" or between individuals and companies directly.

When bonds of another company are acquired, the purchaser has become a creditor of the issuing company, since bonds represent debt owed by the other company similar to a long-term note payable. As the holder of a bond, the investor is entitled to receive interest on the principal of the bond and the principal if held to maturity. In contrast, when shares of capital stock are purchased as an investment, the purchaser becomes one of the owners (frequently called stockholders, shareholders, or equity-holders) of the company that issued the stock. As an owner, the stockholder receives dividends when they are declared and paid by the board of directors of the other company. Since most capital stock confers voting rights, the stockholder is provided an opportunity to exercise some control over the issuing company. The amount of control is dependent upon the number of voting shares owned by the shareholder in relation to the total number of such shares of stock outstanding.

Investments made by one company in the stocks or bonds of another company may be either (1) short-term investments (sometimes called temporary investments) or (2) long-term investments (sometimes called permanent investments). This chapter discusses the measurement and reporting of short-term investments; long-term investments are discussed in Chapter 13.

SHORT-TERM INVESTMENTS DEFINED

To be classified as a short-term (or temporary) investment, a security must meet a twofold test of (1) marketability and (2) a short-term holding period. **Marketability** means that the security must be traded regularly on the market so that there is a continuous market available and a determinable market price. Therefore, short-term investments generally are listed stocks and bonds, or short-term government securities. A **short-term holding period** means that it must be the **intention** of the management to convert the securities into cash in the near future for normal operating purposes.[4] Short term refers to the longer of the normal operating cycle of the business or one year as specified in the definition of current assets (Chapter 2, page 49). The distinction between short-term and long-term investments is important because (1) there are accounting differences that must be observed and (2) short-term investments must be classified as a current asset, whereas the long-term investments are reported under a noncurrent caption, "Investments and funds."

MEASUREMENT OF SHORT-TERM INVESTMENTS

In accordance with the cost principle, short-term investments, when acquired, are measured and recorded at their cost. Cost includes the market price paid plus all additional costs incurred to purchase the security. To illustrate, assume the Brown Corporation had approximately $50,000 in cash that would not be needed for operations for six or more months. In December, Brown purchased 1,000 shares of American Telephone and

---

[4] We shall see later that long-term investments also include marketable securities. Thus, the basic distinction between short-term and long-term investments turns primarily on the intention of management in respect to their expected disposal date. The same kind of security may be a short-term investment in one company and a long-term investment in another company, depending upon the intentions of the respective managements.

Telegraph (AT&T) stock for $56,000, including all broker's fees, transfer costs, and taxes related to the purchase.

The transaction would be recorded in the accounts as follows:

December 19A:

Short-term investments (1,000 shares @ $56) 56,000
   Cash 56,000
   Purchase of 1,000 shares at AT&T stock at $56 as a short-term investment.

Assume that two months after the purchase a quarterly cash dividend of $0.70 per share is received. The revenue on the short-term investment would be recorded as follows:

Cash 700
   Investment revenue 700
   Cash dividend of $0.70 per share on short-term investment (AT&T stock); $0.70 × 1,000 shares = $700.

Short-term investments held at the end of the accounting period are reported, at lower of cost or market (LCM) on the balance sheet as a current asset (lower of cost or market is duscussed in the next section). The current market value at that date should be shown parenthetically. For example, at the end of 19A Brown Corporation would report the short-term investment of AT&T stock as follows, assuming a market value **above** cost of $57 per share at the end of the accounting period:

Balance Sheet
At December 31, 19A

Current assets:
   Cash $62,000
   Short-term investments, at cost (current market value, $57,000) 56,000

When a short-term investment is sold, any loss or gain on the sale must be recognized. To illustrate, assume that during April 19B Brown sold one fourth of the short-term investment in AT&T stock (250 shares) for $14,500 cash; after deducting broker's fees, transfer costs, and taxes it would be recorded as follows:

April 19B:

```
Cash ................................................  14,500
    Short-term investments (250 shares @ $56) ..............       14,000
    Gain on sale of investments ..........................          500
  Sale of 250 shares of AT&T stock at $58 per share = $14,500.
```

When a company owns short-term securities in several other companies, the securities held generally are referred to collectively as the **short-term portfolio**. A portfolio of short-term investments is managed (i.e., acquired, held, and sold) with the objective of maximizing the return while minimizing the risk. Thus, a portfolio of securities tends to be managed and accounted for as a whole rather than as a number of separate investments.

SHORT-TERM INVESTMENTS VALUED AT LOWER OF COST OR MARKET (LCM)

Although short-term investments are measured and recorded at cost when acquired and are measured thereafter in conformity with the cost principle, there is an important exception. The exception occurs when the *current* market value of the portfolio of **shares** (i.e., equity securities only) drops below the recorded acquisition cost.[5]

In Chapter 7, relating to inventories of merchandise, we explained that items of merchandise in the inventory for which the *replacement cost* had dropped below acquisition cost should be measured on a lower of cost or market basis (LCM). The same principle applies to other current assets, including the short-term stock investment portfolio. It is reasoned that because of the drop in market value, the short-term stock investment portfolio has lost a part of its value as a short-term source of cash. The drop in value is viewed as a **holding or unrealized loss** that should be recognized in the period in which the drop occurred. However, a corresponding line of reasoning is not applied when the current market value is *above* the acquisition cost. Although this practice is an exception to both the *cost principle* and the *consistency principle*, the LCM basis in this situation is applied because the **principle of conservatism** (see Exhibit 2–6) is permitted to override the other principles. Thus, the short-term stock investment portfolio is restated on a LCM basis. The LCM rule does not apply to short-term investments in **debt** securities; they are accounted for at cost.

For short-term investments, at the end of the accounting period, any difference between their cost and a **lower** end-of-the-period market value is recorded in the accounts. The entry is a debit to an **expense** account

---

[5] FASB *Statement of Accounting Standards No. 12,* "Accounting for Certain Marketable Securities" (Stamford, Conn. December 1975). The procedures and accounting entries in this section specifically follow the *requirements* of *FASB statement No. 12.* The statement *does not apply LCM to investments in debt securities.*

called "Unrealized Loss on Short-Term Investments" and a credit to a **contra asset** account called "Allowance to Reduce Short-Term Investments to Market." Thus, this entry records the holding (market) loss as an expense in the period in which the market dropped and revalues the short-term investment on an LCM basis.

To illustrate, let's return to the above example. Recall that Brown Corporation still owns 750 shares of AT&T stock at a cost of $42,000 (i.e., $56 per share). Assume that it is the end of the 19B accounting period and the financial statements are to be prepared. Assume further that the current market value of the stock is $55 per share; the total market value, therefore, is 750 shares × $55 = $41,250. Although the stock is not sold at this date, under LCM basis, a **holding loss** would be recognized at the end of the accounting period in an adjusting entry as follows:

December 31, 19B:

Unrealized loss on short-term investments*	750	
Allowance to reduce short-term investments to market		750
To reduce short-term investments to LCM basis ($42,000 − $41,250 = $750).		
*Report on the current income statement as "Financial expense."		

After the write-down illustrated above, the 19B balance sheet would report the short-term investment in equity securities as follows:

Balance Sheet
At December 31, 19B

Current assets:		
Short-term investments (at cost)	$42,000	
Less: Allowance to reduce short-term		
investments to market	750	$41,250

or alternatively:

Current assets:	
Short-term investment, at LCM (cost $42,000)	$41,250

When the LCM basis is applied to short-term investments, the measurement is based upon the *total portfolio cost* versus *total portfolio market* amount rather than on an item-by-item basis. To illustrate, assume Brown Company (see above) had three separate stocks, A, B, and C (rather than AT&T), in its short-term **investment portfolio.** The measurement at the end of the accounting period would be derived as follows:

Security	Portfolio Acquisition cost	Current market
A Company common stock	$10,000	$10,000
B Company preferred stock	25,000	23,000
C Company common stock..............	7,000	8,250
Totals	$42,000	$41,250

Under the LCM basis, the Short-term Investments account would be written down to $41,250 as illustrated above.[6]

In applying the LCM basis, when a short-term investment is sold, any loss or gain on disposal is measured as the difference between its **sales price** and its **original cost** regardless of any balance in the allowance account. Any balance in the allowance account at the end of the accounting period is adjusted (up or down) to reflect any difference between total portfolio cost and a lower total portfolio market of the short-term investments held at the end of the accounting period.

To illustrate, assume that during January 19C Brown Company sold the remaining 750 shares of AT&T stock at $55.50 per share. The sale would be recorded as follows:[7]

January, 19C:

```
Cash (750 shares × $55.50) .................................     41,625
Loss on sale of short-term investments ......................        375
     Short-term investments (750 shares × $56) ..............               42,000
```

CERTIFICATES OF DEPOSIT

In recent years a common short-term investment strategy to employ idle cash has been to purchase debt securities called **certificates of deposit**

---

[6] In contrast, when the LCM rule is applied to merchandise inventories, the item-by-item basis generally is used since merchandise is not viewed "as a single item" but as separate items.

[7] Assuming no short-term investments were held at the end of 19C, the following entry would be made:

December 31, 19C:

```
Allowance to reduce short-term investments to market ........................     750
     Recovery of unrealized loss on short-term investments* .....................          750
```
*Some accountants prefer the title: "Unrealized Gain on Short-Term Investments."

Note that the LCM effect is to record a holding loss in the period that the market dropped below cost and to record an offset (a holding gain) in the period of sale. This anomalous effect occurs because LCM is not consistent with either cost basis accounting or market value accounting for investments.

(CDs). A "CD" is an investment contract (a certificate is received) an investor may purchase from a bank for cash. The contract specifies (1) a limited period of time for the investment, such as 90 days, 6 months, 1 year, and so on; and (2) a guaranteed interest rate. Generally, the larger the amount of the certificate (the amount invested), the higher the interest rate. The interest rate also tends to be higher for longer time periods to maturity. Certificates of deposit and similar commercial paper are used often for the short-term employment of idle cash because of the relatively high interest return and the liquidity factor.

Certificates of deposit are measured and accounted for on the cost basis (not LCM). At the end of the accounting period, an adjusting entry is made for any accrued interest earned yet not collected. CDs are accounted for separately from the regular cash. The interest earned is reported on the income statement as investment revenue. For external reporting purposes, certificates of deposit are reported as a current asset as shown here:

Current assets:
Cash $200,000
Certificates of deposit 300,000

or

Current assets:
Cash and certificates of deposit $500,000

ADJUSTING ENTRIES FOR INVESTMENT REVENUE

At the end of the accounting period, **no adjusting entry** is made for dividend revenue on capital stock held as an investment because dividends (1) do not accrue on the basis of time and (2) are not paid unless formally declared by the board of directors of the issuing corporation. In contrast, when CDs, bonds, or other debt securities are held, an **adjusting entry is required** for accrued interest revenue as for each debt security illustrated in Chapter 4 and in Part C of this chapter.

PART C: MEASURING AND REPORTING RECEIVABLES

Broadly, receivables encompass all claims of the entity against other entities or persons for money, goods, or services. In most businesses there are two types of receivables: trade receivables and special (nontrade) receivables. Either type may include both short-term receivables (i.e., classified as current assets) and long-term receivables (i.e., classified as long-term investments or other assets). For example, a balance sheet may report the following receivables:

Current assets:		
Trade accounts receivable	$40,000	
Less: Allowance for doubtful accounts	3,000	$37,000
Trade notes receivable, short term		5,000
Special receivables:		
Due from employees		400
Equipment note receivable, short term		600
Long-term investments:		
Note receivable, long term		10,000
Special receivable, long term		8,000
Other assets:		
Utility deposits		2,000
Due from company officers		1,000

TRADE RECEIVABLES

Trade receivables include trade accounts receivable (usually called accounts receivable) and trade notes receivable. Either may be short term or long term, although the latter is relatively rare in most situations. Trade receivables arise from the regular operating activities of the business; that is, from the sale of merchandise and/or services.

Trade accounts receivable and the contra account, Allowance for Doubtful Accounts, were discussed in detail in Chapter 6.

Many businesses *factor* their accounts receivable instead of holding them until due date for collection. **"Factoring"** is a term used for the sale of accounts receivable to a financial institution, which usually occurs on the date that the goods and/or services are sold. It is used widely because the business immediately receives the cash for sales; however, the rate of interest for factoring arrangements tends to be high. A discussion of the detailed accounting involved is beyond the objectives of this book.

SPECIAL RECEIVABLES

Special (or nontrade) receivables arise from transactions other than the sale of merchandise and/or service. Special receivables may be short term or long term and should be given descriptive titles similar to those illustrated above. They should not be included in the caption "Accounts receivable." Other than for appropriate classification on the balance sheet, special receivables generally do not involve unusual measurement or reporting problems.

NOTES RECEIVABLE

Notes receivable may be either trade notes receivable or special notes receivable, depending upon the source of the note. A promissory note is an unconditional promise in writing (i.e., a formal document) to pay (1) a specified sum of money on demand or at a definite future date known as the maturity or due date and (2) specified interest at one or more future dates. The person who signs a promissory note is known as the **maker,** and the person to whom payment is to be made is known as the **payee.** The maker views the note as a "note payable," whereas the payee views the note as a "note receivable." A note receivable involves two distinctly different amounts: (1) **principal,** which is the amount loaned; and (2) **interest,** which is the specified amount charged for use of the principal.

Interest calculations. Interest represents the **time cost of money.** To the payee of a promissory note, interest is **revenue;** while to the maker it is **expense.** The formula for computing interest is:

Principal × Annual rate of interest × Fraction of year = Interest amount

It is important to remember that **interest rates** are quoted on an **annual basis** and, therefore, must be restated for time periods of less than one year. Thus, the interest on a $10,000, 12 percent, 90-day promissory note would be calculated as follows:

$$\$10,000 \times 0.12 \times 90/360 = \$300$$

When a note specifies a number of days, the exact days must be counted on the calendar to determine the due date and then related to the number of days in the year. For computing interest, sometimes it is assumed that the year encompasses 360 days, so that each day's interest is $\frac{1}{360}$ of a year rather than $\frac{1}{365}$. This has the effect of making the actual interest cost for a short-term loan slightly higher than the stated amount of interest.[8]

All commercial notes involve interest, either explicitly or implicitly, because money borrowed, or loaned, has a time value that cannot be avoided.[9]

Accounting for notes receivable. Notes receivable usually arise in a business as a result of selling merchandise or services. Although most businesses use open accounts (i.e., accounts receivable), those selling high-priced items on credit frequently require notes from their customers. Assuming a $10,000, 12 percent, interest-bearing promissory note was received from a customer as a result of the sale of goods, the payee would record it on the date of the sale as follows:

Notes receivable (trade)	10,000	
Sales revenue		10,000

To record 90-day, 12 percent, interest-bearing note received from customer.

Note: Assuming the note was in settlement of an open account receivable, which frequently happens, the credit would have been to Accounts Receivable instead of to Sales Revenue.

---

[8] For simplicity throughout this book, interest dates are given in a manner that avoids the needless counting of exact days on a calendar. Most lending institutions use 365 days in the calculations.

[9] An *interest-bearing note* explicitly specifies a stated rate of interest (such as 12 percent) on the face of the note, and the interest is to be paid in addition to the *face amount* of the note. In contrast, a *noninterest-bearing note* does not explicitly state an interest rate on the note because the interest charge is included in the face amount of the note (i.e., the interest is implicit).

When collection is made at maturity date 90 days later, the entry would be:

```
Cash ..................................................  10,300
    Notes receivable (trade) ...............................        10,000
    Interest revenue .......................................           300
    To record collection of a 90-day, 12 percent, interest-bearing
    note receivable plus interest ($10,000 × 0.12 × 90/360 = $300).
```

Default of a note receivable. A note receivable that is not collected at maturity is said to be **dishonored** or **defaulted** by the maker. Immediately after default, an entry should be made by the payee transferring the amount due from the Notes Receivable account to a special account such as Special Receivable—Defaulted Trade Notes. Since the maker is responsible for both the unpaid principal and the unpaid interest, the receivable account should reflect the full amount owed to the payee. To illustrate, assuming the above note receivable was defaulted by the maker, the entry in the accounts of the holder or payee would be:[10]

```
Special receivable—defaulted trade notes ....................  10,300
    Notes receivable (trade) ................................        10,000
    Interest revenue .......................................           300
    To record the principal and interest earned on defaulted note.
```

Special Receivable—Defaulted Trade Notes is reported as a current or noncurrent asset depending upon the probable collection date.

Discounting a note receivable. Many businesses prefer a negotiable note receivable rather than an open account receivable from customers involved in large amounts of credit. The primary reasons are (1) the note provides formal evidence of the receivable and (2) notes often can be sold to a financial institution, such as a bank, or to individuals to obtain needed cash *before* the maturity date. Selling a note receivable to a financial institution frequently is referred to as **discounting** a note receivable.

Promissory notes almost always are negotiable. A **negotiable instrument** is one that can be transferred by endorsement (there are other technical legal requisites for negotiability). The most common negotiable instrument is a check. Notes and a number of other instruments generally can be transferred by endorsement. An endorsement may be simply by signature

---

[10] From date of default, the amount due at that date (principal plus interest) continues to draw interest either at the stipulated rate or the legal rate as specified by the law of the state. There may be a question about the propriety of recognizing the interest revenue until collection is made when there is a reasonable probability that collection will not be made.

of the holder, in which case it is said to be "with recourse." This means that in case of default, as in the case of a "hot" check (i.e., one that the depositor's bank has turned down because of insufficient funds in the depositor's account), the endorser is liable contractually for repayment. In contrast, an endorsement may be made "without recourse" by writing this phrase on the instrument before the endorsement signature. This means that the endorser cannot be held liable contractually in the case of default by the maker.[11] Entities and individuals seldom will accept endorsements without recourse; that is, a discounted note receivable usually is endorsed with recourse and, as a result, the financial institution can rely on both the maker and the endorser. An endorsement with recourse makes the endorser **contingently liable;** that is, if the maker does not pay the note at maturity, the endorser must do so. The full-disclosure principle (Exhibit 2–6) requires that such **contingent liabilities** be reported on the financial statements. This usually is done by means of a note to the financial statements, as illustrated below.

To illustrate the discounting of a note receivable, assume that the $10,000, 12 percent, 90-day interest-bearing note receivable (page 336) was sold to the Capital National Bank after 30 days at a **discount rate** of 15 percent per annum. The discount rate is the annual rate of interest required by the bank and may be more or less than the interest rate specified on the note. The discount rate is applied to the **maturity value**— that is, the principal amount of the note *plus* the amount of interest due at maturity. The discount rate of interest is applied to the number of days the bank will hold the note (in this case, 60 days). Computation of the amount the bank will pay for the note is:

Discounting a note receivable

Note: Principal, $10,000; annual interest rate, 12%; term, 90 days.
Discounted: Thirty days after date; discount rate, 15% per year.

Principal amount	$10,000.00
Plus: Interest due at maturity ($10,000 × 0.12 × 90/360)	300.00
Maturity value—amount subject to discount rate	10,300.00
Less: Discount—interest charged by bank	
($10,300 × 0.15 × 60/360)	257.50
Proceeds—amount the bank pays for the note	$10,042.50

The discounting or sale of the note receivable would be recorded by the payee as follows:[12]

---

[11] The endorser or transferor may not be held liable contractually. However, the transferor may be held liable under *warranty* liability since the endorsement "without recourse" does not disclaim warranties such as title to the instrument. These legal distinctions are beyond the scope of this course.

[12] The credit of $42.50 to Interest Revenue may be explained as follows: Had the note been held to maturity, the payee would have earned $300 interest revenue; however, the bank charged interest amounting to $257.50. The difference is $42.50, which is the

Cash	10,042.50	
Notes receivable (trade)		10,000.00
Interest revenue		42.50

To record discounting of a note receivable.

Although the note was sold, the endorser must disclose the *contingent liability* related to the note by means of a footnote to the financial statements similar to the following:

Note: At December 31, 1981, the company was contingently liable for notes receivable discounted in the amount of $10,300.

EXCEPTION PRINCIPLE

In the preceding chapters, the terms **materiality** (or material amount) and **conservatism** were used often. The principle of conservatism was cited earlier as the reason for using the LCM basis in measuring inventory (page 291) and short-term investments (page 331). These terms, materiality and conservatism, refer to one of the fundamental accounting principles listed in Exhibit 2–6. In that exhibit conservatism is shown as one part of the **exception principle.** The exception principle is comprised of the following three subprinciples: (1) materiality, (2) conservatism, and (3) industry peculiarities.

Although accounting recognizes that measurement and compliance with the fundamental accounting principles (Exhibit 2–6) are essential, from a practical point of view the benefits of extremely high accuracy in measurement and absolute compliance with concepts sometimes are offset by practical considerations. Under certain **limited conditions,** the exception principle may override one or more of the other principles. These conditions are specified in the following three subprinciples:

1. **Materiality**—The fundamental accounting principles must be followed without exception for each transaction when the amount involved in the transaction is material (i.e., significant) in relationship to its overall effect on the financial statements. Although immaterial amounts must be accounted for, they need not be accorded theoretically correct treatment. For example, a pencil sharpener that cost $7.99 and has a five-year estimated life need not be depreciated under the matching principle; rather the $7.99 may be expensed in the period of acquisition because the amount is not material. The clerical cost alone of recording depreciation over the five-year period would exceed, by far, the cost of the

---

net interest earned by the payee for holding it 30 of the 90 days. The discount rate is applied to the maturity value of the note because that is the amount the bank will advance, less the interest required by the bank.

asset. Additionally, the $1.60 annual depreciation amount would not affect any important decisions by statement users.

2. **Conservatism**—This concept holds that where more than one accounting or measurement alternative is permissible for a transaction, the one having the least favorable immediate effect on income or owners' equity usually should be selected. For example, in measuring the amount of a short-term investment or a merchandise inventory, the LCM basis is used. In this case, conservatism overrides the cost principle so that any market or holding loss (but not a gain) that occurs before the asset is sold is recorded and reported.

3. **Industry peculiarities**—This concept holds that the unique characteristics of an industry may require use of special accounting approaches and measurement procedures in order to produce realistic financial reporting. For example, in the insurance and mutual fund industries, investment portfolios are accounted for and reported at market value (rather than at LCM or at cost).

DEMONSTRATION CASE

Dotter's Equipment Company, Incorporated

(Try to resolve the requirements before proceeding to the suggested solution that follows.)

Dotter's Equipment Company has been selling farm machinery for more than 30 years. The company has been quite successful in both sales and repair services. A wide range of farm equipment, including trucks, is sold. The company policy is to seek "high volume and quality service, at the right price." Credit terms with varying conditions are typical. Although most of the credit granted is carried by several financial institutions, Dotter's will carry the credit in special circumstances. As a result, the company occasionally accepts a promissory note and keeps it to maturity. However, if a cash need arises, some of these notes may be sold (i.e., discounted) to the local bank with which Dotter's carries its checking account. This case focuses on two farm equipment notes that were received during 19D. By following these notes from date of sale of farm equipment to final collection, we can see the various measurement problems posed and the accounting for them. The fiscal year for accounting purposes ends December 31, 19D.

The series of transactions in respect to the two notes follows:

Equipment Note No. 1:

19D:

Jan. 15   Sold a farm tractor to S. Scott for $20,000 and received a 25 percent cash down payment plus a $15,000 equipment note receivable for the balance. The note was due in nine months and was interest bearing at 12 percent per annum. A mortgage on the tractor was executed as a part of the agreement.

Apr. 15   The Scott equipment note was sold to the local bank at a 13 percent per annum discount rate. Dotter endorsed the note, with recourse, and the proceeds were deposited in Dotter's checking account.

Oct. 15   Scott paid the bank the face amount of the note plus the interest, $15,000 + ($15,000 \times 0.12 \times \frac{9}{12}) = $16,350.

Required:

a. Give appropriate journal entries on each of the three dates. Show the interest computations and give an explanation for each entry.

b. Assume, that instead of payment on October 15, 19D, S. Scott defaulted on the note. When notified by the bank, Dotter's paid the note and interest in full. Give the appropriate entry for this assumption and one for the further assumption that Scott later paid Dotter's in full on December 1, 19D.

Equipment Note No. 2:

19D:

Oct. 1   Sold a farm truck to B. Day for $7,000; received a down payment of $1,000 and set up an account receivable for the balance; terms, n/30.

Nov. 1   Day came in and wanted an extension on the account receivable "until he sold some products." After some discussion it was agreed to settle the account with a six-month, 12 percent, interest-bearing note. Day signed the $6,000 note and a mortgage on this date.

Dec. 31   End of the fiscal period. An adjusting entry is required.

19E:

Jan. 1   Start of the new fiscal period.

May 1   Since this was the due date, Day came in and paid the note plus interest in full. The note was marked paid and the mortgage was canceled.

Required:

c. Give appropriate journal entries on each date, including any adjusting entries at year-end. Omit closing entries at year-end. Provide an explanation for each journal entry.

Suggested solution

Requirement (a)—Equipment Note No. 1:

January 15, 19D:

```
Cash ..................................................   5,000.00
Equipment notes receivable ..........................  15,000.00
    Sales revenue ...................................               20,000.00
    Sale of tractor to S. Scott for cash and equipment note;
    terms of note, nine months, 12 percent interest, including
    a mortgage.
```

April 15, 19D:

```
Cash ..............................................  15,287.25
    Equipment notes receivable .....................               15,000.00
    Interest revenue ...............................                  287.25
    Discounted Scott equipment note receivable
    at bank discount rate of 13 percent.
    Proceeds computed:
    Principal amount ...........................  $15,000.00
    Interest to maturity ($15,000 × 0.12 × 9/12) .....  1,350.00
    Maturity value ............................  16,350.00
    Discount ($16,350 × 0.13 × 6/12) .............   1,062.75
    Proceeds ..................................  $15,287.25
```

October 15, 19D: No entry required; Scott paid the bank that owned the note. During the period from April 15, 19D, until the note was paid, Dotter's was contingently liable for the note because of the possibility that Scott would default.

Requirement (b)—Equipment Note No. 1:

Under the assumption that Scott defaulted on the note on due date, Dotter's would have to pay the principal plus interest in full and make the following entry:

October 15, 19D:

```
Special receivable (defaulted note—S. Scott) ............  16,350.00
    Cash ..............................................               16,350.00
    Scott note defaulted; payment to bank of the $15,000 prin-
    cipal plus interest ($15,000 × 0.12 × 9/12 = $1,350).
```

December 1, 19D:

```
Cash .............................................  16,350.00
    Special receivable (defaulted note, S. Scott) .........        16,350.00
    Payment received in full on Scott note in default.

    Note: In most states, Dotter's could also have assessed Scott interest at the legal rate on
    the $16,350 amount overdue; in this case, there would be a credit to Interest Revenue.
```

Requirement (c)—Equipment Note No. 2:

October 1, 19D:

```
Cash ......................................................  1,000
Accounts receivable  ......................................  6,000
    Sales revenue  ........................................          7,000
    Sold truck to B. Day; terms of the receivable, n/30.
```

November 1, 19D:

```
Equipment notes receivable ................................  6,000
    Accounts receivable ...................................          6,000
    Settled account receivable with a six-month, 12 percent, interest-
    bearing note.
```

December 31, 19D:

```
Interest receivable .......................................  120
    Interest revenue ......................................          120
    Adjusting entry for two months' interest accrued at 12 percent on
    Day equipment note ($6,000 × 0.12 × 2/12 = $120).
```

January 1, 19E: No entry is required on this date; however, a reversal of the adjusting entry could be made to facilitate the subsequent entry when the interest is collected. The *optional reversing entry* would be (see Chapter 5, Appendix A):

```
Interest revenue ..........................................  120
    Interest receivable ...................................          120
```

May 1, 19E: This entry to record collection of the principal plus interest will vary depending on whether the above reversing entry was made:

a. Assuming reversing entry was not made:

Cash	6,360	
Equipment notes receivable		6,000
Interest receivable ($6,000 × 0.12 × $\frac{2}{12}$)		120
Interest revenue ($6,000 × 0.12 × $\frac{4}{12}$)		240
Collection of Day equipment note plus interest.		

b. Assuming reversing entry was made:

Cash	6,360	
Equipment notes receivable		6,000
Interest revenue ($6,000 × 0.12 × $\frac{6}{12}$)		360
Collection of Day equipment note plus interest.		

SUMMARY

This chapter discussed the measurement and reporting of cash, short-term investments, and receivables. Because cash is the most liquid of all assets and is flowing continually into and out of a business, it can be one of the most critical control problems facing the managers. Also, it may be of critical importance to decision makers who rely on financial statements for relevant information. The measurement and reporting of cash includes such problems as control of cash, safeguarding of cash, reconciliation of bank balances, petty cash, and recording of all cash inflows and outflows.

The use of short-term investments to employ idle cash was discussed. Marketability and the intention of management in respect to the holding period are fundamental in the classification of an investment as short term as opposed to long term. Short-term investments are accounted for in accordance with the **cost principle;** however, in accordance with the **principle of conservatism,** the LCM basis is applied to the short-term investment portfolio of **equity securities** at the end of each accounting period. Debt securities held as short-term investments are accounted for at cost (not LCM). Long-term investments are discussed in Chapter 13.

Receivables include trade receivables (usually called accounts receivable), special receivables, and notes receivable. Each of these should be accounted for separately. Interest calculations and discounting of notes receivable were discussed and illustrated.

The chapter emphasized the importance of careful measurement of these liquid assets and the importance of examining their characteristics before classifying them as current assets for reporting purposes. Financial statement users often are faced with decisions in which these liquid assets are critical; therefore, they should be measured properly and reported adequately.

APPENDIX A: PETTY CASH

A petty cash fund is established to avoid the inconvenience and cost of writing checks for the many small payments that occur daily in some businesses. This appendix discusses and illustrates the detailed accounting and recordkeeping for a petty cash fund (often called an imprest fund).

Establishing the petty cash fund. To establish a petty cash fund, a check should be written for the estimated amount needed to meet the expected payments, say for an average month. The check, made payable to "Petty Cash," is cashed, and the money kept in a safe place under the direct control of a *designated individual* as the *custodian.* The entry to set up a **separate Cash account** and to record the initial check would be:

Petty cash	100	
Cash		100
To record establishment of a petty cash fund.		

Disbursements from the petty cash fund. The policies of the petty cash system should require that the custodian responsible for disbursements from the fund maintain a running record of all disbursements and the amount of cash on hand. No entry is made in the regular accounts at the time each payment is made from the petty cash fund by the custodian. Rather, the custodian maintains a separate *petty cash record* in which each disbursement is recorded when made. This record is supported by signed bills, vouchers, and receipts for each payment made. As an internal control feature, the custodian should expect occasional surprise counts of the fund and examinations of the records of disbursements (audits). "Borrowing" from the fund by the custodian or others should not be allowed. Careless handling of petty cash often leads to defalcations and theft.

Replenishment of the petty cash fund. When the amount of cash held by the custodian gets low, and at the end of each accounting period, the fund should be reimbursed, or replenished, with an amount of cash sufficient to restore it to the original amount (to $100 in the example). Reimbursement is accomplished by having the custodian turn in the petty cash record and the supporting documents. On the basis of these records, a check to "Petty Cash" is written for the amount of cash needed for replenishment. That is, the check for replenishment should be for the sum of the expenditures reported by the custodian. The check is cashed, and the money is given to the custodian, which increases the cash held by the custodian to the original amount ($100 in the example). An entry in the regular accounts for the amount of the check is made to record the expenditures. The petty cash documents turned in by the custodian provide the underlying support for this entry.

To illustrate, assume that by the end of the month, there remained $8.50 petty cash on hand of the $100. This means that cash expenditures by the custodian amounted to $91.50 for the month. Assuming no shortage or overage, the bills, vouchers, and receipts accumulated by the custodian should sum to this amount. They provide the supporting documents for the additional check to petty cash for $91.50. These supporting documents provided the detailed data for recording the replenishment check in the following journal entry:

Telephone and telegraph expense	12.40	
Office expense (coffee)	6.32	
Postage expense	21.45	
Freight-in	6.33	
Taxi fare expense	14.87	
Repair expense, office equipment	5.00	
Supply expense for coffee bar	10.04	
Miscellaneous expenses	15.09	
Cash		91.50

It should be emphasized that the Petty Cash account is debited *only* when the petty cash fund is first established. The Petty Cash account carries a stable balance at all times ($100 in the above example). Expense accounts, not Petty Cash, are debited, and the *regular* Cash account is credited when the fund is replenished. Hence, there will be no further entries in the petty cash fund once it is established unless it is decided by management to discontinue the fund or to increase or decrease the original amount on a permanent basis. The fund must be replenished *(a)* when the balance of cash in the fund is low, and *(b)* always at the end of the accounting period, whether low or not. The latter is necessary in order to *(a)* record the expenses incurred by the fund up to the date of the financial statements and *(b)* have the same amount of cash on hand that is shown in the Petty Cash account and included on the balance sheet (see pages 320–321). The petty cash fund should be subject to rigid internal control procedures to remove all temptations to misuse it.

APPENDIX B: SPECIAL JOURNALS

Up to this point in your study of accounting, we have utilized the *general journal* to record all transactions in chronological order (i.e., by order of date). The general journal is flexible in that any transaction can be recorded in it. However, it is inefficient if used for recording transactions that have a very high rate of occurrence, such as credit sales, credit purchases, cash receipts, and cash payments. It is inefficient in three ways: (1) in recording the same journal entry repeatedly (except for changed amounts), (2) in posting to the ledger, and (3) in facilitating division of labor. Special journals are designed to reduce these inefficiencies as will be demonstrated below.

In discussing and illustrating special journals, we emphasize that no accounting principles or concepts are involved—we are dealing simply with the mechanics of data processing. Although special journals can, and should, be designed to meet a special need when a particular type of data processing problem arises, we will limit this discussion to the four special journals that often are used: credit sales, credit purchases, cash receipts, and cash payments.

Credit sales journal. This journal is designed to accommodate *only credit sales.* Cash sales are entered in the cash receipts journal as explained below. You will recall that the journal entry to record a credit sale (assuming a periodic inventory system) is:[13]

Jan. 3	Accounts receivable (customer's name).....................	100
	Sales	100
	To record credit sale; Invoice No. 324; terms, n/30.	

The credit sales journal is designed specifically to simplify (1) recording only this kind of entry and (2) subsequent posting to the ledger. The design of a credit sales journal is shown in Exhibit 8–4. Observe the saving in space, time, and accounting expertise required to journalize a **credit** sale (all of these are minimized).

Posting the credit sales journal. Posting the special credit sales journal involves two distinct phases. First, the *individual charges* (i.e., debits) must be posted daily to the customers' individual accounts in the *accounts receivable subsidiary ledger* (see Chapter 6, Appendix A). Observe here the potential for division of labor. Second, periodically (usually weekly or monthly), the *totals* are posted to the *general ledger* accounts: Accounts Receivable (debit) and Sales (credit). In this activity, there is a significant saving in time.

Posting on a daily basis to the subsidiary ledger is indicated in the folio column by entering the account number for each individual customer. Daily posting to the subsidiary ledger is necessary because the customer may, on any day, want to pay the current balance then owed.

Thus, the control account and the subsidiary ledger would agree only when both the totals and the daily postings are complete.

---

[13] For instructional purposes, we will utilize simplified amounts, a limited number of transactions and customers, and T-accounts. We remind you again that a manual system and T-accounts are illustrated for instructional purposes. In many companies these procedures are completely computerized.

EXHIBIT 8–4

	CREDIT SALES JOURNAL				Page 9
Date	Customer Name	Terms	Invoice Number	Folio	Amount
Jan. 3	Adams, K. L.	n/30	324	34.1	100
4	Small, C. C.	n/30	325	34.6	60
6	Baker, C. B.	n/30	326	34.2	110
10	Roe, R. R.	n/30	327	34.5	20
11	Mays, O. L.	n/30	328	34.3	200
16	Roe, R. R.	n/30	329	34.5	90
18	Null, O. E.	n/30	330	34.4	30
20	Baker, C. B.	n/30	331	34.2	180
21	Small, C. C.	n/30	332	34.6	150
31	Null, O. E.	n/30	333	34.4	260
	Total				1,200
	Posting				(34) (81)
Feb. 1	Etc.				

The daily posting during January to the accounts receivable subsidiary ledger is shown below.

ACCOUNTS RECEIVABLE SUBSIDIARY LEDGER

Adams, K. L.		34.1		Baker, C. B.		34.2
Jan. 3	9	100		Jan. 6	9	110
				20	9	180	290

Mays, O. L.		34.3		Null, O. E.		34.4
Jan. 11	9	200		Jan. 18	9	30
				31	9	260	290

Roe, R. R.		34.5		Small, C. C.		34.6
Jan. 10	9	20		Jan. 4	9	60
16	9	90	110	27	9	150	210

The second phase in posting the sales journal is to transfer to the general ledger the total credit sales for the month. Thus, the $1,200 total will be posted to the general ledger as (1) a debit to the Accounts Receivable *control account* and (2) as a credit to the Sales account. This posting is shown below; note in the credit sales journal that two ledger account numbers were entered for the $1,200 total to indicate the posting procedure.

Accounts Receivable (control)		34		Sales		81
Jan. 31	9	1,200		Jan. 31	9	1,200

The credit sales journal can be adapted readily to record sales taxes by adding a column headed "Sales Taxes Payable," and separate sales columns can be added to accumulate sales by department or product. You should observe the following efficiencies attained: (1) recording in the credit sales journal is much less time consuming than separately entering each credit sale in the general journal; (2) posting is reduced significantly by transferring the *total* to the ledger as opposed to posting separate debits and credits for each sales transaction; and (3) the potential for division of labor.

Credit purchases journal. Following exactly the same pattern as described above, a credit purchases journal may be designed as shown below to accommodate the entry common to all purchases on credit, viz:

Jan. 8 Purchases* 392
        Accounts payable   392
        To record purchase on credit from C. B. Smith, Purchase Order
        No. 139; invoice dated January 5, 19B; terms, 2/10, n/30.
        Recorded at net of discount, $400 \times 0.98 = $392.

  * This assumes a periodic inventory system; if a perpetual inventory system is used, this account would be Merchandise Inventory.

Only credit purchases would be recorded in the credit purchases journal. Cash purchases would be entered in the cash payments journal as illustrated later. The design of a purchases journal generally is as shown in Exhibit 8–5.

Observe that purchases are recorded net of the purchase discount as explained in Chapter 6, page 231. The cash payments journal will provide for recording the subsequent payment of cash for the purchase including situations where the purchase discount is lost.

Exhibit 8–5 was not completed in detail for illustrative purposes since it follows essentially the same pattern already illustrated for the sales journal, both in respect to entries therein and the two phases in posting. Daily posting would involve transfer to the creditors' individual accounts in the *accounts payable subsidiary ledger.* Periodically, the total would be posted to the *general ledger* as (1) a debit to the Purchases account and (2) a credit to the Accounts Payable control account. The efficiencies cited for the sales journal also are realized by a purchases journal.

EXHIBIT 8–5

			CREDIT PURCHASES JOURNAL			Page _4_	
Date		Creditors Account	Purchase Order No.	Date of Invoice	Terms	Folio	Amount
Jan 8		Smith C.B.	139	Jan. 5	2/10, n/30	91.8	392
		Etc.					Etc.
		Total					784
		Posting					(6) (5)

Cash receipts journal. The design of a special journal to accommodate **all, and only, cash receipts** is more complex since there are a number of different accounts that are *credited* individually when the Cash account is debited. To resolve this problem, more than one credit column is necessary to accommodate the various credits. The number and designation of the debit and credit columns will depend upon the character of the repetitive cash receipts transactions in the particular business.

A typical cash receipts journal with some usual transactions recorded is shown in Exhibit 8–6. Notice in particular that there are separate debit and credit sections. Each column illustrated is used as follows:

1. **Cash debit**—This column is used for *every* debit to cash. The column is totaled at the end of the month and posted as one debit amount to the Cash account in the general ledger. The posting number at the bottom indicates the total was posted to account number "12," which is the Cash account.[14]

2. **Accounts Receivable credit**—This column is used to enter the individual amounts collected on trade accounts which must be posted to the individual customer accounts in the accounts receivable *subsidiary* ledger (as indicated by the posting numbers in the folio columns). The **total** of this column is posted at the end of the month as a credit to the Accounts Receivable control account in the general ledger as indicated by the posting number "34."

3. **Sundry Accounts credit**—This column is used for recording credits to all accounts other than those for which special credit columns are

---

[14] This design assumes that the company correctly records credit sales at net of discounts. If credit sales are recorded at "gross," then a Sales Discount debit column would also be needed in this special journal.

EXHIBIT 8–6

CASH RECEIPTS JOURNAL						Page __14__	

Date		Explanation	DEBITS	CREDITS				
			Cash	Account Title	Folio	Accounts Receivable	Sundry Accounts	Cash Sales
Jan.	2	Cash sales	1,237					1,237
	3	Cash sales	1,482					1,482
	4	Sale of land	2,500	Land	43		2,000	
				Gain on sale of land	91		500	
	4	Cash sales	992					992
	6	Invoice #324	100	Adams, K.L.	34.1	100		
	6	Cash sales	1,570					1,570
	10	Bank loan, 12%	1,000	Notes payable	54		1,000	
	15	Invoice #328	200	Mays, O.L.	34.3	200		
	26	Cash sales	1,360					1,360
	31	Invoice #326	110	Baker, C.B.	34.2	110		
	31	Cash sales	1,810					1,810
		Totals	12,361			410	3,500	8,451
		Posting	(12)			(34)	(NP)	(81)

provided (in this example Accounts Receivable and Sales). The titles of the accounts to be credited are entered under the column "Account Title." Since the Sundry Accounts column represents a number of *accounts*, the *total* is not posted; rather, each individual amount must be posted as a credit directly to the indicated general ledger account. Account numbers entered in the related folio column indicate the posting.

4. **Cash Sales credit**—This column is used to record **all cash sales.** The total at the end of the month is posted as a credit to the Sales account in the general ledger.

Posting the cash receipts journal involves the same two phases explained previously for the sales and purchases journals. The daily posting phase encompasses posting the individual credits to the accounts receivable subsidiary ledger. The second phase involves posting the totals periodically to the accounts in the general ledger, with the exception of the column total for "Sundry Accounts," as explained above.

The individual accounts shown in the "Sundry Accounts" column can be posted daily or at the end of the month. Posting through January is indicated by account code numbers in the illustrated cash receipts journal.

The representative entries shown in the illustrated cash receipts journal are summarized below, in *general journal form,* for convenience in assessing the increased efficiencies of the cash receipts journal approach in journalizing and posting a large number of individual cash transactions.

Jan. 2 Cash 1,237
      Sales 1,237
    To record total cash sales for the day.

3 Cash 1,482
      Sales 1,482
    To record total cash sales for the day.

4 Cash 2,500
      Land 2,000
      Gain on sale of land 500
    To record sale of land for $2,500 that originally cost $2,000.

4 Cash 992
      Sales 992
    To record total cash sales for the day.

6 Cash 100
      Accounts receivable 100
    To record collection of K. L. Adams account for Invoice No. 324 (no discount).

6 Cash 1,570
      Sales 1,570
    To record total cash sales for the day.

10 Cash 1,000
      Notes payable 1,000
    To record bank loan, 90-day, 12 percent.

15 Cash 200
      Accounts receivable 200
    To record collection of O. L. Mays account for Invoice No. 328 (no discount).

26 Cash 1,360
      Sales 1,360
    To record total cash sales for the day.

31 Cash 110
      Accounts receivable 110
    To record collection of C. B. Baker, Invoice No. 326 (no discount).

31 Cash 1,810
      Sales 1,810
    To record total cash sales for the day.

Other debit and credit columns can be added to the cash receipts journal to accommodate repetitive transactions that also involve cash receipts.

Cash payments journal. The special cash payments journal (often called the check register) is designed to accommodate efficiently the recording of **all, and only cash payments.** The basic credit column, of course, is Credits, Cash; other columns are incorporated into the format to accommodate repetitive transactions that involve cash payments. The cash payments journal, of necessity, also must include a column for "Sundry Accounts, Debits" to accommodate the nonrecurring transactions involving cash payments for which a special debit column is not provided.

A typical cash payments journal with some usual transactions recorded is shown in Exhibit 8–7. Observe that in common with the cash receipts journal, there are separate debit and credit sections. Each column illustrated is used as follows:

1. **Cash credit**—This column is for every *credit* to the Cash account. The column is totaled at the end of the month and posted as a credit to the Cash account in the general ledger.
2. **Accounts Payable debit**—This column is used to enter the individual amounts paid on accounts payable. The individual amounts are posted as debits to the accounts payable subsidiary ledger (as indicated by

EXHIBIT 8–7

Date	Check No.	Explanation	CREDITS	DEBITS				
			Cash	Account Title	Folio	Accounts Payable	Sundry Accounts	Cash Purchases
Jan 2	101	Purchased mdse.	1,880					1,880
4	102	Invoice #37	2,970	Ray Mfg. Co.	51.3	2,970		
5	103	Jan. rent	1,200	Rent expense	71		1,200	
8	104	Purchased mdse.	250					250
10	105	Freight on mdse.	15	Freight in	63		15	
14	106	Invoice #42	980	Bows Supply Co	51.1	980		
15	107	Paid note, plus	2,200	Notes payable	54		2,000	
		interest		Interest expense	79		200	
20	108	Insurance premium	600	Prepaid insurance	19		600	
26	109	Purchased mdse.	2,160					2,160
29	110	Invoice #91 - after	500	Myar Corp	51.2	490		
		discount period		Discount lost	80		10	
31	111	Wages	1,000	Wage expense	76		1,000	
		Totals	13,755			4,440	5,025	4,290
		Posting	(12)			(51)	(NP)	(61)
Feb 1		Etc.						

CASH PAYMENTS JOURNAL   Page ___16___

the account numbers under folio), and the total at the end of the month is posted as a debit to the Accounts Payable control account in the general ledger.

3. **Sundry Accounts debit**—This column is used to record all accounts debited for which special columns are not provided (in this example Accounts Payable and Purchases are provided). The titles of the accounts to be debited are entered under the column "Account Titles." Since this column represents a number of accounts, the total cannot be posted; rather, each individual amount is posted as a debit directly to the indicated general ledger account.

4. **Cash Purchases debit**—All cash purchases are entered in this column. The total at the end of the month is posted as a debit to the Purchases account in the ledger.

Posting the cash payments journal involves two phases: (1) daily posting of the individual credit amounts to the accounts payable subsidiary ledger; and (2) periodic posting of the totals to the general ledger, with the exception of the total of "Sundry Accounts." The posting of the individual amounts in the "Sundry Accounts" column can be done during the period, say daily.

The illustrative transactions entered in the cash payments journal were:

Jan. 2 Issued Check No. 101 for cash purchase of merchandise costing $1,880.

4 Issued Check No. 102 to pay account payable owed to Ray Manufacturing Company within the discount period. Discount allowed, 1 percent; Invoice No. 37, $3,000.

5 Issued Check No. 103 to pay January rent, $1,200.

8 Issued Check No. 104 for cash purchase of merchandise costing $250.

10 Issued Check No. 105 for freight-in on merchandise purchased, $15.

14 Issued Check No. 106 to pay account payable owed to Bows Supply Company within the discount period. Discount allowed, 2 percent; Invoice No. 42, $1,000.

15 Issued Check No. 107 to pay $2,000 note payable plus 10 percent interest for one year.

20 Issued Check No. 108 to pay three-year insurance premium, $600.

26 Issued Check No. 109 for cash purchase of merchandise costing $2,160.

29 Issued Check No. 110 to pay account payable to Myar Corporation; terms, 2/10, n/30; Invoice No. 91, $500. Therefore, accounts payable to Myar was credited for $490 at the purchase date (see Chapter 6, page 231). The payment was made after the discount period; hence, the full invoice price of $500 was paid and purchase discount lost of $10 was recorded.

31 Issued Check No. 111 to pay wages amounting to $1,000.

Additional debit and credit columns can be added to the cash payments journal to accommodate other repetitive transactions involving cash disbursements.

Many companies use a *voucher system* for controlling expenditures rather than the purchases and the cash payments journals. A voucher system is particularly adaptable to computerized accounting and provides tight control mechanisms on the sequence of events for each transaction from incurrence until final cash payment. The voucher system is explained and illustrated in Chapter 10, Appendix B.

In summary, special journals do not involve new accounting principles or concepts. Rather, they represent a mechanical technique designed to increase the efficiency in the data processing cycle. Special journals are not standardized; they should be designed especially to fit each particular situation. Although a manual approach has been illustrated for instructional purposes, many companies have computerized fully the procedures represented by special journals. In computerized systems, essentially the same mechanics illustrated for the manual system are accomplished by the computer.

IMPORTANT TERMS DEFINED IN THE CHAPTER (with page citations)

Cash—317
Internal control—317
Bank statement—319
Petty cash—321, 327
Bank reconciliation—321, 323
Outstanding checks—322
Deposits in transit—322
Cash over and short—326
Compensating balances—327
Short-term investments—329
Holding or unrealized loss—331
Lower of cost or market (LCM)—331
Investment portfolio—332

Certificates of deposit (CDs)—333
Receivables, short term—334
Trade receivables—335
Special receivables—335
Notes receivable—335
Default of a note receivable—337
Discounting a note receivable—337, 338
Negotiable instrument—337
Contingent liability—338
Exception principle—339
Materiality—339
Conservatism—340

QUESTIONS FOR DISCUSSION

Part A

1. Define cash in the accounting context and indicate the types of items that should be included.

2. Explain the purpose and nature of internal control.

3. What are the primary characteristics of an effective internal control system for cash?

4. Why should cash-handling and cash-recording activities be separated? Generally, how is it accomplished?

5. What are the purposes and nature of a bank reconciliation? Specifically, what balances are reconciled?

6. Briefly explain how the total amount of cash reported on the balance sheet is computed.

7. What is the purpose of petty cash? How is it related to the regular Cash account?

Questions
Part B

8. Define a short-term investment. What is the twofold test for classification as a short-term investment?

9. Is a marketable security always a short-term investment? Explain.

10. How does the cost principle apply in accounting for short-term investments in (a) debt securities and (b) equity securities?

11. What is the rationale for application of the LCM basis to the short-term investment portfolio of equity securities?

12. Explain the purpose and nature of the account, "Allowance to Reduce Short-Term Investments to Market."

Questions
Part C

13. Distinguish between accounts receivable and special receivables.

14. Define a promissory note indicating the names of the parties and explain what is meant by principal, maturity date, and interest rate.

15. Distinguish between an interest-bearing and noninterest-bearing note.

16. What is a negotiable promissory note?

17. What is a defaulted note? Who is responsible for its payment? Explain.

18. What is meant by discounting a note receivable?

19. What is a contingent liability? How does one arise in respect to a note receivable?

20. Briefly explain the exception principle.

EXERCISES

Part A

E8–1. National Company operates several branches and, as a consequence, has cash at several locations. The general ledger at the end of 1981 showed the following accounts: Petty Cash—Home Office, $500; City Bank—Home Office, $57,300; Cash Held for Making Change, $1,000 (included in the regular Cash account); Petty Cash—Branch A, $50; National Bank—Branch A, $4,458; Petty Cash— Branch B, $75; Southwest Bank—Branch B, $864; Petty Cash—Branch C, $100; State Bank—Branch C, $965; and Metropolitan Bank—Savings account, $7,500; post-dated checks held that were received from two regular customers, $600.

The bank balances given represent the true cash balances as reflected on the bank reconciliations.

Required:

What amount should be reported on the 1981 balance sheet? Explain the basis for your decisions on questionable items.

E8–2. RX Service Company prepared a December 31, 19B, balance sheet that reported cash, $5,849. The following items were found to have been included in the reported cash balance:

(Relates to Exercise 8–2)

a. Balance per bank statement at City Bank	$3,734*
a. A deposit made to the local electric utility	600
b. Postage stamps on hand	40
c. Check signed by a customer, returned for NSF	30
d. Petty cash on hand	150
e. IOUs signed by employees	80
f. Check signed by the company president for an advance to him; to be held until he "gives the word to cash it."	1,000
g. Money orders on hand (received from customers)	45
h. A signed receipt from a freight company that involved a $10 overpayment to them. They have indicated "a check will be mailed shortly."	10
i. A money order obtained from the post office to be used to pay for a special purchase upon delivery; expected within the next five days	160
Total	$5,849

* Items not considered: deposit in transit, $300; checks outstanding, $175; and cash held for making change, $100 (included in the regular Cash account).

Required:

a. The reported cash balance has been questioned. Compute the correct cash amount that should be reported on the balance sheet. Give appropriate reporting for any items that you exclude.

b. Assume the company carries two cash accounts in the general ledger—Cash and Petty Cash. What balance should be reflected in each account at December 31, 19B (end of the accounting period)? Show computations.

E8–3. Stone Company has just received the June 30, 19B, bank statement and the June ledger accounts for cash, which are summarized below:

Required:

a. Reconcile the bank account, assuming that a comparison of the checks written with the checks that have cleared the bank show outstanding checks of $800 and that cash on hand (for making change) on June 30 is $100 (included in the Cash account). Some of the checks that cleared in June were written prior to June; there were no deposits in transit carried over from May.

b. Give any entries that would be made as a result of the bank reconciliation.

c. What is the balance in the Cash account after the reconciliation entries?

(Relates to Exercise 8–3)

	Checks	Deposits	Balance
Balance, June 1			$ 4,800
Deposits during June		$17,000	21,800
Checks cleared through June	$17,700		4,100
Bank service charges	19		4,081
Balance, June 30			4,081

Cash

June	1	Balance	4,400	June Checks written	18,000
June		Deposits	19,000		

Petty Cash

June 30	Balance		75

d. What total amount of cash would be reported on the balance sheet at June 30?

E8–4. RTS Company has just received the September 30, 19D, bank statement and the September ledger accounts for cash, which are summarized below:

Required:

a. Reconcile the bank account. (Hint: You may find an error made by either the bank or the company.)

b. Give any entries that would be made based upon the bank reconciliation.

c. What should be the balance in the Cash account after the reconciliation entries?

(Relates to Exercise 8–4)

	Checks	Deposits	Balance
Balance, September 1			$ 5,100
Deposits recorded during September		$27,000	32,100
Checks cleared during September	$27,300		4,800
NSF check—J. J. Jones	80		4,720
Bank service charges	23		4,597
Balance, September 30			4,597

Cash

Sept.	1	Balance	5,300	Sept.	Checks written	28,000
Sept.		Deposits	29,500			

Petty Cash

Sept. 30	Balance	50	

Cash on hand for making change (included in the Cash account) on September 1 and September 30 amounted to $200. There were no outstanding checks and no deposits in transit carried over from August.

d. What total amount of cash should be reported on the September 30 balance sheet?

E8–5. Rock Company has just received the March 31, 19C, bank statement and the March ledger accounts for cash, which are summarized below:

(Relates to Exercise 8–5)

	Checks	Deposits	Balance
Balance, March 1			$ 8,600
Deposits during March		$28,000	36,600
Note collected for depositor (including $60 interest)		1,060	37,660
Checks cleared during March	$32,200		5,460
Bank service charges	35		5,425
Balance, March 31			5,425

Cash

Mar.	1	Balance	8,220	Mar.	Checks written	32,500
Mar.		Deposits	31,000			

Petty Cash

Mar. 31 Balance	60	

A comparison of deposits recorded with deposits on the bank statement showed deposits in transit of $3,000. Similarly, outstanding checks at the end of March were determined to be $900. Cash on hand for making change (included in the Cash account) was $200 at March 31.

Required:

a. Prepare a bank reconciliation for March. (Hint: A cash overage or shortage is involved; however, the bank figures have been verified as correct.)

b. Give any entries that should be made based on the reconciliation.

c. What amount should be reflected as the ending balance in the Cash account after the reconciliation entries? What total amount of cash should be reflected on the balance sheet at the end of March?

Exercises
Part B

E8–6. Sly Company, in July 19B, had accumulated approximately $10,000 in cash that would not be needed for 10 to 15 months. To employ the idle cash profitably, the management decided to purchase some shares of stock as a short-term investment. This series of transactions occurred:

19B:

July 30   Purchased 5,000 shares of the common stock of XY Corporation on the stock exchange. The cash price, including fees and transfer costs related to the acquisition, amounted to $20,000.

Dec. 15   Received a cash dividend of $0.30 per share on the XY shares.

30   Sold 1,000 of the XY shares at $5 per share for cash.

Required:

a. Give appropriate journal entries on each date for this short-term investment.

b. How would the short-term investment be reported on the balance sheet at December 31, 19B? Assume the same market value as on December 30.

E8–7. Ray Company, to put some idle cash to work, decided to purchase some common stock in RS Corporation as a short-term investment. The following transactions reflect what happened after this decision:

19B:

Feb. 1   Purchased for cash 6,000 shares of RS Corporation common stock at a cost of $36,000.

Aug. 15   Received a cash dividend on the RS stock of $0.30 per share.

Dec. 30   Sold 2,000 shares of the RS stock at $5.80 per share.

31   End of the fiscal year. RS stock was selling at $5.75 per share.

Required:

a. Give appropriate journal entries for each date (including December 31) for the investment in RS stock. Ray Company had no other short-term investments.

b. How would the effects of this short-term investment be reported on the financial statements at December 31, 19B?

c. Give the entry on January 15, 19C, assuming the remaining shares were sold at $5.50 per share.

E8–8. May Company, to use some idle cash, in March 19B acquired 200 shares of common stock in each of three corporations at the following costs: Corporation A, $8,000; Corporation B, $6,000; and Corporation C, $12,000. At the end of the annual accounting period, December 31, 19B, the quoted market prices per share were: Corporation A, $40; Corporation B, $25; and Corporation C, $61.

Required:

a. Give the entry to record the acquisition of these short-term investments in equity securities.

b. Give the entry to record cash dividends of $1,200 received on the short-term investments in November 19B.

c. Give the entry to reflect the investments at LCM at December 31, 19B. Show computations.

d. Show how the investments would be reported on the financial statements at December 31, 19B.

e. Give the entry on January 5, 19C, assuming all of the shares were sold for $25,000 cash.

f. Give any entry required at December 31, 19C, assuming no short-term equity investments are held at that time (disregard any closing entries).

E8–9. Watts Company, to put some idle cash to work, purchased a debt security as a short-term investment at a cost of $12,000 on August 1, 19B. The security (due in 12 months) earns 10 percent annual interest payable on the date of maturity. At the end of the annual accounting period (December 31) the same security could be purchased for $11,500 cash.

Required:

a. Give all of the entries indicated on the following dates and provide an explanation for each date:
   1. August 1, 19B.
   2. December 31, 19B.
   3. July 31, 19C.

b. Show how the security would affect the 19B financial statements.

Exercises
Part C

E8–10. Approximately 40 percent of the merchandise sold by DX Company is on credit. Accounts receivable that are overdue, if material in amount, are "converted" to notes receivable when possible. This case traces one sale through accounts receivable, to notes receivable, and to final collection. The related transactions during 19B were:

Jan. 10 Sold merchandise on account to J. K. Mim for $10,000; terms, n/30.

Mar. 1 The account was unpaid; therefore, DX Company asked Mim to sign a 120-day, 12 percent, interest-bearing note for the account. Mim executed the note on this date.

July 1 Mim paid the note plus interest.

Required:

a. Give the entry required on each of the three dates.

b. Give the entry that would have been made on July 1, 19B, assuming Mim defaulted.

c. Give the entry assuming the default in *b* and also that Mim paid the note in full on July 15, 19B.

E8–11. Royce Company sells a line of products that has a high unit sales price. Credit terms are traditional in the industry; accordingly, Royce frequently takes a promissory note for the sales price. This exercise follows one promissory note, taken at date of sale, through final collection. The fiscal year ends December 31. The series of transactions and events was:

19B:

Dec. 1 Sold merchandise to J. Doe on a 90-day, 15 percent, interest-bearing note for $2,000.

31 End of fiscal period; adjusting entry.

19C:

Jan. 1 Start of new fiscal period.

Mar. 1 Collected the note, plus interest, in full.

Required:

a. Give appropriate entries at each of the four dates; if none, so state.

b. With respect to the note, what item(s) and amount(s) would be reported on the 19B income statement?

c. With respect to the note, what item(s) and amount(s) would be reported on the balance sheet at December 31, 19B?

E8–12. Dilly Company frequently sells merchandise on a promissory note, which later is sold (i.e., discounted) to the local bank to obtain cash needed before maturity date. The following series of transactions relates to one note that followed this pattern:

19B:

Apr. 1 Sold merchandise for $8,000 to C. C. Ney; took a six-month, 12 percent, interest-bearing note.

June 1 Discounted the note at the local bank at an 11 percent discount rate; received the proceeds upon endorsement of the note to the bank.

Oct. 1 Due date of the note plus interest.

Required:

a. Give appropriate journal entries at each of the three dates, assuming Ney paid the bank for the note on due date.

b. Give appropriate entry on October 1, 19B, assuming Ney defaulted on the note and Dilly Company had to make payment plus a $15 protest fee.

c. Give the appropriate entry assuming Ney paid Dilly in full on October 5, 19B.

E8–13. (Based on Appendix A) On January 1, 19B, Exalto Company established a petty cash fund amounting to $150 by writing a check to "Petty Cash." The fund was assigned to J. Wright, an employee, to administer as custodian. At the end of January there was $20 cash remaining in the fund. Signed receipts for expenditures during January were summarized as follows: postage, $43; office supplies, $18; transportation, $41; newspapers, $24; and miscellaneous (coffee for the office), $14.

Required:

a. Give the entry to establish the petty cash fund on January 1, 19B.

b. Give the entry to replenish the fund on January 31, 19B.

c. What balance would be reflected in the Petty Cash account in the ledger at January 31? Explain.

d. How would petty cash be reported on the balance sheet at January 31, 19B?

e. What effect did the petty cash fund have on the January 19B income statement?

f. Assume it is January 5, 19C, and the management has decided to increase the petty cash fund to $200. Give the required entry.

PROBLEMS

Part A

P8–1. Careless Company has one trusted employee who, as the owner said, "handles all of the bookkeeping and paperwork for the company." This also includes counting, verifying, and recording cash receipts and payments, such as making the weekly bank deposit, preparing checks for major expenditures (signed by the owner), making small expenditures from the cash reg-

ister for daily expenses, and making collections on accounts receivable. The owner asked the local bank for a $25,000 loan, whereupon the bank asked that an audit be performed covering the year just ended. The independent auditor (a local CPA), in a private conference with the owner, presented evidence of the following activities of the trusted clerical employee during the past year:

1. Cash sales sometimes were not entered in the cash register, and the trusted employee pocketed approximately $20 per month.
2. Cash taken from the cash register (and pocketed by the trusted employee) was replaced with *expense memos* with fictitious signatures (approximately $10 per day).
3. A $500 collection on an account receivable of a valued out-of-town customer was pocketed by the trusted employee and was covered by making a $500 entry as a debit to Return Sales and a credit to Accounts Receivable.
4. A $200 collection on an account receivable from a local customer was pocketed by the trusted employee and was covered by making a $200 entry as a debit to Allowance for Doubtful Accounts and a credit to Accounts Receivable.

Required:

a. What was the approximate amount stolen during the past year?
b. What would be your recommendations to the owner?

P8–2. (Special case) Hall Manufacturing Company is a relatively small local business that specializes in the repair and renovation of antique jewelry, brass objects, and silverware. The owner is an expert craftsman. Although a number of skilled workers are employed, there is always a large backlog of work to be done. A long-time employee, who serves as clerk-bookkeeper, handles cash receipts, keeps the records, and writes checks for disbursements. The checks are signed by the owner. Small claims are paid in cash by the clerk-bookkeeper, subject to approval of the owner. Approvals generally are made in advance; however, routine payments are approved later. Approximately 100 regular customers regularly are extended credit. Although credit losses are small, in recent years the bookkeeper has established an Allowance for Doubtful Accounts.

Recently, the owner decided to con-

struct a building for the business that would provide many advantages over the presently rented space and would make possible needed expansion of facilities. As a part of the considerations in financing, the financing institution asked for "audited financial statements." There had never been an audit of the company. Early in the audit, the independent CPA found numerous errors and one combinations of amounts, in particular, that worried him. There appeared to be evidence that a job billed at $500 had been charged to a new customer. The account was credited with a $500 collection a few days later. The new account was never active again. The auditor also observed that at about the same time there had been three write-offs of Accounts Receivable balances to Allowance for Doubtful Accounts as follows: Jones, $125.32; Adams, $269.88; and Coster, $104.80. These write-offs triggered the attention of the auditor, who knew the customers involved and believed they would not default on their accounts.

Required:

a. Can you determine what caused the CPA to be "worried"? Explain.
b. What recommendations would you make in respect to internal control procedures for this small company?

P8–3. The bookkeeper at Downhill Company has not reconciled the bank statement with the Cash account, saying, "I don't have time." You have been asked to prepare a reconciliation and review the procedures with the bookkeeper.

The April 30, 19D, bank statement just received and the April ledger accounts for cash showed the following (summation):

(Relates to Problem 8–3)

	Checks	Deposits	Balance
Balance, April 1			$23,550
Deposits during April		$38,000	61,550
Note collected for depositor (including $90 interest)		1,090	62,640
Checks cleared during April	$44,700		17,940
NSF check—A. B. Cage	140		17,800
Bank service charges	30		17,770
Balance, April 30			17,770

Cash

Apr.	1	Balance	22,850	Apr.	Checks written	44,500
Apr.		Deposits	42,000			

Petty Cash

Apr. 30	Balance	$150	

A comparison of checks written before and during April with the checks cleared reflected outstanding checks at the end of April of $600. No deposits in transit were carried over from March. Cash on hand, held for change, at the end of April was $100 (included in the regular Cash account).

Required:

a. Prepare a detailed bank reconciliation for April.
b. Give any entires indicated as a result

of the reconciliation. Why are they necessary?
c. What were the balances in the cash accounts in the ledger at the end of April?
d. What total amount of cash should be reported on the balance sheet at the end of April?

P8–4. Swan Company received the following bank statement for the month of August 19B and the August ledger accounts for cash:

(Relates to Problem 8–4)

		Checks	Deposits	Balance
Aug.	1	....			$16,000
	2	....	$ 300		15,700
	3	....		$7,000	22,700
	4	....	400		22,300
	5	....	200		22,100
	9	....	900		21,200
	10	....	300		20,900
	15	....		9,000	29,900
	21	....	700		29,200
	24	....	21,000		8,200
	25	....		8,000	16,200
	30	....	800		15,400
	31	....		2,180*	17,580
	31	....	30†		17,550

* $2,000 note collected plus interest.
† Bank service charge.

Cash

Aug. 1 Balance	15,250	Checks written:	
Deposits:		Aug. 2	300
Aug. 2	7,000	4	900
12	9,000	15	600
24	8,000	17	550
31	6,000	18	800
		18	700
		23	21,000

Petty Cash

Aug. 31 Balance	75

Cash on hand for making change at the end of August amounted to $150 (included in the regular Cash account). There were three outstanding checks at the end of July: $200, $400, and $300. There were no deposits in transit at that time.

Required:

a. Determine the deposits in transit at the end of August.
b. Determine the outstanding checks at the end of August.
c. Prepare a bank reconciliation for August.

d. Give any entries indicated on the reconciliation that should be made. Why are they necessary?
e. After the reconciliation entries, what balances would be reflected in the cash accounts in the ledger?
f. What total amount of cash should be reported on the August 31, 19B, balance sheet?

P8–5. OK Company received the following bank statement for the month of December 19B and the December ledger accounts for cash:

(Relates to Problem 8–5)

Date	Checks	Deposits	Balance
Dec. 1			$41,000
2	400, 150	16,000	56,450
4	7,000, 80		49,370
6	120, 180, 1,500		47,570
11	900, 1,200, 90	21,000	66,380
13	450, 700, 1,900		63,330
17	17,000, 2,000		44,330
23	40, 23,500	36,000	56,790
26	1,800, 2,650		52,340
28	2,200, 4,800		45,340
30	13,000, 1,890, 200*	19,000	49,250
31	1,650, 1,200, 28‡	6,360†	52,732

* NSF check, J. Doe, a customer.
† Note collected, principal, $6,000 plus interest.
‡ Bank service charge.

Cash

		Checks written during December:		
Dec. 1 Balance	55,850	40	5,000	2,650
Deposits:		13,000	4,800	1,650
Dec. 11	21,000	700	1,890	2,200
23	36,000	4,400	1,500	7,000
30	19,000	1,200	120	150
31	17,000	180	80	450
		17,000	23,500	2,000
		90	900	1,900
		1,800	1,200	

Petty Cash

Dec. 31 Balance	$100

The November 19B, bank reconciliation showed the following: True cash balance at November 30, $55,700; deposits in transit (November 30), $16,000; and outstanding checks ($400 + $900), $1,300. At the end of December 19B, cash held on hand for making change amounted to $150 (included in the regular Cash account).

Required:

a. Determine the deposits in transit December 31, 19B.

b. Determine the outstanding checks at December 31, 19B.

c. Prepare a bank reconciliation at December 31, 19B.

d. Give any entries indicated on the reconciliation that should be made. Why are they necessary?

e. After the reconciliation entries, what balances would be reflected in the cash accounts in the ledger?

f. What total amount of cash should be reported on the December 31, 19B, balance sheet?

Problems
Part B

P8–6. Blue Company, to use idle cash, usually acquires common stocks as a short-term investment. This case focuses on the purchase of three different common stocks during 19B. The annual fiscal period ends December 31. The sequence of transactions was:

19B:

Apr. 2 Purchased for cash, as a short-term investment, the following common stocks:

Corporation	Number of shares	Total price per share
X	300	$50
Y	400	70
Z	100	90

Sept. 8 Received a cash dividend of $3 per share on Corporation Z stock.

Dec. 30 Sold the stock in Corporation Y for $75 per share.

Dec. 31 Quoted market prices on this date were Corporation X stock, $46; Corporation Y stock, $75; and Corporation Z stock, $95.

Required:

a. Give the appropriate entry on each date.

b. Illustrate how the effects of these investments would be reflected on the income statement (single step) and the balance sheet (classified) at December 31, 19B.

c. What was the amount of the 19B holding loss? Explain

d. Assume it is December 31, 19C, and that all of the X and Z share still are held and that their market values per share are X, $50; and Z, $92. Give the required LCM entry.

P8–7. On July 1, 19D, AB Corporation purchased, as a short-term investment, ten $1,000, 10 percent bonds of Lowe Corporation at par (i.e., at $1,000 each). The bonds mature on June 30, 19G. Annual interest is payable on June 30 each year. The accounting period for AB Corporation ends on December 31.

Required:

a. Give entries required on the following dates (if no entry is required, explain why): July 1, 19D and December 31, 19D (adjusting entry).

b. At the end of 19D the bonds were quoted on the market at $990 each. Give any LCM entry required on December 31, 19D. If none is required explain why.

c. Show how this investment would affect the 19D balance sheet and income statement.

d. Give the entry required on June 30, 19E.

P8–8. Smith Manufacturing Company produces and sells one main product. Demand is seasonal, and the unit price is relatively high. Smith's fiscal year ends December 31. Typically, in the high months of the cycle the company generates cash, which is idle during the low months. As a consequence, the company consistently acquires short-term investments to earn a return on what otherwise would be idle cash. Recently, the company purchased 1,000 shares of common stock in each of two other corporations—Corporations A and B. The prices per share, including fees and related costs, were A, $30; and B, $70. In addition, Smith purchased a $10,000 bond of Kamas Corporation. The bond pays 9 percent annual interest on each March 31. The bond was purchased on April 1, 19B, for $10,000 cash (i.e., at par).

The sequence of transactions was:

19B:

Apr. 1 Purchased the 2,000 shares of common stocks and the $10,000 bond. (Hint. Account for the stocks and bonds separately.)

Oct. 3 Received a cash dividend of $0.50 per share on the stock of Corporation B.

Nov. 30 Sold 600 shares of the stock of Corporation A at $26 per share and 600 shares of the stock of Corporation B at $75 per share.

Dec. 31 End of fiscal period. The market prices on this date were A stock, $29; B stock, $69; and Kamas bonds, 100 (i.e., at par). (Hint: Do not overlook accrued interest.)

Required:

a. Give appropriate entries at each of the four dates. Omit any closing entries.

b. Illustrate how the effects of the investment would be reported on the balance sheet at December 31, 19B.

c. What items and amounts would be reported on the 19B income statement?

Problems
Part C

P8–9. Davis Company sells approximately 60 percent of its merchandise on credit; terms, n/30. Occasionally, as a part of the collection process of a delinquent account, a promissory note will be received. This case focuses on two different sales that ultimately generated promissory notes. The annual fiscal period ends December 31. The sequence of transactions was:

Note No. 1:

19B:

Feb. 15 Sold merchandise for $2,000 to B. B. Cox; received $500 cash, and the balance was charged to Accounts Receivable.

Apr. 1 Received an interest-bearing note in settlement of the overdue account of Cox. Terms of the note were four months, 12 percent interest.

July 31 Due date for note; Cox defaulted.

Oct. 1 Cox paid the defaulted note plus interest, plus 8 percent interest on the defaulted amount for the period July 31–October 1. The 8 percent is the legal rate of interest on overdue obligations.

Required:

a. Give appropriate entries on each date. Show interest calculations.

Note No. 2:

19B:

Oct. 1 Sold merchandise for $3,600 to D. D. Day, received $600 cash, and the balance was charged to Accounts Receivable (terms, n/EOM).

Nov. 1 Received an interest-bearing note in settlement of the overdue account from Day. The terms of the note were three months, 12 percent interest.

Dec. 31 End of fiscal period.

19C:

Jan. 1 Start of new fiscal period.

30 Maturity date of the note. Day paid the principal plus interest.

Required:

b. Give appropriate entries on each of the above dates (omit any closing entries). Show interest calculations. Specify any accounting assumptions you make.

c. How much interest revenue (Note No. 2 only) will be reported on the 19B income statement?

d. Show how Note No. 2 will affect the balance sheet at December 31, 19B.

P8–10. Eastern Machinery Company sells heavy machinery. Credit terms are customary and generally involve promissory notes and a mortgage on the machinery sold. Down payments of 20 percent to $33\frac{1}{3}$ percent are required. The annual fiscal period ends December 31. This problem focuses on two different promissory notes that were received in 19B. The transactions were:

Note No. 1:

19B:

Feb. 1 Sold equipment to B. R. Rite for $12,000; received a 25 percent cash down payment and a 120-day, 12 percent, interest-bearing note for the balance.

Mar. 1 Sold the note to the local bank at a 10 percent discount rate; endorsed the note to the bank and received the cash proceeds.

June 1 Due date of the note plus interest; Rite paid the note.

Required:

a. Give appropriate entry on each of the three dates. Show interest computations. Assume that Rite paid the bank for the principal plus interest on due date.

b. Give entry on due date, June 1, 19B, assuming Rite defaulted on the note and Eastern paid the note plus interest, plus a $25 protest fee.

c. How much interest revenue (Note No. 1) will be reported on the income statement for 19B?

Note No. 2:

19B:

Dec. 1 Sold equipment to W. T. Owens for $20,000; received $5,000 cash down payment and a 90-day, 12 percent, interest-bearing note for the balance.

31 End of fiscal period.

19C:

Jan. 1 Start of new fiscal period.

Mar. 1 Due date of the principal plus interest; Owens paid the note plus interest in full.

Required:

d. Give the appropriate entry on each of the four dates (omit any closing entries). State any assumptions you make. Use 30-day months for interest purposes to avoid counting on the calendar.

e. How much interest revenue (Note No. 2) will be reported on the 19B income statement?

f. Show how Note No. 2 will affect the balance sheet at December 31, 19B.

P8–11. (Based on Appendix B) Alexander Company completes a wide variety of transactions each year. A number of them are repetitive in nature; therefore, the company maintains five journals: general, sales, purchases, cash receipts, and cash payments. Selected transactions are listed below that are to be entered in the appropriate journals. To shorten this case amounts have been simplified and the number of transactions limited.

Selected transactions are (use the letter to the left in lieu of the date and use the letter *v* for the last day of the period):

a. Sold merchandise to K. K. May at invoice cost of $250; terms, 2/10, n/20; Invoice No. 38.

b. Received merchandise from Sable Company at invoice cost of $300; credit terms, 1/10, n/20; Purchase Order No. 17.

c. Sold merchandise to B. B. Wise for $200 on credit; terms, 2/10, n/20; Invoice No. 39.

d. Received merchandise from Rex Supply Company at an invoice cost of $200 on credit; terms, 1/10, n/20; Purchase Order No. 18.

e. Sold merchandise to A. B. Cox for $150 cash.

f. Received merchandise from Baker Manufacturing Company at a cost of $360; paid cash (number the checks consecutively starting with No. 81).

g. Purchased an operational asset (machinery) at a cost of $3,000; gave a 90-day, 12 percent, interest-bearing promissory note for the purchase price.

h. Sold a track of land for $9,000 which previously was used as a company parking lot and originally cost $3,000; collected cash.

i. Collected account receivable from B. B. Wise within the discount period; Invoice No. 39.

j. Paid $600 for a three-year insurance premium.

k. Obtained a $5,000 bank loan; signed a one-year, 12 percent, interest-bearing note.

l. Paid account payable to Rex Supply Company within the discount period.

m. Paid monthly rent, $650.

n. Sold merchandise for cash, $1,400.

o. Purchased merchandise for cash, $980.

p. Sold merchandise on credit to C. C. Coe for $700; terms, 2/10, n/20; Invoice No. 40.

q. Received merchandise on credit from Stubbs Company at an invoice cost of $400; terms, 2/10, n/30; Purchase Order No. 19.

r. Collected account receivable from K. K. May after the discount period.

s. Paid account payable to Sable Company after the discount period.

t. Paid monthly salaries, $2,400.

u. By year-end, six months of the prepaid insurance had expired.

Use the following general ledger account code numbers for posting: Cash, 11; Accounts Receivable, 14; Prepaid Insurance, 16; Machinery, 17; Land, 19; Accounts Payable, 21; Notes Payable, 22; Purchases, 31; Purchase Discounts Lost, 33; Sales, 41; Sales Discount Revenue, 43; Expenses, 51; and Gain on Sale of Operational Assets, 53. For journals, use the following page numbers: General, 15; Sales, 18; Purchases, 14; Cash Receipts, 21; and Cash Payments, 34.

Required:

1. Draft a format for each of the journals, including a general journal, following the illustrations included in Appendix B. Include folio columns.
2. Set up T-accounts for the general ledger accounts listed above.
3. Set up T-accounts (with account numbers) for the subsidiary ledgers as follows:

Accounts receivable (14)	*Accounts payable (21)*
Coe—14.1	Sable—21.1
May—14.2	Stubbs—21.2
Wise—14.3	Rex—21.3

4. Enter each transaction in the appropriate journal. Sales and purchases are recorded net of discount.
5. Indicate all postings to the *subsidiary ledgers* by entering appropriate account numbers in the folio columns.
6. Sum the special journals and indicate all postings to the *general ledger* accounts by entering the account code numbers in the folio columns and below totals posted. Use the account code numbers given above.

9

Operational assets— plant and equipment, natural resources, and intangibles

PURPOSE OF THE CHAPTER

Operational assets are the **noncurrent assets** that a business retains more or less permanently (not for sale) for use (physically or in terms of rights) in the course of **normal operations.** Thus, operational assets include land in use, plant and equipment, furniture and fixtures, natural resources, and certain intangibles (such as a patent) used in operating the business. The degree of efficiency in the utilization of the operational assets will influence the earnings of the business. The types and costs of the operational assets, their ages and states of repair, and the future demands for funds needed to replace them loom large in many important decisions. The expense of maintaining and operating these assets often has a major effect on income.

An operational asset is acquired by a business because of the **future services** potentially available from it to generate future revenue through use by the entity. Thus, such an asset can be viewed as a bundle of services that is purchased *in advance of usage* for generating revenue. As those services are used, as in the use of a machine, the **prepaid cost** of the asset, in part, is allocated as an expense of each of the periods of utilization. To illustrate, assume a truck is purchased at a cost of $10,000 for use in the business. The cost is debited to an asset account and, assuming a five-year useful life, each year a part of the prepaid cost is apportioned to expense. This periodic apportionment of the prepaid costs of operational assets to expense is known as **depreciation, depletion,** or **amortization,** depending on the characteristics of the particular asset.

The financial statements provide information in respect to operational assets. The economic impact of operational assets on the balance sheet, income statement, and statement of changes in financial position is useful information to decision makers.

The purpose of this chapter is to discuss and illustrate the measuring, accounting, and reporting of operational assets *(a)* at acquisition, *(b)* during subsequent use, and *(c)* at disposition. To accomplish this purpose the chapter is divided into two parts:

Part A: Property, plant and equipment, and depreciation

Part B: Repairs and maintenance, natural resources, and intangible operational assets

Behavioral and learning objectives for this chapter are provided in the *Teachers Manual.*

CATEGORIES OF OPERATIONAL ASSETS

Effective management of a business requires a combination of assets with different characteristics and purposes. Each type of asset—be it current, long-term investments, or operational—serves a particular purpose not served by the other types of assets. The optimum combination of assets varies with each business, and its determination is a central responsibility of the management. An objective of the financial statements is to report the different assets classified by types and the amount of resources committed to each type. For measuring and reporting purposes, operational assets may be classified as:

1. **Tangible operational assets**—those long-lived tangible assets (i.e., having physical substance) acquired for continued use in carrying on the normal operations of the business and not intended for resale. Examples are land, buildings, equipment, furniture, tools, vehicles, and mineral deposits. There are three kinds of tangible operational assets: *(a)* land—not subject to depreciation; *(b)* plant, equipment, and fixtures—subject to depreciation; and *(c)* natural resources—the wasting assets used in the operation of the business, such as mines, gravel pits, oil wells, and timber tracts. Natural resources are subject to depletion.
2. **Intangible operational assets**—the assets held by the business because of the **special rights** they confer. They have no physical substance. Examples are patents, copyrights, franchises, licenses, and trademarks. Intangible assets are subject to amortization.

PRINCIPLES UNDERLYING ACCOUNTING FOR OPERATIONAL ASSETS

The primary phases of accounting for operational assets are:

1. Measuring and recording the cost of the asset at acquisition date.
2. After acquisition, measurement of the expense of using it during its useful life.
3. Recording disposals of operational assets.

At the date of acquisition, an operational asset is measured and recorded in conformity with the **cost principle**. After acquisition, a portion of the cost of an operational asset (except land) is matched periodically with the revenues generated during its useful life in accordance with the **matching principle**.

PART A: PROPERTY, PLANT AND EQUIPMENT, AND DEPRECIATION

MEASURING AND RECORDING ACQUISITION AND INSTALLATION COST

Under the **cost principle**, all reasonable and necessary costs incurred in acquiring an operational asset and in placing it in its operational setting and ready for use, less any cash discounts, should be recorded in an appropriately designated asset account. Cost represents the net cash equivalent paid or to be paid. **Acquisition cost** can be determined readily when an operational asset is purchased for cash. For example, the acquisition cost of a machine on January 1, 19A, may be measured as follows:

Invoice price of the machine	$10,000
Less: Cash discount ($10,000 × 0.02)	200
Net cash invoice price	9,800
Add: Transportation charges paid by purchaser	150
Installation costs paid by purchaser	200
Sales tax paid ($10,000 × 0.02)	200
Cost—amount debited to the Machinery account	$10,350

The acquisition of this operational asset would be recorded as follows:

January 1, 19A:

Machinery	10,350	
Cash		10,350

When an operational asset is purchased and a *noncash* consideration is included in part, or in full, payment for it, cost is the cash equivalent measured as any cash paid plus the **market value** of the noncash consideration given. Alternatively, if the market value of the noncash consideration cannot be reasonably determined, the market value of the asset purchased is used for measurement purposes. To illustrate, assume a tract of timber (a natural resource) was acquired by Fast Corporation. Payment in full was made as follows: $28,000 cash plus 2,000 shares of Fast nopar capital stock.[1] At the date of the purchase, Fast stock was selling at $12 per share. The cost of the tract would be measured as follows:

Cash paid	$28,000
Market value, noncash consideration given	
(2,000 shares nopar stock @ $12)	24,000
	52,000
Title fees, legal fees, and other costs paid in cash	
(incidental to the acquisition)	1,000
Cost—amount debited to the asset account	$53,000

The journal entry to record the acquisition of this natural resource would be:

January 1, 19A:

Timber tract (#20)	53,000	
Cash		29,000
Capital stock, nopar (2,000 shares @ $12)		24,000

When land is purchased, all of the incidental costs paid by the purchaser, such as title fees, sales commissions, legal fees, title insurance, delinquent taxes, and surveying fees, should be included in the cost of the land.

Not infrequently, an old building or used machinery is purchased for operational use in the business. Renovation and repair costs incurred by the purchaser *prior to use* should be debited to the asset account as a part of the cost of the asset. Repair costs incurred *after* the asset is placed in use usually are normal operating expenses.

Basket purchases. When two or more kinds of operational assets are acquired in a single transaction and for a single lump sum, the cost of each kind of asset acquired must be measured and recorded separately. For example, when a building and the land on which it is located are purchased for a lump sum, at least two separate accounts must be established: one for the building (which is subject to depreciation) and one for the land (which is not subject to depreciation). This means that the single sum must be apportioned between the land and the building on a rational basis.

Relative market value of the several assets at the date of acquisition

---

[1] See Chapter 12 for discussion of capital stock.

is the most logical basis on which to allocate the single lump sum. Appraisals or tax assessments often have to be used as indications of the market values. To illustrate, assume Fox Company purchased a building suitable for an additional plant and the land on which the building is located for a total of $300,000 cash. Since the separate, true market values of the building and land were not known, a professional appraisal was obtained that showed the following *estimated* market values: building, $189,000; and land, $126,000 (apparently the buyer got a good deal). The apportionment of the $300,000 purchase price should be made as follows:

| Asset | Appraised value | | Apportionment of lump-sum acquisition cost | |
	Amount	Ratio	Computation	Apportioned cost
Building	$189,000	0.60*	$300,000 × 0.60 =	$180,000
Land	126,000	0.40†	300,000 × 0.40 =	120,000
	$315,000	1.00		$300,000

* $189,000 ÷ $315,000 = 0.60.
† $126,000 ÷ $315,000 = 0.40.

The journal entry to record the acquisition would appear as follows:

Plant building...	180,000	
Land—plant site	120,000	
Cash		300,000

CAPITALIZATION OF INTEREST AS A COST OF OPERATIONAL ASSETS

In the preceding paragraphs we have discussed application of the cost principle in determining the acquisition cost of an operational asset. In October 1979 *FASB Statement No. 34* was issued, which provided for the inclusion of **interest cost** as a part of the acquisition cost of an operational asset under very limited conditions. A basic concept of accounting is that interest on borrowed funds must be recorded and reported as interest **expense** on the income statement when incurred. Interest is incurred on funds borrowed because of the **passage of time** (rather than when the related cash is paid); that is, interest is the **time cost of money.**

When an operational asset is purchased and a loan is incurred as all, or part, of the payment, periodic interest on the related debt is recorded and reported as interest expense over the term of the loan. However, *FASB Statement No. 34* provided an exception to this principle that relates to the **construction** (by the entity for its own use, or by another entity) of an operational asset that requires an **extended construction** (or production) **period. In such situations, interest during the extended construction period is recorded as a part of the cost of the operational asset,** regardless of whether borrowed for that particular purpose.[2]

To illustrate, assume that on January 1, 19A, X Corporation entered into a construction contract with Y Construction Company to build a new plant building at a contract price of $1,000,000. The construction period started February 1, 19A, and the building was substantially complete and ready for its intended use on December 31, 19A (end of the construction period). X Corporation made the following quarterly cash progress payments on the contract during 19A:

a. March 31, 19A	$ 120,000
b. June 30, 19A	220,000
c. September 30, 19A	480,000
d. December 31, 19A	180,000
Total	$1,000,000

To make these payments, X Corporation borrowed 75 percent of each payment from a financial institution at 10 percent annual interest; the remaining cash needed was from within X Corporation. Total interest cost for the period was $40,000.

Upon completion, December 31, 19A, X Corporation should reflect the following acquisition cost in the operational asset account, Plant Building:

Contract price (paid in full)		$1,000,000
Add interest during the construction period:		
a. $120,000 \times 0.10 \times 9/12 =$	$ 9,000	
b. $220,000 \times 0.10 \times 6/12 =$	11,000	
c. $480,000 \times 0.10 \times 3/12 =$	12,000	
d. $180,000$—no interest	-0-	32,000
Total acquisition cost		$1,032,000

> FINANCIAL Accounting STANdards Board

FASB Statement No. 34 provides the following guidelines that must be observed:

1. Interest is capitalized only during the construction period.
2. Interest is computed on the expenditures during the construction period.
3. The applicable borrowing interest rate for the company is used.
4. Interest is computed regardless of the source of the funds (borrowed or internally generated).
5. Interest added to the cost of the operational assets cannot exceed the

---

[2] *FASB Statement of Financial Accounting Standards No. 34,* "Capitalization of Interest Cost" (Stamford, Conn., October 1979). Under this Statement, interest cannot be capitalized for assets that are (1) in use or ready for their intended use, or (2) not used in the earnings activities of the entity. Interest capitalized in any accounting period cannot exceed the total interest cost in that period.

total amount of interest expense of the entity in that period (for all purposes).

MATCHING THE COST OF AN OPERATIONAL ASSET WITH FUTURE REVENUES

The acquisiton cost of an operational asset having a limited useful life represents the prepaid cost of a bundle of **future services** or benefits (i.e., future economic usefulness to the entity). The **matching principle** requires that the acquisition cost of such assets be apportioned as expense to the periods in which revenue is generated as a result of using those assets. Thus, the acquisition cost of this kind of operational asset is matched in the future with the future revenues to which it contributes by way of services and benefits.

We should make clear the distinction among three different terms that are used to describe the cost apportionment required by the matching principle for the different types of operational assets:

1. **Depreciation**—the systematic and rational apportionment of the acquisition cost of tangible **operational assets** (other than natural resources) to future periods in which the services or benefits contribute to revenue. Example—depreciation of the $10,350 cost of a machine over its estimated useful life of ten years and no residual value (see page 372):

December 31, 19B:

Depreciation expense	1,035	
Accumulated depreciation, machinery		1,035

2. **Depletion**—the systematic and rational apportionment of the acquisition cost of **natural resources** to future periods in which the use of those natural resources contributes to revenue. Example—depletion of the $53,000 cost of a timber tract over the estimated period of cutting based on "cutting" rate of approximately 20 percent per year (see page 373):

December 31, 19B:

Depletion expense	10,600	
Timber tract (No. 20)		10,600
Note: A contra account could be used such as Accumulated Depletion.		

3. **Amortization**—the systematic and rational apportionment of the acquisition cost of **intangible operational assets** to future periods in which

the benefits contribute to revenue. Example—amortization of the cost
of a patent over its estimated economic useful life to the entity:

December 31, 19B:

Patent expense	500	
Patents		500

Note: A contra account could be used such as Accumulated Patent
Amortization.

Each of these terms relates to the same basic objective; namely, the
apportionment of the acquisition cost of an operational asset to the future
periods in which the benefits of its use contribute to the earning of revenue.
The amounts of depreciation, depletion, and amortization measured and
recorded during each period are reported as expenses or costs for the
period. On the balance sheet, the amounts of depreciation, depletion, and
amortization *accumulated since acquisition date* are reported as deductions from
the assets to which they pertain. To illustrate, an operational asset, such
as the machine illustrated above, would be reported on the balance sheet
(at the end of the second year in the example) as follows:

Balance Sheet
At December 31, 19B

Property, plant, and equipment:
Machinery $10,350
Less: Accumulated depreciation 2,070 $8,280

or

Machinery (less accumulated depreciation, $2,070) $8,280

We emphasize that the amounts for operational assets reported on the
balance sheet do not represent their market values at balance sheet date,
rather, they are book, or carrying, values. **Book value** is their acquisition
cost (which was their market value at acquisition date), less the accumulated apportionments to expense of that cost from acquisition date to
the date of the balance sheet. Recording and reporting depreciation is a
process of cost allocation; it is not a process of valuing the asset. This is
in accordance with the cost principle. Under it, the cost of an operational
asset is measured and recorded at acquisition date at the then market
value. The cost is not remeasured on a market value basis at subsequent
balance sheet dates, rather the acquisition cost is reduced by the accumulated expense allocation for depreciation, depletion, or amortization.

OPERATIONAL ASSETS SUBJECT TO DEPRECIATION

Two kinds of operational assets were identified on page 371. In this
section the discussion will be limited to land and those tangible operational

assets subject to depreciation. The term *tangible operational* refers to all kinds of buildings, machinery, furniture, and other equipment used in the operation of the business. Although the term *fixed* asset is used sometimes, more descriptive terms such as **property, plant, and equipment** and **land, plant, and equipment** usually are used in published financial statements.

Buildings, machinery, furniture, and other tangible operational assets (except land) decrease in economic utility to the user because of a number of causative factors, such as wear and tear, the passage of time, effects of the elements (such as the weather), obsolescence (i.e., becoming out-of-date), technological changes, and inadequacy. These causative factors always are bearing down on such assets during the periods in which the assets are being used to generate revenues. Thus, under the **matching principle,** at the end of each accounting period an **adjusting entry** is needed to record these expense-causing effects. In developing the adjusting entry, the fundamental accounting principles require that a *rational and systematic* measurement approach be used to match the acquisition cost of tangible operational assets with periodic revenues.[3]

Because of the wide diversity of operational assets subject to depreciation and the varying effects of the causative factors listed above, a number of **depreciation methods** have been developed that are acceptable for both accounting and income tax purposes. In the paragraphs to follow, we will discuss and illustrate the methods of measuring and recording depreciation that usually are used.

To measure depreciation expense each period, the methods require three amounts for each asset: (1) **actual acquisition cost,** (2) **estimated net residual value,** and (3) **estimated useful life.** It is important to observe that of these three amounts, two are *estimates* (residual value and useful or service life); thus, the depreciation expense that is recorded and reported is an estimate. To illustrate, depreciation expense may be measured as follows:

Actual acquisition cost	$625
Less: Estimated residual value	25
Amount to be depreciated over useful life	$600
Estimated useful life	3 years
Annual depreciation expense: $600 ÷ 3 =	$200

Estimated residual value[4] must be deducted from acquisition cost because it represents that part of the acquisition cost that is expected to

---

[3] AICPA, *Accounting Research Bulletin No. 43* (New York, 1961), chap. C, par. 5, defines depreciation accounting as "a system of accounting which aims to distribute the cost or other basic value of tangible capital assets, less salvage value (if any), over the estimated useful life of the unit (which may be a group of assets) in a systematic and rational manner. It is a process of allocation, not of valuation." Copyright (1961) by the American Institute of CPAs.

[4] Residual value also is called scrap value or salvage value, however, "residual value" is a more descriptive term because the asset may not be scrapped or sold as salvage upon disposition; a subsequent buyer may renovate it and reuse it for many years.

be recovered by the user upon disposal of the asset at the end of its estimated useful life to the entity. *Residual value* is the total estimated amount to be recovered less any estimated costs of dismantling, disposal, and selling. Because these costs may approximately equal the gross residual amount recovered, many depreciable assets are assumed to have no residual value. It is important to realize that the estimated net residual value is not the value of the asset as salvage or scrap, rather, it is the net recovery estimated to be realized at the date on which the *current user* intends to dispose of it. For example, a company whose policy is to replace all trucks at the end of three years normally would use a higher estimated residual value than would a user of the same kind of truck whose policy is to replace the trucks at the end of five years.

Estimated useful or service life should be viewed as the *economic* useful life to the *present owner* rather than as the total useful life to all potential users. In the truck example above, for accounting purposes, one user would use a three-year estimated useful life, whereas the other user would use a five-year estimated useful life.

Estimates are necessary to allocate a known cost amount (the acquisition cost of an operational asset) over a number of future periods during which the asset will be contributing to the generation of revenues. The allocation must be made at the end of each period because it would not be very useful in the measurement of periodic income and asset valuations to defer all cost allocations for the long period of time until the date of disposal of an operational asset which is "used up."

DEPRECIATION METHODS

Several **methods of depreciation** will be discussed and illustrated. For this purpose we will use a common set of facts and notations:

	Symbols	Illustrative amounts
Acquisition cost of a particular operational asset (a productive machine)	C	$625
Estimated net residual value at end of useful life	R	$ 25
Estimated service life:		
Life in years	N*	3
Life in units of productive output	P*	10,000
Depreciation rate	r	
Dollar amount of depreciation expense per period	D	

* Lowercase letters will be used for the current period.

The several depreciation methods commonly used are identical in basic concept; that is, each method allocates a portion of the cost of a depreciable asset to each of a number of future periods in a consistent and rational manner. The methods vary among themselves as to the allocation pattern to each of the future periods.

The discussions to follow will define, illustrate, and evaluate the following commonly used depreciation methods:[5]

1. Straight line.
2. Productive output (units of production).

Accelerated:

3. Sum-of-the-years' digits.
4. Double-declining balance.

Straight-line depreciation. This method has been used widely because of its simplicity and apparent relationship to what actually happens to the **utility** of many kinds of depreciable assets. Under this method, an *equal portion* of the acquisition cost less the estimated residual value is allocated to each accounting period during the estimated useful life. Thus, the annual depreciation expense is measured as follows:

$$D = \frac{C-R}{N} \quad \text{or} \quad D = \frac{\$625-\$25}{3} = \$200 \quad \text{depreciation expense per year}$$

A **depreciation schedule** covering the entire useful life of the machine can be developed as follows:

Depreciation schedule—straight-line method

Year	Periodic depreciation expense	End of year Balance in accumulated depreciation	Book value
At acquisition			$625
1	$200	$200	425
2	200	400	225
3	200	600	25
	$600		

The adjusting entry for depreciation expense on this machine would be the same for each of the three years of the useful life, viz:

	Year 1	Year 2	Year 3
Depreciation expense	200	200	200
Accumulated depreciation, machinery	200	200	200

[5] AICPA, *Accounting Trends and Techniques* (Annual Survey of Accounting Practices Followed in 600 Stockholders' Reports), 3d ed. (New York, 1979), p. 248, reports on the use of the various depreciation methods by the 600 companies surveyed (some companies use more than one method): straight line, 560; declining balance, 67; sum-of-the-years' digits, 35; accelerated method—not specified, 67; and units of production, 44. Copyright (1979) by the American Institute of CPAs.

Observe that *(a)* depreciation **expense** is constant in amount from year to year (often called a **fixed** or constant expense) and *(b)* **accumulated** depreciation increases by an equal amount each year. This is the reason for the designation, straight line.

The straight-line method is simple, rational, and systematic (i.e., logical, stable, consistent, and realistically predictible from period to period). It is especially appropriate where the asset is used essentially at the same rate each period. It implies an approximately equal decline in the economic usefulness of the asset each period. For these reasons, it is used far more often than all of the other methods combined (see footnote 5).

Productive-output method. This method, sometimes called the units-of-production method, is based upon the assumption that the revenue-generating benefits derived each period from a depreciable asset are related directly to the periodic **output** of the asset. For example, many persons believe that certain equipment, such as a delivery truck, should be depreciated on the basis of miles driven each period (i.e., based on a measure of ouput) rather than on the mere passage of time as is assumed by the straight-line method. These persons believe that many productive assets do not contribute to the generation of revenues merely because time is passing, rather, only when they are used productively.

Since the productive-output method relates acquisition cost less estimated residual value to the estimated productive life of the asset in terms of units of output, a **depreciation rate per unit of output** is computed as follows:

$$r = \frac{C - R}{P} \quad \text{or} \quad r = \frac{\$625 - \$25}{10,000 \text{ units}} = \$0.06 \quad \begin{array}{l} \text{depreciation rate per} \\ \text{unit of output} \end{array}$$

for Life

Assuming 3,000 units of actual output from the illustrative machine in Year 1, depreciation expense for Year 1 would be:

$$D = r \times p \quad \text{or} \quad D = \$0.06 \times 3,000 = \$180 \text{ depreciation expense}$$

Assuming actual output to be 5,000 units in Year 2 and 2,000 units in Year 3, the depreciation schedule would be as follows:

Depreciation schedule— productive-output method

Year	Periodic depreciation expense		Balance in accumulated depreciation (End of year)	Book value (End of year)
At acquisition				$625
1	(3,000 × $0.06)	$180	$180	445
2	(5,000 × 0.06)	300	480	145
3	(2,000 × 0.06)	120	600	25
		$600		

The *adjusting entry* for depreciation at the end of each year would be:

	Year 1	Year 2	Year 3
Depreciation expense	180	300	120
Accumulated depreciation, machinery	180	300	120

Observe that depreciation expense varies from period to period directly with the periodic outputs; thus, when the productive-output method is used, depreciation expense is said to be a **variable expense.**

The productive-output method is simple, rational, and systematic. It is appropriate where output of the asset can be measured realistically and where the economic **utility** of the asset to the entity tends to decrease with productive use rather than with the passage of time. Also, where use is significantly variable from period to period, a more realistic measurement of expense which is matched with revenue is attained. Despite these conceptual and practical advantages, it is not used widely (see footnote 5).

Accelerated depreciation methods. Accelerated depreciation is based upon the notion that there should be relatively large amounts of depreciation expense reported in the early years of the useful life of the asset and correspondingly reduced amounts of depreciation expense in the later years. The basis for this conclusion is that a depreciable asset is more efficient in generating revenue in the early years than in the later years of its life. Also, repair expense tends to be lower in the early years and higher in the later years. Therefore, it is contended that the *combined effect* of decreasing depreciation expense and increasing repair expense is relatively constant from period to period over the life of the asset.

Accelerated depreciation has considerable appeal from the **income tax** viewpoint. Higher depreciation expense means lower reported periodic income amounts in the early years and lower income taxes. Of course, the effect reverses in the later years; however, an early tax deduction is to be preferred over a later tax deduction because of the time value of money.[6]

There are several variations of accelerated depreciation; however, the two methods generally used are the sum-of-the-years'-digits method and the double-declining balance method.

Sum-of-the-years'-digits method. This method, sometimes abbreviated as the SYD method, is used primarily because it is simple and produces a significantly accelerated effect compared to straight-line depreciation. Depreciation expense each year is computed by multiplying the acquisition cost, less estimated residual value, by a fraction that is successively *smaller* each

---

[6] The time value of money refers to interest that can be earned on money invested or used in the business.

year. Each of the decreasing fractions is determined by using the sum of the digits comprising the estimated useful life as the denominator and the specific year of life in *inverse order* as the numerator. The computations may be demonstrated, using the illustrative data previously given, as below:[7]

Denominator:
   Sum of digits (comprising the useful life): $1 + 2 + 3 = 6$.
Numerators:
   Digits (specific year of life) in inverse order: 3, 2, 1.

Year of life	Fraction
1	$3/6$
2	$2/6$
3	$1/6$
Total	$6/6$

Therefore, the depreciation expense each year for the useful life of the illustrative machine would be: Year 1, $600 \times 3/6 = 300; Year 2, $600 \times 2/6 = 200; and Year 3, $600 \times 1/6 = 100.[8]

The accelerated effects of SYD depreciation can be readily observed in the following depreciation schedule:

Depreciation schedule—sum-of-the-years'-digits method

Year	Computations	Periodic depreciation expense	Balance in accumulated depreciation (End of year)	Book value (End of year)
At acquisition				$625
1	$600 \times 3/6 =$	$300	$300	325
2	$600 \times 2/6 =$	200	500	125
3	$600 \times 1/6 =$	100	600	25
Total		$600		

---

[7] The sum of the digits can be computed by using the formula:

$$SYD = n\left(\frac{n+1}{2}\right).$$

For example, a five-year life would be:

$$SYD = 5\left(\frac{5+1}{2}\right) = 15.$$

[8] Although somewhat cumbersome, the SYD computation can be expressed as an equation as follows (Year 1 illustrated):

$$SYD = \frac{(C - R)(N + 1 - n^*)}{N\left(\frac{N+1}{2}\right)}$$

$$SYD_1 = \frac{($625 - $25)(3 + 1 - 1^*)}{3\left(\frac{3+1}{2}\right)} = \frac{$1,800}{6} = $300$$

    * Year of life.

384

The **adjusting entry** for depreciation expense by year would be:

	Year 1	Year 2	Year 3
Depreciation expense	300	200	100
Accumulated depreciation, machinery	300	200	100

Comparison of depreciation expense and the increase in the accumulated balance between the straight-line method (page 380) and the above SYD results indicates the significantly different income amounts reported each period.

The SYD method is relatively simple to apply and is considered to be "rational and systematic." Reference to footnote 5 will indicate that it is not used widely.

Double-declining balance method. This accelerated method, known as the DDB method, came directly from a provision in the Internal Revenue Code. For income tax purposes, accelerated depreciation is permitted; however, depreciation expense for each period may not be more than double the rate that would result under the straight-line method, ignoring residual value. Since this approach is permitted for income tax purposes, and because it gives a significant accelerating effect, it has been used widely on tax returns.[9] Although considered by many accountants as unsound conceptually, it is used by some companies for accounting purposes (see footnote 5). This is the only method that **ignores residual value** in computing the depreciation rate (and expense).

Depreciation expense is measured each year by multiplying a constant rate by the decreasing undepreciated cost of the asset (i.e., the book value), ignoring residual value. The rate used is *double* the straight-line rate, ignoring residual value. Depreciation stops when the book value equals (or approximates) the estimated residual value. Thus, depreciation expense would be computed as follows, based on the illustrative data:[10]

Straight-line rate: 3 years = 1 ÷ 3 years = 0.333.
Double straight-line rate: 0.333 × 2 = 0.667.
Annual depreciation: 0.667 × the decreasing book value of the asset.

---

[9] Accelerated depreciation is limited for tax purposes to assets having a useful life of three years or more; the short period was used to simplify the illustrations. There are other related special tax provisions which are too detailed to be considered in this book.

[10] The DDB computation can be expressed as an equation as follows (Year 1 illustrated):

$$DDB = \left[(C)\left(1 - \frac{2}{N}\right)^{n*-1} \right] \frac{2}{N}$$

$$DDB_1 = \left[(\$625)\left(1 - \frac{2}{3}\right)^{1*-1} \right] \frac{2}{3}$$
$$= [\$625]\, 0.667 = \$417$$

* Year of life.

Depreciation schedule— double-declining balance method

| | | | End of year | |
| | | Periodic depreciation | Balance in accumulated | Book |
Year	Computations	expense	depreciation	value
At acquisition				$625
1	0.667 × $625	$417	$417	208
2	0.667 × 208	139	556	69
3	0.667 × 69	44*	600	25

* Although 0.667 × $69 = $46, depreciation expense in the last year is the amount necessary to leave the book value equal to the residual value of $25 (or zero if there is no residual value).

COMPARISON OF DEPRECIATION METHODS

Although the four methods of computing depreciation discussed above are different ways of measuring periodic depreciation expense, the total expense for all periods combined is the same regardless of the method used. The comparative effects of each method on the income statement (depreciation expense) and the balance sheet (book value) for the illustrative data are shown quantatively in the table below and graphically in Exhibit 9–1. The methods have different impacts on the measurement of periodic income, even though the asset cost, estimated life, and estimated residual value are the same. This demonstrates how the selection of a

EXHIBIT 9–1
Depreciation methods— comparative results graphed (including a typical repair curve)

Years

particular accounting approach will cause a difference in the measurement of income for each period (but the same in total for all methods).

Depreciation methods— comparative expense and book value results

Year	Straight line		Productive output		Sum-of-the-years' digits		Double declining	
	Depre-ciation expense	Book value	Depre-ciation expense	Book value	Depre-ciation expense	Book value	Depre-ciation expense	Book value
At acquisition		$625		$625		$625		$625
1	$200	425	$180	445	$300	325	$417	208
2	200	225	300	145	200	125	139	69
3	200	25	120	25	100	25	44	25
At end	$600	$ 25	$600	$ 25	$600	$ 25	$600	$ 25

To date the accounting profession has not provided officially definitive guidelines for selection of a depreciation method which would be preferable for each type of depreciable asset. Therefore, the several methods can be characterized as "open" alternatives for financial reporting purposes.

DEPRECIATION FOR INTERIM PERIODS

The preceding illustrations assumed that depreciation expense for a full year is recorded at the end of each year by means of an adjusting entry. Some businesses record depreciation monthly, quarterly, or semiannually. Also, a depreciable asset may be acquired or disposed of during the year. These situations require that depreciation expense be recorded for periods of less than one year. Therefore, it is customary to compute depreciation on a proportional basis to either the nearest month, quarter, or six-month period. For example, depreciation for a full month may be assumed to start or end at the nearest first of the month. For all of the methods illustrated, except productive output, monthly depreciation normally is determined by computing the annual amount of depreciation as illustrated, then dividing by 12 to obtain the monthly amount.[11] For example, in the above illustration for double-declining balance depreciation, the depreciation for the first year was determined to be $417. Assume the asset was acquired on August 12, 19A, with a December 31 fiscal year ending. The depreciation expense for 19A would be (nearest-month basis):

$$\frac{\$417}{12} \times 5 = \$174$$

Since depreciation expense is an estimate, one should never record depreciation to amounts below one dollar, since to do so would suggest a higher degree of accuracy than is warranted. For this reason, depreciation amounts

[11] Under the productive-output method, monthly depreciation is derived by multiplying the unit depreciation rate by the output for the particular month.

always should be rounded to the nearest amount—one, ten, or hundred dollars—depending upon the cost of the depreciable asset compared with total depreciable assets. The **materiality concept** also applies in this situation.

CHANGE IN DEPRECIATION ESTIMATES

Recall that depreciation is based on two estimates—useful life and residual value—made when a depreciable asset is acquired. It sometimes is necessary to revise one, or both, of these initial estimates as experience with the asset accumulates. When it is clear that either estimate should be revised (to a material degree), the undepreciated balance, less any residual value, at that date should be apportioned over the remaining estimated life. In accounting this is called a "change in estimate."

To illustrate, assume the following for a particular machine:

Cost of machine when acquired	$33,000
Estimated life	10 years
Estimated residual value	$ 3,000
Accumulated depreciation through Year 6	
(assuming the straight-line method is used)	$18,000

Shortly after the start of Year 7, the initial estimates were changed to the following:

Revised estimated total life	14 years
Revised estimated residual value	$1,000

No entry is required when this decision is reached. However, the **adjusting entry** at the **end of Year 7** would be:

Depreciation expense	1,750	
Accumulated depreciation		1,750

Computations:

Acquisition cost	$33,000
Accumulated depreciation, Years 1–6	18,000
Undepreciated balance	15,000
Less: Revised residual value	1,000
Balance to be depreciated	$14,000

Annual depreciation:

$14,000 ÷ (14 years − 6 years) =	$ 1,750

PART B: REPAIRS AND MAINTENANCE, NATURAL RESOURCES, AND INTANGIBLE OPERATIONAL ASSETS

REPAIRS AND MAINTENANCE

After the acquisition of a tangible operational asset, related cost outlays often must be made for such items as ordinary repairs and maintenance, major repairs, replacements, and additions. The central measurement problem is the determination of which of these items should be recorded as an expense of the current period when incurred, and which should be recorded as an asset (i.e., as a prepayment) to be matched with future revenues. In measuring the cost of using operational assets, two basic types of expenditures must be considered. The term **expenditure** means the payment of cash or the incurrence of a debt for an asset or service received. The purchase of a machine or a service, such as repairs on a truck, may be for cash or on credit. In either case there is an expenditure. The *two* types of expenditures are:

1. **Capital expenditures**—These are expenditures for the acquisition of an asset or for the expansion or improvement of an asset already owned. A capital expenditure benefits one or more accounting periods *beyond the current period;* therefore, capital expenditures are recorded in the respective asset accounts. For example, a plant addition costing $90,000 would be recorded as follows:

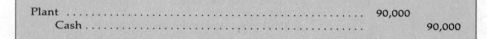

| Plant .... | 90,000 | |
| Cash .... | | 90,000 |

2. **Revenue expenditures**—These are expenditures for normal operating items such as ordinary repairs, maintenance, and salaries which benefit *only* the current period; therefore, revenue expenditures are debited when incurred directly to appropriate expense accounts.[12] For example, the payment of $600 for ordinary repairs to the plant would be recorded in the current period as follows:

| Repair expense .... | 600 | |
| Cash .... | | 600 |

Each expenditure made subsequent to the acquisition of an operational asset must be evaluated carefully to classify it as either capital or revenue. The distinction between capital and revenue expenditures is essential to conform with the matching principle. The expenditures must be matched with the periodic revenues to which they relate. The purpose and nature of the expenditure is the controlling factor in its classification. In the next few paragraphs we will discuss the common types of outlays subsequent to acquisition of a tangible operational asset.

---

[12] The term *revenue expenditure* is widely used. It suggests that the expenditure is to be deducted in the current period from revenue in deriving income. However, a term such as *expense expenditure* would be more descriptive.

Extraordinary repairs. Extraordinary repairs are classified as **capital expenditures;** therefore, each is debited to the related *asset* account and depreciated over the *remaining* life of that asset. *Extraordinary repairs* occur infrequently, involve relatively large amounts of money, and tend to increase the economic usefulness of the asset in the future because of either greater efficiency or longer life, or both. They are represented by major overhauls, complete reconditioning, and major replacements and betterments. For example, the complete replacement of a roof on the factory building would constitute an extraordinary repair, whereas patching the old roof would constitute an ordinary repair.

To illustrate the accounting for extraordinary repairs, assume a machine is being used that originally cost $40,000 and is being depreciated on a straight-line basis over ten years with no estimated residual value. At the beginning of the seventh year, a major reconditioning was completed at a cost of $12,700. The estimated useful life was changed from 10 years to 13 years (i.e., a change in estimate). A typical sequence of entries would be:

At acquisition of the asset:

Machinery	40,000	
Cash		40,000
Purchase of machinery.		

Depreciation—annually at end of Years 1 through 6:

Depreciation expense	4,000	
Accumulated depreciation, machinery		4,000
Adjusting entry to record annual depreciation ($40,000 ÷ 10).		

Extraordinary repair—at start of seventh year:[13]

Machinery	12,700	
Cash		12,700
Expenditure for major repair.		

[13] Some accountants prefer to debit the related asset account, as illustrated above, only when the major repair increases the efficiency above normal. In contrast, when it is estimated that only the useful life is extended, those accountants instead would debit the related accumulated depreciation account. This distinction usually is not made because the distinction is difficult to apply practically. Also, subsequent book value and depreciation expense would be the same, irrespective of which account is debited because the remaining book value to be depreciated would be the same in either instance.

Revised depreciation—annually at end of Years 7 through 13:

Depreciation expense	4,100	
Accumulated depreciation		4,100
Adjusting entry to record annual depreciation.		

Computation:
Original cost	$40,000	
Depreciation, Years 1–6	24,000	
Book value remaining		$16,000
Extraordinary repair		12,700
Balance to be depreciated over remaining life		$28,700

Annual depreciation: $28,700 ÷ (13 − 6) years = $4,100

Additions. Additions are extensions to, or enlargements of, existing assets, such as the addition of a wing to a present building. Since these are **capital expenditures,** the cost of such additions should be debited to the existing account for the asset and depreciated over the remaining life of the asset to which the cost is related.

Ordinary repairs and maintenance. Ordinary repairs and maintenance always are classified as **revenue expenditures** and debited to an appropriate *expense* account in the period in which incurred. *Ordinary* repairs and maintenance are those relatively small recurring outlays essential to keep a tangible operating asset in *normal* operating condition. Ordinary repairs do not add materially to the economic value of the asset or to its estimated useful life. Rather, they tend to restore and repair the effects of normal wear and tear that occurred with usage. As a consequence, normal repair and maintenance tend to assure the expected useful life and operating efficiencies. These reasons justify the matching of current repair and maintenance expenditures (i.e., expense) with revenues of the current period.

NATURAL RESOURCES

A natural resource, such as a mineral deposit, oil well, or timber tract, often is referred to as a "wasting asset" since it is consumed physically, or **depleted,** as it is used. When acquired or developed, a natural resource is measured and recorded in the accounts in accordance with the **cost principle.** As the natural resource is consumed or used up, the acquisition cost, in accordance with the **matching principle,** must be apportioned among the various periods in which the resulting revenues are recognized. The term **"depletion"** is used to describe this process of periodic cost allocation over the period of use of a natural resource. A **depletion rate** per unit of the resource produced is computed by dividing the total acquisition and development cost by the *estimated* units that can be withdrawn economically from the resource. The depletion rate, thus computed, is multiplied each period by the number of units actually withdrawn. This procedure is the same as the productive output method of calculating depreciation (see page 381).

To illustrate, assume that a gravel deposit was developed at a cost of $80,000 and that a reliable estimate was made that 100,000 cubic yards of gravel could be withdrawn economically from it. The depletion rate per unit would be computed as follows:

$$\$80,000 \div 100,000 \text{ cubic yards} = \$0.80 \text{ per cubic yard (depletion rate per unit)}$$

Depletion expense for the first year, assuming 5,000 cubic yards of gravel were withdrawn during the year, would be recorded by means of the following adjusting entry.[14]

Depletion expense	4,000	
Gravel pit		4,000
Depletion for the year, 5,000 cubic yards × $0.80 = $4,000.		

At the end of the first year, this natural resource should be reported as follows:

Balance Sheet

Operational assets:
Gravel pit (cost, $80,000 − $4,000 accumulated depletion) $76,000

Because changes in the estimate of recoverable units from a natural resource are made frequently, the depletion rate must be revised often. This is a "change in estimate"; hence, the undepleted acquisition cost is spread over the estimated remaining recoverable units by computing a new depletion rate. For example, assume in Year 2 that the estimate of recoverable units remaining was changed from 95,000 to 150,000 cubic yards. The depletion rate to be applied to the cubic yards of gravel withdrawn in Year 2 would be:

$$(\$80,000 − \$4,000) \div 150,000 \text{ cubic yards} = \$0.51 \text{ per cubic yard}$$

When buildings and similar improvements are constructed in connection with the development and exploitation of a natural resource, they should be recorded in separate asset accounts and *depreciated*—not depleted. Their estimated useful lives usually cannot be longer than the time required to exploit the natural resource.

---

[14] Consistent with the procedure for recording depreciation, an Accumulated Depletion account may be used. However, as a matter of precedent, the asset account itself generally is credited directly for the periodic amortization. Either procedure is acceptable. The same is true for intangible operational assets, discussed in the next section.

INTANGIBLE OPERATIONAL ASSETS

An intangible operational asset, like any other asset, has value because of certain rights and privileges conferred by law upon the owner of the asset. However, an intangible asset has no corporeal existence (i.e., no material or physical substance) as do tangible assets such as land and buildings. Thus, intangible assets are characterized by their lack of physical substance and the special rights that ownership confers. Examples of intangible operational assets are patents, copyrights, franchises, licenses, trademarks, and goodwill. An intangible asset usually requires the expenditure of resources. For example, an entity may purchase a patent from the inventor. The cost of an intangible asset should be measured and recorded in the accounts and reported on the financial statements of the entity in the same way as a tangible asset.[15]

At acquisition, an intangible operational asset is recorded at its cash equivalent cost in accordance with the cost principle. Cost is defined as the sum of all expenditures made to acquire the rights or privileges.

Each type of intangible operational asset should be recorded in a separate asset account when acquired. To illustrate, assume that on January 1, 19A, Mason Company purchased a patent from its developer, J. Doe, at a cash price of $17,000. The acquisition of this intangible asset would be recorded as follows:

January 1, 19A:

Patents	17,000	
Cash		17,000
Purchase of patent rights from J. Doe.		

Under the cost principle, an intangible right or privilege, although it may have value, is not recorded unless there has been an identifiable expenditure of resources to acquire or develop it. For example, the demise of a competitor's patent may cause the company's patent to be more valuable. This increase in value would not be recorded since there was no expenditure of resources incident to the increase in value.

Research and development (R&D) costs are recorded as expenses in the period incurred, even though they sometimes result in the development of a patent.

AMORTIZATION OF INTANGIBLE OPERATIONAL ASSETS

Intangible operational assets normally have limited lives similar to tangible operational assets; however, such intangible assets seldom, if ever,

---

[15] Intangible operational assets often are referred to as intangible assets.

have a residual value at the ends of their useful lives. Intangible assets have a limited life because the **rights or privileges** that give them value terminate or simply disappear. For example, a patent has a *legal* life of 17 years from the date it is granted; however, the right may cease to have economic utility, although still legally alive, before the end of the legal life. Therefore, the cost of a patent must be allocated to expense over its *economic life,* which cannot be longer (but may be less) than 17 years. The systematic write-off of the cost of an intangible asset over its economically useful life is referred to as **amortization.** To illustrate, assume the patent acquired by Mason Company, recorded above, had an estimated ten-year remaining economic life. At the end of 19A the **adjusting entry** to record amortization for one year would be (see footnote 14):

December 31, 19A:

Patent expense	1,700	
Patents		1,700
Adjusting entry to record amortization of patent over the estimated		
economic life of ten years ($17,000 ÷ 10 years = $1,700).		

The amount of patent amortization expense recorded for 19A is reported on the income statement as an operating expense. The patent would be reported on the December 31, 19A, balance sheet as follows:

Intangible assets:
    Patents (cost, $17,000, less amortization) $15,300

In 1970 the Accounting Principles Board (APB) issued *Opinion No. 17,* which requires that each intangible be amortized over its estimated economic life. The *Opinion* specifies that, for accounting purposes, the estimated useful life of an intangible asset cannot exceed 40 years. The *Opinion* does not permit an arbitrary and immediate write-off of an intangible asset down to, say, a nominal amount of $1. Prior to *Opinion No. 17,* this sometimes was done under the guise of conservatism.

Although an intangible asset may be amortized by using any "systematic and rational" method that reflects the actual expiration of its economic usefulness, the straight-line method is used almost exclusively.

Copyrights. A copyright is similar to a patent. A copyright gives the owner the exclusive right to publish, use, and sell a literary, musical, or artistic piece of work for a period not exceeding 50 years beyond the author's death. The same principles and procedures used in accounting for and reporting the cost of patents also are appropriate for copyrights.

Franchises and licenses. Franchises and licenses frequently are granted by governmental and other units for a specified period and purpose. For example, a city may grant one company a franchise to distribute gas to homes for heating purposes, or a company may sell franchises, such as the right to operate a Kentucky Fried Chicken restaurant to local outlets. Franchises and licenses generally require the expenditure of resources by the franchisee to acquire them; therefore, they represent intangible operational assets that should be accounted for as illustrated earlier for patents.

Leaseholds. Leasing is a common type of business contract whereby one party, the owner or lessor, for a consideration known as rent, extends to another party, the lessee, certain rights to use specified property. Leases may vary from simple arrangements, such as the month-to-month lease of an office or apartment or the daily rental of an automobile, to long-term leases having complex contractual arrangements. The rights granted to a lessee frequently are referred to as a **leasehold.**

In the case of long-term leases, a lump-sum advance rental payment sometimes is required. The lessee should debit the advance payment to an intangible asset account (frequently called Leaseholds) and amortize it to expense over the contractual life of the lease. The true amount of annual rent expense includes the amortization of the leasehold; therefore, the annual amortization is debited to Rent Expense. To illustrate, assume that Favor Company leased a building for its own use on January 1, 19A, under a five-year contract that required, in addition to the monthly rental payments, a single payment in advance of $20,000. The advance payment would be recorded as follows:

January 1, 19A:

Leasehold (or Rent paid in advance) 20,000
    Cash 20,000
    Rent paid in advance.

At the end of 19A, and at the end of each of the remaining four years, the following **adjusting** entry would be made to reflect amortization of this intangible asset:[16]

December 31, 19A:

Rent expense 4,000
    Leasehold (or Rent paid in advance) 4,000
    Adjusting entry to record amortization of leasehold over five years
    ($20,000 ÷ 5 years = $4,000).

---

[16] This discussion presumes the normal or operating type of lease. In some instances, a lease is in effect a sale/purchase agreement. Such leases, known as financing leases, involve complex accounting problems that are deferred to more advanced accounting books.

The monthly rental payments would be debited to Rent Expense when paid each month.

Leasehold improvements. In most instances, when buildings, improvements, or alterations are constructed by the **lessee** on leased property, such assets legally revert to the owner of the property at the end of the lease. The lessee has full use of such improvements during the term of the lease, and they should be recorded in an intangible operating asset account entitled "Leasehold Improvements." These expenditures should be amortized over the estimated useful life of the related improvement or the remaining life of the lease, whichever is shorter.

Goodwill. Usually, a successful business, if sold as a unit, will command a price somewhat in excess of the sum of the market values of the recorded assets less the liabilities. The reason a business may command the excess price is that an intangible operational asset called goodwill attaches to a successful business.

Goodwill represents the potential of a business to earn above a normal rate of return on the recorded assets less the liabilities. It arises from such factors as customer confidence, reputation for dependability, efficiency and internal competencies, quality of goods and services, and financial standing. From the date of organization, a successful business continually is building goodwill. In this context, the goodwill is said to be "generated internally at no identifiable cost." On the other hand, when a business is purchased as an entity, the purchase price will include a payment for any goodwill that exists at that time. *In conformance with the cost principle, goodwill is recorded as an intangible operational asset only when it actually is purchased.*

To illustrate, assume Richard Roe purchased the College Men's Store on January 1, 19A, for $200,000 cash. At date of purchase, it was determined that the recorded assets had a total **market value** of $160,000, comprised of the market values of inventory, $110,000; fixtures, $35,000; prepaid rent, $1,000; and other assets, $14,000 (Roe did not accept any of the liabilities.) The purchase would be recorded by Roe as follows:

January 1, 19A:

Inventory	110,000	
Furniture and fixtures	35,000	
Prepaid rent	1,000	
Other assets	14,000	
Goodwill	40,000	
Cash		200,000
Purchase of College Men's Store.		

The intangible asset—goodwill—must be amortized to expense over its estimated economic life not to exceed 40 years *(APB Opinion No. 17).*

Assuming a 40-year economic life, the amortization for 19A would be recorded in an **adjusting entry** as follows:

December 31, 19A:

Goodwill amortization (expense)	1,000	
Goodwill		1,000
Adjusting entry to record goodwill amortization for one year based on 40-year economic life ($40,000 ÷ 40 years = $1,000).		

Many other types of intangible assets may be observed in financial statements. Examples are formulas, processes, and film rights. These are not discussed in detail since they are accounted for, and reported, in a manner similar to that illustrated above.

DEFERRED CHARGES

An asset category called **deferred charges** is reported occasionally on balance sheets. A deferred charge, like a prepaid expense, is an *expense paid in advance;* that is, goods or services were acquired which will be used to generate future revenues. A deferred charge is a **long-term** prepaid expense and, therefore, cannot be classified as a current asset. A prepaid expense is a short-term prepayment and, for this reason, is classified as a current asset. Thus, the only difference between the two is time. For example, a $1,000 insurance premium for five years' coverage paid at the start of Year 1 would be reported as follows at the end of Year 1:

Income statement:
    Insurance expense $200

Balance sheet:
    Current assets:
        Prepaid insurance 200
    Deferred charges:
        Insurance premium paid in advance 600

Common examples of deferred charges are bond issuance costs (Chapter 11), start-up costs, organization costs, and plant rearrangement costs. In conformance with the matching principle, deferred charges are amortized to expense each period over the future periods benefited.

DISPOSAL OF OPERATIONAL ASSETS

Operational assets may be disposed of in either of two ways: voluntarily by sale, trade-in, or retirement; or involuntarily as a result of a casualty, such as a storm, fire, or accident. Whatever the nature of the disposal, the cost of the asset and any accumulated depreciation, depletion, or amortization must be removed from the accounts at the date of disposal. The difference between any resources received upon disposal of an operational asset and the **book value** of the asset at the date of disposal represents a "gain or loss on disposal of operational assets." To illustrate, assume a machine is sold for $3,500 cash when the account balances showed: Machine, $10,000; and Accumulated Depreciation, Machine, $7,000 (i.e., a book value of $3,000). The entry to record the *voluntary* disposal would be:

Cash	3,500	
Accumulated depreciation, machine	7,000	
Machine		10,000
Gain on disposal of operational asset		500
Gain computed:		
Sale price	$3,500	
Book value at date of sale ($10,000 − $7,000)	3,000	
Difference − gain	$ 500	

When an operational asset is disposed of at any date other than the end of the accounting period, it may be necessary to record depreciation, depletion, or amortization for the fraction of the year to the date of disposal. After this entry is made, the entry to record the disposal may be made. To illustrate, assume a truck which cost $16,000 when acquired on January 1, 1978, was "totaled" in a wreck on June 30, 1981. The truck had been depreciated on a straight-line basis with an estimated useful life of eight years and an estimated residual value of $4,000. The insurance company paid a claim of $10,000 cash (i.e., the market value at date of the wreck). The sequence of entries from date of acquisition to date of **involuntary** disposal would be:

January 1, 1978:

Truck	16,000	
Cash		16,000
Purchase of heavy duty truck.		

Annually December 31, 1978, through 1980:

Depreciation expense	1,500	
Accumulated depreciation		1,500
Adjusting entry to record annual depreciation; repeated each year for eight years ($16,000 − $4,000) ÷ 8 years = $1,500.		

June 30, 1981:

Depreciation expense	750	
Accumulated depreciation		750

Depreciation from end of last accounting period to date of disposal, $1,500 × 6/12 = $750. This assumes depreciation is computed to the nearest month.

June 30, 1981:

Cash	10,000	
Accumulated depreciation: ($1,500 × 3) + $750	5,250	
Casualty loss on operational assets	750	
Truck		16,000

Casualty loss on operational asset, including removal from the accounts of original cost and accumulated depreciation.

In the above illustration, the truck, when wrecked, had a book or carrying value of $16,000 − $5,250 = $10,750. The difference between this book value and the insurance indemnity of $10,000 was the amount of the loss on involuntary disposal ($750).

The gain or loss on involuntary disposal of operational assets is reported on the income statement, and the truck would not be reported on the 1981 balance sheet.

TRADING IN USED ASSETS

It is not unusual when acquiring a new (or used) asset to trade in an old asset. Although there may be a direct trade of two assets, the typical case involves the trading in of an old asset plus the payment of a cash difference (often called "boot"). In such transactions, the asset acquired must be recorded in the accounts and the old asset removed from the account.

Accounting for the exchange of one asset for another asset depends on two factors:[17]

1. Whether the two assets are similar or dissimilar.
2. Whether a cash difference (boot) is paid or received.

The trading in of an old truck on a new truck would involve similar assets. In contrast, the trading in of a plot of land on a new truck would involve dissimilar assets.

---

[17] APB Opinion No. 29, "Accounting for Nonmonetary Transactions" (New York, May 1973), specifies the appropriate accounting for transactions that involve the exchange of assets when either or both of these factors are present.

The basic principle for recording the exchange of assets can be stated as follows: If the assets exchanged are *similar*, the exchange should be recorded on a "book value" basis because there is no completed earning process.[18] If the assets exchanged are *dissimilar*, the exchange should be recorded on a "market value" basis because there is a completed earning process.

Four cases will be presented to illustrate application of the basic principle. The four cases will be based on the following fact situation:

Transaction: Company T acquired new Asset N, and traded in old Asset O. At the date of the transaction, the accounts of Company T reflected the following:

```
Asset O:
    Cost when acquired  . . . . . . . . . . . . .    $5,000
    Accumulated depreciation  . . . . . . . . .      3,000
    Estimated market value  . . . . . . . . . . .    2,200
Asset N:
    Market value  . . . . . . . . . . . . . . . . . .  2,250
```

Case A—*Similar assets* are exchanged; *no* cash boot paid.

Principle applied:
   The asset acquired is recorded at the *book value* of the asset traded in.

Entry:

```
Asset N . . . . . . . . . . . . . . . . . . . . . . . . . . . . . . . . . . . . . . . . . . . . . .    2,000
Accumulated depreciation, Asset O . . . . . . . . . . . . . . . . . . . . . .    3,000
    Asset O . . . . . . . . . . . . . . . . . . . . . . . . . . . . . . . . . . . . . . . . . .              5,000
```

Case B—*Dissimilar assets* are exchanged; *no* cash boot paid.

Principle applied:
   The asset acquired is recorded at the *market value* of the asset traded in.

Entry:

[18] In the case of an exchange of similar productive assets, since the asset acquired performs essentially the same productive function as the asset given up, the exchange is only one step in the earning process. The earning process in these situations is completed when the goods or services are sold that the similar productive assets helped to produce. In contrast, in the case of an exchange of dissimilar productive assets, the earning process is completed because the productive function of the productive asset given up is terminated. The asset acquired serves a different economic purpose for the entity and begins a new earning process of its own.

```
Asset N ............................................................. 2,200
Accumulated depreciation, Asset O ....................... 3,000
    Asset O ..........................................................        5,000
    Gain on disposal of operational asset ..................         200
```

Case C—*Similar assets* are exchanged; $50 cash boot is *paid.*

> Principle applied:
> The asset acquired is recorded at the *book value* of the asset traded in *plus* the cash boot paid.

Entry:

```
Asset N ($2,000 + $50) ................................ 2,050*
Accumulated depreciation, Asset O ....................... 3,000
    Asset O ..........................................................        5,000
    Cash ..............................................................           50
    * This amount cannot exceed the market value of the asset acquired.
```

Case D—*Dissimilar assets* are exchanged; $50 cash boot is *paid.*

> Principle applied:
> The asset acquired is recorded at the *market value* of the asset traded in *plus* the cash boot paid.

Entry:

```
Asset N ($2,200 + $50) ................................ 2,250*
Accumulated depreciation, Asset O ....................... 3,000
    Asset O ..........................................................        5,000
    Cash ..............................................................           50
    Gain on sale of operational asset ....................         200
    * This amount cannot exceed the market value of the asset acquired.
```

These four cases are sufficient for our objective to explain the exchange of assets. Sometimes the terms of the transaction include the *receipt* of boot, in which case the recording becomes more complex. Note particularly that under fundamental accounting principles *(APB Opinion No. 29)* an asset, when acquired, should never be recorded at an amount greater than its market value (i.e., its cash equivalent price). In some instances, this constraint will serve to reduce a gain (or increase a loss) on disposal.

In the above illustration, market value of old Asset O was $200 in excess of book value. Therefore, in Cases B and D (relating to dissimilar assets), this amount was recorded as a gain. In contrast, if the market value of old Asset O were $1,900 (i.e., $100 below book value), a loss of $100 would be reported in Cases B and D. This is true also for Cases A and C (similar assets) when the market value of either asset is below book value because it indicates an impairment of value.

DEMONSTRATION CASE

Diversified Industries

(Try to resolve the requirements before proceeding to the suggested solution that follows.)

Diversified Industries has been in operation for a number of years. It started as a construction firm, and in recent years has expanded into a number of related activities. For example, in addition to heavy construction, its operations now include ready-mix concrete, sand and gravel, construction supplies, and earth-moving services.

The transactions given below were selected from those completed during 19D. They focus on the primary issues discussed in this chapter. Amounts have been simplied for case purposes.

19D:

Jan. 1 The management decided to purchase a building that was approximately ten years old. The location was excellent, and there was adequate parking space. The company bought the building and the land on which it ·was situated for $305,000 cash. A reliable appraiser appraised the property at the following market values: land, $126,000; and building, $174,000.

Jan. 12 Paid renovation costs on the building amounting to $38,100.

June 19 Purchased a third location (designated No. 3) for a gravel pit at a cost of $50,000 cash. The location had been carefully surveyed, and it was estimated that 100,000 cubic yards of gravel could be removed from the deposit.

July 10 Paid $1,200 ordinary repairs on the building.

Aug. 1 Paid $10,000 for costs of preparing the gravel pit, acquired in June 19D, for exploitation.

Dec. 31, 19D (end of the annual accounting period)—the following data were developed as a basis for the adjusting entries:

a. The building will be depreciated on a straight-line basis over an estimated useful life of 30 years. The estimated residual value is $35,000.

b. During 19D, 12,000 square yards of gravel were removed from gravel pit No. 3. Use an Accumulated Depletion account.

c. The company owns a patent right that is used in operations. The Patent account on January 1, 19D, reflected a balance of $3,300. The patent has an estimated remaining life of six years (including 19D).

Required:

1. Give the journal entries for the transactions completed during 19D.
2. Give the adjusting entries on December 31, 19D.

3. Show the December 31, 19D, balance sheet classification and amount for each of the following items: land, building, gravel pit, and patent.

Suggested solution:

Requirement 1—entries during 19D:

January 1, 19D:

Land (building site)	128,100	
Building	176,900	
Cash		305,000

Allocation of purchase price based on appraisal:

Item	Appraisal value	Percent	Computation	Allocation
Land	$126,000	42	× $305,000 =	$128,100
Building	174,000	58	× 305,000 =	176,900
Totals	$300,000	100		$305,000

January 12, 19D:

Building	38,100	
Cash		38,100
Renovation costs on building prior to use.		

June 19, 19D:

Gravel pit (No. 3)	50,000	
Cash		50,000
Purchased gravel pit; estimated production, 100,000 cubic yards.		

July 10, 19D:

Repair expense	1,200	
Cash		1,200

August 1, 19D:

Gravel pit (No. 3) 10,000

    Cash 10,000

Preparation costs.

Requirement 2—adjusting entries, December 31, 19D:

a. Depreciation expense, building 6,000

    Accumulated depreciation 6,000

Computations:

  Cost ($176,900 + $38,100) $215,000

    Less: Residual value 35,000

  Cost to be depreciated $180,000

Annual depreciation: $180,000 ÷ 30 years = $6,000.

b. Depletion expense 7,200

    Accumulated depletion, gravel pit (No. 3) 7,200

Computations:

  Cost ($50,000 + $10,000) $60,000

Depletion rate:

  $60,000 ÷ 100,000 cubic yards = 0.60

Depletion expense:

  $0.60 × 12,000 cubic yards = 7,200

c. Patent expense 550

    Patent 550

Computation:

  $3,300 ÷ 6 years = $550.

Requirement 3—balance sheet, December 31, 19D:

Assets

Operational assets:

Land $128,100

Building $215,000

  Less: Accumulated depreciation 6,000   209,000

Gravel pit................................ 60,000

  Less: Accumulated depletion 7,200   52,800

    Total operational assets $389,900

Intangible assets:

Patent ($3,300 − $550) 2,750

SUMMARY

This chapter discussed accounting for operational assets. These are the noncurrent assets that a business retains for long periods of time for use in the course of normal operations rather than for sale. They include tangible assets and intangible assets. At acquisition, operational assets are measured and recorded in the accounts at cost, in conformity with the cost principle. Cost includes the cash equivalent purchase price plus all reasonable and necessary incidental expenditures made to acquire and make ready the asset for its intended use.

An operational asset is, in nature, a bundle of future services and benefits that has been paid for in advance. As an operational asset is used, this bundle of future services gradually is used up in the generation of revenue. Therefore, in accordance with the matching principle, the asset cost (less any estimated residual value) is allocated to periodic expense over the periods benefited. In this way the expense associated with the use of operational assets is matched with the revenues generated. This allocation process is known as depreciation in the case of plant, equipment, and furniture; as depletion in the case of natural resources; and as amortization in the case of intangibles.

Four methods of depreciation are used widely: straight line, productive output, sum-of-the-years' digits, and double-declining balance.

Expenditures related to operational assets are classified either as:

1. **Capital expenditures**—those expenditures that provide benefits for one or more periods beyond the current period; consequently, they are debited to appropriate asset accounts and depreciated, depleted, or amortized over their useful lives; or
2. **Revenue expenditures**—those expenditures that provide benefits during the current period only; consequently, they are debited to appropriate current expense accounts when incurred.

Ordinary repairs and maintenance costs are revenue expenditures, whereas extraordinary repairs and additions are capital expenditures.

Operational assets may be disposed of voluntarily by sale or retirement, or involuntarily through casualty, such as storm, fire, or accident. Upon disposal, such assets must be depreciated, depleted, or amortized up to the date of disposal. The disposal transaction is recorded by removing the cost of the old asset and the related accumulated depreciation, depletion, or amortization amount from the accounts. Normally, a gain or loss on disposal of an operational asset will result since the disposal price generally is different from the book value of the old asset. Special rules apply to the trade in of an old asset as all, or part, of the consideration given for another asset.

IMPORTANT TERMS DEFINED IN THE CHAPTER (with page citations)

QUESTIONS FOR DISCUSSION

Part A

1. Define operational assets. Explain how they may be considered to be a "bundle of future services."

2. What are the classifications of operational assets? Briefly explain each.

3. Relate the cost principle to accounting for operational assets.

4. Relate the matching principle to accounting for operational assets.

5. Define and illustrate the book value of an operational asset that has an estimated residual value. Relate it to market value.

6. Under the cost principle, what amounts usually should be included in the acquisition cost of an operational asset?

7. What is a "basket purchase"? What measurement problem does it pose?

8. Briefly explain the circumstances under which interest cost can be included in the acquisition cost of an operational asset.

9. Briefly distinguish among depreciation, depletion, and amortization.

10. In computing depreciation, three values must be known or estimated; identify and explain the nature of each.

11. Estimated useful life and residual value of an operational asset relate to the current owner or user rather than to all users. Explain this statement.

12. What kind of a depreciation-expense pattern is provided under the straight-line method? When would its use be particularly appropriate?

13. What kind of depreciation-expense pattern emerges under the productive-output method? When would its use be particularly appropriate?

14. What are the arguments in favor of accelerated depreciation?

15. Explain how monthly depreciation should be computed using the sum-of-the-years'-digits method for an asset having a ten-year life.

Questions
Part B

16. Distinguish between capital expenditures and revenue expenditures.

17. Distinguish between ordinary and extraordinary repairs. How is each accounted for?

18. Over what period should an addition to an existing operational asset be depreciated? Explain.

19. Define an intangible operational asset.

20. What period should be used to amortize an intangible operational asset?

21. Define goodwill. When is it appropriate to record goodwill as an intangible operational asset?

22. Distinguish between a leasehold and a leasehold improvement.

23. Over what period should a leasehold improvement be amortized? Explain.

24. Compare the accounting for a prepaid expense with a deferred charge.

25. When an operational asset is disposed of *during* the accounting period, two separate entries usually must be made. Explain this statement.

EXERCISES

Part A

E9–1. A machine was purchased by X Company on March 1, 19A, at an invoice price of $16,000. On date of delivery, March 2, 19A, X Company paid $10,000 on the machine and the balance was an open account at 10 percent interest. On March 3, 19A, $100 was paid for freight on the machine, and on March 5 installation costs relating to the machine were paid amounting to $600. On September 1, 19A, X Company paid the balance due on the machine plus the interest.

Required:

a. Give the journal entries on each of the above dates through September 19A.
b. Give the adjusting entry for straight-line depreciation at the end of 19A, assuming an estimated useful life of ten years and an estimated residual value of $3,200. Depreciate to the nearest month. The fiscal period ends December 31, 19A.
c. What would be the book value of the machine at the end of 19B?

E9–2. Woody Company purchased a building and the land on which it is located for a total cash price of $180,000. In addition, they paid transfer costs of $600. Renovation costs on the building amounted to $5,000. An independent appraiser provided market values of building, $160,000; and land, $40,000.

Required:

a. Apportion the cost of the property on the basis of the appraised values. Show computations.
b. Give the entry to record the purchase of the property, including all expenditures. Assume all expenditures were cash when purchased at the start of Year 1.
c. Give the entry to record straight-line depreciation at the end of one year assuming an estimated 20-year useful life and no estimated residual value.
d. What would be the book value of the property at the end of Year 2?

E9–3. On January 1, 19A, W Corporation purchased land at a cost of $120,000 and on January 2, 19A, paid transfer fees of $6,000. Construction of an office building for company use was started on March 1, 19A. The company borrowed approximately 80 percent of the funds to purchase the land and construct the office building at a 12 percent interest rate. The remaining cash needed was paid from company funds. Total interest costs for the period, $36,000. The company made the following cash payments at the dates indicated:

January 1, 19A, down payment on the land (20%)	$ 24,000
January 2, 19A, transfer costs on the land	6,000

March 1, 19A, fees for preliminary
surveys and work prior to
start of construction*   12,000

Progress payments to contractor:
May 31, 19A, No. 1   200,000
August 31, 19A, No. 2   300,000
November 30, 19A, No. 3 (end
of the construction period) . .   200,000

* Construction started on April 1, 19A.

Required:

Compute the cost of the tangible operational asset with separate amounts for

(Relates to Exercise 9–5)

Year	Depreciation Expense			
	Straight Line	Productive Output	Sum-of-the-Years' Digits	Double-Declining Balance
1				
2				
3				
4				
Total				

the land and building. Show computations.

E9–4. For each asset listed below, enter a code letter to the left to indicate the allocation procedure for each asset. Use the following letter codes:

A—Amortization   P—Depletion
D—Depreciation   N—None of these

_____ 1. Land   _____ 13. Mineral
_____ 2. Patent   deposit
_____ 3. Building   _____ 14. Machinery
_____ 4. Cash   _____ 15. License
_____ 5. Oil well   right
_____ 6. Trademark   _____ 16. Deferred
_____ 7. Goodwill   charge
_____ 8. Stamps   _____ 17. Inventory
_____ 9. Franchise   of goods
_____ 10. Plant site   _____ 18. Timber
        in use   tract
_____ 11. Copyright   _____ 19. Tools
_____ 12. Invest-   _____ 20. Gravel pit
        ment in
        common
        stock

E9–5. DT Corporation purchased a machine at a cost of $1,350. The estimated useful life

was four years, and the residual value, $150. Assume that the estimated productive life of the machine is 50,000 units and each year's production was Year 1, 20,000 units; Year 2, 15,000 units; Year 3, 9,000 units; and Year 4, 6,000 units.

Required:

a. Determine the amount for each cell in the following table. Show your computations and round to even dollars.

b. Assuming the machine was used directly in the production of a product manufactured and sold by the company, what factors might be considered in selecting a preferable depreciation method?

E9–6. Tabor Company purchased a machine that cost $18,000. The estimated useful life was five years, and the estimated residual value, $3,000. Assume the estimated useful life in productive units to be 50,000. Units actually produced were Year 1, 9,000; and Year 2, 11,000.

Required:

a. Determine the appropriate amounts to complete the table below. Show computations.

$\frac{15,000}{50,000}$

(Relates to Exercise 9–6)

Method of Depreciation	Depreciation expense		Book value at end of	
	Year 1	Year 2	Year 1	Year 2
Straight line	____	____	____	____
Productive output	____	____	____	____
Sum-of-the-years' digits	____	____	____	____
Double-declining balance	____	____	____	____

b. Which method would result in the lowest EPS for Year 1? for Year 2?

E9–7. Raven Company acquired a machine that cost $5,300 on July 1, 19B. The estimated useful life is four years, and the estimated residual value is $500.

Required:

Compute montly depreciation expense for July 19B and September 19C assuming *(a)* the straight-line method and *(b)* the SYD method.

E9–8. AB Company owns the office building occupied by the administrative office. The office building was reflected in the accounts on the December 31, 1981, balance sheet as follows:

Cost when acquired	$250,000
Accumulated depreciation (based on estimated life of 30 years and $40,000 residual value)	105,000

During January 1982, on the basis of a careful study, the management decided that the estimated useful life should be changed to 25 years and the residual value reduced to $35,000.

Required:

a. Give the adjusting entry for straight-line depreciation at the end of 1982. Show computations.

b. Explain the rationale for your response to *(a)*.

Exercises
Part B

E9–9. For each item listed below, enter the appropriate letter to the left to indicate the type of expenditure. Use the following:

A—Capital expenditure
B—Revenue expenditure
C—Neither

____ 1. Paid $500 for ordinary repairs.
____ 2. Paid $6,000 for extraordinary repairs.
____ 3. Addition to old building; paid cash, $10,000.
____ 4. Routine maintenance; cost, $300; on credit.
____ 5. Purchased a machine, $6,000; gave long-term note.
____ 6. Paid $2,000 for organization costs.
____ 7. Paid three-year insurance premium, $600.
____ 8. Purchased a patent, $3,400 cash.
____ 9. Paid $10,000 for monthly salaries.
____ 10. Paid cash dividends, $15,000.

E9–10. WT Company operates a small manufacturing facility as a supplement to its regular service activities. At the beginning of 1982, an operational asset account for the company showed the following balances:

Manufacturing equipment	$70,000
Accumulated depreciation through 1981	48,400

During 1982 the following expenditures were incurred for repairs and maintenance:

1. Routine maintenance and repairs on the equipment	$1,000
2. Major overhaul of the equipment	6,400

The equipment is being depreciated on a straight-line basis over an estimated life of 15 years and a $4,000 estimated residual value. The annual accounting period ends on December 31.

Required:

a. Give the adjusting entry for depreciation for the manufacturing equipment that was made at the end of 1981.

Starting with 1982, what is the remaining estimated life?

b. Give the entries to record appropriately the two expenditures for repairs and maintenance during 1982.

c. Give the adjusting entry that should be made at the end of 1982 for depreciation of the manufacturing equipment assuming no change in the estimated life or residual value. Show computations.

E9–11. At the end of the annual accounting period, December 31, 1981, the records of Ryan Company reflected the following:

Machine A:
Cost when acquired $17,000
Accumulated depreciation   10,000

During January 1982, the machine was renovated extensively including several major improvements at a cost of $7,500. As a result, the estimated life was increased from six years to eight years and the residual value was increased from $2,000 to $2,300.

Required:

a. Give the entry to record the renovation. How old was the machine at the end of 1981?

b. Give the adjusting entry at the end of 1982 to record straight-line depreciation for the year.

c. Explain the rationale for your responses to *(a)* and *(b)*.

E9–12. In February 19A, Kleen Extractive Industries paid $350,000 for a mineral deposit. During March, $130,000 was spent in preparing the deposit for exploitation. It was estimated that 800,000 cubic yards could be extracted economically. During 19A, 30,000 cubic yards were extracted. During January 19B, another $89,000 was spent for additional developmental work. After conclusion of the latest work, the remaining estimated recovery was increased to 950,000 cubic yards over the remaining life. During 19B, a total of 35,000 cubic yards was extracted.

Required:

Give the appropriate journal entry at the following dates:

a. February 19A, for acquisition of the deposit.

b. March 19A, for developmental costs.

c. Year 19A, for annual depletion assuming the company uses a contra account (show computations).

d. January 19B, for developmental costs.

e. Year 19B, for annual depletion (show computations).

E9–13. Reo Manufacturing Company had three intangible operational assets at the end of 1981 (end of the fiscal year):

1. Patent—Purchased from J. Ray on January 1, 1981, for a cash cost of $4,260. Ray had registered the patent with the U.S. Patent Office on January 1, 1976. Amortize over remaining legal life.

2. A franchise acquired from the local community to provide certain services for ten years starting on January 1, 1981. The franchise cost $26,000 cash.

3. On January 1, 1981, the company leased some property for a five-year term. Reo immediately spent $4,800 cash for long-term improvements (estimated useful life, eight years, and no residual value). At the termination of the lease, there will be no recovery of these improvements.

Required:

a. Give entry to record the acquisition of each intangible. Provide a brief explanation with the entries.

b. Give adjusting entry at December 31, 1981, for amortization of each intangible. Show computations. The company does not use contra accounts.

c. Show how these assets, and any related expenses, should be reported on the financial statements for 1981.

E9–14. MB Company acquired three intangible operational assets during 19C. The relevant facts are:

1. On January 1, 19C, the company purchased a patent from C. Cox for $2,550 cash. Cox had developed the patent and registered it with the Patent Office on January 1, 19A. Amortize over the remaining legal life.
2. On January 1, 19C, the company purchased a copyright for a total cash cost of $9,500 and the remaining legal life was 25 years. The company executives estimated that the copyright would be of no value by the end of 20 years.
3. The company purchased a small company in January 19C at a cash cost of $100,000. Included in the purchase price was $16,400 for goodwill; the balance was for plant, equipment, and fixtures. Amortize the goodwill over the maximum period permitted.

Required:

a. Give the entry to record the acquisition of each intangible.
b. Give the adjusting entry that would be required at the end of the annual accounting period, December 31, 19C, for each intangible. The company uses contra accounts. Include a brief explanation and show computations.
c. What would be the book (carrying) value of each intangible at the end of 19D?

E9–15. Vol Company conducts operations in several different localities. In order to expand into still another city, the company obtained a ten-year lease, starting January 1, 19D, on a very good downtown location. Although there was a serviceable building on the property, the company had to construct an additional structure to be used for storage purposes. The ten-year lease required a $12,000 cash advance rental payment, plus cash payments of $1,000 per month during occupancy. During January 19D, the company spent $30,000 cash constructing the additional structure. The new structure has an estimated life of 12 years with no residual value (straight-line depreciation).

Required:

a. Give the entries for Vol Company to record the payment of the $12,000 advance on January 1, 19D, and the first monthly rental.
b. Give the entry to record the construction of the new structure.
c. Give any adjusting entries required at the end of the annual accounting period for Vol Company on December 31, 19D, in respect to (1) the advance payment and (2) the new structure. Show computations.
d. What is the total amount of rental expense resulting from the lease for 19D?

E9–16. Rye Company is in the process of preparing the balance sheet at December 31, 1981. The following are to be included:

Prepaid insurance	$ 450
Long-term investment in common stock of X Corporation, at cost (market $6,200)	6,000
Patent (at cost)	3,400
Accumulated amortization of patents	800
Accounts receivable	20,000
Allowance for doubtful accounts	600
Franchise (at cost)	1,000
Accumulated amortization franchises	300
Land—site of building	10,000
Building	280,000
Accumulated depreciation, building	150,000

Required:

Show how each of the above assets would be reflected on the Rye Company balance sheet at December 31, 1981. Use the following subcaptions: Current assets, Investments and funds, Tangible operational assets, Intangible operational assets, Deferred charges, and Other assets. The company prefers to use the "accumulated" accounts as listed above. (Hint: Intangible operational assets sum to $3,300 on the balance sheet.)

E9–17. Adams Company sold a small truck that had been used in the business for three years. The records of the company reflected the following:

Delivery truck $6,000
Accumulated depreciation   5,000

Required:

   a. Give the entry for disposal of the truck assuming the sales price was $1,000.

   b. Give the same entry but assume that the sales price was $1,200.

   c. Give the same entry but assume that the sales price was $800.

   d. Summarize any conclusions that can be drawn from the three different situations above.

E9–18. The records of the Miller Company on December 31, 1980, reflected the following data in respect to a particular machine:

Machine, original cost $27,000
Accumulated depreciation 16,000*

   * Based on a six-year estimated useful life, a $3,000 residual value, and straight-line depreciation.

On April 1, 1981, the machine was sold for $10,700 cash. The accounting period ends on December 31.

Required:

   a. How old was the machine on January 1, 1981? Show computations.

   b. Give entry, or entries, incident to the sale of the machine.

   c. Give entry, or entries, incident to the sale of the machine assuming the price was $9,300.

E9–19. On August 31, 1981, a delivery truck owned by Prince Corporation was a total loss as a result of an accident. On January 1, 1981, the records reflected the following:

Truck (estimated residual
  value, 10%) $10,000
Accumulated depreciation
  (straight line, two years)   3,000

Since the truck was insured, Prince Corporation collected $6,300 cash from the insurance company on October 5, 1981.

Required:

   a. Compute the estimated useful life and the estimated residual value of the truck.

   b. Give all entries with respect to the truck from January 1 through October 5, 1981. Show computations.

E9–20. Mason Company had a particular machine (designated Machine O for case purposes) which no longer met the needs of the company. On December 31, 1980, the records reflected the following:

Machine O:
  Original cost $30,000
  Accumulated depreciation   17,000

On January 3, 1981, the company acquired a new machine (Machine N) and traded in the old machine. On this date, a reliable estimate of the market value of Machine O was $15,000.

Required:

   a. Give the entry by Mason to record the transaction on January 3, 1981, for each of the following independent cases:

    Case A—The machines were similar and no cash difference was paid or received by Mason.

    Case B—The machines were dissimilar and no cash difference was paid or received by Mason.

   b. For each case, explain the underlying reason for the amount that you recorded as the cost of Machine N.

E9–21. Use the facts and requirements given in Exercise 9–20 except that for each case assume Mason paid a $1,000 cash difference (boot). The market value of Machine N was $16,100.

E9–22. The records of Huber Company reflected the following data in respect to an operational asset:

Equipment—old (at cost) $8,000
Accumulated depreciation 5,000

Huber Company decided to purchase new equipment; the dealer demonstrated new equipment that was suitable. The new equipment had a special list price of $6,800. However, the cash price without a trade-in was $6,400. The dealer required a cash payment of $3,300 in addition to the old asset. No reasonable market value was available for the old equipment.

Required:

a. Give the entry by Huber Company to record the exchange and the cash payment assuming similar assets.
b. Give the entry to record the exchange and the cash payment assuming the two assets were dissimilar.
c. Explain the basis for the amounts recorded as the cost of the new equipment in *(a)* and *(b)*.

PROBLEMS

Part A

P9–1. Dawson Company purchased three used machines from J. Evers for a cash price of $31,400. Transportation costs on the machines amounted to $600. The machines immediately were overhauled, installed, and started operating. Since the machines were essentially different, each had to be recorded separately in the accounts. An appraiser was employed to estimate their market values at date of purchase (prior to the overhaul and installation). The book values reflected on Evers's books also are available. The book values, appraisal results, installation costs, and renovation expenditures were:

	Machine A	Machine B	Machine C
Book value—Evers	$5,000	$ 9,000	$6,000
Appraised value	6,000	15,000	9,000
Installation costs	200	300	100
Renovation costs prior to use	800	500	600

Required:

a. Compute the cost of each machine by making a realistic allocation. Explain the rationale for the allocated basis used.
b. Give the journal entry to record the purchase of the three machines assuming all payments were cash. Set up a separate asset account for each machine.

P9–2. Ace Company purchased a machine that cost $34,375. The estimated useful life is ten years, and the estimated residual value is 4 percent of cost. The machine has an estimated useful life in productive output of 110,000 units. Actual output was Year 1, 15,000; and Year 2, 12,000.

Required:

a. Determine the appropriate amounts for the table below. Show your computations.

(Relates to Problem 9–2)

Depreciation method	Depreciation expense Year 1	Year 2	Book value at end of Year 1	Year 2
Straight line	$_____	$_____	$_____	$_____
Productive output	_____	_____	_____	_____
Sum-of-the-years' digits	_____	_____	_____	_____
Double-declining balance	_____	_____	_____	_____

b. Give the adjusting entries for Years 1 and 2 under each method.

c. In selecting a depreciation method, some companies assess the comparative effect on *cash flow* and EPS. Briefly, comment on the depreciation methods in terms of cash flow and EPS effects.

P9–3. Obie Company purchased a machine that cost $9,200. The estimated useful life was three years, and the residual value, $200. The management is considering several depreciation methods and is concerned about the choice of a method.

Required:

a. You have been asked to prepare a table that will reflect the relevant income statement and balance sheet amounts over the life of the machine. Accordingly, you have designed the following table to be completed (show computations):

and boats. There are two manufacturing operations: one does custom work and the other manufactures standard items that are distributed through retail channels in several states. In January 19A, the company purchased land, including a building that was approximately 15 years old, at a cost of $357,000. Transfer costs, surveys, appraisals, titles, and legal fees amounted to another $8,000.

The property was appraised, at acquisition date, for loan purposes, with the following results: land, $72,000; building, $288,000; estimated remaining life, 20 years; and estimated residual value, $20,000.

Required:

a. Give the entry to record the purchase of the operational assets in January 19A. Show computations.

b. Give the adjusting entry for depreciation on December 31, 19A, assuming:

(Relates to Problem 9–3)

Comparison of depreciation methods

	Relevant amounts		
Depreciation methods and effects	Year 1	Year 2	Year 3
Straight line:			
Depreciation expense on income statement	___	___	___
Income tax expense on income statement	___	___	___
EPS on income statement	___	___	___
Net asset amount reported on balance sheet	___	___	___
Double-declining balance:			
Depreciation expense on income statement	___	___	___
Income tax expense on income statement	___	___	___
EPS on income statement	___	___	___
Net asset amount reported on balance sheet	___	___	___

Additional data:
Income before depreciation and before income tax (average rate, 30 percent): Year 1, $30,000; Year 2, $33,000; and Year 3, $35,000.
Common stock outstanding for all three years, 10,000 shares.

b. Analyze the effect of each method on (1) cash outflow for income tax and (2) EPS.

P9–4. Jack Manufacturing Company was organized a number of years ago. It is a local manufacturer of seat covers, floor mats, and similar items for automobiles

Case A—Straight-line depreciation.
Case B—Sum-of-the-years'-digits depreciation.
Case C—Double-declining balance depreciation.

c. Compute the book value of the building at the end of 19B (after the adjusting entries) for each case.

P9–5. Roe Company owns an existing building that was constructed at an original cost of $95,000. It is being depreciated on a straight-line basis over a 20-year estimated useful life and has a $5,000 estimated residual value. At the end of 1981, the building was one-half depreciated. In January 1982, a decision was made, on the basis of new information, that a total estimated useful life of 25 years, and a residual value of $2,000 would be more realistic. The accounting period ends December 31.

Required:

a. Compute the amount of depreciation expense recorded in 1981 and the book value of the building at the end of 1981.

b. Compute the amount of depreciation that should be recorded in 1982. Show computations. Give the adjusting entry for depreciation at December 31, 1982.

Problems
Part B

P9–6. Kellner Company found it necessary to do some extensive repairs on its existing building and to add a new wing suitable for use during the next ten years. The existing building originally cost $300,000; and by the end of 1980, it was one-half depreciated on the basis of a 20-year estimated useful life and no residual value. During 1981 the following expenditures were made that were related to the building:

1. Ordinary repairs and maintenance expenditures for the year, $9,000 cash.
2. Extensive and major repairs to the roof of the building, $20,000 cash. These repairs were completed on June 30, 1981.
3. The new wing was completed on June 30, 1981, at a cash cost of $170,000. Assume no residual value.

Required:

a. Record each of the 1981 transactions.

b. Give the adjusting entry that would be required at the end of the annual accounting period, December 31, 1981, for the building after taking into account your entries in (a) above. Assume straight-line depreciation. The company computes depreciation to the nearest one-half year.

c. Show how the assets would be reported on the December 31, 1981, balance sheet. (Hint: Depreciation expense for 1981 is $25,000.)

P9–7. Erie Company has five different intangible operational assets to be accounted for and reported on the financial statements. At issue is a decision by the management in respect to amortization of the cost of each of the intangibles. Certain facts concerning each intangible are:

1. Patent—The company purchased a patent for a cash cost of $26,000 on January 1, 1981. The patent had a legal life of 17 years from date of registration with the U.S. Patent Office, which was January 1, 1977. Amortize over the remaining legal life.
2. Copyright—On January 1, 1981, the company purchased a copyright at a cost of $15,000. The legal life remaining from that date is 30 years. It is estimated that the copyrighted item will have little or no value by the end of 25 years.
3. Franchise—The company obtained a franchise from X Company to make and distribute a special item. The franchise was obtained on January 1, 1981, at a cash cost of $10,000 and was for a ten-year period.
4. License—On January 1, 1980, the company secured a license from the city to operate a special service for a period of five years. Total cash expended in obtaining the license was $8,000.
5. Goodwill—The company started business in January 1979 by purchasing another business for a cash lump sum of $400,000. Included in the purchase

price was the item "Goodwill, $80,000." Erie executives believe that "the goodwill is an important long-term asset to us." Amortize over maximum period permitted.

Required:

a. Give the entry to record each of the five acquisitions.
b. Give the adjusting entry for each intangible asset that would be necessary at the end of the annual accounting period, December 31, 1981. Provide a brief explanation and show computations. If no entry is required for a particular item, explain the basis for your conclusion.
c. Determine the book value of each intangible on January 1, 1983. (Hint: The total book value for the five intangibles is $119,000.)

P9–8. On January 1, 19A, Tejas Corporation was organized by five individuals for the purpose of purchasing and operating a successful business known as Kampus Korner. The name was retained and all of the assets, except cash, were purchased for $300,000 cash. The liabilities were not assumed by Tejas Corporation. The transaction was closed on January 5, 19A, at which time the balance sheet of Kampus Korner reflected the book values shown below:

KAMPUS KORNER
January 5, 19A

	Book value	Market value*
Accounts receivable (net)	$ 30,000	$ 30,000
Inventory	180,000	175,000
Operational assets (net)	19,000	50,000
Other assets	1,000	5,000
Total assets	$230,000	
Liabilities	$ 80,000	
Owner's equity	150,000	
Total liabilities and owner's equity	$230,000	

* These values for the assets purchased were provided to Tejas Corporation by an independent appraiser.

As a part of the negotiations, the former owners of Kampus Korner agreed not to engage in the same or similar line of business in the same general region.

Required:

a. Give the entry by Tejas Corporation to record the purchase of the assets of Kampus Korner. Include goodwill.
b. Give the adjusting entries that would be made by Tejas Corporation at the end of the annual accounting period, December 31, 19A, for:
   (a) Depreciation of the operational assets (straight line) assuming an estimated remaining useful life of 20 years and no residual value.
   (b) Amortization of goodwill assuming the maximum amortization period is used.

P9–9. During 1981, Watson Company disposed of three different assets. On January 1, 1981, prior to their disposal, the accounts reflected the following:

(Relates to Problem 9–9)

Assets	Original cost	Residual value	Estimated life	Accumulated depreciation (straight line)
Machine A ...	$20,000	$2,000	10 years	$12,600 (7 years)
Machine B	35,400	3,000	9 years	21,600 (6 years)
Machine C	65,200	6,000	14 years	59,200 (14 years)

The machines were disposed of in the following ways:

Machine A—Sold on January 1, 1981, for $6,400 cash.

Machine B—Exchanged for a new machine of similar type on May 1, 1981. The new machine had a quoted price of $48,000. The old machine was traded in and cash of $30,000 was paid.

Machine C—On January 2, 1981, this machine suffered irreparable damage from an accident. On January 10, 1981, it was given to a salvage company at no cost. The salvage company agreed to remove the machine immediately at no cost. Since the machine was insured, $3,000 cash was collected from the insurance company.

Required:

a. List each machine and its book value on the date of disposal. Show computations. The company computes depreciation to the nearest full month.
b. Give all entries incident to the disposal of each machine. Explain the accounting rationale for the way that you recorded each disposal.

P9–10. Quick Manufacturing Company operates a number of machines. One particular bank of machines consists of five identical machines acquired on the same date. At the beginning of 1981 the operational asset account for the five machines showed the following:

Machinery (Type A, five
   machines) $200,000

Accumulated depreciation
   (Type A machines) 108,000*

   * Based on ten-year estimated useful life and $4,000 residual value per machine and straight-line depreciation.

One of the machines (Type A) was disposed of on September 1, 1981.

Required:

a. How old were the Type A machines at January 1, 1981? Show computations.
b. What was the book value of the machine at date of disposal? Show computations. The company computes depreciation to the nearest full month.
c. Give all entries incidental to disposal of the machine under two independent assumptions:
   1. It was sold outright for $14,000 cash.
   2. It was exchanged for a new machine having a "quoted" price of $47,000; however, it was determined that it could be purchased for $44,000 cash. The old machine was traded in, and $30,000 was paid in cash. Assume the machines were similar. No reasonable market value was determinable for the old machine.

P9–11. (Note: This is a comprehensive problem covering several issues discussed in the chapter.)
   On January 1, 19A, AB Company purchased four identical machines. The costs were:

Invoice price per machine (subject
   to 2% cash discount) $400

Installation costs (total wages paid
  to AB employees for
  installation time) 168
Freight on machines, per machine ... 50

Sales tax paid on invoice price, 4 percent.

Required:

a. Give the entry to record the acquisition
   of the four machines on January 1, 19A
   (round amounts to nearest dollar).
b. Give the adjusting entries to record depreciation for Years A, B, and C. Assume a five-year estimated life, no
   residual value, and the straight-line
   method.
c. On July 1, 19D, three of the machines
   (each in essentially the same condition) were disposed of as follows:

   Machine No. 1—Sold for $215 cash.
     (Hint, there was a gain on disposal
     of $65.)
   Machine No. 2—Traded in on a new
     similar machine (improved) and
     paid $250 cash difference (includ-
     ing sales taxes and other acquisi-
     tion costs).
   Machine No. 3—Since this machine
     was no longer needed, it was
     traded for an electric typewriter
     (assume dissimilar) that had a firm
     cash price of $520 and paid a $200
     cash difference. Assume there was
     no market value for the old ma-
     chine that was as reliable as the
     $520 market price of the type-
     writer.

   Give the entry to record the disposal
   of each machine.
d. During the first week of January 19E,
   a major overhaul of Machine No. 4
   was completed at a cost of $140 which
   extended its estimated useful life by
   an additional two years (over the original estimate).

   Give the entry to record the major
   overhaul of Machine No. 4 and depreciation for 19E. Show computations.

P9–12. (Note: This is a comprehensive problem
   to test your analytical ability.)

   It is the end of the annual fiscal period,
December 31, 1981, for XY Company.
The following items must be resolved before the financial statements can be prepared:

1. On January 1, 1981, a used machine
   was purchased for $3,900 cash. This
   amount was debited to an operational
   asset account, Machinery. Prior to use,
   cash was expended for *(a)* repairing the
   machine, $300, and *(b)* for installation,
   $150; both were debited to Expense.
   The machine has an estimated remaining useful life of five years and a 10
   percent residual value. Straight-line
   depreciation will be used.
2. A small warehouse (and the land site
   on which it is located) was purchased
   on January 1, 1981, at a cash cost of
   $40,000 which was debited to an oper-
   ational asset account, Warehouse. The
   property was appraised for tax purposes near the end of 1980 as follows:
   warehouse, $21,250; and land, $8,250.
   The warehouse has an estimated remaining useful life of ten years and
   a ten percent residual value. Double-
   declining balance depreciation will be
   used.
3. During the year 1981, usual recurring
   repair costs of $1,200 were paid. Dur-
   ing January 1981, major repairs (on the
   warehouse purchased in 2 above) of
   $1,000 were paid. Repair Expense was
   debited $2,200, and Cash was credited.
4. On June 30, 1981, the company purchased a patent for use in the business
   at a cash cost of $2,040. The patent
   was dated July 1, 1976. The Patent account was debited.
5. On December 31, 1981, the company
   acquired a new truck that had a firm
   cash price of $4,300 (estimated life,
   five years; residual value, $300). The
   company paid for the truck with cash,
   $3,000, and traded in an old truck

418

(similar) that had a book value on December 31, 1981, as follows:

Original cost,
    January 1, 1977 .... $3,500
Accumulated depreciation,
    December 31, 1981 ....   2,000*

    * Includes 1981 depreciation, five-year life and $1,500 residual value.

The transaction was recorded as follows:

Truck (new)	4,500	
Accumulated depreciation (old)	2,000	
Truck (old)		3,500
Cash		3,000

Required:

For each of the above items, give the following:

a. Entry or entries that should be made to correct the accounts at December 31, 1981, before the adjusting entries are made. If none is required, so state.
b. Adjusting entry at December 31, 1981, after the corrections in Requirement *(a)* have been made.

10

Measurement and reporting of liabilities

PURPOSE OF THE CHAPTER

A business generates or receives resources from three distinct sources: (a) contributions by owners, (b) extension of credit by creditors, and (c) sale of goods and services. Creditors provide resources to the business through cash loans and by providing property, goods, and services to the entity on credit. These borrowing activities of the entity create **liabilities** to various creditors. *Liabilities can be defined as obligations that result from transactions requiring the future payment of assets or the future performance of services, which are definite as to amount or are subject to reasonable estimation. Liabilities generally have a definite and known payment date known as the maturity or due date.*

From the point of view of the user of the financial statements, the liabilities reported on the balance sheet, and the expense incurred from borrowing funds (i.e., interest expense), reported on the income statement, often are important factors in evaluating the financial performance of an entity. Usually there are a number of different kinds of liabilities and a wide range of creditors; therefore, those interested in the business necessarily must rely on the financial statements for relevant information on this important facet of the financial activities of an entity. The accounting model, coupled with the audit made by an independent accountant, provides the user with a good level of confidence that all liabilities are identified, properly measured, and fully reported.

This chapter discusses the measurement and reporting problems associated with the various classifications of liabilities. Throughout this chapter the discussions emphasize (1) identification of liabilities, (2) measurement of the amount of each liability, (3) accounting for the various types of liabilities, and (4) appropriate reporting. To accomplish this purpose the chapter is divided into two parts:

Part A: Accounting for, and reporting, liabilities

Part B: Measurement of future value and present value

This chapter includes the following Appendixes:

Appendix A: Payroll accounting

Appendix B: The voucher system

Behavioral and learning objectives for this chapter are provided in the *Teachers Manual.*

PART A: ACCOUNTING FOR, AND REPORTING, LIABILITIES

Although there are various ways to classify liabilities, for accounting and reporting purposes the following classifications are used:

1. Current liabilities:
   a. Accounts payable.
   b. Short-term notes payable.
   c. Other short-term obligations.
2. Long-term liabilities:
   a. Long-term notes payable and mortgages.
   b. Bonds payable.
   c. Other long-term obligations.

Bonds payable will be discussed in Chapter 11. Each of the other classifications will be discussed and illustrated in this chapter.

MEASUREMENT OF LIABILITIES

Identification of the specific liabilities of an entity at each balance sheet date generally is not difficult for the accountant; however, aside from identification, the problem of **measurement** of the amount of each liability may be more complex. Conceptually, the amount of a liability, at any point in time, is the **present value** of the future outlays of assets required to pay the liability in full; that is, the present value of the principal plus all future interest payments. This present value amount may be called the **current cash equivalent amount.**[1]

A liability that requires the "going rate of interest" will always have a present value equal to its maturity amount. However, when the stated rate of interest is different from the going rate, or interest is unspecified, the present value will be different from the maturity amount. As such liabilities approach maturity (due date) the present value (current cash

---

[1] Some people find it useful to think of the current cash equivalent amount of a liability as the figure that the two parties involved (the debtor and the creditor) would settle the obligation for at a given date (between the beginning and due date) on a fair and equitable basis. This figure may be constant over the life of the debt, as in the case of an interest-bearing note. In the case of a bond payable, issued at a discount or premium, the carrying amount would be different each date (see Chapter 11).

equivalent amount) approaches the maturity amount. These concepts are discussed and illustrated in Part B.

Fundamentally, liabilities are measured in accordance with the *cost principle*. That is, the amount of a liability, when initially incurred, is equivalent to the current value of the resources received when the transaction occurred. Although the amount of most liabilities is definitely specified in the initial transaction (such as in a note payable), there are situations in which a liability is known to exist but the exact amount is not determinable until a later date. For example, television sets may be sold with a one-year guarantee against defects. For the vendor, the guarantee creates a liability, the actual amount of which depends on the performance of the sets during the year. Thus, liabilities can be said to be comprised of known obligations of a definite amount and known obligations of an estimated amount.

CURRENT LIABILITIES

Current liabilities are short-term obligations that will be paid within the **current operating cycle** of the business or within one year of the balance sheet date, whichever is the longer. Thus, the definition presumes that current liabilities will be paid with existing current assets.[2]

An important financial relationship on the balance sheet is known as working capital. **Working capital is the dollar difference between total current assets and total current liabilities.** The relationship between current assets and current liabilities also is measured as the **working capital ratio** (sometimes called the **current ratio**). The current ratio is computed by dividing total current assets by total current liabilities. To illustrate, assume the balance sheet for XY Company on December 31, 19B, reported total current assets of $900,000 and total current liabilities of $300,000. The amount of working capital would be $900,000 − $300,000 = $600,000. The current ratio would be $900,000 ÷ $300,000 = 3.00, or 3 to 1. That is, at balance sheet date, for each $1 of current liabilities there were $3 of current assets. These relationships often assist creditors and others in assessing the ability of a company to meet its short-term maturing obligations.[3]

Current liabilities commonly encountered are trade accounts payable, short-term notes payable, accrued liabilities (such as wages payable, taxes payable, and interest payable), cash dividends payable, and revenues collected in advance (i.e., deferred or unearned revenues).

---

[2] Current assets and current liabilities were defined and discussed in Chapter 2. Current assets are defined as cash and other resources reasonably expected to be realized in cash or sold or consumed within one year from the date of the balance sheet or during the *normal operating cycle,* whichever is the longer.

The AICPA Committee on Accounting Procedure defined current liabilities as follows: The term "current liabilities" is used principally to designate obligations whose liquidation is reasonably expected to require the use of existing resources properly classifiable as current assets, or the creation of other current liabilities.

[3] Interpretation of financial ratios is discussed in Chapter 16.

Accounts payable

Trade accounts payable were discussed in Chapter 6 because they are created by the purchases of goods and services. The term "accounts payable" is used in accounting to mean *trade* accounts payable. Typical entries are:

March 6, 19B:

Purchases (or Inventory)	980	
Accounts payable		980
Purchase of merchandise on credit; terms, 2/10, n/30. (Invoice price, $1,000 \times 0.98 = \$980$.)		

March 11, 19B:[4]

Accounts payable	980	
Cash		980
Payment of account payable within the discount period.		

Accrued liabilities

Accrued liabilities arise at the end of an accounting period when there are expenses that have been incurred but have not yet been paid or recorded. They appeared in Chapter 4 in the discussion of **adjusting entries.** To illustrate a typical accrued liability, assume it is December 31, 19B, and the annual amount of property taxes for 19B was determined to be $1,600, which had not been paid or recorded. At the end of the accounting period, December 31, 19B, the expense and related current liability must be recorded and reported, although the amount will not be paid until January 15, 19C.[5] Therefore, the following adjusting entry must be made:

December 31, 19B:

Property tax expense	1,600	
Property taxes payable		1,600
Adjusting entry to record property taxes incurred in 19B yet not recorded or paid.		

---

[4] In case of payment after the discount period, the entry would be:

Accounts payable	980	
Purchase discounts lost (or Interest expense)	20	
Cash		1,000

[5] If these taxes already had *been paid* (i.e., Expense debited and Cash credited), there would be no accrued liability to record at year-end. Similarly, if these taxes *already had been recorded but not paid* (i.e., Expense debited and Taxes Payable credited), there would be no accrued liability to record at year-end.

The entry in 19C for payment of the above accrued liability would be:

January 15, 19C:

Property taxes payable 1,600
   Cash 1,600
Payment of liability for property taxes accrued in 19B.

Payroll liabilities

When employees perform services, the employer incurs an obligation that normally is paid on a weekly or monthly payroll basis. In the preceding discussions and illustrations, accounting for wage and salary expense was simplified by disregarding payroll taxes and payroll deductions.

In addition to the obligation to the employee, payrolls create other liabilities that are related directly to the payment of salaries and wages. These additional liabilities generally arise as a result of federal and state laws (social security taxes), and contractual obligations (such as pension plans and union dues). Some of these liabilities are paid by the employee through the employer (as payroll deductions); others must be paid by the employer and are additional expenses to the business.

The take-home pay of most employees is considerably less than the gross salary or wages because of **payroll deductions** for such items as employee income taxes withheld, social security taxes that must be paid by the employee, and other employee deductions such as insurance and union dues. The employer is required to pay the amounts, deducted from the wages, to the designated governmental agencies and other organizations such as the union. From the date of the payroll deduction until the date of payment to the agencies or organizations, the employer must record and report the **current liabilities** that are owed to the designated units. Thus, a typical journal entry for a $100,000 payroll would be as follows:

January 31, 19B:

Salaries expense 60,000
Wages expense 40,000
   Liability for income taxes withheld—employees 21,000
   Liability for union dues withheld—employees 400
   FICA taxes payable—employees 6,000
   Cash (take-home pay) 72,600*
To record the payroll including employee deductions (see Appendix A).

  * Observe that take home pay approximates 73%.

In addition to the payroll taxes that the *employees* must pay through the employer, the *employer* is required by law to pay *additional* specified payroll taxes. These constitute an operating expense for the business.

Therefore, a second entry related to the payroll is needed to record the taxes to be paid by the employer. A typical entry, related to the above payroll, would be as follows:

January 31, 19B:

Payroll tax expense	9,400*	
FICA taxes payable—employer (matching)		6,000
FUTA taxes payable—employer		700
State unemployment taxes payable—employer		2,700
Employer payroll taxes for January payroll.		
* Total payroll expense: $100,000 + $9,400 = $109,400.		

The six current liabilities created in the two entries immediately above will be paid in the near future when the company remits the requisite amounts of cash to the appropriate agencies. Details involved in payroll accounting are discussed and illustrated in Appendix A to this chapter. Payroll accounting does not entail any new concepts or accounting principles; however, there is a significant amount of clerical detail involved.

Deferred revenues

Deferred revenues (frequently called unearned or precollected revenues) arise from revenues that have been collected in advance during the current period but will not be earned until a later accounting period (see Chapter 4). A more descriptive title preferred by many accountants is Revenue Collected in Advance.

Deferred revenues constitute a liability since the cash has been collected but the revenue has not been earned by the end of the accounting period; therefore, there is a *present obligation* to render, in the future, the services or to provide the goods. To illustrate, assume that during November 19B rent revenue collected amounted to $6,000, which was debited to Cash and credited to Rent Revenue. Assume further that at the end of 19B it was determined that $2,000 of this amount was for January 19C rent. Thus, there is a current liability for deferred rent revenue that must be recognized. The sequence of entries for this situation would be as follows:

November 19B:

Cash..	6,000	
Rent revenue		6,000
Collection of rent revenue.[6]		

---

[6] The credit could be made to Rent Revenue Collected in Advance, in which case the adjusting entry to give the same results on December 31, 19B, would be:

Rent revenue collected in advance	4,000	
Rent revenue		4,000

December 31, 19B (adjusting entry):

Rent revenue	2,000	
Rent revenue collected in advance (deferred revenue)		2,000
Adjusting entry to record unearned rent revenue at the end of the accounting period.		

LONG-TERM LIABILITIES

Long-term liabilities encompass all obligations of the entity not properly classified as current liabilities. Long-term liabilities often are incurred in conjunction with the purchase of operational assets or the borrowing of large amounts of cash for asset replacements and major expansions of the business. Long-term liabilities usually are long-term notes payable or bonds payable. Frequently, a long-term liability is supported by a mortgage on specified assets of the borrower *pledged* as security for the liability. A mortgage involves a separate document that is appended to the note payable. A liability supported by a mortgage is said to be a "secured debt." An unsecured debt is one for which the creditor relies primarily on the integrity and general earning power of the borrower.

Long-term liabilities are reported on the balance sheet under a separate caption below "Current liabilities." As a long-term debt approaches the maturity date, the portion of it that is to be paid in the next current period is reclassified as a current liability. To illustrate, assume a five-year note payable of $50,000 was signed on January 1, 1979. Repayment is to be in two installments as follows: December 31, 1982, $25,000; and December 31, 1983, $25,000. The December 31, 1980, 1981, and 1982 balance sheets would report the following:

December 31, 1980:
Long-term liabilities:
Note payable $50,000

December 31, 1981:
Current liabilities:
Maturing portion of long-term note 25,000
Long-term liabilities:
Long-term note 25,000

December 31, 1982:
Current liabilities:
Maturing portion of long-term note 25,000

Alternatively, the entry could have been made on payment date in such a way as to avoid the need for an adjusting entry, viz:

Cash	6,000	
Rent revenue		4,000
Rent revenue collected in advance.................		2,000

Notes payable may be either short term or long term. A short-term note payable usually has a maturity date within one year from the balance sheet date and generally arises as a result of borrowing cash or from purchasing merchandise or services on credit. Bonds payable (see Chapter 11) are always long-term liabilities, except for any currently maturing portion as illustrated above for the long-term note payable.

NOTES PAYABLE

A note payable (short term or long term) is a written promise to pay a stated sum at one or more specified dates in the future. A note payable may require a single-sum repayment at the due or maturity date or it may call for installment payments. To illustrate, assume the purchase of a sailboat for $3,000, with a $1,000 cash down payment and a note payable for the balance which specifies 12 monthly payments which include principal and interest.

Notes payable require the payment of interest and, hence, the recording of interest expense. Interest expense is incurred on liabilities because of the **time value of money.** The word "time" is significant because the longer borrowed money is held, the larger the total dollar amount of interest expense. Thus, one must pay more interest for a two-year loan of a given amount, at a given **interest rate,** than for a one-year loan. To the borrower, interest is an expense; whereas to the lender (creditor), interest is a revenue. In calculating interest we must consider three variables: (1) the principal, (2) the interest rate, and (3) the duration of time. Therefore the formula is:

$$\text{Interest} = \text{Principal} \times \text{Rate} \times \text{Time}$$

To illustrate, assume $10,000 cash was borrowed by Baker Company on November 1, 19A, and a six-month, 12 percent, interest-bearing note payable was given. The interest is payable at the due date of the note. The computation of interest expense would be: $10,000 \times 0.12 \times 6/12 = 600. This note would be recorded in the accounts as follows:

November 1, 19A:

Cash...	10,000	
Note payable, short term		10,000
Borrowed on short-term note; terms, six months at 12 percent per annum; interest is payable at maturity.		

Since interest is an expense of the period when the money is used (unpaid), it is measured, recorded, and reported on a *time basis* rather than when the cash actually is paid or borrowed. This is based on legal as well as on economic considerations. For example, were the $10,000 loan cited above to be paid off in two months instead of in six months, interest amounting to $10,000 \times 0.12 \times 2/12 = \$200$ would have to be paid.

The *adjusting entry* for accrued interest payable would be made at the end of the accounting period on the basis of time expired from the last interest date or from the date of the note. To illustrate, assume the accounting period ends December 31, 19A. Although the $600 interest for the six months will not be paid until April 30, 19B, two months' unpaid interest (i.e., November and December) must be accrued by means of the following adjusting entry by Baker Company:

December 31, 19B:

Interest expense	200	
Interest payable		200
Adjusting entry to accrue two months' interest ($10,000 \times 0.12 \times$ 2/12 = \$200).		

At maturity date the payment of principal plus interest for six months would be recorded as follows:[7]

April 30, 19C:

Notes payable, short term	10,000	
Interest payable (per prior entry)	200	
Interest expense ($10,000 \times 0.12 \times 4/12$)	400	
Cash ($10,000 + \$600$ interest)		10,600
To record payment of note payable including interest.		

The accounting for a note payable is the same whether it is classified as a current or as a long-term liability. Accounting for a note payable also is the same regardless of the purpose for which the note was executed.

Interest on notes. A note may be designated as either "interest bearing" or as "noninterest bearing." Nevertheless, all commercial notes involve interest, either explicitly or implicitly, because money loaned, or borrowed, has a time value that cannot be avoided.

An **interest-bearing note** is one that explicitly specifies (1) a stated rate of interest (such as 12 percent) on the note itself, and (2) that the interest is to be paid at maturity, or in future installments, *in addition to*

---

[7] This assumes no reversing entry was made on January 1, 19C. (See Chapter 5, Appendix.) If a reversing entry of the accrual was made on January 1, 19C, the payment entry would have been:

Notes payable, short term	10,000	
Interest expense	600	
Cash		10,600

the face or principal amount of the note. For example, a $30,000, 12 percent, one-year, interest-bearing note would (1) provide the borrower with $30,000 cash, (2) have a face or principal amount of $30,000, and (3) require the payment of the principal ($30,000) plus interest for one year ($3,600)—a total of $33,600.

In contrast, a **noninterest-bearing note** is one that has implicit interest; that is, it is a note that (1) does not specify a rate of interest on the note itself but (2) includes the interest in the face amount of the note. For example, a $33,600, one-year, noninterest-bearing note (assuming a stated rate of interest of 12 percent) (1) would provide the borrower $30,000 cash (i.e., $33,600 − $3,600 implicit interest) and (2) would require the payment of only the face amount of the note at maturity date ($33,600). Observe that the implicit interest is included in the face amount of the note. The entries for the two different types of notes payable cited above are:

Transactions	Interest bearing		Noninterest bearing	
November 1, 19A, date of note:				
Cash	30,000		30,000	
Discount on note payable			3,600	
Note payable, short term		30,000		33,600
(12% interest; term, one year.)				
December 31, 19A, end of accounting period:				
Interest expense (two months)	600		600	
Interest payable		600		
Discount on note payable				600
Adjusting entry for 2 months' accrued interest; $30,000 × 0.12 × 2/12 = $600.				
October 31, 19B, maturity date of note:*				
Note payable	30,000		33,600	
Interest expense (ten months)	3,000		3,000	
Interest payable	600			
Discount on note payable				3,000
Cash		33,600		33,600
Payment of note at maturity.				

* It would have simplified this entry if a *reversing entry* of the accrual of December 31, 19A, had been made on January 1, 19B.

The above illustration suggests two important concepts in the measurement of liabilities and interest expense. The concept of *present value* is important in the measurement of liabilities. The present value of a note is the value today of its future cash flows. In the case of the interest-bearing note, the present value and the face amount of principal are the same at all dates, that is, $30,000 (at 12 percent). Also, in the case of the noninterest-bearing note, the present value on the date of the note (November 1, 19A) is $30,000, the amount of cash received; however, the face amount is $33,600.

DEFERRED INCOME TAX

Throughout the preceding chapters, income taxes paid by corporations were discussed and illustrated. In those illustrations, income tax expense was reflected on the income statement and income tax payable was reflected as a liability on the balance sheet. In addition to income tax payable, most corporate balance sheets report another tax item called **deferred income tax.**

The concept of deferred income tax is that income tax **expense** should be based on the *taxable* income reported on the income statement, while income tax **payable** necessarily must be based on the taxable income per the **tax return** (i.e., as specified in the tax laws). Often there is a difference between the time when certain revenues or expenses (which affect income taxes) appear on the income statement and when they appear on the tax return. Thus, when a taxable revenue or expense appears on the income statement before or after it appears on the tax return, a deferred income tax amount will result. When it later appears in the other place, the deferred income tax amount automatically will be offset (i.e., it will "reverse" or "turn around").

To illustrate, XY Company reported income tax as follows at the ends of 19A, 19B, and 19C:[8]

	19A	19B	19C
Income statement:			
Income before depreciation expense and before income tax expense	$34,000	$34,000	$34,000
Depreciation expense	4,000	4,000	4,000
Pretax income	30,000	30,000	30,000
Income tax expense (30%)	9,000	9,000	9,000
Net income	$21,000	$21,000	$21,000
Balance sheet:			
Liabilities:			
Income tax payable	$ 8,400	$ 9,000	$ 9,600
Deferred income tax	600	600*	

* Cumulative balance.

Observe that income tax expense (on the income statement) does not agree with income tax payable on the balance sheet in years 19A and 19C. However, the totals for the three years agree ($27,000). Also observe that in 19A and 19B a second tax liability, "Deferred income tax," of $600 was reported; this additional liability disappears in 19C.

The difference between "Income tax expense" on the income statement and "Income tax payable" on the balance sheet in the example above was due to a single expense—depreciation. XY Corporation purchased an asset at the beginning of 19A that cost $12,000 and had a useful life

---

[8] For illustrative purposes and to focus on income taxes only, the illustration has two simplifying assumptions: (1) pretax income is held constant for the three years and (2) income tax payable at the end of each period is paid in the next period.

of three years with no residual value. The company used straight-line depreciation in the accounts (and hence on the income statement) and sum-of-the-years'-digits depreciation on its tax return. This caused a difference between income tax expense and income tax payable as follows:

Year	Straight-line depreciation	SYD depreciation
A	$12,000 × 1/3 = $4,000	$12,000 × 3/6 = $6,000
B	12,000 × 1/3 = 4,000	12,000 × 2/6 = 4,000
C	12,000 × 1/3 = 4,000	12,000 × 1/6 = 2,000

	19A	19B	19C
Computation of tax expense as reported on the income statement:			
Income before depreciation expense and before income tax expense	$34,000	$34,000	$34,000
Less: Depreciation expense (straight line)	4,000	4,000	4,000
Amount subject to tax	30,000	30,000	30,000
Income tax *expense* (30%)	$ 9,000	$ 9,000	$ 9,000
Computation of income tax payable as reported on the tax return:			
Income before depreciation expense and before income taxes	$34,000	$34,000	$34,000
Less: Depreciation expense (SYD)	6,000	4,000	2,000
Amount subject to tax	28,000	30,000	32,000
Income tax *payable* (30%)	$ 8,400	$ 9,000	$ 9,600

Compare these amounts

Since income tax *expense* (on the income statement) in years 19A and 19C is different from income tax *payable* (on the tax return) for years 19A and 19C, *deferred income tax* must be recorded as follows:

	19A	19B	19C
Income tax expense (from income statement)	9,000	9,000	9,000
Income tax payable (from tax return)	8,400	9,000	9,600
Deferred income tax (the difference)	600		600

The liability account, Deferred Income Tax, would appear as follows for the three-year period:

Deferred Income Tax

Dec. 31, 19C	600	Dec. 31, 19A and B	600

Observe that the $600 liability, Deferred Income Tax, recorded in 19A, remained in that account through 19B but reversed or turned around in 19C. This effect occurred because the advantage of the increased depreciation deduction in early years using SYD for tax purposes was offset in 19C. Recall that regardless of the method of depreciation used, only the cost of the asset (less any residual value) can be depreciated for both accounting and tax return purposes ($12,000 in the example above). Also, this illustration demonstrates what has been noted before—the economic advantage of SYD (or DDB) over straight line is only the time value of money. That is, the tax savings resulting from use of SYD in early years can be invested to earn a certain return during 19B and 19C.

From the above illustration, it can be seen that deferred income tax is recorded only when there are one or more items of expense or revenue that appear on the income statement in one period and on the income tax return of another period. Also, observe that Deferred Income Tax may have a debit balance (an infrequent occurrence), in which case it would be reported under Assets as a prepaid expense or deferred charge. This situation would have occurred in the above example had XY Corporation used SYD on the income statement and straight-line depreciation on the tax return (permissible by the tax regulations but not a likely choice by the taxpayer).

APB Opinion No. 11, "Accounting for Income Taxes" (December 1967), specifies that deferred income tax shall be recorded *only* when there is a **timing difference** between the income statement and the tax return. A timing difference occurs only when an item of revenue or expense will be included on *both* the income statement and the tax return in different years so that the deferred tax effect automatically will reverse (as illustrated above). Another type of difference between the income statement and tax return amounts is called a **permanent difference.** A permanent difference does not create deferred income tax because it appears on either the income statement or the tax return but not both. For example, interest revenue on tax-free municipal bonds is included on the income statement of the recipient, but is not reported on the recipient's federal income tax return.

On the balance sheet, the total amount of deferred income tax must be reported in part as a current liability (or asset) and in part as a longterm liability (or asset) depending upon the length of time before it automatically will reverse or turn around.[9]

---

[9] It is unfortunate that the accounting profession adopted the term *deferred income taxes* because it is not descriptive since the item may be reported as either a liability or an asset. More descriptive (but less succinct) titles are:

Liabilities:
Estimated future income taxes payable due to tax timing differences.

Assets:
Estimated future income tax savings due to tax timing differences.

This discussion of deferred income taxes was presented so that you will understand the nature of deferred income tax reported on the balance sheets of most medium and large corporations. Income tax payable (as a liability) is easy to comprehend; however, many statement users have difficulty understanding the other tax item—deferred income tax.

LEASE LIABILITIES

Leases are classified for accounting purposes as operating type leases and financing type leases.

1. **Operating type lease**—a short-term lease in which the owner (called the lessor), for a stated rental, grants the user (called the lessee) the right to use property under specified conditions. The lessor is responsible for the cost of ownership (such as taxes, insurance, and major maintenance), and the lessee pays a monthly rental (and usually the utilities). The lease of an automobile on a daily basis and office space on a monthly basis are typical of operating leases. When the monthly rent is paid, the lessor records rent **revenue** and the lessee records rent **expense.**
2. **Financing type lease**—a long-term, noncancelable lease contract in which the lessor transfers most of the **risks and rewards of ownership** to the lessee during the lease term. Thus, the lessee assumes most of the costs of ownership (such as taxes, insurance, and maintenance) and, in addition, pays a periodic rental. For accounting purposes this type of lease is viewed as a **sale** of the leased property by the lessor and a **purchase** of it by the lessee. Therefore, when a financing type lease is signed, the lessor records a sale of the property (on the installment basis) and the lessor records a purchase of it (on long-term financing).

To illustrate the primary decision-making issues that result in operating and financing types of leases, we will use the case of Daly Construction Company. Assume it is January 1, 19A, and that Daly Construction Company urgently needs a heavy machine which costs $100,000 new. It has an estimated useful life of five years and no residual value. The management of the company is considering three alternative ways of acquiring the machine:

Alternative *(a)*—Purchase the machine outright—Since the company is short of cash, this would entail borrowing practically all of the purchase price at 15 percent interest on a two-year, monthly repayment schedule. If this alternative is selected, purchase of the machine would be recorded in the accounts as follows:

```
Machinery ..........................................  100,000
    Note payable, long term ..........................        100,000
```

The monthly payments on the note would be $4,850 (computed as shown in Part B of this chapter), of which only the interest portion would be deducted for income tax purposes. Also, each period, payments for maintenance, operating, insurance, taxes, and so on, would be made and reported as operating expenses on the income statement and income tax return. Annual depreciation would be deductible on the income statement for income tax purposes.

Alternative *(b)*—Lease the machine on (1) a month-to-month or (2) a year-to-year operating lease basis—It has been determined that the rental payments would be as follows:

> Monthly basis .... $ 5,000 (per month)
> Yearly basis .... 50,000 (per year)

If alternative 1 is selected the monthly entry would be:

Machinery rental expense	5,000	
Cash		5,000

Each period, payments for maintenance and operating expenses (but not for insurance, taxes, and interest; these would be paid by the lessor) would be paid in addition to the rental payment. These payments, and the rental payments in full, would be included on the income tax return.

Alternative *(c)*—Lease the machine on a long-term (five-year), noncancelable lease contract—This contract would provide that Daly be fully responsible for paying all expenses for maintenance, operating, insurance, taxes, and so on, for the full five years and, in addition, would pay 60 monthly rentals of $2,540 each (see footnote 10). At the end of the five years, the machine could be kept by Daly.

In this situation, after preparing comparative cost and cash-flow analyses, the management of Daly Construction Company tentatively selected the third alternative. Let's look at some of the considerations given by the management that influenced the decision. Note that this does not mean that their reasoning was sound in every respect nor that they considered all of the important issues.

Alternative *(a)* was considered undesirable by the management because (1) of the immediate cash demand if borrowing is not feasible; (2) the 15 percent interest rate was unfavorable when compared with the average rate currently being paid by the company; (3) the anticipated difficulty in obtaining a $100,000 loan even at 15 percent; and (4) the undesirability of increasing the long-term liabilities on the balance sheet by $100,000, which could affect their current credit standing with the banks and probably would increase the interest rate on other loans.

Alternative *(b)* was given very little consideration because of the extremely high rental payments required. Although the machine could be returned at any time with no further obligation under this alternative, the high rental payments would cause a significant decrease in income. In the view of the management, the income statement effect and, even more significantly, the high monthly cash outflow would be "more than the company could stand," even though there would be no liability reflected on the balance sheet.

Alternative *(c)* was tentatively selected by the management; the reasons given were (1) no cash down payment would be required to obtain the machine; (2) the rental payment would be deductible in full on the income tax return each period; (3) the amount of the annual rental payment "appears to be reasonable"; and (4) continuing availability of the machine.

The third alternative is typical of many current leasing contracts that involve high-cost machinery and equipment. It is a situation that has caused some difficult accounting and reporting problems. Certain *APB Opinions* and *FASB Statements* specify that the essence of the long-term, noncancelable lease, for the life of the equipment, is in fact a **purchase/sale transaction.** The rationale is that the leasing company is providing **financing** for Daly; therefore, it is a **financing type of lease** rather than an *operating type of lease* [as in alternative *(b)*]. When classified as a financing type of lease, Daly would have to make the following entries:

January 1, 19A—date of inception of the lease:

Asset—machinery	100,000	
Discount on financing lease obligations	52,400*	
Liability—obligations on financing lease ($2,540 × 60		
payments)		152,400*

* The liability is reported on the balance sheet as the net of these two balances.

At date of first rental payment:

Liability—obligations on financing lease	2,540	
Cash		2,540

At year end (adjusting-entries):

Interest expense ($100,000 × 0.12)	12,000	
Discount on financing lease obligations		12,000
Depreciation expense ($100,000 ÷ 5 years)	20,000	
Accumulated depreciation		20,000

We emphasize that correct accounting, as illustrated above, reports both the **asset** and the **long-term liability** on the balance sheet.[10] This result essentially follows the accounting effect of alternative *(a)* in that it reports the financing on the balance sheet.

There was widespread opposition by companies, such as Daly, to accounting for this kind of transaction as a *financing lease* (as opposed to an operating lease) because of the effect on their financial statements. Consistent with the above entries, the lessor company would have to record the long-term lease, outlined in alternative *(c)*, as a **sale** at the date of the lease transaction. There are many related complexities; however, the above illustration should be sufficient to comprehend the basic measurement and reporting issues of long-term noncancelable leases.

CONTINGENT LIABILITIES

A contingent liability is not a legal or effective liability; rather it is a **potential future liability.** The **amount** of a contingent liability may be known or estimated. A contingent liability is defined as a potential liability that has arisen as a result of an event or transaction that *already has occurred* but its conversion to an effective liability is dependent upon the occurrence of one or more *future* events or transactions (i.e., a future contingency). To illustrate, assume that in 19B Baker Company was sued for $100,000 damages arising from an accident involving one of the trucks owned by the company. The suit is scheduled for trial during March 19C. Whether there is a legal liability will depend upon the decision of the court at the termination of the trial. When financial statements are prepared at December 31, 19B, a contingent liability must be disclosed. Because of the accident, the company is contingently liable for the payment of damages.

A contingent liability is *not* recorded in the accounts unless there is a **high probability** of loss. Rather, it is reported in a note to the financial statements. For example, the contingent future liability arising from the lawsuit may be disclosed by a note to the 19B balance sheet similar to the following:

> The company is contingently liable for $100,000 because of a lawsuit based on an accident involving a company vehicle. Legal counsel believes that the suit is lacking in merit. Trial is scheduled for March 19C.

CONTROLLING EXPENDITURES

The purchase of merchandise, services, and operational assets often requires the recording of either a short-term or long-term liability. As a

---

[10] Lease accounting requires the use of present value concepts (see Part B of this chapter). For example, assuming the lessor expected an 18 percent return, the annual rental was computed as $100,000 \div 39.38027 = \$2,540$. The present value of an annuity of 1 for 60 periods at 15 percent $= 39.38027$.

consequence, in addition to the cash transactions a large number of **cash payments,** such as on liabilities, are made in a business. In most companies, control over cash expenditures is essential to prevent the misapplication of cash in the cash-disbursement process. In a very small business it is often possible for the owner to give attention personally to each transaction when it is incurred and to make each cash payment. This personal attention may assure that the business is getting what it pays for, that cash is not being disbursed carelessly, and that there is no theft or fraud involving cash.

As a business grows and becomes more complex, the owner or top executive cannot devote personal attention to each transaction involving the processing of cash disbursements. In such situations these activities must be assigned to various employees. The assignment of these responsibilities to others creates a need for systematic and effective procedures for the control of cash expenditures. This is an important facet of the internal control of a well-designed accounting system.

In Chapter 8 the essential features of effective **internal control** were discussed. That chapter emphasized the control of cash receipts. Similar procedures were discussed in respect to cash disbursements: the separation of duties, disbursement of cash by check, petty cash, and the two special journals—the purchases journal and the cash disbursements journal. In larger companies and in computerized accounting systems, the method usually used for maintaining control over cash expenditures is known as the **voucher system.** This system replaces the cash disbursements journal procedures that were explained in Chapter 8, Appendix B.

The voucher system

The voucher system is designed to establish strict control over the incurrence of every legal obligation to make an expenditure of cash. The system requires that a **written authorization,** called a **voucher,** be approved by one or more designated managers at the time each such transaction occurs. An approved voucher is required regardless of whether the transaction involves the purchase of merchandise or services, the acquisition of operational assets, the payment of a liability, or an investment. The system permits checks to be issued only in payment of properly prepared and approved vouchers. Check writing is kept completely separate from the voucher-approval, check-approval, and check-distribution procedures.

The voucher system requires that every obligation be supported by a voucher and that each transaction be recorded when incurred. The incurrence of each obligation is treated as an independent transaction, and each payment of cash is treated as another independent transaction. This sequence of voucher approval, followed by payment by check, is required even in strictly cash-disbursement transactions. To illustrate, the *cash* purchase of merchandise for resale would be recorded under the voucher system as follows:

1. To record the incurrence of an obligation:

| Purchases (or Inventory) .... | 1,000 | |
| Vouchers payable .... | | 1,000 |

2. To record payment of the obligation by check (immediately thereafter):

| Vouchers payable .... | 1,000 | |
| Cash .... | | 1,000 |

In the voucher system, the account designated **Vouchers Payable** replaces the account entitled Accounts Payable; but "Accounts payable," as the designation on the balance sheet, continues to be used. Entries of the first type are entered in a **voucher register,** and entries of the second type are entered in a **check register.**

The primary objective of the voucher system is to attain continuous control over each step in an expenditure from the incurrence of an obligation to the final disbursement of cash to satisfy the obligation. Thus, every single transaction leading to a cash payment, and the cash payment itself, is reviewed systematically, then subjected to an approval system based on separately designated responsibilities. Appendix B to this chapter discusses and illustrates the *mechanics* of the voucher system.

PART B: MEASUREMENT OF FUTURE VALUE AND PRESENT VALUE

The measurement ar
corded in the accounts
involve application of
These concepts also are
ments in bonds, leases,
applications in accounti
the measurement of a li

1. **Establishment of a f**
amount of cash to b
as to pay off a large
the requirements of a
on the balance sheet
51. They also are disc
2. **Measurement of a lia**
receivables usually inv
The measurement of
of future and present

The concepts of future and present value focus on the **time value of money,** which is another name for **interest.** The time value of money refers to the fact that a dollar received today is worth more than a dollar to be received one year from today (or at any other later date). A dollar received today can be invested, say at 10 percent, so that it grows to $1.10 in one year. In contrast, a dollar to be received one year from today denies one the opportunity to earn the $0.10 interest revenue for the year. The difference is due to interest, which is the cost of the use of money for a specific period of time, just as rent represents the cost for use of a tangible asset for a period of time. Interest may be specified (i.e., it is stated explicitly), as in the case of an interest-bearing note, or it may be unspecified, as in a noninterest-bearing note (but it is paid nonetheless; i.e., it is present implicitly).

For many years the time value of money often was overlooked in accounting for some transactions. In recent years, several *Opinions* issued by the APB have required the application of present value determinations. Of particular significance was *Opinion No. 21,* issued in August 1971, entitled "Interest on Receivables and Payables." This *Opinion* **requires** the application of present value determinations to a number of transactions. For example, the *Opinion* states: "In the absence of established exchange prices for the related property, goods, or service or evidence of the market value of the note, the present value of a note that stipulates either no interest or a rate of interest that is clearly unreasonable should be determined by *discounting* all future payments on the notes using an imputed rate of interest. . . ." To illustrate, assume a machine is purchased for $20,000 and the purchaser is given two years in which to make payment. What amount should be debited to the Machine account in order to conform to the cost principle assuming an imputed interest rate of 12 percent is used? Answer: The present value of the debt, which is the **current cash equivalent cost,** $15,944 (see page 445).

IC CONCEPTS

Time value of money relates to four different concepts that involve interest calculation:

	Symbol
1. Future value of $1	*f*
2. Present value of $1	*p*
3. Future value of an annuity of $1	*F*
4. Present value of an annuity of $1	*P*

using $1 as the base, provide values for each of these situations periods of time *(n)* and at different rates of interest *(i)*. Extracts ables are shown on pages 440 and 441. Let's examine each

Future value of
$1 *(f)*

This concept generally is referred to as **compound interest.** The future value is the amount to which $1 will increase at *i* interest rate for *n* periods. The future amount will be the **principal plus compound interest.**

To illustrate, assume that on January 1, 19A, you deposited $1,000 in a savings account at 10 percent annual interest, compounded annually. How much would you have at the end of three years, that is, on December 31, 19C? We can calculate the compound amount to be $1,331 as follows:

	Amount at start of year +	Interest during the year =	Amount at end of year
Year 1	$1,000	+ $1,000 × 0.10 = $100 =	$1,100
Year 2	1,100	+ 1,100 × 0.10 = 110 =	1,210
Year 3	1,210	+ 1,210 × 0.10 = 121 =	1,331

However, we can avoid the detailed arithmetic by referring to Table 10–1, *"Future value of $1,"* as shown on page 440. For *i* = 10 percent, *n* = 3, we find the value 1.331; therefore, we can compute the balance at the end of Year 3 as $1,000 × 1.331 = $1,331. The increase of $331 was due to the time value of money; it would be interest revenue to you and interest expense to the savings institution. Assuming a positive interest rate, the future value of 1 always will be greater than 1. Exhibit 10–1 presents a summary of the concept.

Present value of
$1 *(p)*

Present value of $1 is the value now (i.e., the present) of one dollar to be received at some date in the future. It can be said to be the inverse of the future value of $1 concept. To compute the present value of a sum to be received in the future, the future sum is subjected to **compound discounting** at *i* interest rate for *n* periods. In compound discounting, the interest is subtracted rather than added, as in compounding. To illustrate, assume that today is January 1, 19A, and that you will receive $1,000 cash on December 31, 19C—that is, three years from now. Assuming an interest rate of 10 percent per year, how much would the $1,000 be worth today; that is, what is its present value (today, on January 1, 19A)? We could set up a discounting computation, year by year, that would be the inverse to the tabulation shown above. However, to facilitate the computation, we can refer to a *"Present value of $1 table,"* like the one shown on page 440, Table 10–2. For *i* = 10 percent, *n* = 3, we find the present value of $1 to be 0.7513. The $1,000, to be received three years hence, has a present value of $1,000 × 0.7513 = $751.30. The difference (i.e., the discount) of $248.70 is due to the time value of money; it is the interest. The concept of the present value of $1 is summarized in Exhibit 10–1.

Future value of
an annuity of $1
(F)

Basically, the future value of an **annuity** of $1 is the same as the future value of $1, except for the addition of the concept of an **annuity.** The word "annuity" refers to a series of periodic payments characterized by

TABLE 10–1
Future value of
$1, $f = (1 + i)^n$

Periods	2%	3%	3.75%	4%	4.25%	5%	6%	7%	8%
0	1.	1.	1.	1.	1.	1.	1.	1.	1.
1	1.02	1.03	1.0375	1.04	1.0425	1.05	1.06	1.07	1.08
2	1.0404	1.0609	1.0764	1.0816	1.0868	1.1025	1.1236	1.1449	1.1664
3	1.0612	1.0927	1.1168	1.1249	1.1330	1.1576	1.1910	1.2250	1.2597
4	1.0824	1.1255	1.1587	1.1699	1.1811	1.2155	1.2625	1.3108	1.3605
5	1.1041	1.1593	1.2021	1.2167	1.2313	1.2763	1.3382	1.4026	1.4693
6	1.1262	1.1941	1.2472	1.2653	1.2837	1.3401	1.4185	1.5007	1.5869
7	1.1487	1.2299	1.2939	1.3159	1.3382	1.4071	1.5036	1.6058	1.7138
8	1.1717	1.2668	1.3425	1.3686	1.3951	1.4775	1.5938	1.7182	1.8509
9	1.1951	1.3048	1.3928	1.4233	1.4544	1.5513	1.6895	1.8385	1.9990
10	1.2190	1.3439	1.4450	1.4802	1.5162	1.6289	1.7908	1.9672	2.1589
20	1.4859	1.8061	2.0882	2.1911	2.2989	2.6533	3.2071	3.8697	4.6610

Periods	9%	10%	11%	12%	13%	14%	15%	20%	25%
0	1.	1.	1.	1.	1.	1.	1.	1.	1.
1	1.09	1.10	1.11	1.12	1.13	1.14	1.15	1.20	1.25
2	1.1881	1.2100	1.2321	1.2544	1.2769	1.2996	1.3225	1.4400	1.5625
3	1.2950	1.3310	1.3676	1.4049	1.4429	1.4815	1.5209	1.7280	1.9531
4	1.4116	1.4641	1.5181	1.5735	1.6305	1.6890	1.7490	2.0736	2.4414
5	1.5386	1.6105	1.6851	1.7623	1.8424	1.9254	2.0114	2.4883	3.0518
6	1.6771	1.7716	1.8704	1.9738	2.0820	2.1950	2.3131	2.9860	3.8147
7	1.8280	1.9487	2.0762	2.2107	2.3526	2.5023	2.6600	3.5832	4.7684
8	1.9926	2.1436	2.3045	2.4760	2.6584	2.8526	3.0590	4.2998	5.9605
9	2.1719	2.3579	2.5580	2.7731	3.0040	3.2519	3.5179	5.1598	7.4506
10	2.3674	2.5937	2.8394	3.1058	3.3946	3.7072	4.0456	6.1917	9.3132
20	5.6044	6.7275	8.0623	9.6463	11.5231	13.7435	16.3665	38.3376	86.7362

TABLE 10–2
Present value of
$1, $p = \dfrac{1}{(1 + i)^n}$

Periods	2%	3%	3.75%	4%	4.25%	5%	6%	7%	8%
1	0.9804	0.9709	0.9639	0.9615	0.9592	0.9524	0.9434	0.9346	0.9259
2	0.9612	0.9426	0.9290	0.9246	0.9201	0.9070	0.8900	0.8734	0.8573
3	0.9423	0.9151	0.8954	0.8890	0.8826	0.8638	0.8396	0.8163	0.7938
4	0.9238	0.8885	0.8631	0.8548	0.8466	0.8227	0.7921	0.7629	0.7350
5	0.9057	0.8626	0.8319	0.8219	0.8121	0.7835	0.7473	0.7130	0.6806
6	0.8880	0.8375	0.8018	0.7903	0.7790	0.7462	0.7050	0.6663	0.6302
7	0.8706	0.8131	0.7728	0.7599	0.7473	0.7107	0.6651	0.6227	0.5835
8	0.8535	0.7894	0.7449	0.7307	0.7168	0.6768	0.6274	0.5820	0.5403
9	0.8368	0.7664	0.7180	0.7026	0.6876	0.6446	0.5919	0.5439	0.5002
10	0.8203	0.7441	0.6920	0.6756	0.6595	0.6139	0.5584	0.5083	0.4632
20	0.6730	0.5534	0.4789	0.4564	0.4350	0.3769	0.3118	0.2584	0.2145

Periods	9%	10%	11%	12%	13%	14%	15%	20%	25%
1	0.9174	0.9091	0.9009	0.8929	0.8850	0.8772	0.8696	0.8333	0.8000
2	0.8417	0.8264	0.8116	0.7972	0.7831	0.7695	0.7561	0.6944	0.6400
3	0.7722	0.7513	0.7312	0.7118	0.6931	0.6750	0.6575	0.5787	0.5120
4	0.7084	0.6830	0.6587	0.6355	0.6133	0.5921	0.5718	0.4823	0.4096
5	0.6499	0.6209	0.5935	0.5674	0.5428	0.5194	0.4972	0.4019	0.3277
6	0.5963	0.5645	0.5346	0.5066	0.4803	0.4556	0.4323	0.3349	0.2621
7	0.5470	0.5132	0.4817	0.4523	0.4251	0.3996	0.3759	0.2791	0.2097
8	0.5019	0.4665	0.4339	0.4039	0.3762	0.3506	0.3269	0.2326	0.1678
9	0.4604	0.4241	0.3909	0.3606	0.3329	0.3075	0.2843	0.1938	0.1342
10	0.4224	0.3855	0.3522	0.3220	0.2946	0.2697	0.2472	0.1615	0.1074
20	0.1784	0.1486	0.1240	0.1037	0.0868	0.0728	0.0611	0.0261	0.0115

TABLE 10–3
Future value of annuity of \$1 (ordinary),

$$F = \frac{(1+i)^n - 1}{i}$$

Period rents*	2%	3%	3.75%	4%	4.25%	5%	6%	7%	8%
1	1.	1.	1.	1.	1.	1.	1.	1.	1.
2	2.02	2.03	2.0375	2.04	2.0425	2.05	2.06	2.07	2.08
3	3.0604	3.0909	3.1139	3.1216	3.1293	3.1525	3.1836	3.2149	3.2464
4	4.1216	4.1836	4.2307	4.2465	4.2623	4.3101	4.3746	4.4399	4.5061
5	5.2040	5.3091	5.3893	5.4163	5.4434	5.5256	5.6371	5.7507	5.8666
6	6.3081	6.4684	6.5914	6.6330	6.6748	6.8019	6.9753	7.1533	7.3359
7	7.4343	7.6625	7.8386	7.8983	7.9585	8.1420	8.3938	8.6540	8.9228
8	8.5830	8.8923	9.1326	9.2142	9.2967	9.5491	9.8975	10.2598	10.6366
9	9.7546	10.1591	10.4750	10.5828	10.6918	11.0266	11.4913	11.9780	12.4876
10	10.9497	11.4639	11.8678	12.0061	12.1462	12.5779	13.1808	13.8164	14.4866
20	24.2974	26.8704	29.0174	29.7781	30.5625	33.0660	36.7856	40.9955	45.7620

Period rents*	9%	10%	11%	12%	13%	14%	15%	20%	25%
1	1.	1.	1.	1.	1.	1.	1.	1.	1.
2	2.09	2.10	2.11	2.12	2.13	2.14	2.15	2.20	2.25
3	3.2781	3.3100	3.3421	3.3744	3.4069	3.4396	3.4725	3.6400	3.8125
4	4.5731	4.6410	4.7097	4.7793	4.8498	4.9211	4.9934	5.3680	5.7656
5	5.9847	6.1051	6.2278	6.3528	6.4803	6.6101	6.7424	7.4416	8.2070
6	7.5233	7.7156	7.9129	8.1152	8.3227	8.5355	8.7537	9.9299	11.2588
7	9.2004	9.4872	9.7833	10.0890	10.4047	10.7305	11.0668	12.9159	15.0735
8	11.0285	11.4359	11.8594	12.2997	12.7573	13.2328	13.7268	16.4991	19.8419
9	13.0210	13.5795	14.1640	14.7757	15.4157	16.0853	16.7858	20.7989	25.8023
10	15.1929	15.9374	16.7220	17.5487	18.4197	19.3373	20.3037	25.9587	33.2529
20	51.1601	57.2750	64.2028	72.0524	80.9468	91.0249	102.4436	186.6880	342.9447

* There is one rent each period.

TABLE 10–4
Present value of annuity of \$1 (ordinary),

$$P = \frac{1 - \dfrac{1}{(1+i)^n}}{i}$$

Period rents*	2%	3%	3.75%	4%	4.25%	5%	6%	7%	8%
1	0.9804	0.9709	0.9639	0.9615	0.9592	0.9524	0.9434	0.9346	0.9259
2	1.9416	1.9135	1.8929	1.8861	1.8794	1.8594	1.8334	1.8080	1.7833
3	2.8839	2.8286	2.7883	2.7751	2.7620	2.7232	2.6730	2.6243	2.5771
4	3.8077	3.7171	3.6514	3.6299	3.6086	3.5460	3.4651	3.3872	3.3121
5	4.7135	4.5797	4.4833	4.4518	4.4207	4.3295	4.2124	4.1002	3.9927
6	5.6014	5.4172	5.2851	5.2421	5.1997	5.0757	4.9173	4.7665	4.6229
7	6.4720	6.2303	6.0579	6.0021	5.9470	5.7864	5.5824	5.3893	5.2064
8	7.3255	7.0197	6.8028	6.7327	6.6638	6.4632	6.2098	5.9713	5.7466
9	8.1622	7.7861	7.5208	7.4353	7.3513	7.1078	6.8017	6.5152	6.2469
10	8.9826	8.5302	8.2128	8.1109	8.0109	7.7217	7.3601	7.0236	6.7101
20	16.3514	14.8775	13.8962	13.5903	13.2944	12.4622	11.4699	10.5940	9.8181

Period rents*	9%	10%	11%	12%	13%	14%	15%	20%	25%
1	0.9174	0.9091	0.9009	0.8929	0.8850	0.8772	0.8696	0.8333	0.8000
2	1.7591	1.7355	1.7125	1.6901	1.6681	1.6467	1.6257	1.5278	1.4400
3	2.5313	2.4869	2.4437	2.4018	2.3612	2.3216	2.2832	2.1065	1.9520
4	3.2397	3.1699	3.1024	3.0373	2.9745	2.9137	2.8550	2.5887	2.3616
5	3.8897	3.7908	3.6959	3.6048	3.5172	3.4331	3.3522	2.9906	2.6893
6	4.4859	4.3553	4.2305	4.1114	3.9975	3.8887	3.7845	3.3255	2.9514
7	5.0330	4.8684	4.7122	4.5638	4.4226	4.2883	4.1604	3.6046	3.1611
8	5.5348	5.3349	5.1461	4.9676	4.7988	4.6389	4.4873	3.8372	3.3289
9	5.9952	5.7590	5.5370	5.3282	5.1317	4.9464	4.7716	4.0310	3.4631
10	6.4177	6.1446	5.8892	5.6502	5.4262	5.2161	5.0188	4.1925	3.5705
20	9.1285	8.5136	7.9633	7.4694	7.0248	6.6231	6.2593	4.8696	3.9539

* There is one rent each period.

EXHIBIT 10–1
Time value of money determinations

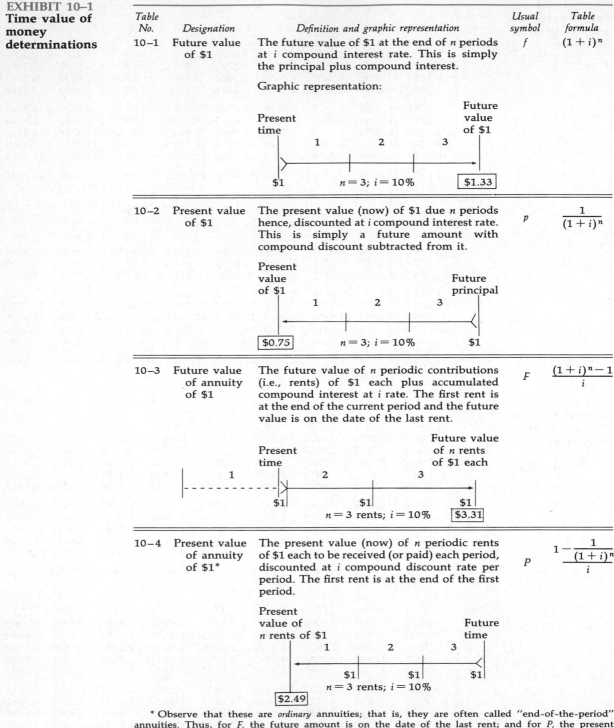

Table No.	Designation	Definition and graphic representation	Usual symbol	Table formula
10–1	Future value of $1	The future value of $1 at the end of n periods at i compound interest rate. This is simply the principal plus compound interest. Graphic representation: Present time ... Future value of $1 1 2 3 $1 $n = 3; i = 10\%$ $1.33	f	$(1 + i)^n$
10–2	Present value of $1	The present value (now) of $1 due n periods hence, discounted at i compound interest rate. This is simply a future amount with compound discount subtracted from it. Present value of $1 ... Future principal 1 2 3 $0.75 $n = 3; i = 10\%$ $1	p	$\dfrac{1}{(1 + i)^n}$
10–3	Future value of annuity of $1	The future value of n periodic contributions (i.e., rents) of $1 each plus accumulated compound interest at i rate. The first rent is at the end of the current period and the future value is on the date of the last rent. Present time ... Future value of n rents of $1 each 1 2 3 $1 $1 $1 $n = 3$ rents; $i = 10\%$ $3.31	F	$\dfrac{(1 + i)^n - 1}{i}$
10–4	Present value of annuity of 1^*	The present value (now) of n periodic rents of $1 each to be received (or paid) each period, discounted at i compound discount rate per period. The first rent is at the end of the first period. Present value of n rents of $1 ... Future time 1 2 3 $1 $1 $1 $n = 3$ rents; $i = 10\%$ $2.49	P	$\dfrac{1 - \dfrac{1}{(1 + i)^n}}{i}$

* Observe that these are *ordinary* annuities; that is, they are often called "end-of-the-period" annuities. Thus, for F, the future amount is on the date of the last rent; and for P, the present value is at the beginning of the period of the first rent. Annuities *due* assume the opposite; that is, they are "beginning-of-the-period" annuities. Ordinary annuity values can be converted to annuities due simply by multiplication of $(1 + i)$. Annuities due are discussed at the next level of accounting sophistication, intermediate accounting.

(1) an *equal amount each period* (for two or more future consecutive periods), (2) equal length of each consecutive period, and (3) an equal interest rate each period. In contrast to an amount of $1, which involves a single contribution at the start, an annuity of $1 involves an equal contribution each period. The future value, of an annuity of $1 involves *compound interest* on *each periodic amount.* To illustrate, assume that you decide to deposit (i.e., contribute) $1,000 cash in a savings account each year for three years at 10 percent interest per year (i.e., a total of $3,000). The first $1,000 contribution is made on December 31, 19A; the second one on December 31, 19B; and the third and last one on December 31, 19C. How much would you have in the savings account at the end of Year 3, that is, immediately after the third (and last) deposit on December 31, 19C? In this situation, the first $1,000 contribution would draw compound interest for two years (19B and 19C); the second deposit would draw interest for one year (19C); and the third deposit would draw no interest (since we desire to know the amount in the savings account *immediately* after the third deposit). We could compute laboriously the interest for each contribution to derive the future value of this annuity. However, we can refer to Table 10–3 (page 441), *"Future value of annuity of $1."* For $i = 10$ percent, $n = 3$, we find the value 3.31.[11] This is the future value of $1 at $i = 10$ percent, $n = 3$. Therefore, the total of your three contributions (of $1,000 each) would have increased to $1,000 × 3.31 = $3,310 on December 31, 19C. The increase of $310 was due to the time value of money; it is interest revenue to you on the $3,000. This concept is summarized in Exhibit 10–1.

Present value of annuity of $1 *(P)*

The present value of an annuity of $1 is the value **now** (i.e., the present time) of a series of *equal amounts* (i.e., rents) to be received each period for some specified number of periods in the future. It can be said to be the inverse of the future value of an annuity of $1 explained immediately above. It involves **compound discounting** of each of the equal periodic amounts.

To illustrate, assume now is January 1, 19A, and that you are to receive $1,000 in cash on each December 31, 19A, 19B, and 19C. How much would these three $1,000 future amounts be worth now, on January 1, 19A (i.e., the present value), assuming an interest rate of 10 percent per year? We could calculate laboriously the discounting on each rent; however, we can compute the present value readily by referring to Table 10–4, *"Present value of annuity of $1."* For $i = 10$ percent, $n = 3$ rents, we find the value 2.4869. This is the present value of an **annuity** of $1 at $i = 10$ percent, and three equal periodic rents. Therefore, your three $1,000 amounts to be received in the future have a present value of $1,000 × 2.4869 = $2,487. The difference (i.e., the discount) of $513 was due to

---

[11] The equal amounts for each period in annuities often are referred to in the literature as "rents."

the interest factor. This concept is summarized in Exhibit 10–1 (page 442).

The preceding illustrations assumed **annual** interest rates and **annual** periods for compounding and discounting. When the interest periods are less than a year, such as semiannually or quarterly, the values of n and i used must be consistent in all computations and selection of table values. Also, interest rates almost always are quoted on an annual basis. To illustrate, 8 percent interest compounded or discounted **semiannually** for five years requires use of, $n = 10$ and $i = 4$ percent, and if quarterly, $n = 20$ and $i = 2$ percent.

SOME MEASUREMENT AND ACCOUNTING APPLICATIONS OF FV AND PV

We have said that there are numerous trasactions where the concepts of future and present value are used for accounting measurements. Below are cited four different situations where they must be employed.

Case A—Company A, on January 1, 19A, set aside $150,000 cash in a special building fund (an asset) to be used at the end of five years to construct a new building. The fund is expected to earn 10 percent interest per year, which will be added to the fund balance each year. On the date of deposit the company made the following entry:

January 1, 19A:

Special building fund	150,000	
Cash		150,000

Required:

1. What will be the balance of the fund at the end of the fifth year?
   Answer: This situation involves the future value of $1 concept.

   Principal × Table 10–1 value ($i = 10\%$; $n = 5$) = Future value
   $150,000 × 1.6105 = $241,575

2. How much interest revenue was earned on the fund during the five years?
   Answer:

   $$\$241,575 - \$150,000 = \$91,575$$

3. What entry would be made on December 31, 19A, to record the interest revenue for the first year?
   Answer: Interest for one year on the fund balance is added to the fund and recorded as follows:

December 31, 19A:

```
Special building fund .................................  15,000
    Interest revenue ($150,000 × 0.10) ..................        15,000
```

4. What entry would be made on December 31, 19B, to record interest revenue for the second year?
   Answer:

December 31, 19B:

```
Special building fund .................................  16,500
    Interest revenue ...................................        16,500
    ($150,000 + $15,000) × 0.10 = $16,500.
```

Case B—On January 1, 19A, Company B purchased a new machine to be used in the plant at a list price of $20,000, which was payable at the end of two years. The going rate of interest was 12 percent.

Required:

1. The company accountant is preparing the following entry:

January 1, 19A:

```
Machinery ...........................................  $  ?
    Account payable (special) ..........................       $  ?
```

What amount should be used in this entry?

Answer: This situation requires application of the present value of $1 concept. Under the cost principle, the cost of the machine is the current cash equivalent price, which is the present value of the future payment. The present value of the $20,000 is computed as follows:

Future amount × Table 10–2 ($i = 12\%$; $n = 2$) = Present value
$20,000 × 0.7972   = $15,944

Therefore, the entry would be as follows:

January 1, 19A:

```
Machinery ...........................................  15,944
    Account payable (special) ..........................       15,944
```

446

2. What entry would be made at the end of the first and second years for interest expense on the accounts payable?

Answer: Interest expense for each year on the amount in the Account Payable account would be recorded by means of an adjusting entry, as follows:

December 31, 19A:

Interest expense	1,913	
Account payable (special)		1,913

$15,944 \times 0.12 = \$1,913$.

Note: The account payable would be reported on the 19A balance sheet at $15,944 + \$1,913 = \$17,857$.

December 31, 19B:

Interest expense	2,143	
Account payable (special)		2,143

$(\$15,944 + \$1,913) \times 0.12 = \$2,143$.

The effect of these two entries is to increase the balance in Account Payable to the new **current cash equivalent amount.** By maturity date the balance will have been increased to the maturity amount, $20,000, which is the current cash equivalent amount at due date. Interest expense was $1,913 + \$2,143 = \$4,056$, or alternatively, $20,000 - \$15,944 = \$4,056$.

3. What entry would be made to record the payment on due date?

Answer: At this date the amount to be paid as the balance of Account Payable is the current cash equivalent amount, which is the same as the maturity amount on the due date; that is, $15,944 + \$1,913 + \$2,143 = \$20,000$.[12]

[12] These entries could also be made as follows with the same results:

January 1, 19A:

Machinery	15,944	
Discount on account payable	4,056	
Account payable (special)		20,000

December 31, 19A:

Interest expense ($15,944 \times 0.12$)	1,913	
Discount on account payable		1,913

At the end of 19A, the liability would be reported at net as $20,000 - \$2,143 = \$17,857$.

December 31, 19B:

Interest expense ($17,857 \times 0.12$)	2,143	
Account payable (special)	20,000	
Cash		20,000
Discount on account payable		2,143

The entry would be:

December 31, 19B:

Account payable (special) 20,000
    Cash   20,000

Case C—Company C decided to make five annual deposits of $30,000 each with a financial institution to create a debt retirement fund. The deposits will be made each December 31, starting December 31, 19A. The fifth and last deposit will be made December 31, 19E. The financial institution will pay 8 percent annual compound interest, which will be added to the fund at the end of each year (also see Exhibit 11–4).

1. What entry should be made to record the first deposit?
   Answer:

   December 31, 19A:

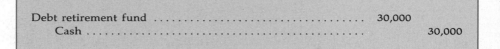

Debt retirement fund 30,000
    Cash   30,000

2. What will be the balance in the fund immediately after the fifth and last deposit (i.e., on December 31, 19E)?
   Answer: This situation requires application of future value of an annuity of $1.

$$\begin{array}{llll} \text{Rent} & \times \text{Table 10–3} \ (i=8\%; \ n=5) & = \text{Future value} \\ \$30{,}000 & \times \ 5.8666 & = \$175{,}998 \end{array}$$

3. What entries would be made at the end of 19B?
   Answer:
   a. Interest for one year on the fund balance would be added to the fund and recorded as follows:

   December 31, 19B:

Debt retirement fund 2,400
    Interest revenue ($30,000 × 0.08)   2,400

   b. The second deposit would be recorded as follows:

   December 31, 19B:

Debt retirement fund	30,000	
Cash		30,000

4. What would be the amount of interest revenue to be recorded at the end of the 19C?

   Answer: Interest would be computed on the increased fund balance as follows:

   $$(\$30,000 + \$2,400 + \$30,000) \times 0.08 = \$4,992$$

Case D—On January 1, 19A, Company D purchased a new machine at a cash price of $40,000. Since the company was short of cash, arrangements were made to execute a $40,000 note payable to be paid off in three equal annual installments. Each installment would include principal plus interest on the unpaid balance at 11 percent per year. The equal annual installments are due on December 31, 19A, 19B, and 19C. The acquisition was recorded as follows:

January 1, 19A:

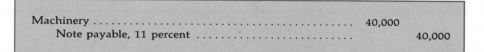

Machinery	40,000	
Note payable, 11 percent		40,000

Required:

1. What would be the amount of each annual installment?

   Answer: The $40,000 is the amount of the debt today; hence, it is the present value of the three future installment payments required (i.e., the rents). Therefore, $n = 3$, $i = 11$ percent, and the present value is $40,000. To compute the amount of each equal rent (payment) required, the present value of an annuity of $1 must be used as follows:

   Rent $\times$ Table 10–4 value ($i = 11\%$; $n = 3$) = Present value
   Substituting:
   Rent $\times$ 2.4437 = $40,000
   Rent = $40,000 ÷ 2.4437
       = $16,369 (amount of each annual payment)

2. What was the amount of interest expense in dollars?
   Answer:

   $$(\$16,369 \times 3) - \$40,000 = \$9,107$$

3. What entry would be made at the end of each year to record the payment on this $40,000 note payable?
   Answer:
   a. To record the first installment payment on the note:

December 31, 19A:

```
Note payable .......................................  11,969
Interest expense ($40,000 × 0.11) ....................   4,400
    Cash (computed above)............................          16,369
```

b. To record the second installment on the note:

December 31, 19B:

```
Note payable .......................................  13,285
Interest expense ($40,000 − $11,969) × 0.11 ............   3,084
    Cash (computed above)...........................          16,369
```

c. To record final installment on the note:

December 31, 19C:

```
Note payable .......................................  14,746
Interest expense ....................................   1,623
    Cash (computed above)...........................          16,369
    Interest: ($40,000 − $11,969 − $13,285) × 0.11 = $1,623
    (rounded to accommodate rounding errors).
```

4. Prepare a debt payment schedule that shows the effect on interest expense and the unpaid amount of principal each period.

Debt payment schedule

Date	Payment of cash (cr.)	Interest expense (dr.)	Reduction of principal (dr.)	Unpaid principal
1/1/A				40,000
12/31/A	16,369 [a]	4,400 [b]	11,969 [c]	28,031 [d]
12/31/B	16,369	3,084	13,285	14,746
12/31/C	16,369	1,623*	14,746	–0–
Total	49,107	9,107	40,000	

* To accommodate rounding error.
Sequential computations:
[a] Annual payment: Computed above.
[b] Interest expense: Unpaid principal, $40,000 × 0.11 = $4,400.
[c] Reduction of principal: Annual payment, $16,369 − Interest, $4,400 = $11,969.
[d] New unpaid balance: Prior Balance, $40,000 − Reduction, $11,969 = $28,031.

Observe in the debt schedule that of each successive payment an increasing amount is payment on principal and a decreasing amount is interest expense. This effect happens because the interest each period is based on a lower amount of unpaid principal.

Although there are many other applications of the concept of the time value of money in the recording and reporting processes, the above examples are typical. The application of these concepts to capital budgeting is deferred to *Fundamentals of Management Accounting.*

SUMMARY

This chapter discussed accounting for three types of obligations: current, long-term, and contingent liabilities. Accounting for bonds payable is deferred to Chapter 11. Liabilities are obligations of either a known or estimated amount. Detailed information concerning the liabilities of an entity is especially important to many decision makers, whether internal or external to the enterprise. Identification by the decision maker of the kinds and amounts of liabilities would be practically impossible without reliable financial statements. The existence and amount of liabilities sometimes are easy to conceal from outsiders. The accounting model and the verification by the independent CPA contstitute the best assurance that all liabilities are disclosed.

Current liabilities are those obligations that will be paid from the resources reported on the same balance sheet as current assets. Thus, they are short-term obligations that will be paid within the coming year or within the normal operating cycle of the business, whichever is longer. All other liabilities (except contingent liabilities) are reported as long-term liabilities. A contingent liability is not a liabilitiy, it is a potential claim due to some event or transaction that has happened already, but whether it will materialize as a legal liability is not certain because it depends upon some future event or transaction. Contingent liabilities must be disclosed fully on the financial statements. Disclosure usually is by note to the financial statements.

APPENDIX A: PAYROLL ACCOUNTING

Accurate and detailed payroll accounting, although it does not involve any new accounting concepts or principles, is particularly important in most enterprises because of the necessity to pay the employees for their services promptly and correctly. In addition, detailed payroll accounting is necessary to fulfill legal requirements under federal and state laws with respect to withholding taxes, social security taxes, and unemployment taxes. Further, the management of an enterprise, for planning and control purposes, need detailed and accurate cost figures for wages and salaries. Frequently, salaries and wages is the largest category of expense in an enterprise. As a consequence of these requirements, payroll accounting is characterized by a large amount of detailed recordkeeping. Payroll accounting often is computerized, including the production of individual checks for the employees.

Payroll accounting requires that a detailed payroll record be maintained for each employee. The payroll record varies with the circumstances in each company; however, it must include for each individual such data as social security number, number of dependents (for income tax withholding), rate of pay, a time record (for hourly paid employees), deductions from gross pay, and so on.

To understand payroll accounting, a distinction must be made between (1) payroll deductions and taxes that must be paid by the *employee* (i.e., deducted from the employee's gross earnings); and (2) payroll taxes that must be paid by the *employer*. Both types of payroll amounts must be transmitted to the governmental unit or other party to whom the amount is owed. Payroll taxes and deductions apply only in situations where there is an employer-employee relationship. Independent contractors that are not under the direct supervision of the client, such as outside lawyers, independent accountants, consultants, and building contractors, are not employees; hence; amounts paid to them are not subject to payroll taxes and related deductions.

An employee generally receives take-home pay that is much less than the gross earnings for the period. This is due to two types of payroll deductions:

1. Deductions for taxes that must be paid by the employee as required by state and federal laws.
2. Deductions authorized by the employee for special purposes.

Deductions for taxes paid by employees

There are two categories of taxes that the employee must pay and thus are deducted from the employee's gross earnings; they are income taxes and social security taxes. The employer must remit the total amount deducted to the appropriate government agency.

Employee income taxes. Practically every employee must submit a federal income tax return annually. Wages and salaries earned during the year must be included on the income tax return as income. For many years, federal laws have required the employer to deduct an appropriate amount of income tax each period from the gross earnings of each employee. The amount of the deduction for income tax is determined from a tax table (provided by the Internal Revenue Service) based upon the earnings and number of exemptions (for self and dependents) of the employee. The amount of income tax withheld from the employee's wages is recorded by the employer as a current liability between the date of deduction and the date the amount withheld is remitted to the government. The total amount withheld must be paid to the Internal Revenue Service within a specified short period of time. An especially designed form to accompany each remittance is provided by the Internal Revenue Service to identify the employees and the amounts withheld. Some states also require withholding for state income tax.

Employee FICA taxes. The social security taxes paid by the employee generally are called FICA taxes since they are a result of the Federal Insurance Contributions Act. This act provides that persons who are *qualified* under the provisions of the act, upon reaching age 62, may retire and receive the minimum monthly benefits for life, plus certain medical benefits after age 65.[13] Retirement at age 65 provides maximum pension benefits. It also provides benefits for the family of a deceased person who was qualified.

The funds required by the government to provide the benefits under the Social Security Act are obtained by payroll taxes, which are imposed in equal amounts on **both the employee and the employer.** Effective January 1, 1980, the FICA rate was 6.13 percent on the first $25,900 paid to each employee during the year. Since FICA rates and the wage maximum change frequently, for convenience in calculations we will use a rounded rate of 6 percent for illustrative and problem purposes.

At the end of each year, the employer is required to provide each employee with a **Withholding Statement, Form W-2,** which reports to the employee (1) gross earnings for the year, (2) earnings subject to FICA taxes, (3) income taxes withheld, and (4) FICA taxes withheld. A copy of this form also is sent to the Internal Revenue Service.

Employee deductions for special purposes

Many companies encourage programs of voluntary deductions from earnings by employees. Typical of these voluntary deductions are savings funds, insurance premiums, charitable contributions, supplementary retirement programs, repayment of loans, stock purchase plans, and the purchase of U.S. savings bonds. The employer agrees to make these deductions, subject to employee authorization, as a matter of convenience to the employees. The amounts deducted are remitted in a short time to the organization or agency in whose behalf the deduction was authorized. Another type of deduction, not voluntary on an individual basis, is for union dues as specified in the union contract. The employer is required to remit the deductions, along with the employee list, to the union each month.

Accounting for employee deductions

The employer must maintain detailed and accurate records of all deductions from the earnings of each employee. From the employer's viewpoint, the employee deductions are *current liabilities* from the date of the payroll deduction to the date of remittance to the government or other entity.

To illustrate the basic accounting entry to be made for the payment of a payroll and the accrual of liabilities for the *employee* deductions, assume

---

[13] To qualify under the act for retirement and medical benefits, the employee must be in "covered" employment for a specified period of time. Covered employment requires payroll deductions for these taxes. The amount of benefits and the FICA tax deductions are frequently changed by the U.S. Congress.

that X Company accumulated the following data in the detailed payroll records for the month of January 19B:

Gross earnings:

Salaries	$60,000
Wages (hourly paid employees)	40,000
Income taxes withheld	21,000
Union dues withheld	400
FICA taxes (assume no maximums were exceeded in January, $100,000 × 6%)	6,000

The entry to record the payroll and employee deductions would be:

January 31, 19A:

Salaries expense	60,000	
Wages expense	40,000	
Liability for income taxes withheld—employees		21,000
Liability for union dues withheld—employees		400
FICA taxes payable—employees ($100,000 × 6%)		6,000
Cash (take-home pay)		72,600
Payroll for January, including employee payroll deductions.		

Payroll taxes paid by employer

Remember that the payroll taxes illustrated above are those levied on the *employees.* The employer simply serves as a tax collector with respect to them. In addition, specific payroll taxes also are levied on the employer. These taxes represent **operating expenses** of the business. The liability for these taxes is extinguished when the taxes are remitted to the designated agencies of the state and federal governments. Generally, three different payroll taxes must be paid by the employer—FICA taxes, FUTA taxes, and state unemployment compensation taxes.

Employer FICA taxes. The employer must pay an additional FICA tax equal to the amount withheld from the employee's wages. Thus, the FICA tax paid by the employer is at the same rate as the FICA employee tax and on the same amount of wages (i.e., for 1980, 6.13 percent on the first $25,900 of gross earnings of each employee).

Employer FUTA taxes. The Social Security Act provides for another program known as unemployment compensation. This program derives its monetary support under the provisions of the Federal Unemployment Tax Act. The FUTA, or unemployment tax, is paid *only by the employer.* Currently, the federal tax amounts to 3.4 percent of the first $6,000 in wages paid to each employee during the year.

State unemployment compensation taxes. The unemployment program specified in the Federal Unemployment Tax Act is a joint federal-state program; consequently, each state participates in the program by sharing both in providing benefits and in funding the program through payroll taxes. Although state laws vary in some respects, 2.7 percent is payable to the state (of employment), and the remaining 0.7 percent is payable to the federal Treasury (i.e., the total of 3.4 percent on the first $6,000 wages paid). Most states have a merit-rating plan that provides for a reduction in the tax rate for employers that establish a record of stable employment over a period of time.

Accounting for employer payroll taxes

Payroll taxes paid by the employer are debited to an expense account and credited to a current liability when the payroll is paid each period. To illustrate, the January entry for the employer's payroll taxes for X Company (data shown on page 453), assuming a 2.7 percent state unemployment tax rate, would be as follows:[14]

Payroll tax expense	9,400*	
FICA taxes payable—employer ($100,000 × 6% matching) . . .		6,000
FUTA taxes payable—employer ($100,000 × 0.7%)		700
State unemployment taxes payable—employer		
($100,000 × 2.7%)		2,700
To record employer payroll taxes.		
* Total payroll expense, $100,000 + $9,400 = $109,400.		

When the taxes are remitted to the government, the liability accounts are debited and Cash is credited.

APPENDIX B: THE VOUCHER SYSTEM

The voucher system is designed to attain strict control over cash expenditures from the point of incurrence of an obligation (by means of purchase of merchandise for resale, services, operational assets, investments, etc.) through the payment of cash. The incurrence of an obligation and the payment of cash to satisfy it are viewed as separate and independent transactions. When a voucher system is used, an account called *Vouchers Payable* replaces the account *Accounts Payable* in the ledger. Similarly, a *voucher register* and a *check register* replace the purchases journal and the cash disbursements journal, respectively (see Chapter 8, Appendix B).

The basic document in the voucher system is the *voucher*. A voucher is a form, prepared and used within the business, on which a transaction is (1) summarized and supported adequately, (2) approved, (3) analyzed for recording, and (4) approved for payment. Thus, it is a comprehensive document that follows a transaction from the transaction date to the final cash payment. A voucher is prepared for *each* transaction involving the payment of cash, such as the purchase of assets, the use of services, the incurrence of expenses, and the payment of debt. The form of a voucher

---

[14] In this and the preceding entries, it was assumed that none of the employees received remuneration above the $25,900 and $6,000 maximums for the year.

varies between companies since it should be designed to meet the internal requirements of the individual company. For control purposes, all voucher forms and checks should be numbered consecutively when printed.

Each voucher, after approval, is entered in the voucher register in order of number. The voucher register is designed to record the basic information from the voucher, including the accounts to be debited and credited.

To illustrate the mechanics of a voucher system, we will follow a purchase of merchandise for resale through the system from the **order date** to the final cash payment date. Each step in the sequence may be illustrated and explained as follows:

19A:

Jan. 10 Merchandise ordered from Box Supply Company, cost $1,000; terms, n/15. A purchase order is prepared and approved.

12 Merchandise ordered from Box Supply Company on January 10 is received; invoice is received. Voucher No. 47 is drawn and the purchase order is attached (see Exhibit 10–2). Goods are checked for quantity and condition; a receiving report is prepared.

12 Receiving report and invoice sent to accounting department; they are attached to the voucher. Voucher is approved, and then recorded in the voucher register (see Exhibit 10–3).

26 Voucher is approved by designated manager for payment on January 27 and sent to disbursements department; Check No. 90 is prepared.

27 Check No. 90 is signed by treasurer and mailed.

28 The accounting department enters Check No. 90 in the check register (see Exhibit 10–4). Enters payment notation in the voucher register (see Exhibit 10–3). Files the voucher in the *Vouchers Paid File.*

For illustrative purposes, two more transactions are recorded in the voucher register, one of which remains unpaid.

At the end of the month the voucher register and the check register are totaled and the equality of the debits and credits is verified. Posting to the ledger from these two special journals follows the same pattern explained in Chapter 8, Appendix B, for the special journals illustrated there. Posting involves two separate phases:

1. Current posting—During the period, and perhaps daily, the details in the Voucher Register columns are posted to *(a)* the selling expense subsidiary ledger (under the selling expense control); *(b)* the administrative expense subsidiary ledger (under the administrative expense control); and *(c)* other accounts to be debited. No current posting is required from the check register as illustrated.

2. Monthly posting—The totals from the voucher register, except for the "Other Accounts to Be Debited" are posted at the end of each month. The account number to which each total is posted is entered below

EXHIBIT 10–2
Voucher

Voucher No. _47_

MAY DEPARTMENT STORE
Boston, Mass.

Date of Voucher _Jan. 12, 19A_   Date Paid _Jan 27, 19A_

Pay to: _Box Supply Company_   Check No. _90_

1119 Brown Street

Philadelphia, Pa.

For the following goods or services: (attach all supporting documents)

Date Incurred	Terms	Explanation of Details	Amount
Jan. 12	n/15	Merchandise, Dept. 8	1,000.00
		Invoice No. 17-8132	
		Receiving Report No. 123	
		Net payable	1,000.00

Approvals:

Voucher Approval: Date _1/12/A_   Signature _R.C. Roe_

Payment Approval: Date _1/26/A_   Signature _A.B. Doe_

Accounting Analysis:

Account Debited:	Acct. No.	Amount
Purchases	91	1,000.00
Office Supplies		
Sales Salaries		
Operational Assets		
Etc.		
Total, Voucher Payable Credit	41	1,000.00

the amount. The column for "Other Accounts to Be Debited" was posted individually; hence, the total should not be posted. The totals from the check register are posted to the accounts at the end of each month as indicated by the account numbers entered below the total.

The balance in the ledger account Vouchers Payable is reported on the balance sheet as a liability and on the financial statement is designated

EXHIBIT 10–3
Voucher register

Date	Vou. No.	Payee	Payment Date	Payment Check No.	Vouchers Payable (Credit)	Purchases (Debit)	Selling Expense Control Account Code	Selling Expense Control Folio	Selling Expense Control Amount (Debit)	Adm. Expense Control Account Code	Adm. Expense Control Folio	Adm. Expense Control Amount (Debit)	Other Accounts to Be Debited Account Name	Other Accounts to Be Debited Folio No. P	Other Accounts to Be Debited Amount (Debited)
Jan 12	47	Box Supply Co	1/27	90	1,000.00	1,000.00									
Jan 14	48	John Day—salary	1/15	89	600.00		64	✓	600.00						
Jan 31	98	Capital Nat'l Bank—note			2,160.00								Notes payable	44 ✓	2,000.00
													Interest expense	82 ✓	160.00
		Totals			27,605.00	14,875.00			7,410.00			3,160.00			2,160.00
		Posting notations			(41)	(91)			(60)			(70)			(✓)

as Accounts Payable. The amount should be allocated and classified between current and long-term liabilities, depending on due dates.

The Vouchers Payable account is a control account, the balance of which represents all of the *unpaid* vouchers at any given time. The total of all vouchers in the *Unpaid Vouchers File* must agree with the balance of the Vouchers Payable account; therefore, the Vouchers Payable account replaces the Accounts Payable control account in the ledger (see Chapter 6, Appendix A).

In studying the mechanics of the voucher system, as illustrated above, you should not overlook its most important aspect—the high degree of **internal control** attained through formalization of the sequence of acquiring operational assets, services, and merchandise, and in making the cash payments. The internal control feature rests upon (1) clear-cut separation and designation of specific approval responsibilities, (2) a prescribed routine for carrying out these responsibilities, and (3) accounting for the results.

EXHIBIT 10–4
Check register

Date	Payee	Voucher No. Paid	Check No.	Vouchers Payable (Debit)*	Cash (Credit)*
Jan. 15	John Day	48	89	600.00	600.00
27	Box Supply Co.	47	90	1,000.00	1,000.00
31	Totals			18,751.00	18,751.00
	Posting notation			(41)	(11)

* These two columns could be combined.

Although a manual approach was illustrated, we emphasize again that these routines are adapted easily to the computer. The computer program is designed to accomplish the same steps and procedures illustrated above. Most companies of any size have computerized the voucher system in order to attain a high degree of control over expenditures and to accelerate the processing of a large volume of transactions, including cash disbursements.

IMPORTANT TERMS DEFINED IN THE CHAPTER (with page citations)

Liabilities—419
Current liabilities—421
Working capital—421
Working capital (current) ratio—421
Accrued liabilities—422
Deferred revenues—424
Long-term liabilities—425
Notes payable—426
Time value of money—426, 438
Interest—426, 438
Interest-bearing note—427
Noninterest-bearing note—428
Deferred income tax—427

Timing difference—431
Permanent difference—431
Lease liabilities—432
Operating type lease—432
Financing type lease—432
Contingent liabilities—435
Voucher system—436
Future value of $1—439, 440
Present value of $1—439, 440
Future value of annuity of $1—439, 441
Present value of annuity of $1—441, 443
Payroll accounting—Appendix A

QUESTIONS FOR DISCUSSION

Part A

1. Define a liability and distinguish between a current liability and a long-term liability.

2. How can external parties be informed in respect to liabilities of an enterprise? Explain.

3. Liabilities are measured and reported at their current cash equivalent amount. Explain.

4. A liability is a known obligation of either a definite or estimated amount. Explain.

5. What is working capital?

6. What is the current ratio? What is another name for the current ratio? How is it related to the classification of liabilities?

7. What is an accrued liability? What kind of an entry generally reflects an accrued liability?

8. What is a deferred revenue? Why is it a liability?

9. Define a note payable and distinguish between a secured and an unsecured note payable.

10. Distinguish between an interest-bearing note and a noninterest-bearing note.

11. Define deferred income tax. Explain why deferred income tax is said to reverse, or turn around, in subsequent periods.

12. What is a lease liability?

13. What is meant by a financing type lease?

14. What is a contingent liability? How is a contingent liability reported?

15. Briefly explain the primary purpose of a voucher system.

Questions

Part B

16. Briefly explain what is meant by the time value of money.

17. Explain the basic difference between future value and present value.

18. What is an annuity?

19. Complete the following schedule:

(Relates to Question 19)

Concept	Symbol	Table Values		
		$n = 4$; $i = 5\%$	$n = 7$; $i = 10\%$	$n = 9$; $i = 15\%$
FV of $1				
PV of $1				
FV of annuity of $1				
PV of annuity of $1				

EXERCISES

Part A

E10–1. Spicer Company is preparing the 19B balance sheet. The company records reflect the following related amounts:

Total current assets	$152,100
Total all remaining assets	665,000
Liabilities:	
Note payable (10%, due in 5 years) ...... *Long-term*	22,000
Accounts payable	60,000
Income tax payable	15,000
Liability for witholding taxes	4,000
Rent revenue collected in advance	3,000
Bonds payable (due in 15 years) ...... *Long term*	200,000
Wages payable	6,000
Property taxes payable	2,000
Note payable, 12% (due in 6 months)	5,000
Interest payable	100

Required:

a. Compute total owners's equity.
b. Compute (1) working capital and (2) the working capital ratio (show computations).
c. Compute the amount of interest expense for 19B on the 12 percent note assuming it was dated September 1, 19B.

E10–2. During 19B, the two transactions given below were completed by TW Company. The annual accounting period ends December 31.

1. Wages paid and recorded during 19B amounted to $70,000; however, at the end of December 19B, there were two days' wages unpaid and unrecorded because the weekly payroll will not be paid until January 6, 19C. Wages for the two days amounted to $700.
2. On December 10, 19B, TW Company collected rent revenue amounting to $600 on some office space that it rented to another party. The rent collected was for the month from December 10, 19B, to January 10, 19C, and was credited to Rent Revenue.

Required:

a. Give (1) the adjusting entry required on December 31, 19B, and (2) the January 6, 19C, entry for payment of any unpaid wages from December 19B.
b. Give (1) the entry for the collection of rent on December 10, 19B, and (2) the adjusting entry on December 31, 19B (compute rent to the nearest ten days).

c. Show how any liabilities related to the above transactions should be reported on the balance sheet at December 31, 19B.

E10–3. Owens Manufacturing Company has completed the payroll for January 19B, reflecting the following data:

Salaries and wages earned	$80,000
Employee income taxes withheld	11,000
Union dues withheld	1,100
FICA payroll taxes*	4,800
FUTA payroll taxes	560
State unemployment taxes	2,160

* Assessed on both employer and employee at a 6 percent rate for each.

Required:

a. Give the entry to record payment of the payroll and employee deductions.

b. Give the entry to record employer payroll taxes.

c. What was the amount of additional labor expense to the company due to tax laws? Explain. What was the employee take-home pay? Explain.

E10–4. On November 1, 19A, Flash Auto Parts Company borrowed $30,000 cash from the City Bank for working capital purposes and gave an interest-bearing note with a face amount of $30,000. The note was due in six months, and the interest rate was 12 percent per annum payable at maturity.

Required:

a. Give the entry to record the note on November 1.

b. Give the adjusting entry that would be required at the end of the annual accounting period, December 31, 19A.

c. Give the entry to record payment of the note and interest on the maturity date, April 30, 19B (disregard reversing entries).

E10–5. On November 1, 19A, Quality Furniture Company borrowed $20,000 cash from the City Bank for working capital pur-

poses and gave a noninterest-bearing note payable. The note was due in six months, and the face amount was $21,200. The going rate of interest was 12 percent per year.

Required:

a. Give the entry to record the note on November 1, 19A.

b. Give the adjusting entry that would be required at the end of the annual accounting period, December 31, 19A.

c. Show how the note should be reported on the December 31, 19A, balance sheet.

d. Give the entry to record payment of the note at maturity on April 30, 19B (disregard reversing entries).

E10–6. Assume you needed to borrow exactly $3,600 cash on a one-year note payable. The City Bank charges 10 percent interest per annum on such loans. You are to respond to the following questions (show computations):

Required:

a. What would be the face amount of the note assuming the bank agreed to accept an interest-bearing note?

b. What would be the face amount of the note assuming the bank insisted on a noninterest-bearing note?

c. Give the journal entries to record the note in (a) and (b). Set the entries in parallel columns.

d. Give the journal entries at date of maturity in (a) and (b).

E10–7. Tandy Company sells a wide range of goods through two retail stores that are operated in adjoining cities. Most purchases of goods for resale are on invoices with credit terms of 2/10, n/30. Occasionally, a short-term note payable is executed to obtain cash for current use. The following transactions were selected from those occurring during 19B:

1. On January 10, 19B, purchased merchandise on credit, $14,000; terms, 2/10, n/30. Record at net; the company uses the periodic inventory system.
2. On March 1, 19B, borrowed $30,000 cash from City Bank and gave an interest-bearing note payable: face amount, $30,000; due at the end of six months, with an annual interest rate of 10 percent payable at maturity.

Required:

a. Give the entry for each of the above transactions. Record purchases and accounts payable at net.
b. Give the entry assuming the account payable of January 10, 19B, was paid within the discount period.
c. Give the entry assuming the account payable of January 10, 19B, was paid after the discount period.
d. Give the entry for the payment of the note payable plus interest on the maturity date.

E10–8. The comparative income statements of TX Company at December 31, 19B, reflected the following data (summarized and excluding income taxes):

	Annual income statement for	
	19A	19B
Sales	$50,000	$60,000
Expenses	40,000	48,000
Pretax income	$10,000	$12,000

Included on the 19B income statement given above was an expense amounting to $4,000 that was deductible on the income tax return in 19A rather than in 19B. Assume an average tax rate of 20 percent.

Required:

a. For each year compute (1) income tax expense, (2) income tax payable, and (3) any deferred tax.

b. Give the entry for each year to record income tax, including any deferred tax.
c. Show how the income tax liabilities would be shown on the balance sheet for each year assuming the tax is paid the following April.

E10–9. The comparative income statement for Moody Company for the years ended December 31, 19A, and 19B, reflected the following data (summarized and excluding income taxes):

	Annual income statement for	
	19A	19B
Revenues	$90,000	$94,000
Expenses	75,000	78,000
Pretax income	$15,000	$16,000

Included on the 19B income statement given above was a revenue item amounting to $6,000 that was included on the income tax return for 19A rather than in 19B. Assume an average income tax rate of 20 percent.

Required:

a. For each year, compute (1) income tax expense, (2) income tax payable, and (3) deferred tax. (Hint: Deferred tax will have a debit balance for 19A.)
b. Give the entry for each year to record income tax, including any deferred tax.
c. Show how income tax would be reported on the balance sheet each year assuming the tax is paid the following April.

E10–10. Redy Corporation reported the following income statement data (summarized):

(Relates to Exercise 10–10)

	Income statement for year ended December 31		
	19A	19B	19C
Revenues	$150,000	$150,000	$150,000
Expenses (including depreciation) . .	110,000	110,000	110,000
Pretax income	$ 40,000	$ 40,000	$ 40,000

Depreciation expense included on the income statement was computed as follows:

Machinery cost (acquired on January 1, 19A), $60,000; estimated useful life, three years, no residual value; annual depreciation (straight line) $60,000 ÷ 3 years, $20,000.

The company uses sum-of-the-years'-digits depreciation on the income tax return and has an average income tax rate of 30 percent.

Required:

a. For each year, compute (1) income tax expense for the income statement and (2) income tax payable for the tax return (show computations).
b. Give the entry for each year to record income tax including any deferred tax.
c. What kind of "tax difference" was involved? Explain.
d. What advantage was gained by using SYD depreciation on the tax return?

Exercises
Part B

E10–11. On January 1, 19A, Hypo Company, completed the following transactions (assume on 8 percent annual interest rate):

1. Deposited $10,000 in a special fund (designated Fund A).
2. Decided to establish a special fund (designated Fund B) by making six equal annual deposits of $2,000 each.

3. Decided to establish a special fund (designated Fund C) by depositing a single amount that will increase to $50,000 by the end of Year 7.
4. Decided to deposit a single sum in a special fund (designated Fund D) that will provide ten equal annual year-end payments of $10,000 to a retired employee (starting December 31, 19A).

Required (show computations and round to the nearest dollar):

a. What will be the balance of Fund A at the end of Year 9?
b. What will be the balance of Fund B at the end of Year 6 (i.e., six rents)?
c. What single amount must be deposited in Fund C on January 1, 19A?
d. What single sum must be deposited in Fund D on January 1, 19A?

E10–12. On January 1, 19A, you deposited $5,000 in a savings account. The account will earn 9 percent annual compound interest, which will be added to the fund balance at the end of each year. You recorded the deposit as follows:

Savings account	5,000	
Cash		5,000

Required:

a. What will be the balance in the savings account at the end of ten years (round to the nearest dollar)?
b. What is the time value of the money in dollars for the ten years?

c. How much interest revenue did the fund earn in 19A? 19B?

d. Give the entry to record interest revenue at the end of 19A and 19B.

E10–13. On December 31, 19A, Parent decided to deposit a single sum in a savings account that will provide $20,000 four years later to send Offspring to Super University. The savings account will earn 9 percent which will be added to the fund each year-end.

Required (show computations and round to the nearest dollar):

a. How much must Parent deposit on January 1, 19A?

b. Give the accounting entry that Parent should make on January 1, 19A.

c. What is the time value of the money for the four years?

d. Give the accounting entry Parent should make on (1) December 31, 19A, and (2) December 31, 19B.

E10–14. On each December 31, you plan to deposit $600 in savings account. The account will earn 9 percent annual interest, which will be added to the fund balance at year-end. The first deposit will be made December 31, 19A.

Required (show computations and round to the nearest dollar):

a. Give the required entry on December 31, 19A.

b. What will be the balance in the savings account at the end of the tenth year (i.e., ten deposits)?

c. What is the time value of money in dollars for the ten deposits?

d. How much interest revenue did the fund earn in 19B? 19C?

e. Give all required entries at the ends of 19B and 19C.

E10–15. You have decided to take a trip around the world upon graduation, four years from now (January 1, 19A). Your grand-

father desires to deposit sufficient funds for this purpose in a savings account for you. On the basis of a carefully drawn budget you estimate the trip now would cost $8,000. To be generous, your grandfather decided to deposit $2,200 in the fund at the end of each of the next four years. The savings account will earn 7 percent annual interest, which will be added to the savings account at each year-end.

Required (show computations and round to the nearest dollar):

a. Give the required entry on December 31, 19A.

b. What will be the balance in the fund at the end of Year 4 (i.e., four deposits)?

c. What is the time value of the money for the four years?

d. How much interest revenue would the fund earn in 19A, 19B, and 19C?

e. Give the accounting entries at the end of 19B and 19C.

E10–16. You have an opportunity to purchase the royalty interest of a land owner in an oil well. Your best estimate is that the royalty income will average $24,000 net per year for five years. There will be no residual value at that time. Assume the cash inflow is at each year-end and that, considering the uncertainty in your estimates, you expect to earn 20 percent per year on the investment.

Required:

a. What should you be willing to pay for this investment on January 1, 19A? Show computations and round to nearest dollar.

b. Give the required entry (cash paid in full) on January 1, 19A.

c. Give the required entry on December 31, 19A, assuming the net cash received was 10 percent above your estimate.

PROBLEMS

Part A

P10–1. Fate Company completed the transactions listed below during 19B. The annual accounting period ends December 31, 19B.

Jan. 8 Purchased merchandise for resale at an invoice cost of $10,000; terms, 2/10, n/60. Record at net (see Chapter 6); assume a periodic inventory system.

17 Paid invoice of January 8.

Apr. 1 Borrowed $20,000 from the National Bank for general use; executed a 12-month, 12 percent, interest-bearing note payable.

June 3 Purchased merchandise for resale at an invoice cost of $30,000; terms, 1/20, n/30; record at net.

July 5 Paid invoice of June 3.

Aug. 1 Rented two rooms in the building owned by Fate and collected six months' rent in advance amounting to $1,800. Record the collection in a way that will not require an adjusting entry at year-end.

Dec. 20 Received a $200 deposit from a customer as a guarantee to return a large trailer "borrowed" for 30 days.

31 Wages earned but not paid on December 31 amounted to $4,000 (disregard payroll taxes).

Required:

a. Prepare journal entries for each of the above transactions.

b. Prepare all adjusting entries required on December 31, 19B.

c. Show how all of the liabilities arising from the above transactions would be reported on the balance sheet at December 31, 19B.

P10–2. Owens Company completed the transactions listed below during 19A. The annual accounting period ends December 31.

May 1 Purchased an operational asset (fixtures) for $60,000; paid $20,000 cash and gave a 12-month, 15 percent, interest-bearing note payable for the balance.

June 5 Purchased an operational asset (machine) at an invoice cost of $10,000; terms, 3/10, n/60.

14 Paid invoice of June 5.

Sept. 1 Collected rent revenue on some office space rented to another company; the rent of $3,000 was for the next six months. Record the collection so as to avoid an adjusting entry at the end of 19A.

Dec. 31 Received a tax bill for property tax for 19A in the amount of $900; the taxes are payable no later than March 1, 19B.

Required:

a. Give the journal entries for each of the above transactions.

b. Prepare any adjusting entries required on December 31, 19A (exclude depreciation).

c. Show how all liabilities arising from the above transactions would be reported on the balance sheet at December 31, 19A.

P10–3. Stereo Retailers' sold a Super-set to a customer for $2,000 cash on December 30, 19A. Stereo gave the customer a one-year guarantee on the Super-set. Experience with this set by Stereo indicates that to maintain the warranty would cost approximately 5 percent of the sales price.

Assume a perpetual inventory system

and that the Super-set cost Stereo $900.

Actual cash for warranty expenditures (parts and labor) to make good the warranty on the set during 19B amounted to $95.

Required:

a. Give entry or entries required on December 30, 19A. Explain the basis for your entries. (Hint: Set up a liability.)
b. Give entry (or entries) required on December 31, 19A, end of the annual accounting period. Explain the bases for your responses.
c. Show how the income statement and balance sheet for 19A would reflect the above data.
d. Give the entry to record the repair made to the set in 19B. Discuss any issues that are evident.

P10–4. On April 1, 19A, Rye Company purchased equipment at a cost of $110,000. A cash down payment in the amount of $30,000 was made. An interest-bearing note (including a mortgage on the equipment) for $80,000 was given for the balance. The note specified 15 percent annual interest. Two payments on principal of $40,000 each plus interest on the unpaid balance on March 31, 19B, and March 31, 19C, are required. (Note: These will be unequal cash payments.)

Required:

a. Give the indicated entries on April 1, 19A, and December 31, 19A (end of the annual accounting period).
b. Show how the liabilities related to the purchase should be shown on the Rye balance sheet on December 31, 19A.
c. Give the indicated entry on March 31, 19B.

P10–5. This situation was designed to illustrate accounting for (a) an interest-bearing note payable and (b) a noninterest-bearing note payable. The annual accounting

period ends December 31 in both cases.

Assume Company T executed a note payable in favor of American Bank for a loan of cash on April 1, 19A. The loan was for 12 months with a maturity date of March 31, 19B. The bank charges a 12 percent annual rate on loans of this type. The amount of cash borrowed was $20,000. We will assume:

Case A—The note was interest bearing—that is, the principal plus the interest is payable at maturity. The face amount of note was $20,000.

Case B—The note was noninterest bearing—that is, the interest was on the cash received and was included in the face amount of the note.

Required:

a. Record the issuance of the note on April 1, 19A, under each of the two cases. Your solution can be simplified by setting up five columns: Account Titles; Case A (debit and credit), and Case B (debit and credit). Thus, the two cases can be presented in your solution in parallel columns.
b. Give the journal entry to record the adjusting entry that would be required for each case on December 31, 19A.
c. Give the entry to record payment of the note under each case at maturity, March 31, 19B; disregard any reversing entries.
d. In respect to each case show the following:
   1. Liabilities that would be reported on the balance sheet at December 31, 19A.
   2. Interest expense that would be reported on the income statements for 19A and 19B (separately).

P10–6. Foster Company is in the process of preparing comparative statements at December 31, 19B. The records reflect the following summarized income statement data, exclusive of income tax expense:

	19A	19B
Revenues	$150,000	$160,000
Expenses	(110,000)	(129,000)
Extraordinary item	(10,000)	4,000
Income before income tax	$ 30,000	$ 35,000

Included in the 19B revenues of $160,000 is an item of revenue amount-

(Relates to Problem 10–7)

1. Revenues $150,000
2. Expenses (including $13,000 depreciation expense) 113,000
3. Depreciation expense was computed as follows for income statement purposes:
   Operational asset cost (acquired January 1, 19A) 52,000
   Four-year useful life (no residual value).
   Depreciation expense per year $52,000 ÷ 4 years 13,000
4. Extraordinary loss 10,000
5. The revenues given in 1 include $3,000 interest on tax-free municipal bonds.
6. Assume an average income tax rate of 20 percent on both ordinary income and extraordinary income.
7. Sum-of-the-years'-digits depreciation on the operational asset will be used on the income tax return and straight line on the income statement.

ing to $10,000 that was required to be included on the income tax return for 19A rather than 19B. Also included in the 19B expenses of $129,000 was an item of expense amounting to $6,000 that had to be deducted on the income tax return for 19A rather than 19B. Assume an average 20 percent income tax rate. Assume there were no deferred taxes in the extraordinary items.

Required:

a. For each year, compute (1) income tax expense, (2) income tax liability, and (3) deferred tax.
b. Give the entry for each year to record income tax expense, including any deferred taxes.
c. Restate the above comparative income statement, including the appropriate presentation of income tax for each year. (Hint: Allocate income tax

expense between operations and extraordinary items.)
d. What kind of "tax difference" was represented by the two items? Explain.

P10–7. At December 31, 19A, the records of XY Corporation provided the following pretax information:

Required:

a. Compute income tax expense.
b. Compute income tax on the tax return.
c. Give the entry to record income tax including any deferred tax.
d. Prepare a single-step income statement.
e. What kind of "tax differences" were involved? Explain the basis for your treatment of them.

Problems
Part B

P10–8. On January 1, 19A, Illustrative Company completed the following transactions (assume a 10 percent annual interest rate):

1. Deposited $20,000 in a special debt retirement fund. Interest will be com-

puted at six-month intervals and added to the fund at those times (i.e., semiannual compounding). (Hint: Think carefully about n and i.)

2. Decided to establish a plant addition fund of $150,000 to be available at the end of Year 5. A single sum will be deposited on January 1, 19A, that will grow to the $150,000.

3. Decided to establish a pension retirement fund of $500,000 by the end of Year 6 by making six equal annual deposits each at year-end, starting on December 31, 19A.

4. Decided to purchase a $100,000 machine on January 1, 19A, and pay cash, $25,000. A three-year note payable is signed for the balance. The note will be paid in three equal year-end payments starting on December 31, 19A.

Required (show computations and round to the nearest dollar):

a. In transaction 1 above, what will be the balance in the fund at the end of Year 4? What is the total amount of interest revenue earned?

b. In transaction 2 above, what single sum amount must the company deposit on January 1, 19A? What is the total amount of interest revenue earned?

c. In transaction 3 above, what is the required amount of each of the six equal annual deposits? What is the total amount of interest revenue earned?

d. In transaction 4 above, what is the amount of each of the equal annual payments that must be paid on the note? What is the total amount of interest expense?

P10–9. Biggie Company has decided to build another plant during 19C which they estimate will cost $800,000. At the present time, January 1, 19A, they have excess cash, some of which they may decide to set aside in a special savings

account to defray $600,000 of the plant cost. The savings account would earn 8 percent annual interest which would be credited to the savings account each year-end.

Required (show computations and round to the nearest dollar):

a. What single amount would have to be deposited in the savings account on January 1, 19A, to create the desired amount by the end of 19C?

b. What will be the time value of the money by the end of 19C?

c. How much interest revenue will be earned each year?

d. Give the following entries:
   1. Interest earned at each year-end.
   2. Use of the fund to pay on the plant (completed December 31, 19C).

P10–10. On January 1, 19A, X Construction Company signed a construction contract with Y Company. X Company was required to deposit with an independent trustee $50,000 cash as a performance guarantee on a construction project. The trustee agreed to pay 7 percent annual interest on the fund and to add it to the fund balance at each year-end. At the end of the third year, the construction project was completed satisfactorily and the trustee returned the balance of the fund to X Construction Company. The entry by X Construction Company to record the deposit was as follows:

Performance fund .   50,000
    Cash   50,000

Required (show computations and round to the nearest dollar):

a. What was the balance of the fund at the end of the three years?

b. What was the time value of the money for the three years?

c. How much interest revenue did the fund earn each year?

d. Give the following accounting entries for X Construction Company:

1. To record interest revenue at each year-end.
2. To record receipt of the fund balance at the end of 19C.

P10–11. On January 1, 19A, the management of Moses Company agreed to set aside a special fund in order to provide sufficient cash to pay off the principal amount of a $55,000 long-term debt which will be due at the end of five years. The single deposit will be made with an independent party (a bank), which will pay 8 percent annual interest on the fund balance. The interest will be added to the fund balance at each year-end.

Required (show computations and round to the nearest dollar):

a. How much must be deposited as a single sum on January 1, 19A, to satisfy the agreement?
b. What was the time value of the money in dollars for the five years?
c. How much interest revenue would the fund earn in 19A? 19B?
d. Give accounting entries for the following for Moses Company:
   1. To record the deposit on January 1, 19A.
   2. To record the interest revenue for 19A and 19B (separately).
   3. To record payment of the maturing liability at the end of the fifth year.

P10–12. On December 31, 19A, the management of Moe Company agreed to set aside, in a special fund, sufficient cash to pay the principal amount of a $50,000 debt which will be due on December 31, 19D. Moe Company will make four equal annual deposits on each December 31, 19A, 19B, 19C, and 19D. The fund balance will earn 7 percent annual interest, which will be added to the balance of the fund at each year-end. The fund trustee will pay the loan principal (to the creditor) upon receipt of the last fund deposit.

Required (show computations and round to the nearest dollar):

a. How much must be deposited each December 31? (Hint: Use Table 10–3 and divide instead of multiply.)
b. What will be the time value of the money in dollars for the fund?
c. How much interest revenue will the fund earn in 19A, 19B, 19C, and 19D?
d. Give accounting entries for the following for Moe Company:
   1. For the first deposit on December 31, 19A.
   2. For all amounts at the ends of 19B and 19C.
   3. For payment of the debt on December 31, 19D.

P10–13. On January 1, 19A, W Company sold to Z Company a new machine for $40,000. A cash down payment of $10,000 was made by Z Company. A $30,000, 12 percent note was signed by Z Company for the balance due. The note is to be paid off in three equal installments due on December 31, 19A, 19B, and 19C. Each payment is to include principal plus interest on the unpaid balance. The sale was recorded by Z as follows:

January 1, 19A:

Machine	40,000	
Cash		10,000
Note payable		30,000

Required (show computations and round to the nearest dollar):

a. What is the amount of the equal annual payment that must be made by Z Company? (Hint: Use Table 10–4 and divide instead of multiply.)
b. What was the time value of the money, in dollars, on the note?
c. Complete the following debt payment schedule:

(Relates to Problem 10–13)

Date	Cash Payment	Interest Expense	Reduction of Principal	Unpaid Principal
1/1/19A				
12/31/19A				
12/31/19B				
12/31/19C				
Total				

d. Give the entries for each of the three payments.

e. Explain why interest expense decreased in amount each year.

P10–14. On January 1, 19A, you purchased a new Super-Whiz automobile for $15,000. You paid a $5,000 cash down payment and signed a $10,000 note, payable in four equal installments on each December 31, the first payment to be made on December 31, 19A. The interest rate is 14 percent per year on the unpaid balance. Each payment will include payment on principal plus the interest.

Required:

a. Compute the amount of the equal payments that you must make (Hint: Use Table 10–4 and divide.)

b. What is the time value of the money in dollars for the installment debt?

c. Complete a schedule using the format below.

(Relates to Problem 10–14)

DEBT PAYMENT SCHEDULE

Date	Cash Payment	Interest Expense	Reduction of Principal	Unpaid Principal
1/1/A				
12/31/A				
12/31/B				
12/31/C				
12/31/D				
Total				

d. Explain why the amount of interest expense decreases each year.

e. Give the payment entries on December 31, 19A, and 19B.

P10–15. (Based on Appendix A) Tappen Company has completed the salary and wage payroll for March 19A. Details provided by the payroll were:

Salaries and wages earned $200,000*
Employee income taxes withheld 42,000
Union dues withheld 2,000
Insurance premiums withheld 900

FICA tax rate, 6%.
FUTA tax rate, 0.7%.
State unemployment tax rate, 2.7% (based on same amount of wages as FUTA taxes).
* Subject in full to payroll taxes.

Required:

a. Give the entry to record the payroll for March, including employee deductions. Show computations.

b. Give the entry to record the employer's payroll taxes.

c. Give a combined entry to reflect remittance of amounts owed to governmental agencies and other organizations.

d. What was the total labor cost for Tappen Company? Explain. What percent of the payroll was take-home pay? Explain.

P10–16. (Based on Appendix B) Holt Company uses a voucher system to attain control of expenditures. The following transactions have been selected from December 19B for case purposes. The accounting year ends December 31.

You are to design a voucher register and a check register similar to those shown in Appendix B. The transactions to follow will be entered in these two special journals.

Dec. 2 Purchased merchandise from AB Wholesalers for resale, $2,000; terms, 2/10, n/30; record purchases at net and assume a periodic inventory system (see Chapter 6); Invoice No. 14; start with Voucher No. 11.

7 Approved contract with Ace Plumbing Company for repair of plumbing, $450; account, Building Repairs, No. 77.

11 Paid Voucher No. 11; start with Check No. 51.

22 Purchased store supplies for future use from Crown Company; Invoice No. 21 for $90; account, Store Supplies Inventory, No. 16.

23 Advertising for pre-Christmas sale $630; bill received from Daily Press and payment processed immediately;

account, Advertising Expense, No. 54.

31 Monthly payroll voucher, total $2,500; $1,500 was selling expense (Sales Salaries, No. 52) and $1,000 was administrative expense (Administrative Salaries, No. 62). The voucher was supported by the payroll record; therefore, one voucher was prepared for the entire payroll. The voucher was approved for immediate payment. Six checks with consecutive numbers were issued.

Required:

a. Enter the above transactions in the voucher register and the check register.

b. Total the special journals and check the equality of the debits and credits. Set up T-accounts and post both registers. Complete all posting notations. The following accounts may be needed:

Account titles	Account No.
Cash	01
Store supplies inventory	16
Vouchers payable	30
Purchases	40
Selling expense control	50
Subsidiary ledger:	
Sales salaries	52
Advertising expense	54
Administrative expense control	60
Subsidiary ledger:	
Administrative salaries	62
Building repairs	77

c. Reconcile the Vouchers Payable account balance with the Unpaid Vouchers File at the end of December.

Measuring and reporting bonds payable

PURPOSE OF THE CHAPTER

The sale (and issuance) of bonds is a primary way of obtaining resources for long-term growth and expansion by businesses, nonprofit organizations (such as colleges), and public subdivisions (such as municipalities and water districts). Bonds are long-term debt instruments. When bonds are sold, they become an investment to the buyer and an obligation of the issuer. Accounting for bonds is complex because of the wide range of characteristics they possess. To be efficient in decision making, both the issuing entity and the investor need to understand the characteristics of bonds and their varying economic effects. Accounting seeks to measure and report these economic effects.

Because of the special characteristics of bonds and the related accounting complexities, bonds were deferred for separate consideration. The purposes of this chapter are to discuss the characteristics of bonds payable and to explain the accounting approaches used to measure, record, and report their economic impact. To provide flexibility the chapter is divided into two parts:

Part A: Fundamentals of measuring, recording, and reporting bonds payable

Part B: Some complexities in accounting for bonds payable

Behavioral and learning objectives for this chapter are provided in the *Teacher's Manual*

PART A: FUNDAMENTALS OF MEASURING, RECORDING, AND REPORTING BONDS PAYABLE

CHARACTERISTICS OF BONDS PAYABLE

Funds required for long-term purposes, such as the acquisition of high-cost machinery or the construction of a new plant, often are obtained by issuing long-term notes payable (discussed in Chapter 10) or bonds payable. Bonds payable represent a long-term liability and may be secured by a mortgage on specified assets. Bonds commonly are issued in denominations of $1,000 or $10,000 and, occasionally, in denominations of $100,000. They usually are negotiable (i.e., transferable by endorsement) and are bought and sold daily by investors. The bonds of most leading companies are quoted on the security exchanges.[1] Two typical bond certificates are shown in Exhibit 11–1.

The **principal** of a bond is the amount payable at the maturity or due date as specified on the bond certificate. This amount also is called its **par value,** maturity value, or its **face amount.** Throughout the life of a bond, the issuing company makes periodic interest payments, usually semi-annually, to the bondholders.

EXHIBIT 11–1
Two typical bond certificates

---

[1] In addition to bonds that are issued by corporations, bonds also are issued by governmental units, such as federal and state governments, cities, counties, school districts, water districts, and by nonprofit institutions. The discussions in this chapter apply to both types, although we will focus mainly on those issued by corporations.

Exhibit 11–1
(*continued*)

A company desiring to sell a **bond issue** must draw up a **bond indenture,** which specifies the legal provisions of the bonds, such as due date, rate of interest to be paid, date of each interest payment, and any conversion privileges (explained later). When a bond is sold, the investor receives a **bond certificate** (i.e., a bond). All of the bond certificates for a single bond issue are identical in that there is specified on the face of each certificate the same maturity date, interest rate, interest dates, and the other provisions. Usually when a company issues bonds, an **underwriter** is engaged to sell them to the public. A third party, called the **trustee,** usually is appointed to represent the bondholders. The duties of an independent trustee are to ascertain that the issuing company fulfills all of the provisions of the bond indenture.

CLASSIFICATION OF BONDS

Bonds may be classified in a number of different ways, depending upon their characteristics. The usual classifications are:

1. On the basis of the underlying security:
   a. **Unsecured bonds**—bonds that do not include a mortgage or pledge of specific assets as a guarantee of repayment at maturity date. These often are called **debentures.**
   b. **Secured bonds**—bonds that include a mortgage or a pledge of specific assets as a guarantee of repayment. Secured bonds tend to be designated on the basis of the type of assets pledged, such as real estate mortgage bonds and equipment trust bonds.
2. On the basis of repayment of principal:
   a. **Ordinary or single-payment bonds**—the principal is payable in full at a single specified maturity date in the future.
   b. **Serial bonds**—the principal is payable in installments on a series of specific dates in the future.
3. On the basis of early retirement:
   a. **Callable bonds**—bonds that may be called for early retirement at the option of the *issuer.*
   b. **Redeemable bonds**—bonds that may be turned in for early retirement at the option of the *bondholder.*
   c. **Convertible bonds**—bonds that may be converted to other securities of the issuer (usually common stock) after a specified date in the future at the option of the *bondholder.*
4. On the basis of payment of interest:
   a. **Registered bonds**—the name and address of the owner must be currently on file (registered) with the issuing company. Payment of interest is made by check, which is mailed only to the person shown in the bond register.
   b. **Coupon bonds**—bonds to which a printed coupon is attached for each interest payment throughout the life of the bond. When an interest date approaches, the bondholder "clips" the coupon, signs it, and mails it to the issuing company. In turn, an interest check is sent to the person and address shown on the completed coupon. Coupon bonds are used widely.

ADVANTAGES OF ISSUING BONDS

To obtain large amounts of funds for long-term use, the advantages of issuing bonds instead of capital stock stem from the fact that the bondholders are **creditors** and not owners, as are stockholders. A bondholder does not share in the management, the accumulated earnings, or the growth in assets, as does the shareholder. Payments of resources to bondholders are limited to (1) the amount of interest specified on the bond and (2) the principal or face amount of the bond at maturity. Depending upon the circumstances, the rate of interest paid to bondholders may be more or less than the dividend rate paid to shareholders.

Using borrowed assets (i.e., assets acquired with funds obtained from creditors) to enhance the return to the owners' equity is called **financial leverage.** When leverage is positive, an important financial advantage to the shareholders occurs. Leverage is positive when the net aftertax interest rate on borrowed funds is less than the aftertax rate of return earned by the company on total assets.

To illustrate, assume X Corporation earned a 15 percent return (after income tax) on total assets (i.e., income, $75,000 ÷ total assets, $500,000 = 0.15) and that the aftertax interest on total debt was 5.4 percent (i.e., aftertax interest expense, $10,800 ÷ total debt, $200,000 = 0.054). There was positive financial leverage in this situation because the creditors provided assets of $200,000 for 5.4 percent interest and the company is earning 15 percent on those (and the other) assets. Since the only return paid to the creditors is 5.4 percent interest, the difference between 15 percent and 5.4 percent (of the $200,000) increases net income, which in turn accrues to the long-term benefit of the company and, therefore, to the shareholders. Exhibit 11–2 presents two comparative cases for X Corporation to illustrate the cause and economic effects of financial leverage. Case A assumes that the company has total assets of $500,000, all of which was provided by shareholders (i.e., it has no debt). In contrast, Case B assumes that of the total amount of assets, $300,000, was provided by shareholders and the remaining $200,000 was provided by creditors (i.e., debt). For illustrative purposes the other variables are held constant in order to demonstrate the cause and economic effects of using debt to help finance a business.

Observe in Exhibit 11–2, Case A, that return on total assets and return on stockholders' equity are the same (15 percent) because there was no debt. The obvious result would be no financial leverage because it is caused only by debt. In contrast, in Case B, the $200,000 of debt caused return on stockholders' equity (21 percent) to be higher than the return on total assets (15 percent); thus there was positive financial leverage, which is measured as the difference (i.e., 21% − 15% = 6%). This illustration demonstrates that financial leverage is caused by the existence of debt and that the economic effect of financial leverage can be measured. Financial leverage will be positive when the overall earnings rate of the company exceeds the average interest rate on debt; if the opposite is the case, negative financial leverage will exist. The significance of the economic effect of financial leverage depends upon (1) the difference between the aftertax interest rate and the earnings rate on total assets and (2) the relative amount of total assets provided by creditors.

EXHIBIT 11–2
Effects of financial leverage

X CORPORATION

Case A: No debt		Case B: Debt, $200,000 @ 9 Percent	
Balance sheet:			
Total assets	$500,000		$500,000
Total debt (9%)	–0–		200,000
Stockholders' equity, par $10	$500,000		$300,000
Income statement:			
Revenues	$300,000		$300,000
Operating expenses	(175,000)		(175,000)
Income tax (40%)	(50,000)		(50,000)
Interest expense		$200,000 × 0.09%	
(net of income tax)	–0–	× (1.00 – 0.40)	(10,800)
Net income	$ 75,000		$ 64,200
Analysis:			
a. Return on total assets		[($64,200 + $10,800)	
($75,000 ÷ $500,000)	15%	÷ $500,000]*	15%
b. Return on stockholders'			
equity ($75,000 ÷			
$500,000)	15%	($64,200 ÷ $300,000)	21%
c. Financial leverage			
([b] – [a])†	0		6%
d. EPS ($75,000 ÷ 10,000			
shares)	$7.50	($64,200 ÷ 6,000 shares)	$10.70

* Interest on debt, net of income tax, is added back to derive total return to all fund providers (also see Chapter 15).
† Also see discussion of financial leverage in Chapter 15.

Dividends normally are paid to stockholders only if earnings are satisfactory. In contrast, interest payments to bondholders legally must be paid each period, regardless of whether the corporation earns income or incurs a loss. This "fixed charge" to expense each period is a distinct disadvantage of bonds; however, there is an important compensating factor for the issuing company. Interest expense is *deductible* on the income tax return of the issuer, whereas dividends paid to stockholders are not deductible for tax purposes. This fact reduces significantly the net cost of funds acquired by issuing bonds. For example, a corporation with an average income tax rate of 40 percent and interest of 9 percent per annum on bonds payable would incur a **net interest cost** on the bonds of 9% × (1.00 – 0.40) = 5.4%. Despite the advantages of financial leverage, sound financing of a large business requires a realistic *balance* between the amounts of debt (including bonds payable) and owners' equity (i.e., common and preferred stock and retained earnings). For example, in Case A, there was no debt, which is the most conservative position. In Case B, the $200,000 of debt was 40 percent of total assets employed (not an unusual situation). However, if X Corporation had $400,000 debt, the 80 percent debt to total assets would be considered too high in most situations.

MEASURING BONDS PAYABLE AND BOND INTEREST EXPENSE

The accounting approach used in measuring, recording, and reporting bonds payable is determined primarily by the **cost** and **matching principles.** When a bond is issued (i.e., sold), the issue price (or proceeds) is the net cash received, plus the market value of any noncash resources received. Under the cost principle, bonds payable are recorded at their issue price, that is, at their **current cash equivalent amount.** Subsequent to issuance, the bonds usually are measured and reported at the **present value** of their future cash flows. This amount will change from period to period if the bonds were issued at a discount or at a premium.

Bonds may be sold at **par;** that is, at the face or maturity amount (these are alternative terms for the same amount). If sold above par, they are said to have been issued at a **premium.** If sold below par, they are said to have been issued at a **discount.** To illustrate, if the issuing corporation received $1,000 cash for a bond with a $1,000 face, maturity, or par value, there would be no premium or discount. Alternatively, if the corporation received $967 for the bond, there would be a discount of $33; or if $1,035 cash were received, there would be a premium of $35. Typically, bond prices are quoted on the security exchanges as a percent of par or face amount. A bond quoted at 100 sells at par; if quoted at 96.7, it sells at a discount of 3.3 percent below its face amount; if quoted at 103.5, it sells at a premium of 3.5 percent above its face amount.

Interest rates on bonds

A bond specifies an **annual** rate of interest based on the par value (face or maturity amount) of the bond. This rate is called variously the **stated, coupon, nominal,** or **contract rate.** The annual interest usually is specified to be paid on a semiannual basis; thus, an 8 percent bond of $1,000 par value will pay semiannual **cash** interest of 4 percent or $40 (i.e., $1,000 × 0.04 = $40) each six months regardless of whether the bond sold at par value, a discount, or a premium. The stated or coupon rate is set by the issuing company to approximate the market rate of interest when the bond issue is authorized. It is printed on each bond certificate and does not change over the term of the bonds.

The stated or coupon rate establishes the fixed amount of cash interest that will be paid each interest period over the entire life of the bond; however, bonds sell at a market rate of interest which often is different from the stated or coupon rate. Whether a bond sells at par, at a discount, or at a premium is determined by the forces of supply and demand in the capital markets. The **market rate** of interest on a bond is the rate that borrowers (issuers) are willing to pay and lenders (investors) are willing to accept on their money taking into consideration the perceived level of risk involved. Market rates tend to fluctuate from day to day. The market rate of interest also is called the yield, effective, or real rate.

When the market and stated (or coupon) rates of interest are the same, a bond will sell at its par value. When the market rate for a bond is higher than the stated rate, the bond will sell at a discount; and when the market rate is lower than the stated rate, a bond will sell at a premium.

When a bond is issued at a discount, the issuer receives less cash than is paid at maturity date. When a bond is issued at a premium, the issuer receives more cash than is paid at maturity. The difference between the market and stated rates of interest on a bond causes a different cash flow on issue date than on maturity date. Recall that the specified cash flow for interest on each interest payment date is not changed by the issue price of a bond.

Each period bond interest is measured, recorded, and reported in conformance with the **matching principle.** Since interest is incurred on the basis of passage of time, at the end of each period the amount of interest unpaid must be accrued and reported as expense so that it will be matched with the revenues in the period in which it was incurred. The measurement and reporting of interest already has been discussed in respect to both notes receivable and notes payable. When bonds are issued at a premium or discount, however, an additional measurement problem arises because these affect both the **price of the bond and the amount of interest expense.** This measurement problem is discussed subsequently.

In the discussions to follow, we will utilize a common set of illustrative data for Mason Corporation. Assume the board of directors and the shareholders of the corporation approved a bond issue with the following provisions:

Bonds payable authorized ($1,000 per bond) $500,000
Date on each bond .... January 1, 1981.
Maturity in ten years, on December 31, 1990.
Interest, 8% per annum, payable 4 percent each six months on
   June 30 and December 31.
Mason Corporation, end of the annual accounting period:
   December 31.

Using the above data, we will discuss and illustrate three different assumed situations in which the bonds are sold (1) at par, (2) at a discount, and (3) at a premium.

Bonds sold at par

Bonds sell at their par value when buyers (investors) are willing to invest in them at the **stated interest rate** on the bond. To illustrate, assume that on January 1, 1981, Mason Corporation issued $400,000 of the bonds payable and received $400,000 in cash for them. The bonds were dated to start interest on January 1, 1981. The entry by Mason Corporation to record the issuance of the bonds would be:

January 1, 1981:

```
Cash ................................................... 400,000
    Bonds payable ......................................              400,000
    Sold $400,000, 8 percent, ten-year bonds payable at par.
```

Subsequent to the sale of the bonds, interest at 4 percent on the face amount of the bonds must be paid each June 30 and December 31 until maturity. The entries to record the interest payments during 1981 would be as follows:

June 30, 1981:

```
Bond interest expense .................................. 16,000
    Cash                                                            16,000
    Paid semiannual interest on bonds payable ($400,000 × 0.04
    = $16,000).
```

December 31, 1981:

```
Bond interest expense .................................. 16,000
    Cash ...............................................             16,000
    Paid semiannual interest on bonds payable ($400,000 × 0.04
    = $16,000).
```

At the end of the accounting period, December 31, 1981, the financial statements would report the following:

```
Income statement:
    Bond interest
        expense ...........................  $ 32,000

Balance sheet:
    Long-term liabilities:
        Bonds payable,
        8% (due December 31, 1990) ..........  400,000
```

In this situation, Mason Corporation received $1,000 cash for *each* $1,000 bond sold and will pay back $1,000, principal + ($40 × 20, semiannual interest payments) = $1,800. The $800 difference is the amount of interest expense for the ten years; therefore, the interest cost was $80 per year and the *yield or effective rate of interest* was $80 ÷ $1,000 = 8 percent per year. The *stated* or *coupon rate* called for on the bond also was 8 percent.

Bonds sold at a discount

Bonds sell at a discount when the buyers (investors) are willing to invest in them only at a yield or market rate of interest that is *higher* than the stated or coupon interest rate on the bonds. To illustrate, assume the capital market established an 8½ percent market rate of interest for the ten-year Mason bonds (stated rate 8 percent, payable semiannual basis), which means the bonds would sell at a discount. At an 8½ percent market (yield or effective) rate, how much cash would a $1,000 bond of Mason Company command if sold on January 1, 1981? To compute the cash issue (sale) price of one bond requires computation of the present value at the market rate, of the **two** future cash flows specified in the bond: *(a)* the principal ($n = 20$, $i = 4¼\%$) and *(b)* the cash interest paid each semiannual interest period ($n = 20$, $i = 4¼\%$). Thus, the cash issue (sale) price of one Mason bond would be computed as follows (refer to Chapter 10, Part B):

	Present value
a. Principal: $1,000 \times p_{n=20;\ i=4\,1/4\%}$ (Table 10–2, 0.4350) =	$435
b. Interest: $40 \times P_{n=20;\ i=4\,1/4\%}$ (Table 10–4, 13.2944) =	532
Issue (sale) price of one Mason bond	$967

When a bond is sold at a discount (i.e., $33 in the above example), the Bonds Payable account is credited for the face or maturity amount and the discount is recorded as a debit to Discount on Bonds Payable. To illustrate, the issuance of 400 of the bonds of Mason Company at a cash sale price of $967 per bond (i.e., an 8½ percent market rate) would be recorded as follows:

January 1, 1981:

Cash (400 bonds × $967)	386,800	
Discount on bonds payable (400 × $33)	13,200*	
Bonds payable (400 × $1,000)		400,000*

Sold $400,000, 8 percent, ten-year bonds payable at 96.7 (i.e., 96.7% × $400,000 = $386,800).

* Note: In effect, the bonds are recorded at their issue price because the liability will be reported on the balance sheet net of these two balances.

In the above entry the amount of the discount was recorded in a separate contra account (Discount on Bonds Payable) as a **debit** because it must be accorded special treatment in the income statement (in measuring interest expense) and on the balance sheet, which reports the bonds payable at their carrying value (maturity amount less any unamortized discount).

Measuring and recording interest expense

The computation and related entry given above indicate that each of the 8 percent Mason bonds issued at an 8½ percent market rate commanded $967 cash and sold at a discount of $33 (i.e., $1,000 — $967). During the ten-year term of the bonds Mason must make 20 semiannual interest payments of $40 each (i.e., $40 × 20 = $800 total interest) and at maturity must pay back the $1,000 cash principal. Therefore, in addition to the cash interest of $800, $33 more cash per bond is paid back than was borrowed. This $33 discount causes the yield or effective rate to be 8½ percent (instead of the 8 percent stated on the bonds). It is an **adjustment** of the amount of interest expense which will be **reported** each period on the income statement. Bond discount, in the economic sense, represents an increase in **bond interest expense.** To give accounting effect to bond discount in periods subsequent to issuance, the $13,200 debit to Discount on Bonds Payable (in the above entry), must be apportioned to each semiannual interest period as an increase in bond interest expense from the date of issuance to maturity date. There are two different methods for doing this: (1) **straight-line amortization** and (2) **effective-interest amortization.** Straight-line amortization is easy to understand and compute; however, it is conceptually deficient. Effective-interest amortization requires use of the future and present value concepts (discussed in Part B of Chapter 10). The effective-interest method is required; however, it or the straight-line method may be used when the difference between the two results is not material in amount each year. Although the difference appears material for Mason Company, to introduce the subject we will use straight-line amortization because it is easy to follow. The more complex **effective-interest method** will be presented in Part B of this chapter.

Straight-line amortization. To amortize the $13,200 bond discount over the period from date of issuance to maturity date on a straight-line basis, an equal dollar amount is allocated to each interest period. Since there are 20 six-month interest periods, the computation would be: $13,200 ÷ 20 periods = $660 amortization on each semiannual interest date. Therefore, the payments of interest on the bonds during 1981 would be recorded as follows:[2]

---

[2] The amount of interest expense recorded each semiannual period may be confirmed as follows:

Cash to be paid out by the borrower:	
Face amount of the bonds—payable at maturity	$400,000
Interest payments ($16,000 × 20 semiannual payments)	320,000
Total cash payments	720,000
Cash received by the borrower	386,800
Total interest expense over ten years	$333,200
Interest expense per semiannual period ($333,200 ÷ 20 periods)	$ 16,660

June 30, 1981:

Bond interest expense......................................	16,660	
Discount on bonds payable ($13,200 ÷ 20)		660
Cash ($400,000 × 0.04).................................		16,000
Payment of semiannual interest on bonds payable and amortization of bond discount for six months.		

December 31, 1981:

Bond interest expense......................................	16,660	
Discount on bonds payable		660
Cash..		16,000
Payment of semiannual interest on bonds payable and amortization of bond discount for six months.		

In accordance with the thrust of *APB Opinion No. 21,* "Interest on Receivables and Payables," bonds payable should be measured and reported on the balance sheet at their *net liability amount,* that is, the maturity amount less any unamortized bond discount or plus any unamortized bond premium. Therefore, at the end of the accounting period, December 31, 1981, the financial statements would report the following:

Income statement:
Bond interest expense ($16,660 × 2) .... $ 33,320

Balance sheet:
Long-term liabilities:
Bonds payable, 8%, due December 31, 1990 .... $400,000
Less unamortized discount 11,800* $388,120

Or, alternatively:

Bonds payable, 8%, due December 31, 1990
(maturity amount, $400,000, less unamortized
discount) .... $388,120†

* $13,200 − $660 − $660 = $11,880.
† This is called the net liability.

Each succeeding year the unamortized discount will *decrease* by $1,320, and as a consequence, the net liability will *increase* each year by $1,320. At the maturity date of the bonds, the unamortized discount (i.e., the balance in the Discount on Bonds Payable account) will be zero. At that time the maturity or face amount of the bonds and the current net liability amount will be the same — $400,000. Amortization of bond discount and premium is shown graphically in Exhibit 11–3.

Bonds sold at a premium

Bonds sell at a premium when the buyers (investors) are willing to invest in them at a market or yield rate of interest that is **lower** than the stated or coupon interest rate on the bonds. To illustrate, assume the capital market established a 7½ percent market rate of interest for the ten-year Mason bonds (stated rate, 8 percent, payable on semiannual basis), which means the bonds would sell at a premium. Computation of the cash issue (sale) price of one Mason bond would be computed as follows (refer to Chapter 10, Part B):

		Present value
a. Principal: $1,000 \times p_{n=20;\ i=3\ 3/4\%}$ (Table 10–2, 0.4789)	=	$ 479
b. Interest: $40 \times P_{n=20;\ i=3\ 3/4\%}$ (Table 10–2, 13.8962)	=	556
Issue (sale) price of one Mason bond		$1,035

When a bond is sold at a premium ($35 in the above example), the Bonds Payable account is credited for the face amount and the premium is recorded as a credit to Premium on Bonds Payable. To illustrate, the issuance of 400 of the bonds of Mason Company at a cash sale price of $1,035 each (i.e., at a 7½ percent market rate) would be recorded as follows:

January 1, 1981:

Cash (400 bonds × $1,035)	414,000	
Premium on bonds payable (400 × $35)		14,000
Bonds payable (400 × $1,000)		400,000
Sold $400,000, 8 percent, ten-year bonds payable at 103.5		
(i.e., 103.5% × $400,000 = $414,000).		

The premium of $14,000 must be apportioned to each of the 20 interest periods. The effective-interest method usually must be used to make the allocation; however, the straight-line method may be used if the results are not different materially from the other method. For illustrative purposes the straight-line method is used because of its simplicity. The amortization of premium each semiannual interest period would be: $14,000 ÷ 20 periods = $700. Therefore, the payments of interest on the bonds during 1981 would be recorded as follows:[3]

---

[3] The amount of interest expense recorded each semiannual period may be confirmed as follows:

Cash paid out by the borrower:	
Face amount of bonds at maturity	$400,000
Interest payments ($16,000 × 20 periods)	320,000
Total cash payments	720,000
Cash received by the borrower	414,000
Total interest expense over ten years	$306,000
Interest expense per semiannual period	
($306,000 ÷ 20 periods)	$ 15,300

June 30, 1981:

Bond interest expense....................................	15,300	
Premium on bonds payable..............................	700	
Cash..		16,000
To record payment of interest for six months ($400,000 × 0.04 = $16,000) and to amortize bond premium for six months ($14,000 ÷ 20 periods = $700).		

December 31, 1981:

Bond interest expense....................................	15,300	
Premium on bonds payable..............................	700	
Cash..		16,000
To record payment of interest for six months and to amortize bond premium for six months as computed above.		

In the entry to record the sale of the bonds, the premium was recorded in a separate account, Premium on Bonds Payable, as a *credit*. The premium has the effect of *decreasing* interest expense; therefore, in each period a portion of it is amortized to interest expense. Observe that in the above illustration Bond Interest Expense is reduced by $700 each semiannual period since straight-line amortization was assumed. At the end of 1981, the financial statements will reflect the following:

Income statement:		
Bond interest expense ($15,300 × 2)		$ 30,600
Balance sheet:		
Long-term liabilities:		
Bonds payable, 8% (due December 31, 1990)	$400,000	
Add unamortized premium	12,600*	412,600
Or, alternatively:		
Bonds payable, 8%, due December 31, 1990 (maturity amount, $400,000, plus unamortized premium)		412,600†

  * $14,000 − $700 − $700 = $12,600.
  † This is called the net liability.

At maturity date, after the last interest payment, the bond premium of $14,000 will be amortized fully and the maturity or face amount and the current net liability for the bonds will be the same—$400,000. At maturity, December 31, 1990, the bonds will be paid off, resulting in the same entry whether originally sold at par, a discount, or a premium, viz:

December 31, 1990:

Bonds payable   400,000
    Cash   400,000
    To retire the 8% bonds payable at maturity date.

The discussions and illustrations in this part of the chapter have focused on the fundamental issues in measuring and reporting bonds payable. This part has provided the background essential to understanding the economic impact of bonds payable on the issuing company and its reporting on the periodic financial statements. The next part discusses some complexities often encountered in accounting for bonds payable.

The effect of amortization of bond discount and bond premium on a $1,000 bond, sold at a premium, at par, and at a discount is shown graphically in Exhibit 11–3.

PART B: SOME COMPLEXITIES IN ACCOUNTING FOR BONDS PAYABLE

This part of the chapter focuses primarily on three complexities commonly encountered in accounting for bonds payable because important

EXHIBIT 11–3
Amortization of bond premium and discount

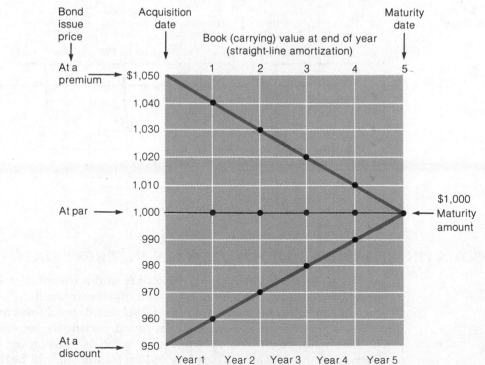

dates related to a bond issue often are not the same as the date of issuance of some or all of the bond certificates or the ending date of the accounting period. Bonds sold between interest dates, adjusting entries for accrued bond interest, and effective interest amortization are discussed and illustrated. Also treated is a related issue—bond sinking funds.

As a basis for the discussions to follow, we will utilize a common set of data for Mendez Corporation. Assume that the following bond issue was approved:

Bonds payable authorized ($1,000 per bond) $200,000
Date on each bond .... June 1, 1981

Maturity in ten years on May 31, 1991.
Interest, 12% per annum, payable 6% each May 31 and November 30.

Additional data:
   Mendez Corporation: End of the annual accounting period, December 31.
   Bonds issued: $100,000 (half of the amount authorized) sold August 1, 1981, for $96,460.

In order to focus on the effect of different dates on the accounting for a bond issue, the bond time scale shown in Exhibit 11–4 may be helpful.

EXHIBIT 11–4
Bond time scale

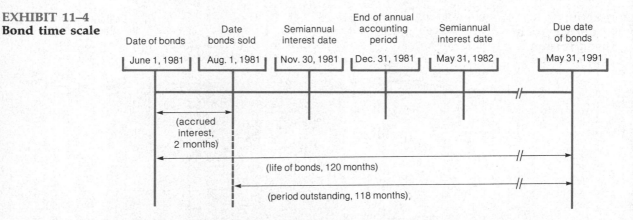

ACCOUNTING FOR BONDS SOLD BETWEEN INTEREST DATES

The bond certificates specify the **date** and **amount** of each cash interest payment. Although bonds may be sold on an interest date, generally market factors cause them to be sold *between* interest dates. Nevertheless, the exact amount of interest specified on the bond certificate for each interest date will be paid, regardless of whether a bond is sold on an interest date or between interest dates. Therefore, when bonds are sold **between** two interest dates, the investor (i.e., the buyer) must **pay the accrued interest since the last interest date** in addition to the market price of the bond. Because the amount of the next interest payment will be for a **full** interest period, the accrued interest then is effectively returned to the buyer. The net effect is that the investor will realize interest revenue only for the number of months the bonds were held by the investor from the date of sale. Similarly, the issuing corporation will incur interest expense for the same period. This situation presents two complexities in accounting for bonds: (1) the amount of accrued interest charged to the buyer must be included in the entry of the issuer to record the sale of bonds; and (2) any premium or discount is amortized by the issuer over the remaining **period outstanding**—that is, the period from date of sale to date of maturity of the bonds.

To illustrate, the above data for Mendez Corporation assume that $100,000 of the bonds (i.e., 100 bonds) were sold for $96,460 (i.e., issued at a discount of $3,540) on August 1, 1981, which was **two** months after the date of the bonds.

On August 1, 1981, date of the sale of the 100 bonds, Mendez Corporation would receive cash for the sales price of the bonds, *plus* two months accrued interest (June 1, 1981, to July 31, 1981), computed as follows (refer to the bond time scale above):

Market price (for 100 bonds)	$96,460
Add accrued interest for 2 months:	
$100,000 × 12% × 2/12	2,000
Total cash received	$98,460

The entry by the issuer, Mendez Corporation, to record the issuance of the 100 bonds payable would be as follows:

August 1, 1981:

Cash (per above)	98,460	
Discount on bonds payable ($100,000 − $96,460)	3,540	
Bonds payable		100,000
Bond interest expense (per above)		2,000
Sale of bonds two months after interest date for $96,460 plus accrued interest ($100,000 × 0.12 × 2/12 = $2,000).		

In this entry, Bond Interest Expense was credited because the $2,000 accrued interest collected will be refunded to the investor when the next interest payment is made. That payment will be recorded as a credit to Cash and a debit to Bond Interest Expense, which is illustrated below.

The $3,540 recorded in the Discount on Bonds Payable account is amortized over the *period outstanding* of 118 months; therefore, straight-line amortization would be \$3,540 ÷ 118 months = \$30 per month. The entry to record the following interest payment would include amortization of discount only for the four months that the bonds have been outstanding. Therefore, the next interest payment would be recorded as follows:

November 30, 1981

Bond interest expense	6,120	
Discount on bonds payable (\$30 × 4 months)		120
Cash (\$100,000 × 0.06)		6,000
Payment of bond interest for six months and amortization of discount for four months.		

After the two preceding entries are posted, the Bond Interest Expense account would reflect a debit balance of \$4,120, which is equivalent to four months' interest (\$100,000 × 12% × 4/12 = \$4,000) plus four months' discount amortization (\$30 × 4 = \$120) = \$4,120, viz:

Bond Interest Expense

11/30/81	6,120	8/1/81	2,000

(Balance, 11/30/81, \$4,120)

ADJUSTING ENTRY FOR ACCRUED BOND INTEREST

To account for notes payable, recall that at the end of each accounting period, an **adjusting entry** must be made for any interest expense accrued since the last interest payment date. The same adjustment procedure must be applied to bonds payable. However, in the case of bonds, the adjusting entry must include **both** the accrued interest and amortization of any bond discount or premium. To illustrate for 1981 for Mendez Corporation, recall that the last interest payment date was November 30, 1981; therefore, on December 31, 1981, there is accrued interest for one month. Bond discount also must be amortized for one more month. The adjusting entry would be:

December 31, 1981:

Bond interest expense	1,030	
Discount on bonds payable		30
Bond interest payable		1,000
Adjusting entry to record bond interest payable for one month, \$100,000 × 12% × 1/12 = \$1,000, and to amortize bond discount for one month, \$30.		

After this entry is posted on December 31, 1981, the Bond Interest Expense account will reflect a debit balance of $5,150, which represents interest expense for the five months that the bonds have been outstanding during 1981 (August 1 to December 31). Prior to closing, the account would appear as follows:

Bond Interest Expense

11/30/81	6,120	8/1/81	2,000
12/31/81	1,030		

(Balance 12/31/81, $5,150)

The ending balance may be verified in this way:

Interest: $100,000 × 12% × 5/12	$5,000
Add discount amortized: $30 × 5	150
Total interest expense for 1981	$5,150

This amount is closed to Income Summary and will be reported on the income statement for 1981 as "Bond interest expense."

BOND SINKING FUND

On the maturity date of bonds payable, the issuing company must have available a large amount of cash to pay off the bondholders. Such a large cash demand might place the issuing company in a severe financial strain. In order to avoid this situation, some companies build up a separate **cash fund** in advance by making equal annual contributions over a period of time in advance of the bond maturity date. Such a separate cash fund customarily is known as a **bond sinking fund.** A bond sinking fund is an asset that is invested pending the due date; it is reported on the balance sheet under the caption "Investments and funds."

A bond sinking fund also adds a measure of security for the bondholders since it assures them that funds will be available for retirement of the bonds at maturity date. Each cash contribution (rent) usually is deposited with an independent trustee, a designated third party such as a bank or another financial institution. The trustee invests the funds received and adds the stipulated earnings to the fund each year. Interest earned on a sinking fund is recorded as an increase in the fund balance (a debit) and as interest revenue (a credit). Thus, a bond sinking fund typically has the characteristics of a regular savings account such as was illustrated in Chapter 10, Part B. At the maturity date of the bonds, the balance of the fund is used to pay off the bondholders. Any excess is returned to the issuing corporation, or, in the case of a deficit, it must be made up by the issuer.

To illustrate a bond sinking fund, assume Mendez Corporation, in order to have the cash needed to pay off the $100,000 bonds payable due May

31, 1991, decided to set up a bond sinking fund. The fund will be built up over the last five years that the bonds are outstanding by making five equal annual deposits each May 31, starting in 1987. The sinking fund contributions will be deposited with City Bank, as trustee, which will pay 8 percent annual interest on the fund balance each May 31. The amount of each deposit required was calculated to be $17,046. This was based on the time value of money concepts discussed and illustrated in Chapter 10, Part B. If the fund earned no interest, obviously each deposit would have to be $100,000 ÷ 5 contributions = $20,000. Instead of $20,000, the annual deposit required is $17,046 because the interest earned each year will be added to the fund balance. The required annual deposit was computed as follows:

Situation:
Future amount needed $100,000
Period of accumulation; equal annual contributions . . . .   5 rents
Assumed interest earnings rate on the fund balance . . . .   8% per year
Computation (application of future value of annuity of $1):
Future value = Periodic rent × $F_{n=5; i=8\%}$
Substituting:
$100,000 =   ?   × 5.8666 (Table 10–3)
Periodic rent = $100,000 ÷ 5.8666
            = $ 17,046

The entries for May 31, 1987, and 1988 to be made by Mendez Corporation for this sinking fund would be:[4]

May 31, 1987 (first deposit):

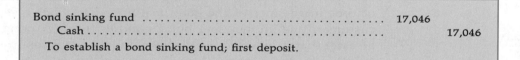

Bond sinking fund 17,046
    Cash   17,046
    To establish a bond sinking fund; first deposit.

May 31, 1988 (interest added to the fund):

Bond sinking fund 1,364
    Interest revenue   1,364
    To record sinking fund earnings during first year ($17,046 × 0.08
    = $1,364).

---

[4] In connection with such funds, a company also may restrict, or appropriate, an equivalent amount of retained earnings as a dividend restriction. The restriction of retained earnings by a corporation is discussed in Chapter 12.

May 31, 1988 (second deposit):

Bond sinking fund 17,046	
Cash	17,046
To record second deposit in bond sinking fund.	

Identical entries with different interest amounts, because of the increasing balance in the fund, would be made for each of the five years of the accumulation period. At maturity date of the bonds, the following entry would be made upon payment to the bondholders:

At maturity date:

Bonds payable 100,000	
Bond sinking fund	100,000
To record payment of bonds payable at maturity from the bond sinking fund.	

Often it is useful to develop a fund accumulation schedule as shown in Exhibit 11–5. Observe that the schedule provides data for (1) the entry on each interest date and (2) the build-up of the fund to maturity date.

EXHIBIT 11–5

FUND ACCUMULATION SCHEDULE

Date	Cash Deposit	Interest Revenue	Increase in Fund Balance	Fund Balance
5/31/87	17,046 [a]		17,046	17,046
5/31/88	17,046	17,046 × 0.08 = 1,364 [b]	18,410 [c]	35,456 [d]
5/31/89	17,046	35,456 × 0.08 = 2,836	19,882	55,338
5/31/90	17,046	55,338 × 0.08 = 4,427	21,473	76,811
5/31/91	17,046	76,811 × 0.08 = 6,143*	23,189	100,000
Totals	85,230	14,770	100,000	

* Rounded $2 to accommodate prior rounding errors.
[a] Computed on page 490.
[b] Interest earned on beginning balance in the fund each period at 8 percent.
[c] Period deposit ($17,046) plus interest earned ($1,364) = $18,410 (etc.).
[d] Prior balance ($17,046) plus increase in fund ($18,410) = $35,456 (etc.).

EFFECTIVE-INTEREST AMORTIZATION ON BONDS PAYABLE

Effective-interest amortization of bond discount or bond premium is the only conceptually sound approach for measuring both (1) the effective-interest expense on bonds and (2) the carrying amount of the bonds (at the current net liability amount). It uses the concept of present value discussed in Chapter 10, Part B.

APB Opinion No. 21, "Interest on Receivables and Payables," requires this approach for amortization of bond discount or premium. However, the straight-line approach is permitted when the difference in amortization results is not material in amount. Conceptually, the effective-interest method is similar to the debt reduction when one purchases an automobile on installment payment basis and equal monthly payments are made on the debt. Each equal payment made on the debt consists of two parts: (1) a payment of principal and (2) a payment of interest (see page 448).

Now let's see how this concept applies to the amortization of discount or premium on **bonds payable,** which also is a debt. A simplified case is used to illustrate this concept and the related entries. Assume the following facts:

EIA Corporation Case:

a. Bonds payable authorized ($1,000 per bond) $10,000
b. Date printed on each bond . . . . January 1, 19A
c. Maturity date (five-year term) . . . . .December 31, 19E
d. Interest, payable per annum each December 31 . . . . 8%
e. End of the accounting period . . . . December 31
f. Issued (sold) all of the bonds on January 1, 19A,
   market interest rate. 12%
g. Sales price (at a discount) $8,558
   Computations:

   $10,000 \times p_{n=5; \ i=12\%}$ (Table 10–2 = 0.5674) = $5,674
   $800 \times P_{n=5; \ i=12\%}$ (Table 10–4 = 3.6048)   = 2,884
   $\overline{\$8,558}$

h. Entry to record issuance:

> Cash 8,558
> Discount on bonds payable 1,442
>   Bonds payable, 8% 10,000
>
> Note: Instead of recording the discount separately, Bonds Payable could have been credited for the gross amount, $8,558. In either case, the $1,442 discount would be amortized and the results would be the same.

Required:

Give the entry to record each of the five interest payments assuming effective-interest amortization.

Case Solution:

The amounts for each of the five interest entries must be computed uniquely. An organized computation approach would be the construction of a bond (debt) payment schedule for the bonds (refer to page 449) because it will provide automatically the amortization and interest expense amounts for each interest period. In contrast to an installment debt (where equal periodic payments are made that include both interest and principal), a bond payment schedule reflects only the periodic cash interest payments because all of the principal is paid at maturity. The bond payment schedule for this case would be as shown in Exhibit 11–6.

EXHIBIT 11–6

BOND PAYMENT SCHEDULE

(a) Date	(b) Cash interest paid on each interest date	(c) Interest expense (based on beginning unpaid liability at market rate)	(d) Effective-interest amortization (increase of liability)	(e) Net liability (unpaid balance)
1/1/19A				8,558
12/31/19A	800	8,558 × 0.12 = 1,027	227	8,785
12/31/19B	800	8,785 × 0.12 = 1,054	254	9,039
12/31/19C	800	9,039 × 0.12 = 1,085	285	9,324
12/31/19D	800	9,324 × 0.12 = 1,119	319	9,643
12/31/19E	800	9,643 × 0.12 = 1,157	357	10,000
Subtotal	4,000		5,442	1,442
12/31/19E	10,000†		10,000	-0-

* Adjusts the net liability to the maturity amount.
† Payment of principal.

Straight-line amortization of the premium each period for EIA Corporation would be $288 (i.e., $1,442 ÷ 5). In contrast, effective interest amortization would be a different amount each period as reflected in Exhibit 11–6, column (d). This column reflects the change in the **net liability amount** each period (which is increased to the maturity amount at the end of the last period, immediately before payment of the principal). Thus, the $1,442 discount is amortized by a different amount each period. Since the interest computation each period in the schedule (column [c]) is based on the increasing unpaid net liability (column[e]) at the market rate of interest, the amortization method is appropriately called effective-interest amortization. The interest entry on each of the five interest dates would be taken directly from the schedule as follows:

	19A	19B	19C	19D	19E
Bond interest expense	1027	1,054	1,085	1,119	1,157
Discount on bonds payable	227	254	285	319	357
Cash	800	800	800	800	800

The entry to retire the entire bond issue would be:

December 31, 19E:

Bonds payable	10,000	
Cash		10,000

The financial statements of EIA Corporation would reflect the following at each year-end (refer to the bond payment schedule):

	19A	19B	19C	19D	19E
Income statement:					
Bond interest expense	$1,027	$1,054	$1,085	$1,119	$1,157
Balance Sheet:					
Bonds payable (maturity amount $10,000) minus unamortized discount	8,785	9,039	9,324	9,643	-0-

The underlying effective-interest concept of the measurement of interest expense is indicated on the income statement above; the dollar amount of interest expense changes each year. Had straight-line amortization been used, interest expense would have been a constant dollar amount each year. The underlying concept of the measurement of the **current net liability amount** of the debit is reflected as an increasing amount when there is a discount (a decreasing amount when there is a premium), on the balance sheet from the issue price to the maturity amount of the bonds at maturity date.

To summarize, effective-interest amortization conceptually is superior to straight-line amortization because, for each period, consistent with the issue price of the bonds, it measures (1) the true amount of interest expense each period on the income statement and (2) the true current net carrying amount of the bonds outstanding (net liability) on the balance sheet each period. Straight-line amortization provides approximations of these amounts and can be used only when the difference between the two methods is deemed not material (refer to exception principle, materiality). In such situations, straight-line amortization is used because it is less complex.

DEMONSTRATION CASE

Reed Company, Inc.

(Try to resolve the requirements before proceeding to the suggested solution that follows.)

In order to raise funds to construct a new plant, the management of Reed Company, Inc., decided to issue bonds. Accordingly, a proposed bond indenture was submitted to the board of directors and approved. The provisions in the bond indenture and specified on the bond certificates were:

Face value of bonds to be issued ($1,000 bonds) $600,000

Date of bond issue—February 1, 1981, due in ten years on
January 31, 1991.

Interest—10% per annum, payable 5% on each July
31 and January 31.

The bonds were sold on June 1, 1981, at 102½ plus accrued interest. The annual accounting period for Reed Company, Inc., ends on December 31.

Required:

a. How much cash was received by Reed Company, Inc., from the sale of the bonds payable on June 1, 1981? Show computations.

b. What was the amount of premium on the bonds payable? Over how many months should it be amortized?

c. Compute the amount of amortization of premium per month and for each six-month interest period; use straight-line amortization. Round to the nearest dollar.

d. Give entry on June 1, 1981, to record the sale and issuance of the bonds payable.

e. Give entry for payment of interest and amortization of premium for the first interest payment on July 31, 1981.

f. Give adjusting entry required on December 31, 1981, at the end of the accounting period.

g. Give the optional reversing entry that could be made on January 1, 1982.

h. Give entry to record second interest payment and amortization of premium on January 31, 1982.

i. Show how bond interest expense and bonds payable would be reported on the financial statements at December 31, 1981.

Suggested solution:

Requirement (a):

Sales price of the bonds: ($600,000 × 102.5%)	$615,000
Add accrued interest for four months (February 1 to May 31) ($600,000 × 10% × 4/12)	20,000
Total cash received for the bonds	$635,000

Requirement (b):

Premium on the bonds payable ($600,000 × 2.5%)	$ 15,000
Months amortized: From date of sale, June 1, 1981, to maturity date, January 31, 1991. 120 months − 4 months = ...	116 months

Requirement (c):

Premium amortization: $15,000 ÷ 116 months = $129 per month, or $774 each six-month interest period (straight line).

Requirement (d):

June 1, 1981:

Cash (per Req. [a] above).................................	635,000	
Premium on bonds payable (per Req. [b] above).........		15,000
Interest expense (per Req. [a] above)...................		20,000
Bonds payable		600,000

To record sale of bonds payable at 102½ plus accrued interest for four months, February 1 to May 31, 1981.

Requirement (e):

July 31, 1981:

Bond interest expense....................................	29,742	
Premium on bonds payable ($129 × 2 months)	258	
Cash ($600,000 × 5%).................................		30,000

To record payment of semiannual interest and to amortize premium for two months, June 1 to July 31, 1981.

Requirement (f):

December 31, 1981:

Bond interest expense....................................	24,355	
Premium on bonds payable ($129 × 5 months)	645	
Bond interest payable ($600,000 × 10% × 5/12)		25,000

Adjusting entry for five months' interest accrued plus amortization of premium, August 1 to December 31, 1981.

Requirement (g):

January 1, 1982:

Bond interest payable	25,000	
Premium on bonds payable		645
Bond interest expense		24,355

Reversing entry; optional.

Requirement (h):

January 31, 1982 (assuming reversing entry [g] was made):[5]

Bond interest expense....................................	29,226	
Premium on bonds payable (per Req. [c])....................	774	
Cash ($600,000 × 10% × 6/12)...........................		30,000
To record payment of semiannual interest and to amortize premium for 6 months.		

Requirement (i):

Interest expense to be reported on the 1981 income statement should be for the period outstanding during the year (i.e., for seven months, June 1 through December 31). Interest expense, per the above entries, is $29,742 + $24,355 − $20,000 = $34,097; or, alternatively, ($600,000 × 10% × 7/12 = $35,000) minus ($129 × 7 months = $903) = $34,097.

Income statement for 1981:		
Interest expense		$34,097
Balance sheet, December 31, 1981:		
Long-term liabilities:		
Bonds payable, 10% (due January 31, 1991)	$600,000	
Add unamortized premium*	14,097	614,097
* $15,000 − ($258 + $645) = $14,097.		

SUMMARY

This chapter discussed bonds payable, the issuance of which is one of the primary ways to obtain funds to acquire long-term assets and to expand the business. An important advantage of bonds payable is that the cost of the funds—interest expense—is deductible for income tax purposes. This reduces the interest cost to the business. Bonds are measured and reported at their current cash equivalent amount.

Bonds may be sold at their face, or par, amount; at a premium; or at a discount, depending upon the stated interest rate on the bonds compared with the market (or yield) rate of interest that the bond buyers demand and the issuer will accept. The price of a bond varies **inversely** with the relationship between the market and stated rates of interest. If the market rate is higher than the stated rate on the bond, the bonds will sell at a

---

[5] If no reversing entry was made on January 1, 1982, this entry would be:

Bond interest payable	25,000	
Premium on bonds payable	129	
Bond interest expense	4,871	
Cash		30,000

discount. Conversely, if the market rate is lower than the stated rate on the bond, the bonds will sell at a premium.

Discount and premium on bonds payable are adjustments of the **cash** interest payments made by the issuing company during the term of the bonds. As a consequence, discount or premium on bonds payable is amortized to interest expense over the *outstanding* life of the bonds (i.e., from issue date to maturity date).

To retire bonds payable at maturity, a company may set aside cash in advance by means of equal periodic contributions to a bond sinking fund. Such a fund is similar to a savings account. The bond sinking fund normally is administered by an independent third party, such as a bank (called the trustee). Interest earned on the fund balance is added to the fund each period. At the maturity date of the bonds, the fund is used to pay off the bondholders. Such a fund is reported on the balance sheet under the caption "Investments and funds." Interest earned on the fund is reported on the income statement as "Interest revenue."

IMPORTANT TERMS DEFINED IN THE CHAPTER (with page citations)

Bonds payable—472
Bond principal (par value, face amount)—472
Par value (bonds)—472, 477, 478
Bond indenture—473
Bond certificate—472, 473
Trustee—473
Registered bonds—474
Coupon bonds—474
Unsecured and secured bonds—477
Ordinary and serial bonds—474
Callable bonds—474
Redeemable bonds—474
Convertible bonds—474

Financial leverage—475, 476
Net interest cost—476
Bond premium—477, 482
Bond discount—477, 480
Bond stated (coupon) rate—477
Bond price—478, 480, 483
Amortization of bond discount—481
Straight-line amortization—481
Effective-interest amortization—481, 491
Bond time scale—486
Period outstanding (bonds)—487
Accrued bond interest—487, 488
Bond sinking fund—489

QUESTIONS FOR DISCUSSION

Part A

1. What is a bond? For what purpose are bonds usually issued?

2. What is the difference between the bond indenture and the bond certificates?

3. Distinguish between secured and unsecured bonds.

4. Distinguish among callable, redeemable, and convertible bonds.

5. Distinguish between registered and coupon bonds.

6. What are some advantages to the issuer in raising funds by the issuance of bonds, as compared with issuing capital stock?

7. The higher the tax bracket, the lower the net cost of borrowing money. Explain.

8. Briefly explain financial leverage.

9. At date of issuance, bonds are recorded at their current cash equivalent amount. Explain.

10. What is the nature of discount and premium on bonds payable?

11. What is the difference between the stated interest rate and the effective interest rate on a bond?

12. Distinguish between the stated and effective rates of interest on a bond (a) sold at par, (b) sold at a discount; and (c) sold at a premium.

Questions
Part B

13. Why is bond discount (and premium) amortized over the outstanding life of the bonds payable rather than the period from the date of the bonds to their maturity date?

14. In respect to bonds payable, what is meant by "current net liability"?

15. Why is the lender (i.e., the purchaser of a bond) charged for the accrued interest from the last interest date to date of purchase of the bonds?

16. What is a bond sinking fund? How should a bond sinking fund be reported in the financial statements?

17. Explain the basic difference between straight-line amortization and effective-interest amortization of bond discount or premium. Explain when each should, or may, be used.

EXERCISES

Part A

E11–1. Lemons, Inc., borrowed $60,000 on a three-year note payable. The interest rate is 12 percent per annum, payable each year. The company computed its return on total assets [i.e., Net income ÷ (Liabilities + Owners' equity)] to be 20 percent. The average tax rate for the company is 40 percent.

Required:

a. What amount of interest would be paid the first year?
b. Considering the effect of income tax, what would be the net interest cost and the net interest rate?
c. Would financial leverage be present in this situation? Explain.
d. List two advantages to Lemons in favor of the note payable versus selling more of its unissued capital stock.

E11–2. Hypo Corporation is planning to issue $100,000, five-year, 8 percent bonds. Interest is payable semiannually each June 30 and December 31. Assume all of the bonds will be sold on January 1, 19A, and that they will mature on December 31, 19E.

Required (round to the nearest dollar):

a. Compute the issue (sale) price on January 1, 19A, for each of the following three cases (show computations).

Case A—The market (yield) rate is 8 percent.
Case B—The market (yield) rate is 6 percent.
Case C—The market (yield) rate is 10 percent.

b. Give the entry to record the issuance for each case.

E11–3. John Corporation had $200,000, ten-year, coupon bonds outstanding on December 31, 19A (end of the accounting period). Interest is payable each June 30 and December 31. The bonds were sold and issued on January 1, 19A. The 19A annual financial statements reflected the following:

Income statement:
Bond interest expense
(straight-line amortization) . . . . $ 18,600

Balance sheet:
Bonds payable (net liability)   194,600

Required (show computations):

a. What was the issue price of the bonds?

b. What was the coupon rate on the bonds?

c. Prepare computations which will indicate whether the above amounts of (1) interest expense and (2) bonds payable (net liability) are correct.

E11–4. The summarized information below was taken from the 19B annual financial statements of two competing companies in the same industry (assume 50,000 shares of common stock outstanding):

	Thousands of dollars	
	Company A	Company B
Balance sheet:		
Total assets	$900	$900
Total liabilities (10% interest)	400	600
Income statement:		
Total revenues	480	421
Total expenses (including income tax)	300	400
Tax rate	40%	20%

Required:

a. Complete a tabulation similar to the following (show computations):

Item	Company A	Company B
Earnings per share		
Return on stockholders' equity		
Return on total assets		
Financial leverage		

b. Interpret and compare the financial leverage figures for the two companies.

E11–5. Adams, Incorporated, sold a $150,000, 8 percent bond issue on January 1, 19A, for $140,372 (9% market rate). The bonds were dated January 1, 19A, and pay interest each December 31. The bonds mature ten years from January 1, 19A.

Required:

a. Give the entry to record the issuance of the bonds.

b. Give the entry to record the interest payment on December 31, 19A. Assume straight-line amortization.

c. Show how the bond interest expense and the bonds payable should be reported on the December 31, 19A, annual financial statements.

d. Verify the sales price of $140,372 (show computations).

E11–6. XY Company, Inc., sold a $60,000, 8 percent bond issue on January 1, 19A, for $64,211 (at a market rate of 7 percent). The bonds were dated January 1, 19A, and interest is paid each December 31. The bonds mature ten years from January 1, 19A.

Required:

a. Give the entry to record the issuance of the bonds.

b. Give the entry for the interest payment on December 31, 19A. Assume straight-line amortization.

c. Show how the bond interest expense and the bonds payable should be reported on the December 31, 19A, annual financial statements.

d. Verify the issue (sale) price of $64,211 (show computations).

E11–7. In order to obtain cash for a purchase of operational assets, Day Corporation, whose annual accounting period ends on December 31, issued the following bonds:

Date of bonds: January 1, 19A.

Maturity amount and date: $100,000, due in ten years (December 31, 19J).

Interest: 9 percent per annum payable each December 31.

Date sold: January 1, 19A.

Required:

a. Give the entry to record the issuance and the first two interest payments under each of three different assumptions (assume straight-line amortization):
   1. The bonds sold at par.
   2. The bonds sold at 96.
   3. The bonds sold at 104.
b. Provide the following amounts to be reported on the financial statements at the end of 19A:

(Relates to Exercise 11–7)

	Assumption 1	Assumption 2	Assumption 3
1. Interest expense	$	$	$
2. Bonds payable			
3. Unamortized premium or discount			
4. Net liability			
5. Stated rate of interest			
6. Cash interest paid			

c. Explain why items 1 and 6 are different in Requirement (b).

Exercises
Part B

E11–8. PB Corporation authorized the issuance of $300,000, 9 percent, ten-year bonds. The date printed on the bond certificates is January 1, 19A, and the interest is payable each June 30 and December 31.

On September 1, 19A, the company issued (sold) $200,000 of the bonds at 96 plus any accrued interest.

Required:

a. How much cash did PB Corporation receive on September 1, 19A? Show computations.
b. Give the entry to record the issuance.
c. How much net cash interest did PB

Corporation pay during 19A on the $200,000 issuance? Show computations.

E11–9. White Corporation issued the following bonds:

Bonds payable authorized	$60,000
Date on each bond	Jan. 1, 19A
Maturity date (ten years)	Dec. 31. 19J
Interest, 10% per year, payable each December 31.	

White sold all of the bonds on March 1, 19A, and received $61,180 cash plus any accrued interest.

Required:

a. What was the amount of discount or premium?
b. Over what period of time should the discount or premium be amortized?
c. What would be the amortization amount per month assuming straight-line amortization?
d. Give the entry to record the issuance.
e. Give the entry on first interest payment date.
f. What amount should be reported as interest expense for 19A?
g. What amount of net liability should be shown on the balance sheet at December 31, 19A?

E11–10. WT Corporation issued $10,000, 9 percent bonds dated April 1, 19A. Interest is paid each March 31. The bonds mature in 3 years on March 31, 19D. The bonds were sold on June 1, 19A, for $9,660 plus accrued interest. The accounting period ends each December 31.

Required:

a. Give the entry to record the issuance on June 1, 19A.
b. Give the adjusting entry required on December 31, 19A; use straight-line amortization.
c. What amount of interest expense should be reported on the income statement for 19A?
d. What amount of net liability should be reported on the balance sheet at December 31, 19A?
e. Give the entry to record the first interest payment on March 31, 19B.

E11–11. Smith Corporation has a $50,000 bond issue outstanding that is due four years hence. It desires to set up a bond sinking fund for this amount by making five equal annual contributions. The first contribution will be made immediately and the last one on the due date (i.e., an ordinary annuity). The corporation will deposit the contributions with a bank as trustee, which will increase the fund at the end of each year for 8 percent on the fund balance that existed at the beginning of the year.

Required:

a. Compute the annual contribution (rent) to the fund.
b. Give the entry for the first and second contributions, including interest.
c. Show how the effects of the fund would be reported on the financial statements at the end of the second year.

E11–12. Small Company has a $90,000 debt that will be due three years hence. The management has decided to deposit three equal year-end amounts of $27,723 in a debt retirement fund (i.e., an ordinary annuity). The fund balance will earn 8 percent interest which will be added to the fund at each year-end.

Required:

a. Prepare a fund accumulation schedule similar to Exhibit 11–5. Round to the nearest dollar and show computations.
b. Give the entry(s) at the end of the second year to record the increase in the fund.
c. Show how the $27,723 was computed.

E11–13. Fluger Corporation issued a $1,000 bond on January 1, 19A. The bond specified an interest rate of 8 percent payable at the end of each year. The bond matures at the end of 19C. It was sold at a market rate of 9 percent per year. In respect to the issuance of the bond, the following schedule was completed:

Date	Cash	Interest	Amortization	Balance
January 1, 19A (issuance)				$ 975
End of Year A ..	$80	$88	$8	983
End of Year B ..	80	88	8	991
End of Year C ..	80	89	9	1,000

Required:

Respond to the following questions:

a. What was the issue price of the bond? What were the coupon and yield rates of interest?
b. Did the bond sell at a discount or a premium? How much?
c. What amount of cash was paid each year for bond interest?
d. What amount of interest expense should be shown each year on the income statement?
e. What amount(s) should be shown on the balance sheet for bonds payable at each year-end (for Year C, show the balance just before retirement of the bond)?
f. What method of amortization was used?

g. Show how the following amounts were computed for Year B: (1) $80, (2) $88, (3) $8, and (4) $983.

h. Is the method of amortization used preferable? Explain why.

E11–14. Toten Company issued a $10,000, 11 percent, three-year bond on January 1, 19A. The bond interest is paid each De-

cember 31. The bond was sold to yield 10 percent (issue price, $10,249).

Required:

a. Complete a bond payment schedule similar to Exhibit 11–6.

b. Give the interest and amortization entry at the end of 19B.

c. Show how the $10,249 issue price was computed.

PROBLEMS

Part A

P11–1. The financial statements of WT Corporation for 19A reflected the following:

Income Statement

Revenues	$200,000
Expenses	(139,000)
Interest expense	(1,000)
Pretax income	60,000
Income taxes (40%)	(24,000)
Net income	$ 36,000

Balance Sheet

Assets	$150,000
Liabilities (average interest rate, 10%)	$ 10,000
Common stock, par $10	100,000
Retained earnings	40,000
	$150,000

To demonstrate leverage, assume that WT Corporation during 19A had $60,000 liabilities (instead of $10,000) and common stock of $50,000 (5,000 shares) instead of $100,000 (10,000 shares). That is, they financed the business more with debt.

Required:

a. Complete a table similar to the following to demonstrate the economic effects of financial leverage.

(Relates to Problem 11–1)

Item	Actual results for 19A	Results assuming an increase in debt of $50,000
a. Total debt		
b. Total assets		
c. Total stockholders' equity		
d. Interest expense (total @ 10%)		
e. Net income		
f. Return on total assets		
g. Earnings available to stockholders:		
1. Amount		
2. Per share		
3. Return on stockholders' equity		

b. Write an explanation of the advantages and disadvantages of higher debt financing (i.e., higher leverage) in this particular situation.

P11–2. On January 1, 19A, XY Corporation sold and issued $100,000, 8 percent, five-year bonds. The bond interest is payable annually each December 31. Assume the bonds were sold under three separate and independent cases: Case A, at par; Case B, at 95; and Case C, at 105.

Required:

a. Complete a tabulation similar to the following for each separate case assuming straight-line amortization of discount and premium. Disregard income tax.

b. For each separate case, respond to each of the following:

1. Total pretax cash outflow
2. Total pretax cash inflow
3. Difference—net pretax cash outflow
4. Total pretax interest expense

c. 1. As among the three cases, explain why the net pretax cash outflows are different.
   2. For each case, explain why the net pretax cash outflow is the same amount as total interest expense.

P11–3. Assume a $200,000, 8 percent bond issue was sold on January 1, 19A. The bonds pay interest each December 31, and will mature ten years from January 1, 19A. For comparative study and analysis, as-

(Relates to Problem 11–2)

	At Start of 19A	At End of 19A	At End of 19B	At End of 19C	At End of 19D	At End of 19E Prior to Payment of Principal	At End of 19E Payment of Principal
Case A—Sold at par (100): Pretax cash inflow	$	$	$	$	$	$	$
Pretax cash outflow							
Interest expense on income statement							
Net liability on balance sheet							
Case B—Sold at a discount (95): Pretax cash inflow							
Pretax cash outflow							
Interest expense on income statement							
Net liability on balance sheet							
Case C—Sold at a premium (105): Pretax cash inflow							
Pretax cash outflow							
Interest expense on income statement							
Net liability on balance sheet							

sume the three separate cases (show computations, assume straight-line amortization, and disregard income tax):

Case A—The bonds sold at par.

Case B—The bonds sold at 97.

Case C—The bonds sold at 103.

(Relates to Problem 11–3)

	Case A	Case B	Case C
1. Cash inflow at issue date	_____	_____	_____
2. Total cash outflow through maturity	_____	_____	_____
3. Difference—total interest expense	_____	_____	_____
Income statement for 19A:			
4. Bond interest expense, pretax	══════	══════	══════
Balance sheet at December 31, 19A:			
Long-term liabilities:			
5. Bonds payable, 8%	_____	_____	_____
6. Unamortized discount	_____	_____	_____
7. Unamortized premium	_____	_____	_____
8. Net liability	══════	══════	══════
9. Stated interest rate	_____	_____	_____
10. Total interest expense, net-of-tax (40% tax rate)	_____	_____	_____

Required:

a. Complete a schedule similar to the one outlined above.

b. Give the entries for each case on January 1, 19A, and December 31, 19A (exclude closing entries).

c. Explain why items 3, 4, and 10 of Requirement *(a)* are the same, or different, as the case may be.

P11–4. Ward Company issued bonds with the following provisions:

Maturity value: $300,000.
Interest: 11% per annum payable semiannually each June 30 and December 31.
Terms: Bonds dated January 1, 19A, due five years from that date.

The annual accounting period for Ward ends December 31. The bonds were sold on January 1, 19A, at a 10 percent market rate.

Required:

a. Compute the issue price of the bonds (show computations).

b. Give the journal entry to record issuance of the bonds

c. Give the journal entries at the following dates (assume straight-line amortization): June 30, 19A; December 31, 19A; and June 30, 19B.

d. How much interest expense should be reported on the income statement for 19A? Show how liabilities relating to the bonds would be reported on the December 31, 19A, balance sheet.

P11–5. May Company issued $75,000 bonds, due in five years, at 7 percent interest. The bonds were dated January 1, 19A, and interest is payable each June 30 and December 31.

The bonds were sold on January 1, 19A, to yield 8 percent interest The annual accounting period ends December 31.

Required:

a. Compute the issue (sale) price of the bonds (show computations).

b. Give the entry to record the issuance of the bonds on January 1, 19A.

c. Give the entry to record the first interest payment and amortization of discount on June 30, 19A. Assume straight-line amortization.

d. Give the amounts that should be reported on the 19A financial statements for:

Interest expense.
Bonds payable.
Unamortized discount or premium.
Net liability.

e. What would be the aftertax net interest cost for 19A (dollars and percent) assuming a 30 percent tax rate? Show computations.

Problems
Part B

P11–6. RT Corporation authorized the following bond issue:

Bonds payable authorized
($1,000 bonds) $100,000
Date printed on each bond . . . . Jan. 1, 19A
Maturity date (ten years) . . . . Dec. 31, 19J
Interest, 9% per year, payable
each June 30 and
December 31.

During 19A, RT Corporation issued (sold) the following bonds:

Date	Issuance (sale)		Market price (does not include any accrued interest)
Jan. 1, 19A	#1 . .	10 bonds	100
May 1, 19A	#2 . .	20 bonds	94
Sept. 1, 19A	#3 . .	30 bonds	106

Required:

a. Complete a schedule for RT Corporation similar to the following (show computations, round to the nearest dollar, and disregard income tax):

	Cash received			Cash disbursed		
Date	#1	#2	#3	#1	#2	#3
Jan. 1, 19A						
May 1, 19A						
June 30, 19A						
Sept. 1, 19A						
Dec. 31, 19A						

b. Give a separate entry to record each of the three issuances.

c. How much net cash interest was paid during 19A to the investors in each of the three issuances? Show computations.

P11–7. Suber Corporation authorized a $300,-000, ten-year bond issue dated July 1, 19A. The bonds pay 8 percent interest each June 30. The accounting period ends December 31. Assume the bonds were sold on August 1, 19A, under three different assumptions as follows:

Case A—Sold at par.
Case B—Sold at 98.
Case C—Sold at 102.

Required:

Complete a schedule for Suber Corporation similar to the following assuming straight-line amortization. Show computations.

(Relates to Problem 11–7)

	Case A par	Case B 98	Case C 102
1. Cash received at issuance (sale) date	$ _____	$ _____	$ _____
2. Cash received for interest at issuance date	_____	_____	_____
3. Amount of premium or discount at issuance date	_____	_____	_____
4. Stated rate of interest (annual)	_____ %	_____ %	_____ %
5. Net cash interest paid during 19A	$ _____	$ _____	$ _____
6. Interest expense reported for 19A	_____	_____	_____
7. Bonds payable reported at end of 19A	_____	_____	_____
8. Unamortized premium or discount reported at end of 19A	_____	_____	_____
9. Net liability reported at end of 19A	_____	_____	_____
10. Interest payable reported at end of 19A	_____	_____	_____

P11–8. In order to expand to a new region, Goode Manufacturing Company decided to construct a new plant and warehouse. It was decided that approximately 60 percent of the resources required would be obtained through a $600,000 bond issue. Accordingly, the company developed and approved a bond indenture with the following provisions:

Date of bonds	March 1, 19A, due in ten years
Amount authorized ..	$600,000 (maturity amount)
Interest	10% per annum, payable 5% each February 28 and August 31

The annual accounting period ends on December 31. The bonds were sold on May 1, 19A, at 102.36.

Required:

a. How much cash was received by Goode on May 1, 19A?
b. What was the amount of the premium? Over how many months will it be amortized?
c. Complete the following tabulation (use straight-line amortization):

	Per month
Interest payment	$ _____
Premium amortization ..	$ _____
Net interest expense	$ _____

d. Give entries, if any, at each of the following dates: May 1, 19A; August 31, 19A; December 31, 19A; January 1, 19B; and February 28, 19B.
e. In respect to the financial statements for December 31, 19A:
   1. How much interest expense would be reported on the income statement?
   2. Show how the liabilities related to the bonds would be reported on the balance sheet.

P11–9. On January 1, 1970, Boston Corporation issued $500,000, 6 percent bonds due at the end of 15 years (December 31, 1984). The bonds specified semiannual interest payments on each June 30 and December 31. The bonds originally sold at par. Additionally, the bond indenture called for the establishment of a bond sinking fund to be accumulated over the last five years by making five equal annual deposits on each December 31, starting in 1980. Interest on the fund balance at 5 percent is to be added to the fund at year-end.

Required:

a. Give the entry for issuance of the bonds on January 1, 1970.

b. Give the entry for the semiannual interest payment on the bonds on June 30, 1980.

c. Give the entry on December 3, 1980, for the first $90,488 contribution of cash to the sinking fund. Show how this amount was computed.

d. Give the sinking fund entry at the end of 1981.

e. Unless instructed otherwise by your professor, prepare a fund accumulation schedule similar to Exhibit 11–5.

f. Give the entry to retire the bonds at maturity assuming the total bond sinking fund accumulation is $500,000.

P11–10. To obtain funds to acquire additional long-term assets, Korn Company approved the following bond indenture:

Maturity value authorized: $600,000 (in $1,000 denominations).
Interest: 8% per annum, payable 4% each May 31 and November 30.
Maturity: Ten years from June 1, 19A.
Bond sinking fund: Starting on July 1 of the eighth bond year, deposit $150,000 annually (three deposits) into a bond sinking fund under the control of Trustee X. Interest earned by the fund will be deposited in the fund. The bond sinking fund will be used only to retire the bonds at maturity.

The annual accounting period for Korn Company ends on December 31. The bonds were sold on August 1, 19A, for $625,700, which included two months' accrued interest (June 1 to July 31).

Required:

a. Give the entry to record the issuance of the bonds on August 1, 19A.

b. Give the entries at the following dates (assume straight-line amortization):
1. First interest date.
2. End of first annual accounting period (19A).
3. Beginning of second accounting period (19B).
4. Second interest date.

c. In respect to the 19A financial statements:
1. How much interest expense would be reported on the 19A income statement?
2. Show how the liabilities related to the bonds would be reported on the December 31, 19A, balance sheet.

d. Give the entry to record:
1. The first contribution to the sinking fund.
2. Interest earned on the sinking fund by December 31, bond Year 8, $6,000 (net of fund expenses).

e. Give the entry to retire the bond issue at the end of the tenth bond year assuming the bond sinking fund has a balance of $510,000. (Note: The fund earnings rate varied from year to year.)

P11–11. Foster Corporation issued bonds and received cash in full for the issue price. The bonds were dated and issued on January 1, 19A. The stated interest rate was payable at the end of each year. The bonds mature at the end of four years. In respect to the issuance of the bonds, the following schedule has been completed:

(Relates to Problem 11–11)

Date	Cash	Interest	Amortization	Balance
January 1, 19A				$5,173
End of Year 19A	$350	$310	$40	5,133
End of Year 19B	350	308	42	5,091
End of Year 19C	350	305	45	5,046
End of Year 19D	350	304	46	5,000

Required:

Respond to the following questions:

a. What was the maturity amount of the bonds?

b. How much cash was received at date of issuance (sale) of the bonds?

c. Was there a premium or a discount? If so, which and how much?

d. How much cash will be disbursed for interest each period and in total for the full life of the bond issue?

e. What method of amortization is being used? Explain.

f. What is the stated rate of interest?

g. What is the yield rate of interest?

h. Show how the following amounts for 19C were computed: (1) $350, (2) $305, (3) $45, and (4) $5,046.

i. What amount of interest expense should be reported on the income statement each year?

j. Show how the bonds should be reported on the balance sheet at the end of each year (show the last year immediately before retirement of the bonds).

k. Why is the method of amortization being used preferable to other methods? When must it be used?

Measuring and reporting owners' equity

PURPOSE OF THE CHAPTER

Owners' equity is defined as the excess of total assets over total liabilities. It is a residual amount that represents the **book value** of the owners' interest in the business enterprise. Owners' equity appears somewhat differently on the balance sheet (and in the accounts) of a sole proprietorship, partnership, and corporation. With the same set of transactions, however, the *total amount* of owners' equity on a given date would be the same (except for income tax effects) regardless of the type of business organization. The accounting entries and financial reporting for the three types of business organizations essentially are the same in all situations, *except for those entries that directly affect owners' equity.* This commonality exists because the underlying fundamentals of accounting (Exhibit 2–6) apply equally to each of the three types of business organizations.

Because of certain legal requirements and the full-disclosure principle, owners' equity for each of the three types of business organizations must be accounted for and reported in a slightly different way. Accounting for the owners' equity of a corporation is more complex than for a sole proprietorship or a partnership.

To accomplish the above purposes the chapter is divided into two parts:

Part A: Stockholders' equity

Part B: Accounting for dividends and retained earnings

Appendix: Owners' equity for sole proprietorship and partnership

Behavioral and learning objectives for this chapter are provided in the *Teachers Manual.*

PART A: STOCKHOLDERS' EQUITY

In terms of volume of business the corporation is the dominant type of business organization in the United States. This is because the corporate form has three important advantages over the sole proprietorship and the partnership. First, the corporate form facilitates the bringing together of large amounts of funds through the sale of ownership interests (capital stock) to the public. Second, it facilitates the transfer of separate ownership interests because the shares can be transferred easily to others. Third, it affords the investor or stockholder limited liability.[1]

In contrast to a sole proprietorship or a partnership, a corporation is recognized in law as a separate legal entity. Legally, it is distinct from the owners and enjoys a continuous existence separate and apart from them. It may own property, sue others, be sued, and execute contracts independently of the stockholder owners.

OWNERSHIP OF A CORPORATION—CAPITAL STOCK

Ownership of a corporation is evidenced by shares of **capital stock,** which are freely transferable without affecting the corporation. The owners of a corporation are known as **stockholders** or **shareholders.**

Each state has laws that govern the organization and operation of corporations. The provisions of these laws vary considerably among the states. The laws of each state establish the requirements that must be met to organize a corporation. To form a corporation, an **application for a charter** must be submitted to the appropriate state official. The application must specify the name of the corporation, the purpose (type of business), kinds and amounts of capital stock authorized, and certain minimum financial contributions that must be made (through the sale of capital stock) at date of organization. Most states require a minimum of three stockholders initially. Upon approval of the application, the state issues a **charter** (sometimes called the **articles of incorporation**). The governing body of a corporation is the **board of directors,** which is elected by the shareholders.

When a person acquires shares of capital stock, a **stock certificate** is received as evidence of ownership interest in the corporation. The certificate designates the name of the stockholder, date purchased, type of stock, number of shares represented, and a description of the characteristics of the stock. Exhibit 12–1 shows a stock certificate for 100 shares of common stock. On the back of the certificate are instructions and blanks to be completed when the shares are sold or transferred to another party.

---

[1] In case of insolvency of a corporation, the creditors have recourse for their claims only to the assets of the corporation. Thus, the stockholders stand to lose, as a maximum, only their equity in the corporation. In contrast, in the case of a partnership or sole proprietorship, creditors have recourse to the personal assets of the owners in case the assets of the business are insufficient to meet the outstanding debts of the business.

EXHIBIT 12–1
Stock certificate

The charter granted by a state specifies the maximum number of shares of stock the corporation can issue. To illustrate, assume the charter of Rogers Corporation specified "authorized capital stock, 10,000 shares; par value, $10 per share." Assume further that the corporation immediately sold and issued 6,000 shares. The following terms are used to describe the status of the 10,000 shares permitted:

1. **Authorized shares**—the maximum number of shares of stock that can be sold and issued as specified in the charter of the corporation. For Rogers Corporation, the number of authorized shares is 10,000.
2. **Issued shares**—the number of shares of capital stock that has been issued by the corporation to date. For Rogers Corporation, the number of issued shares at this time is 6,000.
3. **Unissued shares**—the number of authorized shares of capital stock that have not been issued by the corporation to date. For Rogers Corporation, the number of unissued shares at this time is 4,000.
4. **Subscribed shares**—A corporation may sell some stock on credit and not issue it until payment is received. These are called subscribed shares. To illustrate, assume Rogers Corporation sold 500 shares to an individual and has not issued them because the sales price has not been collected. In this instance there would be 500 subscribed shares.
5. **Treasury stock**—A corporation may buy back some of its own shares previously sold. Shares of the corporation that have been **sold** and **issued** and **repurchased** subsequently and are **held** currently by the issuing corporation are referred to as treasury stock. They are considered

issued but not outstanding. To illustrate, assume Rogers Corporation purchased 200 of its own shares from a stockholder. The corporation then would have 200 shares of treasury stock.

6. **Outstanding shares**— the number of shares currently owned by stockholders. It is the number of shares *issued* to stockholders less the number of shares of treasury stock held currently by the corporation. For example, for Rogers Corporation, outstanding shares would be: Issued shares, 6,000, minus treasury stock (shares), 200, equals outstanding shares, 5,800.

TYPES OF CAPITAL STOCK

The capital stock of a corporation may consist of only one kind of stock, which would be known as **common stock;** or it may consist of two kinds of stock—common stock and **preferred stock.** Common stock may be viewed conveniently as the "usual" or "normal" stock of the corporation. In contrast, preferred stock is distinguished because it grants certain **preferences.** These preferences generally specify that the preferred shareholders must receive their dividends *before* any dividends can be paid to the common shareholders. Because of the important differences between common and preferred stock, they are identified separately in the accounting and reporting processes.

Common stock

When only one class of stock is issued, it must be common. It has the voting rights and often is called the **residual equity** since it ranks after the preferred stock for dividends and assets distributed upon dissolution of the corporation. However, since common stock has no dividend limits comparable with those associated with preferred, it has the possibility of higher dividends and increases in market value. The two primary classifications of common stock are par value and nopar value.

Par value and nopar value stock. Many years ago, all capital stock was par value. Par value is a **nominal** value per share established for the stock in the charter of the corporation and is printed on the face of each stock certificate. Stock that is sold by the corporation to investors above par value is said to sell at a premium, whereas, stock sold below par is said to sell at a discount. In recent years the laws of all states have been changed to forbid the initial sale of stock by the corporation to investors below par value.[2] Originally, the concept of par value was established as a protection to creditors and investors by means of a "cushion" of assets that could not be impaired. Par value does not establish

---

[2] The discussions throughout this chapter in respect to the sale of stock refer to the *initial* sale of the stock by the corporation rather than to later sales between investors as is the common situation in the day-to-day transactions of the stock markets. Since the sale of stock by a corporation at a discount no longer is legal, no further discussion of it is included. The sale of stock among individuals is not recorded in the accounts of the corporation.

market value or worth, and the idea that it represented a financial cushion was ill-conceived. Today, par value, when specified, only serves to identify the stated or legal capital of the corporation.

The par value concept proved to be ineffective in protecting either creditors or stockholders. For that reason, many states enacted legislation permitting **nopar value** stock. Nopar value common stock does not have an amount per share specified in the charter; therefore, it may be issued at any price without involving a **discount** or premium. It also avoids giving the impression of a value that is not present. When nopar stock is used by a corporation, the legal, or stated, capital is as defined by the state law. State laws generally define it as (1) a stated amount per share set by the corporation itself or (2) as the amount for which the stock was sold originally.

In recent years, when par value stock is used, the par value is set at a very low amount (such as $1 per share) and the issuing (asking) price is set much higher (such as $10 per share). This reduces significantly the possibility of a discount.

The term legal capital, or **stated capital,** is specified by the law of the state of incorporation. It varies among states; however, it generally is viewed as the par value of the stock outstanding (in the case of par value stock), or in the case of nopar value stock, the stated value set by the company or the amount for which the stock was sold originally. We shall see later that legal capital generally cannot be used as the basis for dividends. The stock certificate shown in Exhibit 12–1 represents common stock, par $1.

Preferred stock

When one or more classes of stock in addition to common stock are issued, the additional classes are called preferred stock. Preferred stock involves some modification that makes it different from the common stock. The usual modifications, (i.e., characteristics or features) of preferred stock are:

1. Dividend preferences.
2. Conversion privileges.
3. Asset preferences.
4. Nonvoting specifications.

In comparison with common stock, preferred stock generally has both favorable and unfavorable characteristics.[3] For example, **nonvoting** preferred stock would have an unfavorable characteristic. Preferred stock almost always has a par value. For example, a corporation charter may specify "Authorized capital stock: nonvoting, 5 percent preferred stock, 5,000 shares, par value $20 per share; common stock, 100,000 shares, nopar value."

A corporation may choose to issue more than one class of stock to (1)

---

[3] A majority of corporations issue only common stock. Large corporations tend to have both common and preferred in their financial structures. Some large companies also issue more than one class of preferred stock in addition to the common stock.

obtain favorable control arrangements from its own point of view, (2) issue stock without voting privileges, and (3) appeal to a wide range of investors with the special provisions on the preferred stock.

The dividend preferences of preferred stock will be discussed and illustrated later in Part B of the chapter. The other features are briefly explained below.

Convertible preferred stock extends to the preferred stockholders the option to turn in their preferred shares and receive in return shares of common stock of the corporation. The terms of the conversion will specify dates and a conversion ratio. To illustrate, in the example above, the charter could have read: "Each share of preferred stock, at the option of the shareholder, can be converted to two shares of the nopar common stock anytime after January 1, 1984."

Asset preferences almost always are specified for preferred stock. It is a preference as to the distribution of assets in the event that the corporation (1) *dissolves* or (2) "calls" the preferred stock. The asset preference often is higher than the par value. Upon call of the preferred stock or dissolution of the corporation, the preferred stockholders would receive cash equal to the asset preference of their stock before any distribution could be made to the common stockholders. To illustrate, in the above example, the asset preference could have been specified as $25 per share. If it were, then a holder of the preferred stock would be entitled to receive $25 per share on call or dissolution before a shareholder of common stock would receive any assets.

Nonvoting preferred stock is customary, despite the fact that the nonvoting feature is undesirable to the investor. This feature denies the preferred stockholder the right to vote at stockholder meetings. It is one avenue for obtaining capital without lessening the control of the common stockholders.

ACCOUNTING FOR AND REPORTING CAPITAL STOCK

In accounting for and reporting shareholders' equity, accountants follow a **concept of sources.** Under this concept, the capital or owners' equity from different sources is recorded in different accounts and reported separately in the stockholders' equity section of the balance sheet. The three basic sources of stockholders' equity are:

1. **Contributed capital**—the amount invested by stockholders through the purchase of shares of stock from the corporation. It is comprised of two distinct components: *(a)* stated capital—par or stated amounts derived from the sale of capital stock and *(b)* additional contributed capital—excess amounts derived from the sale of stock above par. This often is referred to as **paid-in capital.**
2. **Retained earnings**—the cumulative amount of net income earned since organization of the corporation less the cumulative amount of dividends of the corporation since organization.
3. **Unrealized capital** (discussed in chapter 16).

First, we will discuss and illustrate contributed capital. For illustrative purposes in this section, we will use Siesta Corporation. Assume the charter specified two types of capital stock as follows:

> Authorized capital stock:
> Preferred stock, 6%, 1,000 shares, $10 par value per share.
> Common stock, 200,000 shares, $1 par value per share.

Sale and issuance of capital stock

When par value stock is sold for cash and issued, Cash is debited and an appropriately designated contributed capital account for each type of stock is credited and any difference between the selling price and the par value of the stock is credited to a separate additional contributed capital account entitled "Contributed Capital in Excess of Par." To illustrate, assume Siesta Corporation sold and collected cash for 400 shares of preferred stock at $15 per share and 100,000 shares of common stock at $5 per share. The entry would be:

Cash ($6,000 + $500,000)	506,000	
Preferred stock (400 shares × $10 par value)		4,000
Contributed capital in excess of par, preferred (400 shares × [$15 − $10])		2,000
Common stock (100,000 shares × $1 par value)		100,000
Contributed capital in excess of par, common (100,000 shares × [$5 − $1])		400,000

Observe in the above entry that the two capital stock accounts were credited for the *par value* of the shares sold and the differences between selling prices and the par values were credited to two additional contributed capital accounts. Siesta Corporation recognized **two** different sources—preferred and common stock—and each source was subdivided between the par value and the excess received over par.[4]

Now, assume a balance sheet is prepared after the above entry. The **stockholders' equity** would be reported as follows:

Stockholders' Equity

Contributed capital:		
6% preferred stock, par $10; authorized 1,000 shares, issued and outstanding, 400 shares	$ 4,000	
Common stock, par $1; authorized 200,000 shares, issued and outstanding, 100,000 shares	100,000	
Contributed capital in excess of par:		
Preferred stock	2,000	
Common stock	400,000	
Total contributed capital		$506,000
Retained earnings (illustrated later).		

---

[4] Contributed capital in excess of par sometimes is called premium on stock or paid-in capital above par.

Capital stock sold for noncash assets or services. When noncash considerations, such as buildings, land, machinery, and services (e.g., attorney fees), are received in payment for capital stock issued, the assets received (or expenses, in the case of services) should be recorded by the issuing corporation at the **market value** of the stock issued at the date of the transaction in accordance with the cost principle. Alternatively, if the market value of the stock issued cannot be determined, then the market value of the consideration received should be used. To illustrate, assume Siesta Corporation issued 50 shares of common stock for legal services when the stock was selling at $5 per share. The entry would be:

```
Legal expense (50 shares × $5) .................................   250
    Common stock (50 shares × $1 par) ..........................         50
    Contributed capital in excess of par, common stock (50 shares
        × [$5 − $1]) ............................................        200
```

Accounting for nopar stock. Nopar stock does not have a particular "value" specified in the charter of the corporation. As a consequence, when nopar stock is sold and issued, it may be recorded in one of two ways, depending on the laws of the particular state that granted the charter. In some states the law requires the corporation, after the charter is granted for nopar stock, to set a *stated* value per share. This stated value becomes the *legal* capital and is credited to the Nopar Common (or preferred) Stock and any excess is credited to "Contributed Capital in Excess of Stated Value, Nopar Common Stock." To illustrate, assume that Elgin Corporation sold and issued 1,000 shares of its nopar common stock at $25 per share. Assume also that the corporation established a *stated value* of $20 per share. The sale and issuance of the nopar common stock would be recorded as follows:

```
Cash ..................................................... 25,000
    Nopar common stock (1,000 shares × $20) ...............        20,000
    Contributed capital in excess of stated value, nopar common
        stock ............................................         5,000
    Sale and issuance of 1,000 shares of nopar common stock at
    $25 per share; stated value, $20 per share.
```

In contrast, the corporation may be chartered in a state in which the law requires that the corporation must credit *all* of the proceeds from the sale of its nopar capital stock to the Nopar Capital Stock account. In this situation there would be no "stated" value. To illustrate, under these circumstances, Elgin Corporation would record the sale and issuance of the nopar common stock at $25 per share as follows:

Cash	25,000	
Nopar common stock		25,000
Sale and issuance of 1,000 shares of nopar common stock at $25 per share.		

At this point it may be emphasized that there is no difference in accounting between preferred and common stock, except that they are recorded in separate accounts. On the financial statements, common and preferred stock are reported in the same manner, although separately.

TREASURY STOCK

Treasury stock is a corporation's own capital stock that was sold, collected for, issued, and reacquired subsequently by the corporation. Corporations frequently purchase shares of their own capital stock for sound business reasons—to obtain shares needed for employee bonus plans, to influence the market price of the stock, to increase their earnings per share amount, or to have shares on hand for use in the acquisition of other companies. Treasury stock, while held by the issuing corporation, has no voting, dividend, or other stockholder rights.[5]

When a corporation purchases its own capital stock, the assets (usually cash) of the corporation and the stockholders' equity are reduced by equal amounts. When treasury stock is sold, the opposite effects occur. Purchases of treasury stock generally are recorded by debiting the cost to a *negative* stockholders' equity account called Treasury Stock (by type of stock) and crediting Cash. Since the Treasury Stock account has a debit balance, often it is referred to as a negative (or contra) stockholders' equity account. When treasury stock is sold, the Treasury Stock account is credited at cost and Cash is debited. Generally, the purchase and selling prices will be different, necessitating recognition of the difference in an appropriately designated contributed capital account in the entry to record the sale. To illustrate accounting for treasury stock, assume the balance sheet for May Corporation reflected the following on January 1, 19B:[6]

---

[5] The laws of most states impose certain restrictions on the amount of treasury stock a corporation can hold at any one time since this is an avenue for taking resources out of the corporation by the owners (stockholders), which may jeopardize the rights of creditors. The law in some states limits the cost of treasury stock that can be purchased to the balance reflected in the Retained Earnings account.

[6] There are two alternative approaches to accounting for treasury stock—the cost method and the par value method. We will limit our discussions to the cost method since it is less complex and used more widely. The par value method is discussed in most accounting texts at the intermediate level.

MAY CORPORATION
Summarized Balance Sheet
January 1, 19B

Assets		*Stockholders' Equity*	
Cash	$ 30,000	Contributed capital:	
Other assets	70,000	Common stock, par $10, authorized 10,000 shares, issued 8,000 shares	$ 80,000
		Retained earnings	20,000
Total assets	$100,000	Total stockholders' equity	$100,000

Assume that on January 2, 19B, May Corporation purchased 300 of the outstanding shares of its own common stock at $12 per share. This treasury stock transaction would be recorded as follows:

January 2, 19B:

Treasury stock, common (300 shares at cost)	3,600	
Cash		3,600
Purchased 300 shares of treasury stock at $12 per share.		

The effect of this entry is to reduce both the assets and stockholders' equity by $3,600. Now, assume that on February 14, 19B, one third of the treasury shares were resold at $13 per share. This transaction will have the effect of expanding both assets and stockholders' equity by $1,300. These effects are reflected in the following entry to record the resale of 100 of the treasury shares:

February 14, 19B:

Cash	1,300	
Treasury stock, common (100 shares at cost)		1,200
Contributed capital, treasury stock transactions		100
Sold 100 shares of treasury stock at $13; cost, $12 per share.		

The Treasury Stock account has a debit balance, although owners' equity accounts normally carry a credit balance. Since the balance in the Treasury Stock account reflects a **contraction** of stockholders' equity, it is a negative equity account and is **subtracted** from total stockholders' equity. To illustrate, a balance sheet at February 15, 19B, **assuming no other transactions** by May Corporation, would be: [7]

---

[7] Some persons argue that the debit balance in the Treasury Stock account should be reported on the balance sheet as an asset rather than as a reduction in stockholders' equity. This position is supported by the argument that the treasury stock could be sold for

MAY CORPORATION
Summarized Balance Sheet
February 15, 19B

Assets		*Stockholders' Equity*	
Cash	$27,700	Contributed capital:	
Other assets	70,000	Common stock, par $10, authorized 10,000 shares, issued 8,000, of which 200 shares are held as treasury stock	$ 80,000
		Contributed capital, treasury stock transactions	100
		Total contributed capital	80,100
		Retained earnings	20,000
		Total	100,100
		Less cost of treasury stock held	2,400
Total assets	$97,700	Total stockholders' equity	$ 97,700

Upon resale of the 100 shares of treasury stock, **contributed capital** was increased by $100, which was the difference between cost and sales price of the treasury shares sold [i.e., 100 shares × ($13 − $12)]. Observe that this difference was *not* recorded as a gain as would be done for the sale of an asset. The basic accounting concept is that "gains or losses" on transactions involving a corporation's own stock are balance sheet *(stockholders' equity)* items and not income statement items.

Also observe in the preceding balance sheet that May Company, on February 15, 19B, had both **treasury stock** and **unissued stock;** there were 200 shares of treasury stock held and 2,000 shares of unissued stock. The purchase and/or resale of treasury stock does not affect the number of shares of unissued (or issued) stock; however, the number of shares of *outstanding* stock is affected. The only difference between treasury stock and unissued stock is that treasury stock has been sold at least once and recorded in the accounts.

To illustrate the resale of treasury stock at a price *less than cost,* assume that an additional 50 shares of the treasury stock were resold by May Corporation on April 1, 19B, at $11 per share; that is, $1 per share below cost. The resulting entry would be:

April 1, 19B:

```
Cash...................................................... 550
Contributed capital, treasury stock transactions ..................... 50
    Treasury stock, common (50 shares) ......................... 600
    Sold 50 shares of treasury stock at $11 per share; cost, $12 per share.
```

cash just as readily as the shares of other corporations. The argument is fallacious; all *unissued* stock of the corporation presumably also could be sold for cash, yet unissued shares never are considered to be an asset.

Note that the difference was debited to the same contributed capital account to which the difference in the preceding entry was credited. Retained Earnings would be debited for the amount of the deficiency only if there were no credit balance or there were an insufficient credit balance in the account Contributed Capital, Treasury Stock Transactions.

PART B: ACCOUNTING FOR DIVIDENDS AND RETAINED EARNINGS

A dividend is a distribution to stockholders by a corporation. Dividends must be voted by the board of directors of the corporation (i.e., a dividend declaration) before they can be paid. Dividends may involve the distribution of cash, other assets of the corporation, or the corporation's own stock (i.e., a stock dividend). The term *dividend,* without a qualifier, generally is understood to mean a cash dividend, which is the most common type. Dividends normally are stated in terms of so many dollars per share, or as a percent of par value.

For illustrative purposes in this section, we will use Monarch Corporation and will assume the following capital stock outstanding and retained earnings:

6% preferred stock, par $20, shares outstanding 2,000 .	$40,000
Common stock, par $10, shares outstanding 5,000	50,000
Retained earnings	40,000

To illustrate the payment of a **cash dividend,** assume the board of directors voted the following:

"On December 1, 19E, the Board of Directors of Monarch Corporation hereby declares an annual cash dividend of $2 per share on the common stock and 6 percent per share on the preferred stock to the stockholders on date of record, December 10, 19E, payable on December 15, 19E."

The entry to record the combined declaration and payment of the cash dividend would be:[8]

---

[8] Two entries may be made with the same result (see pages 529 and 530):

December 10:

Dividends declared	12,400	
Dividends payable		12,400

December 15:

Dividends payable	12,400	
Cash		12,400

December 15, 19E:

```
Dividends paid, common stock (or Retained earnings) .........   10,000
Dividends paid, preferred stock (or Retained earnings) .........    2,400
    Cash . . . . . . . . . . . . . . . . . . . . . . . . . . . . . . . . . . . . . . . . . . .            12,400
  To record payment of a cash dividend:
  Computations:
    Common stock, 5,000 shares × $2 = $10,000.
    Preferred stock, $40,000 × 0.06 = $2,400.
```

In the above entry the debits were to a **temporary** account, Dividends Paid. This account is closed directly to Retained Earnings at the end of the period because it is a **temporary** contra account. Many accountants prefer to make the dividend debit directly to Retained Earnings rather than using the temporary Dividends Paid account. The effect is precisely the same in either case. The important point to observe is that the payment of a **cash dividend** has two effects: (1) assets are decreased and (2) retained earnings (i.e., owners' equity) is decreased by the same amount.

NATURE OF A CASH DIVIDEND

An investor disburses cash (and perhaps incurs some debt) to acquire shares of stock as an investment. The incentive for buying the shares is to earn a future economic return on the investment, usually in future cash inflows. The investor's future cash inflows from the stock investment are expected to come from two sources: (1) current cash inflows in the form of dividends on the shares and (2) a cash inflow at the time the stock is sold. Thus, the investor anticipates that the sum of these two cash inflows will be greater than the original investment in the shares. The cash inflow from dividends is considered by the investor as revenue. The other cash inflow, a return of the investment (from sale of the shares), usually will result in a **market** gain or loss, depending on whether the investor sells the shares above or below the acquisition price. The amounts and frequency of dividends paid by a corporation generally have an effect on the market price of the stock.

Now, let's look at a cash dividend from the viewpoint of the corporation. The primary objective of a corporation is to earn income on the resources provided by the stockholders and creditors. The ability to attract and retain resources from present and potential stockholders (and creditors), in the long run, depends in good measure upon the earnings record of the company. The profits of a corporation may be retained in the business for corporate expansion or paid to the shareholders as dividends. One of the significant decisions faced by the board of directors of a corporation is how much of the earnings should be retained and how much should be distributed to the shareholders as dividends each year.

In the entry given above to record a cash dividend, it is significant to note that both assets (i.e., cash) and owners' equity (i.e., retained earnings) were decreased by the amount of the dividend. This fact suggests that there are two fundamental requirements for the payment of a cash dividend, viz:

1. **Sufficient retained earnings**—The corporation must have accumulated a sufficient amount of retained earnings to cover the amount of the dividend. State laws usually place restrictions on cash dividends. For example, the state laws often limit cash dividends to the balance in Retained Earnings. As a matter of financial policy, and to meet growth objectives, corporations seldom disburse more than 40 to 60 percent of the average net income amount as dividends.
2. **Sufficient cash**—The corporation must have access to cash sufficient to pay the dividend and, in addition, adequate cash to meet the continuing operating needs of the business. The mere fact that there is a large *credit* in the Retained Earnings account does not indicate sufficient cash. The cash generated in the past by earnings represented in the Retained Earnings account may have been expended to acquire inventory, purchase operational assets, and/or pay liabilities. There is no necessary relationship between the balance of retained earnings and the balance of cash on any particular date.

DIVIDENDS ON PREFERRED STOCK

Recall that preferred stock grants to its holders certain rights that have precedence over the rights of common stock. The primary distinguishing characteristic of preferred stock is dividend preferences. The **dividend preferences** may be classified as follows:[9]

1. Current dividend preference.
2. Cumulative dividend preference.
3. Participating dividend preference.

Preferred stock may have one or a combination of these three dividend preferences. The charter of the corporation must state specifically the distinctive features of the preferred stock.

Current
dividend
preference

Preferred stock usually carries a current dividend preference. This preference, each year, assures the preferred shareholders that if any *current dividends* are paid, their current dividend must be paid before any dividends can be paid on the common stock. When the current dividend preference is met and no other preference is operative, dividends then can be paid to the common stock shareholders. The current dividend preference almost

[9] A dividend preference does not mean that dividends will be paid automatically. Dividends are paid only when *formally* declared by the corporation's board of directors. Thus, the declaration of a dividend is discretionary. A typical dividend problem involves the allocation of a total amount of dividends declared between the preferred stock and common stock as illustrated in the next section.

always is a specified percent of the par value of the preferred stock. To illustrate, the preferred stock of Monarch Corporation was "6 percent preferred stock, par $20 per share, 2,000 shares outstanding, total par value outstanding, $40,000." The current dividend preference is $20 × 0.06 = $1.20 per share of preferred. Therefore, current dividends paid by Monarch Corporation, under four different assumptions in respect to the total dividends paid, would be divided between the preferred and common shareholders in the following ways:

MONARCH CORPORATION
Current Dividend Preference

		Amount of dividend paid to shareholders of	
Assumptions	*Total dividends paid*	*6% preferred stock (2,000 shares @ $20 par = $40,000)**	*Common stock (5,000 shares @ $10 par = $50,000)*
Case A	$ 1,000	$1,000	-0-
Case B	2,000	2,000	-0-
Case C	3,000	2,400	$ 600
Case D	18,000	2,400	15,600

* Preferred dividend preference, $40,000 × 0.06 = $2,400; or 2,000 shares × $1.20.

Cumulative dividend preference

If preferred stock has the cumulative preference, it is called "cumulative preferred stock." This means that if all or a part of the specified dividend (6 percent in the above example) is not paid in full during a given year, the unpaid amount becomes dividends **in arrears.** If the preferred stock is cumulative, the amount of any dividends in arrears must be paid at subsequent dates before any dividends can be paid to the common shareholders. However, in this situation, the preferred stock in any one year cannot receive total dividends in excess of the current year dividend plus all dividends in arrears. To illustrate, assume in the above example that Monarch Corporation did not declare any dividends during the two preceding years. Therefore, a dividend payment, assuming two years in arrears, under four different assumptions would be divided between the preferred and common stock as follows:

MONARCH CORPORATION
Cumulative Preferred Stock

		Amount of dividend paid to shareholders of	
Assumptions	*Total dividends paid*	*6% preferred stock (2,000 shares @ $20 par = $40.00)**	*Common stock (5,000 shares @ $10 par = $50,000)*
Case A	$ 2,400	$2,400	-0-
Case B	7,200	7,200	-0-
Case C	8,000	7,200	$ 800
Case D	30,000	7,200	22,800

* Current dividend preference, $40,000 × 0.06 = $2,400; dividends in arrears preference, $2,400 × 2 years = $4,800; and current dividend plus dividends in arrears = $7,200.

Of course, if the preferred stock is **noncumulative,** dividends never can be in arrears and, in effect, are lost permanently to the preferred stockholders. Because of this highly unfavorable feature for the preferred stockholders, preferred stock usually is cumulative.

Participating dividend preference

Preferred stock may be (1) nonparticipating, (2) fully participating, or (3) partially participating. These features relate to dividends that could be paid to preferred shareholders *above* the current dividend preference (i.e., above the 6 percent of par value in the above example) and above any cumulative dividends in arrears.

Most preferred stock is **nonparticipating;** that is, the amount of dividends payable to preferred shareholders in any one year is limited, in the absence of dividends in arrears, to the current preference rate or amount. If the stock is nonparticipating but cumulative, the preferred dividends are limited to any amount in arrears plus the current dividend preference. To illustrate, assume Monarch 6 percent preferred stock is **non**participating and **non**cumulative. Under this assumption, dividends on the preferred stock would be limited to a maximum of 6 percent of par (i.e., $1.20 per share) in any one year. However, if Monarch preferred stock were **nonparticipating** but **cumulative,** the preferred shareholders would be limited to the $1.20 per share for the current preference *plus* any dividends in arrears.

Alternatively, preferred stock may be **fully participating.** This means that the preferred stock receives a first priority for the current preference, and then participates *pro rata* with common stock, and, since it "fully" participates, it has no specified upper limit to the annual dividend amount. This means that when the preferred stock is **fully** participating, after the specified preference on the preferred stock is satisfied each year, the common stockholders then would receive an equivalent percentage amount, after which each group of stockholders would participate on an equivalent pro rata basis. If the participating preferred stock also is cumulative, any dividends in arrears must be paid **before** any participation is effective. To illustrate dividends under the two different assumptions as to the preferred stock of Monarch Corporation, total dividends declared between the preferred and common shareholders would be divided as follows (observe the sequential steps which are necessary):

MONARCH CORPORATION
Distributions on Participating Preferred Stock and Common Stock

	Amount of dividend paid to		
Assumptions	*Preferred shareholders (total par, $40,000)*	*Common shareholders (total par, $50,000)*	*Total dividends paid*
Case A—Preferred stock is fully participating and noncumulative (two years in arrears). Total dividends paid, $7,200:			
Current dividend ($40,000 × 0.06)	$ 2,400		$ 2,400
Equivalent amount to common ($50,000 × 0.06)		$3,000	3,000
Subtotal			5,400
Full participation—balance dividend in ratio of par values:			
($40,000/$90,000) × ($7,200 − $5,400)	800		800
($50,000/$90,000) × ($7,200 − $5,400)		1,000	1,000
Totals	$ 3,200	$4,000	$ 7,200
Case B—Preferred stock is fully participating and cumulative (two years in arrears). Total dividends paid, $16,500:			
Arrears ($2,400 × 2 years)	$ 4,800		$ 4,800
Current preference	2,400		2,400
Equivalent amount to common ($50,000 × 0.06)		$3,000	3,000
Subtotal			10,200
Full participation—balance dividend in ratio of par:			
($40,000/$90,000) × ($16,500 − $10,200)	2,800		2,800
($50,000/$90,000) × ($16,500 − $10,200)		3,500	3,500
Totals	$10,000	$6,500	$16,500

Partially participating preferred stock essentially is the same as fully participating, except that the participating preference above the current dividend rate is limited to a stated percent of par. For example, the charter may read, ". . . and partially participating only up to an additional two percent." Fully participating and partially participating preferred stock preferences are rather rare.[10]

STOCK DIVIDENDS

Instead of paying a cash dividend, the board of directors of a corporation may decide to distribute to the stockholders, on a *pro rata basis*, additional shares of the corporation's own unissued stock. This is known as a **stock dividend.** Stock dividends almost always consist of common stock distrib-

---

[10] Refer to more advanced books for additional discussion and illustrations of the participating features and the payment of a dividend in assets other than cash, such as property and stock of other corporations being held as an investment.

uted to holders of common stock. To illustrate, assume Monarch Corporation distributed a 10 percent stock dividend to the common shareholders; for each ten shares of common stock held, one additional common share will be issued.

In contrast to a cash dividend, a stock dividend does *not affect the assets* of a corporation or the *total* amount of stockholders' equity. A stock dividend causes only an internal change in stockholders' equity. In accounting for a stock dividend, *Retained Earnings* is decreased (i.e., debited) and *Contributed Capital* is increased (i.e., credited) by the amount of the stock dividend. The 10 percent stock dividend of Monarch Corporation requires the company to issue 500 additional shares (i.e., 5,000 shares outstanding × 10 percent) of the unissued common stock. The entry to record the distribution of the stock dividend, assuming a current market value of $15 per share, would be:[11]

Retained earnings (500 shares × $15)	7,500	
Common stock (500 shares × $10 par)		5,000
Contributed capital in excess of par, common stock		
(500 shares × $5)		2,500
Common stock dividend of 10 percent distributed when market value per share was $15 per share.		

The transfer of retained earnings to permanent or contributed capital by means of a stock dividend often is referred to as **capitalizing earnings.** To reiterate, the only effects on the corporation issuing a stock dividend are to *(a)* reduce retained earnings and increase contributed capital by the same amount and *(b)* increase the number of shares outstanding. From the viewpoint of the stockholder, additional shares of stock are received; however the stockholder owns the same *proportion* of the total common shares outstanding after the stock dividend as before.

Observe in the above illustration that the amount for the stock dividend transferred from Retained Earnings to Contributed Capital was the *current market value* of the shares issued (i.e., $15 × 500 shares = $7,500). This amount is considered appropriate when the stock dividend is "small"; that is, when it is less than 25 percent of the previously outstanding shares. In those cases where a stock dividend is "large" (i.e., more than 25 percent), some accountants believe that the amount transferred should be the par value of the shares issued. Par value is considered to be the absolute minimum since stock cannot be issued at a discount. Market value is preferred by many accountants in all situations primarily because (1) it is the amount that would be credited to Contributed Capital if the

---

[11] Some accountants prefer to debit an account called "Stock Dividends Distributed," which is closed to Retained Earnings at the end of the period. The effect is precisely the same.

stock were sold at the current price and (2) it is the amount that would be debited to Retained Earnings for all other types of dividends.

Reasons for stock dividends. Stock dividends often are distributed because they serve useful purposes both from the viewpoint of the corporation and the individual stockholder. The two primary purposes of a stock dividend are:

1. **To maintain dividend consistency**—Many corporations prefer to declare dividends each year. In the case of a cash shortage, the dividend record may be maintained by issuing a stock dividend. Stock dividends tend to satisfy the demands of stockholders for continuing dividends and yet avoid the demand on cash. Also, a stock dividend is not considered as revenue to the shareholder for income tax purposes. Shareholders view stock dividends as quite different from cash dividends.

2. **To "capitalize" retained earnings**—A stock dividend is used to transfer retained earnings to permanent capital and thus remove such earnings from cash dividend availability. When a corporation consistently retains a substantial percent of its earnings for growth, the related funds are, more or less, invested permanently in long-term assets such as plant and other property. Therefore, it is considered realistic to transfer those accumulated earnings to permanent capital. A stock dividend is a convenient approach for doing this. In profitable corporations that are expanding rapidly, this may be the fundamental reason for stock dividends.

Stock splits. We will digress for the moment to consider **stock splits** because they are *(a)* similar in some respects to a stock dividend, *(b)* often confused with a stock dividend, and *(c)* quite different from a stock dividend as to their internal effects upon stockholders' equity of the issuing corporation. In a stock split, the total number of authorized shares is increased by a specified amount, such as a two-for-one split. In this instance, each share held is called in and two new shares are issued in its place. A stock split is accomplished by reducing the par or stated value per share of all authorized shares, so that the total par value (in dollars) of all authorized shares is unchanged. For example, assuming $20 par value stock before a split, a two-for-one split would involve reducing the par value of each new share to $10 and issuing twice as many new as the number of old shares called in. In contrast to a stock dividend, a stock split does not result in a transfer of retained earnings to contributed capital. No transfer is needed in view of the change in the par value per share to accomplish the increased number of shares. The primary reason for a stock split is to reduce the market price *per share*, which tends to increase the market activity of the stock. Sometimes a corporation desires to **reduce** the number of shares outstanding. One way to do this is to implement a **reverse** stock split. A stock dividend requires a journal entry while a stock split does not.

The comparative effects of a stock dividend versus a stock split may be summarized as follows:

	Stockholders' equity		
	Before a stock dividend or split	After a 100% stock dividend	After a 2 for 1 stock split
Contributed capital:			
Number of shares outstanding	30,000	60,000	60,000
Par value per share	$ 10	$ 10	$ 5
Total par value outstanding	300,000	600,000	300,000
Retained earnings	650,000	350,000	650,000
Total stockholders' equity	950,000	950,000	950,000

DIVIDEND DATES

The preceding discussions assumed that a dividend was paid immediately after its declaration by the board of directors. Almost always, by necessity, there is a time lag between declaration and payment. For example, a typical dividend declaration is as follows: "On November 20, 19B, the Board of Directors of XY Corporation hereby declare a $0.50 per share cash dividend on the 200,000 shares of nopar common stock outstanding. The dividend will be paid to stockholders of record at December 15, 19B, on January 15, 19C." In this declaration there are three identified dates. Strict accounting in respect to each date would be:

1. **Declaration date—November 20, 19B:** This is the date on which the board of directors officially voted the dividend. As soon as public announcement of the declaration is made, legally it is irrevocable; hence, a dividend *liability* immediately comes into existence. Accordingly, on this date the **declaration** by XY Corporation would be recorded as follows:

November 20, 19B:

Dividends declared (or Retained earnings)	100,000	
Dividends payable		100,000
Cash dividend declared: 200,000 shares × $0.50 =$100,000.		

The December 31, 19B, balance sheet would report Dividends Payable as a current liability and Dividends Declared would reduce Retained Earnings.

2. **Date of record—December 15, 19B:** This date follows the declaration date, usually by about one month, as specified in the declaration. It is the date on which the corporation takes from its **stockholders' records**

the list of individuals owning the outstanding shares. The dividend is payable only to those names listed on the record date. Thus, share transfers between buyers and sellers reported to the corporation before this date result in the dividend being paid to the new owner. Changes reported after this date are not recognized for this particular dividend; they will be effective for subsequent dividends. No accounting entry would be made on this date.

3. **Date of payment—January 15, 19C:** This is the date on which the cash is disbursed to pay the dividend liability. It follows the date of record as specified in the dividend announcement. The entry to record the cash disbursement by XY Corporation would be as follows:

January 15, 19C:

Dividends payable	100,000	
Cash		100,000
To pay the liability for a cash dividend declared and recorded on November 20, 19B.		

For instructional purposes this time lag customarily is disregarded since it does not pose any substantive issues. Also, when all of the dates fall in the same accounting period, a single entry on the date of payment usually is made in practice for purely practical reasons.

STOCKHOLDER RECORDS

A corporation must maintain a record of each stockholder. The record includes at least the name and address of each stockholder, number of shares purchased of each type of stock, certificate numbers, dates acquired, and shares sold. Such a record is known as the **stockholders' subsidiary ledger.** The Capital Stock account serves as the **controlling account** in the general ledger for this subsidiary ledger. Sales of shares by a stockholder to others must be reported to the corporation so that new stock certificates can be issued and the stockholders' subsidiary ledger can be changed accordingly. Dividends are sent only to the names and addresses shown in the stockholders' subsidiary ledger. Large corporations with thousands of stockholders generally pay an independent **stock transfer agent** to handle the transfer of shares, to issue new stock certificates, and to maintain the equivalent of a stockholders' subsidiary ledger.

A particularly important record that must be maintained by all corporations is called the **minute book.** This is an official record of the actions taken at all meetings of the board of directors and of the stockholders. The independent auditor is required to inspect the minute book as a part of the audit program.

REPORTING RETAINED EARNINGS

The preceding chapters have emphasized that the income statement reports two income amounts: (1) income before extraordinary items and (2) net income (i.e., after extraordinary items). Net income is closed to the Income Summary account. Net income is reflected on the statement of retained earnings. For the income statement, *APB Opinion No. 30* (dated June 1973) defines extraordinary items as those transactions and events that meet two criteria; that is, to be classified as extraordinary, a gain or loss must be both (1) unusual in nature for the business and (2) infrequent in occurrence. They are set out separately on the income statement to enable statement users to focus on the usual and frequent results; that is, income before extraordinary items because it is a much better measure of future earnings and cash inflow than is net income (i.e., after extraordinary items).

In several prior chapters we have discussed and illustrated the statement of retained earnings. Although not a required statement, it almost always is presented to conform with the full-disclosure principle. Since retained earnings is one of two basic components of stockholders' equity, we should extend our knowledge of it at this point. A typical statement of retained earnings is shown in Exhibit 12–2.

EXHIBIT 12–2

FERRARI CORPORATION
Statement of Retained Earnings
For the Year Ended December 31, 19C

Retained earnings balance, January 1, 19C		$226,000
Prior period adjustment:		
Deduct adjustment for correction of prior		
accounting error (net of tax)		10,000
Balance as restated		216,000
Net income for 19C		34,000
Total		250,000
Deduct dividends declared in 19C:		
On preferred stock	$ 6,000	
On common stock	12,000	18,000
Retained earnings balance, December 31, 19C (see Note 5)		$232,000

Note 5. Restrictions on retained earnings; total, $137,400:
    a. Treasury stock—The corporation has treasury stock that cost $37,400. The state law requires that retained earnings equal to the cost of all treasury stock held be restricted from dividend availability.
    b. Bonds payable—The bond indenture requires that retained earnings be restricted in accordance with an agreed schedule. The schedule amounts for 19B and 19C total $100,000.

The statement of retained earnings shown in Exhibit 12–2 reports two kinds of items that have not been discussed: (1) prior period adjustments and (2) restrictions on retained earnings.

Prior period adjustments. This category of events is defined in *FASB Statement No. 16,* paragraph 11, as follows:

Items of profit and loss related to the following shall be accounted for and reported as prior period adjustments and excluded from the determination of net income for the current period:

a) Correction of an error in the financial statements of a prior period and

b) Adjustments that result from realization of income tax benefits of preacquisition operating loss carryforwards of purchased subsidiaries.[12]

Prior period adjustments must be reported on the statement of retained earnings (as an adjustment of the beginning balance of Retained Earnings) and not on the income statement. Prior period adjustments should be recorded in specially designated gain and loss accounts, which are closed at the end of the period directly to the Retained Earnings account. Examples of prior period adjustments would be corrections of errors made in a prior period such as in depreciation, revenues, operational assets, liabilities, and expenses. Exhibit 12–2 illustrates reporting of a prior period adjustment.[13] Observe that prior period adjustments are defined and reported quite differently than extraordinary items.

Restrictions on retained earnings. Corporations frequently have restrictions on retained earnings. Basically, such a restriction temporarily removes the restricted amount of retained earnings from availability for dividends. When the restriction is removed, the amount that was restricted resumes dividend-availability status. Restrictions on retained earnings may be voluntary or involuntary. For example, the two restrictions reported on Exhibit 12–2 are considered involuntary; one was imposed by law (i.e., the treasury stock restriction) and the other was imposed by contract. On occasion, the management or the board of directors may voluntarily establish a restriction on retained earnings for expansion of the business which is financed by using internally generated funds. The amount of retained earnings restricted for this purpose often is called "Retained earnings appropriated for earnings invested in plant and equipment." Of course, this restriction can be removed at will by the management.

The full-disclosure principle requires that restrictions on retained earnings be reported on the financial statements or in a separate note to the financial statements. The approach most widely used uses a note as illustrated in Exhibit 12–2.

A practice used widely in past years, but used now infrequently, was to set up a special retained earnings account for each appropriation. Such accounts, somewhat illogically, often were called "reserves." To illustrate, had Ferrari Corporation followed this approach, it would have made the following entry:

---

[12] *FASB Statement No. 16,* "Prior Period Adjustments" (New York, 1977), par. 11. Copyright © by the Financial Accounting Standards Board, High Ridge Park, Stamford, Conn. 06905, U.S.A. Quoted (or excerpted) with permission. Copies of the complete document are available from the FASB.

[13] Discussion of the second category of prior period adjustments, which relates to certain tax benefits due to loss carryforwards, is deferred to more advanced accounting books.

Retained earnings	137,400	
Reserve for cost of treasury stock*		37,400
Reserve for bonds payable		100,000

* A much more descriptive title would be preferable, such as "Retained earnings appropriated equal to the cost of treasury stock held."

In preparing the statement of retained earnings, these two accounts would be listed on the statement of retained earnings and Note 5 would be unnecessary. When the restrictions are removed, the above entry is reversed.

ACCOUNTING AND REPORTING FOR UNINCORPORATED BUSINESSES

Most unincorporated businesses are **sole proprietorships** (one owner) or **partnerships** (two or more owners). The accounting and reporting for these two types of businesses (also see pages 5 and 6) are the same as for a corporation except for owners' equity. Typical account structures and reporting of owners' equity on the balance sheet for the three primary types of business organizations may be outlined as shown in Exhibit 12–3.

EXHIBIT 12–3
Comparative account structures and owners' equity

A. TYPICAL ACCOUNT STRUCTURE FOR OWNERS' EQUITY		
Corporation	Sole proprietorship	Partnership
Stockholders' equity	Proprietor's equity	Partners' equity
Capital stock	Doe, Capital	Able, Capital
Contributed capital in excess of par		Baker, Capital
Dividends paid	Doe, Drawings	Able, Drawings
Retained earnings	None—use capital account	Baker, Drawings
Income summary (close to Retained earnings)	Income summary (close to capital account)	None—use capital accounts
		Income summary (close to capital accounts)
B. TYPICAL OWNERS' EQUITY ON BALANCE SHEET		
Stockholders' equity:	Proprietor's equity:	Partners' equity:
Capital stock	Doe, Capital	Able, Capital
Contributed capital in excess of par		Baker, Capital
Retained earnings		

Accounting and reporting for sole proprietorships and partnerships are discussed and illustrated in the Appendix to this chapter.

DEMONSTRATION CASE

Shelly Corporation

(Try to resolve the requirements before proceding to the suggested solution that follows.)

This case focuses on the organization and operations for the first year of Shelly Corporation, which was organized officially on January 1, 19A, the date on which the charter was granted by the state. The laws of the state specify that the legal or stated capital for nopar stock is the full sales amount. The corporation was promoted and organized by ten local entrepreneurs for the purpose of operating a hotel supply business. The charter authorized the following capital stock:

Common stock, nopar value, 20,000 shares authorized.
Preferred stock, 5 percent, $100 par value, 5,000 shares authorized (cumulative, non-participating, and nonvoting; liquidation value, $110).

The following summarized transactions, selected from 19A, were completed on the dates indicated:

1. Jan.   Sold a total of 7,500 shares of nopar common stock to the ten promoters for cash at $52 per share. Credit the Nopar Common Stock account for the total sales amount.

2. Feb.   Sold 1,890 shares of preferred stock at $102 per share; cash collected in full.

3. Mar.   Purchased land for a store site and made full payment by issuing 100 shares of preferred stock. Early construction is planned. Debit Land (store site). Assume the preferred stock is selling at $102 per share.

4. Apr.   Paid cash for organization costs amounting to $1,980. Set up and debit an intangible asset account entitled "Organization Cost."

5. May   Issued ten shares of preferred stock to A. B. Cain in full payment of legal services rendered in connection with organization of the corporation. Assume the preferred stock is selling regularly at $102 per share. Debit Organization Cost.

6. June   Sold 500 shares of nopar common stock for cash to C. B. Abel at $54 per share.

7. July   Purchased 100 shares of preferred stock that had been sold and issued earlier. The stockholder was moving to another state and "needed the money." Shelly Corporation paid the stockholder $104 per share.

8. Aug.   Sold 20 shares of the preferred treasury stock at $105 per share.

9. Dec. 31 Purchased equipment at a cost of $600,000; paid cash. Assume no depreciation expense in 19A.

10. Dec. 31   Borrowed $20,000 cash from the City Bank on a one-year, interest-bearing note. Interest is payable at a 12 percent rate at maturity.

11. Dec. 31   Gross revenues for the year amounted to $129,300; expenses, including corporation income tax but excluding organization costs, amounted to $98,000. Assume, for simplicity, that these summarized revenue and expense transactions were cash. Since the equipment and the bank-loan transactions were on December 31, no related adjusting entries at the end of 19A are needed.

12. Dec. 31   Shelly Corporation decided that a "reasonable" amortization period for organization costs, starting as of January 1, 19A, would be ten years. This is an intangible asset that must be amortized to expense over a reasonable period.

Required:

a. Give appropriate entries, with a brief explanation for each of the above transactions. Include the adjusting entry to amortize organization cost for a full year in 19A.

b. Give appropriate closing entries at December 31, 19A.

c. Prepare a balance sheet for Shelly Corporation at December 31, 19A. Emphasize full disclosure of stockholders' equity.

Suggested solution:

Requirement (a)—journal entries:

1. January 19A:

```
Cash ........................................... 390,000
     Nopar common stock (7,500 shares) ..............        390,000
     Sale of nopar common stock ($52 × 7,500 shares =
     $390,000).
```

2. February 19A:

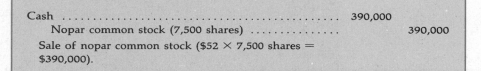

```
Cash ........................................... 192,780          .
     Preferred stock, 5 percent, par $100 (1,890
     shares) ......................................        189,000
     Contributed capital in excess of par, preferred
     stock [1,890 shares × ($102 − $100)].............          3,780
     Sale of preferred stock ($102 × 1,890 shares = $192,780).
```

3. March 19A:

Land (store site)	10,200	
Preferred stock, 5 percent, par $100 (100 shares)		10,000
Contributed capital in excess of par, preferred stock		200
Purchased land for future store site; paid in full by issuance of 100 shares of preferred stock; implied market value ($102 × 100 shares = $10,200).		

4. April 19A:

Organization cost	1,980	
Cash		1,980
Paid organization cost.		

5. May 19A:

Organization cost	1,020	
Preferred stock, 5 percent, par $100 (10 shares)		1,000
Contributed capital in excess of par, preferred stock		20
Organization cost (legal services) paid by issuance of ten shares of preferred stock; implied market value ($102 × 10 shares = $1,020).		

6. June 19A:

Cash	27,000	
Nopar common stock (500 shares)		27,000
Sold 500 shares of the nopar common stock ($54 × 500 shares = $27,000).		

7. July 19A:

Treasury stock, preferred (100 shares at $104)	10,400	
Cash		10,400
Purchased 100 shares of preferred treasury stock ($104 × 100 shares = $10,400).		

8. August 19A:

Cash (20 shares at $105) 2,100
    Treasury stock, preferred (20 shares at $104) 2,080
    Contributed capital from treasury stock
      transactions 20
Sold 20 shares of the preferred treasury stock at $105.

9. December 31, 19A:

Equipment 600,000
    Cash... 600,000
Purchased equipment.

10. December 31, 19A:

Cash 20,000
    Note payable 20,000
Borrowed on one-year, 12 percent, interest-bearing note.

11. December 31, 19A:

Cash 129,300
    Revenues 129,300

Expenses 98,000
    Cash.. 98,000
To record summarized revenues and expenses.

12. December 31, 19A:

Expenses 300
    Organization cost 300
Adjusting entry to amortize organization cost for one year
($1,980 + $1,020) ÷ 10 years = $300.

Requirement (b)—closing entries:

13. December 31, 19A:

Revenues	129,300	
Income summary		129,300
Income summary	98,300	
Expenses ($98,000 + $300)		98,300
Income summary	31,000	
Retained earnings		31,000
($129,300 − $98,300 = $31,000).		

Requirement (c):

SHELLY CORPORATION
Balance Sheet
At December 31, 19A

Assets

Current assets:		
Cash		$ 50,800
Tangible assets:		
Land	$ 10,200	
Equipment (no depreciation assumed in the problem)	600,000	610,200
Intangible assets:		
Organization cost (cost, $3,000 less amortization, $300)		2,700
Total Assets		$663,700

Liabilities

Current liabilities:		
Note payable, 12%		$ 20,000

Stockholders' Equity

Contributed capital:		
Preferred stock, 5%, par value $100, authorized 5,000 shares, issued 2,000 shares of which 80 shares are held as treasury stock	$200,000	
Common stock, nopar value, authorized 20,000 shares, issued and outstanding 8,000 shares	417,000	
Contributed capital in excess of par, preferred stock	4,000	
Contributed capital from treasury stock transactions	20	
Total contributed capital	621,020	
Retained earnings	31,000	
Total.......................................	652,020	
Less cost of preferred treasury stock held (80 shares)	8,320	
Total stockholders' equity		643,700
Total liabilities and stockholders' equity		$663,700

SUMMARY

This chapter discussed accounting for and reporting of owners' equity for corporations, sole proprietorships, and partnerships. Other than owners' equity, the accounting and reporting basically is unaffected by the type of business organization. Accounting for owners' equity is based upon the concept of **source:** each specific source of owners' equity should be accounted for and reported separately. The two basic sources of owners' equity for a corporation are contributed capital and retained earnings. Separate accounts are maintained for each type of capital stock.

The earnings of a corporation that are not retained in the business for growth and expansion are distributed to the stockholders by means of dividends. Dividends are paid only when formally declared by the board of directors of the corporation. A cash dividend results in a decrease in assets (cash) and a commensurate decrease in stockholders' equity (retained earnings). In contrast, a stock dividend does not change either total assets or total stockholders' equity. Significantly, a stock dividend results in a transfer of retained earnings to the permanent or contributed capital of the corporation by the amount of the stock dividend.

Not infrequently a corporation purchases its own stock in the marketplace. Such stock, having been sold and issued by the corporation and subsequently reacquired, is known as **treasury stock.** The purchase of treasury stock is viewed as a contraction of corporate capital, and the subsequent resale of the treasury stock is viewed as an expansion of corporate capital.

APPENDIX: OWNERS' EQUITY FOR SOLE PROPRIETORSHIP AND PARTNERSHIP

Owners' equity for a sole proprietorship

A sole proprietorship is a business owned by one person. As a consequence, accounting for owner's equity is simple. The only owner's equity accounts needed are (1) a capital account for the proprietor (for example, J. Doe, Capital; or J. Doe, Owner's Equity), and (2) a drawing account for the proprietor (for example, J. Doe, Drawings; or J. Doe, Withdrawals). The capital account is used to record investments by the owner and to absorb the net income (or loss) for each period. Thus, the **Income Summary** account is closed to the capital account at the end of each accounting period. The drawing account is used to record withdrawals of cash or other assets by the owner from the business or the payment of the owner's personal obligations with assets of the business. The drawing account is closed to the capital account at the end of each accounting period; thus, the capital account cumulatively reflects all investments by the owner, plus all earnings of the entity, less all withdrawals of resources from the entity by the owner. In all other respects the accounting for a sole proprietorship is the same as for a corporation.

The following sequence of selected entries for Doe's Retail Store is presented to illustrate the accounting and reporting of owner's equity for a sole proprietorship:

January 1, 19A:

J. Doe started a retail store by investing $150,000 of personal savings. The accounting entry would be as follows:

```
Cash ........................................... 150,000
    J. Doe, Capital ...............................        150,000
    Investment by owner.
```

During 19A:

Each month during the year, Doe withdrew $1,000 cash from the business for personal living costs. Accordingly, each month the following entry was made:

```
J. Doe, Drawings ...................................... 1,000
    Cash ..............................................        1,000
    Withdrawal of cash by owner for personal use.
        Note: At December 31, 19A, after the last withdrawal, the drawings account will
    reflect a debit balance of $12,000.
```

December 31, 19A:

Usual accounting entries for the year, including adjusting and closing entries for the revenue and expense accounts, resulted in an $18,000 *credit balance* in the Income Summary account (i.e., $18,000 net income). The next closing entry will be:

```
Income summary ..................................... 18,000
    J. Doe, Capital ...................................        18,000
    Closing entry to transfer net income for the year to the
    owner's equity account.
```

December 31, 19A:

The entry required on this date to close the drawings account would be:

```
J. Doe, Capital ...................................... 12,000
    J. Doe, Drawings ...............................        12,000
    Closing entry to transfer drawings for the year to the capi-
    tal account.
```

The financial statements of a sole proprietorship basically follow the same format as for a corporation, **except in respect to owner's equity** on the balance sheet. In conformity with the full-disclosure principle, the balance sheet at December 31, 19A, for Doe's Retail Store would report the owner's equity as follows:[14]

Owner's Equity

J. Doe, capital, January 1, 19A	$150,000	
Add: Net income for 19A	18,000	
Total	168,000	
Less: Withdrawals for 19A	12,000	
J. Doe, capital, December 1, 19A		$156,000

Since a sole proprietorship, as a business entity, does not pay income taxes, the financial statements will not reflect income tax expense or income taxes payable. The net income of a sole proprietorship must be included on the personal income tax return of the owner. Also, since an employer/employee contractual relationship cannot exist with only one party involved, a "salary" to the owner is not recognized as an expense of a sole proprietorship.

Owners' equity for a partnership

The Uniform Partnership Act, which has been adopted by most states, defines a partnership as "an association of two or more persons to carry on as co-owners of a business for profit." The partnership form of business is used by small businesses and professional people, such as accountants, doctors, and lawyers. A partnership is formed by two or more persons reaching mutual agreement as to the terms of the partnership. The law does not require an application for a charter as in the case of a corporation. The agreement between the partners constitutes a **partnership contract,** and it should be in writing. The partnership contract or agreement should specify such matters as division of periodic income, management responsibilities, transfer or sale of partnership interests, disposition of assets upon liquidation, and procedures to be followed in case of the death of a partner. The primary advantages of a partnership are (1) ease of formation, (2) complete control by the partners, and (3) no income taxes on the business itself. The primary disadvantage is the unlimited liability feature discussed in Chapter 1.

As with a sole proprietorship, accounting for a partnership follows the same underlying fundamentals of accounting as any other form of business organization, **except for those entries that directly affect owners' equity.** Accounting for partners' equity follows the same pattern as illustrated earlier for a sole proprietorship, except that **separate** partner capital and

---

[14] Alternatively, the balance sheet may reflect only "J. Doe, capital, December 31, 19A, $156,000," with a supplemental or supporting *statement of owner's equity* that would be the same as this illustration.

drawings accounts must be established for **each** partner. Investments by each partner are credited to separate capital accounts. Withdrawals of cash and other resources from the partnership by each partner are debited to the respective drawings accounts. The net income for a partnership is divided between the partners in the **profit ratio** specifield in the partnership contract. The Income Summary account is closed to the respective partner capital accounts in accordance with the division of income. The respective drawings accounts also are closed to the partner capital accounts. Therefore, after the closing process, the capital account of each partner cumulatively reflects all investments of the individual partner, plus the partner's share of all partnership earnings, less all withdrawals by the partner.

The following sequence of selected entries is presented to illustrate the accounting and reporting of partners' equity.

January 1, 19A:

The AB Partnership was organized by A. Able and B. Baker on this date. Able contributed $60,000 and Baker $40,000 cash in the partnership and agreed to divide net income (and net loss) 60 percent and 40 percent, respectively. The accounting entry to record the investment would be:

Cash	100,000	
A. Able, Capital		60,000
B. Baker, Capital		40,000
Investment to initiate a partnership.		

During 19A:

It was agreed that in lieu of salaries, Able would withdraw $1,000 and Baker $650 per month in cash. Accordingly, *each month* the following entry for the withdrawals was made:

A. Able, Drawings	1,000	
B. Baker, Drawings	650	
Cash		1,650
Withdrawal of cash by partners for personal use.		

December 31, 19A:

Assume the normal closing entries for the revenue and expense accounts resulted in a $30,000 *credit balance* in the Income Summary account (i.e., $30,000 net income). The next closing entry would be:

Income summary 30,000
    A. Able, Capital 18,000
    B. Baker, Capital 12,000
Closing entry to transfer net income to the respective capital accounts. Net income divided as follows:
A. Able: $30,000 × 0.60 = $18,000
B. Baker: $30,000 × 0.40 = 12,000
       Total $30,000

December 31, 19A:

The entry required to close the drawings accounts would be:

A. Able, Capital 12,000
B. Baker, Capital 7,800
    A. Able, Drawings 12,000
    B. Baker, Drawings 7,800
Closing entry to transfer drawings for the year to the respective capital accounts.

After the closing entries the partners' accounts would reflect the following balances:

Income summary .... -0-
A. Able, Drawings .... -0-
B. Baker, Drawings .... -0-
A. Able, Capital $66,000
B. Baker, Capital 44,200

The financial statements of a partnership follow the same format as for a sole proprietorship and a corporation, except (1) the income statement includes an additional section entitled "Distribution of net income," and (2) the partners' equity section of the balance sheet is detailed for each partner in conformity with the principle of full disclosure. To illustrate, the income statement and balance sheet for the AB Partnership for 19A would reflect the following additional information:

Income statement:
  Net income .... $ 30,000

Distribution of net income:
  A. Able (60%) $18,000
  B. Baker (40%) 12,000
                          $30,000

Balance sheet:

Partners' Equity

A. Able, capital	$66,000
B. Baker, capital	44,200
Total partners' equity	$110,200

A separate statement of partners' capital similar to the following customarily is prepared to supplement the balance sheet:

AB PARTNERSHIP
Statement of Partners' Capital
For the Year Ended December 31, 19A

	A. Able	*B. Baker*	*Total*
Investment, January 1, 19A	$60,000	$40,000	$100,000
Add: Additional investments during the year	-0-	-0-	-0-
Net income for the year	18,000	12,000	30,000
Totals	78,000	52,000	130,000
Less: Drawings during the year	12,000	7,800	19,800
Partners' equity, December 31, 19A	$66,000	$44,200	$110,200

IMPORTANT TERMS DEFINED IN THE CHAPTER (with page citations)

Charter of a corporation—511
Stock certificate—511
Authorized shares—512
Issued shares—512
Unissued shares—512, 520
Subscribed shares—512
Treasury stock—512, 518, 520
Outstanding shares—513
Common stock—513
Preferred stock—513
*Par value—513
Nopar value—513, 517
Legal or stated capital—514
Convertible preferred stock—515
Concept of sources—515
Paid-in capital—515
Dividend distribution—521
Cash dividend—521
Dividend preferences—523
Current dividend preference—523
Cumulative dividend
  preference—523, 524

Participating dividend
  preference—523, 525
Dividends in arrears—524
Stock dividends—526
Stock splits—528
Dividend dates:
  Declaration date—529
  Date of record—529
  Date of payment—530
Stockholders' subsidiary
  ledger—530
Minute book—530
Stock transfer agent—530
Retained earnings—531
Prior period adjustments—531
Restrictions on retained
  earnings—532
Sole proprietorships—533
Partnerships—533

QUESTIONS FOR DISCUSSION

Part A

1. Define a corporation and cite its primary characteristics.

2. What is the charter of a corporation?

3. Briefly explain each of the following terms: *(a)* authorized capital stock, *(b)* issued capital stock, *(c)* unissued capital stock, and *(d)* outstanding capital stock.

4. Briefly distinguish between common stock and preferred stock.

5. Briefly explain the distinction between par value stock and nopar value capital stock.

6. What are the usual characteristics of preferred stock?

7. What are the two basic sources of stockholders' equity? Explain them briefly.

8. Owners' equity is accounted for by source. Explain what is meant by source.

9. Define treasury stock. Why do corporations acquire treasury stock?

10. How is treasury stock reported on the balance sheet? How is the "gain or loss" on treasury stock which has been sold reported on the financial statements?

Questions
Part B

11. What are the fundamental requirements to support a cash dividend? What are the effects of a cash dividend on assets and stockholders' equity?

12. Distinguish between cumulative and noncumulative preferred stock.

13. Distinguish between participating and nonparticipating preferred stock.

14. Define a stock dividend. In what major respects does it differ from a cash dividend?

15. What are the primary purposes in issuing a stock dividend?

16. Identify and briefly explain the three important dates in respect to dividends.

17. Define retained earnings. What are the primary components of retained earnings?

18. Define prior period adjustments. How are they reported?

19. Explain what is meant by restrictions on retained earnings.

20. List and explain the basic purposes of each owners' equity account for a partnership (based on the Appendix).

EXERCISES

Part A

E12–1. MK Corporation was organized in 19A for the purpose of operating an engineering service business. The charter authorized the following capital stock: common stock, par value $20 per share, 10,000 shares. During the first year the following selected transactions were completed:

1. Sold 5,000 shares of common stock for cash at $24 per share; the stock was issued on the sale date.

2. Issued 200 shares of common stock for a piece of land that will be utilized as a facilities site; construction was started immediately. Assume the stock was selling at $26 per share. Debit Land

3. Sold 1,000 shares of common stock for cash at $26 per share; issued the stock.

4. At year-end, the Income Summary account reflected a $7,000 loss. Since a loss was incurred, no income tax expense was recorded.

Required:

a. Give the indicated journal entry for each of the transactions listed above.

b. Assume it is the year-end and the financial statements must be prepared. Show how stockholders' equity would be reported on the balance sheet.

E12–2. RN Corporation was organized in January 19A by ten stockholders to operate an air conditioning sales and service business. The charter issued by the state authorized the following capital stock:

Common stock, $10 par value, 30,000 shares.
Preferred stock, $20 par value, 5 percent, nonparticipating, noncumulative, 5,000 shares.

During January and February 19A, the following stock transactions were completed:

1. Collected $25,000 cash from each of the ten organizers and issued 1,000 shares of common stock to each of them.
2. Sold 2,000 shares of preferred stock at $30 per share; collected the cash and immediately issued the stock.

Required:

a. Give the journal entries to record the above stock transactions.

b. Assume it is the end of the annual accounting period, December 31, 19A, and net income for the year was $32,000; also assume that cash dividends declared and paid at year-end amounted to $15,000. Prepare the stockholders' equity section of the balance sheet at December 31, 19A.

E12–3. Video Systems, Incorporated, was issued a charter on January 15, 19A, that authorized the following capital stock:

Common stock, nopar, 40,000 shares.
Preferred stock, 5 percent, par value $10 per share, 10,000 shares.

The board of directors established a stated value on the nopar common stock of $5 per share.

During 19A, the following selected transactions were completed in the order given:

1. Sold 20,000 shares of the nopar common stock at $40 per share. Collected the cash and issued the shares.
2. Sold 4,000 shares of preferred stock at $15 per share. Collected the cash and issued the shares.
3. At the end of 19A the Income Summary account reflected a credit balance of $25,000.

Required:

a. Give the entry indicated for each of the above transactions.

b. Prepare the stockholders' equity section of the balance sheet at December 31, 19A.

E12–4. Mixon Corporation obtained a charter at the start of 19A that authorized 20,000 shares of common stock, par value $20 per share, and 5,000 shares of nonvoting preferred stock, par value $10. The corporation was promoted and organized by five individuals who "reserved" 50 percent of the common stock shares for themselves. The remaining shares were to be sold to the public at $50 per share on a cash basis. During 19A the following selected transactions occurred:

1. Collected $20 per share cash from each of the five organizers and issued 2,000 shares of common stock to each of them.
2. Sold 5,000 shares of common stock to an "outsider" at $50 per share. Collected the cash and issued the stock.
3. Sold 4,000 shares of preferred stock at $15 per share. Collected the cash and issued the stock.
4. At the end of 19A, the Income Summary account, after income taxes, reflected a credit balance of $30,000.

Required:

a. Give journal entries indicated for each of the transactions listed above.

b. Prepare the stockholders' equity section of the balance sheet at December 31, 19A.

E12–5. The stockholders' equity section on the December 31, 19D, balance sheet of JA Corporation was:

Stockholders' Equity

Contributed capital:

Preferred stock, par value $30, authorized 5,000 shares; ? issued, of which 500 shares are held as treasury stock	$165,000
Common stock, nopar, authorized 10,000 shares; issued and outstanding 7,000 shares	630,000
Contributed capital in excess of par, preferred.........................	7,150
Contributed capital, treasury stock transactions ....:	2,000
Retained earnings	40,000
Cost of treasury stock, preferred	16,000

Required:

Complete the following statements and show your computations.

a. The number of shares of preferred stock issued was _____.

b. The number of shares of preferred stock outstanding was _____.

c. The average sales price of the preferred stock when issued apparently was $ _____ per share.

d. Have treasury stock transactions (1) increased corporate resources _____; or (2) decreased resources _____? By how much? $ _____.

e. How much did the treasury stock held cost per share? $ _____.

f. Total stockholders' equity is $ _____.

E12–6. The balance sheet (summarized) for JAN Corporation reflected the information at the bottom of the page.

During the next year, 19C, the following selected transactions affecting stockholders' equity occurred:

Feb. 1 Purchased for cash, in the open market, 500 shares of Jan's own common stock at $40 per share.

(Relates to Exercise 12–6)

JAN CORPORATION
Balance Sheet
At December 31, 19B

Assets		*Liabilities*	
Cash	$100,000	Current liabilities	$ 60,000
All other assets	412,000	Long-term liabilities	80,000
			140,000

		Stockholders' Equity	
		Contributed capital:	
		Common stock, par $20, authorized 20,000 shares; outstanding 12,000 shares	240,000
		Contributed capital in excess of par	72,000
		Retained earnings	60,000
	$512,000		$512,000

July 15 Sold 100 of the shares purchased on February 1, 19C, at $41 per share.

Sept. 1 Sold 20 more of the shares purchased on February 1, 19C, at $38 per share.

Dec. 31 The credit balance in the Income Summary account was $31,140.

Required:

a. Give the indicated entries for each of the four transactions.

b. Prepare the stockholders' equity section of the balance sheet at December 31, 19C.

Exercises
Part B

E12–7. The records of Dement Supply Company reflected the following balances in the stockholders' equity accounts at December 31, 19H:

Common stock, par $5 per share, 30,000 shares outstanding.

Preferred stock, 5 percent, par $10 per share, 3,000 shares outstanding.

Retained earnings, $150,000.

On September 1, 19H, the board of directors was considering the distribution of a $42,000 cash dividend. No dividends had been paid during 19F and 19G. You have been asked to determine the total and per-share amounts that would be paid to the common stockholders and to the preferred stockholders assuming (show computations):

a. The preferred stock is noncumulative and nonparticipating.

b. The preferred stock is cumulative and nonparticipating.

c. The preferred stock is cumulative and fully participating.

E12–8. Rare Manufacturing Company has outstanding 50,000 shares of $5 par value common stock and 15,000 shares of $10 par value preferred stock (6 percent). On December 1, 19B, the board of directors voted a 6 percent cash dividend on the preferred stock and a 10 percent common stock dividend on the common stock (i.e., for each ten shares of common stock held one additional share of common stock is to be issued as a stock dividend). At the date of declaration, the common stock was selling at $32 and the preferred at $20 per share.

Required:

a. Give the entry to record the payment of the cash dividend. Assume immediate payment.

b. Give the entry to record the distribution of the stock dividend. (Hint: Transfer retained earnings on the basis of market values.)

E12–9. On December 31, 19E, the stockholders' equity section of the balance sheet of LN Corporation reflected the following:

Common stock, par $10, shares authorized 50,000; shares outstanding 20,000	$200,000
Contributed capital in excess of par	15,000
Retained earnings	103,000

A 20 percent stock dividend is declared and issued (that is, one additional share will be issued for each five shares now outstanding). The market value of the stock is $16 per share. Assume the market value is capitalized.

Required:

a. Give the entry to record the distribution of the stock dividend.

b. Reconstruct the stockholders' equity section of the balance sheet (1) immediately before the stock dividend and (2) immediately after the stock dividend. (Hint: Use two amount columns.)

c. How much did total stockholders' equity change as a result of the stock dividend? Explain.

E12–10. The following account balances were selected from the records of Zee Corporation at December 31, 19E, after all adjusting entries were completed:

(Relates to Exercise 12–10)

Common stock, par $5, authorized 200,000 shares; issued 120,000 shares, of which 500 shares are held as treasury stock	$600,000
Contributed capital in excess of par	280,000
Bond sinking fund	70,000
Dividends declared and paid in 19E	24,000
Retained earnings, January 1, 19E	90,000
Correction of prior period accounting error (a debit, net of tax)	10,000
Treasury stock at cost (500 shares)	3,000
Income summary for 19E (credit balance)	45,000

Restriction on retained earnings equal to the cost of treasury stock held is required by law in this state.

Required:

Based upon the above data, prepare *(a)* the statement of retained earnings for 19E and *(b)* the stockholders' equity section of the balance sheet at December 31, 19E. (Hint: Total stockholders' equity is $978,000.)

E12–11. The data at the bottom of the page were taken from the records of Kellog Company at December 31, 19B.

Required:

Based upon the above date, prepare *(a)* the statement of retained earnings for 19B and *(b)* the stockholders' equity section of the balance sheet at December 31, 19B.

E12–12. At December 31, 19E, the records of Reedy Corporation provided the following data:

Common stock, par $5:
Shares authorized, 300,000
Shares issued, 150,000—issue price $12 per share
Shares held as treasury stock, 2,000 shares—cost $15 per share
Net income for 19E, $76,000.
Dividends declared and paid during 19E, $30,000.
Bond sinking fund balance, $20,000.
Prior period adjustment—correction of 19B accounting error, $14,000 (a credit, net of tax).
Retained earnings balance, January 1, 19E, $180,000.
State law places a restriction on retained earnings equal to the cost of treasury stock held.

Required:

a. Prepare a statement of retained earnings for 19E.
b. Prepare the stockholders' equity section of the balance sheet at December 31, 19E.

E12–13. Assume that at the beginning of 19D the stockholders' equity accounts of Roe Corporation reflected the following:

(Relates to Exercise 12–11)

Common stock, par $2, authorized 300,000 shares, issued 110,000 shares of which 1,000 are held as treasury stock (purchased at $8 per share)	$220,000
Preferred stock, par $10, authorized 20,000 shares, issued and outstanding 15,000 shares	150,000
Contributed capital in excess of par:	
Common stock	230,000
Preferred stock	120,000
Dividends declared and paid during 19B	24,000
Net income for 19B	64,000
Retained earnings balance, January 1, 19B	130,000
Prior period adjustment (gain, net of tax)	10,000

Common stock, $5 par, 50,000 shares
outstanding $250,000
Retained earnings (including a $50,000 re-
striction on retained earnings for bonds
payable) 185,000

Assume the following transactions were completed in the order given:

1. Declared and paid cash dividends during 19D amounting to $3 per share.
2. During 19D discovered that land acquired in 19C was debited incorrectly to expense ($5,000) at that time (assume there was no error on the tax return).
3. The Income Summary account on December 31, 19D, after closing all revenue and expense accounts, reflected a credit balance of $50,000.

Required:

a. Give the appropriate entries for each of the above items.
b. Prepare a statement of retained earnings, after taking into account the entries made in *(a)*.

PROBLEMS

Part A

P12–1. Jet Corporation received its charter during January 19A. The charter authorized the following capital stock:

Preferred stock, 5 percent, par $10, authorized 10,000 shares.
Common stock, par $2, authorized 150,000 shares.

During 19A the following transactions occurred in the order given:

1. Issued a total of 60,000 shares of the common stock to the six organizers at $5 per share. Cash was collected in full, and the stock was issued immediately.
2. Sold 3,000 shares of the preferred stock at $22 per share. Collected the cash and issued the stock immediately.
3. Sold 2,000 shares of the common stock at $7 per share and 1,000 shares of the preferred stock at $30. Collected the cash and issued the stock immediately.
4. Revenues for 19A totaled $206,000, and expenses (including income tax) totaled $160,000.

Required:

a. Give all entries, including closing entries, for the above items.
b. Prepare the stockholders' equity section of the balance sheet at December 31, 19A.

P12–2. Greenspan Corporation began operations in January 19A. The charter authorized the following capital stock:

Preferred stock, 5 percent, $10 par, authorized 20,000 shares.
Common stock, nopar, authorized 100,000 shares.
The corporation, in conformance with state laws, established a stated value per share of $5 for the nopar common stock.

During 19A, the following transactions occurred in the order given:

1. Issued 20,000 shares of the nopar common stock to each of the three organizers. Collected $8 per share in full and issued the stock immediately.
2. Sold 4,000 shares of the preferred stock at $15 per share. Collected the cash and issued the stock immediately.
3. Sold 200 shares of the preferred stock at $16 and 1,000 shares of the nopar common stock at $10 per share. Collected the cash and issued the stock immediately.

4. Operating results at the end of 19A, were reflected as follows:

Revenue accounts $150,800
Expense accounts, includ-
  ing income taxes 115,000

Required:

a. Give the entries indicated, including closing entries, for each of the above transactions.
b. Prepare the stockholders' equity section of the balance sheet at December 31, 19A.

P12–3. Keely Company was issued a charter in January 19A, which authorized 50,000 shares of common stock. During 19A, the following selected transactions occurred in the order given:

1. Sold 10,000 shares of the stock for cash at $70 per share. Collected the cash and issued the stock immediately.
2. Acquired land to be used as a future plant site; made payment in full by issuing 500 shares of stock. Assume a market value per share of $70.
3. At the end of 19A, the Income Summary account reflected a credit balance of $30,000.

Three independent cases are assumed as follows:

Case I—Assume the stock was $30 par value per share.
Case II—Assume the stock was nopar and that the total selling price is credited to the Nopar Capital Stock account.
Case III—Assume the stock is nopar with a stated value, specified by the board of directors, of $10 per share.

Required:

  For each case:

a. Give the entries for the three transactions.
b. Prepare the stockholders' equity sec-

tion of the balance sheet at December 31, 19A. (Hint: Total stockholders' equity is the same amount in each case.)

P12–4. Stephanie Company obtained a charter from the state in January 19A, which authorized 100,000 shares of common stock, $1 par value. The stockholders comprised 20 local citizens. During the first year the following selected transactions occurred in the order given:

1. Sold 80,000 shares of the common stock to the 20 shareholders at $5 per share. Collected the $400,000 cash and issued the stock.
2. During the year, one of the 20 stockholders moved to another state and wanted to "get the investment back." Accordingly, the corporation purchased the investor's 5,000 shares at $5.20 per share.
3. Two months later, 3,000 of the shares purchased from the departing stockholder were resold to another individual at $5.50 per share.
4. On December 31, 19A, the end of the first year of business, the Income Summary account reflected a credit balance of $28,500.

Required:

a. Give the indicated journal entry for each of the above items.
b. Prepare the stockholders' equity section of the balance sheet at December 31, 19A.

P12–5. Summers Manufacturing Company was granted a charter that authorized the following capital stock:

Common stock, nopar, 50,000 shares. Assume the nopar stock is not assigned a stated value per share.
Preferred stock, 5 percent, par value $10, 10,000 shares.

  During the first year, 19A, the following selected transactions occurred in the order given:

1. Sold 20,000 shares of nopar common stock at $30 per share and 3,000 preferred stock at $22 per share. Collected cash and issued the stock immediately. For the nopar stock, credit the full selling price to the Nopar Common Stock account.
2. Issued 1,000 shares of preferred stock as full payment for a plot of land to be used as a future plant site. Assume the stock is selling at $22.
3. Purchased 300 shares of the nopar common stock sold earlier; paid cash, $26 per share.
4. Sold all of the treasury stock (common) purchased in 3 above. The sales price was $28 per share.
5. Purchased 200 shares of preferred stock at $24 per share at the request of a stockholder who was moving to another state.
6. At December 31, 19A, the Income Summary account reflected a credit balance of $21,200.

Required:

a. Give the entries indicated for each of the above transactions.
b. Prepare the stockholders' equity section of the balance sheet at December 31, 19A, end of the annual accounting period.

Problems
Part B

P12–6. Farm Equipment Company had the following stock outstanding and retained earnings at December 31, 19E:

Common stock, $10 par, outstanding 20,000 shares	$200,000
Preferred stock, 5%, $20 par, outstanding 5,000 shares	100,000
Retained earnings	240,000

The board of directors is considering the distribution of a cash dividend to the two groups of stockholders. No dividends were declared in 19C or 19D. Four different case situations are assumed:

Case A—The preferred is noncumulative and nonparticipating; the total amount of dividends is $35,000.

Case B—The preferred is cumulative and nonparticipating; the total amount of dividends is $15,000.

Case C—Same as Case B, except the amount is $50,000.

Case D—The preferred is cumulative and fully participating; the total amount of dividends is $49,000.

Required:

a. Compute the amount of dividends, in total and per share, that would be payable to each class of stockholders for each case. Show computations.
b. Give the entry to record the cash dividends paid in Case C. Reflect a separate dividends paid account for each class of stock.
c. Give the required entry assuming, instead of a cash dividend, the declaration and issuance of a 10 percent common stock dividend on the outstanding common stock. Assume the market value per share of common stock was $22.

P12–7. The accounts of RK Company reflected the following balances on January 1, 19C:

(Relates to Problem 12–7)

Preferred stock, 5%, $50 par value, cumulative, authorized 10,000 shares, issued and outstanding 2,000 shares	$100,000
Common stock, $10 par value, authorized 100,000 shares, outstanding 20,000 shares	200,000
Contributed capital in excess of par, preferred	5,000
Contributed capital in excess of par, common	10,000
Retained earnings	200,000
Total stockholders' equity	$515,000

The transactions during 19C relating to the stockholders' equity are listed below in order:

1. Purchased 200 shares of preferred treasury stock at $120 per share.
2. The board of directors declared and paid a cash dividend to the preferred shareholders only. No dividends were declared during 19A or 19B. The dividend was sufficient to pay the arrears plus the dividend for the current year.
3. The board of directors declared a one-for-ten (i.e., 10 percent) common stock dividend on the outstanding common stock. Market value of $15 per share is to be capitalized.
4. Net income for the year was $50,000.

Required:

a. Give the entry for each of the above transactions, including the closing entries. Show computations.
b. Prepare a statement of retained earnings for 19B and the stockholders' equity section of the balance sheet at December 31, 19C. (Hint: Total stockholders' equity is $527,500.)

P12–8. Walker Company is in the process of completing its year-end accounting, including the preparation of the annual financial statements, at December 31, 19E. The stockholders' equity accounts reflected the following balances at the end of the year:

Common stock, par $10, shares
outstanding 50,000 .... $500,000
Contributed capital in excess
of par 50,000
Retained earnings, January 1, 19E
(credit) 300,000
Cash dividends declared and paid
during 19E (debit) 30,000
Income summary account for 19E
(credit balance; after tax) 60,000

The following selected transactions occurred near the end of 19E; they are not included in the above amounts:

1. During 19D Walker Company was sued for $35,000, and it was clear that the suit would be lost. Therefore, in 19D Walker should have debited a loss and credited a liability for this amount. This accounting error was found in 19E. (Hint: Credit Liability for Damages. Disregard income tax effects.)
2. The board of directors voted a voluntary restriction on retained earnings of $100,000. It is to be designated as "Earnings appropriated for plant expansion" effective for the 19E financial statements.
3. A 10 percent stock dividend (i.e., one share was issued for each ten shares outstanding) was issued on December 31, 19E. Capitalize the market value at $16 per share.

Required:

a. Give the appropriate entries for the events listed immediately above. If no entry is given, explain why not.
b. Give the appropriate closing entries, based upon the above data and Requirement (a), at December 31, 19E.
c. Prepare a statement of retained earnings for 19E and the stockholders' equity section of the balance sheet at December 31, 19E.

P12–9. Rye Company has completed all of the annual information processing at December 31, 19D, except for preparation of the financial statements. The following account balances were reflected at that date:

(Relates to Problem 12–9)

Adjusted Trial Balance
December 31, 19D

	Debit	Credit
Cash	$ 57,000	
Accounts receivable (net)	58,000	
Merchandise inventory, December 31, 19D	120,000	
Long-term investment in Company Y	20,000	
Bond sinking fund	40,000	
Land	20,000	
Buildings and equipment (net)	738,000	
Other assets	29,200	
Accounts payable		$ 86,000
Income tax payable		18,000
Bonds payable, 7%, payable Dec. 31		100,000
Preferred stock, par $10, authorized 50,000 shares		100,000
Common stock, par $5, authorized 200,000 shares		660,000
Contributed capital in excess of par, preferred		6,100
Contributed capital in excess of par, common		19,900
Treasury stock, preferred, 10 shares at cost	1,100	
Retained earnings, January 1, 19D		163,300
19D net income		40,000
19D cash dividends on preferred	26,000	
19D common stock dividends distributed (10,000 shares)	70,000	
19D, discovered an accounting error made in 19A in recording a purchase of land (the correction required a net credit to land of $14,000)	14,000	
	$1,193,300	$1,193,300

Note: Retained earnings is restricted in an amount equal to the bond sinking fund per the provisions of the bond indenture.

Required:

Prepare a statement of retained earnings for 19D and a classified balance sheet at December 31, 19D. (Hint: Total stockholders' equity is $1,082,200.)

P12–10. The bookkeeper for Careless Company prepared the following balance sheet:

(Relates to Problem 12–10)

CARELESS COMPANY
Balance Sheet
For the Year 19X

Assets

Current assets	$ 45,000
Fixed assets (net of depreciation reserves, $70,000)	125,000
Other assets	50,000
Total debits	$220,000

Liabilities

Current liabilities	$ 32,000
Other debts	25,000

Capital

Stock, par $10, authorized 10,000 shares	60,000
Stock premium	30,000
Earned surplus	58,000
Treasury stock (500 shares)	(10,000)
Reserve for treasury stock (required by law)	10,000
Correction of prior year error (a credit, net)	7,000
Cash dividends paid during 19X	(12,000)
Net profit for 19X	20,000
Total credits	$220,000

Required:

a. What basic objections do you have of the above statement? Assume the amounts given are correct.

b. Prepare a statement of retained earnings for 19X.

c. Recast the above balance sheet in good form; focus especially on stockholders' equity.

P12–11. You are to refer to the financial statements of J. C. Penney Company, Inc., shown in Chapter 2, and respond to the following:

a. What name was used for the statement of retained earnings?

b. What items caused retained earnings to change during 1979?

c. In which year were dividends higher?

d. Approximately what percent of net income was declared as dividends each year? Show computations.

P12–12. (Based on Appendix) KL Partnership is owned and operated by J. Kay and H. Low. The annual accounting period ends December 31, 19B. At the end of December 19B, the accounts reflected the following:

Credit balance in capital accounts (January 1, 19B):	
J. Kay	$50,000
H. Low	30,000
Credit balance in Income Summary account	23,000
Debit balance in drawings accounts:	
J. Kay	7,000
H. Low	6,000

The partners divide net income equally.

Required:

a. Give the closing entries indicated.

b. Prepare the December 31, 19B, statement of partners' capital.

P12–13. (Based on Appendix) Assume for each of the three separate cases below that the annual accounting period ends on December 31, 19X, and that the Income Summary account at that date reflected a debit balance of $30,000 (i.e., a loss).

Case A—Assume that the company is a sole proprietorship owned by Proprietor A. Prior to the closing entries, the capital account reflected a credit balance of $70,000 and the drawings account a balance of $6,000.

Case B—Assume that the company is a partnership owned by Partner A and Partner B. Prior to the closing entries, the owners' equity accounts reflected the following balances: A, Capital, $50,000; B, Capital, $45,000; A, Drawings, $7,000; and B, Drawings, $6,000. Profits and losses are divided equally.

Case C—Assume that the company is a corporation. Prior to the closing entries, the stockholders' equity ac-counts showed the following: Capital Stock, par $20, authorized 20,000 shares, outstanding 4,000 shares; Contributed Capital in Excess of Par, $2,000; and Retained Earnings, $40,000.

Required:

a. Give all of the closing entries indicated at December 31, 19X, for each of the separate cases.

b. Show how the owners' equity section of the balance sheet would appear at December 31, 19X, for each case.

7,336,732

13

Measuring and reporting long-term investments

PURPOSE OF THE CHAPTER[1]

One corporation may invest in another corporation by acquiring either **debt securities** (e.g., bonds) or **equity securities** (e.g., capital stock) of the other corporation. These investments are classified by the investing entity for measuring and reporting purposes as either short-term investments or long-term investments, depending upon the investment **intentions** of the management. In Chapter 8, short-term investments were defined as those which meet two tests: (1) **ready marketability** and (2) **management intention** to convert them to cash in the short run. Those not meeting these two tests are classified as long-term investments. Short-term investments are classified on the balance sheet as a current asset. Long-term investments are classified on the balance sheet under the asset caption "Investments and funds."

The purpose of this chapter is to discuss measuring and reporting of long-term investments, except for those situations in which *consolidated statements* must be prepared (a parent and subsidiary relationship). Consolidated statements are discussed in Chapter 14. To accomplish this purpose the chapter is subdivided into two parts:

Part A: Long-term investments in equity securities (stocks)

Part B: Long-term investments in debt securities (bonds)

Behavioral and learning objectives for this chapter are provided in the *Teachers Manual.*

---

[1] We suggest that you review the discussion of short-term investments in Chapter 8 prior to studying this chapter.

PART A: LONG-TERM INVESTMENTS IN EQUITY SECURITIES (STOCKS)

An entity may invest in the equity securities (either the common or preferred stock) of one or more corporations for various reasons such as to use idle cash, to exercise influence or control over the other company, to attain growth through sales of new products and new services, to gain access to new markets and new sources of supply, or to attain other economic purposes. Basically, one entity may acquire capital stock of a corporation by purchasing outstanding shares from other shareholders for cash (or other assets); or if the investor is a corporation, by exchanging some of its own capital stock for outstanding capital stock of the other corporation.

It is important to remember that when one company purchases *outstanding* shares of stock of another company, the transaction is between the acquiring company and the *shareholders* of the other company (not the other company itself). Thus, the accounting problems in focus here are those of the acquiring entity only. The accounting of the other company is unaffected.

The purchasing entity (i.e., the investor) may acquire *some or all* of either the preferred or the common stock *outstanding* of the other corporation (often called the investee). If the purpose is to gain influence or control, the typical situation involves investment in the *common stock* because it is the voting stock. The number of shares of outstanding stock of a corporation acquired by another entity generally depends upon the investment objectives of the investing company (i.e., the acquiring company). For measuring and reporting purposes, **three different levels of ownership** are recognized. Each of these calls for different measuring and reporting approaches. The three levels generally are related to the percentage of shares of voting capital stock owned by the investing company in relation to the total number of such shares that are outstanding.

MEASURING LONG-TERM INVESTMENTS IN VOTING COMMON STOCK

For long-term investments in voting common stock, measuring the investment amount which should be reported on the balance sheet and the periodic investment revenue which should be reported on the income statement depend upon the **relationship** between the investor and the investee company. The periodic financial statements of companies reporting long-term investments can be used with efficacy by decision makers who understand the measuring approaches used.

In accordance with the cost principle, long-term investments in the capital stock of another company are measured and recorded, at the dates of acquisition of the shares, as the total consideration given to acquire them. This total includes the market price, plus all commissions and other buying costs. Subsequent to acquisition, measurement of the investment amount and the investment revenue depends upon the extent to which the investing company can exercise **significant influence or control over the operating and financial policies** of the other company. Significant influence and control are related to the number of voting shares owned of the investee company in proportion to the total number of such shares outstanding.

For measuring and reporting long-term investments in the voting capital stock of another company, *APB Opinion No. 18* defines the two terms "significant influence" and "control" essentially as:

1. **Significant influence**—the ability of the investing company to affect, in an important degree, the operating and financing policies of another company in which it owns shares of the voting stock. Significant influence may be indicated by *(a)* membership on the board of directors of the other company, *(b)* participation in the policy-making processes, *(c)* material transactions between the two companies, *(d)* interchange of management personnel, or *(e)* technological dependency. In the absence of a clear-cut distinction based upon these factors, **significant influence is presumed** if the investing company owns at least 20 percent but not more than 50 percent of the outstanding shares of the other company.

2. **Control**—the ability of the investing company to determine the operating and financing policies of another company in which it owns shares of the voting stock. For all practical purposes, control is assumed when the investing company owns more than 50 percent of the outstanding voting stock of the other company.

The way these terms relate to the measuring and reporting of long-term investments in voting capital stock is as follows:

Level of ownership	Measuring and reporting approach
1. Neither significant influence nor control	Cost method
2. Significant influence but not control	Equity method
3. Control	Consolidated statement method

Each of these approaches is outlined in Exhibit 13–1. The first two are discussed in this chapter and the third is discussed in Chapter 14.

COST METHOD—NO SIGNIFICANT INFLUENCE OR CONTROL

When the investment by one entity in the **voting** capital stock of a corporation does not give the former the ability to exercise significant influence or control, the **cost method** of accounting and reporting must be used. Under this method of accounting, the investment is measured

EXHIBIT 13–1
Measuring and reporting long-term investments in capital stock

Status of ownership	Designation of method	Measurement at date of acquisition	Measurement after date of acquisition	
			Investment	Revenue
1. Investor can exercise no significant influence or control. Presumed if investor owns less than 20% of the outstanding voting stock of the investee company.	Cost method	Investor records the investment at cost. Cost is the total outlay made to acquire the shares.	Investor reports the investment on the balance sheet at LCM by recognizing unrealized losses.	Investor recognizes revenue each period when dividends are declared by the investee company. A realized gain or loss is recognized when the investment is sold.
2. Investor can exercise significant influence, but not control, over the operating and financing policies of the investee company. Presumed if the investor owns at least 20% but not more than 50% of the outstanding voting stock of the investee company.	Equity method	Same as above.	Investor measures and reports the investment at cost *plus* the investor's share of the earnings (or less the losses) and *minus* the dividends received from (i.e., declared by) the other company. (Dividends received are not considered revenue. To recognize them as revenue, rather than as a reduction in the investment, would involve double counting.)	Investor recognizes as revenue each period the investor's proportionate share of the earnings (or losses) reported each period by the investee company.
3. Investor can exercise control over the operating and financing policies of the investee company. Control is presumed if the investor owns more than 50% of the outstanding voting stock of the investee company.	Consolidated financial statement method	Same as above.	Consolidated financial statements required each period. Discussed in Chapter 14.	

at acquisition date in the accounts at cost in accordance with the cost principle. Subsequent to acquisition, the investment amount is considered to be the **current lower of cost or market** (LCM), and this amount is reported under "Investments and funds" on the balance sheet for each period. Cash dividends declared by the investee corporation are reported by the investing entity as "Revenue from investments" in the period declared. The cost method is essentially the same as the accounting and reporting previously discussed and illustrated for short-term investments in Chapter 8.

FASB Statement No. 12, "Accounting for Certain Marketable Securities" (December 1975), requires that long-term equity investments accounted for under the cost method be valued at LCM after acquisition. Thus, at the end of each accounting period, the *entire portfolio* of long-term equity investments, accounted for under the cost method, must be calculated at both total cost and total market. If total market is less than total cost, the difference must be recorded as a credit to a contra account called Allowance to Reduce Long-Term Investments to Market; the offsetting debit is to a contra owners' equity account called Unrealized Loss on Long-Term Investments. If, at the end of a subsequent period, market exceeds the valuation reported the prior period, the portfolio is written up to the new market not to exceed the acquisition cost of the securities portfolio. (To repeat, only the recovery to acquisition cost is recognized as a recovery of the unrealized loss previously recorded.) *Market* is measured as the number of shares owned multiplied by the actual market price per share at the balance sheet date.

When long-term securities are sold, the difference between the sales price and acquisition cost is recorded and reported as a *realized* gain or loss.

To illustrate application of the cost method, assume the following transactions by Able Corporation over a two-year period:

February 1, 19A: Purchased the following long-term investments:

> Baker Corporation common stock (nopar), 1,000 shares at $12 per share (this is 10 percent of the shares outstanding).
> Cox Corporation, nonvoting, 5 percent preferred stock (par $20), 500 shares at $40 per share (this is 1 percent of the shares outstanding).

Entry:

```
Long-term investments .....................................  32,000
    Cash ..................................................             32,000
    Computations:
      Baker common stock, 1,000 shares × $12 = $12,000
      Cox preferred stock, 500 shares × $40  =  20,000
          Total acquisition cost .............  $32,000
```

November 30, 19A: The following dividends on the long-term investments were declared by Baker and Cox payable in January 19B:

> Baker common stock, $1 per share.
> Cox preferred stock, 5 percent of par.

Entry:

Dividends receivable	1,500
Revenue from investments	1,500

Computations:
  Baker common stock, 1,000 shares × $1   = $1,000
  Cox preferred stock, 500 shares × $20 × 5% =   500
       Total dividends $1,500

December 31, 19A: Quoted market prices at year-end:

Baker common stock, $13.
Cox preferred stock, $36.

Entry:

Unrealized loss on long-term investments	1,000
Allowance to reduce long-term investments to market	1,000

Computations:

	Shares	Market Dec. 31, 19A	Acquisition cost	Market Dec. 31, 19A
Baker common stock	1,000	$13	$12,000	$13,000
Cox preferred stock	500	36	20,000	18,000
			$32,000	$31,000

LCM: $32,000 − $31,000 = $1,000 (balance required in the allowance account).

January 15, 19B: Received cash for the November 30, 19A, dividends of Baker and Cox Corporations:

Entry:

Cash	1,500
Dividends receivable	1,500

June 15, 19B: Sold 300 shares of the Cox preferred stock at $41:

Entry:

Cash (300 shares × $41)	12,300
Long-term investments (300 × $40)	12,000
Gain on sale of investment	300

November 30, 19B: Dividends declared on this date; payable December 30, 19B:

Baker common stock, $0.90 per share.
Cox preferred stock, 5 percent of par.

Entry:

Cash..	1,100	
Revenue from investments		1,100

Computations:
    Baker common stock, 1,000 shares × $0.90 = $ 900
    Cox preferred stock, 200 shares × $20 × 5% =   200
        Total dividends........................ $1,100

December 30, 19B: Cash received for the November 19B dividends:

Entry:

Cash..	1,100	
Dividends receivable		1,100

December 31, 19B: Quoted market price at year-end:

    Baker common stock, $11.
    Cox preferred stock, $43.

Entry:

Allowance to reduce long-term investments to market 600
    Unrealized loss on long-term investments...................... 600

Computations:

	Shares	Market Dec. 31, 19B	Acquisition cost	Market Dec. 31, 19B
Baker common stock........	1,000	$11	$12,000	$11,000
Cox preferred stock.........	200	43	8,000	8,600
			$20,000	$19,600

LCM: $20,000 − $19,600 = $400 (balance required in the allowance account). Reduction in the allowance account: $1,000 − $400 = $600.

The income statement and balance sheet for each year would report the following:

	19A		19B	
Income statement:				
Revenue from investments		$ 1,500		$ 1,100
Gain on sale of investment...............				300
Balance sheet:				
Current assets:				
Dividends receivable		1,500		
Investments and funds:				
Investments in equity securities.........	$32,000		$20,000	
Less: Allowance to reduce long-term				
investments to market	1,000	31,000	400	19,600
Stockholders' equity:				
Unrealized loss on long-term				
investments		(1,000)		(400)

The preceding entries reflect application of the cost principle at acquisition and application of LCM subsequent to that time. The investment is carried continuously at LCM, and revenue is recognized from the investment *only* in periods in which dividends are declared.

Recall that the discussion above pertains only to the **investing entity**—Able Corporation. The fact that Able Corporation purchased 10 percent of the outstanding voting common shares of Baker Corporation and 1 percent of the outstanding preferred shares of Cox Corporation had absolutely no affect on the accounting and reporting by either Baker or Cox Corporations.

All *nonvoting* stock owned as a long-term investment, regardless of the level of ownership, is accounted for under the cost method as described above.

EQUITY METHOD—SIGNIFICANT INFLUENCE EXISTS (BUT NOT CONTROL)

When significant influence can be exercised over the dividend policies of an investee corporation, the income of the investee corporation can be obtained, almost at will (by means of dividends), by the investor company. To prevent the investor company from manipulating its income by manipulating dividends, under the equity method, each year the investor company recognizes its proportionate part of the **net income** (or net loss) of the investee corporation as a part of its own net income rather than awaiting the declaration of dividends. At the time of recognition of income, since no cash is received, the offsetting debit is to the investment account (an asset increase). Thus, under the equity method, both the **investment account** and **investment revenue account** of the investor company reflect the investor's proportionate share of the income (and losses) of the other corporation. When dividends are received (i.e., declared), they are debited to Dividends Receivable or Cash and credited to the investment account.[2] Thus, dividends declared reduce the investment account balance; they are *not* credited to Revenue from Investments. The revenue already was recognized by the investor in the same period in which the investee corporation earned the income.

To illustrate the accounting and reporting under the equity method, assume that Crown Corporation (the investor company), on January 15, 19E, purchased from other investors 3,000 shares of the outstanding common stock of Davis Corporation (often called the investee company) at a cash price of $120 per share. At the date of purchase, Davis Corporation

---

[2] If cash dividends are declared in one year and paid in the following year, such a dividend is recognized by the investor when declared by debiting Dividends Receivable (a current asset) instead of Cash. Subsequently, when the cash is received, the Cash account is debited and Dividends Receivable is credited. In contrast, dividends declared and paid in the same year may be recorded by the investor on payment date as a debit to Cash and credit to Investment Revenue.

had outstanding 10,000 shares of common stock (par $100 per share). Since Crown Corporation purchased **30 percent** of the outstanding voting stock of the other corporation, **the equity method must be used.** At the date of acquisition, the investment would be recorded by Crown Corporation **at cost** as follows:[3]

January 15, 19E:

Investment in common stock, Davis Corporation
   (3,000 shares) 360,000
      Cash   360,000
Purchased 3,000 shares (30 percent) of the common stock of
Davis Corporation at $120 per share.

After the acquisition date, each year when the other corporation reports income (or loss), the investor company records its percentage share (i.e., equity) of the investment revenue. To illustrate, assume that at the end of 19E, Davis Corporation reported an income of $50,000. The entry by Crown Corporation (the investor company) to recognize its proportionate share of the net income would be:

December 31, 19E:

Investment in common stock, Davis Corporation 15,000
   Revenue from investments   15,000
To record the proportionate share of 19E income reported by
Davis Corporation ($50,000 × 30% = $15,000). The credit often
is called Equity in Earnings of Partially Owned Company.

The proportionate share of the net income of Davis Corporation was taken up by Crown Corporation as revenue and as an *increase* in the investment account. Therefore, when a dividend is received, to avoid counting the income twice, it is recorded as a debit to Cash and as a **credit to the investment account.** This entry reflects the fact that a dividend represents the conversion of a part of the investment account balance to cash. To illustrate, assume that on December 31, 19E, Davis Corporation declared and paid a cash dividend amounting to $10,000, of which 30 percent, or $3,000, was received by Crown Corporation. Crown Corporation would record the dividend as follows:

---

[3] This example assumes that the investment was purchased at "book value." The accounting and reporting procedures for other situations are more complex since they involve asset write-ups and write-downs and, perhaps, the recognition of "goodwill." This chapter presents the fundamentals devoid of this complexity. More advanced books devote considerable attention to these complexities.

December 31, 19E:

> Cash   3,000
>   Investment in common stock, Davis Corporation   3,000
>   To record the receipt of a cash dividend from Davis Corporation
>   ($10,000 × 30% = $3,000).

To recapitulate, under the equity method, the balance in the **investment account** initially starts at cost. Subsequently, the account balance is increased on a proportionate basis by the earnings (or decreased by losses) of the investee company and decreased by the proportionate share of the dividends declared by that company. The investment and revenue accounts on the books of the investor company, Crown Corporation, would reflect the following:

Investment in Common Stock, Davis Corporation

1/15/E	Purchased 3,000 shares	360,000	12/31/E	Proportionate share of dividends of Davis Corp.	3,000
12/31/E	Proportionate share of 19E income of Davis Corp.	15,000			

(debit balance, $372,000)

Revenue from Investments

		12/31/E	Revenue from Davis Corp. 15,000

The financial statements for Crown Corporation, the investor company, at the end of 19E would report the following:

CROWN CORPORATION
Balance Sheet
At December 31, 19E

Investments and funds:
  Investment in common stock, Davis Corporation,
  equity basis (cost, $360,000; market, $369,000)* $372,000

Income Statement
For the Year Ended December 31, 19E

Revenue from investments . . . . $ 15,000

  * Market is measured as the number of shares owned multiplied by the actual market price per share on the balance sheet date.

Recall that when the cost method is applied to the investment, LCM is used at the end of each period (pages 561–563). LCM is not used with the equity method (hence there is no "allowance" account) because under it the investment, after acquisition, is accounted for and reported at equity, not cost.

In interpreting and using financial statements that report long-term investments, information in respect to the method of measuring the investment and the related investment revenue is important. The financial statement must disclose the method used. In addition, regardless of whether the cost or the equity method is used, the original cost, current market value, and carrying value of the investment should be disclosed; this disclosure was illustrated in the preceding paragraphs.

The different methods used represent a compromise on the part of the accounting profession in respect to measuring the effects of long-term investments. Although not currently acceptable, many accountants believe that marketable securities should be measured and reported at their **market values** at each balance sheet date. Under this approach, both dividends received and changes in the market value of the stock since the last period would be reported as revenue (or loss) on the income statement. Accountants who take this position believe that it meets most closely the objective of reporting the **economic consequences** of holding an investment in marketable securities. The *cost method* measures only the dividends received by the investor as revenue, but these may have absolutely no relationship to the earnings of the investee company for the period. The cost method does not indicate to the investor or statement user the earnings pattern of the other company. The equity method tends to overcome this objection; however, it does not reflect the economic impact on the entity of market changes in the investment shares held. The effect of such market changes is significant to the investor. After consideration of these and other factors, the accounting profession, for the present time, has accepted the three different measurement approaches for long-term investments in shares that are outlined in Exhibit 13–1.

PART B: LONG-TERM INVESTMENTS
IN DEBT SECURITIES (BONDS)

In Chapter 11, measuring and reporting of bonds as long-term liabilities of the issuing corporation were discussed. This part of the chapter discusses bonds of another company held as a **long-term investment.** Bonds purchased as a long-term investment offer significantly different investment risks than does capital stock. Although bonds held as an investment do not confer voting privileges, as does capital stock, they do provide a stated rate of interest (which determines the dollar amount of interest that will be received on each interest date) and a specified maturity value (which will be received in cash at maturity date). As debt, they rank above shares as a claim for both interest and principal. For example, assume that Smith Company issued $100,000, 8 percent, 20-year bonds. At the specified maturity date, the investors in the bonds (i.e., the bondholders) will receive exactly $100,000 cash in retirement of the bonds. The 8 percent stated interest on the face amount of the bonds is received in cash each year (usually 4 percent semiannually, which is $4,000) regardless of the market price of the bonds or the earnings of the issuing company. The owner (i.e., the investor) of one or more of these bonds has no right to vote in the annual stockholders' meeting as would be the case if some of the common stock of Smith Company were owned.

Similar to capital stock, bonds are bought and sold in the regular security markets. The market price of bonds fluctuates **inversely** with changes in the **market rate** of interest since the **stated rate** of interest, paid on the face amount of the bonds, remains constant over the life of the bonds (see Chapter 11).

MEASURING AND REPORTING BOND INVESTMENTS

Investors may buy bonds as an investment at their date of issuance or at subsequent dates during the life of the bonds. Regardless of the timing of their acquisition, at the end of each period the investor must measure the (1) cost plus any unamortized discount or minus any unamortized premium which is reported on the balance sheet, and (2) interest revenue earned, which is reported on the income statement. An understanding of the measurement approaches used is helpful in interpreting and using financial statements.

At date of acquisition, a bond investment is measured, recorded, and reported in accordance with the **cost principle.** The purchase cost, including all incidental acquisition costs (such as transfer fees and broker commissions), is debited to an investment account such as "Long-Term Investment, Bonds of X Corporation." The cost recorded under the cost principle is the **current cash equivalent amount;** and it may be the same as the maturity amount (if acquired at par), less than the maturity amount (if acquired at a discount), or more than the maturity amount (if acquired at a premium).[4] The premium or discount on a bond investment usually is not recorded in a separate account as is done for bonds payable; rather, the investment account reflects the current book or carrying amount. However, a separate discount or premium account can be used with precisely the same results.

Subsequent to acquisition, a bond investment is measured as the acquisition cost plus or minus any unamortized **discount** or **premium** at each subsequent date. If the bond investment was acquired at maturity value (at par), the carrying value amount remains constant over the life of the investment because there is no premium or discount to be amortized. In this situation, revenue earned from the investment each period is measured as the amount of cash interest collected (or accrued).

---

[4] Fees, commissions, and other incidental costs decrease the discount, or increase the premium; hence, they are amortized over the remaining period to maturity. Alternatively, such costs sometimes are recorded separately and amortized on the same basis as the discount or premium.

When a bond investment is acquired at a current cash equivalent amount that is either more or less than the maturity amount (i.e., at a premium or discount), measurement of the carrying value of the investment after date of acquisition necessitates adjustment of the investment account balance from acquisition cost to maturity amount each period over the life of the investment. This adjustment is the periodic amortization of the premium or discount. The periodic amortization is made as a debit or credit to the investment account, depending on whether there was a premium or discount at acquisition, so that the investment account at the end of each period reflects the *then current carrying amount.*

When a bond investment is acquired at a premium or discount, the revenue from interest each period is measured as the cash interest collected (or accrued) plus or minus the periodic amortization of premium or discount. As was illustrated in Chapter 11 for bonds payable, bond premium or discount may be amortized by using either the straight-line or effective-interest approach. The former is simpler, whereas the latter conceptually is preferable. In the paragraphs to follow, we will assume straight-line amortization; effective-interest amortization is explained at the end of this part. In contrast to long-term investments, premium or discount is not amortized on bonds held as a short-term investment since the bonds will be converted to cash (i.e., sold) within the coming year (or the operating cycle if longer) instead of being held to maturity.

The concepts of the carrying value of a bond investment and amortization of a premium and discount may be portrayed graphically in the following manner:

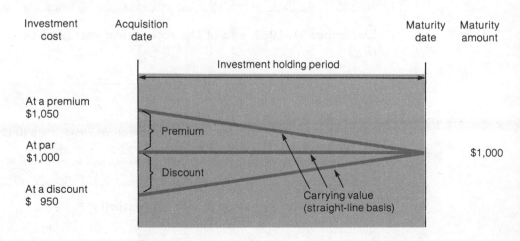

Observe that when effective-interest amortization is used, the carrying value lines, when there is a premium or discount, will be curved instead of straight.

Accrual of interest revenue. After date of acquisition, interest revenue must be accrued (by means of an adjusting entry) for periods between the last date on which interest revenue was collected and the end of the accounting period. The procedure for accruing interest expense and interest revenue was discussed and illustrated in several prior chapters.

BONDS PURCHASED AT PAR

To illustrate a long-term investment in the bonds of another company, purchased at par, assume that on July 1, 1982, Roth Company purchased $10,000, 8 percent, 20-year bonds of Smith Company in the open market at a cost of $10,000 cash (i.e., purchased at par). The bonds were issued originally by Smith Company on July 1, 1967, and mature on June 30, 1987; thus, Roth Company purchased the bonds at 100, five years before the maturity date. The bonds call for 8 percent annual interest payable each June 30. Roth Company adjusts and closes its book each December 31. The sequence of entries on the books of Roth Company to account for this long-term investment in bonds follows:[5]

July 1, 1982:

Long-term investment, bonds of Smith Company	10,000	
Cash		10,000
Purchased at par, $10,000 maturity value, 8 percent bonds of Smith Company. (Note: Since the bonds were purchased on an interest date, there was no accrued interest.)		

December 31, 1982, end of the accounting year (and each year until maturity):

Bond interest receivable	400	
Revenue from investments*		400
Adjusting entry to accrue six months interest revenue on Smith Company bonds ($10,000 × 0.08 × 6/12 = $400).		
* Alternate titles are Interest Revenue and, sometimes, Interest Income.		

June 30, 1983 (and each year until maturity):[6]

---

[5] Bonds generally pay interest semiannually. Annual interest is used in this illustration to reduce the number of repetitive entries. The concepts are applied the same way in either case.

[6] This entry presumes that there was no reversal on January 1, 1983, of the prior adjusting entry. A reversing entry is optional since it serves only to facilitate the subsequent entry (see Chapter 5).

```
Cash ($10,000 × 0.08) ...........................................  800
      Bond interest receivable (from December 31 entry) ............       400
      Revenue from investments ...................................       400
      Receipt of annual interest payment on the Smith Company bonds.
```

June 30, 1987:

```
Cash ...............................................  10,000
      Long-term investment, bonds of Smith Company .........       10,000
      Retirement of bonds at maturity date (assumes last interest re-
      ceipt already recorded).
```

Since the bond investment was purchased at par or maturity value, there was no premium or discount to be amortized.

At the end of 1982, the financial statements of Roth Company would report the following:

Balance Sheet

Current assets:
   Bond interest receivable .... $ 400
Investments and funds:
   Investment in bonds, at cost (market, $10,125) 10,000

Income Statement

Revenue from investments .... $ 400

BONDS PURCHASED AT A DISCOUNT

When investors demand a *higher* rate of interest on bonds than the **stated rate,** bonds will sell in the market at a **discount.** When a bond investment is purchased at a discount, say at 98 (this means 98 percent of the bond's par value), the investor receives back in cash the periodic interest payments stated on the bond plus the maturity value (i.e., at 100). The discount increases the interest revenue earned on the bond investment. To illustrate, assume that on July 1, 1982, Roth Company purchased a $10,000, 8 percent bond issued by Smith Company for $9,800 cash. The bond will mature in five years. Interest revenue of $10,000 × 0.08 = $800 will be collected annually. This investment can be analyzed to show that although $800 cash is collected each year, the annual revenue *earned* from the investment is $840; the additional $40 is due to amortization of the discount. The analysis, assuming straight-line amortization, is as follows:

```
Cash inflows from the investment:
  Annual interest collected, July 1, 1982, through
    June 30, 1987 ($10,000 × 0.08 × 5 years) ..............   $ 4,000
  Collection of bond at maturity date, June 30, 1987 ........   10,000   $14,000
Cash outflow for the investment:
  July 1, 1982—purchase of bond .......................              9,800
        Difference—net increase in cash (this is the
          total interest earned) ............................        $ 4,200
Revenue from investment per year: $4,200 ÷ 5 years = $840
(assuming straight-line amortization).
```

When a bond is purchased as a long-term investment, the long-term investment account is debited for the current cash equivalent amount in accordance with the cost principle. Therefore, when a bond investment is purchased at a discount, the investment account balance at purchase date will be less than par or maturity value. Through **amortization** of the discount, the balance of the investment account must be *increased* each period so that the carrying value will be at the par amount on maturity date. Amortization of the discount each period over the **remaining life** of the bond also *increases* the amount of interest revenue earned. To accomplish this effect, the amount of discount amortized each period is debited to the investment account and credited to Interest Revenue. The effects of this periodic amortization, over the life of the investment, are (1) to reflect the investment account balance at the end of each period at the then current carrying amount and (2) to increase interest revenue earned each year by the amount of the amortization.

To illustrate, in the preceding example, Roth Company each year must amortize a part of the discount ($10,000 − $9,800 = $200), so that the total discount ($200) will be amortized over the remaining life of the bond investment. Assuming straight-line amortization, the amount of discount amortized each full year will be $200 ÷ 5 years = $40 per year.

The sequence of entries by Roth Company, from the date of acquisition of the bond investment through maturity date, would be:

July 1, 1982:

```
Long-term investment, bonds of Smith Company (at cost) ........   9,800
  Cash ................................................              9,800
  Purchased $10,000 maturity value, 8 percent bonds of the Smith
  Company at 98.
  Note: This entry records the investment at its cost; that is, net of any discount or premium.
Some accountants prefer to record it at gross as follows with the same end result:

Long-term investment ...........................................  10,000
  Discount on long-term investment ..............................              200
  Cash ..........................................................            9,800
```

December 31, 1982 (and each year until maturity):

Bond interest receivable ($10,000 × 0.08 × 6/12) 400
Long-term investment, bonds of Smith Company
  (amortization: $40 × 6/12) 20
    Revenue from investments 420
  Adjusting entry to (1) accrue interest revenue for six months and
  (2) to amortize discount on the bond investment for six months (July
  1 to December 31).

June 30, 1983 (and each year until maturity):

Cash ($10,000 × 0.08) 800
Long-term investment, bonds of Smith Company
  (amortization: $40 × 6/12) 20
    Bond interest receivable (from December 31 entry) 400
    Revenue from investments 420
  Receipt of annual interest on Smith Company bonds and amortization
  of discount for six months (January 1 to June 30).

June 30, 1987:

Cash... 10,000
    Long-term investment, bonds of Smith Company 10,000
  Retirement of bonds at maturity (assumes last interest receipt
  already recorded).

The increase in the balance of the long-term investment account from
cost at date of purchase to par value at maturity date which results from
the amortization of the bond discount is reflected in the investment ledger
account in Roth's accounts as follows:[7]

Long-Term Investment, Bonds of Smith Company

July 1, 1982 At acquisition	9,800	June 30, 1987 Retirement	10,000
Yearly amortizations by:			
Dec. 31, 1982	20		
31, 1983	40		
31, 1984	40		
31, 1985	40		
31, 1986	40		
June 30, 1987	20		
	10,000		10,000

[7] Observe that the amortization of discount or premium on bond investments conceptually is the same as the amortization discussed and illustrated in Chapter 11 in the issuer's
accounts. Here, we simply are looking at the other side of the transaction. A minor procedural difference may be noted. In Chapter 11, premium or discount was recorded in a
separate account; in this chapter, the *net amount* (i.e., the cost) was recorded in the investment
account. Either procedure can be used in either situation with the same results. Common
practice follows the procedures illustrated in the respective chapters.

At the end of 1982, the financial statements of Roth Company would report the following:

Balance Sheet

Current assets:
Bond interest receivable .... $ 400

Investments and funds:
Investment in bonds, at amortized cost (market, $10,125) 9,820

Income Statement

Revenue from investments .... $ 420

BONDS PURCHASED AT A PREMIUM

When investors are willing to invest at a rate of interest *less* than the **stated rate** of interest on bonds, the bonds will sell at a **premium.** When bonds are purchased at a premium, the investment account is debited for an amount greater than the par or maturity value. Therefore, the premium must be **amortized** over the **remaining life** of the bonds as a *decrease* in the balance in the investment account so that the balance of the investment account will be at par value on maturity date. The procedure parallels that illustrated above for a discount, except that each period the investment account is credited and the premium amortization *decreases* interest revenue.

To illustrate the accounting and reporting where there is a premium, assume that in the preceding example, Roth Company purchased Smith Company bonds for $10,200 cash. The cash outflow and inflows for this investment, assuming straight-line amortization, may be analyzed to illustrate the effect of the premium on interest revenue as follows:

Cash inflows from the investment:
Annual interest collected, July 1, 1982, through
June 30, 1987 ($10,000 × 0.08 × 5 years) .... $ 4,000
June 30, 1987, collection of bond at maturity 10,000 $14,000

Cash outflow for the investment:
July 1, 1982—purchase of bond   10,200

Difference—net increase in cash (this is the total
interest revenue earned) $3,800

Revenue from investment, per year: $3,800 ÷ 5 years = $760

The amount of premium amortization each full year, on a straight-line basis would be $200 ÷ 5 years = $40. The sequence of entries by Roth Company for the bond investment, purchased at a premium, would be:

July 1, 1982:

Long-term investment, bonds of Smith Company (at cost) 10,200
    Cash   10,200
    Purchased $10,000 maturity value, 8 percent bonds of Smith
    Company at 102.

December 31, 1982, end of accounting year (and each year until maturity):

```
Bond interest receivable ($10,000 × 0.08 × 6/12) ...................   400
    Long-term investment, bonds of Smith Company
        (amortization: $40 × 6/12).................................           20
    Revenue from investments ....................................          380
Adjusting entry to (1) accrue interest revenue for six months and
(2) amortize premium on the investment for six months (July 1 to
December 31).
```

June 30, 1983 (and each year until maturity):

```
Cash ($10,000 × 0.08) .........................................   800
    Bond interest receivable (per December 31 entry) ..............         400
    Long-term investment, bonds of Smith Company
        (amortization: $40 × 6/12)................................           20
    Revenue from investments ....................................          380
Receipt of annual interest revenue on Smith Company bonds and
amortization of premium for six months (January 1 to June 30, 1983).
```

June 30, 1987:

```
Cash .........................................................   10,000
    Long-term investment, bonds of Smith Company .........              10,000
Retirement of bonds at maturity (assuming the last interest re-
ceipt has been recorded).
```

At the end of 1982, the financial statements of Roth Company would report the following:

Balance Sheet

Current assets:
Bond interest receivable .... $ 400

Investments and funds:
Investment in bonds, at amortized cost (market, $10,225)   10,180

Income Statement

Revenue from investments .... $ 380

BOND INVESTMENT PURCHASED BETWEEN INTEREST DATES

Investors generally purchase bond investments between the interest dates specified on the bonds. In these situations the investor must pay the amount of **interest accrued** since the last interest date in addition to the purchase price of the bond. The bond market operates in this fashion because the holder of the bond receives on the interest date interest for the full period between interest dates, regardless of the purchase date. The former owner of the bond is entitled to interest for the period of time that the bond was held (see Chapter 11). To illustrate, assume P Company purchased a $1,000 bond, 12 percent interest, payable 6 percent each March 31 and September 30. The bond was purchased on June 1, 1982, at 100 plus accrued interest. The purchase of the bond investment would be recorded by P Company as follows:

June 1, 1982:

Long-term investment, 12 percent bond	1,000	
Revenue from investments ($1,000 × 0.12 × 2/12)*	20	
Cash [$1,000 + ($1,000 × 0.12 × 2/12)]		1,020

Purchase of a $1,000, 12 percent bond as a long-term investment at 100 plus accrued interest for two months, March 31 to June 1, 1982.

* Alternatively, an account, "Bond Interest Receivable," could have been debited on June 1 for $20 and then credited for that amount on September 30. The net effect would have been the same. When the end of the accounting period falls between the purchase date and the next interest date, such a procedure may be less complex.

It is important to observe in this entry that the long-term investment account is debited for the *cost* of the investment, which **excludes** the accrued interest. The $20 accrued interest was paid for in cash by the purchaser; however, it will be returned to the investor at the next interest date, September 30, 1982. At that time, the investor will receive the full amount of cash interest for six months, although the new investor has owned the bond for only four months (i.e., June 1 to September 30, 1982).

The entry to record the first interest collection after the purchase would be:

September 30, 1982:

Cash	60	
Revenue from investments		60

Collected interest for six months on bond investment ($1,000 × 0.06 = $60).

After these two entries are posted, the Revenue from Investments account on the books of P Company will reflect $20 interest earned for the four months since purchase as follows:

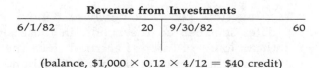

Revenue from Investments

6/1/82		20	9/30/82		60

(balance, $1,000 × 0.12 × 4/12 = $40 credit)

SALE OF A BOND INVESTMENT

When bonds are acquired as a long-term investment, they are accounted for with the expectation that they will be held to maturity. This expectation is the basis for amortizing any premium or discount over the period from the date of purchase to the maturity date. Nevertheless, such a long-term investment may be sold prior to the maturity date. When a bond investment is sold prior to maturity of the bonds, the difference between the sale price and the balance in the investment account (i.e., the book or carrying value) is recorded as a "Gain (or Loss) on the Sale of Investments."

To illustrate, assume Carson Corporation has two $1,000, 12 percent bonds of Drake Company that are being held as a long-term investment. Each bond was purchased at 104; therefore, the long-term investment account was debited for $2,080. Because of amortization to January 1, 1982, the investment account balance is $2,040. On that date one of the bonds was sold at 100. The entry by Carson Company to record the sale would be as follows:

Cash	1,000	
Loss on sale of investments	20	
Long-term investment, Drake Company bonds		1,020
Sale of long-term investment.		

EFFECTIVE-INTEREST AMORTIZATION ON BOND INVESTMENTS

Effective-interest amortization of the discount or premium on a bond investment is identical conceptually with that discussed for bonds payable in Chapter 11 (page 491). This method of amortization is superior conceptually because the **effective-interest rate** is used; therefore, (1) interest revenue is measured correctly each period for income statement purposes, and (2) the carrying amount of the investment is measured correctly for balance sheet purposes at the end of each period. Each interest revenue collection (in cash) is assumed to be part principal and part interest. To illustrate the effective-interest approach, assume that on January 1, 19A, Company A purchased all of the five-year, $10,000, 8 percent bonds of EIA Corporation as a long-term investment. The purchase price, based on a 12 percent effective-interest rate, was 85.58. Therefore, the cash paid was $8,558, that is, at a $1,442 discount. The bonds carried a stated rate of interest of 8 percent per year, payable each December 31. The acquisition was recorded by Company A as follows:[8]

---

[8] Given the effective rate of 12 percent, the price of the bonds can be determined from a bond table or computed as follows:

$$\$10,000 \times p_{n\,=\,5,\,i\,=\,12\%} = \$10,000 \times 0.5674 \text{ (Table 10–2)} = \$5,674$$
$$\$800 \times P_{n\,=\,5,\,i\,=\,12\%} = \quad \$800 \times 3.6048 \text{ (Table 10–4)} = \underline{2,884}$$
$$\text{Bond price (PV of future cash flows)} \quad \underline{\$8,558}$$

January 1, 19A:

> Long-term investment, EIA Corporation bonds
> (maturity amount $10,000) 8,558
>   Cash 8,558
> Purchase of long-term investment.

Company A decided to use effective-interest amortization of the discount rather than straight line. The entries for a bond investment are the same regardless of the amortization method used, except for some of the **amounts** in the interest entries.

Computation of effective-interest amortization is shown in Exhibit 13–2. Observe that the effective rate of interest of 12 percent, rather than the 8 percent stated rate, is used to compute the interest revenue amounts.

EXHIBIT 13–2
Bond investment—Schedule of effective-interest amortization

Date	Cash interest received each interest date	Interest revenue (based on beginning balance of investment)	Amortization (increase investment)*	Net investment
1/1/19A (acquisition)				8,558
12/31/19A	800	8,558 × 0.12 = 1,027	227	8,785
12/31/19B	800	8,785 × 0.12 = 1,054	254	9,039
12/31/19C	800	9,039 × 0.12 = 1,085	285	9,324
12/31/19D	800	9,324 × 0.12 = 1,119	319	9,643
12/31/19E	800	9,643 × 0.12 = 1,157	357	10,000
Totals	4,000	5,442	1,442	

Note: This example is identical to the illustration of the issuer's situation shown in Exhibit 11–6, p. 493. Computation of the sale price of the bonds at an effective rate of 12 percent was shown in that illustration.

* Adjusts the net investment balance to the maturity amount.

The first amount column reflects the cash inflow each period for interest (at the stated rate); the second column shows the interest revenue amount to be reported on the income statement each period (i.e., the effective rate on the net investment); and the last column shows the amount of the investment (i.e., the unamortized principal) that will be reported on the balance sheet at the end of each period under "Investments and Funds." The entry for interest revenue each period can be taken directly from the schedule (Exhibit 13–2), viz:

	Year 1	Year 2	Etc.
Cash	800	800	
Long-term investment	227	254	
Revenue from investments	1,027	1,054	

Conceptually, this method derives the true- or effective-interest revenue earned during each period and the correct current carrying value of the investment at the end of each period. The straight-line approach provides only approximations of these amounts. When the amortization amounts between the two methods are material, *APB Opinion No. 21*, "Interest on Receivables and Payables," requires use of the effective-interest method. Straight-line amortization often is used because it is simple to apply and the different amounts of premium or discount amortized each period are not material. In such a case, the departure from the conceptually superior method is justified by the exception (i.e., materiality) principle of accounting.

DEMONSTRATION CASE

Howell Equipment, Incorporated

(Try to resolve the requirements before proceeding to the suggested solution that follows.)

Howell Equipment, Incorporated, has been in operation for 18 years. The company sells a major line of farm equipment. In recent years its service department has expanded significantly. Both sales and services have been quite profitable. At the beginning of 19A, the company had considerable excess cash. At that time the management decided to invest in some securities of two of the manufacturers that supply most of the equipment purchased by Howell for resale. The annual accounting period ends on December 31.

This case focuses on the two long-term investments made in 19A. One investment was in equity securities, and the other in debt securities. The transactions follow:

19A

a. Jan. 1 Purchased 2,000 shares of common stock of Dear Company at $40 per share. This was 1 percent of the shares outstanding.

b. Aug. 1 Purchased $100,000, 9 percent bonds payable of the Massy Company at 102, plus accrued interest. The bonds pay semiannual interest each May 31 and November 30. The bonds mature on May 31, 19F (i.e., 5 years from June 1, 19A). Brokerage fees amounted to $900.

c. Nov. 30 Received semiannual interest on Massey Company bonds. Use straight-line amortization.

d. Dec. 28 Received $4,000 cash dividend on the Dear Company stock.

e. Dec. 31 Adjusting entry for accrued interest on the Massey Company bonds.

f. Dec. 31 The current market price of the Dear stock is $39 and 103 for the Massey bonds.

g. Dec. 31 Closed the Revenue from Investments to Income Summary.

Required:

a. Give the journal entry for each of the above transactions.

b. Show how the two investments, the accrued interest receivable and the related revenue, would be reported on the balance sheet and income statement at December 31, 19A.

Suggested solution:

Requirement (a):

a. January 1, 19A:

> Long-term investment, stock of Dear Company
>   (2,000 shares)   80,000
>   Cash   80,000
> Purchased 2,000 shares Dear Company common stock
> at $40 per share.

b. August 1, 19A:

> Long-term investment, bonds of Massey Company   102,900
> Revenue from investments ($100,000 × 0.09 × 2/12) . . .   1,500
>   Cash   104,400
> Purchased $100,000 bonds of the Massey Company.
>
> Computations:
>   Cost ($100,000 × 1.02) + $900 = $102,900
>   Accrued interest for 2 months
> $100,000 × 0.09 × 2/12   =   1,500
>   Total cash paid $104,400

c. November 30, 19A:

> Cash   4,500
>   Long-term investment, bonds of Massey Company .   200
>   Revenue from investments   4,300
>
> Computations:
>   Semiannual interest: $100,000 × 0.045 = $4,500
>   Amortization of premium:
> $2,900 ÷ 58 months = $50
>   per month; $50 × 4 months*   =   200
>   Revenue from investments $4,300
> * August 1, 19A, to May 31, 19 F = 58 months remaining life.

d. December 28, 19A:

> Cash   4,000
>   Revenue from investments   4,000
> Received dividend on Dear Company stock.

e. December 31, 19A:

Interest receivable   750
    Long-term investment, bonds of Massey Company .   50
    Revenue from investments   700
Adjusting entry for accrued interest and premium
amortization for one month on Massey Company bonds.
  Computations:
    Accrued interest receivable:
      $100,000 × 0.09 × 1/12   = $750
    Amortization of premium:
      $50 × 1 month   =   50
      Revenue from investments .. $700

f. December 31, 19A:

Unrealized loss on long-term investment   2,000
    Allowance to reduce long-term investment to LCM   2,000
  To record LCM on Dear stock:
  2,000 shares × ($40 − $39) = $2,000.

g. December 31, 19A:

Revenue from investments   7,500
    Income summary   7,500
  Closing entry: ($4,300 − $1,500 + $4,000 + $700 = $7,500).

Requirement (b):

HOWELL EQUIPMENT, INCORPORATED
Balance Sheet
At December 31, 19A

Current assets:
  Interest receivable .... $ 750
Investment and funds:
  Stock of Dear Company, at LCM, 2,000 shares
    (cost, $80,000)....................................... $ 78,000*
  Bonds of Massey Company, at amortized cost
    ($100,000 maturity value; market, $103,000) .... 102,650†   180,650
Stockholders' equity:
  Unrealized loss on long-term investments ....   (2,000)

Requirement (b) continued:

Income Statement
For the Year Ending December 31, 19A

Revenue from investments		$ 7,500
* Cost of equity securities	80,000	
Less: Allowance to reduce long-term investment to LCM	2,000	
Equity investment at LCM	$ 78,000	
† Cost of debt securities	$102,900	
Less: Amortization of premium ($200 + $50)	250	
Debt investment at amortized cost ..	$102,650	

SUMMARY

This chapter discussed the measuring and reporting of two types of long-term investments: the capital stock (equity securities) and the bonds (debt securities) of another company. An entity (investor) may acquire a part or all of the outstanding capital stock of a corporation by **purchase** of the shares or, if the investor is a corporation, by **exchange** of its own stock for shares in the other company. The measuring and reporting for a long-term investment in shares of capital stock of another company are determined by the percent of shares owned in relation to the total number outstanding.

If the ownership level of **voting** shares is less than 20 percent, or if the ownership is of nonvoting stock, the **cost method** must be used. Under this method the investment amount reported by the investor company is LCM, and dividends declared by the investee corporation are recognized as investment revenue.

If the ownership is at least 20 percent but not more than 50 percent, the **equity method** must be used. Under this method the investment is recorded at cost by the investor company at date of acquisition. Each period thereafter, the investment amount is increased (or decreased) by the proportionate interest in the income (or loss) reported by the investee corporation and decreased by the proportionate share of the dividends declared by the investee corporation. Each period, the investor company recognizes as revenue its proportionate share of the income (or loss) reported by the other company.

When there is a controlling interest—that is, more than 50 percent ownership of the outstanding voting stock is held by the investor—the financial statements of the affiliated companies (investor and investee) are **consolidated.** The subject is discussed in Chapter 14.

An entity may purchase the bonds of another entity as a long-term investment. In contrast to capital stock, bonds are a liability of the issuing company, therefore they (1) have a specified maturity date and face amount, (2) require the payment of a stated rate of interest at regular specified interest dates, and (3) do not convey voting privileges. At the date of purchase, a long-term investment in bonds is recorded at cost, which may be at par, at a discount, or at a premium. When purchased at a premium or a discount, amortization of such premium or discount over the **remaining life** of the bonds is required. The periodic amortization adjusts (1) the investment amount to a carrying value which is reported on the balance sheet and (2) the interest revenue which is reported on the income statement.

IMPORTANT TERMS DEFINED IN THE CHAPTER (with page citations)

Debt securities—557, 567
Equity securities—557
Significant influence (investments)—559, 560, 564
Control (investments)—559, 560
Cost method of accounting for investments—559, 560
Lower of cost or market (LCM)—560
Equity method of accounting for investments—560, 564

Cost principle—568
Current cash equivalent amount—568
Discount on bonds—568, 591
Premium on bonds—568, 574
Stated interest rate—571, 574
Amortization—572, 574, 577
Effective-interest rate—577
Effective-interest amortization—577

QUESTIONS FOR DISCUSSION

Part A

1. Explain the difference between a short-term investment and a long-term investment.

2. Match the following:

    Measurement method
    _____ Cost method.
    _____ Equity method.
    _____ Consolidation.

    Level of ownership of capital stock
    a. More than 50% ownership.
    b. Less than 20% ownership.
    c. At least 20% but not more than 50%.

3. Explain the application of the cost principle to the purchase of shares of capital stock in another company.

4. Under the cost method, why is revenue measured by the investor company only in periods during which the other company declares a cash dividend?

5. Under the equity method, why is revenue measured on a proportionate basis by the investor company when income is reported by the other company, rather than when dividends are declared?

6. Under the equity method, dividends received from the investee company are not recorded as revenue. To record dividends as revenue would involve double counting. Explain.

7. Match the following relating to the balance of the long-term investment amount reported on the balance sheet of the investor company:

    Measurement method
    _____ Cost method.
    _____ Equity method.

    Explanation of balance in the investment account
    a. LCM.
    b. Original cost plus proportionate part of the income of the investee, less proportionate part of the dividends declared by investee.

Questions
Part B

8. Explain the difference between an equity security and a debt security.

9. Explain why interest revenue must be accrued on a long-term investment in bonds but not on a long-term investment in capital stock.

10. Under what conditions will a bond sell at (a) par, (b) a discount, and (c) a premium?

11. Distinguish between a long-term investment in bonds versus a long-term investment in capital stock of another company.

12. Why is it necessary to amortize premium or discount that arises from the purchase of a long-term bond investment above or below par? Over what period should the premium or discount be amortized?

13. When a bond investment is purchased between interest dates, the purchaser must pay accrued interest plus the purchase price of the bond. Explain why the accrued interest must be paid.

EXERCISES
Part A

E13–1. Company P purchased a certain number of the outstanding voting shares of Company S at $15 per share as a long-term investment. Company S had outstanding 10,000 shares of $10 par value stock. On a separate sheet complete the following matrix relating to the measurement and reporting by Company P after acquisition of the shares of Company S stock.

(Relates to Exercise 13–1)

Questions	Method of Measurement	
	Cost Method	Equity Method
a. What is the applicable level of ownership by Company P of Company S to apply the method?	Percent	Percent
For (b), (e), (f), and (g) which follow, assume: Number of shares acquired of Company S stock Net income reported by Company S in first year Dividends declared by Company S in first year Market price at end of first year, Company S stock, $13.50	1,000 $40,000 $10,000	3,000 $40,000 $10,000
b. At acquisition, the investment account on the books of Company P should be debited at what amount?	$	$
c. On what basis should Company P recognize revenue earned on the stock of Company S? Explanation required.		
d. After acquisition date, on what basis should Company P change the balance of investment account in respect to the stock of Company S owned (other than for disposal of the investment)? Explanation required.		

(Relates to Exercise 13–1—Continued)

Questions	Method of Measurement	
	Cost Method	Equity Method
e. What would be the balance in the investment account on the books of Company P at the end of the first year?	$	$
f. What amount of revenue from the investment in Company S will Company P report at the end of the first year?	$	$
g. What amount of unrealized loss will Company P report at the end of the first year?	$	$

E13–2. Adams Company acquired some of the 60,000 shares of the common stock, par $10, of Cox Corporation as a long-term investment. The following transactions occurred during 19B. The accounting period for both companies ends December 31.

19B
July 2 Purchased 6,000 shares of Cox common stock at $20 per share.

Dec. 31 Received a copy of the 19B annual financial statement of Cox Corporation that reflected an income of $40,000.

31 Cox Corporation declared and paid a cash dividend of $0.50 per share.

31 Market price of Cox stock, $19.

Required:

a. What accounting method should be used? Why?
b. Give the required entries by Adams Company for each transaction. If no entry is required, explain why.
c. Show how the long-term investment and the related revenue would be reported on the 19B financial statements of Adams Company.

E13–3. May Company acquired some of the 40,000 shares of outstanding common stock (nopar) of Noe Corporation during

19E as a long-term investment. The annual accounting period for both companies ends December 31. The following transactions occurred during 19E:

19E
Jan. 10 Purchased 12,000 shares of Noe stock at $30 per share.

Dec. 31 Received the 19E financial statement of Noe Corporation which reported net income was $70,000.

31 Noe Corporation, declared and paid a cash dividend of $1.25 per share.

31 Market price of Noe stock, $28.

Required:

a. What method of accounting should be used? Why?
b. Give the entries by May Company for each of the above transactions. State if no entry is required and explain why.
c. Show how the long-term investment and the related revenue would be reported on the 19E financial statements of May Company.

E13–4. During 19H, Ross Company purchased some of the 100,000 shares of common stock, par $10, of Salt Marine, Inc., as a long-term investment. The annual accounting period for each company ends

December 31. The following transactions occurred during 19H.

19H

Jan. 7 Purchased 15,000 shares of Salt stock at $15 per share.

Dec. 31 Received the 19H financial statement of Salt Marine, which reported net income was $70,000.

    31 Salt declared and paid a cash dividend of $1.10 per share.

    31 Market price of Salt stock, $14.50.

Required:

a. What method of accounting is required? Why?

b. Give the entries for Ross Company for each of the above transactions. State if no entry is required and explain why.

c. Show how the long-term investment and the related revenue would be reported on the 19H financial statements of Ross Company.

E13–5. You are to use the same situation and data given in Exercise 13–4, *except* for the January 7, 19H, transaction. Assume it to be as follows:

19H

Jan. 7 Purchased 30,000 shares of Salt stock at $15 per share.

(The data for December 31 are unchanged.)

Required:

a. What method of accounting is required? Why?

b. Give the entries for Ross Company for each transaction (refer also to transactions given in Exercise 13–4). State if no entry is required and explain why.

c. Show how the long-term investment and the related revenue would be reported on the 19H financial statements of Ross Company.

Exercises
Part B

E13–6. On July 1, 19A, AB Company purchased at par a $10,000, 9 percent, 20-year bond of CD Corporation as a long-term investment. The annual bond interest is payable each year on June 30. The accounting period for AB Company ends December 31. At the date of purchase, the bond had five years remaining before maturity.

Required:

Give the following entries on the books of AB Company in respect to the long-term investment:

a. July 1, 19A, for acquisition.

b. December 31, 19A, adjusting entry at the end of the accounting period.

c. June 30, 19B, collection of first interest.

d. Maturity date of the bond, June 30, 19F.

E13–7. On April 1, 19A, GP Company purchased at par eight $1,000, 9 percent, ten-year bonds of HI Corporation as a long-term investment. The bond interest is payable semiannually each March 31 and September 30. The accounting period ends for GP Company on December 31. At the date of purchase, the bonds had six years remaining before maturity.

Required:

Give the entry for each of the following dates in the accounts of GP Company in respect to the long-term investment: April 1, 19A; September 30, 19A; December 31, 19A; March 31, 19B; and the maturity date.

E13–8. On February 1, 19A, Ham Company purchased at par a $12,000, 10 percent, 20-year bond of Lam Corporation as a long-term investment. The bond interest is payable semiannually each January 31 and July 31. The accounting period for

Ham Company ends December 31. At the date of purchase, the bonds had four years remaining life.

Required:

Give all entries required in the accounts of Ham Company for the period February 1, 19A, through January 31, 19B, and on the maturity date.

E13–9. On July 1, 19B, Ray Company purchased three different bonds as long-term investments. Data with respect to the three bonds and the purchase prices were:

(Relates to Exercise 13–9)

Bond designation	Face of bond	Annual interest	Payable semiannually	Remaining years to maturity	Market purchase price*
A	$1,000	10%	Dec. 31 and	5	$1,000
B	1,000	9	June 30	5	970
C	1,000	12	each year	5	1,020

* These amounts do not include any accrued interest.

Required:

a. Give the entries to record separately the purchase of each bond.
b. Give the entries to record separately collection of interest on the first interest date after purchase. Use straight-line amortization of any discount or premium.
c. Give the entries to record separately the maturity of each bond.

E13–10. On May 1, 19B, Noe Company purchased $9,000 maturity value bonds of Opel Corporation at 96.25 (plus any accrued interest) as a long-term investment. The bond interest rate is 12 percent per annum payable 6 percent each April 30 and October 31. The bonds mature in four years from May 1, 19B.

Required:

a. Give the entries for Noe Company on May 1, 19B; October 31, 19B; and December 31, 19B (adjusting entry

for accrued interest). Use straight-line amortization and round all amounts to the nearest dollar.
b. Show how this long-term investment and the related revenue would be shown on the December 31, 19B, annual financial statements of Noe Company. (Hint: Include the investment, interest receivable, and any revenue.)

E13–11. On May 1, 19B, KC Company purchased $6,000, 8 percent bonds of Cook, Inc., at 104 (plus any accrued interest) as a long-term investment. The bonds pay interest each April 30 and October 31. The bonds mature in four years on April 30, 19F.

Required:

a. Give the entries for KC Company on May 1, 19B; October 31, 19B; and December 31, 19B (adjusting entry for accrued interest). Use straight-line amortization.
b. Show how this long-term investment would be shown on the December 31, 19B, annual financial statements of KC Company.

E13–12. On March 1, 19B, ST Corporation purchased $6,000, 10 percent bonds of TU Corporation as a long-term investment. The bonds pay 5 percent interest each June 30 and December 31. The bonds mature in ten years on December 31, 19K. The purchase price was $6,236, plus any accrued interest.

Required:

a. Give the entry by ST Corporation to record the purchase on March 1, 19B.

b. Give the entry to record the interest received on June 30 and December 31, 19B. Use straight-line amortization.

c. What was the amount of interest revenue in 19B? At what amount would the bonds be reported on the balance sheet at December 31, 19B?

E13–13. On January 1, 19A, Cotton Company purchased, as a long-term investment, a $3,000 bond of Devons Company for $2,922 (plus any accrued interest). The bond had a stated interest rate of 7 percent, payable each January 1. The bond matures in three years. Cotton Company uses effective-interest amortization. As a consequence, the amortization table at the bottom of the page was developed.

Required:

Respond to the following questions:

a. How much was the discount or premium?

b. What was the total cash outflow and the total cash inflow over the life of this investment? What does the difference represent? Explain.

c. How much interest revenue will be recognized on the income statement each year and in total?

d. What amounts will be shown on the balance sheet each year? Give the last year just prior to collection of the maturity amount.

e. What was the effective rate of interest per year? Show computations.

f. How were the four different amounts computed that are listed on the line 19B"?

g. Show how the price of the bond of $2,922 was computed.

E13–14. On January 1, 19A, Indian Company purchased, as a long-term investment, a $10,000 face value, 12 percent bond issued by Jackson Corporation. The bond pays interest each year on December 31 and has five years' remaining life from January 1, 19A, until maturity. The accounting period ends December 31.

The bond was purchased to yield a 10 percent effective rate of interest; therefore, the price of the bond was computed as follows:

$$\$10,000 \times p_{n=5; i=10\%} \, (0.6209) = \$\ 6,209$$
$$\$1,200 \times P_{n=5; i=10\%} \, (3.7908) = \underline{4,549}$$
$$\text{Sales price} \ldots\ldots\ldots \underline{\underline{\$10,758}}$$

Required:

a. Give the entry for Indian Company to record the purchase of the bond on January 1, 19A.

b. Prepare a schedule of effective-interest amortization similar to Exhibit 13–2.

c. Give the entries for the collection of interest on the bond investment for 19A and 19B.

d. Complete the following (show computations):

(Relates to Exercise 13–13)

Date	Cash inflow	Interest revenue	Investment change	Investment balance
January 1, 19A				$2,922
End Year 19A	$210	$234	$24	2,946
End Year 19B	210	236	26	2,972
End Year 19C	210	238	28	3,000

	December 31	
	19A	19B
Income statement:		
Revenue from bond investment	$_____	$_____
Balance sheet:		
Bond interest receivable	_____	_____
Long-term investment, bond of Jackson corporation	_____	_____

PROBLEMS

Part A

P13–1. During January 19A, Seven Company purchased 10,000 shares of the 100,000 outstanding common shares (nopar value) of Eleven Corporation at $40 per share. This block of stock was purchased as a long-term investment. Assume the accounting period for each company ends December 31.

Subsequent to acquisition, the following data were available:

Required:

a. What accounting method should be used by Seven Company? Why?

b. Give the entries required in the accounts of Seven Company for each year (use parallel columns) for the following (if none, explain why):

1. Acquisition.
2. Net income reported by Eleven Corporation.
3. Dividends received.
4. Market value effects.

c. For each year show how the following amounts should be reported on the financial statements for Seven Company:

1. Long-term investment.
2. Stockholders' equity—unrealized loss.
3. Revenues.

P13–2. During January 19A, Doe Corporation acquired the shares listed below as a long-term investment:

(Relates to Problem 13–1)

	19A	19B
Income reported by Eleven Corporation at December 31	$60,000	$70,000
Cash dividends declared and paid by Eleven Corporation during year	20,000	30,000
Market price per share of Eleven common stock on December 31	37	38

(Relates to Problem 13–2)

		Number of shares		
Corporation	Stock	Outstanding	Acquired	Cost per share
M	Common (nopar)	80,000	12,000	$10
N	Preferred, nonvoting (par $10)	10,000	4,000	15

Assume the accounting period of each company ends on December 31.

Subsequent to acquisition, the following data were available:

	19A	19B
Net income reported at December 31:		
Corporation M	$20,000	$22,000
Corporation N	30,000	31,000
Dividends declared and paid per share during the year:		
Corporation M common stock	$ 1.00	$ 1.10
Corporation N preferred stock	0.20	0.20
Market value per share at December 31:		
Corporation M common stock	8.00	9.00
Corporation N preferred stock	16.00	15.00

Required:

a. What accounting method should be used by Doe for the M common stock? N preferred stock? Why?

b. Give the following entries for the accounts of Doe Corporation for each year in parallel columns (if none, state why):
  1. Acquisition of the investments.
  2. Income reported by Corporations M and N.
  3. Dividends received.
  4. Market value effects.

c. For each year, show how the following amounts should be reported on the financial statements for 19A:
  1. Long-term investment.

2. Stockholders' equity—unrealized loss.
3. Revenues.

P13–3. Company S had outstanding 20,000 shares of common stock, par value $10 per share. On January 1, 19B, Company P purchased some of these shares at $20 per share. At the end of 19B, Company S reported the following: income, $30,000; and cash dividends declared and paid, $10,000. The market value of Company S stock at the end of 19B was $17 per share.

Required:

a. For each case given below, identify the method of accounting that should be used by Company P. Explain why.

b. Give the entries required in the accounts of Company P at the dates indicated below for each of the two independent cases. If no entry is required, so indicate and explain.

c. Give the separate amounts that would be reported on the financial statements of Company P, for 19B, in respect to the investment in Company S as indicated on page 591:

(Relates to Problem 13–3)

Items	Case A—2,000 shares purchased	Case B—8,000 shares purchased
1. Entry to record the acquisition at January 1, 19B.		
2. Entry to recognize the income reported by Company S for 19B.	————	————
3. Entry to recognize the dividends declared and paid by Company S for 19B.	————	————
4. Entry to recognize market value effect at end of 19B.	————	————

	Dollar amounts	
	Case A	Case B
Balance sheet:		
Investments and funds	_____	_____
Stockholders' equity..................	_____	_____
Income statement:		
Revenue from investments	_____	_____

d. Explain why assets, stockholders' equity, and revenues are different between the two cases.

P13–4. Fortner Company purchased, as a long-term investment, some of the 100,000 shares of the outstanding common stock of Towns, Inc. The annual accounting period for each company ends December 31. The following transactions occurred during 19E.

19E

Jan. 10 Purchased shares of common stock of Towns at $11 per share as follows:

Case A—10,000 shares purchased.

Case B—30,000 shares purchased.

Dec. 31 Received financial statements of Towns, Inc., for the year ended December 31, 19E. The reported net income was $70,000.

31 Received cash dividend of $0.30 per share from Towns, Inc.

31 Market price of Towns stock, $10.

Required:

a. For each case, what accounting method should be used by Fortner? Explain why.

b. Give the entries for Fortner Company for each case for the above transactions. State if no entry is required and explain why. (Hint: You can save time by using parallel columns for Case A and Case B.)

c. Give the amounts for each case that would be reported on the financial statements of Fortner Corporation at December 31, 19E. Use the following format:

	Case A	Case B
Balance sheet:		
Investments and funds:		
Investment in common stock, Towns, Inc.	_____	_____
Stockholders' equity:		
Unrealized loss	_____	_____
Income statement:		
Revenue from investments .	_____	_____

P13–5. Sub Corporation had outstanding 200,000 shares of nopar value common stock. On January 10, 19B, Par Company purchased a block of these shares in the open market at $20 per share. At the end of 19B, Sub Corporation reported net income of $100,000 and cash dividends of $0.30 per share. At December 31, 19B, the Sub stock was selling at $19.50 per share. This problem involves two separate cases:

Case A—Par Company purchased 30,000 shares of Sub stock.

Case B—Par Company purchased 60,000 shares of Sub stock.

Required:

a. For each case, what accounting method should be used by Par Company? Explain why.

b. For each case, give, in parallel columns, entries in the accounts of Par Company for (if no entry is required, explain why):

1. Acquisition.
2. Revenue recognition.
3. Dividends received.
4. Market value effects.

c. For each case, show how the following should be reported on the 19B financial statements for Par Company:

1. Long-term investments.
2. Any market effects.
3. Revenues.

d. Explain why the amounts reported (in Requirement [c]) are different as between the two cases.

Problems
Part B

P13–6. On January 1, 19B, Ace Company purchased $60,000, 9 percent bonds of Bye Company as a long-term investment, at 100 (plus any accrued interest). Interest is payable annually on December 31. The bonds mature in six years from December 31, 19A. The annual accounting period for Ace Company ends December 31. In addition, on January 2, 19B, Ace Company purchased in the market 5 percent of the 10,000 shares of outstanding common stock of Bye Company at $30 per share.

Required:

a. Give the entry by Ace Company for the purchase of the bonds on January 1, 19B.
b. Give the entry to record the purchase of the common stock on January 2, 19B.
c. Give the entry assuming a cash dividend of $2.50 per share was received on the Bye stock on December 28, 19B.
d. Give the entry for the receipt of the interest on the Bye bonds on December 31, 19B.
e. Show how the long-term investments and the related revenues would be reported on the annual financial statements of Ace Company at December 31, 19B. Market price of Bye stock, $31.

P13–7. On May 1, 19B, Sun Company purchased $30,000 maturity value, 8 percent bonds of Taylor Company, as a long-term investment. The interest is payable each April 30 and October 31. The bonds mature in four years from May 1, 19B. The bonds were purchased at 96 (plus any accrued interest). In addition, brokerage fees of $240 were paid by Sun Company.

Required:

a. Give the 19B entries for Sun Company on the following dates:

May 1 Purchase.
Oct. 31 First interest date. Use straight-line amortization.
Dec. 31 Adjusting entry for accrued interest at the end of the annual accounting period.

b. Show how the investment, interest receivable, and related revenue would be reported on the annual financial statements of Sun Company on December 31, 19B.
c. Give the entry at the maturity date of the bonds.

P13–8. On June 1, 19B, Fry Company purchased $30,000, 9 percent bonds of Gray Company, as a long-term investment. The interest is payable each April 30 and October 31. The bonds mature in five years from the issue date, May 1, 19B. The bonds were purchased at 103 (plus any accrued interest). In addition, Fry Company paid brokerage fees of $280. The annual accounting period for Fry Company ends December 31.

Required:

a. Give the entries for Fry Company on the following dates:

June 1 Purchase plus accrued interest.
Oct. 31 First interest date. Use straight-line amortization.
Dec. 31 Adjusting entry for accrued interest.

b. Show how the investment, interest receivable, and related revenue would be reported on the annual financial statements of Fry Company on December 31, 19B.

c. Give the entry at the maturity date of the bonds, April 30, 19G.

P13–9. During 19A, Akers Company purchased the following bonds of Bounds Corporation as a long-term investment:

(Relates to Problem 13–9)

	Series A	Series B	Series C	Series D
Maturity amount	$10,000	$10,000	$10,000	$10,000
Date purchased	7/1/19A	7/1/19A	7/1/19A	9/1/19A
Interest per annum	8%	7%	9%	9%
Interest dates, annual	June 30	June 30	June 30	June 30
Maturity date	6/30/19F	6/30/19F	6/30/19F	6/30/19F
Purchase price*	100	95	106	100

* Plus any accrued interest.

Required:

a. Record separately the purchase on the books of Akers Company for each series.

b. Give the adjusting entries required on the books of Akers Company for December 31, 19A, assuming this is the end of the accounting period. Make a separate entry for each series. Use straight-line amortization.

c. Give the entry on the books of Akers Company for each separate series that should be made on June 30, 19B, for collection of the first interest payment.

d. Compute the following amounts that should be reflected on the December 31, 19A, financial statements:

Income statement (19A):
  Revenue from investments .... $_____

Balance sheet (at December 31, 19A):
  Long-term investment,
  bonds of Bounds
  Corporation .... $_____

P13–10. On January 1, 19A, Evans Corporation purchased, as a long-term investment, a bond of Fable Corporation. The fol-

lowing table was prepared based on the investment (table captions have been omitted intentionally):

January 1, 19A				$10,339
End Year 19A	$800	$724	$76	10,263
End Year 19B	800	718	82	10,181
End Year 19C	800	713	87	10,094
End Year 19D	800	706	94	10,000

Required:

Respond to the following in respect to Evans Corporation:

a. What was the maturity amount of the bond?

b. What was the acquisition price of the investment?

c. Give the entry which was made at acquisition date by Evans Corporation.

d. Was the bond acquired at a premium or discount? How much?

e. What was the stated rate of interest per year? Show computations.

f. What method of amortization apparently will be used? Explain.

g. What was the effective rate of interest?

h. What were the total cash inflow and total cash outflow on the investment? What does the difference represent? Explain.

i. How much interest revenue will be reported each period on the income statement? How does this relate to the difference in *(h)*?

j. What amount will be reported on the balance sheet at the end of each year? (Show Year 19D just before collection of the maturity amount.)

k. How were the amounts in each of the

four columns computed that are in the table? Use Year 19B and show computations.

l. Why is the method of amortization being used conceptually superior?

P13–11. On January 1, 19A, Austin Corporation purchased $50,000, 9 percent bonds of Boston Company to yield an effective rate of 10 percent. The bonds pay the interest on June 30 and December 31 and will mature on December 31, 19C.

This long-term investment was recorded by Austin Corporation as follows:

January 1, 19A:

Long-term investment, Boston Company bonds	48,730	
Cash		48,730

Computations:
Principal—$50,000 × $p_{n=6;i=5\%}$ (0.7462) = $37,310
Interest—$2,250 × $P_{n=6;i=5\%}$ (5.0757) = 11,420
Bond price $48,730

Required:

a. What were the stated and effective rates of interest?

b. What was the amount of discount or premium? What would be the amount of discount or premium amortization each interest period assuming straight-line amortization?

c. Prepare a schedule of effective-interest amortization similar to Exhibit 13–2.

d. Give the interest entries (including amortization) on June 30 and December 31, 19A, assuming (1) straight-line and (2) effective-interest amortization.

e. Explain when it is appropriate to use each method of amortization.

14

Consolidated statements— measuring and reporting

PURPOSE OF THE CHAPTER

The preceding chapter discussed long-term investments in equity securities when one company owns 50 percent or less of the outstanding voting stock of another corporation. This chapter discusses those situations in which there is a controlling interest evidenced by ownership of more than 50 percent of the outstanding voting stock of another corporation. Prior to studying this chapter you should reread Chapter 13.

A general understanding of a controlling interest, consolidation concepts, and consolidated financial statements is important at this level of your study of accounting. Those persons who do not plan to study accounting beyond the introductory level need this general background in order to understand and evaluate the economic and accounting implications of business combinations. In most business courses, financial statements are encountered in various situations, and most of them will be consolidated statements. Outside the classroom, you frequently will encounter consolidated statements. For those persons who plan to study accounting further, this background will be quite useful. An understanding of the broad issues, measurement approaches, and underlying concepts of consolidated statements also is important to the statement user. This chapter has as its primary objective the presentation of these basic issues.

When an investor company owns more than 50 percent of the outstanding voting stock of another corporation, a **parent** and **subsidiary** relationship is said to exist. The **investing** company is known as the **parent** company, and the **other** corporation is called a **subsidiary.** Both corporations continue as **separate legal entities,** and separate financial statements for each are prepared. However, because of their special relationship, they are viewed as a **single economic entity** for **financial measuring** and **reporting purposes.** They generally are called related or affiliated companies, and the parent company (but not the subsidiary) is required to prepare **consolidated financial statements.** To accomplish this, the individual financial statements of the parent and each of its subsidiaries are combined into one overall or consolidated set of financial statements, as if there were only one entity. The three required statements—balance sheet, income statement, and statement of changes in financial position—are consolidated by the parent company.

This chapter discusses the interpretation and use of consolidated financial statements. Measuring approaches and reporting on a consolidated basis are accorded primary attention. The important differences that result between a pooling of interests and a combination by purchase are identified and discussed. For those who desire to gain a greater depth of understanding of the measurement and consolidation procedures involved. Appendixes A and B have been included.

To accomplish the broad purpose of this chapter, two parts and two appendixes are presented:

Part A: Acquiring a controlling interest

Part B: Reporting consolidated operations after acquisition

Appendix A: Procedures for deriving consolidated statements—100 percent ownership

Appendix B: Procedures for deriving consolidated statements— Controlling interest of less than 100 percent ownership

Behavioral and learning objectives for this chapter are provided in the *Teachers Manual.*

PART A: ACQUIRING A CONTROLLING INTEREST

There are a number of operating, economic, and legal advantages to the parent-subsidiary relationship. As a consequence, most large corporations, and many medium-sized corporations, own more than 50 percent of the outstanding voting stock of one or more other corporations.

Consolidated statements are prepared in situations in which two basic elements that relate to two or more different corporations are present. The two basic elements are control and economic compatibility.

Control is presumed to exist when more than 50 percent of the voting stock of an entity is owned by one investor. The nonvoting stock is not included in this determination because it does not extend any avenue for control to the investor. In special circumstances, effective control may not exist, even though more than 50 percent of the voting stock is owned. This situation may exist when the subsidiary is located in a foreign country where **governmental restrictions** are such that the parent company is powerless to exert meaningful control regardless of the number of shares of voting stock owned by the parent company. In such circumstances, since control is lacking, consolidated statements would be inappropriate.

Economic compatibility means that the operations of the companies are related so that one complements the other. For example, a company manufacturing a major item and a subsidiary manufacturing a component part of the major item would have economic compatibility. On the other hand, a manufacturing company and a bank may lack economic compatibility and would not be consolidated.

When one company owns more than 50 percent of the voting stock of another company, but because of lack of either *(a)* meaningful control or *(b)* economic compatibility it does not qualify for consolidation, the subsidiary is reported as a long-term investment on the balance sheet of the parent as "Investment in unconsolidated subsidiary." In this case the investment is accounted for under the **equity method** as discussed in Chapter 13 and is not consolidated.

The concept of consolidated statements relates **only to reporting** by the parent company of the financial results of the parent and its subsidiaries as one economic unit. Otherwise, the accounting for each business is unaffected. The fact that another company owns a controlling interest has no affect on the accounting and reporting by a subsidiary. At the end of the accounting period, the subsidiary prepares its own financial statements. Similarly, the parent company carries out the accounting for its own operations in the normal manner and prepares its own financial statements at the end of each period.

Under the concept of consolidated statements, when consolidation is appropriate, the financial statements of the parent and the subsidiaries, prepared in the normal manner, are combined, or aggregated, by the parent company on an **item-by-item basis** to develop the consolidated financial statements. Thus, the consolidated statement concept does not affect the recording of transactions by the parent and the subsidiaries but affects only the **reporting phase** of the combined entity represented by the parent company.

At the end of the chapter, a set of actual consolidated statements is presented for study.

METHODS OF ACQUIRING A CONTROLLING INTEREST

One corporation may acquire a controlling interest in another corporation either *(a)* by organizing a new entity and *retaining* more than 50 percent of the capital stock of the new corporation or *(b)* by *acquiring* more than 50 percent of the outstanding stock of an existing corporation. Both approaches of acquiring a controlling interest (to establish a parent-subsidiary relationship) are used widely. Basically, the parent company may acquire more than 50 percent of the voting capital stock of the other entity in either of two ways as follows:[1]

1. **Exchanging shares by the parent of its own unissued capital stock (and sometimes treasury stock) for more than 50 percent of the outstanding voting shares of capital stock of the subsidiary (owned by the shareholders of the subsidiary)**—Under certain circumstances, this is known as a combination by a **pooling of interests.** In this situation, the shareholders of the subsidiary give up their subsidiary shares and become shareholders only of the parent company.

2. **Purchasing by the parent, using cash, other assets, or debt, of more than 50 percent of the outstanding voting shares from the shareholders of the subsidiary**—This is known as a **combination by purchase.** In this situation, the shareholders of the subsidiary sell more than 50 percent of their voting shares and subsequently they are not shareholders of either the parent or the subsidiary.

The pooling and purchase methods have significantly different impacts on the consolidated income statement and balance sheet. The next few paragraphs discuss these major impacts, the problems of measuring, and reporting on the consolidated financial statements.

Throughout the chapter we will use a continuing example to illustrate the measuring approaches involved and the effects on the consolidated financial statements. We will use data for Company P (the parent) and Company S (the acquired subsidiary). Assume that on January 1, 19A (just prior to the acquisition), the separate balance sheets for Company P and Company S reported the data shown in Exhibit 14–1.

POOLING OF INTERESTS

When one corporation acquires a controlling interest in the voting stock of another corporation by **exchanging** some of its own shares, a purchase/sale transaction between the parties often is deemed not to have been consummated.[2] The parent company simply has issued its own stock certif-

---

[1] This is the basic distinction between pure combination by pooling of interest and a pure purchase. However, a controlling interest may be acquired in part by a stock exchange and in part by a cash purchase. In these "nonpure" situations, a rigid list of criteria must be met to qualify as a pooling of interest (see footnote 2); otherwise, the combination must be accounted for as a combination by purchase.

[2] AICPA, *APB Opinion No. 16*, "Business Combinations" (New York, August 1970), states precise conditions under which a business combination *must* be measured and reported as a pooling of interests. Copyright (1970) by the American Institute of CPAs. The *Opinion* states: "The combination of existing voting common stock interests by the exchange of stock is the essence of a business combination accounted for by the pooling of interests." The *Opinion* specifies a number of additional conditions that if present *require* use of the pooling of interests method. Because of these conditions, many stock exchanges (particularly if cash also is involved) do not qualify for the pooling of interests method. All combinations not meeting the specified conditions for pooling of interests must be accounted for by the purchase method. The usual, although not exclusive, mode of combina-

EXHIBIT 14–1

COMPANY P AND COMPANY S
Separate Balance Sheets
January 1, 19A, Immediately before Acquisition

	Company P		Company S	
Assets				
Cash		$205,000		$ 35,000
Accounts receivable (net)*		15,000		30,000
Receivable from Company S		10,000		
Inventories		170,000		70,000
Plant and equipment (net)*		100,000		45,000
Total assets		$500,000		$180,000
Liabilities and Shareholders' Equity				
Liabilities:				
Accounts payable		$ 60,000		$ 20,000
Payable to Company P				10,000
Stockholders' equity:				
Common stock, Company P (par $6)	$300,000			
Common stock, Company S (par $10)			$100,000	
Retained earnings	140,000	440,000	50,000	150,000
Total liabilities and shareholders' equity		$500,000		$180,000

* Accounts receivable, less the allowance for doubtful accounts; and plant and equipment, less accumulated depreciation. The net amounts are used to simplify the example. The end results will be the same as they would have been had the separate contra accounts been used.

icates for the stock certificates of the subsidiary company. Because there was no purchase/sale transaction, the cost principle is not applied. Thus, under the consolidation concept, the exchange of stock, in many cases, is viewed as a combination by a **pooling of interests** rather than as a purchase. As a consequence, when the financial statements of the parent and subsidiary are combined by the parent company, the **book values** of each, as shown on their respective financial statements, are added together with no consideration for the current market values of the assets of the subsidiary.

Assume that on January 2, 19A, Company P (the parent) acquired all of the outstanding voting stock of Company S (the subsidiary) by exchanging with the shareholders of Company S one share of Company P stock for each share of Company S stock. Thus, the shareholders of Company S turned in all of their 10,000 shares and received in return 10,000 shares of unissued Company P stock. They are now shareholders of Company P and no longer shareholders of Company S. After the exchange, Company P owns all of the outstanding voting shares of Company S; that is, it owns a 100 percent interest in Company S. Accordingly, **Company P** would make the following journal entry in its accounts:

tion in these latter situations is by disbursement of cash or by incurrence of debt for the stock.

January 2, 19A:

Investment in Company S stock (10,000 shares; 100 percent) ...	150,000	
Common stock (10,000 shares par $6)		60,000
Contributed capital from pooling of interests		90,000
Acquisition by pooling of interests.		

Observe that the long-term investment account of Company P was debited for the **book value** of the Company S stock as shown on the books of Company S ($100,000 + $50,000). This amount was used because that is the book value of the owners' equity in Company S, which Company P now controls. The Common Stock account of Company P was credited for the number of shares issued times the par value per share, and Contributed Capital from Pooling of Interests was credited for the difference. The cost principle was not involved in the debit to the investment account (an asset) because there was no *purchase* of the stock, only a pooling of interests by exchanging "paper." The exchange of shares of stock had no effect on the accounts of the subsidiary, Company S.

After the above journal entry is posted to the ledger accounts of Company P, the two separate balance sheets then would be changed as shown in Exhibit 14–2.

Now, let's combine the two separate balance sheets shown in Exhibit 14–2 into a single **consolidated balance sheet** as if there were a single

EXHIBIT 14–2

COMPANY P AND COMPANY S
Separate Balance Sheets (pooling of interests basis)
January 2, 19A, Immediately after Acquisition

	Company P	Company S
Assets		
Cash	$205,000	$ 35,000
Accounts receivable (net)	15,000	30,000
Receivable from Company S	10,000	
Inventories	170,000	70,000
Investment in Company S (100%)	150,000*	
Plant and equipment (net)	100,000	45,000
Total assets	$650,000	$180,000
Liabilities and Shareholders' Equity		
Accounts payable	$ 60,000	$ 20,000
Payable to Company P.....................................		10,000
Common stock, Company P	360,000*	
Common stock, Company S		100,000
Contributed capital from pooling of interests	90,000*	
Retained earnings, Company P	140,000	
Retained earnings, Company S		50,000
Total liabilities and shareholders' equity	$650,000	$180,000

* Amounts changed from precombination balance sheets given in Exhibit 14–1.

entity represented by the parent company. To combine the two, we must be careful not to double count or to include any items that are strictly between the two companies. There are two such items in this situation:

a. The debit balance in the investment account of $150,000 shown in the accounts of Company P will be replaced with the assets (less the liabilities) of Company S; therefore, to prevent double counting, it must be eliminated (dropped out). The credit balance in the common stock account of $100,000 shown in the accounts of Company S is now owned by Company P; therefore, it is an intercompany item that must be eliminated. Finally, the difference between the balances in the investment account and the common stock account of Company P ($150,000 − $100,000 = $50,000) must be offset in the account on Company P's books, Contributed Capital from Pooling of Interests. This offset is necessary because it is an intercompany amount included in the investment account balance (refer to the acquisition entry). These three eliminations or offsets of intercompany items must be made by Company P to avoid double counting; they can be summarized as follows:[3]

	Eliminations	
	Consolidated assets	*Consolidated shareholders' equity*
Investment account—decrease	−$150,000	
Common stock, Company S—decrease		−$100,000
Contributed capital from pooling of interests—decrease (for the difference)		− 50,000

b. The accounts of Company P show a receivable of $10,000 from Company S, and the accounts of Company S show this as a debt to Company P. This is called an **intercompany debt.** When the two balance sheets are combined into a single consolidated balance sheet, this intercompany debt must be eliminated because there is no debt owed by the combined entity. Thus, the following elimination or offset must be made when combining the two balance sheets:

	Eliminations	
	Consolidated assets	*Consolidated liabilities*
Receivable from Company S—decrease	−$10,000	
Payable to Company P—decrease		−$10,000

---

[3] This also can be viewed in the debit/credit format as follows (see appendixes):

Common stock, Company S	100,000	
Contributed capital from pooling of interests	50,000	
Investment in Company S		150,000

The two balance sheets are shown separately in Exhibit 14–3 and in the last column are combined (aggregated) on a line-by-line basis, after deducting the "Eliminations," to develop the **"Consolidated balance sheet."** In an external consolidated financial statement, only the last column—the "Consolidated balance sheet" (and not the "Separate balance sheets")—would be reported by the parent company.

In the "Consolidated balance sheet" on the pooling basis, as shown

EXHIBIT 14–3

COMPANY P and Its Subsidiary, COMPANY S (100 percent owned)
Consolidated Balance Sheet (pooling of interests basis)
At January 2, 19A, Immediately after Acquisition

| | Separate balance sheets | | | Consolidated balance sheet |
	Company P*	Company S*	Eliminations*	
Assets				
Cash	$205,000	$ 35,000		$240,000
Accounts receivable (net)	15,000	30,000		45,000
Receivable from Company S	10,000		*(b)* — 10,000	–0–
Inventories	170,000	70,000		240,000
Investment in Company S	150,000		*(a)* — 150,000	–0–
Plant and equipment (net)	100,000	45,000		145,000
Total assets	$650,000	$180,000		$670,000
Liabilities				
Accounts payable	$ 60,000	$ 20,000		$ 80,000
Payable to Company P		10,000	*(b)* — 10,000	–0–
Shareholders' Equity				
Common stock, Company P	360,000			360,000
Common stock, Company S		100,000	*(a)* — 100,000	–0–
Contributed capital from pooling	90,000		*(a)* — 50,000	40,000
Retained earnings, Company P	140,000			190,000
Retained earnings, Company S		50,000		
Total liabilities and shareholders' equity	$650,000	$180,000		$670,000

* Included for instructional purposes only. A worksheet usually is used to derive the consolidated amounts. See Appendixes A and B.

in the last column of Exhibit 14–3, the following measurement procedures are evident: (1) the amounts on each line for the combined assets, liabilities, and shareholders' equity are the **combined book values** of the parent and the subsidiary as were reflected on the separate balance sheets; (2) the intercompany amounts for investment, subsidiary common stock, a part of contributed capital from pooling, and the intercompany debt are eliminated; and (3) the consolidated retained earnings is the sum of the two separate retained earnings amounts ($140,000 + $50,000 = $190,000).[4]

---

[4] The pooling of interests approach also requires that all comparative statements presented for prior years must be restated as if consolidated statements had been prepared.

The capital stock balance reflected in the accounts of Company S is eliminated because it is an intercompany item (all of it is owned by Company P). Retained earnings of Company S is not eliminated because it is not an intercompany item; the old shareholders of Company P plus the new shareholders of Company P (the former Company S shareholders) have dividend claims on the **total** of retained earnings for the combined unit.

The pooling of interests results are compared on page 607 with those that occur when the acquisition is by purchase instead.

COMBINATION BY PURCHASE

When one corporation acquires a controlling interest in the voting stock of another corporation by *purchase* rather than by an exchange of shares of stock, a purchase/sale transaction is deemed to have occurred.[5] This purchase/sale transaction requires application of the **cost principle** by the parent company in recording the long-term investment. That is, the investment account on the books of the parent company must be debited **at cost, which is the market value of the shares purchased** (i.e., the cash or cash equivalent paid). The stock of the subsidiary, purchased by the parent from the subsidiary's former shareholders, may be paid for in cash or a combination of cash, other assets, and debt. The stockholders of the subsidiary are paid off and are no longer shareholders in either the parent or the subsidiary.

At this point, the basic measuring (and reporting) distinction between a combination by pooling of interests and by purchase becomes apparent. Recall that in a pooling of interests the **book values** of the subsidiary's balance sheet accounts are added to the book values of the parent's accounts. In contrast, to prepare consolidated financial statements when the purchase method is used, the subsidiary company's *market values* (measured at date of acquisition) are added to the book values of the parent company.

Since the *market values* of the subsidiary must be recognized in a combination by purchase and its *book values* must be used in a pooling of interests (as explained above), the economic and reporting impacts between pooling and purchasing differ significantly.

To illustrate a combination by *purchase*, the example of Companies P and S as given in Exhibit 14–1 is used. Instead of the change of shares, we will assume that on January 2, 19A, Company P **purchased** 100 percent of the 10,000 shares of outstanding stock of Company S, from Company S's shareholders, at $16.50 per share (i.e., for $165,000) and paid cash. On this date, Company P would make the following entry in its accounts:

---

[5] Refer to footnote 2. In some instances, stock exchanges do not qualify for the pooling approach. In these instances, the purchase approach must be used, in which case the parent company must recognize the *market values* for the subsidiary assets in conformity with the cost principle, just as if cash and/or debt were exchanged for the stock of the subsidiary. These complexities are beyond the scope of this book.

January 2, 19A:

Investment in stock of Company S (10,000 shares, 100 percent)	165,000	
Cash		165,000
Acquisition by purchase.		

Note that Company P paid $165,000 cash for 100 percent of the owners' equity of Company S, although the **total book value** of the shareholders' equity of Company S that was purchased was only $150,000. Thus, Company P paid $15,000 more than "book value." In consolidating the two balance sheets, this $15,000 difference must be taken into account as explained below. Also, Company P determined that the plant and equipment owned by Company S at this date had a market value of $50,000 (compared with the book value of $45,000 reported by Company S).

The purchase by Company P will have no effect on the accounting and reporting by the subsidiary Company S since the stock was sold (and cash was received) by the stockholders of Company S (and not by Company S itself).

After the above entry is posted to the accounts of Company P, the two separate balance sheets then would be changed as shown in Exhibit 14–4.

The consolidated balance sheet of Company P and its subsidiary, Company S, immediately after acquisition, is shown in Exhibit 14–5 on the

EXHIBIT 14–4

COMPANY P AND COMPANY S
Separate Balance Sheets (purchase basis)
January 2, 19A, Immediately after Acquisition

	Company P	Company S
Assets		
Cash	$ 40,000*	$ 35,000
Accounts receivable (net)	15,000	30,000
Receivable from Company S	10,000	
Inventories	170,000	70,000
Investment in Company S (100%)	165,000*	
Plant and equipment (net)	100,000	45,000
Total assets	$500,000	$180,000
Liabilities and Shareholders' Equity		
Accounts payable	$ 60,000	$ 20,000
Payable to Company P		10,000
Common stock, Company P	300,000	
Common stock, Company S		100,000
Retained earnings, Company P	140,000	
Retained earnings, Company S		50,000
Total liabilities and shareholders' equity	$500,000	$180,000

* Amounts changed from precombination balance sheets (given in Exhibit 14–1).

EXHIBIT 14–5

COMPANY P and Its Subsidiary, COMPANY S (100 percent owned)
Consolidated Balance Sheet (purchase basis)
At January 2, 19A, Immediately after Acquisition

	Separate balance sheets			Consolidated balance sheet
	Company P*	Company S*	Eliminations*	
Assets				
Cash	$ 40,000	$ 35,000		$ 75,000
Accounts receivable (net)	15,000	30,000		45,000
Receivable from Company S	10,000		(b) — 10,000	–0–
Inventories	170,000	70,000		240,000
Investment in Company S	165,000		(a) — 165,000	–0–
Plant and equipment (net)	100,000	45,000	(a) + 5,000	150,000
Goodwill†			(a) + 10,000	10,000
Total assets	$500,000	$180,000		$520,000
Liabilities				
Accounts payable	$ 60,000	$ 20,000		$ 80,000
Payable to Company P		10,000	(b) — 10,000	–0–
Shareholders' Equity				
Common stock, Company P	300,000			300,000
Common stock, Company S		100,000	(a) — 100,000	–0–
Retained earnings, Company P	140,000			140,000
Retained earnings, Company S		50,000	(a) — 50,000	–0–
Total liabilitites and shareholders' equity	$500,000	$180,000		$520,000

* Included for instructional purposes only. A worksheet usually is used to derive the consolidated amounts. See Appendixes A and B.

† A title preferred by most accountants is "Excess of purchase price over the current value of the net assets of the subsidiary" rather than "Goodwill." However, the length of this term causes the shorter term to be used extensively.

purchase basis. The two separate balance sheets, given in Exhibit 14–4, were combined, to develop the consolidated balance sheet of Company P, in a manner similar to the previous illustration (Exhibit 14–3) for the pooling of interests basis. There are two intercompany items that require eliminations similar to those illustrated for the pooling of interests approach; however, the first one differs significantly. The two eliminations or offsets are:

a. The investment account debit balance of $165,000, on the books of Company P, is at *market value* (i.e., at cost). It is eliminated or offset against the shareholders' equity of the subsidiary, which is at *book value*. In this case there is a difference, and it must be recognized in the consolidated statement. The difference may be analyzed as follows:

Purchase price for 100% interest in Company S		$165,000
Net assets purchased, valued at market:		
Book value, $180,000 + market value increment of plant and equipment, $5,000 =	$185,000	
Less liabilities assumed	30,000	
Total market value purchased		155,000
Goodwill purchased		$ 10,000

Company P paid $165,000 cash for Company S, which had net assets (total assets minus liabilities) with a **market** value of $155,000; therefore, the goodwill of Company S cost $10,000. **Goodwill** is the amount that Company P actually paid for the good reputation, customer appeal, and general acceptance of the business that Company S had developed over the years. All successful companies enjoy a measure of goodwill. Its "value" is never known except when a business is purchased, as it was in this instance.

To eliminate the investment account on the books of Company P and the owner's equity accounts on the books of Company S, the following steps must be completed:

1. Increase the plant and equipment from the book value to market value; the increase is $5,000.
2. Recognize as an asset the $10,000 goodwill purchased.
3. Eliminate the investment account balance of $165,000.
4. Eliminate the Company S common stock balance of $100,000.
5. Eliminate the Company S retained earnings balance of $50,000.

Recognition of these items is as follows:[6]

	Eliminations	
	Consolidated assets	Consolidated shareholders' equity
Plant and equipment—increase	+$ 5,000	
Goodwill—increase	+ 10,000	
Investment—decrease	− 165,000	
Common stock Company S—decrease		−$100,000
Retained earnings, Company S—decrease		− 50,000

b. The intercompany debt must be eliminated, viz:

	Eliminations	
	Consolidated assets	Consolidated liabilities
Receivable from Company S—decrease	−$10,000	
Payable to Company P—decrease		−$10,000

In contrast to the pooling of interests method, when the purchase method is used, the balance of Retained Earnings of the subsidiary at acquisition

---

[6] This can also be viewed in the debit-credit format as follows (see appendixes):

Plant and equipment	5,000	
Goodwill	10,000	
Common stock, Company S	100,000	
Retained earnings, Company S	50,000	
Investment, Company S		165,000

is eliminated because it was in effect paid out to the former shareholders of Company S when they were reimbursed in cash for the market value of their shares (they are no longer shareholders of either company).

The accounts of Company S are not affected by a purchase since the transactions were between the parent company and the former shareholders of the subsidiary (and not the subsidiary itself).

The two "Separate balance sheets" are shown on Exhibit 14–5 and, using the eliminations, are combined on a line-by-line basis to develop the "Consolidated balance sheet" of Company P shown in the last column. In an external consolidated financial statement of Company P, only the "Consolidated balance sheet" shown in the last column (and not the "Separate balance sheets") would be reported.

To reemphasize the measurements for consolidated purposes: observe that the *market values* at date of acquisition of the subsidiary's assets are added on an item-by-item basis to the **book values** of the parent, Company P.

COMPARISON OF THE EFFECTS ON THE BALANCE SHEET OF POOLING VERSUS PURCHASE

To gain some insight into the differences in measurement of balance sheet amounts that arise when the pooling of interests approach is used versus the purchase approach, we can compare several of consolidated amounts shown in Exhibits 14–3 and 14–5 as follows:

	Acquisition approach		
	Pooling basis	Purchase basis	Difference
1. Cash	$240,000	$ 75,000	$(165,000)
2. Plant and equipment (net)	145,000	150,000	5,000 *
3. Goodwill		10,000	10,000 *
4. Common stock Company P	360,000	300,000	(60,000)
5. Contributed capital from pooling	40,000		(40,000)
6. Retained earnings Company P	190,000	140,000	(50,000)*

* These three amounts reflect the basic differences between the two methods (see footnote 7).

We can observe that when a company elects the purchase approach, the cash position generally suffers; the $165,000 difference in cash was the purchase price. The $100,000 difference in the amount of common stock is due to the effect of issuing stock under pooling of interests rather than paying cash when the purchase approach is elected.[7] The plant and

---

[7] In the example of the purchase method, the subsidiary stock was purchased by Company P for cash without borrowing or selling unissued stock. Had Company P borrowed the $165,000, the cash position would have been unaffected; however, there would have been an increase in debt by the same amount.

Alternatively, Company P could have sold the 10,000 shares of its common stock for

equipment amount is higher when the purchase approach is used than when pooling of interests is used, because the former requires application of the cost principle so that *market value* at date of acquisition rather than book value must be recognized for the assets of the subsidiary. Goodwill usually arises in purchase but does not in pooling of interests. These higher amounts for assets, of course, mean higher expenses will be reported on the income statements in the future periods when the combination is by purchase; that is, for depreciation expense and amortization expense (for goodwill). Finally, under the pooling of interests approach, the reported retained earnings amount is higher because the amount of retained earnings of the subsidiary must be added to that of the parent as shown in Exhibit 14–3.

Thus, when one compares the basic differences between the pooling of interests and purchase methods, three items usually stand out on the consolidated balance sheet, viz:

1. Operational assets almost always are higher in valuation under the purchase method because they are valued at market rather than at the subsidiary's book values.
2. Goodwill almost always is recorded under the purchase method but is never recorded under the pooling of interests method.
3. Retained earnings is lower under the purchase method because under this method only the parent company's retained earnings is reflected, while under the pooling of interests method consolidated retained earnings always is the sum of the parent and subsidiary retained earnings.

Part B will discuss and illustrate other significant differences that are reflected on the consolidated income statement of the parent company.

PART B: REPORTING CONSOLIDATED OPERATIONS AFTER ACQUISITION

The preceding discussions and illustrations focused on the impact of the pooling of interests approach versus the purchase approach on the **balance sheet** immediately after acquisition. The comparative impact of the two approaches on the income statement, for periods following the date of acquisition, is even more significant. Exhibit 14–6 presents the consolidated income statement and balance sheet for Company P and its subsidiary, Company S, after one year of operations (i.e., for the year ended December 31, 19A). The underlying data and consolidation procedures used to derive these two statements are shown in Appendix A, Exhibits 14–10 and 14–11.

The consolidation amounts, one-year after acquisition on a purchase

---

$165,000 cash and then purchased the 10,000 shares of Company S stock with that cash. In this scenario the cash position and the contributed capital accounts would have been the same under both methods.

basis, are based on the annual financial statements prepared by the parent and the subsidiary shown in Exhibit 14–11.

EXHIBIT 14–6

COMPANY P and Its Subsidiary, COMPANY S (100% Owned)
Consolidated Financial Statements
Pooling and Purchase Approaches Compared
At December 31, 19A, One Year after Acquisition

	Consolidated statements	
	Pooling basis	Purchase basis
Income statement (for the year ended December 31, 19A):		
Sales revenue	$510,000	$510,000
Expenses:		
Cost of goods sold	(279,000)	(279,000)
Expenses (not detailed)	(156,500)	(156,500)
Depreciation expense	(14,500)	(15,000)
Amortization expense (goodwill)		(500)
Income tax expense	(26,000)	(26,000)
Net income (carried down to retained earnings)	$ 34,000	$ 33,000
Balance sheet (at December 31, 19A):		
Assets		
Cash	$271,500	$106,500
Accounts receivable (net)	46,000	46,000
Inventories	250,000	250,000
Plant and equipment (net)	130,500	135,000
Goodwill		9,500
Total assets	$698,000	$547,000
Liabilities		
Accounts payable	$ 74,000	$ 74,000
Shareholders' Equity		
Common stock	400,000*	300,000
Retained earnings	190,000	140,000
Add: Net income (from above)	34,000	33,000
Total liabilities and shareholders' equity	$698,000	$547,000

* Includes contributed capital from pooling, $40,000.

Recall that the operational assets of Company S, the subsidiary, at date of acquisition, had a current market value of $5,000 in excess of their book value. These assets are being depreciated over a remaining life of ten years by Company S. Recall also that the acquisition of Company S resulted in $10,000 goodwill to be recognized in consolidation under the purchase basis. This goodwill is to be amortized over the next 20 years.[8]

---

[8] AICPA, *APB Opinion No. 17,* "Accounting for Intangible Assets" (New York, August 1970), states: "The cost of each type of intangible asset [including goodwill] should be amortized on the basis of the estimated life of that specific asset. . . ." The *Opinion* limits the amortization to a maximum of 40 years. Copyright (1970) by the American Institute of CPAs.

The differences in impact between the pooling basis and the purchase basis on the consolidated statements of Company P and its subsidiary, Company S, after one year of operations are as shown in Exhibit 14–7.

EXHIBIT 14–7
Comparison of pooling of interests and purchase methods one year after acquisition.

| | Acquisition approach | | |
	Pooling basis	Purchase basis	Difference
Income statement:			
1. Depreciation expense	$ 14,500	$ 15,000	$ 500*
2. Amortization expense (goodwill)		500	500*
3. Net income.............................	34,000	33,000	$ 1,000*
Balance sheet:			
4. Cash	271,500	106,500	$165,000
5. Plant and equipment (net).................	130,500	135,000	(4,500)
6. Goodwill		9,500	(9,500)
7.　　　Total	698,000	547,000	$151,000
8. Common stock	360,000	300,000	$ 60,000
9. Contributed capital from pooling of interests	40,000		40,000
10. Retained earnings	224,000	173,000	51,000
11.　　　Total	698,000	547,000	$151,000

* Basic differences on the income statement.

The above comparison shows that 11 amounts were different between the two methods. Net income was $1,000 less under the purchase basis than under pooling of interests. This difference was due to *additional* depreciation expense and amortization expense (goodwill) that must be recognized in consolidation when the assets of the subsidiary are recognized at their market values, as is done in consolidation under the purchase basis (but not under pooling of interests). The causes of the $1,000 difference are:

	Items	Difference
a. Depreciation expense on pooling of interests basis (on parent and subsidary assets at book value)	$14,500	
Add depreciation on the increased asset amount of the subsidiary to market value from book value ($5,000 ÷ 10 years)	500	$ 500
Depreciation expense on purchase basis (on parent assets at book value and subsidiary assets at market value)	$15,000	
b. Amortization expense on the intangible asset, goodwill, of $10,000, which is to be amortized over the next 20 years ($10,000 ÷ 20 years)		500
(There is no goodwill recognized under pooling of interests.)		
Total of the differences		$1,000

The additional expenses that must be recognized on the consolidated income statement in future periods cause less net income to be reported when the purchase basis is used. Businesses generally do not like this unfavorable impact of the purchase method.

Likewise, the $151,000 difference in the balance sheet totals is an important issue. In the example, this difference in results is caused by the different way in which the stock was acquired (shares exchanged versus cash payment) and the accounting measurements implicit in each of the two methods. These differences may be explained as follows:

Cash—The $165,000 difference reflects the cash price paid for the stock of the subsidiary purchased under the purchase basis as opposed to the exchange of shares under pooling of interests (see footnote 7).

Plant and equipment (net)—This difference reflects the effects of including the operational assets of the subsidiary at book value under the pooling of interests basis, compared with including them at *acquisition* market value under the purchase basis. The $4,500 difference in plant and equipment may be explained as follows:

Difference between market value and book value of subsidiary assets at date of acquisition	$5,000
Deduct depreciation on the difference for one year ($5,000 ÷ 10 years)	500
Difference: Operational assets (higher under purchase basis)	$4,500

Common stock—The common stock of Company P is greater by $60,000 under a pooling of interests because of the issuance of shares in exchange for the shares of Company S. Note that it is the same as at acquisition.

Contributed capital from pooling of interests—This value arises only under pooling of interests as a result of the exchange of shares. In consolidation, a part or all of it is eliminated. If the percent of ownership remains constant, the amount eliminated each year is constant.

Retained earnings—Retained earnings is $51,000 more under the pooling of interests basis than under the purchase basis. This difference is due to two factors, viz:

Amount of retained earnings eliminated:		
Under pooling of interests basis	$ –0–	
Under purchase basis	50,000	$50,000
Amount of consolidated net income:		
Under pooling of interests basis	34,000	
Under purchase basis	33,000	1,000
Difference: Retained earnings (higher under pooling of interests basis)		$51,000

Now, let's assess some of the economic and motivational impacts of pooling of interests versus combination by purchase. Primarily, these impacts are related to the differences in measurement and reporting procedures used under each of these two accounting approaches. A comparison of these impacts may make clear why pooling of interests generally is preferred by the acquiring company, and also why the accounting profession found it necessary to establish specific criteria for limiting its use. The pooling of interests method usually is preferred because it (1) requires little or no disbursement of cash, other assets, or the creation of debt; (2) causes a higher net income to be reported on the consolidated income statement than does purchase accounting; (3) reports higher retained earnings; and (4) is susceptible to manipulation, which was evidenced by numerous abuses prior to the issuance of *APB Opinion No. 16* (August 1970). The pooling of interests approach generally is preferred because of the "favorable" reporting impacts cited above. However, in the opinion of many persons, the opportunities for manipulation of net income are overriding. Four fairly common practices of the past may be cited and illustrated:

1. **Instant earnings**—To illustrate, assume Company P acquired Company S through an exchange of stock; that is, by a pooling of interests. At acquisition date, Company S owned three separate plants, each of which had a relatively low book value of, say, $100,000 and a high market value of, say, $600,000. Following the pooling of interests approach, the $100,000 book value of each plant was reported on the subsequent consolidated balance sheet as an asset. Assume that during the next year one of the plants was sold for the $600,000 market value. The result was a *gain* on the sale of operational assets of $500,000 (disregarding income taxes), which then was reported on the income statement. This came to be referred to, in a derogatory way, as making "instant earnings." The reported gain would significantly increase *net income* and EPS and often caused the price of the shares of Company P to rise. At the higher stock prices, shares were sold to the public and/or used for another round of mergers following the same pattern and so on. Many persons believe that there was no gain because the **cost** of the plant, to the acquiring company, was the market value of the shares given in exchange (and that it should have been recorded at this amount), that is, $600,000. Under this view (i.e., it would be the purchase basis), no gain would be reported when the plant was sold.

2. **Funny money**—This term, intended to be derogatory, refers to the use of peculiar and **"innovative securities"** that were designed to "qualify" an acquisition as a pooling of interests, when, in fact, its substance was an acquisition by purchase. These innovative securities were used because (1) the company wanted to use pooling of interests accounting, and (2) the shareholders of the acquired company (the subsidiary) wanted cash, not shares of stock of the acquiring company. Both objectives were accomplished by issuing a peculiar type of security (i.e., "funny money"). Typically, the security provided that, say, after one year, it could be turned in for either voting common stock of Company P or cash, at the option of the holder. This qualified superficially as an exchange of shares (i.e., for pooling of interests accounting), while at the same time it made cash available in the short run to the sharehold-

ers of the subsidiary, as would be the case in a combination by purchase. Thus, a purchase transaction was accounted for as a pooling of interests. *APB Opinion No. 16* largely stopped this practice.

3. **Escalating EPS**—This term refers to what was a common practice of seeking out smaller successful companies, usually near year-end, to acquire through a pooling of interests exchange, so that their earnings could be **added** to those of the parent. Thus, by the simple expedient of year-end pooling acquisitions, at no cash cost, the acquiring company could escalate net income and EPS reported on a consolidated basis by the parent company. Many of the year-end acquisitions for this purpose were consummated *after* the end of the year but before publication of the financial statements, in which case they were allowed for inclusion in the consolidated statements of the past year. This became a favorite way to "doctor" net income and EPS at year-end.

4. **Tricky mixes**—This situation represented the ultimate in misleading and illogical accounting. It was referred to as "part-purchase, part-pooling accounting." A corporation, in acquiring another company by pooling, often found a number of shareholders of the other company who would not accept shares in exchange; they wanted cash immediately. For example, it often worked out that, say, two thirds of the shares of the subsidiary would be acquired by exchange of shares and the remaining third would be purchased for cash. In order to derive some of the "reporting benefits" of pooling of interests accounting, two thirds of the acquisition would be accounted for on that basis and one third on the purchase basis—thus part-purchase, part-pooling accounting. This mixture of accounting approaches not only was theoretically untenable but also was misleading and not subject to any rational explanation; it was stopped by *APB Opinion No. 16.*

Thus, the "merger movement" that reached its zenith in the 1960s came under considerable criticism because pooling of interests accounting often was used in situations that were, in substance, purchases. In response to extensive criticism the APB issued *Opinions No. 16,* "Business Combinations," and *No. 17,* "Intangible Assets," which tended to stop the abuses cited above. *Opinion No. 16* states very specific conditions under which pooling of interests accounting is applicable. It is interesting to note that a number of the members of the APB strongly believed, both for conceptual and practical reasons, that pooling of interests accounting should be disallowed completely. The conceptual argument against pooling of interests reporting is that it ignores the market values on which the parties traded shares and substitutes, in violation of the cost principle, wholly irrelevant amounts—the book values carried in the accounts of the seller (i.e., the subsidiary). The practical argument against pooling of interests reporting is that it leads to abuses of the kinds cited above.

The primary arguments in favor of the pooling of interests method of reporting are (1) it avoids the problems of measuring the market value of the different assets of the subsidiary at acquisition date; (2) it avoids the necessity of recognizing goodwill, then having to amortize it as an expense in future periods; and (3) the exchange of shares is not a purchase/ sale transaction but, rather, is a joining of common interests and risks. Many accountants project that the FASB eventually will eliminate the pooling of interests method altogether.

DEMONSTRATION CASE

This actual case, showing selected parts of the consolidated financial statements, is presented for study and dicussion of the reporting of consolidated and nonconsolidated subsidiaries (see Exhibit 14–8).

Refer to Exhibit 14–8 and respond to the following questions:

a. What was the amount of the short-term investments at the end of 1979? How were they valued on the 1979 balance sheet?
b. What were the long-term investments at the end of 1979? How were they valued on the 1979 balance sheet?
c. What was the amount of goodwill at the end of 1979? What was its source?
d. What was the amount of the minority interest at the end of 1979? Explain what this amount represents and the reason for its particular classification on the balance sheet.
e. Explain how the 1979 income statement reflects (1) revenue from the short-term investments, (2) revenue from consolidated subsidiaries, and (3) revenue from long-term investments not consolidated.

Suggested Solution:

a. The short-term investment amount is $177,814,000 for 1979. The short-term investments are valued at LCM. Since market approximates cost at the end of 1979, the short-term investments were reported at cost (refer to Chapter 8).
b. Two different long-term investments were reported for 1979:
   1. Associated companies, $221,659,000. These investments were valued using the equity method because the parent company owned at least 20 percent but not more than 50 percent of the voting stock of each investee company.
   2. Other long-term investments, $7,225,000. These investments were valued using the cost method because the company owned less than 20 percent of the voting stock of the investee company.
c. Goodwill at the end of 1979 was $8,006,000. The goodwill was a result of the parent company's purchasing the controlling interest in the voting stock of the subsidiary at an amount in excess of the market value of the identifiable tangible and intangible operational assets of the subsidiary.

EXHIBIT 14–8

CORNING GLASS WORKS
Consolidated Financial Statements
($000)

Consolidated Balance Sheets

December 30, 1979, and December 31, 1978	1979	1978
Assets		
Current Assets		
Cash	$ 33,113	$ 12,378
Short-term investments, at cost which approximates market value	177,814	182,682
Receivables, net of doubtful accounts and allowances—		
$10,683/1979; $10,632/1978	197,361	173,467
Inventories	204,151	186,866
Prepaid expenses including deferred taxes on income	60,496	59,358
Total current assets	672,935	614,751
Investments		
Associated companies, at equity	221,659	180,997
Other, at cost	7,225	7,889
	228,884	188,886
Plant and Equipment, at Cost		
Land	15,768	15,430
Buildings	187,292	184,010
Equipment	784,534	691,760
Accumulated depreciation	(521,702)	(488,958)
	465,892	402,242
Goodwill	8,006	8,899
Other Assets	9,446	9,663
	$1,385,163	$1,224,441
Liabilities and Stockholders' Equity		
Current Liabilities		
Loans payable	$ 55,217	$ 24,877
Accounts payable	79,163	55,210
Taxes on income payable	65,895	36,579
Wages and employee benefits accrued	66,930	62,364
Other accrued liabilities	66,636	49,405
Advance payments on long-term contracts, net	528	9,553
Total current liabilities	334,369	237,988
Accrued Furnace Repairs	19,630	26,560
Other Liabilities and Deferred Credits	27,971	17,334
Loans Payable Beyond One Year	147,146	163,398
Deferred Investment Credits and Deferred Taxes on Income	23,020	34,596
Minority Interest in Subsidiary Companies	5,063	2,848
Common Stockholders' Equity		
Common stock, including excess over par value—		
Par value $5 per share; authorized—25,000,000 shares	95,956	100,281
Retained earnings	732,008	641,436
Total common stockholders' equity	827,964	741,717
	$1,385,163	$1,224,441

EXHIBIT 14–8
(continued)

CORNING GLASS WORKS
Consolidated Financial Statements
($000)

Historical Comparison

Consolidated Statements of Income	1979	1978	1977	1976	1975
Net sales	$1,421,598	$1,251,728	$1,119,630	$1,025,905	$938,959
Cost of sales	983,907	849,710	762,424	701,647	708,455
Gross Margin	437,691	402,018	357,206	324,258	230,504
Selling, general and administrative expenses	247,537	217,874	187,756	166,773	151,819
Research and development expenses	75,804	63,570	54,812	48,857	42,285
	323,341	281,444	242,568	215,630	194,104
Income from Operations	114,350	120,574	114,638	108,628	36,400
Royalty, interest and dividend income	38,846	27,061	20,572	18,038	11,317
Interest expense	(22,016)	(18,312)	(18,465)	(19,704)	(21,802)
Other income (deductions), net	12,260	8,195	7,611	3,745	(5,211)
Income before taxes on income	143,440	137,518	124,356	110,707	20,704
Taxes on income	61,539	60,531	53,201	51,874	7,723
Income before minority interest and equity earnings	81,901	76,987	71,155	58,833	12,981
Minority interest in (earnings) loss of subsidiaries	(2,202)	(1,566)	(1,174)	(595)	2,617
Equity in earnings of associated companies	45,244	28,942	22,102	25,475	15,539
Net Income	$ 124,943	$ 104,363	$ 92,083	$ 83,713	$ 31,137
Per Share of Common Stock					
Net income	$7.05	$5.89	$5.20	$4.74	$1.76
Dividends	$1.94	$1.73	$1.56	$1.50	$1.40
Average shares outstanding (thousands)	17,725	17,732	17,696	17,648	17,635
Consolidated Statements of Financial Condition					
Working capital	$ 338,566	$ 376,763	$ 342,387	$ 296,240	$243,294
Investments	228,884	188,886	164,361	146,203	124,517
Plant and equipment, at cost (net)	465,892	402,242	360,664	346,445	358,884
Goodwill and other assets	17,452	18,562	16,991	19,843	23,689
	1,050,794	986,453	884,403	808,731	750,384
Loans payable beyond one year	147,146	163,398	158,767	167,173	172,686
Other liabilities and deferred credits	75,684	81,338	59,196	41,049	35,384
Stockholders' equity	$ 827,964	$ 741,717	$ 666,440	$ 600,509	$542,314
Additions to plant and equipment	$ 137,860	$ 103,232	$ 69,600	$ 48,742	$ 62,072
Depreciation and amortization	$ 62,449	$ 57,428	$ 50,923	$ 52,493	$ 54,916
Dividends paid	$ 34,371	$ 30,690	$ 27,622	$ 26,492	$ 24,705
Current earnings retained in the business	$ 90,572	$ 73,673	$ 64,461	$ 57,221	$ 6,432
Number of stockholders at last dividend date	14,486	15,583	16,164	16,059	16,472
Owens-Corning Fiberglas Corporation unremitted earnings:					
Total	$ 17,750	$ 24,760	$ 24,051	$ 15,054	$ 7,624
Per share	$1.00	$1.40	$1.36	$ .85	$ .43

Dollars in thousands, except per share amounts

EXHIBIT 14–8
(concluded)

CORNING GLASS WORKS
Consolidated Financial Statements
($000)

Statement of Accounting Policies

Principles of Consolidation

The consolidated financial statements include the accounts of all significant subsidiary companies. The major foreign subsidiaries are consolidated as of dates up to four weeks earlier than the consolidated balance sheet dates.

The equity method of accounting is used for all investments in associated companies in which the company's interest is 20% or more, except Owens-Corning Fiberglas Corporation. The company, under a 1949 consent decree, is enjoined from exercising any control over Owens-Corning Fiberglas Corporation (see Note 6). Under the equity method, the company recognizes its share in the net earnings or losses of these associated companies as they occur rather than as dividends are received. Investments in Owens-Corning Fiberglas Corporation and in companies in which the ownership interest is less than 20% are carried at cost.

Translation of Foreign Currencies

Foreign inventories, investments, goodwill, property and equipment, and depreciation are expressed in U.S. dollars at rates of exchange prevailing when the assets were acquired. All other foreign assets and liabilities are translated at year-end rates. Revenue and expenses (other than depreciation) are translated at rates prevailing during each year.

Gains and losses resulting from exchange rate fluctuations and changes in the market value of unperformed forward exchange contracts are reflected in current earnings.

Inventories

Inventories are valued at the lower of cost or market. The LIFO (last-in, first-out) method of determining cost is used for substantially all inventories.

Property and Depreciation

Land, buildings and equipment are recorded at cost. Renewals and betterments are charged to the property accounts while replacements of molds, maintenance and repairs (except furnace rebuilding) are charged to income as incurred. The cost of assets retired is offset against accumulated depreciation; undepreciated cost (net of any proceeds) is charged to income.

In accordance with industry practice, the estimated cost of periodic rebuilding of glassmelting furnaces is provided from current operations, in advance, over the interval between renewals.

Depreciation is provided over the estimated useful lives of the properties, using accelerated methods for substantially all assets.

Goodwill

Differences between investment cost and the fair value of net assets acquired of subsidiary companies accounted for by the purchase method are amortized over 20 years from their respective dates of acquisition unless earlier diminution in value occurs.

Taxes on Income

Income tax expense shown in Corning's Statement of Income is computed on the basis of the revenue and expenses shown in that statement. Since revenue and expenses shown in Corning's tax returns may be different from amounts shown in the Statement of Income, income tax expense will not equal income taxes payable. These differences result from including certain items in the Statement of Income in one year and in the tax return in a different year. Certain charges (principally provisions for furnace repairs, employee benefits, inventories and depreciation) are not deductible in the tax return in the year in which they are recognized as expenses in the financial statements; certain income (including that from equity basis companies and foreign subsidiaries) is included in net income when it is earned but is not included in the U.S. federal tax return until received by Corning (timing differences).

Corning and its subsidiaries and associated companies provide income taxes on their earnings at applicable rates. Additional income taxes which would be payable by Corning upon remittance of subsidiaries' earnings to the parent company are provided to the extent that future remittance is anticipated.

Investment tax credits are deferred for financial statement purposes and used to reduce income tax expense in equal installments over the lives of the related properties.

Employee Retirement Plans

Corning Glass Works and its subsidiary companies have pension plans covering domestic employees and certain employees in foreign countries. The company accrues and generally funds pension costs in accordance with actuarial estimates, on the basis of normal cost and 30-year amortization of unfunded prior service cost.

Earnings Per Share

Earnings per share are computed by dividing net income by the weighted average number of common shares outstanding during each year.

Long-Term Contracts

Corning has contracts, extending over several years, to provide know-how, technical assistance, equipment and construction management services. Income under these contracts is recognized on the percentage of completion method. Funds received in excess of costs incurred and income recognized are recorded as current liabilities. When costs incurred and income recognized on any contract exceed funds received, the net amount is included in current assets.

d. At the end of 1979 the "Minority Interest in Subsidiary Companies" was $5,063,000. This item means that the parent company, although it owned a controlling interest in the voting stock of one or more of the subsidiaries, did not own 100 percent. This amount represents the portion of the stockholders' equity of the subsidiary allocated to the minority shareholders.

e. The 1979 income statement reports three different sources of revenue (often inappropriately called income) from the investments:

1. From short-term investments—royalty, interest, and dividend income, $38,846,000. This amount is reported under the caption "Income from operations."
2. Revenue from consolidated subsidiaries—This amount is not reported separately since the revenues of the consolidated subsidiaries are added to the revenues of the parent.
3. Revenue from long-term investments not consolidated. This revenue is reported in two ways:

   (a) Cost method—included in the item "Royalty, interest, and dividend income, $38,846,000."
   (b) Equity method—included in the investment account "Associated companies, at Equity, $221,659,000."

SUMMARY

This chapter discussed the use of consolidated statements that must be prepared in most situations when one corporation owns more than 50 percent of the outstanding voting stock of another corporation. The concept of consolidated statements is based upon the view that a parent company and its subsidiaries constitute one economic entity. Therefore, the separate income statements, balance sheets, and statements of changes in financial position should be combined each period on an item-by-item basis as a single set of financial statements for the parent company.

Ownership of a controlling interest (i.e., more than 50 percent of the outstanding voting stock) of another corporation may be accounted for and reported as either a pooling of interests or combination by purchase. The measurement of amounts reported on the consolidated financial statements of the parent company is influenced to a significant degree by these two quite different accounting approaches.

The pooling of interests method generally is used when the parent company exchanges shares of its own voting stock for more than 20 percent of the voting shares of the subsidiary. In this situation it usually is deemed that there was no purchase/sale (exchange) transaction. Rather, there was merely a joining of interests by exchanging stock certificates and the cost principle was not applied. Therefore, in preparing consolidated statements on a pooling of interests basis, the book values (i.e., those amounts reflected on the books) of each related company are added together and market values are disregarded.

In a combination by purchase, the parent company usually pays cash and/or uses debt for the shares of the subsidiary. In these circumstances, a purchase/sale transaction has been affected and the acquisition is accounted for in conformance with the cost principle. Therefore, to prepare consolidated statements under the purchase basis, the assets of the subsidiary must be measured at their acquisition market values when combined with the statements of the parent company.

Consolidation on a pooling of interests basis versus consolidation on a purchase basis causes significant differences on the consolidated financial statements. The pooling of interests basis in the past led to many abuses.

A large percentage of published financial statements of corporations are consolidated statements. It is important, therefore, that statement users understand the basic concept of consolidated statements and the measurement distinctions between the pooling basis and the purchase basis in reporting the results of business combinations.

The differences between pooling of interests and purchasing in measuring and reporting the results of business combinations by the parent company may be generalized, for the usual case, as follows (the acquisition of a controlling interest does not affect the accounting and reporting of the subsidiary company):

Item	Pooling of interests	Purchasing
1. Measuring and recording at date of acquisition by the parent company.	Acquisition is accomplished by exchanging shares of stock. A purchase/sale transaction is not assumed; hence, the cost principle is not applied. The investment account is debited for the book value of the subsidiary stock acquired.	Acquisition usually is accomplished by purchasing the shares with cash and/or debt. A purchase/sale transaction is assumed; hence, the cost principle is applied. The investment account is debited for the market value of the resources acquired.
2. Goodwill	No goodwill is recognized by the parent company.	Goodwill is recognized by the parent company to the extent that the purchase price exceeds the sum of market values of the assets (less the liabilities) of the subsidiary.
3. Method of aggregating or combining to derive the consolidated balance sheet of the parent company.	Assets and liabilities (less any eliminations) of the subsidiary are added, at book value, to the book values of the parent.	Assets and liabilities (less any eliminations) of the subsidiary are added, at their market values (as of the date of acquisition), to the book values of the assets and liabilities of the parent.
4. Method of aggregating or combining to derive the consolidated income statement of the parent company.	Revenues and expenses as reported by each company, less any eliminations, are aggregated.	Revenues as reported, less any eliminations, are aggregated. Expenses, plus additional depreciation and amortization of goodwill, less any eliminations, are aggregated.

Item	Pooling of interests	Purchasing
5. Eliminations.	Eliminate all intercompany debts, revenues, and expenses. Eliminate investment account on parent's books and owners' equity of the subsidiary, excluding retained earnings.	Eliminate all intercompany debts, revenues, and expenses. Eliminate the investment account on parent's books and common stock and retained earnings of the subsidiary.
6. Usual comparative effects on the consolidated financial statements.	Expenses—lower Net income—higher EPS—higher Assets—higher cash Noncash assets—lower Liabilities—same Capital stock—higher Retained earnings—higher	Expenses—higher Net income—lower EPS—lower Assets—lower cash Noncash assets—higher Liabilities—same Capital stock—lower Retained earnings—lower

APPENDIX A: PROCEDURES FOR DERIVING CONSOLIDATED STATEMENTS—100 PERCENT OWNERSHIP

This appendix discusses in more depth the measurement procedures used in **preparing** consolidated financial statements. To accomplish this objective, we use a *consolidation worksheet* because, through it, the underlying concepts and measurement procedures come into sharp focus. The worksheet should be viewed as a learning device and not something only to be mastered mechanically. At the outset we remind you that the worksheet and the entries made on it are *supplemental* to the accounts and the reports. *The worksheet entries are not recorded in the accounts under any circumstances because the worksheet is an analytical device only.* We will consider the various topics in the same order they were presented in the body of the chapter. The example for Company P and its subsidiary, Company S, given in Exhibit 14–1, will be continued for all of the illustrations in this appendix.

Consolidated balance sheet immediately after acquisition

The consolidated balance sheets for Company P and its subsidiary, Company S, immediately after acquisition, were shown on the pooling of interests basis in Exhibit 14–3 and on the purchase basis in Exhibit 14–5. Those exhibits indicated in the first three columns the worksheet procedures essential to development of the statements. There is no need to repeat those discussions.

Developing consolidated statements for periods subsequent to acquisition

At the end of each accounting period after acquisition, a **consolidated** balance sheet, income statement, and statement of changes in financial position must be prepared by the parent company. This section discusses the application of consolidation principles in the development of both a consolidated balance sheet and a consolidated income statement for periods subsequent to acquisition. We will illustrate a single worksheet that will meet this dual need.

To illustrate the development of a consolidation worksheet for both the balance sheet and the income statement, we will continue the situation involving the *purchase* with cash of Company S stock by Company P given in Exhibit 14–4. Recall that on January 2, 19A, Company P acquired 100 percent of the outstanding stock of Company S. To adapt the example, we will assume that it is now December 31, 19A, and after operating for a year, each company has just prepared its separate income statement and balance sheet as shown in Exhibit 14–9.

EXHIBIT 14–9

COMPANY P AND COMPANY S
Separate Financial Statements for 19A (unclassified)

At December 31, 19A

	Company P		Company S
	Pooling basis	*Purchase basis*	
Income statement (for 19A):			
Sales revenue	$400,000	$400,000	$110,000
Revenue from investments			
(dividend from Company S)	10,000	10,000	
Cost of goods sold	(220,000)	(220,000)	(59,000)
Expenses (not detailed)	(130,000)	(130,000)	(26,500)
Depreciation expense	(10,000)	(10,000)	(4,500)
Income tax expense	(20,000)	(20,000)	(6,000)
Net income	$ 30,000	$ 30,000	$ 14,000
Balance sheet (at December 31, 19A):			
Cash	$226,000	$ 61,000	$ 45,500
Accounts receivable (net)	18,000	18,000	28,000
Receivable from Company S	6,000	6,000	
Inventories	185,000	185,000	65,000
Investment in Company S			
(by purchase, at cost)	150,000*	165,000*	
Plant and equipment (net)	90,000	90,000	40,500
	$675,000	$525,000	$179,000
Accounts payable	$ 55,000	$ 55,000	$ 19,000
Payable to Company P			6,000
Common stock (par $10)	360,000	300,000	100,000
Contributed capital in excess of par	90,000		
Beginning retained earnings*	140,000	140,000	50,000
Dividends declared and paid during 19A			(10,000)
Net income for 19A (per above)	30,000	30,000	14,000
	$675,000	$525,000	$179,000

* Balance at date of acquisition.

At the end of 19A, the following data relating to intercompany eliminations were available:

a. The Investment in Company S balance of $165,000 was the same as at date of acquisition; the balance of Retained Earnings of Company S at acquisition was $50,000.

b. At date of purchase, January 2, 19A, the plant and equipment of Company S had a market value of $5,000 above book value and goodwill purchased amounted to $10,000 (see page 604 and 605).

622

c. The intercompany debt owed by Company S to Company P was $6,000 at the end of 19A.

d. The plant and equipment owned by Company S had a ten-year remaining life from January 1, 19A, for depreciation purposes. The company uses straight-line depreciation.

e. Goodwill is to be amortized from January 1, 19A, over 20 years on a straight-line basis.

f. During December 19A, Company S declared and paid a $10,000 cash dividend to Company P. Accordingly, each company made the following entry in its accounts:

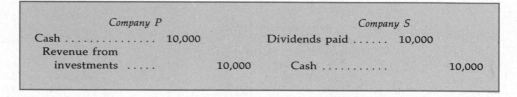

	Company P		Company S	
Cash	10,000	Dividends paid	10,000	
Revenue from investments	10,000	Cash		10,000

A consolidated income statement and balance sheet must be developed at the end of 19A. These statements were shown in Exhibit 14–6, assuming (1) pooling of interests basis and (2) consolidation by purchase. A separate consolidation worksheet is shown for each: Exhibit 14–10, pooling of interests; and Exhibit 14–11, purchase. Each worksheet will be explained.

Pooling of interests basis—income statement and balance sheet. This worksheet (Exhibit 14–10) has side captions for each income statement and balance sheet account, and columns for the parent company, subsidiary, eliminations, and final column for the *"Consolidated Balances."* The amounts entered in the first two money columns are taken directly from the separate financial statements of 19A prepared by the parent and the subsidiary as given in Exhibit 14–9. The last column of this worksheet provided the first column of data for the consolidated income statement and balance sheet shown in Exhibit 14–6.

The worksheet is designed so that the eliminations are entered in debit and credit format. This provides an excellent check on the accuracy of the work. We remind you, however, that the elimination entries are *worksheet entries only;* they are never entered into the accounts of either the parent or the subsidiary. This is because reporting with consolidated statements is a *reporting concept* and does not affect the accounts of either the parent or the subsidiaries.

To complete the worksheet, the elimination entries first must be developed; then each line is accumulated horizontally to derive the consolidated amount in the last column for each item to be reported on the consolidated income statement and the balance sheet. At the end of 19A, three elimination entries are reflected on the worksheet on the pooling of interests basis. They are identified briefly at the bottom of the worksheet; however, we will elaborate on them as follows:

a. Eliminate the investment in Company S with offsets to the accounts for (1) Common Stock, Company S, and (2) Contributed Capital from Pooling (see page 601). These eliminations can be accomplished by means of the following intercompany elimination entry on the worksheet:

Common stock, Company S	100,000	
Contributed capital from pooling of interests	50,000	
Investment in Company S		150,000

b. Eliminate the intercompany debt of $6,000 owed by Company S to Company P (see page 601). These two eliminations can be accomplished by means of the following intercompany elimination entry on the worksheet:

Payable to Company P	6,000	
Receivable from Company S		6,000

c. During the year, Company S declared and paid dividends amounting to $10,000. Since Company P owned 100 percent of the outstanding stock, all of the dividends were paid to Company P. This is another intercompany item that must be eliminated. The Revenue from Investments account of Company P is debited on the worksheet and the Dividends Declared and Paid account of the subsidiary credited for $10,000. Observe that separate lines are set up on the worksheet for dividends and net income. This is simply a matter of convenience and clarity. The worksheet entry to accomplish these two eliminations is:

Revenue from investments	10,000	
Dividends declared and paid (Retained earnings,		
Company S)		10,000

Purchase basis—income statement and balance sheet. In this situation there will be a few more eliminations because the market values for the subsidiary must be recognized when the consolidation is by purchase. The intercompany eliminations on Exhibit 14–11, purchase basis, are identified at the bottom of the worksheet; however, we will elaborate on them as follows:

a. Eliminate the investment account, reported on the parent's balance sheet, against the owners' equity accounts, reflected on the balance

EXHIBIT 14–10

COMPANY P and Its Subsidiary, COMPANY S
Consolidation Worksheet (pooling of interests) for the Balance Sheet and Income Statement
December 31, 19A (100 percent ownership)

| Items | Statements | | Intercompany Eliminations | | Consolidated Balances |
	Company P	Company S	Debit	Credit	
Income statement:					
Sales revenue	400,000	110,000			510,000
Revenue from investments	10,000		(c) 10,000		
Cost of goods sold	(220,000)	(59,000)			(279,000)
Expenses (not detailed)	(130,000)	(26,500)			(156,500)
Depreciation expense	(10,000)	(4,500)			(14,500)
Income tax expense	(20,000)	(6,000)			(26,000)
Net income (carried down)	30,000	14,000			34,000
Balance sheet:					
Cash	226,000	45,500			271,500
Accounts receivable (net)	18,000	28,000			46,000
Receivable from Company S	6,000			(b) 6,000	
Inventories	185,000	65,000			250,000
Investment in Company S	150,000*			(a) 150,000	
Plant and equipment (net)	90,000	40,500			130,500
	675,000	179,000			698,000
Accounts payable	55,000	19,000			74,000
Payable to Company P		6,000	(b) 6,000		
Common stock, Company P	360,000*				360,000
Common stock, Company S		100,000	(a) 100,000		
Contributed capital from pooling	90,000*		(a) 50,000		40,000
Beginning retained earnings, Company P	140,000				140,000
Beginning retained earnings, Company S		50,000			50,000
Dividends declared and paid during 19A		(10,000)		(c) 10,000	
Net income, 19A (from above; not added across)	30,000	14,000			34,000
	675,000	179,000	166,000	166,000	698,000

Explanation of eliminations:
(a) To eliminate Investment in Company S against Common Stock of Company S and Contributed Capital from Pooling of Interests.
(b) To eliminate the intercompany debt.
(c) To eliminate the intercompany revenue and dividends (paid by the subsidiary to the parent).
* These amounts are based upon the pooling of interests approach. The parent would have made the following entry at acquisition date:

Investment in Company S 150,000
    Common stock, Company P   60,000
    Contributed capital from pooling of interests   90,000

EXHIBIT 14–11

COMPANY P and Its Subsidiary, COMPANY S
Consolidation Worksheet (by purchase) for the Balance Sheet and Income Statement
December 31, 19A (100 percent ownership)

Items	Statements Company P	Statements Company S	Intercompany Eliminations Debit	Intercompany Eliminations Credit	Consolidated Balances
Income statement:					
Sales revenue	400,000	110,000			510,000
Revenue from investments	10,000		(e) 10,000		
Cost of goods sold	(220,000)	(59,000)			(279,000)
Expenses (not detailed)	(130,000)	(26,500)			(156,500)
Depreciation expense	(10,000)	(4,500)	(c) 500		(15,000)
Amortization expense (goodwill)			(d) 500		(500)
Income tax expense	(20,000)	(6,000)			(26,000)
Net income (carried down)	30,000	14,000			33,000
Balance sheet:					
Cash	61,000	45,500			106,500
Accounts receivable (net)	18,000	28,000			46,000
Receivable from Company S	6,000			(b) 6,000	
Inventories	185,000	65,000			250,000
Investment in Company S (at cost)	165,000			(a) 165,000	
Plant and equipment (net)	90,000	40,500	(a) 5,000	(c) 500	135,000
Goodwill			(a) 10,000	(d) 500	9,500
	525,000	179,000			547,000
Accounts payable	55,000	19,000			74,000
Payable to Company P		6,000	(b) 6,000		
Common stock, Company P	300,000				300,000
Common stock, Company S		100,000	(a) 100,000		
Beginning retained earnings, Company P	140,000				140,000
Beginning retained earnings, Company S		50,000	(a) 50,000		
Dividends declared and paid during 19A		(10,000)		(e) 10,000	
Net income, 19A (from above; not added across)	30,000	14,000			33,000*
	525,000	179,000	182,000	182,000	547,000

* Carried down from above.
Explanation of eliminations:
(a) To eliminate the investment account against the subsidiary stockholders' equity and to allocate the difference between purchase price and book value purchased to the appropriate accounts.
(b) To eliminate the intercompany debt.
(c) To record additional depreciation for one year on the asset increase resulting from the acquisition.
(d) To record amortization for one year on the goodwill recognized.
(e) To eliminate intercompany revenue and dividends (paid by the subsidiary to the parent).

sheet of the subsidiary. This eliminating entry will be the same as at date of acquisition for each succeeding period since it is based upon the values recognized at the date of acquisition. The $15,000 difference between the purchase price and the book value must be allocated to the assets (including goodwill as shown in the analysis of the purchase transaction given on page 605).

The worksheet entry is as follows:

```
Common stock, Company S ...........................   100,000
Retained earnings, Company S ........................    50,000
Plant and equipment .................................     5,000
Goodwill ............................................    10,000
    Investment in Company S ..........................            165,000
```

b. Eliminate the intercompany debt of $6,000 with the following elimination entry:

```
Payable to Company P ......................................   6,000
    Receivable from Company S ...........................            6,000
```

c. Since the plant and equipment amount for Company S was increased by $5,000, for consolidation purposes we must record on the worksheet additional depreciation on that amount. The depreciation reflected on the statements of Company S does not include this $5,000 increase to market value. Accordingly, the worksheet entry must be:

```
Depreciation expense (Company S) .......................   500
    Plant and equipment (Company S)
        (or accumulated depreciation) ....................          500
    $5,000 ÷ 10 years = $500.
```

d. Goodwill is an intangible asset (see Chapter 9) that must be amortized over a period not longer than 40 years (APB Opinion No. 17). Company P decided to use a 20-year life. Since $10,000 goodwill was recognized in entry (a) above, for consolidated statement purposes it must be amortized on the worksheet in the same manner as the depreciation in entry (c). Therefore, the worksheet entry to accomplish this effect is:

Amortization expense (goodwill) 500
    Goodwill 500
  $10,000 ÷ 20 years = $500.

e. During the year, Company S declared and paid dividends amounting to $10,000. Since Company P owned 100 percent of the outstanding stock, all of the dividends were paid to Company P. This is an intercompany item that must be eliminated. The Revenue from Investments account of Company P must be debited on the worksheet and the Dividends Declared and Paid account of the subsidiary credited for $10,000. Observe that separate lines are set up on the worksheet for dividends and net income. This is simply for convenience and clarity. The worksheet entry to accomplish these eliminations is:

Revenue from investments 10,000
    Dividends declared and paid (retained earnings,
      Company S) 10,000

All of the intercompany eliminations have been effected. The worksheet is completed for the consolidated balances by cumulating the amounts horizontally for each item. The consolidated balances taken directly from the last column of the worksheet are classified in the normal manner in preparing the consolidated income statement and balance sheet.

APPENDIX B: PROCEDURES FOR DERIVING CONSOLIDATED STATEMENTS—CONTROLLING INTEREST OF LESS THAN 100 PERCENT OWNERSHIP

When the parent company owns a controlling interest that is less than 100 percent, the consolidation procedures are identical, except that certain consolidation worksheet eliminations must be based upon the *proportionate* ownership level. When there is less than 100 percent ownership, there will be a group of stockholders of the subsidiary company known as the **minority stockholders.** Their interest in the subsidiary is unaffected by the parent's interest; therefore, the minority stockholders' interest must be accorded appropriate measurement and reporting recognition. This gives rise to a new kind of owners' equity on the consolidated statements referred to as the **minority interest.** It includes their proportionate share of both the earnings and the contributed capital of the subsidiary.

Ownership interests of less than 100 percent generally are on the purchase basis since *APB Opinion No. 16* does not permit use of the pooling of interests basis when the ownership interest held by the parent company is less than 90 percent.

To illustrate the measurement of amounts for consolidated statements for a controlling interest of less than 100 percent, we will adapt the data for Company P and Company S given in Exhibit 14–1, page 599. Assume that on January 2, 19A, Company P purchased 80 percent of the 10,000 shares of outstanding capital stock of Company S for $132,000 cash. At that date, Company P recorded the purchase of the 8,000 shares of capital stock as follows:

January 2, 19A:

Investment, stock of Company S (80 percent ownership) 132,000	
Cash	132,000
Acquisition of 8,000 shares (80 percent) of the capital stock of Company S at $16.50 per share.	

On the date of purchase, the owners' equity accounts of Company S reflected the following amounts: Capital Stock, $100,000; and Retained Earnings, $50,000. Company P paid $132,000 cash for 80 percent of the owners' equity of Company S, or $150,000 × 0.80 = $120,000. Thus, it paid $12,000 more than the book value of Company S. Of this amount, $4,000 (i.e., $5,000 × 80 percent) was for the greater market value of the plant and equipment. The remaining amount, $8,000, was for *goodwill.* The analysis of the purchase transaction, at date of acquisition, follows:[9]

Purchase price for 80% interest in Company S	$132,000
Stockholders' equity (book value) of Company S purchased	
($100,000 + $50,000) × 0.80	120,000
Difference—excess paid over book value	12,000
Analysis of the difference:	
To plant and equipment ($50,000 − $45,000) × 0.80	4,000
Remainder—goodwill purchased	$ 8,000

Assume it is December 31, 19A, and both companies have experienced one year's operations as affiliated companies. Each company has prepared the separate 19A financial statements as shown in Exhibit 14–12.

---

[9] Some accountants believe, on the basis on conservatism, that the plant and equipment difference should be 100 percent (i.e., $5,000) rather than 80 percent (i.e., $4,000). This difference in opinion has not been resolved; however, it appears that most companies currently use the lower amount.

EXHIBIT 14–12

COMPANY P AND COMPANY S
Separate Financial Statements for 19A

	Company P	Company S
Income statement (for 19A):		
Sales revenue	$400,000	$110,000
Revenue from investments (dividends from Company S)	8,000	
Cost of goods sold	(220,000)	(59,000)
Expenses (not detailed)	(130,000)	(26,500)
Depreciation expense	(10,000)	(4,500)
Income tax expense	(20,000)	(6,000)
Net income	$ 28,000	$ 14,000
Balance sheet (at December 31, 19A):		
Cash	$ 92,000	$ 45,500
Accounts receivable (net)	18,000	28,000
Receivable from Company S	6,000	
Inventories	185,000	65,000
Investment in Company S (80%, at cost)	132,000	
Plant and equipment	90,000	40,500
	$523,000	$179,000
Accounts payable	$ 55,000	$ 19,000
Payable to Company P		6,000
Common stock (par $10)	300,000	100,000
Beginning retained earnings	140,000	50,000
Dividends declared and paid during 19A		(10,000)
Net income for 19A (from above)	28,000	14,000
	$523,000	$179,000

Additional data developed for the consolidation worksheet:

a. Investment account balance of $132,000 to be eliminated against 80 percent of stockholders' equity of subsidiary.

b. Plant and equipment of Company S to be increased by $4,000 to market value (i.e., the increment attributable to ownership by Company P). Goodwill to be recognized, $8,000 (see analysis of purchase transaction above).

c. Company S owed Company P $6,000 on December 31, 19A.

d. The plant and equipment is being depreciated on a straight-line basis over a remaining life of ten years by Company S.

e. Goodwill will be amortized over 20 years.

f. Company S declared and paid $10,000 cash dividends on December 15, 19A.

The consolidation worksheet, on the purchase basis, is shown in Exhibit 14–13. It is the same as the worksheet shown in Exhibit 14–11 for 100 percent ownership, except for elimination entries (a), (c), (d), and (e). These intercompany eliminations differ only as to *the amounts. They have been reduced to the 80 percent ownership level.*

EXHIBIT 14–13

COMPANY P and Its Subsidiary, COMPANY S
Consolidation Worksheet (combination by purchase) for the Balance Sheet and Income
Statement
December 31, 19A (80 percent ownership)

Items	Statements		Intercompany Eliminations		Consolidated Balances
	Company P	Company S	Debit	Credit	
Income statement:					
Sales revenue	400,000	110,000			510,000
Revenue from investments	8,000		(e) 8,000		
Cost of goods sold	(220,000)	(59,000)			(279,000)
Expenses (not detailed)	(130,000)	(26,500)			(156,500)
Depreciation expense	(10,000)	(4,500)	(c) 400		(14,900)
Amortization expense (goodwill)			(d) 400		(400)
Income tax expense	(20,000)	(6,000)			(26,000)
Net income	28,000	14,000			33,200
Carried down:					
Minority interest ($14,000 × 20%)					2,800M*
Parent interest income					30,400
Balance sheet:					
Cash	92,000	45,500			137,500
Accounts receivable (net)	18,000	28,000			46,000
Receivable from Company S	6,000			(b) 6,000	
Inventories	185,000	65,000			250,000
Investment in Company S (at cost)	132,000			(a)132,000	
Plant and equipment (net)	90,000	40,500	(a) 4,000	(c) 400	134,100
Goodwill			(a) 8,000	(d) 400	7,600
	523,000	179,000			575,200
Accounts payable	55,000	19,000			74,000
Payable to Company P		6,000	(b) 6,000		
Common stock, Company P	300,000				300,000
Common stock, Company S		100,000	(a) 80,000		20,000M

Exhibit 14–13
(continued)

Items	Statements		Intercompany Eliminations		Consolidated Balances
	Company P	Company S	Debit	Credit	
Beginning retained earnings, Company P	140,000				140,000
Beginning retained earnings, Company S		50,000	(a) 40,000		10,000M
Dividends declared and paid during 19A		(10,000)		(e) 8,000	(2,000)M
Net income, 19A (from above; not added across)	28,000	14,000			2,800M 30,400
	523,000	179,000	146,800	146,800	575,200

M—Minority interest.

* The minority interest in the earnings of the subsidiary is unaffected by the consolidation procedures of the parent company. Thus, the minority interest in the earnings is $14,000 \times 20\% = $2,800. This amount is subtracted from consolidated income to derive the amount of consolidated income identifiable with the controlling interest. The two separate amounts then are carried down to the balance sheet section.

Explanation of eliminations:

(a) To eliminate the investment account against 80 percent of the owners equity of the subsidiary and to allocate the difference between purchase price and book value to the appropriate accounts.

(b) To eliminate the intercompany debt.

(c) To record depreciation for one year on the asset increase resulting from the acquisition.

(d) To amortize goodwill recognized (one year).

(e) To eliminate intercompany revenue arising from dividends declared and paid by the subsidiary.

On the worksheet the 20 percent representing the minority interest is designated with an "M." In the income statement portion of the worksheet, 20 percent of the net income (i.e., $2,800) of the subsidiary is coded "M" and the remainder ($30,400) is identified with the parent. These consolidated balances, on the worksheet, are carried down to the balance sheet section. The 20 percent of subsidiary stockholders' equity was not eliminated; therefore, it is carried across as the minority interest and coded "M." Aside from these adaptations, the "Consolidated Balances" column is completed as previously explained.

The consolidated income statement and balance sheet, based on the data in the "Consolidated Balances" column of the worksheet, are shown in Exhibit 14–14. The *minority* interest share of net income is identified separately on the income statement. Similarly, the minority interest share of stockholders' equity is identified separately on the balance sheet. The minority interest share of stockholders' equity often is shown as a special caption between liabilities and stockholders' equity rather than as illustrated in Exhibit 14–14.

EXHIBIT 14–14

COMPANY P and Its Subsidiary, COMPANY S
Consolidated Income Statement (purchase basis)
For the Year Ended December 31, 19A

Sales revenue		$510,000
Cost of goods sold		279,000
Gross margin		231,000
Less:		
Expenses (not detailed)	$156,500	
Depreciation expense	14,900	
Amortization expense (goodwill)	400	
Income tax expense	26,000	197,800
Consolidated net income		33,200
Less: Minority interest in net income		2,800
Controlling interest in net income		$ 30,400

EPS of common stock ($33,200 ÷ 30,000 shares) = $1.107
(some accountants prefer to use $30,400 as the numerator).

COMPANY P and Its Subsidiary, COMPANY S
Consolidated Balance Sheet (purchase basis)
At December 31, 19A

Assets

Current assets:		
Cash	$137,500	
Accounts receivable (net)	46,000	
Inventories	250,000	$433,500
Tangible operational assets:		
Plant and equipment (net)		134,100
Intangible operational assets:		
Goodwill (or excess of cost over market value of assets of subsidiary)		7,600
Total assets		$575,200

Liabilities

Current liabilities:		
Accounts payable		$ 74,000

Stockholders' Equity

Contributed capital:		
Common stock, par $10, 30,000 shares outstanding	$300,000	
Retained earnings	170,400	
Total	470,400	
Minority interest	30,800*	
Total stockholders' equity		501,200
Total liabilities and stockholders' equity		$575,200

* $20,000 + $10,000 + $2,800 − $2,000 = $30,800.

IMPORTANT TERMS DEFINED IN THE CHAPTER (with page citations)

Parent company—595
Subsidiary company—595
Control—596
Economic compatibility—597
Pooling of interests—598, 610, 622
Purchase (merger)—598, 603, 610, 623
Book value—599, 604

Consolidated balance sheet—600, 610, 631
Cost principle—603
Goodwill—605, 629
Consolidated income statement—610, 631
Minority stockholders interest)—627, 629

QUESTIONS FOR DISCUSSION

Part A

1. Explain what is meant by a parent-subsidiary relationship.

2. Explain the basic concept underlying consolidated statements.

3. What two basic elements must be present before consolidated statements are appropriate?

4. The concept of consolidated statements relates only to reporting as opposed to entries in the accounts. Explain.

5. Explain briefly what is meant by pooling of interests.

6. Explain briefly what is meant by combination by purchase.

7. When one corporation acquires a controlling interest in another corporation, the acquiring corporation debits a long-term investment account. In the case of a pooling of interests, basically, what amount is debited to the investment account?

8. Explain what is meant by intercompany eliminations, or offsets, in consolidation procedures.

9. Explain why the investment account must be eliminated against stockholders' equity.

10. Explain why the "book values" of the parent and subsidiary are aggregated on consolidated statements when there is a pooling of interests, but market values of the subsidiary assets are used when the combination is by purchase.

11. Why is goodwill not recognized in a pooling of interests? Why is it recognized in a combination by purchase?

Questions

Part B

12. Explain why additional depreciation expense generally must be recognized on consolidation when the combination was by purchase.

13. Explain what is meant by goodwill when the combination was by purchase.

14. Explain why pooling of interests has been much more popular in the merger movement than combination by purchase.

15. Explain the basis for each of the following statements:
    a. Pooling of interests, given the same situation basically, reports a higher net income than does combination by purchase.
    b. The cash position, other things being equal, usually is better when there is a combination by pooling than when there is a combination by purchase.
    c. Pooling of interests, other things being equal, reports a higher amount of retained earnings than does combination by purchase.

EXERCISES

Part A

E14–1. On January 2, 19A, Company P acquired all of the outstanding voting stock of Company S by exchanging, on a share-for-share basis, its own unissued stock for the stock of Company S. Immediately after the stock exchange entry was posted by Company P, the separate balance sheets showed the following:

	Balances, January 2, 19A, immediately after acquisition	
	Company P	Company S
Cash	$ 38,000	$12,000
Receivable from Company S .	7,000	
Inventory	35,000	18,000
Investment in Company S (100%)	60,000	
Operational assets (net of accumulated depreciation) .	80,000	50,000
Total	$220,000	$80,000
Liabilities	$ 25,000	$13,000
Payable to Company P		7,000
Common stock (Company P, par $5) (Company S, par $5)	140,000	40,000
Contributed capital from pooling of interests	20,000	
Retained earnings	35,000	20,000
Total	$220,000	$80,000

Required:

a. Is this a pooling of interests or a combination by purchase? Explain why.
b. Give the entry that was made by Company P to record the acquisition.
c. Prepare a consolidated balance sheet immediately after the acquisition. Follow the format of Exhibit 14–3.
d. Were the assets of the subsidiary added to those of the parent, in the consolidated balance sheet, at book value or at market value? Explain why.
e. What were the balances in the accounts of Company P immediately prior to the acquisition for (1) investment and (2) common stock? Were any other account balances for either Company P or Company S changed by the acquisition? Explain.

E14–2. On January 1, 19A, Company P acquired 100 percent of the outstanding common stock of Company S. At date of acquisition, the balance sheet of Company S reflected the following book values (summarized):

Total assets (market value, $220,000)*	$180,000
Total liabilities	30,000
Stockholders' equity:	
Common stock, par $10	100,000
Retained earnings	50,000

* One half subject to depreciation; ten-year remaining life and no residual value.

Two separate and independent cases are given below which indicate how Company P acquired 100 percent of the outstanding stock of Company S, viz:

Case A—Exchanged two shares of its own common stock (par $1) for each share of Company S stock.

Case B—Paid $20 per share for the stock of Company S.

Required:

For each case, answer the following:

a. Was this a combination by pooling of interests or by purchase? Explain.
b. Give the entry in the accounts of Company P to record the acquisition. If none, explain why.
c. Give the entry in the accounts of Company S to record the acquisition. If none, explain why.
d. Analyze the transaction to determine the amount of goodwill purchased. If no goodwill was purchased, explain why.
e. In preparing a consolidated balance sheet, at what amounts would the subsidiary assets be included? Explain.

E14–3. On January 1, 19A, Company P purchased 100 percent of the outstanding shares of Company S in the open market for $70,000 cash. On that date, prior to the acquisition, the separate balance sheets (summarized) of the two companies reported the following book values:

Prior to acquisition

	Company P	Company S
Cash	$ 80,000	$18,000
Receivable from Company P .		2,000
Operational assets (net)	80,000	60,000
Total	$160,000	$80,000
Liabilities	$ 28,000	$20,000
Payable to Company S	2,000	
Common stock:		
Company P (nopar)	100,000	
Company S (par $10)		50,000
Retained earnings	30,000	10,000
Total	$160,000	$80,000

It was determined on date of acquisition that the market value of the operational assets of Company S was $66,000.

Required:

a. Was this a combination by pooling of interests or by purchase? Explain why.
b. Give the entry that should be made by Company P at date of acquisition. If none is required, explain why.
c. Give the entry that should be made by Company S at date of acquisition. If none is required, explain why.
d. Analyze the acquisition to determine the amount of goodwill purchased.
e. At what value will the assets of Company S be included on the consolidated balance sheet? Explain.
f. Prepare a consolidated balance sheet immediately after acquisition. Follow the format of Exhibit 14–5.

E14–4. On January 4, 19A, Company P acquired all of the outstanding stock of Company S for $10 cash per share. At the date of acquisition the balance sheet of Company S reflected the following:

Common stock, par $5	$50,000
Retained earnings	30,000

Immediately after the acquisition entry was posted, the balance sheets reflected the following:

Balances, January 4, 19A, immediately after acquisition

	Company P	Company S
Cash	$ 13,000	$17,000
Receivable from Company P .		3,000
Investment in Company S (100%), at cost	100,000	
Operational assets (net)	122,000	70,000*
Total	$235,000	$90,000
Liabilities	$ 22,000	$10,000
Payable to Company S	3,000	
Common stock (par $5)	150,000	50,000
Retained earnings	60,000	30,000
Total	$235,000	$90,000

* Determined by Company P to have a market value of $78,000 at date of acquisition.

Required:

a. Was this a combination by pooling of interests or by purchase? Explain why.
b. Give the entry that should be made by Company P to record the acquisition.
c. Analyze the acquisition to determine the amount of goodwill purchased.
d. At what value will the assets of Company S be included on the consolidated balance sheet? Explain.
e. Prepare a consolidated balance sheet immediately after acquisition. Follow the format of Exhibit 14–5.

Exercises
Part B

E14–5. On January 1, 19A, Company P acquired all of the outstanding stock of Company S by exchanging one share of its own stock for each share of Company S stock. At the date of the exchange, the balance sheet of Company S showed the following:

Common stock, par $10	$40,000
Retained earnings	10,000

One year after acquisition the two companies prepared their separate financial statements as shown on the following worksheet:

COMPANY P and Its Subsidiary, COMPANY S (100 percent owned)
Consolidated Balance Sheet and Income Statement

(Relates to Exercise 14–5)   December 31, 19A

Items	Separate Statements		Eliminations	Consolidated Statements
	Company P	Company S		
Income statement (for 19A):				
Sales revenue	96,000	42,000		
Revenue from investments	4,000			
Cost of goods sold	(60,000)	(25,000)		
Expenses (not detailed)	(17,000)	(10,000)		
Net income	23,000	7,000		
Balance sheet (at December 31, 19A):				
Cash	21,000	19,000		
Receivable from Company P		2,000		
Investment in Company S (100%)	50,000			
Operational assets (net)	59,000	47,000		
Total	130,000	68,000		
Liabilities	17,000	15,000		
Payable to Company S	2,000			
Common stock, Company P (par $10)	50,000			
Contributed capital from pooling of interests	10,000			
Common stock, Company S (par $10)		40,000		
Beginning retained earnings, Company P	28,000			
Beginning retained earnings, Company S		10,000		
Dividend declared and paid, 19A; Company S		(4,000)		
Net income, 19A (from above)	23,000	7,000		
Total	130,000	68,000		

Required:

a. Give the entry that was made by Company P to record the pooling of interests on January 1, 19A.

b. Complete the Eliminations column in the above worksheet, then combine the two sets of statements in the last column to develop the consolidated income statement and balance sheet. (Hint: To complete the two columns, follow the pattern and approaches shown in Exhibit 14–3. Eliminate the revenue from investments against the dividends declared and paid because this represents intercompany revenue.

The consolidated net income is $26,000.)

E14–6. (Analytical) On January 1, 19A, Company P purchased all of the outstanding stock of Company S at $2.50 per share. At that date the balance sheet of Company S reflected the following:

> Common stock, par $1 .. $20,000
> Retained earnings   10,000

One year after acquisition each company prepared its separate financial statements and Company P set up the following consolidation worksheet (partially completed):

(Relates to Exercise 14–6)

Items	Separate Statements		Intercompany Eliminations		Consoli-dated Balances
	Company P	Company S	Debit	Credit	
Income statement (for 19A):					
Sales	99,000	59,000			
Revenues from investments	6,000		(e) 6,000		
Expenses (not detailed)	(71,000)	(40,400)			
Depreciation expense	(9,000)	(3,600)	(c) 1,200		
Amortization expense (goodwill)			(d) 400		
Net income	25,000	15,000			
Balance sheet (at Dec. 31, 19A):					
Cash	16,000	6,000			
Receivable from Co. P		4,000		(b) 4,000	
Investment in Co. S	50,000			(a) 50,000	
Operational assets (net)	90,000	40,000*	(a) 12,000	(c) 1,200	140,800
Goodwill (amortize over 20 years)			(a) 8,000	(d) 400	
Totals	156,000	50,000			170,400
Liabilities	15,000	11,000			
Payable to Co. S	4,000		(b) 4,000		
Common stock, Co. P	80,000				
Common stock, Co. S		20,000	(a) 20,000		
Beginning retained earnings, Co. P	32,000				
Beginning retained earnings, Co. S		10,000	(a) 10,000		
Dividends declared and paid, Co. S, 19A.		(6,000)		(e) 6,000	
Net income, 19A (per above)	25,000	15,000			32,400†
Totals	156,000	50,000	81,600	81,600	

* Market value of the operational assets at acquisition was $12,000 above book value and their remaining useful life was 10 years.

† Carried down.

Required:

a. Give the purchase entry made by Company P on January 1, 19A.

b. Show how the $8,000 of goodwill was computed.

c. Complete the last column of the worksheet (Note that under "Eliminations" debit/credit instead of +/− were used).

d. Give a brief explanation of eliminations *(c), (d),* and *(e).*

PROBLEMS

Part A

P14–1. During January 19A Company P acquired all of the outstanding voting shares of Company S by exchanging one share of its own unissued voting common stock for two shares of Company S stock. Immediately prior to the acquisition, the separate balance sheets of the two companies reflected the following:

	Company P	Company S
	Balances immediately prior to acquisition	
Cash	$200,000	$ 32,000
Receivable from Company P .		3,000
Inventory	75,000	5,000
Operational assets (net of accumulated depreciation) ..	75,000	80,000
Total	$350,000	$120,000
Liabilities	$ 57,000	$ 30,000
Payable to Company S	3,000	
Common stock, Company P (par $4)	180,000	
Common stock, Company S (par $5)		50,000
Contributed capital from pooling		
Retained earnings	110,000	40,000
Total	$350,000	$120,000

Additional data:

At the date of acquisition, Company S stock was quoted on the market at $16 per share; there was no established market for Company P stock.

The operational assets of Company S were appraised independently at the date of acquisition at $130,000.

Required:

a. Is this a purchase or a pooling of interests? Explain why.

b. What account balances would be changed by the exchange of shares on each of the above balance sheets? List each account and amount.

c. Give the entry that should be made by each company to record the exchange; if no entry is required, explain why.

d. How much goodwill should be recognized? Why?

e. Prepare a consolidated balance sheet immediately after the acquisition. Use the format in Exhibit 14–3.

f. Did you use any market values in solving the above requirements? Explain why.

P14–2. Assume the same facts given in Problem 14–1 except that instead of an exchange of shares of stock, Company P purchased for cash from the shareholders individually 100 percent of the outstanding shares of Company S at a total market price of $160,000.

Required:

a. Is this a purchase or a pooling of interests? Explain why.

b. What account balances would be changed by the purchase of the shares on each of the balance sheets? List each account and amount.

c. Give the entry that should be made by each company to record the exchange; if no entry is required, explain why.

d. How much goodwill should be recognized? Why?

e. Prepare a consolidated balance sheet immediately after acquisition.

f. Did you use any market values in solving the above requirements? Explain why.

P14–3. On January 1, 19A, the separate balance sheets of two corporations showed the following:

	Company P	Company S
	Balances, Jan. 1, 19A	
Cash	$ 21,000	$ 9,000
Receivable from Company P		4,000
Operational assets (net)	99,000	32,000
Total	$120,000	$45,000
Accounts payable	$ 16,000	$10,000
Payable to Company S	4,000	
Common stock (par $20)	60,000	20,000
Retained earnings	40,000	15,000
Total	$120,000	$45,000

On January 3, 19A, Company P acquired all of the outstanding shares of Company S by exchanging one share of its own stock for two shares of Company S stock.

Required:

a. Was this a combination by pooling of interests or by purchase? Explain why.

b. Company P made the following entry on its books, at date of acquisition, to record the investment:

January 3, 19A:

Investment in Co. S	35,000	
Common stock		10,000
Contributed capital from pooling of interests		25,000

Explain the basis for each of the three amounts in this entry.

c. Will any goodwill be recognized on the consolidated balance sheet? Explain why.

d. Prepare a consolidated balance sheet immediately after the acquisition. Follow the format shown in Exhibit 14–3.

P14–4. On January 2, 19A, Company P acquired all of the outstanding stock of Company S by exchanging its own stock for the stock of Company S. One share of Company P stock was exchanged for two shares of Company S stock. Immediately after the acquisition was recorded by Company P, the balance sheets reflected the following:

	Balances, Jan. 2, 19A, immediately after acquisition	
	Company P	Company S
Cash	$ 38,000	$26,000
Receivable from Company S .	6,000	
Inventory	30,000	10,000
Investment in Company S (100%)	70,000	
Operational assets (net)	90,000	50,000
Other assets	6,000	4,000
Total	$240,000	$90,000
Liabilitites	$ 16,000	$14,000
Payable to Company P		6,000
Common stock (par $5)	125,000	50,000
Contributed capital from pooling of interests	45,000	
Retained earnings	54,000	20,000
Total	$240,000	$90,000

Required:

a. Was this a combination by pooling of interests or by purchase? Explain why.

b. Give the journal entry that was made by Company P to record the acquisition on January 2, 19A. Explain the basis for each amount included in the entry.

c. At what amounts will the assets of Company S be included on the consolidated balance sheet? Explain.

d. Will any goodwill be recognized on the consolidated balance sheet? Explain why.

e. Prepare a consolidated balance sheet immediately after acquisition. Follow the format illustrated in Exhibit 14–3.

P14–5. On January 5, 19A, Company P purchased all of the outstanding stock of Company S for $100,000 cash. Immediately after the acquisition the separate balance sheets of the two companies reflected the following:

	Jan. 5, 19A, immediately after acquisition	
	Company P	Company S
Cash	$ 22,000	$ 9,000
Accounts receivable (net)	14,000	6,000
Receivable from Company S .	4,000	
Inventory	50,000	25,000
Investment in Company S (at cost)	100,000	
Operational assets (net)	153,000	67,000
Other assets	7,000	3,000
Total	$350,000	$110,000
Accounts payable	$ 20,000	$ 16,000
Payable to Company P		4,000
Bonds payable	90,000	
Common stock (par $5)	180,000	60,000
Contributed capital in excess of par	8,000	
Retained earnings	52,000	30,000
Total	$350,000	$110,000

The operational assets of Company S were estimated to have a market value at date of acquisition of $71,000.

Required:

a. Was this a combination by pooling of interests or by purchase? Explain why.
b. Give the entry that would be made in the accounts of Company P at date of acquisition.
c. Analyze the acquisition to determine the amount of goodwill purchased.
d. At what amounts will the assets of Company S, the subsidiary, be included on the consolidated balance sheet immediately after acquisition? Explain.
e. Prepare a consolidated balance sheet immediately after acquisition. Follow the format illustrated in Exhibit 14–5.

P14–6. On January 4, 19A, Company P purchased 100 percent of the outstanding common stock of Company S for $240,000 cash. Immediately after the acquisition, the separate balance sheets for the two companies were prepared as shown in the worksheet below.

It was determined at date of acquisition that on the basis of market value compared with the book value, the assets as reflected on the books of Company S should be adjusted as follows: (a) inventories should be reduced by $3,000, (b) plant and equipment should be increased to $148,000, and (c) land should be increased by $2,000.

Required:

a. Was this a combination by pooling of interests or by purchase? Explain why.
b. Give the entry that was made on the books of Company P to record the acquisition.
c. Analyze the acquisition transaction to determine the amount of goodwill purchased. Use data from the worksheet below if needed.
d. At what amount will the assets of Company S be included on the consolidated balance sheet? Explain.
e. Complete the "Eliminations" column in the form below and then extend the amounts for the consolidated balance sheet.

(Relates to Problem 14–6)

COMPANY P and Its Subsidiary, COMPANY S
Consolidated Balance Sheet
January 4, 19A, Immediately after Acquisition

	Separate balance sheets			Consolidated
	Company P	Company S	Eliminations	balance sheet
Assets				
Cash	$ 80,000	$ 40,000	_____	_____
Accounts receivable (net)	26,000	19,000	_____	_____
Receivable from Company P		8,000	_____	_____
Inventories	170,000	80,000	_____	_____
Long-term investment, bonds, Z Company	15,000		_____	_____
Long-term investment, Company S ..	240,000		_____	_____
Land	12,000	3,000	_____	_____
Plant and equipment (net)	157,000	130,000	_____	_____
Goodwill			_____	_____
Total assets	$700,000	$280,000	_____	_____

Liabilities				
Accounts payable	$ 22,000	$ 40,000	_____	_____
Payable to Company S	8,000		_____	_____
Bonds payable, 5%	100,000	30,000	_____	_____
Shareholders' Equity				
Common stock, Company P	500,000		_____	_____
Common stock, Company S (par $10)		150,000	_____	_____
Retained earnings, Company P	70,000		_____	_____
Retained earnings, Company S		60,000	_____	_____
Total liabilities and shareholders' equity	$700,000	$280,000	_____	_____

Problems
Part B

P14–7. (Analytical) On January 1, 19A, Company P acquired 100 percent of the outstanding stock of Company S for $106,000 cash. At date of acquisition the balance sheet of Company S reflected the following:

Total assets (including operational assets*)	115,000
Total liabilities	25,000
Common stock, par $10	60,000
Retained earnings	30,000

  * Book value, $42,000; market value, $48,000 (20-year remaining life).

One year after acquisition the two companies prepared their December 31, 19A, financial statements. Company P developed the following consolidation worksheet (partially completed):

(Relates to Problem 14–7)

COMPANY P AND ITS SUBSIDIARY, COMPANY S
Consolidated Worksheet
Income Statement and Balance Sheet, December 31, 19A (100% ownership)

Items	Separate Statements		Eliminations				Consolidated balances
	Company P	Company S	Debit		Credit		
Income statement:							
Sales	80,000	47,000					
Revenue from investments	4,000		(e)	4,000			
Cost of goods sold	(45,000)	(25,000)					
Expenses (not detailed)	(15,000)	(10,000)					
Depreciation expense	(4,000)	(2,000)	(c)	300			
Amortization of goodwill			(d)	500			
Net income	20,000	10,000					
Balance sheet:							
Cash	15,000	10,000					
Accounts receivable (net)	19,000	9,000					
Receivable from Co. P		1,000			(b)	1,000	
Inventories	70,000	50,000					
Investment in Co. S (100%)	106,000				(a)	106,000	
Plant and equipment (net)	80,000	40,000	(a)	6,000	(c)	300	
Goodwill			(a)	10,000	(d)	500	
	290,000	110,000					
Accounts payable	26,000	14,000					
Payable to Co. S	1,000		(b)	1,000			
Common stock, Co. P	200,000						
Common stock, Co. S		60,000	(a)	60,000			
Beginning retained earnings, Co. P	50,000						
Beginning retained earnings, Co. S		30,000	(a)	30,000			
Dividends declared and paid during 19A, Co. P	(7,000)						
Dividends declared and paid during 19A, Co. S		(4,000)			(e)	4,000	
Net income (from above)	20,000	10,000					
	290,000	110,000	111,800		111,800		308,200

Required:

a. Was this a purchase or pooling? Explain.

b. Give the entry made by each company to record the acquisition.

c. Complete the last column of the worksheet to develop the consolidated income statement and balance sheet.

d. How much goodwill was recognized? How was it computed?

e. Briefly explain each of the elimination "entries" shown on the worksheet. Note that debit and credit rather than plus and minus were used in the "Elimination" column.

P14–8. (Analytical) This problem presents the income statement and the balance sheet on a consolidated basis for Company P and its subsidiary, Company S, one year after acquisition, under two different assumptions: Case A—pooling of interests basis, and Case B—purchase basis. The two different assumptions are used so that we can compare and analyze the differences.

On January 2, 19A, Company P acquired all of the outstanding common stock of Company S. At that date the shareholders' equity of Company S showed the following: common stock, par $10, $50,000; and retained earnings, $20,000. The entry made by Company P to record the acquisition under each case was as follows:

Case A—Pooling of interests basis:

Investment in Co. S		
(5,000 shares, 100%)	70,000	
Common stock, par $8		40,000
Contributed capital from		
pooling		30,000

Case B—Purchase basis:

Investment in Co. S		
(5,000 shares, 100%)	80,000	
Cash		80,000

On January 2, 19A, the acquisition by purchase (Case B) was analyzed to determine the goodwill as follows:

Purchase price paid for 100% interest in	
Company S	$80,000
Net assets purchased, valued at market:	
Book value of net assets ($50,000 +	
$20,000 = $70,000 + increase of	
$2,000 in operational assets to	
market value)	72,000
Goodwill purchased	$ 8,000

For consolidated statement purposes the operational assets are being depreciated over 10 years' remaining life and the goodwill will be amortized over 20 years.

One year after acquisition, the two companies prepared separate income statements and balance sheets (December 31, 19A). These separate statements have been consolidated under each case as reflected on page 644.

Required:

a. Prepare a schedule of amounts that shows what items are different between each statement for Case A, compared with Case B.

b. Explain the reasons why net income is different under pooling versus purchase. Use amounts from the two statements in your explanation and tell why they are different.

c. Explain why the cash balance is different between the two cases.

d. What was the balance in the account "Investment in Company S" in each case prior to its elimination? Explain.

e. Explain why the operational asset (net) amounts are different between the two cases.

f. Why is there a difference in goodwill between the two cases? Provide computations.

g. How much was eliminated for intercompany debt? Why was it eliminated?

h. What amount of "Common stock, Company S," was eliminated? Why was it eliminated?

i. Why was only $20,000 of the $30,000 of contributed capital from pooling of interests eliminated?

j. Explain why the account "Contributed capital in excess of par, $10,000," was not eliminated.

k. Explain why "Beginning retained earnings, Company S, $20,000," is shown under Case A (pooling) but not under Case B (purchase).

(Relates to Problem 14–8)

COMPANY P and Its Subsidiary, COMPANY'S (100% owned)
Consolidated Income Statement and Balance Sheet
December 31, 19A

	Consolidated statements December 31, 19A	
	Pooling basis (Case A)	Purchase basis (Case B)
Income statement (for the year ended December 31, 19A):		
Sales revenue	$236,000	$236,000
Revenue from investments ($4,000, eliminated)		
Cost of goods sold	(112,000)	(112,000)
Expenses (not detailed to simplify)	(75,500)	(75,500)
Depreciation expense	(12,500)	(12,700)
Amortization expense (goodwill)		(400)
Net income	$ 36,000	$ 35,400
Balance sheet (at December 31, 19A):		
Assets		
Cash	$128,000	$ 48,000
Accounts receivable (net)	53,000	53,000
Receivable from Company S ($5,000, eliminated)		
Inventory	37,000	37,000
Investment in Company S (eliminated)		
Operational assets (net)	125,000	126,800
Goodwill		7,600
Total	$343,000	$272,400
Liabilities		
Current liabilities	$ 30,000	$ 30,000
Payable to Company P (eliminated)		
Bonds payable	50,000	50,000
Shareholders' Equity		
Common stock, Company P	140,000	100,000
Common stock, Company S (eliminated)		
Contributed capital in excess of par	10,000	10,000
Contributed capital from pooling of interests ($20,000, eliminated)	10,000	
Beginning retained earnings, Company P	47,000	47,000
Beginning retained earnings, Company S	20,000	
Dividends declared and paid in 19A (eliminated)		
Net income, 19A (from income statement above)	36,000	35,400
Total	$343,000	$272,400

P14–9. This problem is an extension of the decision case in the chapter. Refer to Exhibit 14–8 (Corning Glass Works) and respond to the following questions:

a. At the end of 1979, the balance sheet reported, "Associated companies, at equity, $221,659,000." How was this amount derived? Does LCM apply to it? Explain.

b. At the end of 1979, the balance sheet, under investments, reported, "Other, at cost, $7,225,000." How was this amount derived? Does LCM apply to it? Explain.

c. At the end of 1979, the balance sheet reported, "Goodwill, $8,006,000." How was this amount determined?

Explain why it is less in 1979 than in 1978.

d. At the end of 1979, the balance sheet reported, "Minority interest in subsidiary companies, $5,063,000." Explain how this was derived (including its probable components).

e. The 1979 income statement reported the following item, "Minority interest in (earnings) loss of subsidiary, ($2,202,000)." Explain how this amount was determined. Why is it shown on the consolidated income statement as "earnings" yet as a deduction?

f. The 1979 income statement reported, "Equity in earnings of associated companies, $45,244,000." Explain what this amount represents. Basically, how was it computed?

P14–10. (Based on Appendix A)   On January 1, 19A, Company P purchased 100 percent of the outstanding capital stock of Company S for $98,000 cash. At that date the stockholders' equity section of the balance sheet of Company S reflected the following:

Capital stock, $10 par, 5,000 shares outstanding	$50,000
Retained earnings	30,000
	$80,000

At the date of acquisition, it was determined that the market values of certain assets of Company S, in comparison with the book values of those assets as reflected on the balance sheet of Company S, should be reflected by (a) decreasing inventories by $2,000 and (b) increasing equipment by $8,000.

It is now one year after acquisition, December 31, 19A, and each company has prepared the following separate financial statements (summarized):

(Relates to Problem 14–10)

	Company P	Company S
Balance sheet (at December 31, 19A):		
Cash	$ 52,000	$ 30,000
Accounts receivable (net)	31,000	10,000
Receivable from Company P		3,000
Inventories	60,000	70,000
Investment in Company S (at cost)	98,000	
Equipment	80,000	20,000
Other assets	9,000	17,000
	$330,000	$150,000
Accounts payable	$ 42,000	$ 30,000
Payable to Company S	3,000	
Bonds payable, 10%	70,000	30,000
Capital stock ($10 par)	140,000	50,000
Beginning retained earnings	50,000	30,000
Dividends declared and paid during 19A	(10,000)	(5,000)
Net income, 19A (from income statement)	35,000	15,000
	$330,000	$150,000
Income statement (for 19A):		
Sales revenue	$360,000	$140,000
Revenue from investments	5,000	
Cost of goods sold	(220,000)	(80,000)
Expenses (not detailed)	(106,000)	(44,000)
Depreciation expense	(4,000)	(1,000)
Net income	$ 35,000	$ 15,000

Additional data during 19A:

1. Near the end of 19A, Company S declared and paid a cash dividend amounting to $5,000.
2. The equipment is being depreciated on the basis of a 20-year remaining life (no residual value).
3. Goodwill is to be amortized over a 40-year period.

Required:

a. Give the entry on the books of Company P to record the acquisition of the capital stock of Company S on January 1, 19A.
b. Analyze the acquisition of the stock to determine the purchased goodwill.
c. Prepare a consolidation worksheet (purchase basis) for the year 19A as a basis for the 19A income statement and balance sheet. (Hint: Consolidated net income is $44,300.)

d. Prepare a consolidated income statement and balance sheet based on the data provided by the consolidation worksheet.

P14–11. (Based on Appendix B) On January 1, 19A, Company P purchased 90 percent of the outstanding voting stock of Company S for $100,000 cash. At the date of acquisition, the stockholders' equity accounts of Company S reflected the following: Capital Stock (par $10), $60,000; Contributed Capital in Excess of Par, $10,000; and Retained Earnings, $20,000. At that date it was determined that the book value of the operational assets was $10,000 less than their market value.

It is now December 31, 19A, and each company has prepared the following separate financial statements (summarized):

(Relates to Problem 14–11)

	Company P	Company S
Balance sheet (at December 31, 19A):		
Cash	$ 23,000	$ 11,000
Accounts receivable (net)	57,000	13,000
Receivable from Company P		7,000
Inventories	110,000	24,000
Investment in Company S (at cost; 90% owned)	100,000	
Operational assets (net)	120,000	50,000
Other assets	6,000	5,000
	$416,000	$110,000
Accounts payable	$ 30,000	$ 8,000
Payable to Company S	7,000	
Bonds payable, 9%	80,000	10,000
Capital stock ($10 par)	200,000	60,000
Contributed capital, in excess of par	4,000	10,000
Beginning retained earnings	80,000	20,000
Dividends declared and paid, 19A	(15,000)	(8,000)
Net income (from income statement)	30,000	10,000
	$416,000	$110,000
Income statement (for 19A):		
Sales revenue	$195,000	$ 75,000
Revenue from investments	7,200	
Cost of goods sold	(115,000)	(43,000)
Expenses (not detailed)	(52,200)	(19,500)
Depreciation expense	(5,000)	(2,500)
	$ 30,000	$ 10,000

Required:

a. Give the entry on the books of Company P to record the acquisition of the stock of Company S.

b. Analyze the stock purchase to determine the amount of goodwill purchased.

c. Prepare a consolidation worksheet (purchase basis) for a balance sheet and income statement for 19A. Assume the operational assets of Company S have a 10-year remaining life and that any goodwill will be amortized over 20 years. (Hint: Consolidated net income is $31,400.)

d. Prepare a classified income statement and balance sheet for 19A based upon the data provided by the consolidation worksheet.

e. What is the minority interest claim to earnings and shareholders' equity at December 31, 19A?

The statement of changes in financial position

PURPOSE OF THE CHAPTER

The previous chapters emphasized that three basic statements must be presented for external reporting purposes: (1) an income statement, (2) a balance sheet, and (3) a statement of changes in financial position (SCFP).[1] In the past, the third statement, previously called a statement of sources and uses of funds, was prepared by many companies, although it was not required by GAAP. The modern title, "Statement of Changes in Financial Position," is used almost exclusively. It must be based on an **all-resources concept** and has been required since the issuance of *APB Opinion No. 19*, "Reporting Changes in Financial Position," dated March 1971.[2]

This chapter discusses the **statement of changes in financial position** (for convenience referred to as the SCFP) as required by *APB Opinion No. 19*. To accomplish this purpose the chapter is subdivided as follows:

Part A: Purpose and concept of the SCFP

Part B: SCFP, cash basis

Part C: SCFP, working capital basis

---

[1] Other supporting schedules, such as a statement of cost of goods sold, statement of retained earnings, statement of changes in capital, and a schedule of lease commitments, are essential in certain circumstances to meet the requirements of the full-disclosure principle.

[2] AICPA, *APB Opinion No. 19*, "Reporting Changes in Financial Position" (New York, 1971), states: "The Board concludes that information concerning the financing and investing activities of a business enterprise and the changes in its financial position for a period is essential for financial statement users. . . . A statement summarizing changes in financial position should be presented as a basic financial statement for each period for which an income statement is presented." Copyright (1971) by the American Institute of CPAs.

Appendix: Worksheet preparation of the SCFP. The preparation techniques are set out separately for the convenience of those who desire to extend the study to the worksheet procedures that are used in complex situations.

Behavioral and learning objectives for this chapter are provided in the *Teachers Manual.*

PART A: PURPOSE AND CONCEPT OF THE SCFP

The income statement reports on the entity's operating performance (revenues and expenses) over a period of time, and the balance sheet reports on the financial position (assets, liabilities, and owners' equity) at a specific date. Both of these statements are developed on the **accrual basis.** Although practically all of an entity's transactions during the accounting period are reflected in the income statement and the balance sheet, many of the entries are not reported on those statements in a way that reflects their full significance to investors, creditors, and other external users of the financial statements. Specifically, the income statement and balance sheet do not report the sources of funds and the uses of funds during the period. They do not report on the **liquidity** of the entity.

The SCFP is designed to report *(a)* the **liquidity** dimension of entity performance, that is, on the entity's **financing** activities (the sources or inflows of funds) and **investing** activities (the uses or outflows of funds) and the effects of those activities on the financial position of the entity; and *(b)* the changes in financial position during the period.[3] Fundamentally, the SCFP reports financial information on a funds flow basis (such as cash or working capital) rather than on the accrual basis which is used in the income statement and balance sheet. A periodic report of the **sources and uses** of funds is of particular significance to investors, creditors, and other external users of financial statements because those groups need relevant information to help make useful predictions about the ability of the entity to generate cash in the future.[4] The general format, primary sources of funds and primary uses of funds, of a SCFP is illustrated in Exhibit 15–1.

The income statement and balance sheet usually do not identify specific

---

[3] *APB Opinion No. 19* states: "The funds statement cannot supplant either the income statement or the balance sheet but is intended to provide information that the other statements either do not provide or provide only indirectly about the flow of funds and changes in financial position during the period."

[4] *FASB Statement of Financial Accounting Concepts No. 1,* "Objectives of Financial Reporting by Business Enterprises" (Stamford, Conn., November 1978), states: "Since investors' and creditors' cash flows are related to enterprise cash flows, financial reporting should provide information to help investors, creditors, and others assess the amounts, timing, and uncertainty of prospective net cash inflows to the related enterprise." Copyright © by the Financial Accounting Standards Board, High Ridge Park, Stamford, Conn. 06905, U.S.A. Quoted (or excerpted) with permission. Copies of the complete document are available from the FASB.

EXHIBIT 15–1

ILLUSTRATIVE CORPORATION
Statement of Changes in Financial Position
For the Year Ended December 31, 19B

Sources (inflows) of funds:

1. Regular operations (based on the income statement)	$64,000	
2. Sale of nonfund assets (such as machinery)	6,000	
3. Borrowing (such as on a long-term note)	30,000	
4. Sale and issuance of capital stock	20,000	
Total funds generated		$120,000

Uses (outflows) of funds:

1. Purchase of assets (such as machinery)	$35,000	
2. Payment of debt (such as bonds payable)	50,000	
3. Payment of dividends (such as on common stock)	10,000	
4. Purchase of treasury stock	15,000	
Total funds used		110,000
Net increase in funds during the period		$ 10,000

transactions such as the acquisition of a particular operational asset, an investment in securities, the creation of a receivable, the incurrence of a debt, or the payment of a debt. Although the income statement or balance sheet may report one portion of some of those transactions, such as the gain or loss on disposal of an operational asset, the remaining portions of the transaction (such as the amount of cash received or paid) ordinarily are obscured completely. Comparison of two consecutive balance sheets indicates, for example, the net increase or decrease in total cash, but it tells nothing about the specific sources and uses of cash or working capital. Similarly, the income statement reflects how much better off the entity is in terms of revenues, expenses, and income on the accrual basis, but it reflects little about the related amounts of cash inflow and outflow during the period.

To complement the income statement and balance sheet, the SCFP is designed to report on the liquidity of the enterprise and to reflect the relation between the sources and uses of funds during the period. Consequently, it is designed to provide information that is particularly useful to external users of the financial statements in answering questions such as:

1. How much cash (or working capital) was provided by the regular **operations** of the entity?
2. What were the primary sources of funds from such activities as borrowing, issuance of capital stock, and sale of operational assets?
3. How much cash was derived from **nonrecurring** transactions?
4. How much cash was used to pay long-term debts?
5. How much cash was used to acquire operational assets?
6. Why were large borrowings necessary? What uses were made of the cash borrowed?
7. What are the causes of the persistent liquidity problems of the entity? Does a disastrous cash-flow problem appear imminent?

8. Does the company have idle cash? How does the company "use" idle cash?
9. What was the financial effect of noncash exchanges (such as the settlement of a debt by issuing company shares)?
10. What is the potential ability of the company to generate cash in the long term?

To the extent that the SCFP can assist external users of the financial statements in answering the above questions, better than they would be doing without the SCFP, it serves a very useful and significant purpose.

Funds defined. The terms *funds, cash,* and *working capital* were used in the above paragraphs. Although these terms sometimes are used interchangeably, clarity and precision are essential when they are used in accounting, and in particular, in respect to the SCFP. **Cash** was defined in Chapter 8, and **working capital** was defined in Chapter 2. In contrast, the term *funds* is used widely as a generic term with several different connotations. With respect to the SCFP, *APB Opinion No. 19* specifies that **funds may be measured as either:**[5]

1. **Cash**—As defined in Chapter 8 (also refer to Part B of this chapter).
2. **Working capital**—Working capital always is defined as current assets minus current liabilities. The usual current assets are cash, short-term investments, accounts receivable, inventory, and prepaid expenses. The current liabilities are short-term debts that are expected to be paid out of the current assets.

In contrast to cash, which can be handled, counted, and used to purchase goods and services, to pay debts, and to invest, working capital is an abstract concept because it is the arithmetical difference between the sum of the several current assets and the sum of the several current liabilities.

Generally accepted accounting principles require that a SCFP clearly disclose whether funds are measured as cash or as working capital.

The all-resources concept. The SCFP must be based on the all-resources concept which means that it must report all of the **financing and investing** activities, not just those that cause an inflow or outflow of funds (cash or working capital). Transactions that do not cause an inflow or outflow of funds are called **direct exchanges** because they involve the exchanges of **nonfund** assets, liabilities, or capital stock. Direct exchanges occur when a transaction does not include an increase (a debit) or a decrease (a credit) to at least one fund account (i.e., to cash or working capital). Common examples of direct exchanges are discussed in the cases below.

---

[5] The word "funds" also is used in other ways by accountants. It has been used to refer to assets, generally cash, set aside for specific future use, such as a building fund or a bond sinking fund; and in governmental accounting, it has an entirely different meaning. This wide range of inconsistent usage of the term suggests the desirability of using more descriptive terms, such as *cash* and *working capital,* and the use of more descriptive titles, such as "statement of changes in financial position," rather than the older title, "funds-flow statement."

Case A—AB Company acquired a machine and paid in full by issuing 100 shares of its own common stock, par $50 per share. The stock was selling regularly at $60 per share; therefore, the company recorded the transaction in the accounts as follows:

Machine (100 shares × $60)	6,000	
Common stock, par $50 (100 shares × $50)		5,000
Contributed capital in excess of par		
(100 shares × $10)		1,000

The above entry does not reflect a debit or credit to any fund account because neither cash nor working capital was affected. However, the transaction involved both a financing activity (the issuance of the stock) and an investing activity (the acquisition of the machine). Consequently, the all-resources concept holds that there was an implied (though not explicit) and concurrent inflow and outflow of funds. To illustrate this point, instead of the direct exchange, assume that the company sold the common stock for $6,000 cash and immediately purchased the machine and paid the $6,000 cash cost. Under this assumption, the sale of the common stock was a financing activity and the debit to cash of $6,000 reflected a source (inflow) of funds (cash or working capital). In contrast, the purchase of the machine was an investing activity and the credit to Cash of $6,000 reflected a use (outflow) of funds (cash or working capital). The all-resources concept views direct exchanges in this way; therefore, in Case A the direct exchange of the shares for the machine must be reported on the SCFP "as if" **two separate transactions** occurred concurrently. That is, the SCFP must report (1) a **source** of funds and (2) a **use** of funds for each direct exchange. AB Company would report the following on the SCFP:

Sources of funds:
Sale and issuance of common stock (Note A) $6,000

Uses of funds:
Purchase of machine (Note A) 6,000

Note A: This was a direct exchange. A machine was acquired at a cost of $6,000; payment was made by issuing 100 shares of common stock, par $50 per share, that had a market value of $6,000.

Similar direct exchanges would occur if AB company had made payment by signing a note payable (principal $6,000) or by transferring **nonfund** assets.

Case B—AB Company owed a $30,000 note payable which was paid off in full by issuing 500 of its own common shares, par $50, with a

$60 market value per share. The company would record the direct exchange as follows:

Note payable	30,000	
Common stock, par $50 (500 shares × $50)		25,000
Contributed capital in excess of par		
(500 shares × $10)		5,000

Although no fund accounts (cash or working capital) were debited or credited (i.e., there was no inflow or outflow of funds), the SCFP would report the $30,000 as if it were (1) a source of funds and (2) a use of funds in a manner similar to the example in Case A.

A direct exchange also is illustrated in the exhibits for Fina Company which follow in Parts B and C.

The SCFP is a **change statement.** The income statement was identified in Exhibit 4–1 (page 143) as a **change** statement because it reports the detailed causes (revenues, expenses, and extraordinary items) of the major change (i.e., net income) in the Retained Earnings account between two consecutive balance sheets. However, the income statement has limited scope for this purpose because it "explains" only one change in one balance sheet account—Retained Earnings. The remaining balance sheet accounts usually change during the period, and the **causes** of those changes constitute important information to statement users. The SCFP, in addition to reporting on the **liquidity** of the entity, also explains the causes of the changes in the **nonfund** asset, liability, and owners' equity accounts during the period. This is the primary reason for inclusion of the term "changes" in the title of the statement.

The way in which the SCFP reports the causes of the changes in the nonfund balance sheet accounts can be demonstrated simply because the sources and uses of funds (including the direct exchanges) represent those changes. To illustrate, refer to the SCFP given in Exhibit 15–1 for Illustrative Company. That statement was developed by analyzing the increases and decreases during the period in each of the nonfund balance sheet accounts. Exhibit 15–2 is presented to illustrate the relations among (1) the beginning balance sheet, (2) the sources and uses of funds reported on the SCFP, and (3) the ending balance sheet. Observe for each balance sheet account that the **sources** and **uses** listed report (account for) the change that occurred during the period and, therefore, reconcile the net change in each account during the period. These relations will be used as the basis for preparation of the SCFP as described in Parts B and C of this chapter.

EXHIBIT 15–2

Illustrative company (SCFP given in Exhibit 15–1)—The SCFP as a *CHANGE* statement

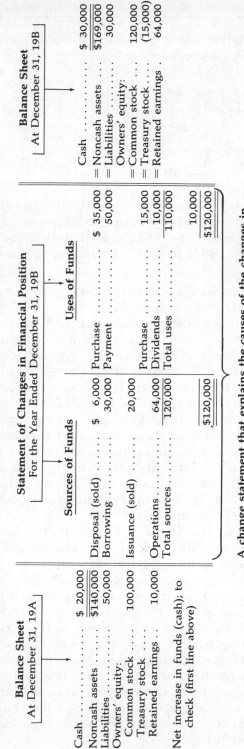

Balance Sheet
At December 31, 19A

Cash	$ 20,000	
Noncash assets	$140,000	
Liabilities	50,000	
Owners' equity:		
Common stock	100,000	
Treasury stock		
Retained earnings	10,000	

Net increase in funds (cash); to check (first line above)

Statement of Changes in Financial Position
For the Year Ended December 31, 19B

Sources of Funds

Disposal (sold)	$ 6,000	
Borrowing	30,000	
Issuance (sold)	20,000	
Operations	64,000	
Total sources	120,000	
	$120,000	

Uses of Funds

Purchase	$ 35,000	
Payment	50,000	
Purchase	15,000	
Dividends	10,000	
Total uses	110,000	
	10,000	
	$120,000	

Balance Sheet
At December 31, 19B

Cash		$ 30,000
= Noncash assets		$169,000
= Liabilities		30,000
= Owners' equity:		
= Common stock		120,000
= Treasury stock		(15,000)
= Retained earnings		64,000

A change statement that explains the causes of the changes in the *NONFUND* balance sheet accounts—assets, liabilities, and owners' equity (Assumptions: Funds measured as cash and no direct exchanges.)

PART B: SCFP, CASH BASIS

APB Opinion No. 19 specifies that the SCFP can be prepared on *either* a cash or a working capital basis. In applying either alternative, the concepts underlying the SCFP are identical except for the manner of measuring "funds." Prior to the issuance of *Opinion No. 19* (1971), the working capital basis was used exclusively, and it continues to be the most popular with statement issuers. However, the recent quotations given below appear to be in contrast to the current choice by issuers.

> Investors and creditors therefore need information about the sources and uses of enterprise cash, and financial statements should provide information about each major source, each major use, and relations between them.[6]

> Potential users of financial information most directly concerned with a particular business enterprise are generally interested in its ability to generate favorable cash flows because their decisions relate to amounts, timing, and uncertainties of expected cash flows.[7]

The **SCFP, cash basis,** is presented before the working capital basis because it (1) is easier to comprehend (everyone knows what cash is!) and (2) appears to be recognized as of more significance to financial statement **users.**

CASH BASIS CONCEPT

The fundamental concept underlying the SCFP, **cash basis,** is that it reports only, but all, of the cash inflows and cash outflows of the period. This concept means that all of the items reported on the income statement and balance sheet must be **converted** from the accrual basis to a current cash basis.

The SCFP, cash basis, defines, measures, and reports the sources and uses of funds in terms of cash.[8] Fundamentally, cash is used as the measure of funds because investors, creditors, and other external statement users need the most relevant information that can be provided to help them **project the ability of the company to generate favorable net cash inflows**

---

[6] FASB, "Tentative Conclusions on Objectives of Financial Statements of Business Enterprises" (Stamford, Conn., December 1976), par. 145. Copyright © by the Financial Accounting Standards Board, High Ridge Park, Stamford, Conn. 06905, U.S.A. Quoted (or excerpted) with permission. Copies of the complete document are available from the FASB.

[7] *FASB Statement of Financial Accounting Concepts No. 1,* "Objectives of Financial Reporting by Business Enterprises" (Stamford, Conn., November 1978), par. 25. Copyright © by the Financial Accounting Standards Board, High Ridge Park, Stamford, Conn. 06905, U.S.A. Quoted (or excerpted) with permission. Copies of the complete document are available from the FASB.

[8] For SCFP purposes, any short-term investments held almost always are added to cash because such investments are very near to cash and can be converted to cash easily at any time (this is permitted by *APB Opinion No. 19*).

in the future. The SCFP reports on the liquidity of the entity, and cash is the most liquid of all assets. Cash represents the concept of funds that circulate through a business daily; a company deals in terms of cash, and it is generated and used continuously. Also, cash is accounted for separately (in the Cash account), and it can be physically counted. Cash inflows and outflows are understood and communicated easily (via the SCFP). In contrast, working capital is an elusive concept to many persons, particularly because it includes numerous assets (all of the different current assets) and numerous offsets (all of the different current liabilities).

The SCFP, cash basis, reports all of the **cash sources,** all of the **cash uses,** and the **difference** between the total cash inflows and total cash outflows of the period. Therefore, the "bottom line" of the SCFP reports the net increase or decrease in cash during the period, which also is the same amount as the change in Cash account balance between the two consecutive balance sheets.

The SCFP, cash basis, reports the following primary captions:

Sources of cash:
  Cash flow from regular operations (including cash receivables less cash expenses)
  Cash flow from extraordinary items
  Other inflows of cash:
    From disposal of *noncash* assets
    From borrowing
    From sale and issuance of capital stock
    Direct exchanges (the financing activity)

Uses of cash:
  Cash outflows to acquire noncash assets
  Cash outflows to pay nontrade liabilities
  Cash outflows to purchase treasury stock
  Direct exchanges (the investing activity)

The above sources and uses of cash are illustrated on a typical SCFP, cash basis, in Exhibit 15–6.

PREPARING THE SCFP, CASH BASIS

Knowledge of the technical preparation of a SCFP is not essential to be able to use it effectively. However, as with the income statement and balance sheet, a general understanding of the procedures used to prepare the SCFP often is helpful in understanding it.[9] The SCFP can be prepared by using either of two alternative approaches:

1. **T-account approach**—This procedure traditionally has been used for instructional purposes because students are familiar with T-account

---

[9] The discussions of the T-account and worksheet approaches which follow can be omitted without significantly impinging upon the remaining discussions.

analyses of various sorts. For that reason it is illustrated in Parts B and C.

2. **Worksheet approach**—This procedure is used almost exclusively in practical situations because it is a sophisticated (although simple) approach, and it is efficient in situations which involve large amounts of data and complex transactions. The worksheet approach is illustrated in the Appendix.

Illustrative case.   Throughout Parts B and C the Fina Company case is used as a basis for discussion and illustration. Assume it is December 31, 19B, the end of the annual accounting period, and that Fina Company has completed all of the year-end procedures, including the preparation of the income statement and the balance sheet. The remaining requirement is preparation of a SCFP for 19B.

The income statement for 19B is shown in Exhibit 15–3.

Comparative balance sheets for the current and past year are shown in Exhibit 15–4. The prior balance sheet, at December 31, 19A, is needed for analytical purposes, as discussed later.

Cash flow from regular operations

The typical sources of cash listed on page 656 do not need further elaboration, with one exception. **Cash flow from regular operations,** which may be a net cash inflow or a net cash outflow, reflects the **net cash effect** of all of the revenues and expenses. This means that the accrual revenues, accrual expenses, and accrual income must be converted to a **strictly current cash basis** for reporting on the SCFP, cash basis. Cash flow from regular operations sometimes is referred to as the "cash throw-off from the income statement" or more appropriately, "cash generated by the income statement." Full disclosure requires that the **conversion** adjustments of accrual income to cash inflow or outflow from operations be shown in detail on the SCFP.

Operations (i.e., as reflected by the income statement) generally is the primary single source of cash for all businesses over the long term. Income reflects the effect of operations for the period on the **accrual basis.** As goods and services are sold during the period, there is an inflow of cash from *revenues* (i.e., customers); however, the cash inflow from the revenues is conditioned by the credit sales of the current and prior periods. To illustrate, assume a company sold goods during Year 1 amounting to $100,000, of which $5,000 remained uncollected at year end. In this case, the cash inflow would be $100,000, minus the $5,000 in accounts receivable, equals $95,000. Similarly, if sales for a later period totaled $100,000 and at the same time the balance in accounts receivable increased during the year by $5,000, cash inflow would be $95,000 for the period. Alternatively, if accounts receivable decreased by $5,000, cash inflow during the period would be $105,000.

During the period, *expenses* are incurred that cause a cash outflow; however, the cash outflow for expenses is conditioned by the amount of ex-

EXHIBIT 15–3

FINA COMPANY
Income Statement
For the Year Ended December 31, 19B

Sales		$100,000
Cost of goods sold		60,000
Gross margin		40,000
Less expenses:		
Expenses (not detailed)	$23,800	
Depreciation expense	6,000	
Amortization expense (patent)	200	
Income tax	2,000	32,000
Net income		$ 8,000

penses incurred on credit in the current and prior periods. To illustrate, assume a company incurred expenses during Year 1 of $92,000, of which $2,000 was unpaid at year-end. In this case, the cash outflow would be $92,000, minus the $2,000 increase in accounts payable, equals $90,000. Alternatively, if expenses for the current period totaled $92,000 and at the same time accounts payable decreased by $2,000 (because payments of old accounts exceeded new accounts), cash outflow for the current period would be $94,000.

Depreciation expense and amortization expense (e.g., patents) are **noncash expenses** which are deducted on the income statement to derive accrual income. Therefore, to measure cash flow from the income statement such expenses must be added to the amount of accrual income. To illustrate, assume Company T sold goods for cash $100,000, paid cash for all current expenses of $86,000, and reported depreciation expense of $6,000. Accrual income reported on the income statement would be $100,000 − $86,000 − $6,000 = $8,000. However, the cash inflow from the income statement (i.e., from operations) would be $8,000 (accrual income) + $6,000 (depreciation expense) = $14,000 (or alternatively, $100,000 − $86,000 = $14,000).

In a similar manner a decrease in inventory during the period would be a current **noncash** expense (cost of goods sold) because the amount of goods sold which were withdrawn from inventory was acquired and paid for in the prior period. Therefore, a decrease in inventory would be added to accrual income to derive net cash flow. Conversely, an increase in inventory during the period would cause a current cash outflow; therefore, the amount of the increase would be subtracted from accrual income to derive net cash flow.

The amount of net cash inflow (or outflow) from operations, therefore, generally will be different from accrual income because of the effect of **noncash revenues and noncash expenses.**

To illustrate the income additions and deductions for the period to derive cash inflow (or cash generated) from operations, refer to Fina Company. The income statement shown in Exhibit 15–3 reported income of $8,000. On the basis of an **analysis** of the revenues and expenses, including noncash depreciation and amortization expenses, income was converted to **cash flow from operations** as follows:

Income (as reported on the income statement; accrual basis) $8,000
Add (deduct) adjustments to convert to cash basis:
    Accounts receivable increase ....   (5,000)
    Depreciation expense   6,000
    Amortization expense   200
   *Merchandise inventory decrease   4,000
   *Accounts payable increase   2,000
    Income tax payable decrease ....   (500)
Net cash inflow from operations during the period $14,700

     * These two items may be combined as a conversion of cost of goods sold on the accrual basis to a cash basis as follows:

    CGS—accrual basis (Exhibit 15–3) $60,000
    Inventory change—decrease (Exhibit 15–4) ....   (4,000)
    Purchases—accrual basis   56,000
    Accounts payable change—increase (Exhibit 15–4) ....   (2,000)
    CGS—cash basis $54,000
    Adjustment (add) for conversion of CGS to
      cash basis ($60,000 − $54,000) = ... $ 6,000

EXHIBIT 15–4

FINA COMPANY
Balance Sheets
At December 31, 19B, and 19A

	December 31, 19B		December 31, 19A [a]	
Assets				
Current assets:				
Cash	$41,300		$31,000	
Accounts receivable (net) [b]	25,000		20,000	
Inventory (periodic)	20,000	$ 86,300	24,000	$ 75,000
Long-term investments:				
Common stock of X Corporation		1,000		6,000
Operational assets: [b]				
Equipment (net) [c]	59,000			
Patent (cost, $3,400 − amort., $200)	3,200	62,200		60,000
Total assets		$149,500		$141,000
Liabilities				
Current liabilities:				
Accounts payable	$22,000		$20,000	
Income tax payable	500		1,000	
Short-term note payable (nontrade)	10,000	$ 32,500	14,000	$ 35,000
Long-term liabilities:				
Long-term note payable	10,000			
Bonds payable	32,000	42,000		40,000
Stockholders' Equity				
Stockholders' equity:				
Common stock (par $10)	60,000		50,000	
Contributed capital in excess of par	6,000		5,000	
Treasury stock (at cost)	(3,000)			
Retained earnings [d]	12,000	75,000	11,000	66,000
Total liabilities and stock-				
holders' equity		$149,500		$141,000

    [a] An alternate dating would be January 1, 19B, since the ending balance sheet for the past period is the beginning balance sheet for the current period.

    [b] In analyzing and reporting changes in financial position, accounts receivable and operational assets generally are shown *net* of the contra accounts as a matter of convenience.

    [c] A machine which cost $5,000 was acquired on January 1, 19B, and payment in full was made by exchanging $5,000 of the investment in the common stock of X Corporation (the carrying value of these shares was the same as their current market value).

    [d] Dividends declared and paid during 19B amounted to $7,000.

The computation on page 659 is reported on the statement of changes in financial position, cash basis, as shown in Exhibit 15–6.

Observe in the computation on page 659 that the net cash inflow from operations ($14,700) was *greater* than income ($8,000). In some instances net cash inflow will be less than income.[10]

T-account approach for preparing the SCFP

Preparing a SCFP, **cash basis,** involves five procedural steps which are illustrated for Fina Company in Exhibits 15–5 (T-account analysis) and 15–6 (the formal SCFP). Preparing the SCFP requires data from the (1) **current** income statement (Exhibit 15–3), (2) **comparative** balance sheets (Exhibit 15–4), and (3) selected data about certain transactions. The preparing procedures, using either the T-account or the worksheet approach, require an *analysis of all of the* **noncash** *balance sheet accounts.* The **net increase or decrease** in each of these noncash accounts, between the two consecutive balance sheets, must be analyzed to identify the cash inflows and cash outflows during the period. The results of such an analysis are to identify and measure the (1) amount of each cash source and each cash use (liquidity) and (2) changes in the noncash balance sheet accounts during the period that were due to cash inflows and outflows (including all direct exchanges). Recall that these are the two purposes of the SCFP.

The five relatively simple procedural steps in preparing the SCFP, cash basis, as illustrated in Exhibits 15–5 and 15–6, may be outlined as follows:

Step 1—Data collection. Obtain the current income statement and comparative balance sheets.

Step 2—Set up the T-account format (or worksheet) as shown in Exhibit 15–5. In the upper part set up a T-account for each **noncash** account reported on the comparative balance sheets. In the lower part set up a special T-account for "Sources and Uses of Cash." The sources will be represented by debits in this special account and the uses by credits. Provide for two sections, "From Operations" and "From Other."

---

[10] The adjustments to convert income to cash flow from operations are quite varied. Although careful analysis is required, the following tabulation may be useful for checking purposes:

Item	When item increases	When item decreases
Accounts receivable (trade)	−	+
Accounts payable (trade)	+	−
Accrued liability and unearned revenue	+	−
Prepaid asset and revenue receivable	−	+
Inventory	−	+
Depreciation, depletion, and amortization	+	
Amortization of discount on bonds payable	+	
Amortization of premium on bonds payable	−	
Amortization of discount on bond investment	−	
Amortization of premium on bond investment	+	

Plus and minus adjustments to convert income to net cash flow from operations

Step 3—Enter the net increases and decreases (NC) in each T-account. To illustrate, Fina Company's comparative balance sheet (Exhibit 15–4) reflected that accounts receivable increased from $20,000 to $25,000; therefore, in Exhibit 15–5 (T-account analysis) the following **debit** was entered in that account: "NC, $5,000." Had this been a decrease, a **credit** would have been entered as "NC, $5,000." Next draw a horizontal line under the "NC" amount in each account.

Step 4—Record **analytical entries** in the T-accounts. The analytical entries follow the pattern of the regular entries and must be made to account for all of the net increases and net decreases in each T-account in the upper part of the analysis. The offsetting debits and credits to **Cash** are recorded in the special T-account in the lower part of the analysis. When all of the NC amounts are accounted for, the analysis is complete and the special T-account will reflect each source and use of cash during the period. One check of accuracy is indicated in Exhibit 15–5; that is, the balance in the **special** T-account should agree with the net change in the Cash account during the period. The analytical entries entered in the T-accounts in Exhibit 15–5 are repeated and explained in Exhibit 15–7 for study purposes.

Step 5—Prepare the formal SCFP. All of the information needed to prepare the formal SCFP is reflected in the special T-account in the lower part of the T-account analysis. The SCFP, cash basis, for Fina Company (Exhibit 15–6) was prepared directly form Exhibit 15–5. Some variations in terminology and minor classifications may be observed in actual practice.

The relative advantages and disadvantages of the SCFP, cash basis, are outlined in the chapter summary.

The illustration of Fina Company does not include transactions involving the disposal of nonfund assets, such as the sale of an operational asset (e.g., equipment). Because of such transactions, net income (accrual basis) often includes a gain or loss. The **cash inflow** from such transactions should be reported on the SCFP, "From other sources." This requires that the gain or loss be removed from the "Net income amount" as one of the conversion adjustments. To illustrate, assume in the Fina illustration that an operational asset (say, equipment) that had a book (carrying) value of $2,000 was sold for $3,000 cash. The conversion adjustment would deduct the $1,000 gain from net income and the $3,000 cash inflow would be reported under "From other sources." The **analytical entry** would be:

Sources of cash, from other sources	3,000	
Equipment (net)		2,000
Sources of cash (income deduction)		1,000

EXHIBIT 15–5

FINA COMPANY
T-Account Approach to Develop Sources and Uses of Cash
Noncash Balance Sheet Accounts

Accounts Receivable (net)		Inventory		LT Investment— Stock X Corp.	
NC 5,000			NC 4,000		NC 5,000
(d) 5,000			(e) 4,000		(f-1) 5,000

Equipment (net)		Patent (net)		Accounts Payable	
	NC 1,000	NC 3,200			NC 2,000
(f-2)Pur. 5,000 (b)	6,000	(g) Pur. 3,400	(c) Amort. 200		(h) 2,000

Income Tax Payable		ST Note Payable (nontrade)		LT Note Payable	
NC 500		NC 4,000			NC 10,000
(i) 500		(j) 4,000			(k) 10,000

Bonds Payable		Common Stock, Par $10		Cont. Cap. in Excess of Par	
NC 8,000			NC 10,000		NC 1,000
(l) 8,000			(m) 10,000		(m) 1,000

Treasury Stock (cost)		Retained Earnings	
NC 3,000			NC 1,000
(n) 3,000		(o) Div. 7,000	(a) NI 8,000

NC = Net change from 19A to 19B.

Sources and Uses of Cash

From Operations

Sources		Uses	
Income Plus Additions		*Income Reductions*	
(a) Net income	8,000	(d) Accounts receivable increase	5,000
(b) Depreciation expense	6,000	(i) Income tax payable decrease	500
(c) Amortization of patent	200		
(d) Inventory decrease	4,000		
(h) Accounts payable increase	2,000		

From Other

Sources		Uses	
(f-1) Exchange of investment for equipment	5,000	(f-2) Exchange of investment for equipment	5,000
(k) LT note payable	10,000	(g) Purchased patent	3,400
(m) Sold and issued common stock	11,000	(j) ST note payable (nontrade)	4,000
		(l) Payment on bonds payable	8,000
		(n) Purchased treasury stock	3,000
		(o) Paid cash dividend	7,000
		Check: Change in Cash account ($41,300 − $31,000)	10,300
Totals	46,200		46,200

EXHIBIT 15–6

FINA COMPANY
Statement of Changes in Financial Position, Cash Basis
For the Year Ended December 31, 19B [a]

Sources of Cash: [b]
  From operations:
    Net income .... $ 8,000
      Add (deduct) adjustments to convert to cash basis:
        Accounts receivable increase .... (5,000)
        Depreciation expense 6,000
        Amortization expense (patent) 200
        Merchandise inventory decrease 4,000
        Accounts payable increase 2,000
        Income tax payable decrease .... (500)
          Net cash generated from operations .... $14,700 [c]

  From other sources:
    Borrowing on long-term note 10,000
    Sale of unissued common stock 11,000
    Disposal of long-term investment (Note A) 5,000
      Total cash generated from other sources   26,000

      Total cash generated during the period   40,700

Uses of Cash: [b]
  Payment of cash dividend on common stock 7,000
  Payment on bonds payable 8,000
  Payment on notes payable, short term (nontrade) 4,000
  Purchase of patent 3,400
  Purchase of treasury stock 3,000
  Acquisition of equipment (Note A) 5,000
    Total cash used during the period   30,400

Net increase of cash during the period $10,300

  Note A: Equipment was acquired in exchange for common stock of X Corporation, which was being held as a long-term investment.

  [a] Source of data. Exhibit 15–5.

  [b] Sometimes referred to as "Cash generated" and "Cash applied," respectively.

  [c] Some persons prefer to set the computations above this line to separate revenues from expenses, which has two distinct advantages: (1) separate computing and reporting of the cash inflows from revenues and the cash outflows for expenses and (2) no implication that depreciation and amortization expenses are sources of cash. To illustrate:

Revenues $100,000
  Add (deduct) adjustments to convert to cash basis:
    Accounts receivable increase .... (5,000)
      Cash generated from revenues $95,000
Expenses ($60,000 + $32,000) 92,000
  Add (deduct) adjustments to convert to cash basis:
    Depreciation expense .... (6,000)
    Amortization expense .... (200)
    Merchandise inventory decrease .... (4,000)
    Accounts payable increase .... (2,000)
    Income tax payable decrease 500
      Cash disbursed for expenses   80,300
Net cash inflow from operations $14,700

EXHIBIT 15–7
**Analytical entries
with explanation
(reference Exhibit
15–5)**

Code	Data source	Analytical entry with explanation

(a) Income statement
(Exhibit 15–3)

Sources of cash (income) 8,000
    Retained earnings 8,000

This analytical entry (1) partially accounts for the $1,000 net credit increase in retained earnings and (2) reflects income as a source of cash. Because net income of $8,000 is an *accrual basis* amount, additions and subtractions must be made in subsequent analytical entries to convert it to a *strictly current cash basis* (see entries [b], [c], [d], [e], [h], and [i]).

(b) Income statement
(Exhibit 15–3)

Sources of cash (income addition) 6,000
    Equipment (or accumulated depreciation) 6,000

This analytical entry (1) accounts for the $6,000 credit increase in the equipment account and (2) adds the $6,000 to income as a source of cash because depreciation is a noncash expense which was deducted to derive accrual income.

(c) Income statement
(Exhibit 15–3)

Sources of cash (income addition) 200
    Patent (or Accumulated amortization) ... 200

This analytical entry accomplishes the same effects as entry (b) except that the asset account is different.

(d) Balance sheet
(Exhibit 15–4 or
analytical
T-account)

Accounts receivable (trade) 5,000
    Sources of cash (income deduction) 5,000

This analytical entry (1) accounts for the $5,000 net debit increase in accounts receivable and (2) deducts the $5,000 from accrual income because credit sales were more than cash sales by this amount; it represents noncash sales for the period.

(e) Balance sheet
(Exhibit 15–4 or
analytical
T-account)

Sources of cash (income addition) 4,000
    Merchandise inventory 4,000

This analytical entry (1) accounts for the net credit decrease in inventory and (2) adds the $4,000 to income as a source of cash because that amount of goods was withdrawn from inventory in excess of purchases. Thus, it represents a noncash expense (cost of goods sold) for this period which was deducted to derive accrual net income.

(f) Balance sheet
(Exhibit 15–4 and
related data)

(f-1) Sources of cash (direct exchange) 5,000
    LT investment, stock of X Corp. 5,000
(f-2) Machine 5,000
    Uses of cash (direct exchange) 5,000

This was a direct exchange; therefore two entries were required. Analytical entry (f-1) reflects the *financing activity;* the debit recognizes the implied "as if" source of cash and the credit accounts for the net credit decrease in the investment account. Analytical entry (f-2) reflects the *investing activity;* the credit recognizes the implied use of cash and the debit accounts for the increase in the asset account. This $5,000 debit increase and the $6,000 credit decrease for depreciation expense (entry b) account fully for the $1,000 net credit decrease in the equipment account.

(g) Balance sheet
(Exhibit 15–4 and
related data)

Patent 3,400
    Uses of cash (purchase of patent) 3,400

This analytical entry (1) accounts for a $3,400 debit increase in the patent account (which was its cost) and (2) recognizes a use

EXHIBIT 15–7
(continued)

Code	Data source	Analytical entry with explanation

of cash. This $3,400 debit increase and the $200 credit decrease for amortization (entry [c]) account fully for the net credit increase of $3,200 in the patent account.

(h) Balance sheet (Exhibit 15–4 or analytical T-account)

Sources of cash (income addition) 2,000
   Accounts payable 2,000

This analytical entry (1) accounts for the $2,000 credit increase in accounts payable and (2) adds the $2,000 to income as a source of cash because the accrual expenses deducted to derive income amounted to $2,000 more than the cash currently paid; thus, this amount is recognized as a noncash expense for the period.

(i) Balance sheet (Exhibit 15–4 or analytical T-account)

Income tax payable 500
   Sources of cash (income deduction) 500

This analytical entry (1) accounts for the net debit increase in income tax payable and (2) deducts $500 from income because income tax expense deducted to derive accrual income was $500 less than the cash currently paid for income taxes; thus, this amount represented an additional *cash* expense for the current period.

(j) Balance sheet (Exhibit 15–4 or analytical T-account)

ST note payable (nontrade) 4,000
   Uses of cash (payment of debt) 4,000

This analytical entry (1) accounts for the net debit decrease in note payable and (2) reflects a use of cash to pay debt.

(k) Balance sheet (Exhibit 15–4 or analytical T-account)

Sources of cash (LT note) 10,000
   LT note payable 10,000

This analytical entry (1) accounts for the $10,000 net credit increase in LT note payable and (2) reflects a source of cash.

(l) Balance sheet (Exhibit 15–4 or analytical T-account)

Bonds payable 8,000
   Uses of cash (payment on bonds) 8,000

This analytical entry (1) accounts for the $8,000 net debit decrease in bonds payable and (2) reflects a use of cash to pay debt.

(m) Balance sheet (Exhibit 15–4 or analytical T-account)

Sources of cash (issued capital stock) 11,000
   Common stock, par $10 10,000
   Contributed capital in excess of par..... 1,000

This analytical entry (1) accounts for the credit increases in the two capital stock accounts and (2) reflects a cash source.

(n) Balance sheet (Exhibit 15–4 or analytical T-account)

Treasury stock 3,000
   Uses of cash (purchase of treasury stock) 3,000

This analytical entry (1) accounts for the debit increase in the treasury stock account and (2) reflects a use of cash.

(o) Statement of retained earnings

Retained earnings 7,000
   Uses of cash (payment of cash dividend) 7,000

This analytical entry (1) accounts for a $7,000 debit decrease in retained earnings and (2) reflects a use of cash. When this $7,000 debit decrease is combined with the $8,000 credit increase (entry [a]) the net credit increase in the retained earnings account is fully accounted for.

PART C: SCFP, WORKING CAPITAL BASIS

CONCEPT OF WORKING CAPITAL

Recall that the only difference between the SCFP prepared on a working capital basis and one prepared on a cash basis is the way in which "funds" are measured. The former measures sources and uses of funds in terms of working capital instead of cash. Compared with cash, working capital is a much broader, and a significantly different, concept of funds because it is only a computed difference—total current assets minus total current liabilities. Thus, working capital is an abstraction because it does not represent a single asset, or group of similar assets; rather it includes an offset—total current liabilities. It cannot be counted, handled, or used to settle receivables and payables. For these reasons it often is not understood fully by statement users. Although working capital is used widely as the current SCFP measurement basis, two related pronouncements of the FASB scarcely mention it.[11]

To understand and interpret properly the SCFP prepared on the working capital basis, one should understand clearly the concept of working capital as a measurement of **funds.** As a basis for discussion, observe in Exhibit 15–4, for Fina Company, that the comparative balance sheets reported working capital as follows:

	December 31		Working capital increase (decrease)
	19B	19A	19A to 19B
Current assets:			
Cash	$41,300	$31,000	$10,300
Accounts receivable	25,000	20,000	5,000
Inventory	20,000	24,000	(4,000)
Total current assets	86,300	75,000	
Current liabilities:			
Accounts payable	22,000	20,000	(2,000)
Income tax payable	500	1,000	500
Short-term note payable (nontrade)	10,000	14,000	4,000
Total current liabilities	32,500	35,000	
Working capital (at year-end)	$53,800	$40,000	$13,800

Examination of the working capital tabulation given above reveals two fundamental relationships that relate directly to the SCFP, working capital basis:

1. Increases in current assets and decreases in current liabilities **increase working capital,** and decreases in current assets and increases in current liabilities **decrease working capital** (i.e., an inverse relationship).
2. A transaction which affects **only** working capital accounts during a

---

[11] Refer to footnotes 6 and 7.

given year does not change the amount of working capital for that year; therefore, the amount of working capital during a given year is changed only by transactions that affect one or more **noncurrent** (i.e., nonworking capital) accounts—noncurrent assets, noncurrent liabilities, and owners' equity accounts (see page 670). This relationship may be demonstrated by using the basic accounting model $(A = L + OE)$, where CA = current assets, NA = noncurrent assets, CL = current liabilities, NL = noncurrent liabilities, and OE = owners' equity:

a. CA + NA = CL + NL + OE; transposing

$\underbrace{\text{Working capital}}$ $\underbrace{\text{Noncurrent accounts}}$

b. CA − CL =   NL + OE − NA

Therefore, changes in NL, OE, and NA (the noncurrent accounts) represent sources and uses of working capital. From this we can develop the following summary of the effects of increases and decreases in the noncurrent accounts on the **uses and sources of working capital:**

Noncurrent (nonworking capital) accounts	Working capital	
	Sources	Uses
Assets—increase		x
—decrease	x	
Liabilities—increase	x	
—decrease		x
Owner's equity—increase	x	
—decrease		x

Thus, an analysis of the **noncurrent** balance sheet accounts is used to develop a SCFP on the working capital basis (see Exhibits 15–8 and 15–9).

SOURCES OF WORKING CAPITAL

Transactions that increase working capital represent sources of working capital. Transactions of this type involve a debit to a current asset or current liability account and a credit to one or more nonworking capital accounts. The four primary sources of working capital are:

1. **Current operations**—Net income reflects the net results of operations. It is composed of *total revenues less total expenses.* As goods and services are sold during the period, there is an inflow of cash and/or accounts receivable (both working capital items). Also, during the period, as expenses are incurred, usually there is a decrease in working capital occasioned by cash payments and/or the incurrence of current liabilities (both working capital items). Therefore, a reported net income generally results in an increase (source) of working capital. In the case of a loss, working capital generally will decrease.

EXHIBIT 15–8

FINA COMPANY
T-Account Approach to Develop Sources and Uses of Working Capital
Nonworking Capital Balance Sheet Accounts*

LT Investment—Stock X Corp.			Equipment (net)			Patent (net)	
NC	5,000			NC	1,000	NC 3,200	
(f-1)	5,000	(f-2) Pur. 5,000		(b)	6,000	(g) Pur. 3,400	(c) Amort. 200

LT Note Payable		Bonds Payable		Common Stock, Par $10	
NC	10,000	NC	8,000		NC 10,000
(k)	10,000	(l)	8,000		(m) 10,000

Cont. Capt. in Excess of Par		Treasury Stock		Retained Earnings	
NC	1,000	NC	3,000		NC 1,000
(m)	1,000	(n)	3,000	(o) Div. 7,000	(a) NI 8,000

NC = Net change from 19A to 19B.

Sources and Use of Working Capital*
From Operations

Sources		Uses	
Income Plus Additions		*Income Reductions*	
(a) Net income	8,000		
(b) Depreciation expense	6,000		
(c) Amortization of patent	200		

From Other

Sources		Uses	
(f-1) Exchange of invest. for equip.	5,000	(f-1) Exchange of invest. for equip.	5,000
(k) LT note payable	10,000	(g) Purchased patent	3,400
(m) Sold and issued common stock	11,000	(l) Payment on bonds payable	8,000
		(n) Purchased treasury stock	3,000
		(o) Declared cash dividend	7,000
		Check: Change (increase) in working capital($53,800 − $40,000)	13,800
Totals	40,200		40,200

* Analytical entry codes used are the same as in Exhibit 15–5 (cash basis) to facilitate comparison and study. Not all of the analytical entries for cash are used in working capital analysis.

EXHIBIT 15–9

FINA COMPANY
Statement of Changes in Financial Position, Working Capital Basis
For the Year Ended December 31, 19B

Part A: Sources and uses of working capital during the period

Sources of working capital:
From operations:

Net income	$ 8,000	
Add (deduct) to convert to working capital basis:		
Depreciation expense	6,000	
Amortization expense (patent)	200	
Total working capital generated by operations		$14,200
From other sources:		
Borrowed on long-term note	10,000	
Sale of unissued common stock	11,000	
Disposal of long-term investment (Note A)	5,000	
Total working capital generated from other sources		26,000
Total working capital generated during the period		40,200

Uses of working capital:

Declaration of cash dividend on common stock	7,000	
Payment on bonds payable	8,000	
Purchase of patent	3,400	
Purchase of treasury stock	3,000	
Acquisition of equipment (Note A)	5,000	
Total working capital used during the period		26,400
Net increase in working capital during the period		$13,800*

Part B: Changes in working capital during the period

Changes in working capital accounts	Balances, December 31 19B	Balances, December 31 19A	Working capital increase (decrease)
Current assets:			
Cash	$41,300	$31,000	$10,300
Accounts receivable (net)	25,000	20,000	5,000
Merchandise inventory	20,000	24,000	(4,000)
Total current assets	86,300	75,000	
Current liabilities:			
Accounts payable	22,000	20,000	(2,000)
Income tax payable	500	1,000	500
Note payable, short term (nontrade)	10,000	14,000	4,000
Total current liabilities	32,500	35,000	
Working capital	$53,800	$40,000	$13,800*

Part A—source of data, Exhibit 15–8.
Part B—source of data, Exhibit 15–4.
Note A: Equipment was acquired in exchange for common stock of X Corporation, which was being held as a long-term investment.
* These two amounts must agree.

The increase in working capital from operations normally is somewhat more than the amount of income for the period. This is due to the fact that the income statement usually includes some expenses that do not involve the use of working capital during the period—depreciation and depletion of tangible assets and amortization of intangible assets. For example, the income statement for Fina Company, Exhibit 15–3, shows that there was an inflow of working capital of $100,000 from sales during the year. It also shows that there were outflows of working capital for cost of goods sold, $60,000; expenses, $23,800; and income tax, $2,000 (resulting in a net working capital inflow of $14,200). In this computation no deductions were made for depreciation expense of $6,000 and amortization expense of $200 because these two items were **nonworking** capital expenses. This latter point is evident if we recall the two expense entries:

Depreciation expense	6,000	
Accumulated depreciation		6,000
Amortization expense	200	
Patent		200

These entries neither increased nor decreased working capital, since no working capital account was debited or credited; however, income was decreased. The **working capital increase from operations,** therefore, would be reported as follows:*

Net income	$ 8,000
Add (deduct) to convert to working capital basis:	
Depreciation expense	6,000
Amortization expense	200
Net working capital from operations	$14,200

* See Exhibit 15–9.

2. **Sale of capital stock for cash or short-term receivables**—A sale of capital stock is a source of working capital because cash or a short-term receivable flows in for the sales price of the stock.

3. **Sale of noncurrent assets**—When a long-term investment, an operational asset, or an "other" asset is sold, working capital is increased by the amount of the cash and/or short-term receivable that results from its disposition (not by the amount of the disposal gain or loss).

4. **Long-term borrowing**—When a loan is obtained on a long-term basis, working capital (cash) is increased by the proceeds of the loan. In contrast, when a short-term loan is obtained, working capital is not increased because a working capital account (Cash) is increased and another working capital account (a current liability) is increased by the same amount. Since the two changes offset each other, working capital (current assets minus current liabilities) does not change. To illustrate, assume Fina Company borrowed $5,000 cash on a 90-day loan near the end of 19B. The working capital effect would be as follows (data from page 666):

	Before short-term loan	Effect of short-term loan	After short-term loan
Current assets	$86,300	+5,000	$91,300
Current liabilities	32,500	+5,000	37,500
Working capital	$53,800	-0-*	$53,800

* Effect on working capital = (+ $5,000) − (+ $5,000) = 0.

USES OF WORKING CAPITAL

Transactions that decrease working capital represent uses of working capital. Transactions of this type involve a credit to a working capital account and a debit to a nonworking capital account. The three primary uses of working capital are:

1. **Purchase operational assets and other noncurrent assets for cash or short-term debt**—Transactions of this type generally require a payment of cash and, sometimes, the creation of a short-term debt. To the extent that cash is paid or short-term debt is incurred, working capital is reduced.
2. **Declare cash dividends**—This transaction causes the creation of a current liability; therefore, working capital is reduced (used) by that amount.[12]
3. **Pay a long-term liability**—Payments on long-term notes, bonds, and other long-term obligations involve an outflow of cash; hence, they represent uses of working capital. In contrast, the payment of a *current liability* does not change working capital for the same reason explained above in respect to borrowing (source) on a short-term debt basis; that is, the two working capital effects offset one another.

To summarize, the above explanations should make it clear that (1) working capital is not increased or decreased by any transaction that involves debits and credits to working capital accounts *only*, and (2) working capital usually is increased or decreased by each transaction that involves debits and/or credits to working capital accounts and debits and/or credits *also* to nonworking capital accounts.

SCFP FORMAT, WORKING CAPITAL BASIS

The SCFP, working capital basis, for Fina Company is shown in Exhibit 15–9. Because working capital is a combination of current assets and current liabilities, the SCFP **standard format** includes two distinct parts (in contrast to the SCFP, cash basis, which needs only the first part):

[12] When a dividend is declared, working capital is reduced by the amount of the dividend even though payment in cash is in a later period. In this situation the dividend payable is recorded as a current liability on declaration date. The cash payment in the later period does not affect working capital at that time since equal debits and credits to working capital accounts will be made. This distinction is important only when declaration and payment dates fall in different accounting periods.

Part A—Sources and uses of working capital

Part B—Changes in the working capital during the period

Part A reports the financing activities (sources of working capital) and the investing activities (uses of working capital) during the period. Part A is the basic report because Part B simply lists each current asset and current liability, the resulting increases and decreases, and the net change in working capital during the period.[13] The format in Part A of the statement follows the cash-basis format, except that it relates only to the sources and uses of **working capital.**

PREPARING THE SCFP, WORKING CAPITAL BASIS

Preparing the SCFP, working capital basis, essentially follows the cash basis approach discussed in Part B, and either the T-account approach or the worksheet approach (see Appendix) may be used. The five consecutive preparation steps are:

Step 1—Collect data. Obtain the current income statement and comparative balance sheets.

Step 2—Set up the T-account (or worksheet) format as shown in Exhibit 15–8. In the upper part set up a T-account for each noncurrent (i.e., nonworking capital) account reported on the comparative balance sheets. In the lower part set up a special T-account for "Sources and Uses of Working Capital." Provide two sections, "From Operations" and "From Other."

Step 3—Enter the net increase or net decrease (NC) in each T-account.

Step 4—Record analytical entries in the T-accounts. The analytical entries follow the pattern of regular entries and must account for all of the net increases and decreases entered in the upper part of the analysis. The offsetting debits and credits for increases and decreases in **working capital** are recorded in the special T-account in the lower part of the analysis.

Step 5—Prepare the formal SCFP. The lower portion of the analysis completed in Step 4 provides all of the data needed to complete the "Sources and uses" part of the SCFP. The second part of the SCFP is copied directly from the comparative balance sheets.

The detailed discussions and illustrations provided in Part B of the chapter for the cash basis apply exactly the same for the working capital basis with two exceptions: (1) the working capital analysis is limited to only the nonworking capital asset, liability, and owners' equity accounts

---

[13] Part B is copied directly from the related comparative balance sheets. For this reason, some accountants consider Part B to be redundant; however, it is required by *APB Opinion No. 19.* The two parts of the SCFP, working capital basis, are not called "Part A and Part B" in actual practice; this designation is used here only for instructional convenience.

(hence there are fewer analytical entries); and (2) the term *working capital* is used instead of *cash.*

Preparation of the SCFP, working capital basis, for Fina Company is illustrated in Exhibits 15–8 and 15–9. The analytical entry codes used in Exhibit 15–5 (cash basis) also were used in Exhibit 15–8 (working capital basis) to facilitate study and comparison. You should reread the explanations in Exhibit 15–7 for entries *(a), (b), (c), (f), (g), (k), (l), (m), (n),* and *(o)* (i.e., the working capital analytical entries).

SUMMARY

The annual financial statements of publicly held companies must include, as a minimum, a balance sheet, income statement, and statement of charges in financial position. The purpose of a SCFP is to provide investors, creditors, and other external statement users information not provided by the other two statements which will help them project the ability of the company to generate cash. To accomplish this purpose the SCFP reports on the **liquidity** of the company in terms of the sources and uses of funds; it also reports the **causes** of the changes in the nonfund balance sheet accounts. The SCFP may be prepared using **either** (1) cash or (2) working capital as the measure of funds. When prepared on a cash basis, the sources and uses of funds are measured in terms of a specific asset, cash. When prepared on a working capital basis, the sources and uses of funds are measured in abstract terms because working capital is the difference between the total current assets and total current liabilities.

The primary source of funds during each period generally is normal operations (i.e., the amount of funds generated through the income statement). Other common sources of funds are borrowing, sale of operational assets, and the sale and issuance of capital stock. Typical uses of funds are payment on debt, purchase of operational assets, long-term investments, and distribution of cash dividends.

Because *APB Opinion No. 19* permits the SCFP to be based on either cash or working capital, there is a question as to which approach better serves the typical external users of financial statements. The summary on page 674 may provide some insights into this issue:

SCFP—Cash and working capital bases compared

Comparative Criteria	Evaluation		Comments
	Cash Basis	Working Capital Basis	
Choice of users	Very low	High	Most companies elect to use working capital basis.
Relevance in projecting future cash flows	High	Lower	Cash basis focuses only on cash sources and uses; working capital basis merges current assets and current liabilities into a difference. Working capital basis not accorded much attention in recent FASB statements of "concepts" and "objectives."
Measurement basis	Specific	Broad	Because it is a broad measure, working capital basis tends to obscure the primary concern of users—cash flows.
Reports liquidity	Short term Long term	Long term	Working capital focuses primarily on the long-term assets and liabilities.
Complexity in preparing SCFP	Low	Low	Both methods involve use of either a T-account or worksheet approach during preparation.
Extent of preparation analyses	More	Less	Because there are more noncash accounts than nonworking capital accounts, the cash basis requires somewhat more analysis.
Understandability of SCFP	High	Low	External users (other than security analysts) tend to have problems with the abstract concept of working capital; most people understand cash.
Objectivity (and not subject to manipulation)	High	Low	Cash is easy to define, identify, and classify; it **excludes** all estimates, such as bad debt expense, depreciation, estimates of current assets (such as certain prepayments) and current liabilities (such as current portions of deferred tax, warranties, lease liabilities, pension liabilities, and accruals). Working capital often **includes** a number of these estimates; also, working capital is plagued with subjectivity in classification of many items (such as marketable securities).
Redundancies	Very low	High	The current asset and current liability sections on the comparative balance sheets are repeated item by item on the SCFP, working capital basis. There are no such redundancies on the cash basis statement.
Information content related to the kind of "funds" that circulate throughout a business entity	High	Low	It has been said that a properly prepared and detailed cash flow SCFP "bears the financial soul of a company." Working capital is said to combine too many diverse items and thereby not reveal many critical financing and investing activities. Potential failure of an entity almost always is first revealed in the cash flows.
Used by all industries	Permitted in *all* industries	Not permitted in some industries	The cash basis must be used in certain types of companies such as real estate development and financial institutions.

APPENDIX: WORKSHEET PREPARATION OF THE SCFP

Parts A and B indicated that the SCFP, on either the cash or working capital basis, can be prepared using the (1) T-account approach or (2) worksheet approach. The T-account approach traditionally has been used for instructional purposes, while the worksheet approach is used almost exclusively in practice and in situations characterized by complexity and large amounts of data. The worksheet approach is effective also for instructional purposes and is viewed by many persons as a more sophisticated and more efficient approach than the simple T-account approach.

This Appendix presents two worksheets—one illustrating the cash basis and the other the working capital basis. The illustrative case used in the chapter (Fina Company) also is used in the Appendix. The worksheets presented in this Appendix are very efficient, and they closely parallel the T-account approach in all respects. Each account is analyzed in a straightforward debit = credit manner, and the **analytical** entries are identical with those used in the T-account approach. The worksheet is designed so that the bottom portion may suffice for the formal SCFP in many problem and examination situations (see Exhibit 15–10, pp. 676–77).

Worksheet for SCFP, cash basis

The SCFP worksheet, cash basis (Exhibit 15–10), is designed to reflect all of the accounts reflected on the comparative balance sheets in the upper portion including the current year's **beginning** balances (i.e., the ending balances from the prior period) and the **ending** balances (i.e., the ending balances for the current period). The prior year's balances are entered in the first amount column, and the current year's balances are entered in the last (fourth) amount column. Two inner amount columns are used for the debits and credits of the **analytical** entries. **The amounts entered in the two inner amount columns represent only the analytical entries and must account fully for the difference on each line between the beginning (first column) and ending balances (last column).** Observe that this is the same process as used in the T-account approach (Exhibit 15–5) and the analytical entries are exactly the same in the worksheet approach as in the T-account approach.

The bottom portion of the worksheet represents the SCFP; therefore, it is set up with the following side captions (leaving sufficient space under each caption to complete the analytical entries):

Sources of cash:
  From operations
  From other sources

Uses of cash:

Net increase in cash

The "Analysis of Interim Entries" has as its purpose the analysis (in summary fashion) of all changes during the period in each **noncash** account entered on the worksheet. These changes are analyzed to determine those that (1) generated (increased) cash, (2) used (decreased) cash, and (3) those that did not affect cash. The analytical entries are entered directly on the worksheet in the normal debit-credit fashion; however, instead of entering amounts in the Cash account the normal debits to cash are entered in the lower section "Sources of cash" and the credits are entered as "Uses of cash."

The final step in completing the worksheet is to record the *analytical entries* on the worksheet. The analytical entries are based upon data provided by the two balance sheets, the income statement, and other accounting records. The analytical entries entered, on the worksheet for Fina Company (Exhibit 15–10) are entered as explained in Exhibit 15–7.

After the above entries are made on the worksheet, a careful check should be made to ascertain whether the change between the beginning and ending balances on each line (i.e., each balance sheet accounts) is accounted for fully. This check indicates that the worksheet analysis is

EXHIBIT 15–10

FINA COMPANY
Worksheet to Develop Statement of Changes in Financial Position, Cash Basis
For the Year Ended December 31, 19B

Items	Balances, Dec. 31, 19A	Analysis of Interim Entries†		Ending Balances, Dec. 31, 19B
		Debit	Credit	
Debits				
Cash account	31,000	(✓) 10,300		41,300
Noncash accounts:				
Accounts receivable (net)	20,000	(d) 5,000		25,000
Inventory	24,000		(e) 4,000	20,000
LT investment, X Corp. stock	6,000		(f-1) 5,000	1,000
Equipment (net)	60,000	(f-2) 5,000	(b) 6,000	59,000
Patent (net)		(g) 3,400	(c) 200	3,200
Total	141,000			149,500
Credits				
Accounts payable	20,000		(h) 2,000	22,000
Income tax payable	1,000	(i) 500		500
Short-term note payable (nontrade)	14,000	(j) 4,000		10,000
Long-term note payable			(k) 10,000	10,000
Bonds payable	40,000	(l) 8,000		32,000
Capital stock (par $10)	50,000		(m) 10,000	60,000
Contributed capital in excess of par	5,000		(m) 1,000	6,000
Treasury stock		(n) 3,000		(3,000)
Retained earnings	11,000	(o) 7,000	(a) 8,000	12,000
Total	141,000	46,200	46,200	149,500

EXHIBIT 15–10
(continued)

Items	Analysis of Interim Entries†	
	Debit	**Credit**
	Income and additions	*Income deductions*
Sources of cash:		
From operations:		
Net income	(a) 8,000	
Depreciation expense	(b) 6,000	
Amortization of patent	(c) 200	
Accounts receivable increase		(d) 5,000
Inventory decrease	(e) 4,000	
Accounts payable increase	(h) 2,000	
Income tax payable decrease		(i) 500
	Sources	*Uses*
From other sources:		
Exchange of investment for equipment*	(f-1) 5,000	
LT note payable	(k) 10,000	
Sold and issued common stock	(m) 11,000	
Uses of cash:		
Exchange of investment for equipment*		(f-2) 5,000
Purchase of patent		(g) 3,400
Payment on ST note		(j) 4,000
Payment on bonds payable		(l) 8,000
Purchase of treasury stock		(n) 3,000
Declared cash dividend		(o) 7,000
Net increase in cash (per line 1 above)		(✓) 10,300
	46,200	46,200

* Equipment was acquired in exchange for common stock of X Corporation, which was being held as a long-term investment.

† These entries are keyed for ready reference to the text discussions; see Exhibit 15–5.

complete. At this point the change in the Cash account during the period (as indicated on the first line) can be entered at the bottom of the worksheet and the debit and credit columns in the bottom portion of the worksheet summed to test for equality. This provides a partial check on the accuracy of the results.

The data provided at the bottom of the worksheet, with appropriate captions added, are used directly in preparing the formal SCFP, cash basis, as reflected in Exhibit 15–6.

Worksheet for SCFP, working capital basis

The worksheet presented in Exhibit 15–10 for the cash basis, adapted slightly, will accommodate conveniently the analysis necessary to develop a statement of changes in financial position on a working capital basis. The adapted worksheet on a working capital basis, completed for Fina Company, is shown in Exhibit 15–11. It maintains all of the desirable mechanical features of the former worksheet. The analytical entries on the worksheet focus on the conversion from an accrual basis to a working capital basis.

The worksheet, working capital basis, is somewhat shorter than the

EXHIBIT 15–11

FINA COMPANY
Worksheet to Develop Statement of Changes in Financial Position—Working Capital Basis
For the Year Ended December 31, 19B

Items	Balances Dec, 31, 19A	Analysis of Interim Entries†		Ending Balances Dec. 31, 19B
		Debit	Credit	
Debits				
Working capital	40,000	(✓) 13,800		53,800
Noncurrent accounts:				
LT investment, X				
Corp. stock	6,000		(*f*-1) 5,000	1,000
Equipment (net)	60,000	(*f*-2) 5,000	(b) 6,000	59,000
Patent (net)		(g) 3,400	(c) 200	3,200
Total	106,000			117,000
Credits				
LT note payable				
(nontrade)			(k) 10,000	10,000
Bonds payable	40,000	(l) 8,000		32,000
Common stock				
(par $10)	50,000		(m) 10,000	60,000
Contributed capital in				
excess of par	5,000		(m) 1,000	6,000
Treasury stock		(n) 3,000		(3,000)
Retained earnings	11,000	(o) 7,000	(a) 8,000	12,000
Total	106,000	40,200	40,200	117,000

		Income and additions	Income deductions	
Sources of working capital:				
From operations:				
Net income		(a) 8,000		
Depreciation expense		(b) 6,000		
Amortization expense		(c) 200		
		Sources	Uses	
From other sources:				
Exchange of investment for				
equipment*		(*f*-1)† 5,000		
LT note payable		(k) 10,000		
Sold and issued common stock		(m) 11,000		
Uses of working capital:				
Exchange of investment for				
common stock*			(*f*-2)† 5,000	
Purchased patent			(g) 3,400	
Payment on bonds payable			(l) 8,000	
Purchased treasury stock			(n) 3,000	
Declared cash dividend			(o) 7,000	
Increase in working capital (line 1)			(✓) 13,800	
		40,200	40,200	

* Equipment acquired in exchange for common stock of X Corporation, which was being held
as a long-term investment.

† These entries are keyed for ready references to the text discussions; see Exhibit 15–8. The
analytical entries for working capital do not include all of the analytical entries for cash; therefore,
some of the code letters are not reflected here.

cash-basis worksheet because only the working capital accounts must be analyzed to determine the *causes* of the inflows and outflows of the working capital. The worksheet is set up with four column headings identical to those of the cash basis worksheet: (1) Beginning Balances; (2) Analysis of Interim Entries, debit; and (3) credit; and (4) Ending Balances (see Exhibits 15–10 and 15–11). The side captions also are identical except for the identification "working capital," viz:

> *Working capital*
>
> *Noncurrent accounts*
>
> *Sources of working capital:*
> From operations
> From other sources
>
> *Uses of working capital*
>
> *Net increase (or decrease) in working capital*

The noncurrent (i.e., nonworking capital) accounts and their beginning and ending balances are entered in the worksheet. Next, the analytical entries are entered in the worksheet (they are identical with those entered in the T-account analysis, Exhibit 15–8); all debits and credits to working capital accounts reflected in the analytical entries are entered in the bottom part of the worksheet under **sources** and **uses** of working capital. Upon completion of the analytical entries the worksheet should be checked to assure that all differences between the beginning and ending balances of the noncurrent accounts are accounted for fully. The net change in working capital, indicated on the first line of the worksheet, may be entered as the last item on the worksheet to test the equality of the sources and uses (refer to Exhibit 15–11).

The bottom portion of the completed worksheet provides all of the data needed to complete the SCFP, working capital basis, as reflected in Exhibit 15–9.

IMPORTANT TERMS DEFINED IN THE CHAPTER (with page citations)

QUESTIONS FOR DISCUSSION

Part A

1. What are the basic statements that now are required to be included in the annual financial statements? Fundamentally, what does each report?

2. What are the primary sources and uses of funds in a business?

3. What is the essential difference between a SCFP prepared on a *(a)* cash basis and *(b)* working capital basis?

4. Company X acquired a tract of land in exchange for a $10,000 bond payable. How does this relate to the SCFP all-recources concept?

5. What is a direct exchange? How does a direct exchange affect the SCFP?

6. Why is the SCFP called a "change" statement?

7. Explain what is meant by each of the following terms. Give two examples of each.
   a. Nonfund assets.
   b. Nonfund liabilities.

8. Explain why net income (i.e., operations) is often the primary source of funds in a business in the long term.

9. In developing "sources of funds, from operations (cash or working capital)," on the SCFP, why are depreciation, amortization of intangible assets, and depletion added back to net income?

Questions
Part B

10. What is the basic reason why the SCFP, cash basis, is particularly relevant to the average external statement user?

11. Explain why the SCFP, cash basis, requires the conversion of net income to another amount.

12. Assume you are completing a SCFP, cash basis, and have the data listed below. On a separate sheet, complete the blanks to the right.

		Cash basis
Net income		$10,000
Increase in accounts receivable	$1,400	_____
Depreciation expense	1,500	_____
Amortization of patent	200	_____
Decrease in merchandise inventory	2,200	_____
Decrease in accounts payable	1,000	_____
Net cash inflow from operations for the period		$_____

13. Total sales revenue for 19B amounted to $300,000, of which one third was on credit. The balances in accounts receivable at year's end were 19B, $15,000; and 19A, $23,000. The cash inflow from sales during 19B was $_____.

14. Total expenses for 19B amounted to $200,000, of which $10,000 was depreciation expense and $30,000 was on credit (accounts payable). The balances in accounts payable at year's end were 19A, $16,000; and 19B, $12,000. The cash outflow for expenses during 19B was $_____.

15. Assume that you are preparing a SCFP, cash basis, and have the data listed below. On a separate sheet, complete the blanks to the right.

		Cash basis
Net income		$20,000
Decrease in accounts receivable	$2,000	_____
Decrease in accounts payable	3,000	_____
Depreciation expense	8,000	_____
Gain on sale of operational asset (cash sales price, $3,000, book value, $2,000)	1,000	_____
Net cash inflow		$_____

16. Company X is preparing the SCFP for 19B. During the year the company acquired a tract of land and paid in full by issuing 1,000 shares of its own capital stock, par $10 per share (market value $15 per share). Show how this transaction should be reported on the SCFP. Explain.

Questions

Part C

17. Complete the following tabulation:

	Working capital	
Transaction	Source	Use
a. Collected on account receivable, $150	$	$
b. Sold land for $4,000, one half collected in cash and the balance on one-year note; gain, $500	_____	_____
c. Paid a bond payable, $1,000	_____	_____
d. Sold and issued common stock, $2,500 cash	_____	_____
e. Paid short-term note payable, $1,300	_____	_____

18. Complete the following tabulation:

	Working capital
Net income, $32,000	$
Depreciation expense, $5,000	_____
Inventory increase, $10,000	_____
Working capital from operations	$

19. Company T reported working capital at year-end of 19A, $90,000; and 19B, $75,000. During 19B the company (a) paid a $5,000 short-term note and (b) paid a $15,000 long-term note. Disregarding interest, how much did each of these transactions change working capital during 19B? Explain.

20. Company S purchased a machine which cost $30,000; payment was made as follows: cash, $10,000; short-term note payable, $4,000; and long-term note payable, $16,000. How much did working capital change? Explain.

21. What are the two basic parts of a SCFP, working capital basis? Why is the second part considered by some to be redundant?

22. As a statement user interested in the statement of changes in financial position, would you prefer the (a) cash basis or (b) working capital basis? Explain.

EXERCISES

Part A

E15–1. Below is listed a number of transactions of Rye Company during 19B. Enter a letter to the right which indicates whether the transaction is a source or use of funds. Use S for source, U for use, and N for neither. Assume cash unless otherwise stated.

Transaction	Effect on funds
a. Net income	_____
b. Write off of a bad debt	_____
c. Purchased an operational asset	_____
d. Depletion expense	_____
e. Declared and issued a cash dividend	_____
f. Depreciation expense	_____
g. Collection on a long-term note	_____
h. Issued a stock dividend	_____
i. Sold a long-term investment	
j. Borrowed cash on a long-term note	
k. Sold an operational asset	_____
l. Amortization of discount on bonds payable	_____
m. Purchased treasury stock	_____
n. Payment on bonds payable	_____
o. A stock split	_____
p. Extraordinary gain	_____
q. Amortization of premium on bond investment	_____
r. Purchased a long-term investment	_____
s. Exchange of unissued stock for operational asset	_____
t. Exchange of land for equipment	_____
u. Sale of treasury stock	_____
v. Payment of debt by issuance of company shares	_____
w. Net loss	_____
x. Amortization of patent	_____
y. Bad debt expense	_____
z. Declared and paid a property dividend	_____

E15–2. The SCFP must be based on the all-resources concept. During 19B, Starter
Corporation completed the two transactions given below on which they have
asked your assistance:

1. A large machine was acquired that
had a list price of $25,000. Starter was
short of cash; therefore, it paid for
the machine in full by giving a
$10,000, 15 percent, interest-bearing
note due at the end of two years and
200 shares of its capital stock, par $50
(market value $60).
2. A small machine was acquired (list
price $9,995), and full payment was
made by transferring a tract of land
that had a market value of $9,500
(surprisingly, this was also its book
value).

Required:

For each machine show what should
be reported on the SCFP under *(a)*
sources of funds and *(b)* uses of funds.
Briefly, explain the basis for your responses.

Exercises
Part B

E15–3. Ross Company has completed its income
statement and balance sheet at December 31, 19B. The following data were
taken from a worksheet or T-account
analysis completed as a basis for the
SCFP:

Net income (Revenues, $150,000 −</br>Expenses, $128,000)	$22,000
Depreciation expense	4,000
Purchase of operational assets for cash	15,000
Sale of long-term investment (sold at</br>book value for cash, $6,000)	6,000
Inventory increase during the period	3,000
Declared and paid cash dividends	8,000
Borrowed on short-term note	20,000
Accounts payable decrease	2,000
Payment of long-term note	30,000
Acquired land for future use; issued</br>capital stock in payment	24,000

Required:

Prepare the SCFP, cash basis, properly classified. (Although not required,
the T-account approach or the worksheet approach may be helpful.)

E15–4. The accounting department of Bear
Company assembled the following unclassified SCFP data at December 31,
19B, end of the accounting period, as
a basis for preparing a SCFP, cash basis:

(Relates to Exercise 15–4)

Transactions	Cash* Sources	Uses
Net income (Revenues, $200,000 − Expenses, $169,000)	$ 31,000	
Depreciation expense	7,000	
Purchase of operational assets for cash		$ 42,000
Wages payable increase	5,000	
Inventory decrease	3,000	
Accounts payable decrease		8,000
Declared and paid a cash dividend on common stock		20,000
Amortization of patent	1,000	
Payment on short-term note payable (nontrade)		25,000
Sale of common stock for cash	15,000	
Sale of operational assets for cash (sold at book value, $9,000)	9,000	
Accounts receivable increase		6,000
Long-term borrowing during the period	50,000	
Purchase of long-term investment, stock of X Co. (paid cash)		30,000
Difference—decrease in cash	10,000	
	$131,000	$131,000

* Including income additions and deductions.

Required:

Use the above data to prepare a SCFP, cash basis, properly classified. Assume all of the above amounts are correct. (Although not required, the T-account approach or the worksheet approach may be helpful.)

E15–5. Below is a tabulation that gives information relating to both cash and working capital for Shaky Company.

Required:

a. Provide appropriate amounts for each of the blanks in the above tabulation; if none, enter a zero.
b. Briefly compare the total of cash with the total of working capital and explain why they are different.
c. Which result do you think would be of most use to statement users? Why?

(Relates to Exercise 15–5)

Transactions	(a) Cash basis	(b) Working capital basis
Net income reported (accrual basis)	$17,000	$17,000
Depreciation expense, $2,700	_____	_____
Increase in wages payable, $500	_____	_____
Decrease in trade accounts receivable, $6,800	_____	_____
Increase in merchandise inventory, $9,300	_____	_____
Amortization of patents, $300	_____	_____
Increase in bonds payable, $10,000	_____	_____
Decrease in trade accounts payable, $7,400	_____	_____
Sale of unissued common stock, $5,000	_____	_____
Total cash generated from operations	$ _____	
Total working capital generated from operations		$20,000

E15–6. The following actual statement was taken from the annual financial statements of Lazy Corporation:

(Relates to Exercise 15–6)

LAZY CORPORATION
Funds Statement
Year, December 31, 19B

Funds generated:

Sales and service	$85,000	
Depreciation	6,000	
Accounts receivable decrease	700	
Merchandise decrease	3,000	
Borrowing (short-term note)	20,000	
Sale of unissued stock	15,000	
Total cash		$129,700

Funds used:

Cost of sales	48,000	
Expenses (including depreciation and income tax)	20,000	
Accounts payable decrease	1,000	
Income tax payable decrease	300	
Payment on long-term mortgage	25,000	
Acquisition of operational asset	9,000	
Dividends (cash)	7,000	
Total		110,300
Increase in funds		$ 19,400

Required:

a. Is this a cash basis or a working capital basis statement? Give the basis for your conclusion.

b. Did Lazy give adequate attention to the communication of financial information to shareholders?

c. What was the amount of net income (or loss) reported for 19B?

d. Recast the above statement in good form (and preferred terminology).

e. Did operations generate more or less cash than net income? Explain what caused the difference.

E15–7. Situation *(a)*—Super Corporation reported net income of $100,000 and $20,000 depreciation expense. To compute cash generated from operations, the corporation **added** the depreciation expense (straight-line basis) to net income deriving a cash basis amount of $120,000 because "depreciation is one of the largest sources of cash in our company." Assume the company could have used accelerated depreciation and reported $30,000 depreciation expense. Would this change increase the cash inflow (disregarding any income tax considerations)? Explain and illustrate your response.

Situation *(b)*—Super Corporation sold a machine (an operational asset) for $6,000 cash. At date of sale the account records reflected the following:

Machine No. 12 (cost)	$30,000
Accumulated depreciation (Machine No. 12)	20,000

At year-end the income statement (summarized) reported the following:

Revenues (all cash)	$900,000
Expenses (all cash except depreciation expense, of $60,000)	(796,000)
Loss on sale of operational asset	(4,000)
Net income	$100,000)

Explain and illustrate how the disposal (sale) of the machine and depreciation expense should be reflected on the SCFP, cash basis.

E15–8. Stinger Company is developing the annual financial statements at December 31, 19B. The statements are complete except for the SCFP, cash basis. The completed balance sheet and income statement are summarized below:

6. Declared and paid a $2,400 cash dividend on capital stock.
7. Accounts receivable decrease—from balance sheets.
8. Merchandise inventory decrease—from balance sheets.
9. Accounts payable increase—from balance sheets.
10. Wages payable decrease—from balance sheets.

(Relates to Exercise 15–8)

	19A	19B
Balance sheet at December 31:		
Cash	$ 20,000	$ 31,500
Accounts receivable (net)	26,000	25,000
Merchandise inventory	40,000	38,000
Operational assets (net)	64,000	67,000
	$150,000	$161,500
Accounts payable	$ 24,000	$ 27,000
Wages payable	500	400
Notes payable, long term	35,000	30,000
Capital stock (nopar)	70,000	80,000
Retained earnings	20,500	24,100
	$150,000	$161,500
Income statement for 19B:		
Sales		$ 90,000
Cost of goods sold		(52,000)
Expenses (including depreciation expense, $4,000)		(32,000)
		$ 6,000

Required:

a. Set up either the T-account approach or the worksheet approach to develop the SCFP, cash basis. Analytical entries should be made for the following:
   1. Net income—from income statement.
   2. Depreciation expense—from income statement.
   3. Purchased operational assets for cash, $7,000.
   4. Paid $5,000 on the long-term note payable.
   5. Sold unissued common stock for $10,000 cash.

b. Based upon the analysis completed in Requirement *(a)*, prepare the formal SCFP, cash basis.

Exercises
Part C

E15–9. The following "Funds Statement" was taken from the annual financial statements of TM Corporation:

(Relates to Exercise 15–9)

TM CORPORATION
Funds Statement
December 31, 19B

Funds generated:

Net profit (plus $10,000 depreciation)	$18,000
Common stock	9,000
Long-term note	10,000
Total	$37,000

Funds applied:

Equipment	$15,000
Dividend	8,000
Debt	12,000
Change	2,000
Total	$37,000

Working capital	19B	Change
Cash	$ 3,200	$ 6,500
Receivables	7,500	5,000*
Inventory	30,000	13,500*
Payables (trade)	(4,800)	2,500*
Notes	(12,000)	7,500*
Total	$23,900	$ 2,000*

* Increase.

Required:

a. What was the amount of income?

b. Is this a working capital or cash basis statement? Explain the basis for your response.

c. Did working capital increase or did it decrease? By how much?

d. Did "operations" generate more or less working capital than income? Explain why.

e. Explain why the amount of the change in working capital was different than income.

f. Assess the soundness of the cash dividend.

g. Can you spot any potential future problems for TM Corporation? Explain why.

h. Did TM Corporation give adequate attention to communication of financial information to shareholders? Explain the basis for your response.

i. Was the dividend paid or only declared? Explain.

j. Compare and explain the amounts of change in working capital versus cash.

k. Was the equipment purchased on credit? Explain.

l. Recast the above statement in good form consistent with your comments in Requirement (h).

E15–10. The following statement has just been prepared by Dow Company:

(Relates to Exercise 15–10)

DOW COMPANY
Statement of Changes in Financial Position, Working Capital Basis
For the Year Ended December 31, 19B

Sources of working capital:
From operations:

Net income	$ 2,000	
Add expenses not requiring working capital:		
Depreciation expense	4,000	
Patent amortization expense	1,000	
Total working capital generated by operations		$ 7,000

From other sources:

Sale of unissued stock	10,000	
Long-term loan	33,000	
Sale of land (at cost)	5,000	
Total working capital from other sources		48,000
Total working capital generated during the period		55,000

Uses of working capital:

Acquisition of machinery	22,000	
Payment of mortgage	20,000	
Cash dividend declared and paid	12,000	
Total working capital applied during the period		54,000
Net increase in working capital during the period		$ 1,000

Changes in working capital accounts:

	Balances at December 31		Working capital increase (decrease)
	19B	19A	
Current assets:			
Cash	$ 1,000	$ 9,000	$ (8,000)
Accounts receivable......................	31,000	24,000	7,000
Inventory	38,000	21,000	17,000
Total current assets	70,000	54,000	
Current liabilities:			
Accounts payable	18,000	15,000	(3,000)
Short-term notes payable.................	22,000	10,000	(12,000)
Total current liabilities	40,000	25,000	
Working capital	$30,000	$29,000	$ 1,000

Required:

a. Was there an increase or decrease in working capital? How much? What were the primary source and the major uses of working capital?

b. Explain how working capital of $55,000 was generated when income was only $2,000.

c. Explain the fact that while working capital increased $1,000 cash decreased $8,000.

d. How much cash was generated and how much was used? How much cash was generated by operations?

e. What current asset increased the most? What current liability increased the most? How were these two changes related to cash?

f. Assess the soundness of the cash dividend.

g. Can you identify a potential problem in respect to liabilities? Explain.

E15–11. Blue Company has completed preparation of the income statement and the balance sheet at year-end, December 31, 19A. A statement of changes in financial position must be developed. The following data are available:

Required:

Prepare a SCFP, working capital basis. Because the data are simplified you should not need to develop a T-account or worksheet analysis.

E15–12. WH Company has never prepared a SCFP. At the end of 19B the company bookkeeper assembled the data given below (which have been determined to be correct) for such a statement:

(Relates to Exercise 15–11)

	Balances at Dec. 31	
	19A	*19B*
1. From balance sheet:		
Current assets:		
Cash	$ 8,000	$15,000
Accounts receivable (net)	17,000	12,000
Inventory	15,000	18,000
Current liabilities:		
Accounts payable..................................	10,000	12,000
Notes payable, short term	18,000	13,000
2. From income statement:		
Net income		$20,000
Depreciation expense		6,000
3. From other records:		
Purchase of long-term investment		15,000
Payment of long-term note		5,000
Sale of unissued capital stock		10,000
Declaration of cash dividend		8,000
Purchased land for future plant site, issued		
capital stock as payment		25,000

(Relates to Exercise 15–12)

	Balances at Dec. 31	
	19A	*19B*
From the balance sheet:		
Current assets:		
Cash	$15,000	$20,000
Accounts receivable (net).........................	24,000	17,000
Merchandise inventory............................	30,000	27,000
Current liabilities:		
Accounts payable	(19,000)	(15,000)
Notes payable, short term	(10,000)	(12,000)
Working capital	$40,000	$37,000

(*Relates to Exercise 15–12—Continued*)

	Balances at Dec. 31	
	19A	*19B*

2. From the worksheet:

Net income	$21,000
Depreciation expense	4,500
Amortization of patent	500
Purchase of operational assets	(6,000)
Sale of operational assets (at book value)	2,000
Payment of long-term note payable	(40,000)
Issuance of bonds payable........................	30,000
Sale and issuance of common stock	10,000
Declaration of dividend on common stock	(25,000)
Difference	$ (3,000)

Required:

Use the above data to prepare a SCFP, working capital basis, for 19B. Because the information is simplified, you should not need a T-account or worksheet analysis.

E15–13. Huber Company is developing the annual financial statements at December 31, 19B. The income statement and balance sheet have been completed, and the SCFP, working capital basis, is to be developed. The income statement and the balance sheet are summarized below:

(*Relates to Exercise 15–13*)

	19A	19B
Balance sheet at December 31:		
Cash..	$12,800	$10,800
Accounts receivable (net)	9,000	10,500
Merchandise inventory	6,600	5,000
Operational assets (net)	40,000	43,000
Patent	3,000	2,700
	$71,400	$72,000
Accounts payable	$11,000	$ 9,000
Income tax payable	400	500
Notes payable, long term	10,000	5,000
Capital stock (nopar)	42,000	45,000
Retained earnings	8,000	12,500
	$71,400	$72,000
Income statement for 19B:		
Sales...		$60,000
Cost of goods sold		35,000
Gross margin		25,000
Expenses (including depreciation, $4,000, and patent amortization, $300)		18,000
Net income		$ 7,000

Additional data for 19B:
Purchased operational assets for cash, $7,000.
Paid $5,000 on long-term note payable.
Sold and issued capital stock for $3,000 cash.
Declared and paid a $2,500 dividend on capital stock.

Required:

a. Based upon the above data, prepare a T-account or worksheet to develop the SCFP, working capital basis.

(Hint: Working capital decreased $200.)

b. Prepare the formal SCFP, working capital basis.

PROBLEMS

Part A

P15–1. Below is a list of ten transactions that involve sources and uses of funds. Some of the transactions relate only to sources and uses of cash; others relate to sources and uses of both cash and working capital. You are to analyze each transaction and enter its dollar effect in the spaces to the right. Assume cash transactions unless stated otherwise.

P15–2. This problem illustrates the distinction between cash and working capital. Recall that cash is only one component of working capital and that the SCFP may measure *funds* on the basis of either cash or working capital.

a. Provide the missing amounts in the schedule given at the top of page 691 of working capital:

(Relates to Problem 15–1)

	Cash		Working Capital	
Transaction	Sources	Uses	Sources	Uses
a. Sold a short-term investment, $500.	$_____	$_____	$_____	$_____
b. Sold an operational asset and received a short-term note, $600.	_____	_____	_____	_____
c. Prepaid a one-year insurance premium, $200.	_____	_____	_____	_____
d. Purchased a small machine (an operational asset) and gave a short-term note, $150.	_____	_____	_____	_____
e. Sold a patent for $700 (book value, $500; gain, $200).	_____	_____	_____	_____
f. Purchased land, $9,900.	_____	_____	_____	_____
g. Sold a long-term investment, $6,000; collected cash, $1,000, short-term note, $2,000, and long-term note, $3,000.	_____	_____	_____	_____
h. Purchased an operational asset, $9,000; paid cash, $4,000, short-term note, $3,000, and long-term note, $2,000.	_____	_____	_____	_____
i. Declared and paid a cash dividend, $3,000.	_____	_____	_____	_____
j. Declared a cash dividend, $4,000; payable half in current year and the balance during next year.	_____	_____	_____	_____

(Relates to Problem 15–2, Req. a)

Current (Working Capital) Accounts	December 31		Working Capital
	19B	19A	Increase (Decrease)
1. Cash	$?	$30,000	($29,000)
2. Short-term investment in securities	5,000	20,000	?
3. Accounts receivable (net)	70,000	?	30,000
4. Inventory	95,000	70,000	?
5. Prepaid expense (e.g., insurance)	?	2,000	1,000
6. Accounts payable	74,000	?	(4,000)
7. Income tax payable	4,000	6,000	?
8. Revenue collected in advance (unearned)	?	1,000	(1,000)
9. Product warranty liability (estimated)	3,000	4,000	?
10. Working capital	?	?	10,000

b. Provide the appropriate dollar amounts in the blank spaces to the right on the following schedule: Assume cash transactions unless otherwise stated.

c. Provide the cash inflow (sources) for each of the transactions given at the top of page 692.

(Relates to Problem 15–2, Req. b)

Transaction	Cash		Working Capital	
	Sources	Uses	Sources	Uses
1. Sold and issued capital stock, $5,000.	$	$	$	$
2. Declared and paid a cash dividend, $3,000.				
3. Sold a short-term investment, $2,000.				
4. Borrowed on a long-term note, $8,000.				
5. Sold an operational asset, $7,500.				
6. Purchased an operational asset; gave a one-year interest bearing note, $6,000.				
7. Declared a cash dividend (payable next year), $1,500.				
8. Paid a short-term note, $2,500.				
9. Collected a short-term note, $1,800.				
10. Collected a long-term note, $7,000.				

(Relates to Problem 15–2, Req. c)

	Cash inflow
1. An operational asset was sold at a gain on disposal of $500; it originally cost $10,000 and was 75 percent depreciated (straight line).	$_____
2. Sales revenue during 19B amounted to $100,000; the balances in Accounts Receivable at year's end were 19A, $20,000; and 19B, $14,000.	_____
3. Sold and issued 1,000 shares of common stock, par $10; credited Contributed Capital in Excess of Par in the amount of $5,500.	_____

Problems
Part B

15–3. The following statement has just been prepared by Down Corporation:

DOWN CORPORATION
Funds Flow Statement
Year, December 31, 19E

Funds earned:

Sales and other incomes	$90,000
Accounts receivable decrease	4,200
Expenses (including depreciation and income tax)	(70,000)
Depreciation	2,000
Inventory increase	(3,000)
Accounts payable increase	1,000
Prepaid insurance increase	(100)
Income tax payable decrease	(100)
Capital stock	5,000
Total cash generated	29,000

Funds spent:

Equipment	(7,000)
Bonds payable	(30,000)
Dividends	(2,000)
Total cash used	$10,000

Required:

a. Is the above on a working capital or cash basis? How did you determine the basis on which the statement was prepared?

b. List the format and terminology deficiencies on the statement.

c. Recast the above statement using preferred format and terminology.

P15–4. Brown Company prepared the tabulation given below at December 31, 19E. Provide an appropriate amount for each blank. Use parentheses for deductions and enter a zero if no adjustment is required.

Sources of cash	SCFP, cash basis
From operations:	
Net income (accrual basis)	$150,000
Add (deduct) adjustments to convert to cash basis:	
Depreciation expense, $2,000	_____
Increase in trade accounts receivable, $6,000	_____
Decrease in inventory, $11,000	_____
Amortization of patent, $1,000	_____
Decrease in rent revenue receivable, $1,500	_____
Increase in prepaid insurance, $4,000	_____
Decrease in trade accounts payable, $7,000	_____
Decrease in income tax payable, $2,500	_____
Gain on sale of operational asset, $2,000 (sold for cash, $8,000)*	_____
Net cash generated from operations	$_____

* Hint: This should be classified as "other sources."

P15–5. The income statement of JT Corporation is given below. Provide the appropriate amounts for the blanks given to the right. Use parentheses to indicate cash deductions and enter a zero for no change. Prove the results.

(Relates to Problem 15–5)

JT CORPORATION
Income Statement for the Year Ended December 31, 19C
Accrual Basis

		Cash flow
Sales revenue (one third on credit; accounts receivable year's end—19A, $11,000; 19B, $15,000)	$300,000	$ _____
Cost of goods sold (one fourth on credit; accounts payable year's end—19A, $9,000; 19B, $8,000 (net); inventory at year's end—19A, $50,000; 19B, $45,000	180,000	_____
Gross margin on sales	120,000	
Expenses:		

Salaries and wages (including accrued wages payable at year's end—19A, $500; 19B, $300)	$44,000		
Depreciation expense	8,000		_____
Rent expense (no accruals)	6,000		_____
Bad debt expense	300		_____
Remaining expenses (no accruals)	11,700		_____
Income tax expense (income tax payable at year's end—19A, $2,000; 19B, $3,000)	10,000		_____
Total expenses		80,000	
Net income		$ 40,000	
Cash generated from operations			$ _____

Proof of results:

Net income (accrual basis)	$ 40,000	
Add (deduct) adjustments to convert to cash basis:		
Accounts receivable decrease		_____
Accounts payable decrease		_____
Inventory decrease		_____
Wages payable increase		_____
Depreciation expense		_____
Income tax payable increase		_____
Cash generated from operations	$ _____	

Note: This problem depicts two somewhat different approaches to derive cash generated from operations; the proof of results approach above is the one usually used (and illustrated in the chapter).

P15–6. The following statement has just been prepared by ST Corporation:

(Relates to Problem 15–6)

ST CORPORATION
Statement of Changes in Financial Position, Cash Basis
For the Year Ended December 31, 19B

Sources of cash:

From operations:

Net loss	($10,000)	
Add (deduct) adjustments to convert to cash basis:		
Accounts receivable decrease	2,000	
Depreciation expense	3,000	
Amortization expense	300	
Inventory increase	(1,500)	
Accounts payable decrease	(1,000)	
Prepaid insurance decrease	200	
Cash generated from (used in) operations		($ 7,000)

From other sources:

Sale of capital stock	10,000	
Long-term note payable	30,000	
Land (exchanged for machinery)	7,000	
Cash from other sources		47,000
Total cash generated during the period		40,000

Uses of cash:

Machinery (acquired in exchange for land)	7,000	
Payment on mortgage	6,000	
Cash dividends paid	12,000	
Total cash expended during the period		25,000
Net increase in cash during the period		$15,000

Required:

a. Explain why the net loss was $3,000 more than the cash "used" in operations.

b. Explain how the company showed a net increase in cash of $25,000 more than the net loss.

c. Explain the land transaction. Why is it reported twice on the above SCFP?

d. Explain why the decrease in accounts receivable is "added" as an adjustment to the net loss.

e. Explain why the inventory increase is "deducted" as an adjustment to the net loss.

P15–7. The following statement was prepared by BO Corporation:

(Relates to Problem 15–7)

BO CORPORATION
Funds Statement
December 31, 19D

Sources:

Operations:

Revenues	$180,000	
Accounts receivable decrease	15,000	
Expenses (including depreciation and income tax)	(160,000)	
Depreciation	14,000	
Inventory increase	(6,000)	
Accounts payable increase	7,000	
Income tax payable decrease	(3,000)	
Total		$ 47,000
Sale of permanent assets (at book value)		17,000
Issuance of common stock for land		25,000
Borrowing—short-term note		40,000
Total cash		$129,000

Uses:

Dividends paid	20,000	
Payment on long-term mortgage	80,000	
Machinery	15,000	
Land (5,000 shares of stock)	25,000	
Funds (decrease)	(11,000)	
Total		$129,000

Required:

a. Is this a cash basis or a working capital basis statement? Explain the basis for your answer.

b. What was the amount of net income reported for 19D?

c. Did cash increase or decrease? Explain.

d. Did the company give adequate attention to communication of financial information to the shareholders? Explain the basis for your response.

e. Recast the above statement using preferred format and terminology.

f. What was the amount of the difference between net income and cash generated from operations? Why were they different?

g. Do you suspect any potential problems for this company? Explain the basis for your response.

P15–8. Sureshot Oil Company prepared the following income statement:

Income Statement
For the Year Ended December 31, 1982

		Millions
a. Revenue from sale of crude oil and natural gas		$40
b. Depletion of crude oil and natural gas reserves	$ 5	
c. Depreciation of production equipment	1	
d. Salaries and wages	4	
e. Remaining expenses	20	30
f. Net income		$10

Additional information:

a. Accounts receivable balance at year's end: 1981, $0.5; 1982, $2.5.

b. This is cost depletion and is based on an old and low "finding cost" incurred in 1955. It is expected that the production will cease at the end of 1990 because the remaining reserves will be uneconomical to produce. The company is involved in the risk and high cost of searching for new reserves.

c. Depreciation is computed using the straight-line method and the equipment is very old and inefficient.

d. Salaries and wages unpaid (in millions) at year's end: 1981, $1.5; 1982, $0.5.

e. All cash (including income tax).

f. The board of directors is considering declaring a $5 million cash dividend which the company president opposes.

Required:

a. Prepare a SCFP, cash basis (from operations only). You should be able to do this directly; if not, use either of the T-account or worksheet analytical approaches.

b. Compare the income statement and the SCFP results. Which statement best indicates the ability of the company (1) to pay the dividend, (2) search for new reserves, and (3) replace the equipment? Give the primary arguments for and against the dividend. Suppose $11 million should be spent in 1982–83 for new equipment and well workover projects.

P15–9. Dawson Company is preparing the 19B financial statements, which include the following information:

	19A	19B
Balance sheet:		
Cash	$ 40,000	$ 52,000
Inventory	30,000	37,000
Accounts receivable (net) ..	20,000	17,000
Long-term investment, stock Co. A	10,000	3,000
Machinery and equipment (net)	80,000	75,000
	$180,000	$184,000

Accounts payable	$ 15,000	$ 11,000
Income tax payable	4,000	6,000
Note payable, long term ...	20,000	10,000
Bonds payable	30,000	10,000
Capital stock, par $10	100,000	110,000
Contributed capital in excess of par	8,000	11,000
Retained earnings	3,000	26,000
	$180,000	$184,000

Income statement:	
Revenue	$140,000
Cost of goods sold	(65,000)
Depreciation expense	(8,000)
Patent expense	(600)
Remaining operating expenses	(28,400)
Income tax expense	(9,000)
Gain on disposal of machine (net of tax)	1,000
Net income	$ 30,000

Additional data:

1. Machinery which had a book value of $10,000 was sold for $11,000 cash.
2. Long-term investment (shares of Company A stock) was sold for $7,000 cash, which had a carrying value of $7,000.
3. Equipment was acquired and payment in full was made by issuing 1,000 shares of capital stock which had a market value of $13 per share.
4. Payments on debt: long-term note, $10,000; bonds payable, $20,000.
5. Declared and issued a stock dividend, $7,000.

Required:

a. Prepare a T-account or worksheet to develop a SCFP, cash basis.

b. Prepare the SCFP, cash basis.

P15–10. Brown Company is developing the 19B annual reports. A SCFP, cash basis, is being developed. The following worksheet has been set up to develop the statement:

(Relates to Problem 15–10)

		BROWN COMPANY		
		Worksheet to Develop Statement of Changes in Financial Position, Cash Basis		
		For the Year Ended December 31, 19B		

Items	Ending Balances, Dec. 31, 19A	Analysis of Interim Entries		Ending Balances, Dec. 31, 19B
		Debit	Credit	
Debits				
Cash account	24,000			32,200
Noncash accounts:				
Accounts receivable (net)	26,000			30,000
Inventory	30,000			28,000
Prepaid insurance	1,200			800
Investments, long term	10,800			8,000
Operational assets (net)	30,000			39,000
Patent (net)	3,000			2,700
	125,000			140,700
Credits				
Accounts payable	21,000			18,000
Wages payable	3,000			2,000
Income tax payable	1,000			1,200
Note payable, long term	25,000			20,000
Capital stock (par $10)	60,000			70,000
Contributed capital				
in excess of par	1,000			3,000
Retained earnings	14,000			26,500
Sources of cash:	125,000			140,700
Uses of cash				
Change in cash				

Additional data for 19B:

a. Revenues, $120,000 — Expenses, $100,000 = Net income, $20,000.

b. Depreciation expense, $3,000.

c. Amortization of patent, $300.

d. Sale of long-term investment at cost, $2,800.

e. Purchased operational assets, and issued 1,000 shares of capital stock as full payment (market value, $12 per share).

f. Paid cash dividend, $7,500.

g. Increase in accounts receivable balance during the period.

h. Decrease in inventory during the period.

i. Decrease in prepaid insurance balance during the period.

j. Decrease in accounts payable balance during the period.

k. Decrease in wages payable balance during the period.

l. Increase in income tax payable balance during the period.

Required:

Complete the above worksheet on a cash basis (refer to the Appendix), or, if you prefer, use the T-account approach.

Problems
Part C

P15–11. The following statement was prepared by Ware Corporation:

(Relates to Problem 15–11)

WARE CORPORATION
Statement of Changes in Financial Position—Working Capital Basis
December 31, 19E

Sources of Funds:
From operations:

Net income			$ 40,000
Add expenses not requiring working capital:			
Depreciation expense	$12,000		
Patent amortization expense	1,000		
Goodwill amortization expense	3,000	16,000	
Total funds generated by operations			$ 56,000

From other sources:

Bonds payable, maturity value $100,000	98,000	
Sale of land (at cost)	25,000	
Common stock (issued for plant site)	40,000	
Total funds from other sources		163,000
Total funds generated during the period		219,000

Uses of funds:

Pay mortgage	20,000	
Construct new plant	150,000	
Purchase plant machinery	20,000	
Plant site (for stock issued)	40,000	
Cash dividend declared	6,000	
Total funds used during the period		236,000
Net decrease in working capital during the period		$ 17,000

(Relates to Problem 15–11)

Changes in working capital accounts:

	Balances at December 31		Working capital increase (decrease)
	19E	19D	
Current assets:			
Cash	$ 6,000	$33,000	$(27,000)
Accounts receivable	13,000	9,000	4,000
Inventory	52,000	40,000	12,000
Total current assets	71,000	82,000	
Current liabilities:			
Accounts payable	8,000	13,000	5,000
Short-term notes payable	16,000	5,000	(11,000)
Total current liabilities	24,000	18,000	
Working capital	$47,000	$64,000	$(17,000)

Required:

a. List any communication deficiencies that you observe.

b. Did working capital and cash each increase or decrease? By how much?

c. What was the primary source of working capital?

d. What was the primary use of working capital?

e. Explain the nonworking capital exchange. Did it directly affect working capital? Why should it be reported on the statement?

f. Explain why working capital decreased although there was a net income for the period.

g. Assess the soundness of the cash dividend.

h. Assess the cash position compared with the working capital position.

i. Can you spot any potential problems with respect to the future? Explain.

P15–12. The following actual statement was taken from the published annual financial statements of Laird Corporation:

Required:

a. Did working capital and cash each change? In what direction and by how much?

b. Explain why the amount of the change in working capital was different from the amount of net income.

c. What were the largest source and use of working capital?

d. Is the working capital position sound? Explain the basis for your decision.

(Relates to Problem 15–12)

LAIRD CORPORATION
Statement of Working Capital
December 31, 19B

Working capital generated:

Net income	$14,000	
Add: Depreciation	15,000	
Patent amortization	1,000	
Total	30,000	
Bonds issued	50,000	
Common stock (for equipment)	15,000	
Total working capital generated		$95,000

Working capital applied:

Pay mortgage	60,000	
Acquired equipment	15,000	
Dividends declared and paid	10,000	
Total working capital applied		85,000
Net increase in working capital		$10,000

Working capital changes:

	19B	Change
Cash	$ 7,400	$(12,400)
Accounts receivable	9,000	6,000
Inventory	24,900	19,900
Accounts payable	(7,000)	(4,000)
Other short-term debt	(1,400)	500
Total	$32,900	$10,000

e. Compare the cash position with the working capital position.

f. List all of the communication deficiencies in the above format.

g. Recast the above statement to correct it for the deficiencies you listed in Requirement *(f)*.

P15–13. Star Company is completing the 19B financial statements. The following information has been developed:

(Relates to Problem 15–13)

Balance sheet:	19A	19B
Cash	$ 10,000	$ 2,000
Accounts receivable (net)	16,600	21,000
Inventory	17,000	25,000
Prepaid expenses	1,400	400
Operational assets (net)	59,000	68,000
Plant site		20,000
Long-term investment	16,000	7,000
	$120,000	$143,400
Accounts payable	$ 8,000	$ 12,000
Wages payable	1,000	1,500
ST note payable (interest, Dec. 31)	6,000	3,000
LT note payable (interest, Dec. 31)	10,000	4,000
Bonds payable (interest, Dec. 31)	30,000	50,000
Capital stock, par $10	60,000	60,500
Contributed capital in excess of par ...	3,000	3,400
Retained earnings	2,000	9,000
	$120,000	$143,400

Income statement:	
Revenues	$135,000
Depreciation expense	(15,000)
Remaining expenses	(95,000)
Loss on sale of long-term investment ..	(3,000)
Net income	$ 22,000

Additional data:

1. Purchased operational asset (cash), $24,000.
2. Sold long-term investment for $6,000, carrying value $9,000.
3. Sold 50 shares of capital stock at $18 per share (cash).
4. Declared and paid cash dividend, $15,000.
5. Payment on short-term note, $3,000.
6. Payment on long-term note, $6,000.
7. Acquired plant site and issued bonds, $20,000, for full purchase price (the bonds sell at par).

Required:

a. Prepare a T-account or worksheet analysis for SCFP, working capital basis.
b. Prepare the SCFP.

P15–14. Kirk Company is preparing the 19B annual financial statements. The data given below have been developed.

(Relates to Problem 15–14)

Balance sheet:	19A	19B
Cash	$ 10,000	$ 1,000
Accounts receivable (net)	30,000	48,500
Inventory	20,000	21,400
Short-term investments	7,000	
Long-term investments	5,000	
Operational assets (net)	50,000	57,000
Patent (net)	4,000	3,600
Land		7,500
	$126,000	$139,000

(Relates to Problem 15–14—Continued)

Accounts payable	$ 43,500	$ 40,000
Income tax payable	500	
Wages payable	2,000	3,000
Bonds payable	15,000	10,000
Capital stock, par $1	40,000	54,000
Contributed capital in excess of par ...		3,500
Retained earnings	25,000	28,500
	$126,000	$139,000

Income statement:	
Revenue	$ 80,000
Depreciation expense	(2,000)
Amortization expense	(400)
Remaining expenses	(73,600)
Gain on sale of long-term investment ..	3,000
Net income	$ 7,000

Additional data:

1. Sold long-term investment that cost $5,000 for $8,000 cash.
2. Annual payment on bond principal, $5,000.
3. Sold and issued 8,000 shares of capital stock at $1.25 per share (cash).
4. Declared and paid cash dividends, $3,500.
5. Purchased operational asset, $9,000 (cash).
6. Acquired land for future use and paid in full by issuing 6,000 shares of capital stock, market value $1.25 per share.

Required:

a. Prepare a T-account or worksheet analysis to develop the SCFP, working capital basis.
b. Prepare the SCFP, working capital basis.

P15–15. (Based on Appendix) Ware Company is preparing the annual financial statements, including a SCFP, in working capital basis, at December 31, 19B. The balance sheet and the income statement and some additional data are summarized below:

(Relates to 15–15)

	Balances	
	19B	*19A*
Balance sheet at December 31:		
Cash...	$ 21,500	$ 15,000
Accounts receivable (net)	23,000	20,000
Merchandise inventory	27,000	22,000
Prepaid insurance	300	600
Investments, long term (S Corp. stock)	12,000	
Operational assets (net)	220,000	134,000
Patent (net)	16,000	
	$319,800	$191,600

(Relates to Problem 15–15—continued)

	Balances	
	19B	19A
Accounts payable	$ 18,000	$ 12,000
Note payable, short term (nontrade)	10,000	18,000
Wages payable	800	1,000
Income tax payable	1,000	600
Note payable, long term	10,000	30,000
Bonds payable	100,000	
Capital stock (par $10)	140,000	100,000
Contributed capital in excess of par	6,000	5,000
Retained earnings	34,000	25,000
	$319,800	$191,600

Income statement for 19B:

Sales		$200,000
Cost of goods sold		126,000
Gross margin on sales		74,000
Expenses (not detailed)	$39,000	
Depreciation expense	14,000	
Amortization of patent	1,000	
Income tax expense	7,000	61,000
Net income		$ 13,000

Additional data for 19B:

1. Purchased patent on January 1, 19B, for $17,000 cash.
2. Purchased stock of S Corporation as a long-term investment for cash, $12,000.
3. Paid $20,000 on the long-term note payable.
4. Sold and issued 4,000 shares of capital stock for $41,000 cash.
5. Declared and paid a $4,000 cash dividend.
6. Acquired a building (an operational asset) and paid in full for it by issuing $100,000 bonds payable at par to the former owner—date of transaction was December 30, 19B.

Required:

a. Based upon the above data, prepare a worksheet to develop the SCFP, working capital basis. (Hint: The increase in working capital was $16,000.)
b. Based upon the completed worksheet, prepare the SCFP, working capital basis.

Using and interpreting financial statements

PURPOSE OF THE CHAPTER

Throughout the preceding chapters, primary attention was given to developing an understanding of the financial reports prepared for use by external parties. The rationale and conceptual basis for the major phases of the accounting process and the resulting financial statements were presented. Throughout those discussions, we also emphasized the use and interpretation of the various items and classifications reported on the income statement, balance sheet, and statement of changes in financial position (SCFP).

The preceding chapters presented the fundamentals underlying financial accounting and reporting. These fundamentals were summarized in Exhibit 2–6. We emphasized these fundamentals because an understanding of them and their impacts on financial statements is essential to the statement users. The interpretation of financial reports and an appreciation of both their advantages and limitations rest basically on a knowledge of the broad fundamentals. They emphasize valuations, measurements, and the basic distinctions in the measuring and reporting processes. As a decision maker who necessarily must rely on financial statements, your understanding of these broad fundamentals should serve you to advantage.

The purpose of this chapter is to discuss (a) uses of external financial statements by decision makers and (b) some analytical techniques that are used widely to interpret those financial statements.

Behavioral and learning objectives for this chapter are provided in the *Teachers Manual.*

FINANCIAL REPORTS IN THE DECISION-MAKING PROCESS

The basic objective of financial statements is to help the users make better economic decisions. Decision makers who use financial statements

703

constitute two broad groups. The management of the business (i.e., internal decision makers) relies on financial data in making important managerial decisions. This aspect of accounting is considered in *Fundamentals of Management Accounting.*

The second broad group that uses financial reports frequently is referred to as "external" decision makers. This group consists primarily of investors (both present and potential owners), investment analysts, creditors (both short term and long term), government, labor organizations, and the public at large. Financial accounting and the external financial reports discussed in the preceding chapters are oriented toward serving this particular group of decision makers.

Regardless of the particular decision maker, there are three primary uses of financial data:

1. **Measurement of past performance**—The decision maker needs to know how the business has performed in the past. Information concerning such items as income, sales volume, extraordinary items, cash and working capital flows, and return earned on the investment helps assess the success of the business and the effectiveness of the management. Such information also helps the decision maker compare one entity with others.

2. **Measurement of the present condition of a business**—The decision maker must have data on how the entity stands today. Relevant questions include: What types of assets are owned? How much debt does the business owe, and when is it due? What is the cash position? How much of the earnings have been retained in the business? What is the debt/equity ratio? What is the inventory position? Answers to these and similar economic questions help the decision maker assess the successes and failures of the past; but, more importantly, they provide useful information in assessing the potentials of the business.

3. **Prediction of the future performance of the business**—Statement users make decisions by selecting from among several alternative courses of action. Each course of action will cause different effects *in the future* for the decision maker. Many of these future effects are financial in nature. In decision making, one is faced with the problem of predicting the probable future impacts of the alternatives under consideration. All decisions are future oriented because they do not (and cannot) affect the past. However, in predicting the probable future impact of a decision, reliable measurements of what has happened in the recent past are valuable. This is particularly true when the decision relates to a business entity. The recent sales and profit trends of a business are good indicators of what might be expected reasonably in the future. The primary value of purposes 1 and 2 is to aid in purpose 3.

Thus, decision makers must rely substantially on the past data presented in financial reports in making assessments and predictions of probable future performance. Generally, this is the most important use of financial statements by decision makers.

Some decisions are made intuitively and without much supporting data. In such cases there is no systematic attempt to collect measurable data such as those provided in financial reports. The decision maker does not attempt to array, measure, and evaluate the advantages and disadvantages of each alternative. There are numerous reasons for intuitive decisions of this sort. Time and cost may prevent a careful analysis. Sometimes the decision maker is unsophisticated and consequently does not understand the systematic approach to decision making and is not aware of the basic factors bearing on the decision. Unsophisticated decision makers tend to oversimplify the decision-making process, disregard basic information, and quite frequently overlook the financial impacts.

In contrast, a sophisticated decision maker will make a systematic analysis of each alternative. Information that bears on each alternative will be collected. In decisions relating to a business, the financial statements generally provide critical financial data bearing on the various alternatives. We must emphasize, however, that the financial impact is only one of several important factors that should be evaluated in most decisions.

To use financial information effectively, one must understand what it represents and how the measurements were made. With a reasonable level of understanding of the fundamentals of the accounting process, one is able to evaluate effectively the **strengths and weaknesses** (and limitations) of the financial data presented in the financial reports of a business. Your study of the preceding chapters should enable you to appreciate and evaluate these aspects.

The three basic financial statements—income statement, balance sheet, and statement of changes in financial position (SCFP)—and the related disclosure notes have evolved primarily to meet the special needs of external decision makers. Because of the varied needs of these users, special and supplementary financial data and analyses frequently are needed.

INVESTORS

Investors constitute a primary group to which external financial statements are addressed. As a group they include present owners (shareholders in the case of a corporation), potential owners (those who may become interested in purchasing shares), and investment analysts (since they advise investors). Investors include individuals, other businesses, and institutions, such as your university.

When purchasing shares of stock, most investors do not seek a controlling interest. Instead, they do so in the anticipation of (1) receiving revenue in the form of dividends during the investment period and (2) subsequent increases in the market value of the shares over the amount invested. Thus, when making an investment of this type or in selling an investment already held, the investor is faced with the problem of predicting the future **income** and **growth** of the enterprise. Investors are interested in enterprise income because it is the "source" of future dividends. They are interested in enterprise growth because it tends to cause the share market price to increase. In making these predictions, the investor should look at several different considerations, such as the nature of the industry, the characteristics of the company, and its financial track record. The income statement provides significant data for the investor, such as revenue from products and services, extraordinary items, income tax impacts, net income, and earnings per share. Other relationships, such as gross margin, profit margin, and expense relationships, can be computed. Similarly, the balance sheet and the statement of changes in financial position, buttressed by the notes to the financial statements, provide a measurement of past profit performance, funds flow, and current financial position. These data constitute an important base from which predictions of future income and growth can be made. These data are particularly valuable when available for recent past periods (see Exhibit 16–1).

CREDITORS

Financial institutions, and other parties to some extent, grant long-term and short-term credit to businesses. Those that grant credit do so in order to earn a return, that is, interest revenue. They expect to collect periodic interest during the credit period and the principal at maturity. As a consequence, in granting credit to a business, the creditor is concerned basically about items such as the

1. Profit potentials of the business because a profitable entity is much more likely to meet its maturing obligations.
2. Ability of the business to generate cash consistently from recurring operations because it will be in a more favorable position to pay its debts.
3. Financial position (assets owned and debts owed) of the business because the assets comprise security for the debts and the debts indicate the future demand for cash at debt maturity dates.

Credit grantors almost always look to the financial reports for information bearing on these matters. Not infrequently the financial institution requires that it be provided with "certified" financial statements prior to making a loan and throughout the credit period. In addition to the financial statements, the disclosure notes and the "auditors' opinion" convey important information because they often provide detailed quantified facts to support the reported amounts and other nonquantified explanations such as certain future contingencies (e.g., major lawsuits pending).

ANALYSIS OF FINANCIAL STATEMENTS

Financial statements include a large volume of quantitative data supplemented by disclosure notes. The notes are intended to be particularly helpful to users in interpreting the statements; therefore, they should be viewed as an integral part of the financial statements. They elaborate on

EXHIBIT 16–1
Comparative statements illustrated

PACKARD COMPANY
Comparative Income Statements (simplified for illustration)
For the Years Ended December 31, 1982, and 1981

	Year ended Dec. 31		Increase (decrease) 1982 over 1981	
	1982	1981*	Amount	Percent
Sales	$120,000	$100,000	$20,000	20.0
Cost of goods sold	72,600	60,000	12,600	21.0
Gross margin on sales	47,400	40,000	7,400	18.5
Operating expenses:				
Distribution expenses	22,630	15,000	7,630	50.9
Administrative expenses	11,870	13,300	(1,430)	(10.8)
Interest expense	1,500	1,700	(200)	(11.8)
Total expenses	36,000	30,000	6,000	20.0
Pretax income	11,400	10,000	1,400	14.0
Income taxes	2,600	2,000	600	30.0
Net income	$ 8,800	$ 8,000	$ 800	10.0

* Base year for computing percents.

PACKARD COMPANY
Comparative Balance Sheets (simplified for illustration)
At December 31, 1982, and 1981

	At December 31		Increase (decrease) 1982 over 1981	
	1982	1981*	Amount	Percent
Assets				
Current assets:				
Cash	$ 13,000	$ 9,000	$ 4,000	44.4
Accounts receivable (net)	8,400	7,000	1,400	20.0
Merchandise inventory	54,000	60,000	(6,000)	(10.0)
Prepaid expenses	2,000	4,000	(2,000)	(50.0)
Total current assets	77,400	80,000	(2,600)	3.3
Investments:				
Real estate	8,000	8,000		
Operational assets:				
Equipment and furniture	82,500	75,000	7,500	10.0
Less accumulated depreciation	(23,250)	(15,000)	8,250	55.0
Total operational assets	59,250	60,000	(750)	(1.3)
Other assets	1,900	2,000	(100)	(5.0)
Total assets	$146,550	$150,000	$ (3,450)	(2.3)
Liabilities				
Current liabilities:				
Accounts payable	$ 13,200	$ 12,000	$ 1,200	10.0
Notes payable, short term	15,000	20,000	(5,000)	(25.0)
Accrued wages payable	7,200	8,000	(800)	(10.0)
Total current liabilities	35,400	40,000	(4,600)	(11.5)
Long-term liabilities:				
Notes payable, long term	7,150	10,000	(2,850)	(28.5)
Total liabilities	42,550	50,000	(7,450)	(14.9)
Shareholders' Equity				
Common stock (par $10)	85,000	85,000		
Retained earnings	19,000	15,000	4,000	26.7
Total shareholders' equity	104,000	100,000	4,000	4.0
Total liabilities and shareholders' equity	$146,550	$150,000	$ (3,450)	(2.3)

* Base year for computing percents.

accounting policies, major financial effects and events, and certain events not directly affecting the current quantitative measurements, but which may bear on the continued success of the firm. An example of the latter situation would be a major lawsuit that is pending. The notes are intended to contribute to an understanding of the significance of such factors.

In respect to the quantitative data presented in the financial statements there are four techniques that are used widely to assist decision makers in understanding and interpreting the external financial statements: (1) comparative statements, (2) long-term summaries, (3) graphic presentations, and (4) ratio analyses.

COMPARATIVE STATEMENTS

For a number of years, the accounting profession has required the presentation of **comparative financial statements** covering, as a minimum, the current year and the immediately prior year.

Practically all financial statements present, side by side, the results for the current and the preceding years (similar to the statements shown in Exhibit 16–1). As published, only two amount columns generally are shown. However, two additional columns may be added for (1) the amount of change for each item and (2) the percent of change. These additional **variance** columns (amount and percent) are illustrated in Exhibit 16–1. The two variance columns facilitate **interpretation** by the statement user. Frequently the percent of change from the prior period is more helpful, for interpretative purposes, than the absolute dollar amount of change. Observe that the percents are determined independently on each line by dividing the amount of the change by the amount for the preceding year. For example, in Exhibit 16–1, the percentage on the Cash line was computed as $4,000 \div $9,000 = 44.4$ percent. Thus, the earlier year was used as the base.

LONG-TERM SUMMARIES

To assure **full disclosure,** many companies also include in the annual report 5-, 10-, and even 20-year summaries of basic data, such as sales, net income, total assets, total liabilities, total owners' equity, and selected ratios. This kind of reporting is encouraged from the standpoint of the statement user. Data for a series of years are particularly important in interpreting the financial statements for the current period. There is considerable likelihood of misinterpretation and unwarranted conclusions when the user limits consideration to only the last one or two periods. The vagaries of transactions, economic events, and accounting are such that the financial reports for one relatively short period of time generally do not provide a sound basis for assessing the long-term potentials of an enterprise. Sophisticated financial analysts typically use data covering a number of periods so that significant **trends** may be identified and interpreted.

However, in interpreting long-term summaries the decision maker must exercise judgment because data for a long period in the past may not be comparable, or even useful, because of changes in the company, industry, and environment. For example, IBM is a very different company now than it was before the advent of electronic computers.

In analyzing and interpreting comparative data, the items showing significant increases and decreases should receive special attention. Care should be exercised to identify evidence of significant **turning points,** either upward or downward, in trends for important items such as net income and cash flow. The turning points often indicate significant future trends. Fundamental to the interpretation is the need to determine the **underlying causes** for significant changes in either direction (favorable or unfavorable). An excellent ten-year financial summary is shown in Exhibit 16–4.

RATIO AND PERCENTAGE ANALYSIS

Some amounts on financial statements, such as income, are highly significant in and of themselves; however, the significance of many amounts is highlighted by their relationships to other amounts. These **significant relationships** can be pinpointed and isolated effectively in many instances through the use of an analytical tool known as **ratio** or **percentage analysis.** A ratio or percent simply expresses the proportionate relationship between two different amounts. A ratio or percent is computed by dividing one quantity by another quantity; the divisor is known as the *base* amount. For example, the fact that a company earned income of $500,000 assumes greater significance when that amount is compared with the stockholders' investment in the company. Assume stockholders' equity is $5,000,000 (i.e., the base amount); the relationship of earnings to shareholder investment would be $500,000 ÷ $5,000,000 = 0.1, or 10 percent. Clearly, this ratio may have significant information content for the decision maker. It enables one to compare companies more realistically than the income amount standing alone.

Fundamentally, there are two aspects of ratio analysis: (1) relationships **within one period** and (2) relationships **between periods.** In addition, ratios may be computed between amounts within one statement, such as the income statement, or between statements, such as the income statement and the balance sheet. In Exhibit 16–1, for Packard Company, the percents of change represent a percentage analysis between periods within each statement.

There is no particular list of ratios or percentages that can be identified as appropriate to all situations. Each situation usually will evidence a need for particular ratios; however, there are a number of ratios or percentages which usually are used because they are appropriate to many situations. The next paragraphs will discuss and illustrate the ratios and percentages which are used often.

COMPONENT PERCENTAGES

A widely used technique, known as component percentages, expresses each item on a particular statement as a percentage of a single base amount. Exhibit 16–2 presents a component analysis for the 1982 and 1981 income statements and balance sheets for Packard Company. On the income statement, the base amount used is **net sales.** Thus, each expense is expressed as a proportionate part of net sales. On the balance sheet, the base amount is **total assets.** The percents are derived by dividing the amount on each line by the base amount (total assets).

Component percentages often are useful in interpreting and evaluating the reported financial data. Percents have the distinct characteristic of revealing important proportional relationships. For example, on the income statement in Exhibit 16–2, observe that distribution expenses were 18.9 percent of sales in 1982, compared with 15 percent in 1981. On the balance sheet, for example, we may note that at the end of 1982 merchandise inventory was 36.8 percent of total assets, compared with 40 percent for 1981. These changes in important relationships often suggest the need for further inquiry because they tend to indicate potentials and problems. Component percentage analysis often is called vertical analysis.

SOME WIDELY USED RATIOS

Numerous ratios can be computed from a single set of financial statements; however, only a selected number may be useful in a given situation. Thus, a common approach is to compute certain widely used ratios and then decide which additional ratios are relevant to the particular type of decisions contemplated. Since balance sheet amounts relate to one instant in time, while the income statement figures refer to transactions and events over a period of time, care must be exercised in calculating ratios that use amounts from both statements. Thus, when an income statement amount is compared with a balance sheet amount, a balance sheet **average** amount often is used to compensate for the difference in time periods. In the examples to follow, the selected balance sheet average usually is computed as one half of the sum of the amounts shown on the beginning and ending balance sheets. When additional information is available, such as monthly data, an average of the monthly data often is more representative.

Commonly used financial ratios can be grouped loosely into the following five categories:[1]

Tests of profitability:
1. Return on owners' investment.
2. Return on total investment.
3. Financial leverage.

---

[1] The numbers to the left are maintained in the subsequent discussions to facilitate reference.

EXHIBIT 16–2
Component percentages illustrated

PACKARD COMPANY
Income Statements (simplified for illustration)
For the Years Ended December 31, 1982, and 1981

	For the year ended			
	Dec. 31, 1982		Dec. 31, 1981	
	Amount	Percent	Amount	Percent
Sales*	$120,000	100.0	$100,000	100.0
Cost of goods sold	72,600	60.5	60,000	60.0
Gross margin on sales	47,400	39.5	40,000	40.0
Operating expenses:				
Distribution expenses	22,630	18.9	15,000	15.0
Administrative expenses	11,870	9.9	13,300	13.3
Interest expense	1,500	1.2	1,700	1.7
Total expenses	36,000	30.0	30,000	30.0
Pretax income....................	11,400	9.5	10,000	10.0
Income taxes	2,600	2.2	2,000	2.0
Net income	$ 8,800	7.3	$ 8,000	8.0

* Base amount.

PACKARD COMPANY
Balance Sheets (simplified for illustration)
At December 31, 1982, and 1981

	At			
	Dec. 31, 1982		Dec. 31, 1981	
	Amount	Percent	Amount	Percent
Assets				
Current assets:				
Cash	$ 13,000	8.9	$ 9,000	6.0
Accounts receivable (net)	8,400	5.7	7,000	4.6
Merchandise inventory	54,000	36.8	60,000	40.0
Prepaid expenses	2,000	1.4	4,000	2.7
Total current assets	77,400	52.8	80,000	53.3
Investments:				
Real estate.....................	8,000	5.5	8,000	5.3
Operational assets:				
Equipment and furniture	82,500	56.3	75,000	50.0
Less accumulated depreciation	(23,250)	(15.9)	(15,000)	(10.0)
Total operational assets	59,250	40.4	60,000	40.0
Other assets	1,900	1.3	2,000	1.4
Total assets*	$146,550	100.0	$150,000	100.0
Liabilities				
Current liabilities:				
Accounts payable	$ 13,200	9.0	$ 12,000	8.0
Notes payable, short term	15,000	10.2	20,000	13.3
Accrued wages payable	7,200	4.9	8,000	5.3
Total current liabilities	35,400	24.1	40,000	26.6
Long-term liabilities:				
Notes payable, long term	7,150	4.9	10,000	6.7
Total liabilities	42,550	29.0	50,000	33.3
Shareholders' Equity				
Common stock (par $10)	85,000	58.0	85,000	56.7
Retained earnings	19,000	13.0	15,000	10.0
Total shareholders' equity ...	104,000	71.0	100,000	66.7
Total liabilities and shareholders' equity* ..	$146,550	100.0	$150,000	100.0

* Base amount.

4. Earnings per share (EPS).
5. Profit margin.

Tests of liquidity:
6. Working capital or current ratio.
7. Quick or "acid-test" ratio.
8. Receivable turnover ratio (or average collection period).
9. Inventory turnover ratio (or average days' supply).

Tests of solvency and equity position:
10. Debt/equity ratio.
11. Owners' equity to total equities.
12. Creditors' equity to total equities.

Market tests:
13. Price/earnings ratio (P/E ratio).
14. Dividend yield ratio.

Miscellaneous ratio:
15. Book value per common share.

Tests of profitability

Continuing profitability is a primary measure of the overall success of a company; it is a necessary condition for survival. Investors and others would like to be able to rely on a *single measure* of profitability that would be meaningful in all situations. Unfortunately, no single amount can be devised to meet this comprehensive need. Tests of profitability focus on measuring the adequacy of income by comparing it with one or more primary activities or factors that are measured in the financial statements. Five different tests of profitability commonly used are explained below.

1. Return on owners' investment. This ratio generally is regarded as a fundamental test of true profitability. It relates income to the amount of investment that was committed to earning the income. To measure the profitability of any investment, whether for a company, a project, or for an individual investment, the amount of income must be gauged against the resources invested. Investors commit their funds to an enterprise because they expect to earn a return (i.e., a profit) on those funds. Fundamentally, the return on owners' investment ratio is computed as follows:

$$\text{Return on owners' investment} = \frac{\text{Income*}}{\text{Average owners' equity\dagger}}$$

$$\text{Packard Company, 1982} = \frac{\$8,800*}{\$102,000\dagger} = 8.6\%$$

Based on Exhibit 16–2.
* Income *before* extraordinary items generally should be used.
† Average owners' equity is preferable when available; that is, (\$100,000 + \$104,000) ÷ 2 = \$102,000.

Thus, Packard Company can be said to have earned 8.6 percent, after income taxes, on the investment provided by the **owners**. Return on owners' investment is a particularly useful measure of profitability from the viewpoint of the owners because it relates the two fundamental factors in any investment situation—the amount of the owners' investment and the return earned for the owners on that investment. Clearly, it focuses on the viewpoint of the investor.

2. Return on total investment. Another view of the return on investment concept relates income to **total assets** used (i.e., the same as total owners' equity plus total liabilities) rather than to owners' investment only. Under this broader concept, return on total investment would be computed as follows:

$$\text{Return on total investment} = \frac{\text{Income* + Interest expense (net of tax)}}{\text{Average total assets†}}$$

$$\text{Packard Company, 1982} = \frac{\$8,800^* + (\$1,500 \times 0.77)}{\$148,275†} = 6.7\%$$

Based on Exhibit 16–2.

* Income before extraordinary items should be used. This illustration assumes an average income tax rate of 23 percent.

† Average total assets should be used; that is: ($150,000 + $146,550) ÷ 2 = $148,275.

Thus, it can be said that Packard Company earned 6.7 percent on **all** of the **resources** employed during the year. This concept views *investment* as the amount of resources provided by both owners and creditors. Thus, it is viewed often as a fundamental measure of the **management's performance** in using all of the resources available.

To compute return on *total* investment, interest expense (net of tax) must be added back to income because it is the return on the creditors' investment and was deducted in deriving income. The denominator represents *total* investment; therefore, interest expense must be added back to raise the numerator (income) to a *total* return basis. Interest net of tax must be used because that is the net cost to the corporation of the funds provided by creditors.

Return on total investment reflects the combined effect of both the operating and the financing activities of a company as illustrated in Exhibit 16–3.

Most analysts compute return-on-investment ratios for both total investment and owners' equity as illustrated above. Return on total investment is viewed as the preferable measure of **management performance,** that is, management performance in using all of the resources available to the company. The return on owners' equity is viewed as particularly relevant to the owners since it tends to measure the return that has accrued to them.

3. Financial leverage. Financial leverage is the advantage, or disadvantage, which derives from earning a return on total investment (total assets) that is different from the return earned on owners' equity. Most companies

EXHIBIT 16–3
Components of
return on
investment

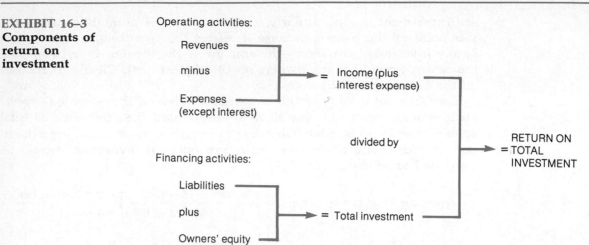

Operating activities:

Revenues

minus

Expenses
(except interest)

= Income (plus
interest expense)

divided by

Financing activities:

Liabilities

plus

Owners' equity

= Total investment

RETURN ON
= TOTAL
INVESTMENT

earn a higher rate on owners' equity than on total equity and thus enjoy a positive leverage. This is because the net interest cost of borrowed funds (debt) is less than the company's earnings rate overall (also, some current liabilities have no measurable interest cost).

The financial leverage of a company can be measured by comparing the two return-on-investment ratios discussed above. The measurement is realistic because the two rates differ only because of the effect of liabilities. The measurement of financial leverage is as follows:

$$\text{Financial leverage} = \frac{\text{Return on}}{\text{owners' investment}} - \frac{\text{Return on}}{\text{total assets}}$$

Packard Company, 1982 = 8.6% − 6.7% = 1.9% (positive leverage)

When the cost of total debt (interest expense, net of tax) is lower as an average rate than the rate of return on total investment earned by the company, the difference accrues to the benefit of the owners. Of course, this is the primary reason why most companies adopt a strategy of obtaining a significant amount of the resources needed from creditors rather than the total investment amount from the sale of capital stock.

4. Earnings per share (EPS). This ratio was illustrated in preceding chapters. This test of profitability is strictly from the common stockholders' point of view. Rather than being based on investment it is based on the number of shares of common stock outstanding. It is intended to provide a measure of profitability that can be adjusted readily for the number of shares owned. Basically, EPS on common stock is computed as follows:

$$\text{Earnings per share} = \frac{\text{Income}}{\text{Average number of shares of}}$$
$$\text{common stock outstanding}$$

$$\text{Packard Company, 1982} = \frac{\$8,800}{\$8,500} = \$1.04 \text{ per share}$$

EPS is computed on *(a)* income before extraordinary items (required), *(b)* extraordinary items (optional), and *(c)* net income (required). Of the three EPS amounts, the first one generally is considered the most relevant.

5. Profit margin. This ratio relates only to the income statement. It is computed as follows:

$$\text{Profit margin} = \frac{\text{Income (before extraordinary items)}}{\text{Net sales}}$$

$$\text{Packard Company, 1982} = \frac{\$8,800}{\$120,000} = 7.3\%$$

This profitability test simply is the percent of each sales dollar, on the average, that represents profit. For Packard Company it may be interpreted as follows:

a. Income was 0.073 of net sales.
b. Income was 7.3 percent of net sales.
c. $0.073 of each $1 of sales was income.

This ratio also is reflected in the component percentages illustrated in Exhibit 16–2. Some persons view this profitability test as the most important measure of overall profitability and, hence, as the fundamental indicator of management performance. This view is erroneous because the ratio does not take into account the amount of resources employed (i.e., total investment) to produce the income. For example, the income statements of Company A and Company B may reflect the following:

	Company A	Company B
a. Sales	$100,000	$150,000
b. Income	$ 5,000	$ 7,500
c. Profit margin *(b) ÷ (a)*	5%	5%
d. Total investment	$ 50,000	$125,000
e. Return on total investment* *(b) ÷ (d)*	10%	6%

* Assuming no interest expense.

In this example, both companies reported the same profit margin (5 percent). Company A, however, appears to be doing much better because it is earning a 10 percent return on the total investment against the 6 percent earned by Company B. The profit margin percents do not reflect the effect of the $50,000 total investment in Company A against a $125,000 total investment in Company B. The effect of the different amounts of investment in each company is reflected in the return on investment percents. Thus, the profit margin ratio omits one of the two important factors that should be used in evaluating return on the investment.

Tests of liquidity

Current liquidity refers to a company's ability to meet its currently maturing obligations; therefore, tests of liquidity focus on the relationship between current assets and current liabilities. The ability of a company to meet its current liabilities is an important factor in short-term financial strength. Recall that working capital is measured as the difference between total current assets and total current liabilities. There are two ratios that are used to measure **current liquidity;** they are the working capital (or current) ratio and the quick (or acid-test) ratio.

6. Working capital ratio. This ratio measures the relationship between total current assets and total current liabilities at a specific date. It is computed as follows:

$$\text{Working capital ratio} = \frac{\text{Current assets}}{\text{Current liabilities}}$$

$$\text{Packard Company, 1982} = \frac{\$77,400}{\$35,400} = 2.2 \text{ times or 2.2 to 1}$$

The working capital ratio tends to measure the adequacy of working capital as well as liquidity. For Packard company it can be said that at year-end current assets were 2.2 times current liabilities or, alternatively, that for each $1 of current liabilities there were $2.20 of current assets. Thus, the working capital ratio measures the cushion of working capital maintained in order to allow for the inevitable unevenness in the flow of "funds" through the working capital accounts.[2]

7. Quick ratio. This ratio is similar to the working capital ratio except that it is a much more stringent test of current liquidity. It is computed as follows:

$$\text{Quick ratio} = \frac{\text{Quick assets}}{\text{Current liabilities}}$$

$$\text{Packard Company, 1982} = \frac{\$21,400}{\$35,400} = 0.60 \text{ times or 0.60 to 1}$$

Quick assets include cash, short-term investments held in lieu of cash, and accounts receivable (net of the allowance for doubtful accounts). Quick assets are those assets that are presumed to be readily convertible into cash at approximately their stated amounts. Inventories generally are omit-

---

[2] Occasionally, "working capital" is taken to mean total current assets. This is confusing and unnecessary since "total current assets" is a perfectly good term. Sometimes the term *net working capital* is used to describe the difference between current assets and current liabilities. Throughout this book, we have followed the more general usage of working capital to mean the difference between current assets and current liabilities.

ted because of uncertainty of when the cash will be received because of the length of the period between their acquisition and the ultimate time when the related accounts receivable will be collected. However, if they typically turn to cash very quickly, they should be included. Prepaid expenses do not "convert" to cash; rather their prepayment means that there will be no related cash outflow in the future; therefore, they are excluded. Thus, the quick or acid-test ratio is much more *severe* test of current liquidity than is the working capital ratio.

8. Receivable turnover. The **current liquidity position** is related to the specific items of working capital. Nearness to cash of a current asset often is measured in terms of **turnover.** There are two ratios, in addition to the two illustrated above, that help show nearness to cash: the receivable turnover and the inventory turnover.

The receivable turnover focuses on measuring the effectiveness of credit and collections. It is computed as follows:

$$\text{Receivable turnover} = \frac{\text{Net credit sales*}}{\text{Average net receivables}}$$

Packard Company, 1982 (net credit sales assumed to be $77,000 for 1982) $= \dfrac{\$77,000}{(\$7,000 + \$8,400) \div 2} = 10 \text{ times}$

* When the amount of credit sales is not known, total sales may be used as a rough approximation.

This is a **turnover ratio** since it reflects how many times the receivables, on the average, were recorded, collected, then recorded again during the period. It expresses the relationship of the average balance in Trade Accounts Receivable including Trade Notes Receivable) to the transactions that generated those receivables—credit sales. This turnover ratio tends to measure the effectiveness of the credit-granting and collection activities of the company. The higher the turnover ratio, the better. Granting credit to poor credit risks and ineffective collection efforts will cause this ratio to be low. The receivable turnover often is converted to a time basis known as the average age of the receivables. The computation is as follows:

$$\text{Average age of receivables} = \frac{\text{Days in year}}{\text{Receivable turnover}}$$

Packard Company, 1982 $= \dfrac{365}{10} = 36.5 \text{ average days to collect}$

The effectiveness of credit and collection activities sometimes is judged by a "rule of thumb" that the *average days to collect* should not exceed 1½ times the credit terms. For example, if the credit terms are 2/10, n/30, the average days to collect should not exceed 45 days (i.e., not more than 15 days past due). Like all rules of thumb, this one is rough and has many exceptions. However, an increase or decrease in the receivable turnover or average days to collect, from one period to the next, would suggest that there were changes in the implementation of credit policies and/or changes in collection efficiency. An increase in the average collection period would indicate an increasing time lag between credit sales and cash realization.

9. Inventory turnover. Inventory turnover tends to measure the liquidity (i.e., nearness to cash) of the inventory. It is the relationship of the inventory to the volume of goods sold during the period. The computation is as follows:

$$\text{Inventory turnover} = \frac{\text{Cost of goods sold}}{\text{Average inventory}}$$

$$\text{Packard Company, 1982} = \frac{\$72{,}600}{(\$60{,}000 + \$54{,}000) \div 2} = 1.3 \text{ times}$$

The inventory may be said to have "turned over" 1.3 times on the average during the year since cost of goods sold was 1.3 times the average inventory level. Typically, this ratio is high for grocery stores and relatively low for heavy equipment dealers. Since a profit normally is realized each time the inventory is sold (i.e., turned over), an increase in the ratio is favorable, up to a point. The higher the ratio, the shorter the average "shelf span" for the items stocked. On the other hand, if the ratio is too high, sales may be lost because of items that are out of stock. The turnover ratio often is converted to a time-basis expression called the **average days' supply in inventory.** The computation would be:

$$\text{Average days' supply in inventory} = \frac{\text{Days in year}}{\text{Inventory turnover}}$$

$$\text{Packard Company, 1982} = \frac{365}{1.3}$$

$$= 281 \text{ average day's supply in inventory}$$

(Another example: A turnover ratio of 12.0 would convert as $365 \div 12.0 = 30 +$ average days' supply in inventory.) Turnover ratios are used widely because they are easy to understand.

Tests of solvency and equity position

We noted above that current liquidity refers to the current assets and current liabilities. In contrast, **solvency** (as often used) refers to the ability of a company to meet its **long-term obligations** on a continuing basis. **Equity position** refers to the relative amount of resources provided by the two equities: creditors' equity (i.e., debt capital) and owners' equity (i.e., equity capital). Since the sum of these two equities equals total equities (i.e., total investment), certain critical relationships are significant. The three ratios discussed below are used to reflect these relationships in different ways.

10. Debt/equity ratio. This ratio expresses the direct proportion between debt and owners' equity. It is computed as follows:

$$\text{Debt/equity ratio} = \frac{\text{Total liabilities (i.e., creditors' equity)}}{\text{Owners equity}}$$

$$\text{Packard Company, 1982} = \frac{\$42,550}{\$104,000} = 0.41 \text{ (or 41\%)}$$

In effect, this ratio states that for each $1 of owners' equity, there was $0.41 of liabilities.

11. Owners' equity to total equities. Instead of the single ratio (debt/equity), some persons prefer two ratios that in combination measure the same relationship. The two ratios are owners' equity to total equities and creditors' equity to total equities.

Owners' equity to total equities is computed as follows:

$$\text{Owners' equity to total equities} = \frac{\text{Owners' equity}}{\text{Total equities (i.e., liabilities plus owners' equity)}}$$

$$\text{Packard Company, 1982} = \frac{\$104,000}{\$146,550} = 0.71 \text{ (or 71\%)}$$

12. Creditors' equity to total equities. This ratio is computed as follows:

$$\text{Creditors' equity to total equities} = \frac{\text{Creditors' equity (i.e., liabilities)}}{\text{Total equities}}$$

$$\text{Packard Company, 1982} = \frac{\$42,550}{\$146,550} = 0.29 \text{ (or 29\%)}$$

Obviously, the latter two ratios are complements of each other; they will always sum to 1.00 or 100 percent. They indicate the relative amount of total resources provided by each of the two groups of suppliers of capital to the business. Debt capital is risky for the company because there are (a) specific maturity dates for the principal amounts and (b) specific interest payments that must be made. Both claims are enforceable by law and do not depend upon the earning of income by the company. In contrast, capital supplied by owners does not give rise to similar obligations; that is, it is not fixed as to amounts and dates of principal and dividend payments. Thus, equity capital generally is viewed as much less risky for the company.

In the long run, earnings rates on stockholders' equity normally must be higher than interest rates paid to creditors. Despite the element of debt risk to the company, because of financial leverage, it may be advantageous to the stockholders if the company derives significant amounts of capital through borrowing. For example, assume a company is earning 15 percent return on total equities (i.e., on total investment), while its borrowing rate on debt is 7 percent on the average. To the extent that there is capital provided by debt, the 8 percent difference between the earnings rate on total resources (15 percent) and the interest paid to the creditors (7 percent) accrues to the benefit of the stockholders.[3] In the long run, the stockholders benefit by the 15 percent earned on the resources provided by them, plus the difference between the 15 percent return and the 7 percent interest rate paid on the resources provided by the creditors. This effect is known as financial leverage, as discussed on page 713. A company with a high proportion of debt (such as bonds payable) is said to be **highly levered.** The debt/equity ratio or, alternatively, the two equity ratios indicate the balance that the management has attained between these two sources of capital.

Market tests

A number of ratios have been developed to measure the "market worth" of a share of stock. Basically, these market tests attempt to relate the current market price of a share of stock to some indicator of the profit (or gain) that might accrue to an investor. The tests focus on the *current market price* of the stock because that is the amount the buyer would have to invest. There are two market test ratios that are quoted widely by analysts, stockbrokers, investors, and others. They are the price/earnings ratio and the dividend yield ratio.

13. Price/earnings ratio. This ratio measures the relationship between the current market price of the stock and its earnings per share. Assuming a current market price of $15.60 per share for Packard Company common stock in 1982, it is computed as follows:

$$\text{Price/earnings ratio} = \frac{\text{Current market price per share}}{\text{Earnings per share}}$$

[3] Interest expense on debt is a deductible expense on the income tax return; in contrast, payments to stockholders by means of dividends are not. Thus, in addition to the lower stated rate for debt, funds obtained by means of debt tend to be less costly because of the tax saving. The real cost of debt in the above example depends upon the income tax rate.

$$\text{Packard Company, 1982} = \frac{\$15.60}{\$1.04^*} = 15 \text{ (or 15 to 1)}$$

* Page 715.

Thus, this stock was selling at 15 times the EPS. This ratio frequently is referred to as the **multiple.** The P/E ratio is used widely as an indicator of the future performance of the stock. It changes with each change in the current market price per share and with each earnings report.

Sometimes the components of this ratio are inverted, giving what is referred to as the capitalization rate. This is said to be the rate at which the stock market apparently is capitalizing the current earnings. For example, computation of the capitalization of current earnings per share would be $1.04 ÷ $15.60 = 6.67 percent (called the capitalization rate).

14. Dividend yield ratio. This ratio measures the relationship between the dividends per share paid in the past and the market price of the stock. Assuming dividends paid by Packard Company of $0.75 per share for 1982, it is computed as follows:

$$\text{Dividend yield ratio} = \frac{\text{Dividends per share}}{\text{Market price per share}}$$

$$\text{Packard Company, 1982} = \frac{\$0.75}{\$15.60} = 0.0481 \text{ (or 4.81\%)}$$

The dividend yield ratio measures the current return to the investor, based upon the dividends declared per share (which is revenue to the investor), against the cost of the investment as indicated by the current market price per share. Like the P/E ratio, it is a volatile measure since the price of stock may change materially over short periods of time, and each change in market price changes the ratio. This ratio frequently is referred to simply as the "yield."

Miscellaneous ratios

15. Book value per share. The book value per share of stock measures the owners' equity in terms of each share outstanding. The two different situations are as follows:

Situation 1—Only common stock. Assume total owners' equity of $250,000 and 10,000 outstanding shares of common stock, par $10.

Book value per common share: $250,000 ÷ 10,000 shares = $25

Situation 2—Both common and preferred stock. In this situation total owner's equity must be allocated between the common and preferred shares outstanding. The allocation is made to the preferred, based on its preferences, and the remainder is allocated to the common shares outstanding.

Assume total owners' equity of $273,000; 5 percent preferred stock, par $20, cumulative, (no dividends in arrears for past years), and liquidation value of $22 per share, 1,000 shares outstanding; and 10,000 outstanding shares of common stock, par $10.

Allocation:

Total owners' equity		$273,000
Less equity allocated to preferred stock:		
Liquidation value preference (1,000 shares × $22)	$22,000	
Cumulative dividend preference for the current year (1,000 shares × $20 × 5%)	1,000	23,000
Equity allocation to common stock		$250,000

Book value per share:
Preferred, $23,000 ÷ 1,000 shares = $23
Common, $250,000 ÷ 10,000 shares = $25

Book value per share has limited significance because it has no necessary relationship to market value. Because it is a low conservative amount (historical cost basis) some persons consider a market value below book value to imply underpriced shares.

INTERPRETING RATIOS

In using ratios computed by others, one must realize that the computation of a particular ratio is not standardized. Neither the accounting profession nor security analysts have prescribed the manner in which a ratio should be computed (except for earnings per share). Thus, each user of a financial statement should compute the various ratios in accordance with the specific objectives in mind. There are no agreed-upon standards in this respect. As a consequence, before relying on a ratio or a series of ratios, the user should be informed as to the basic computational approach used. The discussions and illustrations in this section follow the approaches commonly used.

Ratio analyses, along the lines discussed in the preceding paragraphs, catch the attention of many people; however, ratios pose significant interpretative problems to the user. To evaluate a ratio, it must be compared, at least in the mind of the user, with some *standard* that represents an optimal or desirable level. For example, the return-on-investment ratio may be compared with a long-range objective expressed in this manner. Some ratios, by their characteristics, are unfavorable if they are *either* too high or too low. For example, in a certain company a working capital ratio of approximately 2:1 may be considered optimal. In this situation, a ratio of 1:1 would tend to indicate a danger of being unable to meet maturing obligations, whereas, a ratio of 3:1 may indicate that excess funds are being left idle rather than being employed profitably. Furthermore, an optimal ratio for one company frequently will not be the same as the optimal ratio for another company. Thus, comparisons of ratios among companies frequently are of questionable validity, particularly when there are important differences among companies, such as industry and nature of operations.

Another limitation is that most ratios represent *averages* and, therefore, may tend to obscure large variations in the underlying causative factors above and below the average.

In view of these difficulties there are four types of "standards" against which ratios and percents frequently are compared:

1. **Comparison of the current ratios with the historical ratios of the same company**—Particular attention is given to changes in the *trend* of each ratio over time.
2. **Experience of the analyst who has a subjective feel for the right relationships in a given situation**—These subjective judgments of an experienced and competent observer tend to be more reliable than purely mechanical comparisons.
3. **Comparison of the present ratios with planned goals and objectives expressed as ratios**—Many companies prepare comprehensive profit plans (i.e., budgets) on a continuing basis that incorporate realistic plans for the future. These plans generally incorporate planned goals for significant ratios, such as profit margin and return on investment. These internally developed standards clearly have less inherent difficulties than any of the other comparisons; however, they seldom are available to external parties.
4. **Comparison with external standards**—These comparisons include the use of ratios and percents from other similar companies and from industry averages. Industry averages are published by many trade associations, governmental agencies, and others. For example, a variety of ratios will be found in the publications of Dun & Bradstreet, Inc., Moody's *Manual of Investments,* and Standard and Poor's *Corporation Records.*

SUMMARY

In summary, interpretation of amounts reported on financial statements may be enhanced by expressing certain relationships as ratios or percents. Although a great many ratios can be calculated, a few usually will suffice for a given decision that is under consideration. Having selected the relevant ratios, the analyst has the central problem of evaluating the results. This evaluation involves the task of selecting one or more realistic standards with which to compare the results. Four types of standards frequently are used: (1) historical standards, (2) experience, (3) planned standards, and (4) external standards. Experience and competence are particularly important. The interpretation of ratios often may suggest strengths and weaknesses in the operations and/or the financial position of the company that should be accorded in-depth investigation and evaluation if significant decisions are contemplated.

Selected ratios commonly are presented in published financial statements. For example, the ten-year summary shown in Exhibit 16–4 reports the following ratios: (1) earnings per share, (2) return on shareholders'

EXHIBIT 16–4
ABBOTT LABORATORIES AND SUBSIDIARIES
Ten-year Summary of Selected Financial Data

TEN-YEAR SUMMARY OF SELECTED FINANCIAL DATA

ABBOTT LABORATORIES AND SUBSIDIARIES

MILLIONS OF DOLLARS YEAR ENDED DECEMBER 31	1979	1978	1977	1976	1975	1974	1973	1972	1971	1970
SUMMARY OF OPERATIONS										
Net sales	$1,683.2	1,445.0	1,245.0	1,084.9	940.7	765.4	620.4	521.8	458.1	457.5
Cost of products sold	$ 943.5	810.2	694.5	614.1	527.2	419.6	331.2	275.8	248.4	214.7
Research and development	$ 85.4	76.2	66.7	59.6	50.6	42.2	36.3	31.2	28.8	26.9
Selling, general and administrative	$ 379.6	331.8	291.0	264.8	245.8	209.7	176.5	150.3	141.8	138.2
Interest expense	$ 40.2	31.1	31.6	28.2	29.9	24.9	13.8	9.5	8.7	6.4
Interest and dividend income	$ (36.8)	(27.4)	(20.1)	(15.9)	(11.0)	(7.6)	(4.6)	(1.5)	(1.5)	(1.1)
Other (income) expense	$ (5.4)	(10.6)	(2.1)	(3.9)	(4.2)	(3.1)	(1.5)	(3.6)	(1.7)	(0.1)
Earnings before taxes	$ 276.7	233.7	183.4	138.0	102.4	79.7	68.7	60.1	33.6	72.5
Taxes on earnings	$ 97.7	85.1	65.6	45.5	31.7	24.7	22.7	20.7	10.2	32.5
Net earnings	$ 179.0	148.6	117.8	92.5	70.7	55.0	46.0	39.4	23.4(b)	40.0
Earnings per share (in dollars)(a)	$ 2.97	2.48	1.98	1.63	1.28	1.00	.84	.72	.43(b)	.73
FINANCIAL POSITION										
Current assets	$ 805.4	667.5	590.4	563.6	475.2	445.1	354.7	270.7	233.9	230.1
Current liabilities	$ 525.5	421.4	336.0	259.1	256.7	219.0	210.6	128.0	84.0	118.2
Working capital	$ 279.9	246.1	254.4	304.5	218.5	226.1	144.1	142.7	149.9	111.9
Property and equipment—net	$ 467.0	403.5	365.5	331.5	309.7	279.3	250.7	233.4	219.2	200.8
Long-term debt	$ 210.4	186.0	183.5	198.2	214.9	201.6	97.6	91.7	90.2	47.2
Shareholders' investment	$ 896.0	773.5	663.7	574.9	413.0	362.5	325.8	293.4	267.5	258.8
Return on shareholders' investment	% 21.4	20.7	19.0	18.7	18.3	16.0	14.9	14.1	8.9	16.2
Book value per share (in dollars)(a)	$ 14.86	12.88	11.19	9.75	7.56	6.65	5.98	5.40	4.95	4.79
OTHER STATISTICS										
Capital expenditures—net	$ 103.4	74.1	61.5	48.3	52.1	46.6	33.5	28.8	31.6	27.9
Depreciation & amortization	$ 39.9	36.1	27.5	26.5	21.6	18.0	16.2	14.7	13.2	12.3
Dividends declared per common share (in dollars)(a)	$ 1.00	.78	.575	.455	.38	.33	.30	.275	.275	.275
Common shares outstanding (in thousands)(a)	60,295	60,078	59,291	58,958	54,614	54,494	54,494	54,284	54,064	54,024
Number of common shareholders	25,058	24,852	22,669	22,305	21,905	21,565	21,372	21,336	21,252	21,004
Number of employees	27,765	27,003	26,102	25,444	23,699	22,829	21,320	19,213	18,386	18,394
Sales per employee (in dollars)	$ 60,622	53,510	47,700	42,640	39,690	33,530	29,100	27,160	24,920	24,870

Notes:
(a) On July 25, 1975 and April 21, 1978, the Company effected common stock splits by means of share-for-share stock dividends. All per share data have been adjusted to reflect the above-mentioned common stock splits.

(b) The results of operations for 1971 were adversely affected by, among other things, the March 1971 recall of the Company's domestic intravenous solutions products and temporary restriction on their manufacture and sale. Special one-time expenses directly related to the recall were approximately $19 million before taxes, or 18 cents per common share after taxes. Earnings also suffered from the loss of sales resulting from these restrictions.

equity, and (3) book value per share. Ratios frequently are presented in graphic format in published financial statements.

IMPORTANT TERMS DEFINED IN THE CHAPTER (with page citations)

Comparative financial
  statements—707
Long-term summaries—708
Ratio or percentage analysis—
  709, 722
Component percentages—710
Tests of profitability—712
Return on owners' investment—
  712
Return on total investment—713
Financial leverage—713
Earnings per share (EPS)—714
Profit margin—715
Tests of liquidity—716
Working capital ratio—716
Quick ratio—716
Receivable turnover—717

Turnover ratio—717
Average age of receivables—717
Inventory turnover—718
Average days' supply in
  inventory—718
Tests of solvency and equity
  position—718
Debt-equity ratio—719
Owners' equity to total equities—
  719
Creditors' equity to total
  equities—719
Market tests—720
Price/earnings ratio—720
Dividend yield ratio—721
Book value per share—721

QUESTIONS FOR DISCUSSION

1. What are the three fundamental uses of external financial statements by decision makers?

2. What are some of the primary items on financial statements about which creditors are concerned?

3. Explain why the notes to the financial statements are particularly important in use and interpretation.

4. What is the primary purpose of comparative financial statements?

5. Why are statement users especially interested in financial summaries covering a number of years? What is the primary limitation of long-term summaries?

6. Explain what is meant by ratio analysis. Why are ratio analyses useful?

7. What are component percentages? Why are component percentages useful?

8. Explain the two concepts of return on investment.

9. What is financial leverage?

10. Is profit margin a useful measure of profitability? Explain.

11. Contrast the working capital ratio with the quick ratio.

12. What does the debt/equity ratio reflect?

13. Explain what is meant by the term "market tests."

14. What are the primary problems in using ratios?

EXERCISES

E16–1. The comparative financial statements prepared at December 31, 1982, for Doan Company reflected the following data (summarized):

(Relates to Exercise 16–1)

	1982	1981
Income statement:		
Sales	$150,000*	$140,000
Cost of goods sold	90,000	85,000
Gross margin	60,000	55,000
Operating expenses and interest expense	43,000	40,500
Pretax income	17,000	14,500
Income tax	5,000	4,500
Net income	$ 12,000	$ 10,000
Balance sheet:		
Cash	$ 8,000	$ 11,000
Accounts receivable (net)	12,000	14,000
Inventory	30,000	28,000
Operational assets (net)	50,000	43,000
	$100,000	$ 96,000
Current liabilities (no interest)	$ 15,000	$ 17,000
Long-term liabilities (10% interest)	35,000	35,000
Common stock (par $10)	40,000	40,000
Retained earnings†	10,000	4,000
	$100,000	$ 96,000

* One third were credit sales.
† During 1982, cash dividends amounting to $6,000 were declared and paid.

Required:

a. Complete the following columns for each item in the above comparative financial statements:

Increase (decrease)
1982 over 1981

Amount	*Percent*

b. Respond to the following:
   1. What were the percentage increases in sales, net income, cash, inventory, liabilities, and owners' equity?
   2. By what amount did working capital change?
   3. Did the average income tax rate change? What was the percentage change in the rate?
   4. What was the amount of cash inflow from revenues for 1982?
   5. Did the average markup realized on goods sold change?
   6. Did the book value per share change?

E16–2. Use the data given in Exercise 16–1 for Doan Company.

Required:

a. Present component percentages for 1982 only.
b. Respond to the following for 1982:
   1. What was the average percentage markup on sales?
   2. What was the average income tax rate?
   3. What was the profit margin? Is it a good or poor indicator of performance? Explain.

4. What percent of total resources was invested in operational assets?
5. What was the debt/equity ratio? Does it look good or bad? Explain.
6. What was the return on owners' equity?
7. What was the return on total equities?
8. What was the financial leverage factor? Was it positive or negative? Explain.
9. What was the book value per share?

E16–3. Use the data given in Exercise 16–1 for Doan Company. Use a separate sheet and complete the following tabulation for 1982 only (assume a common stock price of $33 per share); compute the ratios which should be included under each category:

Name and Computation of the Ratio (show computations)	Brief Explanation of the Ratio
A. *Tests of profitability:* (1) Return on stock-holders' investment (2) Etc.	
B. *Tests of liquidity:* (1) Working capital ratio (2) Etc.	
C. *Tests of solvency and equity position:* (1) Debt/equity ratio (2) Etc.	
D. *Market tests:* (1) Price/earnings ratio (2) Etc.	
E. *Miscellaneous ratio:* (1) Book value per share	

E16–4. Match the following by entering the appropriate letters in the blanks.

(Relates to Exercise 16–4)

Ratio or percent	Computation
_____ Profit margin	A. Income + Interest expense (net of tax) ÷ Total assets
_____ Inventory turnover ratio	B. Income (before extraordinary items) ÷ Net sales
_____ Average collection period	C. Days in year ÷ Receivable turnover
_____ Creditors' equity to total equities	D. Income ÷ Average owners' equity
_____ Dividend yield ratio	E. Income ÷ Average number of shares of common stock outstanding
_____ Return on owners' investment	F. Return on owners' equity − Return on total assets
_____ Working capital ratio	G. Quick assets ÷ Current liabilities
_____ Debt/equity ratio	H. Current assets ÷ Current liabilities
_____ Price/earnings ratio	I. Cost of goods sold ÷ Average inventory
_____ Financial leverage	J. Net credit sales ÷ Average net receivables
_____ Receivable turnover ratio	K. Creditors' equity (debt) ÷ Total equities
_____ Average days' supply of inventory	L. Days in year ÷ Inventory turnover
_____ Owners' equity to total equities	M. Total liabilities ÷ Owners' equity
_____ Earnings per share	N. Dividends per share ÷ Market price per share
_____ Return on total investment	O. Owners' equity ÷ Total equities
_____ Quick ratio	P. Current market price per share ÷ Earnings per share
_____ Book value per share	Q. Owners' equity ÷ Shares outstanding

E16–5. Situation A—Current assets totaled to $60,000 and the working capital ratio was 2.00. Assume the following transactions were completed: (1) purchased merchandise for $3,000 of which ⅓ was on short-term credit and (2) purchased a delivery truck for $8,000 paid $2,000 cash and signed a two-year interest bearing note for the balance.

Compute the cumulative working capital ratio after each transaction.

Situation B—Sales for the year amounted to $600,000 of which one half was on credit. The average gross margin rate was 40 percent on sales. Account balances were:

	Beginning	Ending
Accounts receivable (net)	$30,000	$20,000
Inventory	20,000	16,000

Compute the turnover for accounts receivable and inventory, the average age of the receivables and the average day's supply of inventory.

Situation C—The financial statements reported the following at year-end:

Total assets	$100,000
Total debt (10% interest)	60,000
Net income (average tax rate 20%)	12,000

Compute the financial leverage and indicate whether it is positive or negative.

E16–6. Ryan Retail Company has just prepared the comparative annual financial statements for 1982.

(Relates to Exercise 16–6)

RYAN RETAIL COMPANY
Income Statement
For the Years Ended December 31, 1982, and 1981

		For the year ended	
		1982	1981
Sales (one half on credit)		$100,000	$ 95,000
Cost of goods sold		48,000	46,000
Gross margin		52,000	49,000
Expenses (including $3,000 interest expense each year)		34,000	33,000
Pretax income		18,000	16,000
Income tax on operations (22%)		3,960	3,520
Income before extraordinary items ..		14,040	12,480
Extraordinary loss	$3,000		
Less income tax saved	660	2,340	
Extraordinary gain		$1,000	
Applicable income tax		220	780
Net income		$ 11,700	$ 13,260

Balance Sheet
At December 31, 1982, and 1981

	1982	1981
Assets		
Cash	$ 47,200	$ 20,000
Accounts receivable (net) (terms 1/10, n/30)	35,000	30,000
Inventory	30,000	40,000
Operational assets (net)	90,000	100,000
Total assets	$202,200	$190,000

(continued)   *Liabilities*

Accounts payable	$ 60,000	$ 50,000
Income tax payable	1,500	1,000
Note payable, long term	25,000	25,000

Stockholders' Equity

Capital stock (par $10)	80,000	80,000
Retained earnings	35,700	34,000
Total liabilities and stockholders' equity	$202,200	$190,000

Required (round percents and ratios to two places):

a. Compute for 1982 the tests of (1) profitability, (2) liquidity, (3) solvency, and (4) market. Assume the quoted price of the stock was $26.50 for 1982. Dividends declared and paid during 1982 amounted to $10,000.

b. Respond to the following for 1982:

1. What were the percentage changes in sales, income before extraordinary items, net income, cash, inventory, and debt?
2. What appears to be the pretax interest rate on the note payable?

c. Identify at least two problems of the company suggested by your responses to *(a)* and *(b)*.

PROBLEMS

P16–1. Speedy Sales Corporation had just completed the comparative statements for the year ended December 31, 1982. At this point, certain analytical and interpretative procedures are to be undertaken. The completed statements (summarized) are as follows:

Income statement:

	1982	1981
Sales	$400,000*	$390,000
Cost of goods sold	220,000	218,000
Gross margin	180,000	172,000
Operating expenses (including interest on bonds)	147,000	148,000
Pretax income	33,000	24,000
Income tax	9,000	7,000
Net income	$ 24,000	$ 17,000

Balance sheet:

Cash	$ 5,400	$ 2,700
Accounts receivable (net)	44,000	30,000
Merchandise inventory	30,000	24,000
Prepaid expenses	600	500
Operational assets (net)	120,000	130,000
	$200,000	$187,200
Accounts payable	$ 19,000	$ 20,000
Income tax payable	1,000	1,200
Bonds payable (10% interest rate)	50,000	50,000
Common stock (par $10)	100,000†	100,000
Retained earnings‡	30,000	16,000
	$200,000	$187,200

* Twenty-five percent were credit sales.
† The market price of the stock at the end of 1982 was $24 per share.
‡ During 1982 the company declared and paid a cash dividend of $10,000.

Required:

a. Complete a tabulation similar to the following (show computations, round percents and ratios to two places):

Name and Computation of the 1982 Ratio	Brief Explanation of the Ratio
Tests of profitability: (1) Return on stockholders investment (2) Etc. *Tests of liquidity:* (1) Working capital ratio (2) Etc. *Tests of solvency and equity position:* (1) Debt/equity ratio (2) Etc. *Market tests:* (1) Price earnings ratio (2) Etc.	

b. Respond to the following for 1982:
   1. Evaluate the financial leverage amount and explain what it means by using the computed amount(s).
   2. Evaluate the profit margin amount and explain how a shareholder might use it.
   3. Explain to a shareholder why the working capital ratio and the quick ratio are different. Do you observe and liquidity problems? Explain.

4. Assuming credit terms are 1/10, n/30, do you perceive an unfavorable situation related to credit sales? Explain.

P16–2. The information given was taken at the bottom of the page from the annual financial statements of OK Company, which started business January 1, 19A (assume account balances only in Cash and Capital Stock on this date; all amounts are in thousands of dollars).

Required (show computations and round to two decimal places):

a. Complete a tabulation similar to the tabulation on page 731.
b. Evaluate the results of the three related ratios 1, 2, and 3, to identify the favorable or unfavorable factors. Give your recommendations.
c. Evaluate the results of the last four ratios (4, 5, 6, and 7) and identify any favorable or unfavorable factors. Give your recommendations.

(Relates to Problem 16–2)

	19A	19B	19C	19D
Accounts receivable (net) (terms, n/30)	$ 8	$10	$ 16	$ 22
Merchandise inventory	10	12	20	25
Net sales (¾ on credit)	40	60	100	120
Cost of goods sold	26	36	64	80
Net income (loss)	(10)	6	14	10

(Relates to Problem 16–2)

Items	19A	19B	19C	19D
1. Profit margin—percent				
2. Gross margin—ratio				
3. Expenses as a percent of sales excluding cost of goods sold				
4. Inventory turnover				
5. Day's supply in inventory				
6. Receivable turnover				
7. Average days to collect				

P16–3. The 1982 financial statements for two companies are summarized below:

(Relates to Problem 16–3)

	Able Company	Baker Company
Balance sheet:		
Cash	$ 25,000	$ 11,000
Accounts receivable, net	30,000	17,000
Inventory	80,000	20,000
Operational assets, net	125,000	300,000
Other assets	40,000	252,000
Total assets	$300,000	$600,000
Current liabilities	$ 90,000	$ 40,000
Long-term debt (10%)	50,000	60,000
Capital stock, par $10	120,000	400,000
Contributed capital in excess of par	10,000	60,000
Retained earnings	30,000	40,000
Total liabilities and owners' equity	$300,000	$600,000
Income statement:		
Sales (on credit)	(⅓) $600,000	(⅑) $900,000
Cost of goods sold	(350,000)	(450,000)
Expenses (including interest and income tax)	(205,000)	(360,000)
Net income	$ 45,000	$ 90,000
Selected data from the 1981 statements:		
Accounts receivable, net	$ 25,000	$ 19,000
Inventory	70,000	24,000
Long-term debt	50,000	60,000
Other data:		
Per share price at end of 1982 (offering price)	$ 30	$ 18
Average income tax rate	30%	30%
Dividends declared and paid in 1982	$ 25,800	$150,400

Able and Baker companies are in the same line of business and are direct competitors in a large metropolitan area. They have been in business approximately ten years, and each has experienced a relatively steady growth. The two managements have essentially different viewpoints in many respects; however, Baker is considered to be the more conservative and, as the president said, "We avoid what we consider to be undue risks." Neither company is publicly held. Able Company has an annual audit by a CPA.

portunity to purchase 10 percent of the shares in one or the other company at the per share prices given above. Your client has decided to invest in one of the companies. Based on the data given, prepare a comparative evaluation of the ratio analyses (and any other available information) and give your recommended choice with the supporting explanation.

P16–4. The 1982 financial statements for two companies are summarized below:

(Relates to Problem 16–4)

	Doe Company	Roe Company
Balance sheet:		
Cash	$ 20,000	$ 40,000
Accounts receivable, net	60,000	10,000
Inventory	120,000	30,000
Operational assets, net	500,000	150,000
Other assets	155,000	54,000
Total	$855,000	$284,000
Current liabilities	$100,000	$ 20,000
Long-term debt (10%)	200,000	50,000
Capital stock, par $10	500,000	200,000
Contributed capital in excess of par	25,000	2,000
Retained earnings	30,000	12,000
Total	$855,000	$284,000
Income statement:		
Sales (on credit)	($\frac{1}{2}$) $900,000	($\frac{1}{3}$) $300,000
Cost of goods sold	(522,000)	(180,000)
Expenses (including interest and income tax)	(288,000)	(84,000)
Net income	$ 90,000	$ 36,000
Selected data from the 1981 statements:		
Accounts receivable, net	$ 40,000	$ 14,000
Long-term debt (10% interest)	200,000	50,000
Inventory	100,000	40,000
Other data:		
Per share price at end of 1982	$ 12.75	$ 10.50
Average income tax rate	30%	20%
Dividends paid in 1982	$ 40,000	$ 10,000

Required:

a. Complete a schedule that reflects a ratio analysis of each company. As a minimum, compute the 15 ratios discussed in the chapter.

b. Assume a client of yours has the op-

These two companies are in the same line of business and in the same state but in different cities. Each company has been in existence for approximately ten years. Doe Company is audited by one of the "big-8" accounting firms and Roe Company is audited by a local accounting firm. Both companies received an unqualified opinion (i.e., the independent auditors found nothing wrong) on the financial statements. Doe Company wants to borrow $75,000 cash, and Roe Company needs $30,000. The loans will be for a two-year period and are needed for "working capital purposes."

Required:

a. Complete a schedule that reflects a ratio analysis of each company. As a minimum compute the 15 ratios discussed in the chapter.

b. Assume you work in the loan department of a local bank. You have been asked to analyze the situation and recommend which loan is preferable. Based on the data given, your analysis

prepared in *(a)*, and any other information give your choice and the supporting explanation.

P16–5. Refer to financial statements of J. C. Penney Company, Inc., given in Chapter 2. Obtain per share data from the *Wall Street Journal* or estimate what you deem to be a realistic price.

Required:

a. Compute each of the 15 ratios (for the year ended January 26, 1980) listed in the chapter. If you are unable to compute a particular ratio, explain why.

b. Evaluate the ratios and identify any potential problems that you think exist. Comment on any suggestions you may have.

Financial reporting and changing prices

PURPOSE OF THIS CHAPTER

In recent years a characteristic of the economy of the United States (and practically all other countries) has been significantly increasing prices of most commodities and services. This fact has important, and often adverse, effects on most people because the price increases are not uniform among different goods, services, and individuals. Therefore, some groups suffer more from inflation than other groups. Also, measurements of economic events and effects in terms of the monetary unit (dollars in the United States) become distorted. For example, from 1967 to 1979 the dollar declined in **purchasing power** (i.e., its command over real goods and services) by approximately 130 percent; that is, in 1979 it required more than two dollars to purchase what one dollar would purchase in 1967.

The rapid and continuing increase in the rate of inflation has caused most users of financial statements to question the dollar measurements of assets, liabilities, revenues, and expenses reported in the traditional historical cost (HC) basis financial statements. In periods of inflation, such financial statements typically consist of aggregated amounts which include dollars from a number of different years, each of which is dollars·of a different purchasing power. This aggregation of "apples and oranges" tends to produce unrealistic measurements of accounting values.

The impact of inflation upon HC basis financial statements is difficult to assess by statement users, particularly when the related price change information is not reported. Many accountants, economists, governmental agencies, and persons in business are not in agreement as to what should be done to make the financial statements more useful under conditions of significant price changes.

For financial reporting purposes and analysis of the nature of price changes of commodities and services, two distinctly different price-level changes usually are identified, viz:

1. **General price level changes**—These changes occur when the general level (i.e., the average) of the prices of commodities and services changes, which means that the purchasing power (i.e., command over goods and services) of the monetary unit changes. Such changes are characterized as **inflation** when the general price level increases (i.e., the purchasing power of the monetary unit decreases) and **deflation** when the general price level decreases (i.e., the purchasing power of the monetary unit increases). Part A of this chapter discusses general price level (GPL) changes.

2. **Specific price level changes**—These changes occur when the price of a **specific** commodity or service changes at a rate that is higher or lower than the general price level change. Such changes cause **real value changes.** Part B of this chapter discusses current cost (CC), which involves the reporting of real value changes.

This chapter discusses the economic effects of price changes and the two reporting approaches which were initiated recently by the accounting profession to improve the quality of financial statements under conditions of significant price changes. To discuss the issues and approaches, this chapter is divided into two parts as follows:

Part A: Reporting general price level (GPL) changes

Part B: Reporting current cost (CC) changes

Behavioral and learning objectives for this chapter are provided in the *Teachers Manual.*

PART A: REPORTING GENERAL PRICE LEVEL (GPL) CHANGES

Reporting the effects of general price level (GPL) changes on financial statements requires that the traditional historical cost (HC) basis financial statements be **restated** from that basis to the latest **GPL dollars** (often called common or current dollars). This restatement requires use of **general price level (GPL) index numbers.**[1]

USING PRICE LEVEL INDEX NUMBERS

Price level index numbers must be used to develop financial statement amounts which are restated for price changes. A price level index is a

---

[1] Throughout this chapter the descriptive term *restated* is used because the HC basis amounts simply are restated to current GPL dollars. Alternatively, the term *adjusted* sometimes is used. It is less descriptive and suggests the notion of "adjusting" entries, which is based on a completely different concept.

statistical value that expresses the relative price level of each of a series of periods. To construct a price level index, the prices of one specific item, or a group of items, for a number of periods are expressed in relative terms as a series of index numbers. A base year is selected and assigned the base index value of 100. Subsequent changes in prices are expressed in relationship to this base. Two kinds of indexes are used widely:

1. **General price level (GPL) index**—A GPL price index is computed on the basis of an average "market basket" of commodities and services. The average index is computed by collecting the prices of each of the many items that make up the average market basket. Each period the average price of the basket is computed and then related to the base year index of 100. A GPL index is intended to measure **general inflation** (cheaper dollars) and **general deflation** (dearer dollars). A GPL index is used in accounting to measure the effects of general price level (GPL) changes and to restate the financial statements to the latest GPL (common) dollar basis. To illustrate, assume a tract of land was purchased in 1967 at a cost of $10,000 when the GPL index was 100. It is now the end of 1979, the land is still owned, and the GPL index is 229.9 (a decline in purchasing power of 130 percent). The $10,000 cost of the land would be reported on a **GPL restated balance sheet** at $10,000 × 229.9/100 = $22,990.[2]

2. **Specific price level index**—A specific price level index is computed in the same manner as a GPL index except that it is related to a **single item** (or group of homogeneous items). Specific price index values often are used to estimate the current replacement cost of **specific** commodities or services. To illustrate, assume the land example given in 1 above (cost, $10,000) has a **specific** price index of 240 at the end of 1979. The estimated current replacement cost of the land could be computed as $10,000 × 240/100 = $24,000. This indicates that the specific value of the land increased by $14,000, which was more than the GPL increase of $12,990. A specific price index does not measure **general** inflation; rather, it measures the change in price of the specific item to which it relates. Use of specific index numbers is illustrated in Part B of this chapter.

The pervasiveness of **general inflation** (i.e., as indicated by a GPL index) in recent years is reflected in the following selected index values from the Consumer Price Index for all Urban Consumers (CPI-U), which is a widely used GPL index in accounting:

---

[2] The two GPL index series usually used are the Gross National Product Deflator (which is published quarterly) and the Consumer Price Index for all Urban Consumers (CPI-U) (which is published monthly). Both indexes are published by the U.S. Department of Labor.

	CPI-U index*	
Year	Average for the Year	At Year-end
1967 (base year)	100.0	
1970	116.3	
1971	121.3	
1972	125.3	
1973	133.1	
1974	147.7	
1975	161.2	166.3
1976	170.5	174.3
1977	181.5	186.1
1978	195.4	202.9
1979	217.4	229.9

* Source: Economic Indicators Joint Economic Committee, U.S. Government Printing Office (monthly).

Another application of the GPL index may be illustrated by indicating the effect of general inflation on the cost of attending college. In 1967 the average cost of attending "State University" for two semesters was $4,000 per student. This amount included all typical costs such as housing, food, modest recreation, fees, tuition, books, and travel. Using the CPI-U index amounts given above, general inflation would increase the total cost as follows:

Year	CPI-U index (average)	Restatement computation	Average cost per student
1967	100.0		$4,000
1970	116.3	$4,000 × 116.3/100.0 =	4,652
1975	161.2	$4,000 × 161.2/100.0 =	6,448
1979	217.4	$4,000 × 217.4/100.0 =	8,696

THE STABLE MONETARY UNIT ASSUMPTION

In Chapter 2 (page 65) one of the underlying assumptions of GAAP was identified as the **unit-of-measure assumption,** which states: "With many diverse items and transactions to be accounted for, it is necessary that a single unit of measure be adopted. Accounting assumes the monetary unit—the dollar—as the common denominator in the measurement process." Implicit in this assumption is that the dollar has a constant value, which is a necessary measurement characteristic (a "meterstick" is always one meter long!). However, when there is inflation or deflation, the constant value assumption breaks down—the monetary unit literally becomes a "rubber" measuring unit (it stretches and contracts).

The dollar is the common denominator used for accounting measurements because it is used by the society as a measure of value. That is, the dollar will command a certain amount of real goods and services in the marketplace at a given time. Unfortunately, the dollar, or any monetary unit, does not maintain a stable value in terms of the real goods and services it can command.

Over time, one unit of money (e.g., one dollar) will command fewer goods and services in the case of inflation or, alternatively, more goods and services in the case of deflation; that is, its purchasing power changes. In applying the GAAP concept of historical cost (i.e., the cost principle), transactions are recorded in the accounts and reported subsequently on the financial statements in historical cost basis dollars. Some of those dollar amounts (such as the cost of an old operational asset) remain in the accounts and are reported in the financial statements over many years. Thus, over a period of time, the accounting system accumulates and reports dollars that have different purchasing power, given inflation or deflation. Under the GAAP concept of HC, dollars having different real values are **aggregated** on the balance sheet and **matched** on the income statement. Thus, during periods of significant inflation or deflation, the accounting amounts are apt to reflect considerable distortion because of the effects of the changing value of the monetary unit.

To illustrate, assume a company purchased a building for $200,000 when the GPL index was 100. Assuming straight-line depreciation, no residual value, and a 40-year life, the annual depreciation would be $5,000 per year. Let's assume that the current year is Year 30 (since acquisition) and that the current GPL index is 300. At the end of Year 30, the financial statements would show the following amounts, based on historical cost (HC) as recorded in the accounting system:

```
Balance sheet:
  Operational assets:
    Building (at cost) ...........................   $200,000
    Accumulated depreciation
      ($5,000 × 30 years) .......................    150,000
        Carrying value .........................              $50,000

Income statement:
  Depreciation expense .........................              5,000
```

All of the amounts shown above represent dollars "valued" at acquisition date (30 years earlier). Those dollars had a purchasing power equivalent of 100 (the GPL index). With the current GPL index at 300, these amounts are aggregated with other dollar amounts which have different purchasing power equivalents. On the income statement, depreciation expense, expressed in dollars of acquisition cost (index 100), are matched with revenue, which is in current dollars (index 300). The current GPL index of 300 means that each current dollar will command (buy) only one third (i.e., 100/300) as much real goods and services as when the index was 100. One could **restate** the above amounts in common dollars for the GPL change (inflation in this case). The restatement can be accomplished by multiplying the HC amount by a **GPL index ratio.** Using the data given above, the GPL index ratio would be 300/100, or 3.00. Multiplication of the historical dollar amounts by the GPL index ratio raises the HC basis amount to the current GPL basis. The calculations and the resultant GPL restated amounts for the data given above would be as follows:

Item	HC basis	Restatement computation		GPL restated amount
Balance sheet amounts:				
Operational assets:				
Building	$200,000	× 300/100	=	$600,000
Accumulated depreciation	150,000	× 300/100	=	450,000
Carrying value	$ 50,000	× 300/100	=	$150,000
Income statement amount:				
Depreciation expense...........	$ 5,000	× 300/100	=	$ 15,000

If all the other revenues and expenses already were expressed in current GPL dollars, the effect of this increase in depreciation expense would be to decrease reported pretax income by $10,000.

CONCEPTS UNDERLYING GPL RESTATEMENT OF THE FINANCIAL STATEMENTS

GPL restatement of financial statements does not involve the recording of entries in the journal and ledger; rather, it is a **supplementary reporting approach.** The traditional HC basis financial statements are prepared each period in accordance with GAAP. The HC statements continue as the basic periodic reports of the entity. When GPL restatement is used, the HC basis financial statements simply are restated in current end-of-the-period dollars (usually called GPL restated or common dollars). Thus, the GPL restated financial statements continue to be cost basis statements except that all dollar amounts are in **common dollars;** that is, current end-of-the-period GPL dollars (instead some companies prefer to use the average index amount for the period). The GPL restatement computations are simple and straightforward. They are based upon the following underlying concepts:

1. At the end of each accounting period the appropriate financial statement actual HC amounts are restated for the GPL financial statements by multiplying the HC amounts reported on the traditional financial statements by the current end-of-the-period GPL index divided by the GPL index that existed at the date of the transaction on which the item was recorded.
2. Each HC amount considered for restatement is classified as either a **monetary item** or a **nonmonetary item.** The **monetary items are not**

restated on the GPL financial statements, while the **nonmonetary items are restated** on the GPL financial statements.

3. The **monetary** items cause a "GPL purchasing power gain (loss) on monetary items" during each period in which there is inflation or deflation. This gain or loss is measured as the difference between the actual HC basis amount and the restated amount of each monetary item. It is reported on the GPL income statement.

4. The **nonmonetary** items do not cause GPL gains or losses. The differences between their actual HC basis amounts and the GPL restated amounts often are referred to as **fictional changes.** These differences are not reported on the GPL financial statements because they are not **real value** changes; they simply represent the number of dollars which is necessary to keep up with inflation (or deflation).

Each of these underlying concepts is discussed and illustrated in the remainder of Part A of this chapter.

GPL RESTATEMENT—ILLUSTRATIVE CASE

A simplified situation is used as the basis for discussing and illustrating the four underlying concepts, and the related computations, used to develop the amounts reported on a **GPL RESTATED** set of financial statements.[3]

Assume ACE Corporation was organized January 1, 19A, at which time the GPL index was 120. The accounting period ends December 31 and the company develops its financial statements following GAAP; that is, it prepares the conventional HC basis financial statements. Restatement of the HC financial statements of ACE Corporation to a GPL restated basis is discussed and illustrated in the paragraphs to follow. Exhibit 17–1 presents the following 19A data for ACE Corporation:

1. All transactions completed during 19A (summarized) and the GPL index at the date of each transaction.
2. Balance sheet at December 31, 19A (HC basis).
3. Income statement for the year ended December 31, 19A (HC basis).
4. Statement of retained earnings at December 31, 19A (HC basis).
5. Selected GPL index data during 19A.

Monetary and nonmonetary items

Restatement of HC basis financial statements to a GPL restated basis requires that a careful distinction be maintained between two distinctly different types of items on the financial statements. These two types are

---

[3] The illustrative situation for ACE Corporation is simplified by using small amounts, GPL index computations that result in even $10, a small number of accounts and, most importantly, it is limited to the first year's operations. The latter simplification avoids the complexities of comparative statements (which involve only arithmetical computations rather than any additional concepts) and, therefore, enables us to concentrate on the basic concepts of reporting under conditions of changing prices.

known as **monetary items** and **nonmonetary items.** They cause significantly different economic effects on their holder (owner) when the real value of the monetary unit (the dollar) changes (i.e., inflation or deflation occurs).

Monetary items may be either assets or liabilities (but not revenues or expenses). Their basic characteristic is that they have dollar amounts which by their nature, or by contract, are fixed in terms of the number of dollars they will represent in the future. Cash and receivables are monetary assets because their dollar amounts in the future are fixed and those amounts (i.e., the number of dollars they will command) are totally unaffected by inflation or deflation: A dollar held through a period of inflation is still a dollar, although it will command fewer real goods at the end of the period. A receivable of a given amount, held through a period of inflation, will continue to call for the same number of dollars (although the dollars at the later date will command fewer real goods). Therefore, monetary **assets** cannot be restated on the GPL financial statements; however, during a period of inflation the holder (owner) will incur a **real purchasing power loss** because the holder will end with a "cheaper" dollar. This loss usually is called "GPL purchasing power loss on monetary assets."

Liabilities are monetary items because their dollar amounts in the future remain constant and those amounts (i.e., the number of dollars they will command) are totally unaffected by inflation or deflation. A dollar owed through a period of inflation is still a dollar owed, although it will command fewer real goods at the end of the period. Therefore, monetary liabilities cannot be restated on the GPL financial statements; however, during a period of inflation the debtor will incur a **real purchasing power gain** because the debt will be paid with "cheaper" dollars. This gain usually is called "GPL purchasing power gain on monetary liabilities."

In summary, monetary items (i.e., monetary assets and monetary liabilities) **are not restated on the GPL financial statements and their existence can cause the holder (or debtor) to incur a real gain or loss during each period of inflation and deflation. The GPL purchasing power gain or loss on monetary items is reported on the GPL income statement.**

Observe in Exhibit 17–2 that the three **monetary items** (cash, accounts receivable, and note payable) are not restated. Also, a "GPL purchasing power loss on monetary items" of $3,050 is reported on the GPL income statement (this loss is computed in Exhibit 17–3).

Nonmonetary items may be assets, owners' equity, revenues, and expenses (but not cash, receivables, or debt). All items on the financial statements are nonmonetary except for the monetary assets and liabilities. The basic characteristics of nonmonetary items are that they have dollar amounts which are free to move up and down in respect to the number of dollars they may command in the marketplace and they do not have amounts that are fixed in the future by their nature or by contract. Nonmonetary items tend to move up and down with inflation and deflation in respect to their values in the marketplace. For example, a tract of land purchased for $6,350 (see Exhibit 17–2) when the GPL index was 127 would **tend** to increase in market value to $7,500 as a result of an increase of the GPL price index to 150 (i.e., $6,350 × 150/127 = $7,500). Thus, if this happened, the owner would **not experience a real gain** on this nonmonetary asset due to the GPL change (inflation). Under the assumption of no change in real value in this situation, the owner could sell the land that cost $6,350 for $7,500. The $7,500 then would purchase, at the date of sale of the land, the same quantity of real goods and services that the $6,350 would have bought at the earlier purchase date of the land. Of course, the land may have changed in "dollar value" more or less than the GPL, in which case there would have been a real value change (this situation is discussed later). Examples of nonmonetary items are inventories, investments in common stock, operational assets, patents, revenues, expenses, and the common stock accounts.[4]

Thus, the nonmonetary items are restated on the GPL financial statements and they do not cause the holder to incur a real gain or loss as a result of changes only in the GPL.

Observe in Exhibit 17–2 that ten **nonmonetary items** are restated on the GPL balance sheet and income statement. Also, observe that there never will be a GPL purchasing power gain or loss on the **nonmonetary** items reported on the GPL financial statements.

Exhibit 17–2 presents the GPL restatement computation for each nonmonetary item. For example, the Land account was restated as follows:

$$\text{Historical cost basis amount} \times \frac{\text{End-of-current-period index (now)}}{\text{Transaction date index (then)}} = \text{GPL restated amount}$$

$$\text{(numerator index)} \div \text{(denominator index)}$$

$$\text{Land, } \$6,350 \times \frac{150}{127} = \$7,500$$

GPL RESTATEMENT OF HC FINANCIAL STATEMENTS ILLUSTRATED

Now, let's return to our illustration of ACE Corporation and the three HC basis financial statements given in Exhibit 17–1. GPL restatement of each HC financial statement in terms of the current GPL index of 150 is shown in Exhibit 17–2.

Balance sheet restatement. The ACE Corporation balance sheet reflects three monetary items: cash, accounts receivable, and the note payable. As explained above, these three **monetary items** were not restated because each has a fixed monetary amount in the future that is not affected by

---

[4] Preferred stock usually is classified as a monetary item because it usually has a fixed redeemable value. In contrast, receivables and liabilities which can be settled with goods and services (rather than cash) are classified as nonmonetary items.

inflation or deflation. Therefore, the three monetary HC amounts were extended across on the balance sheet to the GPL restatement column. In contrast, the four nonmonetary **asset** amounts on the balance sheet were GPL restated because their future commands over real goods and services change with the GPL index. The HC basis amount of each nonmonetary asset was restated by multiplying each amount by the GPL index number at the end of the current period (150) divided by the GPL index number at the date of the transaction.

Stockholders' equity can be restated as a single balancing (plug) amount. That is, for ACE Corporation, total GPL restated assets of $124,550 — total liabilities of $40,000 = $84,550. However, it is preferable to GPL restate the capital stock accounts (which are nonmonetary items) and the statement of retained earnings. Observe on the balance sheet (Exhibit 17–2) that GPL retained earnings (ending balance) was computed as a balancing (plug) amount ($9,550), which is the same as the ending balance computed in the GPL statement of retained earnings.

Restatement of retained earnings. Retained earnings is a nonmonetary item; therefore, each amount in it is GPL restated. The beginning balance always is restated by using the ending GPL index divided by the beginning GPL index (150/120 in the illustration). Dividends declared during the period are restated. The GPL restated net income is taken directly from the GPL restated income statement ($12,550 in the illustration). The ending GPL restated balance of retained earnings ($9,550) is carried to the GPL restated balance sheet which then balances (as in the illustration at $124,550).

Restatement of the income statement. All items on the income statement are **nonmonetary;** therefore, each item is restated. The numerator is the ending GPL index, and the denominator customarily used is the average GPL index for the period because it is assumed often that the operating activities occur approximately equally during the period. Observe that depreciation expense always is restated using the same GPL index amounts that were used to restate the related asset (150/120 in the illustration). The only unique feature of the income statement is inclusion of the "GPL purchasing power gain (loss) on monetary items." This **real gain or loss** must be computed separately on the monetary assets and monetary liabilities.

Computation of GPL purchasing power gains and losses on monetary items. Computation of this real gain or loss requires restatement of each monetary asset and each monetary liability. Generally, this is the most tedious phase of GPL restatement. Of course, monetary items that have identical numerator indexes and identical denominator indexes can be grouped for computation purposes with the same results.

Computation of the GPL purchasing power gain (loss) on the monetary items for ACE Corporation is shown in Exhibit 17–3. Observe in this exhibit that the HC amount of each monetary item (first money column) is GPL restated by using the appropriate numerator and denominator in-

EXHIBIT 17–1
Historical cost basis data of Ace Corporation for the year 19A

Summary of transactions during 19A:

a. January 1, 19A: Sold and issued capital stock (nopar) for $60,000 cash (GPL index, 120).

b. January 1, 19A: Borrowed $40,000 cash from a local bank; signed a $40,000 interest-bearing note due December 31, 19C (GPL index, 120).

c. February 19A: Purchased equipment for use in the business at a cash cost of $60,000 (GPL index, 125).

d. March 19A: Purchased land for use in the business at a cash cost of $6,350 (GPL index, 127).

e. During 19A: Purchased merchandise (evenly throughout the year) at a cash cost of $121,500 (average GPL index for 19A, 135). Assume a perpetual inventory system (average costing), cost of goods sold, $108,000, and an ending inventory of $13,500 (i.e., total, $121,500).

f. During 19A: Sales revenue, $162,000, sold evenly throughout the year (average GPL index for 19A, 135). Assume total cash collections on sales of $129,600 and accounts receivable at year-end of $32,400 (i.e., total, $162,000).

g. During 19A: Expenses paid in cash $27,000, which included interest expense and income tax expense, but excluded depreciation expense (average GPL index for 19A, 135).

h. July 1, 19A: Declared and paid a cash dividend, $2,700 (GPL average index, 135).

i. December 31, 19A: Depreciation expense on equipment (estimated five-year life and no residual value), $60,000 ÷ 5 years = $12,000.

Balance sheet, at December 31, 19A (HC basis amounts):

Assets		Liabilities	
Cash	$ 12,050	Note payable, long term	$ 40,000
Accounts receivable (net)	32,400		
Inventory	13,500	*Stockholders' Equity*	
Equipment	60,000	Capital stock (nopar)	60,000
Accumulated depreciation	(12,000)	Retained earnings	12,300
Land	6,350		
Total	$112,300	Total	$112,300

Income statement, for the year ended December 31, 19A (HC basis amounts):

Sales revenue	$162,000
Cost of goods sold	(108,000)
Depreciation expense	(12,000)
Remaining expenses	(27,000)
Net income	$ 15,000

Statement of retained earnings, at December 31, 19A (HC basis amounts):

Beginning balance, January 1, 19A	$ 0
Add: Net income of 19A	15,000
Deduct: Dividends of 19A	(2,700)
Ending balance, December 31, 19A	$12,300

GPL index data during 19A:

January 1, 19A	120
Average during 19A	135
December 31, 19A	150

EXHIBIT 17–2
GPL Restatement of financial statements—Ace Corporation

	HC basis	Restatement computations	GPL restated basis
Balance sheet, at December 31, 19A:			
Assets			
Cash	$ 12,050	Monetary, not restated	$ 12,050
Accounts receivable (net)	32,400	Monetary, not restated	32,400
Inventory	13,500	Nonmonetary, $13,500 × 150/135	15,000
Equipment	60,000	Nonmonetary, $60,000 × 150/125	72,000
Accumulated depreciation (credit)	(12,000)	Nonmonetary, $12,000 × 150/125	(14,400)
Land	6,350	Nonmonetary, $6,350 × 150/127	7,500
Total	$112,300		$124,550
Liabilities			
Note payable, long term	$ 40,000	Monetary, not restated	$ 40,000
Stockholders' Equity			
Capital stock (nopar)	60,000	Nonmonetary, $60,000 × 150/120	75,000
Retained earnings	12,300	Nonmonetary, plug, $124,550 −	
		$40,000 − $75,000	9,550
Total	$112,300		$124,550
Income statement, for the year ended December 31, 19A:			
Sales revenue (credit)	$162,000	Nonmonetary, $162,000 × 150/135	$180,000
Deduct:			
Cost of goods sold	108,000	Nonmonetary, $108,000 × 150/135	120,000
Depreciation expense	12,000	Nonmonetary, $12,000 × 150/125	14,400
Remaining expenses	27,000	Nonmonetary, $27,000 × 150/135	30,000
Income from continuing operations	$ 15,000		15,600
GPL purchasing power gain (loss) on monetary items		Computed, per Exhibit 17–3	(3,050)
Income, GPL restated (common dollars)		Carry to statement of retained earnings	$ 12,550
Statement of retained earnings, at December 31, 19A:			
Beginning balance, January 1, 19A	$ -0-	Nonmonetary, $0 × 150/120	$ -0-
Add: Income of 19A	15,000	Nonmonetary, from restated income statement	12,550
Deduct: Dividends of 19A (debit)	(2,700)	Nonmonetary, $2,700 × 150/135	(3,000)
Ending balance, December 31, 19A	$ 12,300	Proof: check per balance sheet plug amount	$ 9,550

dexes. The gain or loss on each monetary item simply is the difference between its *ending* actual HC basis amount and its *ending* GPL restated amount (i.e., for cash, $12,050 − $21,500 = $9,450, loss).

In the restatement of monetary items (to compute the GPL purchasing power gain or loss), three different situations generally are encountered, viz:

1. A monetary item may reflect two or more amounts during the period at different GPL index amounts. In these situations the beginning bal-

ance of the monetary account, and each transaction in the account which involves a different GPL index number, must be GPL restated. This situation is illustrated for *Cash* in Exhibit 17–3.

EXHIBIT 17–3
Computation of purchasing power gain (loss) on monetary items—Ace Corporation

	HC basis	Restatement computations	GPL restated basis	GPL purchasing power gain (loss) on monetary items
Cash: [a]				
Beginning balance	$100,000	$100,000 × 150/120	$125,000	
Debits:				
Sales and accounts receivable	129,600	129,600 × 150/135	144,000	
Credits:				
Purchase of equipment	(60,000)	60,000 × 150/125	(72,000)	
Purchase of land	(6,350)	6,350 × 150/127	(7,500)	
Merchandise, expenses, and dividends ($121,500 + $27,000 + $2,700)	(151,200)	151,200 × 150/135	(168,000)	
Ending balance	$ 12,050		$ 21,500	$ (9,450)
Accounts receivable: [b]				
Ending balance	$ 32,400	32,400 × 150/135	$ 36,000	(3,600)
Note payable: [c]				
Beginning balance	$ 40,000	40,000 × 150/120	$ 50,000	10,000
GPL purchasing power net gain (loss) on net monetary items (to income statement)				$ (3,050)

Explanation:

[a] Restatement of an account that has several changes during the period at *different* GPL ratios requires restatement of each increase and decrease separately. Thus, the beginning balance and each change (grouped by GPL index numbers) are restated. An alternative, and perhaps more understandable, computation follows (i.e., a T-account approach).

Cash Account

Cost basis	Restated basis	Cost basis	Restated basis	Balance
100,000 × 150/120 =	125,000	60,000 × 150/125 =	72,000	
129,600 × 150/135 =	144,000	6,350 × 150/127 =	7,500	
		121,500 × 150/135 =	135,000	
		27,000 × 150/135 =	30,000	
		2,700 × 150/135 =	3,000	
Total 229,600		217,550		$12,050 (HC)
Total	269,000		247,500	21,500 (GPL)

GPL purchasing power gain (loss) on monetary item—Cash account $ (9,450)

[b] Accounts receivable can be restated in this case on the basis of the ending balance because (1) there was no beginning balance and (2) the increases and decreases during the year were at the **average** GPL index (135).

[c] Note payable can be restated in this case on the basis of the beginning balance because there were no increases or decreases in the account during the year (the beginning balance was recorded on January 1, 19A, when the GPL index was 120).

2. A monetary item may reflect no beginning balance, but it reflects several transactions during the period at the same GPL index number. In this

situation the ending balance is GPL restated as illustrated for **accounts receivable** in Exhibit 17–3.

3. A monetary item may reflect only a beginning balance with no changes during the period. In this situation the beginning balance is GPL restated as illustrated for **note payable** in Exhibit 17–3.

In the illustration of ACE Corporation, the total GPL purchasing power loss of $3,050 is the algebraic sum of the purchasing power **losses on monetary assets** and the purchasing power **gains on monetary liabilities.** In the illustration, the $3,050 is a loss during a period of inflation because the monetary assets exceeded the monetary liabilities (in the opposite case, there would have been a gain). This amount is carried to the income statement (as illustrated in Exhibit 17–2) because it represents a real economic (purchasing power) gain or loss.

In summary, GPL restated financial statements are prepared by restating the **nonmonetary** HC-items on the balance sheet, income statement, and statement of retained earnings. The monetary items, since they cannot be restated, are included in the GPL financial statements at their HC basis amounts. However, the **monetary** assets and liabilities are restated separately to compute the GPL purchasing power gain or loss on monetary items, which is reported on the income statement. The GPL restated net income is carried to the GPL statement of retained earnings, and the GPL restated ending balance of retained earnings is reported on the GPL balance sheet.[5] Changes in prices often cause two kinds of differences between HC basis amounts and the price change amounts:

1. **GPL purchasing power gain (loss) on monetary items**—This is a **real** economic gain or loss that is reported on the income statement. It is a real gain or loss because monetary assets held during a period of inflation create economic losses and monetary liabilities create economic gains since the amounts of dollars that they represent become "cheaper."

2. **GPL fictional changes and real value changes on nonmonetary items**—The market value (specific price) of a **nonmonetary** item may be more than, or less than, its GPL restated cost at dates subsequent to acquisition. This occurs when the nonmonetary asset changes in market value at a rate which is more, or less, than the inflation (or deflation) rate. The difference between its GPL restated cost (on a nonmonetary asset) and its actual HC acquisition cost is a **fictional change,** which is the amount of dollars necessary to keep up exactly with infla-

---

[5] In view of GPL restatement on the balance sheet of only the nonmonetary items (not the monetary items), the question always arises as to why a GPL balance sheet "balances." Technically, the reason is that the monetary assets and monetary liabilities are not restated on the balance sheet, but total *owners' equity* is restated. Therefore, the residual, owners' equity (A − L = OE) *includes* a restatement amount for *both* the nonmonetary and monetary items. Inclusion of the GPL purchasing power gain (loss) on monetary items on the income statement (and hence in retained earnings on the balance sheet) provides the mathematically necessary amount to bring the equation A − L = OE into balance on the GPL restated balance sheet.

tion. Thus, it is a fictional (rather than a real value) change. In contrast, the difference between the market value of a **nonmonetary** asset and its GPL restated cost is a **real value holding change,** because the asset has changed in market value by an amount which is more or less than the number of GPL dollars necessary to compensate exactly for inflation or deflation. These two differences (fictional changes and real value changes) between the HC of a nonmonetary asset and its **market value** at a later date may be illustrated simply by assuming a tract of land was acquired for $10,000 on January 1, 19A, at which time the GPL index was 100. At the end of the 19E (five years later) the GPL index was 150 and the land had a market value of $17,000. The "dollar" change of $7,000 (i.e., $17,000 − $10,000) may be analyzed as follows:

GPL restated cost ($10,000 × 150/100)	$15,000
Actual HC acquisition cost	10,000
Difference—the amount of price change necessary to keep exactly even with inflation; a fictitious change rather than a real value change	$5,000
Real value change of the land (market price, $17,000 − GPL restated cost, $15,000)	2,000
Total change in "dollar" values ($17,000 − $10,000)	$7,000

Thus, the specific price (market value) of the land increased more than the GPL effect (which was necessary simply to keep up with inflation), by $2,000, which is the real value change.

OVERVIEW

A comparison of the two balance sheets presented in Exhibit 17–2 shows that the GPL restatement increased total assets from $112,300 to $124,500, which was a 10.9 percent increase. In contrast, the income statement reflected a decrease in reported income of $15,000 to $12,550, which was a 16.3 percent decrease. When there is an inflationary trend, and the relationship between monetary assets and monetary liabilities remain essentially constant, GPL restated income usually will be lower than the cost basis amount.

Now that the concept and related procedures to derive GPL restated financial statements are understood, let's examine them in overall perspective. The HC basis financial statements discussed and illustrated throughout the prior chapters rest on the unit-of-measure assumption (Chapter 2), which holds that each transaction should be measured in dollars which "existed" at the date of each transaction. In the case of GPL changes (i.e., inflation or deflation), the HC basis financial statements report dollar amounts that had different purchasing powers when recorded than exist at the current date. The concept of GPL restated financial statements retains the HC basis amounts **except** that they are restated in common GPL dollars. That is, the HC amounts are restated for the effects of changes in the value of the monetary unit (inflation or deflation) that have occurred since each transaction was recorded. This means that all nonmonetary HC dollar amounts reflected in the HC statements are restated to common (current) dollars each having the same purchasing power. The GPL restated income statement includes a new type of item—GPL purchasing power gain or loss on monetary items.

Those who support the concept of GPL restated financial statements strongly believe that two sets of financial statements should be presented: (1) one set, which is prepared on the traditional HC basis, and (2) another set, which is prepared on the GPL restated basis. The primary arguments for presenting GPL restated financial statements are (1) during periods of significant inflation or deflation, HC basis statements contain serious distortions that are not revealed; (2) the GPL restated amounts, including the GPL purchasing power gain or loss on monetary items, are important to users of financial statements; and (3) the HC approach basically is retained with all amounts stated in terms of current GPL dollars. In contrast, the primary arguments against GPL restated statements are (1) two sets of financial statements (one not restated and one restated) confuse statement users, (2) it is difficult to defend a particular price index to use for restatement purposes, (3) statement users would not find the restated amounts particularly useful, and (4) GPL effects and real value changes on *nonmonetary* items are not revealed separately (discussed in Part B).

The Financial Accounting Standards Board *(FASB)* issues *Statement of Financial Accounting Standards No. 33,* "Financial Reporting and Changing Prices," in September 1979. This Statement, which applied only to very large companies, states that

> for fiscal years ended on or after December 25, 1979, enterprises are required to report:
> a. Income from continuing operations adjusted for the effects of general inflation.
> b. The purchasing power gain or loss on monetary items.[6]

These minimum requirements usually are met by including the two required amounts in the notes to the financial statements. *FASB Statement No. 33* does not require a complete set of GPL restated financial statements, although complete and comprehensive GPL reporting (as illustrated on Exhibit 17–2) is to be encouraged.

PART B: REPORTING CURRENT COST (CC) CHANGES

Accounting academicians and professional accountants (in public practice and in industry) long have discussed the concept of reporting "current

---

[6] *FASB Statement No. 33,* "Financial Reporting and Changing Prices" (Stamford, Conn., September 1979). Copyright © by the Financial Accounting Standards Board, High Ridge Park, Stamford, Conn. 06905, U.S.A. Quoted (or excerpted) with permission. Copies of the complete document are available from the FASB.

values" rather than HC basis amounts on the financial statements. The primary argument in favor of reporting current values is that statement users (investors, creditors, and others) are more interested in the "worth" of the assets at the date of the financial statements than in the HC amounts now reported under GAAP (as presented in the preceding chapters). The use of current values is in a state of indecision as to implementation. Opinions are varied as to exactly what "current value" means and also how the selected current values should be incorporated into the financial statements. On this latter point two basic implementation approaches are under consideration, viz:

1. Report **current value** amounts in the financial statements **instead** of HC amounts. This view is that current value would be a substitute for, and not supplementary information to, the traditional HC statements. A second view, which prevails currently, is that two different sets of financial statements should be presented each period: *(a)* one set on the traditional HC basis and *(b)* another set on the current value basis.
2. Report a **combination** of current value and GPL restated amounts. In effect, under this approach current values are restated so that both current value and GPL effects are reported.

In the discussions to follow the **combination reporting approach** is assumed because it provides considerable information on both current value and GPL effects.

DEFINITION OF CURRENT VALUE IN FINANCIAL REPORTING

The term *current value,* as used in financial reporting, is a generic term that encompasses three different concepts of value; that is the:—

1. **Present value** of the expected net future cash inflow which is attributable to an asset (such as inventories, equipment, and land). This concept of the valuation of an asset was discussed briefly in Part B of Chapter 10. The expected net future cash inflow is discounted to the present at an appropriate interest rate. Conceptually, this approach is superior; however, it is not used widely to determine "current value" in financial statements because of uncertainty in *(a)* projecting the future net cash inflow by period, and *(b)* selecting an appropriate discount rate.
2. **Net realizable value** of an asset, which is the expected price at which it could be sold in present condition, less all costs of disposal. This concept of valuing an asset was discussed in Part B of Chapter 7 in respect to inventories. This method of asset valuation is used in circumstances in which current cost (CC) cannot be determined reasonably by other approaches.[7]

---

[7] *FASB Statement No. 33* (cited on page 749) specifies that current cost cannot exceed net realizable value for financial statement reporting purposes.

3. **Current cost (CC),** which is the cost, at the current balance sheet date, of replacing the identical asset in its present operating condition. Estimating the CC of some assets (such as a plant, because there seldom is an established market for a one-of-a-kind plant) is a complex problem. For operational assets current cost often is defined as the resources required to acquire the same "service potential" as the old asset. In contrast, CC may be estimated reasonably for some assets, such as merchandise inventory, because there is an established market. For inventory, CC is defined as the resources that currently would be required to purchase or produce the goods held. Approaches often used to estimate CC are use of current price lists, prices in established markets for used items, specific price indexes, and professional appraisals.

CONCEPTS UNDERLYING CC FINANCIAL REPORTING

CC financial reporting does not require the recording of CC valuations in the accounts; however, because it is a concept significantly different from HC basis accounting, many accountants view it as a full-blown accounting and reporting method to replace the current GAAP historical-cost valuation model in both the accounts and the financial statements. The discussions and illustrations which follow assume that HC basis financial statements will be reported, and in addition, that CC financial statements will be prepared for supplementary reporting purposes without entering the CC values in the accounts.

When CC financial statements are prepared, the HC amounts are converted to CC amounts. Primarily, CC reporting involves changes in the asset and income statement amounts. For **monetary items** the HC carrying amounts and CC carrying amounts usually will be the same (e.g., cash, receivables, and payables). Development of CC financial statements is simple and straightforward. The following concepts are applied in CC financial statements:

1. At the end of each period a CC valuation is derived for each financial statement amount to be reported. These valuations are developed using the approaches listed above.
2. On the CC balance sheet, the **monetary** items usually are not changed from the HC amounts. The CC **nonmonetary** amounts are changed from the HC amounts and are reported on the CC balance sheet in common or current (GPL) dollars, which means that certain amounts, such as the balance in the contributed capital accounts, must be GPL restated. CC retained earnings is computed as a balancing amount.
3. On the CC income statement, revenues are reported at their HC amounts restated for the GPL change. Expenses are reported at their CC amounts when different from the HC basis amounts (e.g., cost of goods sold and depreciation expense). Expenses for which the HC and CC amounts

are the same must be GPL restated (e.g., remaining expenses in the illustrative problem).

4. A new item "CC real holding gain (loss) on **nonmonetary** items," is computed and reported on the income statement. This holding gain is the difference between the GPL restated HC amounts and the CC amounts (on both the balance sheet and income statement). Thus, it is the total amount that the items changed because CC at the end of the period was different from the GPL restated HC amounts. These amounts usually are aggregated and then reported on the income as a single amount.[8]

5. CC reporting restates those CC amounts which are not already in current or common end-of-the-period dollars. This approach usually is called the CC or common dollar approach.[9] This combination approach (see page 750) has the distinct advantage of reporting both CC and GPL effects; therefore, it is discussed and illustrated in the next section.

CC FINANCIAL REPORTING—ILLUSTRATIVE CASE

The simplified situation of ACE Corporation used in Part A will be continued for the CC illustrations and discussions in this part. The HC basis financial statements were shown in Exhibit 17–1. Current cost (CC) amounts at December 31, 19A, which are different from HC amounts are:

Item	Current cost determination*	CC valuation amount (in common dollars at Dec. 31, 19A)
Ending inventory, December 31, 19A	The **specific** price index at year's end of the inventory based on CC, was 120 percent of HC. $13,500 × 1.20 = ...	$ 16,200
Equipment	The **specific** price index at year's end of the equipment, based on estimated current cost in present condition, was 130 percent of HC. $60,000 × 1.30 = ...	78,000
Accumulated depreciation, equipment	Same as the related equipment, at year's end. $12,000 × 1.30	15,600
Land	Professionally **appraised** at year's end.	6,985
Cost of goods sold	The **average specific** price index, based on the current cost when the goods were **sold,** was 108 percent of HC. $108,000 × 1.08 × 150/135 = ...	129,600

---

[8] This amount can be separated into two amounts: (1) unrealized, which relates to assets still owned (i.e., the first four items in Exhibit 17–4) and (2) realized, which relates to assets sold during the period (last four items in Exhibit 17–4).

[9] Another variation of CC reporting does not include the GPL (or common) dollar feature.

Item	Current cost determination*	CC valuation amount (in common dollars at Dec. 31, 19A)
Depreciation expense	The **average specific** price index, based on the current cost when the related equipment was **used,** was 108⅓% of HC. $12,000 × 1.0833 × 150/125 = ...	15,600
Remaining expenses	HC average and CC average were the same for the year. $27,000 × 150/135 = ...	30,000

* For GPL data—refer to Exhibits 17–1 and 17–2.

Exhibit 17–4 presents *(a)* the HC financial statements (as illustrated previously in Exhibit 17–1) and *(b)* converted CC financial statements (and GPL restated). The basis used to determine each CC amount also is shown in Exhibit 17–4. In particular, note the following: (1) the difference between the CC treatment of monetary and nonmonetary items, (2) the several approaches used to determine the CC values of the nonmonetary items (e.g., specific indexes and appraisals), and (3) restatement of all items in **year-end common dollars** (e.g., capital stock, revenue, and expenses).

In Exhibit 17–4, the monetary assets (cash and accounts receivable) were reported at their HC carrying values, because HC and CC are the same (they already are expressed in common dollars). Inventory, equipment, and accumulated depreciation were CC valued (in common dollars) by using specific year's end price indexes; and land was CC valued by year end appraisal (in common dollars). The monetary liabilities were reported at their HC carrying values, which are the same as CC (they already are expressed in common dollars). The capital stock account at HC is the same as CC but it must be GPL restated to express it in common dollars.

On the CC income statement, HC sales revenue is GPL restated to express it in common dollars at year-end. CC cost of goods sold was determined by using the average CC specific price index (108) when the goods were sold; the CC then is expressed in year-end common dollars by using the ending GPL index of 150 and the average GPL index of 135. CC depreciation expense is determined by using the average specific price index of 108⅓ (when the related asset, equipment, was used) and then is restated in year-end common dollars. The CC income statement, after "Income from continuing operations," is completed by entering the two different **real gains or losses;** one is based on the **monetary items** and the other is based on **nonmonetary items,** viz:

1. **GPL purchasing power gain (loss) on monetary items, $(3,050)**—this real gain or loss occurs when **monetary** items are held during a period of inflation or deflation. It was discussed and illustrated in Part A (Exhibit 17–3).

EXHIBIT 17–4
Current cost (in common dollars) financial statements—Ace Corporation

	HC basis	Basis of determination	Current cost (in common dollars) Amount
Balance sheet, at December 31, 19A:			
Assets			
Cash	$ 12,050	Monetary—HC and CC are the same	$ 12,050
Accounts receivable (net)	32,400	Monetary—HC is net realizable value	32,400
Inventory	13,500	× specific price index (at year's end), 1.20	16,200
Equipment	60,000	× specific price index (at year's end), 1.30	78,000
Accumulated depreciation (credit)	(12,000)	× specific price index (at year's end), 1.30	(15,600)
Land	6,350	Per professional appraisal (in common dollars)	6,985
Total	$112,300		$130,035
Liabilities			
Note payable, long term	$ 40,000	Monetary—HC and CC are the same	$ 40,000
Stockholders' Equity			
Capital stock (nopar)	60,000	× GPL index, 150/120 (to restate in common dollars)	75,000
Retained earnings	12,300	To balance (plug) $130,035 − $40,000 − $75,000	15,035
Total	$112,300		$130,035
Income statement, for the year ended December 31, 19A:			
Sales revenue (credit)	$162,000	× GPL index, 150/135 (to restate in common dollars)	$180,000
Deduct:			
Cost of goods sold (debit)	108,000	× specific price index, 1.08 × 150/135 (to restate in common dollars)	129,600
Depreciation expense (debit)	12,000	× specific price index, 1.0833 × 150/125 (to restate in common dollars)	15,600
Remaining expenses (debit)	27,000	× GPL index, 150/135 (to restate in common dollars; HC and CC are the same as given)	30,000
Income from continuing operations	$ 15,000		4,800
GPL purchasing power gain (loss) on monetary items (Exhibit 17–3)			
CC real holding gain (loss) on nonmonetary items (Exhibit 17–5)			(3,050)
CC income (in common dollars)			16,285
			$ 18,035
Statement of retained earnings, at December 31, 19A:			
Beginning balance	$ –0–	Per income statement	$ –0–
Add: Income of 19A	15,000	× GPL index, 150/135 (to restate in common dollars)	18,035
Deduct: Dividends of 19A	(2,700)		(3,000)
Ending balance, December, 31, 19A	$ 12,300	Carried to balance sheet	$ 15,035

2. **CC real holding gain (loss) on nonmonetary items, $16,285**—this real gain or loss occurs when **nonmonetary assets, which are still owned** at the end of the period, and revenues and expenses of the period, change in dollars more or less than the GPL index. Computation of this amount is illustrated in Exhibit 17–5.

COMPUTATION OF CC REAL HOLDING GAINS AND LOSSES ON NONMONETARY ITEMS

Computation of CC real **holding** gains and losses on **nonmonetary** items (Exhibit 17–5) is based on the conceptual differences between **GPL fictional changes** and **CC real value changes,** viz:

1. **GPL fictional changes on nonmonetary items** are increases (or decreases) from the HC amounts due solely to changes in the GPL. These are not real value changes because they represent only the number of dollars required to exactly keep even with general inflation (GPL).
2. **CC real holding gains (losses) on nonmonetary items** are increases (or decreases) between CC amounts and the related GPL restated amounts. These differences represent real value changes because they measure the extent to which CC changed more (or less) than the GPL restated amounts.

To illustrate these concepts, the ending inventory in Exhibit 17–4 was reported as follows: HC, $13,500; and CC, $16,200. The total price difference between these two amounts, $2,700, represents the effects of two different kinds of price changes:

1. GPL fictional change:
   GPL restated, $15,000 − HC, $13,500 = $1,500 fictional gain
2. CC real holding gain:
   CC, $16,200 − GPL restated, $15,000 = <u>1,200</u> real gain
   Total price change . . . . <u>$2,700</u>

The above analysis may be presented graphically as follows:

HC Basis	GPL Basis	CC Basis
|	|	|
$13,500	($13,500 × 150/135) = $15,000	($13,500 × 1.20) = $16,200

Total price change: $16,200 − $13,500 = $2,700

GPL fictional change $15,000 − $13,500 = $1,500	CC real holding gain $16,200 − $15,000 = $1,200

(Check: $1,500 + $1,200 = $2,700)

EXHIBIT 17-5
Computation of CC holding gains (losses) on nonmonetary items—Ace Corporation

	HC Basis A	GPL Restated Common Dollar Basis (See Exhibit 17-2) B	CC Common Dollar Basis C		Total Change HC to CC C − A	GPL Fictional Change Gain (Loss) B − A	CC Real Holding Gain (Loss) C − B
Nonmonetary assets:							
Inventory	$ 13,500	A × 150/135 $ 15,000	A × 1.20	$ 16,200	$ 2,700	$ 1,500	$ 1,200
Equipment	60,000	A × 150/125 72,000	A × 1.30	78,000	18,000	12,000	6,000
Accumulated depreciation (credit)	(12,000)	A × 150/125 (14,400)	A × 1.30	(15,600)	(3,600)	(2,400)	(1,200)
Land	6,350	A × 150/127 7,500	Appraisal	6,985	635	1,150	(515)
Operations:							
Sales revenue (credit)	(162,000)	A × 150/135 (180,000)	A × 150/135*	(180,000)	(18,000)	(18,000)	–0–
Deduct:							
Cost of goods sold	108,000	A × 150/135 120,000	A × 1.08 × 150/135†	129,600	21,600	12,000	9,600
Depreciation expense	12,000	A × 150/125 14,400	A × 1.0833 × 150/125†	15,600	3,600	12,000	1,200
Remaining expenses	27,000	A × 150/135 30,000	A × 150/135*	15,600 30,000	3,600 3,000	2,400 3,000	1,200 –0–
Totals	$ 52,850	$ 64,500		$ 80,785	$27,935	$11,650	$16,285

* No CC change specified in the problem; to convert to common dollars.

† Observe that the related assets (e.g., inventory and equipment) are "CC valued" at the *year's end specific index*, while the expenses (i.e., cost of goods sold and depreciation expense, etc.) are "CC valued" at the *average specific index* when incurred and then are GPL restated to year-end.

Based on these concepts, we can turn our attention to Exhibit 17–5, which illustrates their application to compute the CC **real holding gains and losses on nonmonetary items** as reported on the CC financial statements (Exhibits 17–4). In Exhibit 17–5, the **nonmonetary** items (nonmonetary assets and the revenues and expenses) are listed at their HC amounts in Column A. Following the concepts as diagrammed above, the GPL restated HC amounts are computed in Column B and the CC (common dollar) amounts are computed in Column C. In respect to the CC amounts, observe that all items are restated to year-end common dollars (i.e., in 19A ending dollars).

The remaining columns in Exhibit 17–5, reflect the differences caused by the price changes of each item—total change, GPL fictional, and the CC real holding gains and losses. In particular, observe that the **CC real holding gain (loss) on nonmonetary items** (the last column) is the difference between the CC common dollar amounts and the GPL restated HC amounts. The CC real holding gain (loss) on nonmonetary items is reported as shown on the CC income statement (Exhibit 17–4). The GPL fictional gain (loss) (the fifth column) is not reported separately on the CC financial statements because the GPL effects are included in the various nonmonetary CC amounts. Therefore, the fourth and fifth column in Exhibit 17–5 (i.e., the total and fictional changes) do not have to be computed to develop the CC financial statements.

OVERVIEW

Now that you understand the "content" of the three different sets of financial statements—HC, GPL restated, and CC—it is appropriate to view them in the perspective of the needs of investors, creditors, and other users of such statements, given the expectation of continuation of the current inflationary trend.

HC financial statements carry a very heavy burden during periods of significant GPL changes because the measuring unit (the dollar in our case) fluctuates in purchasing power. Large changes in purchasing power cause serious distortions in the "dollars" reported in the financial statements—aggregating "apples and oranges" is not very meaningful for measuring financial results. Simply stated, **HC reporting disregards both GPL and CC effects.** On the other hand, HC reporting is quite **objective** because the HC dollars recorded are those established by transactions between two or more parties with adversary economic interests (i.e., the buyer is motivated to buy low while the seller is motivated to sell high, and they strike a bargain).

GPL restated financial statements (in contrast to HC statements) attempt to report the effects of inflation and deflation by restating the HC amounts in terms of the current GPL (i.e., in common dollars). GPL restatement retains the HC model; however, it adds two features that the HC model does not incorporate: (1) restatement of the HC amounts to common (i.e., GPL) dollars and (2) measurement of the purchasing power gains and losses on monetary assets and monetary liabilities held during periods of inflation and deflation. Thus, it fulfills its objective to resolve one of the deficiencies of HC reporting (i.e., the GPL measurement problem). However, it does not report CC effects. Also, some people argue that GPL restated financial statements necessitate two separate sets of financial statements (e.g., HC and GPL restated). The basic argument against the two sets is that the decision makers would be confused by an "information overload."

CC financial statements (in common dollars), attempt to correct the two basic deficiencies of HC financial statements—the GPL and CC effects. CC financial statements attempt to do this by (1) reporting all amounts at their current CC values and (2) expressing the CC values in terms of GPL (i.e., common or current) dollars.[10] The conceptual objective of CC reporting (i.e., to tell the decision maker the current "worth" of each item reported) generally is agreed upon because decision makers necessarily base their decisions on (1) the current situation and (2) their expectations (projections) about the future. For example, a person considering the purchase of a 20-year-old office building would be concerned primarily about (1) its value today and (2) its potential to generate net cash inflows during the expected holding period and the probable residual value upon ultimate disposal. The fact that it cost X dollars 20 years earlier, or that its current HC book value is Y dollars, should be of little, or no, concern in the decision of whether to purchase.

Although CC conceptually is an ideal financial reporting model, it is burdened heavily with an implementation problem; that is, attaining objectivity and accuracy in determining the CC of each item at the end of each accounting period. This burden of attaining **objective measurement** of CC values is not easy to resolve. Of course, it may be relatively easy in some situations but extremely difficult in others. If it can be resolved so that CC values are reasonably accurate and believable, the CC model should replace the need for both HC and GPL restated financial statements.

REPORTING THE EFFECTS OF CHANGING PRICES

The 1979 financial statements of some companies reported the effects of changing prices in a manner similar to the discussions and illustrations in this chapter (i.e., GPL and CC reporting). Exhibit 17–6 presents an excellent example of one such report. Observe that the income statement in that exhibit reflects the three different approaches compared in this chapter—HC (Col. 1); GPL (Col. 2); and CC (Col. 3). Also, observe the following reported effects of price changes (in this particular situation GPL exceeded CC):

---

[10] *FASB Statement No. 33* specifies that the GPL (common dollars) may be expressed as (1) at year-end or (2) the average for the year.

EXHIBIT 17–6
Reporting the effects of changing prices (unaudited)
HOUSTON INDUSTRIES INCORPORATED

Supplementary Information To Disclose The Effects of Changing Prices

The following unaudited supplementary information is supplied in accordance with requirements of Financial Accounting Standards Board (FASB) Statement No. 33, Financial Reporting and Changing Prices, for the purpose of providing certain information regarding the effects of both general inflation and changes in specific prices. It should be viewed only as an estimate of the approximate effect of inflation.

Statement of Consolidated Income From Continuing Operations Adjusted For Changing Prices

For the Year Ended December 31, 1979
(In Thousands of Dollars)

	Conventional Historical Cost	Constant Dollar Average 1979 Dollars	Current Cost Average 1979 Dollars
Revenues	$1,854,159	$1,854,159	$1,854,159
Expenses:			
Electric	1,284,773	1,284,773	1,284,773
Cost of fuel sold	82,170	82,170	82,170
Oil and gas operating expenses	6,755	6,755	6,755
Depreciation, depletion and amortization	109,445	181,191	195,365
Income taxes	109,013	109,013	109,013
Fixed charges and other income — net	100,157	100,157	100,157
Income from continuing operations (excluding reduction to net recoverable cost)	$ 161,846	$ 90,100*	$ 75,926
Income per share from continuing operations (after dividend requirements on preferred stock and excluding reduction to net recoverable cost)	$4.84	$2.69	$2.27
Increase in specific prices (current cost) of property, plant and equipment held during the year**			$ 410,147
Less increase in cost of property, plant, and equipment adjusted for changes in general price level			678,397
Excess of increase in general price level over increase in specific prices			(268,250)
Reduction of utility property to net recoverable cost		$(317,780)	(44,192)
			(312,442)
Gain from decline in purchasing power of net amounts owed		265,527	265,527
Net		$ (52,253)	$ (46,915)

Note: This computation may be compared with Exhibit 17–5 in which the ($268,250) would be computed as: C, $410,147 minus B, $678,397 = $268,250, loss.

* Including the reduction to net recoverable cost, loss from continuing operations on a constant dollar basis would have been $227,680 for 1979.

** At December 31, 1979, current cost of property, plant and equipment, net of accumulated depreciation was $5,847,801, while historical cost was $3,488,863. Net assets at December 31, 1979 at net recoverable cost for constant dollar and current cost were $1,210,743 and $1,211,064, respectively, in average 1979 dollars.

1. CC real holding gain (loss) on nonmonetary items (identified as "Excess of increase in general price level over increase in specific prices"), $268,250,000. Note that this amount was computed as the difference between GPL restated ($678,397,000) and CC ($410,147,000) which equals a loss of $268,250,000.

2. GPL purchasing power gain (loss) on monetary items (identified as "Gain from decline in purchasing power of net amounts owed"), $265,527,000.

Observe that the CC/GPL adjustments changed "Income from continuing operations, $75,926,000," to a loss of $46,915,000.

IMPORTANT TERMS DEFINED IN THE CHAPTER (with page citations)

General price level changes—735
Specific price level changes—735
General price level (GPL) index— 735, 736
Specific price level index—736
Consumer price index for all urban consumers (CPI-U)—736
Unit-of-measure assumption— 737
GPL restatement—739
Common (current) dollars—739, 753

Monetary items—739, 747
Nonmonetary items—739, 747
GPL purchasing power gain (loss) on monetary items—740, 747
GPL fictional changes—740, 755
Current values—750
Present value—750
Net realizable value—750
Current cost (CC)—751
CC real holding gain (loss) on nonmonetary items—752, 755

QUESTIONS FOR DISCUSSION

Part A

1. Explain the difference between general price level changes and specific price level changes.

2. What is a price level index? Explain the difference between a general price level index and a specific price level index.

3. What happens to the "value" of a dollar when there is inflation, and alternatively, when there is deflation?

4. A tract of land was acquired for $15,000 when the GPL index was 150. Five years later the GPL index was 270. At what price would the land have to sell for the owner to keep up exactly with inflation? Explain.

5. Define monetary items and nonmonetary items. Explain why a careful distinction be-

tween them is essential when financial statements are restated on a GPL basis.

6. At the beginning of the current period the Land account reflected a balance of $18,000 (GPL index at acquisition date, 100), and the Note Payable account reflected no beginning balance but had an ending balance of $30,000 (GPL index at transaction date, 150). The GPL index at the end of the current period was 200. Compute the GPL purchasing power gain (loss) on monetary items. Explain the nature of this gain or loss.

7. There never will be a GPL purchasing power gain or loss on nonmonetary items reported on the GPL financial statements. Explain why this is true.

8. Items on the balance sheet may be either monetary or nonmonetary, while all items

on the income statement are nonmonetary. Is this statement true or is it false? Explain why.

9. Explain the difference between a GPL purchasing power gain or loss on monetary items and GPL fictional changes.

Questions
Part B

10. Briefly define each of the following concepts of "current value": (a) present value, (b) net realizable value, and (c) current cost (CC).

11. Are CC amounts usually entered into the journal and ledger? Explain.

12. Explain the nature and composition of the item "CC real holding gain (loss) on nonmonetary items." Contrast it with the "GPL purchasing power gain (loss) on monetary items."

13. Contrast "GPL fictional changes" with "CC real value changes."

14. Explain the difference between an unrealized and a realized gain (loss) on nonmonetary items (refer to footnote 7).

15. A tract of land was purchased at a cost of $10,000 when the GPL was 100. At the end of year five, the GPL was 240 and the appraised value of the land was $27,000. Prepare a diagram that exhibits the price change effects.

EXERCISES
Part A

E17–1. During 1967 a Quality Stereo set sold at $200. Assume that this particular set increased in price exactly the same as the changes in the GPL index through 1978. However, in 1979 it sold at $395.

Required:

   a. What was the selling price in 1970, 1975, and 1978? Use the average CPI-U index values given in the chapter and round to the nearest dollar. Show computations.

   b. Analyze the change in price during 1979.

E17–2. In 1960, Klassen Company purchased a plant site for $23,100. Immediately thereafter, construction of a plant building was started. The building was completed in December 1961, at a cost of $336,000. The building is being depreciated on a straight-line basis assuming an estimated useful life of 30 years and no residual value.

   Assume the GPL index in 1960 was 110, in 1961 it was 112, and at the end of 1980 it was 240.

Required:

   a. Complete a tabulation similar to the following:

	Amount to be reported assuming	
	HC basis	GPL restated
Balance sheet at December 31, 1980:		
Operational assets:		
Land		
Building		
Less accumulated depreciation (20 years) . .		
Income statement for 1980:		
Depreciation expense		

   Show your computations.

   b. Would the GPL change affect income tax expense for the company? Explain. Do you think it should? Explain.

E17–3. The balance sheet for Wells Company, prepared on the conventional HC basis at December 31, 19A, has been completed. Supplemental statements are to be developed on a "GPL restated basis." The following four items were selected from the balance sheet:

(Relates to Exercise 17–3)

Items	HC basis (when acquired)	GPL index (when acquired or incurred)
Receivables	$69,000	115
Investment, common stock	42,000	105
Land, plant site	15,000	100
Payables	99,000	110

The GPL at the end of 19A was 120.

Required:

a. Indicate which are monetary and which are nonmonetary items.
b. Set up a table to derive the amount "GPL restated basis" that should be shown on the supplementary GPL balance sheet for each item. Show computations.
c. Compute the GPL purchasing power gain (loss) that should be reported on the GPL income statement. Show computations.
d. Explain why certain items were omitted from your computation in (c).

E17–4. The items listed below were taken from the December 31, 19A, balance sheet of Smokey Company (HC basis). This is the end of the first year of operations. The GPL index at January 1, 19A, was 200 and at December 31, 19A, it was 220.

Required:

a. Prepare a GPL restated balance sheet. Use a format similar to Exhibit 17–2 and round all amounts to the nearest dollar.
b. What was the amount of GPL restated income for 19A? Explain.
c. Compute the amount of GPL restated income before the GPL purchasing power gain on monetary items of $1,333. Verify the amount of this gain.

E17–5. At the end of 19A (the first year of operations), Strawn Company prepared the summarized HC basis income statement shown below. At January 1, 19A, the GPL index was 220; and at December 31, 19A, it was 260.

(Relates to Exercise 17–4)

	Debits	Credits	GPL index transaction date
Cash	$ 21,000		210†
Accounts receivable (net)	32,000		210†
Investments, common stock	12,000		215
Land	15,000		205
Equipment	80,000		200
Accumulated depreciation		$ 8,000	
Accounts payable		18,000	210†
Notes payable		30,000	200
Capital stock (nopar)		90,000	200
Retained earnings*		14,000	
	$160,000	$160,000	

* Dividends declared and paid on December 31, 19A, amounted to $5,000.
† Average.

STRAWN COMPANY
Income Statement
For the Year Ended December 31, 19A

	Amount	GPL index at average transaction date
Sales revenue	$330,000	234
Cost of goods sold	(165,000)	234
Depreciation expense*	(11,000)	
Remaining expenses	(94,000)	230
Pretax income	60,000	
Income tax expense	18,000	260
Net income	$ 42,000	

* The related asset was acquired when the GPL index was 220.

Required:

a. Prepare a GPL restated income statement. Use a format similar to Exhibit 17–2. The monetary items and their GPL indexes at transaction dates were: receivables, $32,000 (index 234), and liabilities, $16,000 (index 220). Round all amounts to the nearest dollar.

b. Prepare a GPL restated statement of retained earnings assuming dividends of $4,000 were declared on December 31, 19A.

E17–6. This exercise illustrates computation of the GPL purchasing power gains and losses on accounts in situations which involve numerous transactions during the period. Two related accounts are used. At December 31, 19D, the following summary data were taken from the ledger:

Required:

Compute the GPL purchasing power gain or loss for each account separately. Round all amounts to the nearest dollar. You may use the schedule approach or the T-account approach (see Exhibit 17–3).

Exercises
Part B

E17–7. On January 1, 19A, SG Company acquired a tract of land which cost $12,000 when the GPL was 120. Payment was made in cash, $5,000, plus a $7,000 three-year, interest-bearing note. One year later the note was still outstanding and the GPL was 150. The specific index, related to the land, at the end of 19A was 160. The land and the note will be included on the December 31, 19A, CC financial statements.

Required (show computations and round to the nearest dollar):

a. The CC value for the land that should be reported on the 19A, CC balance sheet is $_____.

b. The GPL purchasing power gain (loss) on the monetary liability which should be reported on the 19A, CC income statement, is $_____.

c. The CC real holding gain (loss) on the nonmonetary asset which should be

(Relates to Exercise 17–6)

Transaction	GPL at transaction date	Cash	Payable
Beginning balance	118	$ 30,000	$18,000
Purchased land	125		+ 12,000
Sales revenue	130	+ 150,000	
Borrowing on note	120	+ 60,000	+ 60,000
Payment	122	− 15,000	− 15,000
Payment	132	− 42,000	− 42,000
Expenses paid	130	− 90,000	
Dividends paid	132	− 10,000	
Equipment purchased	120	− 80,000	
Payment	125		− 13,000
Ending balance..................		$ 3,000	$20,000

Note: GPL index numbers: January 1, 19D, 118; December 31, 19D, 132.

reported on the 19A, CC income statement is, $_____.

d. The amount of the GPL fictional change on the land was $_____.

e. Diagram the above responses in respect to the land (not the note payable).

E17–8. On January 1, 19A, WRY Company purchased a machine (an operational asset) which cost $15,000. Cash paid was $10,000 and a $5,000, three-year, interest-bearing note was given to the seller. On January 1, 19A, the GPL index was 100. At the end of 19A the Accumulated Depreciation account reflected $1,500 (i.e., straight-line depreciation; estimated life ten years and no residual value). At the end of 19A the GPL index was 125; the specific price index for the machine was 130, and the average specific price index for depreciation expense (use) was 104. The machine, accumulated depreciation, and note payable will be reported on the 19A CC financial statements.

Required (show computations and round to the nearest dollar):

a. Complete the following tabulation of the amounts which should be reported on the 19A financial statements:

Item	HC basis	CC basis
Balance sheet:		
Machine		
Accumulated depre-		
ciation		
Note payable		
Income statement:		
Depreciation expense		

b. The GPL purchasing power gain (loss) on monetary items which should be reported on the CC income statement is $_____.

c. The CC real holding gain (loss) on non-monetary items which should be reported on the income statement is $_____.

d. The amounts of the GPL fictional changes were:
   1. Machinery, net, $_____.
   2. Depreciation expense, $_____.

E17–9. Tyler Company purchased merchandise for resale during 19A (the first year of operations) which cost $76,000. Payment was in cash except for an $11,400 ending balance in Accounts Payable. The purchases, and payments on accounts payable, occurred evenly throughout the year. The average GPL index for 19A was 190 and at the end of 19A it was 200.

The ending inventory was $15,200; therefore, cost of goods sold was $60,800. Current cost of the ending inventory was $17,000 and $68,000 for cost of goods sold. Accounts payable, inventory, and cost of goods sold will be reported on the 19A CC financial statements.

Required (show computations and round to the nearest dollar):

a. Complete the following tabulation of amounts which should be reported at the end of 19A:

Item	HC basis	CC basis
Balance sheet:		
Inventory		
Accounts payable ...		
Income statement:		
Cost of goods sold ..		

b. The GPL purchasing power gain (loss) on monetary items which should be reported on the CC income statement is $_____.

c. The CC real holding gain (loss) on the nonmonetary items which should be reported on the CC income statement is $_____.

d. The amounts of the GPL fictional changes were:
   1. Inventory, $_____.
   2. Cost of goods sold, $_____.

PROBLEMS

Part A

P17–1. Ford Company has prepared the annual historical cost basis financial statements at December 31, 1981. The company is considering the development of supplemental statements on the "GPL restated basis." The following seven items were selected from the balance sheet:

(Relates to Problem 17–1)

Items	HC basis (when acquired)	GPL index (when acquired or incurred)
1. Cash:		
Beginning balance	$ 20,000	141.5
Debits	38,800	146*
Credits	(44,600)	147*
2. Merchandise inventory (average cost)	58,000	145
3. Accounts receivable, net	28,800	144*
4. Land (no changes during 1980)	12,000	100
5. Building, net (no changes during 1980)	157,500	105
6. Accounts payable	42,000	140*
7. Bonds payable (no changes during 1980)	88,000	110

At the end of 1981 the price-level index was 150.
* Average GPL index for these items.

Required:

a. Group the above items into two categories: monetary and nonmonetary.

b. Set up a table and compute the amount "GPL restated basis" that should be shown on the GPL balance sheet for each of the items. Show calculations. Round to the nearest $100 in the restatement.

c. Compute the GPL purchasing power gain or loss on monetary items that will be shown on the GPL restated income statement. Show calculations and round to the nearest $100.

d. Explain why certain of the seven items were omitted from your computations in (c).

e. Assume the land had a market value of $20,000 on December 31, 1981. Analyze the changes in dollar value since acquisition.

P17–2. At the end of the first year of operations, DE Company prepared the following balance sheet and income statement (HC basis):

DE COMPANY
Balance Sheet
At December 31, 19A
Assets

Cash	$ 3,330
Accounts receivable (net)	5,650
Inventory	46,000
Operational assets (net)	55,000
Total	$109,980

Liabilities

Accounts payable	$ 3,480
Bonds payable	23,000

Stockholders' Equity

Capital stock (nopar)	66,000
Retained earnings	17,500
Total	$109,980

Income Statement
For the Year Ended December 31, 19A

Revenues	$ 69,000
Expenses (not detailed)	(46,000)
Depreciation expense	(5,500)
Net income	$ 17,500

GPL Data

Items	GPL (when acquired or incurred)
GPL at start of year—110	
GPL at end of year—120	
Cash (no beginning balance)	111*
Accounts receivable	113*
Inventory	115
Operational assets	110
Accounts payable	116
Bonds payable	115
Revenues	115*
Expenses	115*
Depreciation expense	110
Capital stock (nopar)	110

* Average GPL index for all items in the account.

Required:

a. Restate the income statement and balance sheet; use the following headings: (1) HC Basis, (2) Restatement Computations, and (3) GPL Restated Basis. Round to the nearest $10.

b. Explain why net income is different between the two statements; identify amounts.

c. Why were the nonmonetary items, but not the monetary, restated on the balance sheet?

d. Does the GPL income statement better match expenses with revenues? Explain.

e. Assume the operational assets had a market value of $75,000 on December 31, 19A. Analyze the dollar changes since acquisition. Explain.

P17–3. After operating for one year, DO Company completed the following income statement and balance sheet:

DO COMPANY
Balance Sheet
At December 31, 19A
Assets

Cash	$ 42,300*
Accounts receivable (net)	29,580
Long-term investment, common stock	7,400
Land	11,200
Plant (net)	140,000
Total	$230,480

Liabilities

Accounts payable	$ 5,880
Bonds payable	28,000

Stockholders' Equity

Capital stock (nopar)	182,000
Retained earnings	14,600
Total	$230,480

Income Statement
For the Year Ended December 31, 19A

Revenues	$ 87,000
Expenses (not detailed)	(58,400)
Depreciation expense	(14,000)
Net income	$ 14,600

* Beginning balance, $58,800 (GPL index, 140); debits $49,600 (GPL index, 148) credits, $66,100 (GPL index, 145.3).

Items	GPL (when acquired or incurred)
GPL index at start of year—140	
GPL index at end of year—150	
Cash	* above
Accounts receivable	141†
Long-term investment purchased, common stock	148
Land purchased	140
Plant acquired	140
Accounts payable	147†
Bonds payable	140
Capital stock (nopar)	140
Revenues	145†
Expenses	146†
Depreciation expense	140

† Average GPL for these amounts.

Required:

a. Restate the income statement and balance sheet with the following headings: (1) Historical Cost Basis, (2) Restatement Computations, and (3) GPL Restated Basis. Round to the nearest $10.

b. Explain why net income is different between the two statements; identify amounts.

c. Why were the nonmonetary items, but not the monetary, restated on the balance sheet?

d. Does the GPL restated income statement better match expenses with revenues? Explain.

e. Assume the land had a market value of $20,000 on December 31, 19A. Analyze the dollar changes since acquisition. Explain.

P17–4. The transactions summarized below were completed by Jan Company during its first year of operations. The accounting period ends December 31. The GPL index on January 1, 19A, was 100, on December 31, 19A, it was 144, and the average was 120.

January 1, 19A: Issued 10,000 shares of capital stock (nopar) for $60,000 cash and borrowed $36,000 cash on a two-year, interest-bearing note (GPL index, 100).

February 1, 19A: Purchased equipment for use in the business, $75,000 cash (GPL index, 105).

During 19A: Purchased merchandise on credit for resale (evenly throughout the year), $180,000 (GPL average index, 120).

During 19A: Sales revenue (evenly throughout the year), $300,000, all cash (GPL average index, 120).

During 19A: Paid expenses (evenly throughout the year), $80,000; includes all expenses except depreciation expense (GPL average index, 120).

During 19A: Paid accounts payable, $161,200 (GPL average index on payments, 124).

December 1, 19A: Declared and paid a cash dividend of $6,900 (GPL index, 138).

December 31, 19A: Depreciation on equipment based on estimated life of ten years and a $5,000 residual value.

December 31, 19A: Cost of goods sold, $170,000 (GPL average index for cost of goods sold and ending inventory, 120).

The above entries resulted in the following preclosing account balances at December 31, 19A:

Debits	
Cash	$ 72,900
Inventory	10,000
Equipment	75,000
Cost of goods sold	170,000
Expenses	80,000
Depreciation expense	7,000
Retained earnings (dividend declared)	6,900
Total	$421,800

Credits	
Accumulated depreciation	$ 7,000
Accounts payable	18,800
Note payable	36,000
Capital stock (nopar)	60,000
Revenues	300,000
Total	$421,800

Required:

a. Set up a format similar to Exhibit 17–2 to derive GPL restated financial statements. Enter thereon the HC basis amounts for each statement.

b. Restate each item on each statement on a GPL basis. Prepare a separate schedule similar to Exhibit 17–3 to compute the GPL purchasing power gain or loss on monetary items. Round all amounts to the nearest dollar. (Hint: There was a $32,083 loss on cash.)

c. Assume the ending inventory had a current cost (CC) of $15,000 on December 31, 19A. Prepare an analysis, with a brief explanation, of the "dollar" value changes related to the inventory.

P17–5. Small Company was organized on January 1, 19A, at which time the GPL index was 150. The accounting period ends December 31. The transactions completed during 19A were:

a. January 1, 19A: Sold and issued 10,000 shares of capital stock (par $10) for $150,000 cash (GPL index, 150).

b. January 1, 19A: Purchased merchandise on credit for resale, $60,000 (GPL index, 150).

c. February 1, 19A: Purchased equipment

for use in the business; paid cash, $31,000, and gave a $46,500, interest-bearing note due December 31, 19C (GPL index, 155).

d. During 19A: Sales revenue, $180,000 (sold evenly throughout the year); one third was on credit (GPL average index, 165).

e. During February–December 19A: Purchased merchandise on credit (evenly throughout the year) for resale, $44,000 (GPL index, 165).

f. During 19A: Collected accounts receivable, $50,000 (average GPL index for collections, 170).

g. During 19A: Paid accounts payable, $84,000 (average GPL index for payments, 160).

h. During 19A: Paid expenses in cash (evenly throughout the year), $61,000, which included interest, income tax, and all other expenses except depreciation expense (average GPL index, 165).

i. July 1, 19A: Invested $96,000 cash for common stock of X Corporation (GPL index, 160).

j. December 31, 19A: Declared and paid a dividend of $10,000 (GPL index, 180).

k. December 31, 19A: Depreciation expense on equipment, $14,000.

l. December 31, 19A: Cost of goods sold, $84,000 (average GPL index for cost of goods sold and ending inventory, 156).

The above transactions resulted in the following preclosing account balances:

Debits

Cash	$ 38,000
Accounts receivable (net)	10,000
Inventory	20,000
Investment, common stock	96,000
Equipment	77,500
Cost of goods sold	84,000
Expenses	61,000
Depreciation expense	14,000
Retained earnings (dividend)	10,000
	$410,500

Credits

Accumulated depreciation	$ 14,000
Accounts payable	20,000
Note payable	46,500
Capital stock (par $10)	100,000
Contributed capital in excess of par	50,000
Revenues	180,000
	$410,500

Required:

a. Set up a format similar to Exhibit 17–2 to derive GPL restated financial statements. Enter thereon the historical cost basis amounts for each statement. The GPL index at December 31, 19A, was 180.

b. Restate each item on each statement on a GPL basis. Prepare a separate schedule similar to Exhibit 17–3 to compute the GPL purchasing power loss or gain on monetary items. (Hint: there was a $10,805 loss on cash). Round all amounts to the nearest dollar.

d. Assume that the investment in common stock had a market value of $110,000 on December 31, 19A. Prepare an analysis, with a brief explanation, of the "dollar" value changes related to the investment.

Problems
Part B

P17–6. This problem is based on the data given in Problem 17–3 (DO Company). The balance sheet and income statement (HC basis) and the GPL index numbers are not changed. Current cost (CC) information is as follows:

(Relates to Problem 17–6)

Item	Current cost (CC) data, December 31, 19A
Long-term investment, common stock	Based on stock market quotation . . . . . . $ 8,500
Land	Per professional appraisal 14,000
Plant (net)	Specific index, 1.10 of carrying value.
Expenses (not detailed)	HC average and CC average the same.
Depreciation expense	Average specific (use) index, 1.0267.

(GPL index at start of year, 140; at end of year, 150)

Required (show computations and round all amounts to the nearest $10):

a. Set up a schedule similar to Exhibit 17–4 to develop a CC balance sheet and income statement at December 31, 19A. Enter the HC data and complete the CC amounts through "Income from continuing operations." The GPL purchasing power loss on monetary items was $2,500.

b. Compute the CC real holding gains (losses) on nonmonetary items.

c. Use the amounts computed in *(b)* to complete the CC income statement. (Hint: The CC balance sheet totals are, $248,380.)

P17–7. This problem is based on the data given in Problem 17–4 (Jan Company). The HC amounts are unchanged, and the GPL index numbers are to be used as given in the original problem. The GPL index at the start of the year, January 1, 19A, was 100, at December 31, 19A, it was 144, and the average was 120. The HC financial statements for 19A were:

(Relates to Problem 17–7)

Balance Sheet

Cash	$ 72,900	Accounts payable	$ 18,800
Inventory	10,000	Notes payable	36,000
Equipment	75,000	Capital stock (nopar)	60,000
Accumulated depreciation . .	(7,000)	Retained earnings	36,100
Total	$150,900	Total	$150,900

Income Statement		Statement of Retained Earnings	
Revenues	$300,000	Beginning balance	$ –0–
Cost of goods sold	(170,000)	Add: Income of 19A	43,000
Expenses	(80,000)	Deduct: Dividends of 19A .	(6,900)
Depreciation expense	(7,000)	Ending balance	$ 36,100
Income	$ 43,000		

Current cost (CC) information is as follows:

(Relates to Problem 17–7)

Item	Current cost (CC) data, December 31, 19A	
Inventory	Specific index, 1.25 of HC carrying value	
Equipment	Per professional appraisal	$120,000
Accumulated depreciation	Per professional appraisal	11,000
Cost of goods sold	Average specific price index, 1.041667 of HC	212,500
Expenses	HC average and CC average are the same	
Depreciation expense	Average specific price index (use), 1.1458	11,000

Required (show computations and round all amounts to the nearest dollar):

a. Set up a schedule similar to Exhibit 17–4 to develop a CC balance sheet, income statement, and statement of retained earnings. Enter the HC data and complete the CC amounts through "Income from continuing operations." The GPL purchasing power loss on monetary items was $6,243.
b. Compute the CC real holding gains

(Hint: The CC balance sheet totals are $194,400.)

P17–8. Thu Company began operations on January 1, 19A, at which time the GPL index was 130. The 19A balance sheet and income statement, along with relevant GPL index numbers and CC information, are given below. The 19A average GPL index was 143, and it was 156 at December 31, 19A.

(Relates to Problem 17–8)

	HC basis	GPL Index at transaction date	CC valuations (which are different from HC) at December 31, 19A
Balance sheet:			
Assets:			
Cash	$ 14,300	143	
Accounts receivable	28,600	143	
Inventory (average)	57,200	143	Specific index, 165/143 of HC
Equipment, net	70,200	130	Appraisal, $90,000
Other assets	19,500	130	Specific index, 160/130 of HC
Total	$189,800		
Liabilities:			
Accounts payable	$ 14,300	143	
Note payable	39,000	130	
Stockholders' equity:			
Capital stock	130,000	136.84	
Retained earnings	6,500		
Total	$189,800		
Income statement:			
Revenue	$114,400	143	
Cost of goods sold	(71,500)	143	Average specific price index, 1.0577 of HC
Depreciation expense*	(7,800)		Average specific price index (use), 1.068 of HC
Remaining expenses	(28,600)	143	HC and CC averages are the same
Net income	$ 6,500		

* Straight-line depreciation, ten-year estimated life and no residual value (Cost, $78,000 ÷ 10 years = $7,800).

(losses) on nonmonetary items. Set up a schedule similar to Exhibit 17–5.
c. Use the amounts computed in b to complete the CC income statement.

Required:

Based on the above data, the company desires to construct a CC balance sheet and income statement at December 31,

19A. Show all computations and round to the nearest $10.

a. Set up a schedule similar to Exhibit 17–4 to develop CC statements. Enter the HC data given above and complete the CC amounts through "Income from continuing operations."

b. The GPL purchasing power gain on monetary items was $5,200. Show how this was computed (refer to Exhibit 17–3).

c. Compute the CC real holding gain (loss) on nonmonetary items. (1) unrealized and (2) realized (refer to Exhibit 17–5).

d. Use the amounts computed in (b) and (c) to complete the CC income statement. (Hint: The CC balance sheet totals are $222,900.)

Index